America's Economic Heritage

America's Economic Heritage

A Mature Economy,
Post 1900

Meyer Weinberg

GREENWOOD PRESS
Westport, Connecticut • London, England

Library of Congress Cataloging in Publication Data

Weinberg, Meyer, 1920-
  America's economic heritage.

  Includes bibliographies and indexes.
  Contents: v. 1. From a colonial to a capitalist
economy, 1634-1900 -- v. 2. A mature economy, post 1900.
    1. United States--Economic conditions--Sources.
I. Title.
HC103.W38 1983   016.330973   83-10877
ISBN 0-313-23751-4 (lib. bdg. : set)
ISBN 0-313-24135-X (lib. bdg. : v. 1)
ISBN 0-313-24136-8 (lib. bdg. : v. 2)

Library of Congress Catalog Card Number: 83-10877
ISBN: 0-313-24136-8

First published in 1983

Greenwood Press
A division of Congressional Information Service, Inc.
88 Post Road West
Westport, Connecticut 06881

Printed in the United States of America

10 9 8 7 6 5 4 3 2 1

Copyright Acknowledgments

Grateful acknowledgment is given for permission to use the following:

A quotation from *American Scientist,* Vol. 48, No. 1, journal of Sigma Xi, The Scientific Research Society, C.E.H. Bawn, "Some Impressions of Soviet Science." Reprinted by permission.

Extracts from the book entitled *Building an American Industry . . . An Autobiography* by Jacob Dolson Cox, Jr. published in 1951 © the Cleveland Twist Drill Company. Reprinted by permission.

Reprinted with permission from "The Case for More Basic Research," in *Chemical and Engineering News XXXVII* (January 19, 1959) by Walter J. Murphy. Copyright 1959 American Chemical Society.

From *Farm Boy to Financier* by Frank A. Vanderlip, copyright 1935 by Hawthorn Properties. Permission to reprint given by Frank A. Vanderlip, Jr.

From *Father of Radio: The Autobiography of Lee de Forest.* Copyright © 1950 by Lee de Forest. Used by permission of Follett Publishing Company.

From *Fifty Billion Dollars, My Years with the RFC, 1932-45* by Jesse Jones and Edward Angly. Reprinted with permission of Macmillan Publishing Co., Inc. Copyright 1951 by The Chronicle Company, renewed 1979 by Houston Endowment Inc.

CONTENTS

FOREWORD

HAROLD D. WOODMAN

The economic history of the United States is an astonishing success story. It's a story that began inauspiciously in 1607 when a handful of English settlers founded Jamestown on the coast of present-day Virginia—and somehow managed to survive. Or at least the settlement survived, for most of the first settlers and many of those who followed succumbed to the rigors of weather, inadequate food, and disease or the attacks of unfriendly Indians. In the decades that followed, other settlements along the North American coast survived the initial difficult years and, like the Virginia colony, became thriving communities. Most of the residents were English, but some Dutch, French, and others chose to settle in the English colonies and a growing number of enslaved black Africans became unwilling residents.

Virginians found that their tobacco had a ready market in Europe; merchants from Boston, New York, Philadelphia, and other cities in the northern colonies, protected by the English navy and by legislation excluding foreigners from trade with the English colonies, provided the ships to carry the tobacco to markets abroad. Grains and other foodstuffs, ships stores, and other commodities also entered the trade to Europe and the West Indies. Earnings from these exports helped to pay for the import of manufactured goods from England and elsewhere. By 1776, when the thirteen colonies declared their independence from England, their population had reached about two and a half million. Most of the people were farmers, but commerce and trade supported a growing urban population of merchants, artisans, sailors, dockworkers, and others.

By the standards of the day, the new nation was wealthy. Although exact figures are unavailable, historians agree that the wealth of the United States at the time of the Revolution about equalled that of every western European nation save England. In the decades that followed, Americans pushed westward, carving out new states from the lands ceded by England following the Revolution and from lands bought from the French and taken from the Spanish, the Mexicans, and the Indians. As the nation extended its geographic boundaries, it diversified its economy. By the middle of the nineteenth century, the United States had become a major producer of industrial commodities. Agriculture still remained the primary economic sector, providing work for the majority of the population, a market and the raw materials for much of the industrial output, and the nation's leading exports.

By the end of the nineteenth century the United States had become the world's leading industrial nation. Twentieth century Americans could and did boast that they lived in the richest nation on earth. The nation's businessess provided a bewildering array of goods to stores and mail order houses that distributed them to a growing population. And an increasing volume of American industrial and agricultural exports entered world markets.

When economic historians speak of this economic success story they usually use terms such as economic growth and economic development, gross national product (GNP) or national income, and per capita product or income. (National product and national income are measures of different things, but when translated into dollar values they become equivalent terms: everything produced earns income for someone—workers, stockholders, bankers, corporations, etc.) Although economists developed these terms and measures for the twentieth century, economic historians have attempted to gather the necessary data to use them to describe the past. It is important, therefore, to understand their meaning.

Economic growth refers to the increase in the output of the economy. Because output is in the form of a variety of goods and services that cannot be compared and totaled—bushels of corn, tons of steel, patients treated by doctors, etc.—it must be converted into comparable numbers. Economists use dollars to make the conversion. Each good and service is assigned to a dollar value, its market value at the time it was produced. The sum of the values of the economy's output of all goods and services is the gross national product. (Items are counted only once in calculating GNP. For example, the value of automobiles includes the value of the steel used in producing them. The value of the steel that is included in the value of automobiles is excluded from the total steel output so as to avoid double-counting.) When economists compare the GNP for two or more time periods they can determine the amount and the rate of economic growth. The same procedure can be used to compare the economic growth of one area or region with another and one nation with another—the latter comparison, of course, requiring that the value of goods in the two nations be converted into a single currency.

Although valuable for some purposes, this measurement is pretty crude and apt to be misleading. If, for example, the years between the two periods being compared were marked by inflation, the GNP for the second period would be higher than that of the first even if output did not increase. The same amount of goods and services would now have a higher value simply because of price increases. To avoid this problem, economists deflate the second figure by the inflation rate. For example, if prices increased by 10 percent, this 10 percent is subtracted from the GNP in the second period. The result would be a new figure which more accurately measured the real output of goods and services.

Still, the figures remain too crude for certain kinds of measurements. The missing ingredient is population. Suppose, for example, that the GNP (adequately adjusted for inflation or deflation) doubled between period A and period B, but during the same time the population also doubled. Growth would have taken place, but insofar as the people were concerned, little change had occurred. Twice the amount of goods and services now had to be distributed to twice the number of people. To deal with this problem, economists use per capita figures when making comparisons. By dividing the population into the GNP they get a per capita GNP. Comparing per capita GNP's gives a more precise comparison if the relative wealth and the well-being of the population over time is the comparison sought. (Per capita GNP figures clearly reveal what is called the "population problem." A nation may experience an increase in its GNP, but if the growth rate of the population exceeds that of the GNP, the result will be increasing poverty.)

When significant per capita economic growth occurs, economists usually refer to the change as economic *development* rather than simply *growth* because the figures reveal that for some reason or set of reasons, production has become more efficient, that is, the output per person has increased. This increase may result from the discovery and exploitation of new or better resources as, for example, occurs with the movement onto more fertile land allowing farmers using the same techniques to increase their output or with the discovery of oil which increases the value of the output from a parcel of land. Unless additional new or better resources are constantly being discovered and exploited, this source of economic development is apt to be a one-time occurrence without lasting results.

Innovation is another source of economic development. Its most obvious form is technological innovation—new machines that increase the productivity of a worker. Important also, however, is organizational innovation—new methods to organize the production and distribution of goods. Such innovations, when they are widespread and recurring, usually bring structural changes in economic organization, changes in the nature of work, and social changes, as, for example, occurred when production of clothing moved out of the home and into the factory.

Thus, new discoveries and innovations might have very different long-term effects. If the change involves only a small part of the economy, its effects will be slight. But if a discovery or innovation stimulates others which in turn stimulate still others, the effects will be profound. The building of the railroad, for example, created a market for iron, steel, coal, lumber, and tools, thereby stimulating the growth of manufacturing and mining and an increase in employment. The railroad also opened new areas to commercial production which created markets for equipment and consumers goods. Innovations that have this ripple effect (economists term the connections "linkages") will usually bring long term economic development. The long run changes may prove to be beneficial, but often their immediate effect will be extremely disruptive, producing structural unemployment and bankruptcies in some areas as the economy adjusts to the changes.

When economic historians gather the necessary figures they can provide concrete data to describe America's economic success story. At the same time, however, there is much that these figures do not reveal. Per capita income figures provide no information about the *distribution* of income, and therefore high per capita income figures may hide the existence of poverty among sections of the population. Nor do the figures provide information about the costs of economic development in the form of such things as polluted air and water, repetitious, meaningless work, over-crowded cities, and added health hazards to workers and consumers—to name but a few. And finally, although the figures show *what* happened, they can at best only suggest *why* it happened.

Economic historians must be able to show the record of economic change, but they must also seek to explain why that change occurred. At first glance, the task seems easy enough. Machines replace hand labor which increases output or the railroad replaces wagons which lowers transportation costs or the assembly line replaces stationary work stations which speeds assembly time. But such explanations usually prove inadequate because they are incomplete. Usually many innovations take place simultaneously, and therefore the historian faces the task of explaining the relative importance of each. Furthermore, innovations are usually inter-related and interdependent. The trucking industry, highway construction, and the businesses providing fuel, repairs, and other services cannot be viewed in isolation from one another or apart from the extent of the demand for over-the-road transportation facilities.

But explaining the cause and effect and mutual interaction, difficult as it often is, is only part of the historian's task. To an American living in the late twentieth century, it may appear obvious that if a new machine is developed which cuts labor costs and increases output that new machine will be purchased and used by a manufacturer. Let us examine some of the assumptions implicit in our finding it obvious that the new machine will be used.

One set of assumptions concerns the costs involved. We assume that the new machine will produce savings that exceed the cost of the machine. The machine's cost will include more than its purchase price; maintenance and training costs must also be counted. If the new machine requires that workers using it have extensive training or if maintenance and repair of the new machine requires the expansion of maintenance facilities including training maintenance workers and purchasing maintenance supplies and equipment, the real cost of the new machine increases, perhaps far beyond its purchase price. If the new machine replaces an old one, then the cost of the new must include the loss involved in scrapping the old. Other possible new costs might include costs of reorganizing the shop to accommodate the new machine, of providing new power sources that might be needed, or changing other equipment and procedures so that the new machine fits into the flow of production. The list could easily be extended, but the point should be clear: when we assume that the new machine will be introduced we assume that the costs of introduction will not exceed the benefits. But we make another cost assumption as well. We assume that a manufacturer can afford to introduce the new machine. Even if the long-term benefits exceed the costs, the manufacturer may lack the funds or the credit needed to buy the machine.

Another set of assumptions concerns the market. We assume the existence of competition which impels a manufacturer to introduce a cost cutting machine in order to get an edge on his competition. If producers have arranged a cartel or some other form of agreement dividing the market and thereby avoiding competition or if the producer has a monopoly, especially one with government support, the inducement to introduce the new machine will be diminished. Another assumption about the market is that there will be a demand for the increased output from the new machine. If the demand for the commodity being produced is saturated, increased production might merely create a surplus that drives prices down and destroys the advantages of the new machine. And finally, we assume the existence of an adequate supply of machines, replacement parts, power, and raw materials.

These assumptions about the costs and the market may appear to be purely economic in nature, but they are only partly so because they really rest upon other assumptions that are political, social, and psychological. Or, to put the matter in a different way, they are based upon assumptions concerning human behavior. Ultimately understanding this behavior becomes the most difficult task faced by the economic historian seeking to explain economic development—or the lack of development.

People raised in the twentieth century United States take certain behavior patterns for granted. Because we share so many perceptions, expectations, and attitudes we behave in fairly predictable ways. We know what is expected of us as workers, employers, landlords, tenants, students, teachers, consumers, and voters—and we act accordingly. We respond to certain kinds of market signals by buying, selling, investing, and saving in response to price, advertising, fad and fashion, interest rates, retirement goals, and the like. Of course our actions are not completely predictable and different people will respond in different ways to various market signals. But most of the variation occurs within a rather narrow range, making the behavior socially acceptable and reasonably predictable. Those whose actions transcend the boundaries of acceptable behavior are deemed odd or dangerous and are punished by ridicule, ostracism, or by the force of the law, depending upon the nature of their deviant behavior.

In brief, most Americans have what some have called a "modern" (in contrast to a "traditional") outlook or what others have termed a "bourgeois ideology." Our behavior is fairly predictable because we share this ideology, that is, because we interpret the world in which we live in similar ways. Because so much of this behavior is automatic we consider it natural rather than learned. But in fact, of course, it is learned from our parents, our peers, our teachers and from what we read and see about us as we grow up—in short, from what the sociologists call the "socialization process." Consider how much of our early training and schooling is concerned with teaching characteristics such as promptness, reliability, individualism, and self reliance, and how early we learn the difference between mine and thine, a difference that gradually becomes enshrined as the idea of private property and the rights and privileges associated with it. We learn to be consumers by having our wants stimulated by enticing advertising and store displays and by seeing the possessions of the people in the books used to teach us to read.

People born and raised in other societies or in other times learn to behave in different ways because they are socialized in different cultures with different ideologies. Behavior which seems natural to us may look odd, deviant, even illegal to such people.

When the socialization process is described in this way the world appears static. There seems to be little room for substantial change. If everyone is brought up to learn to live within the society in which he or she is born, how does change occur? We may expect that in any given society at any given time certain individuals will not behave according to the social norms. But in some instances such people are scorned or ignored or even destroyed, while in other places they gain support and begin the process of change. How can the difference be explained?

More specifically, why did England in the eighteenth century and the United States in the nineteenth century become modernized, industrialized, and thoroughly bourgeois while Spain and China did not? We can point to inventions such as the steam engine, to improved transportation facilities such as canals and railroads, to improvements in the organization of production such as the factory system, and to the development of necessary credit facilities such as banks. These and other changes promoted rapid economic development in England and the United States. Their absence in other countries hindered development.

But the historian must confront the problem of explaining why these development producing institutions arose in England and the United States and not in Spain and China. The complexity of the problem becomes evident when we notice that latecomers to the development process could benefit from the example of others that came earlier, as indeed they often do. But not always. If Japan and Germany entered the development process, many of their neighbors did not. Today, many of the leaders of undeveloped or less developed nations are eager to move their countries onto the path of economic development (or, at least, they say they are) but find the task very difficult.

Obviously there is no easy answer to this problem. If there were, it would not be a problem because people in less developed nations would simply adopt the methods used in the successful nations and thereby achieve the economic development and the wealth they seek. Instead, some seem to cling to older, traditional ways of doing things while others seem to discard growth inhibiting traditions with relative ease. The problem is not one of individual psychology or even national character, although both of these are involved; nor are traditional ways merely the product of habit or inertia. They are grounded in political, social, and economic relations in which certain groups or classes reap benefits in the form of wealth, power, and status. Therefore, discarding traditional ways means discarding the traditional social organization and altering class relations. This makes the change truly revolutionary and it is often marked by violent and bloody upheavals. The change, in short, is political as well as economic, and its success or failure depends upon the relative strengths of those opposing and those favoring change.

Economic historians cannot provide nations seeking economic development with a simple, easily followed success formula. Such a formula might have to include the suggestion that the traditional ruling class commit suicide, a bit of advice that is unlikely to be followed. But this need not concern us. Historians are not policy makers, although we would like to believe that our investigations may prove valuable to those who make or influence policy.

By investigating the history of a country that achieved rapid economic development, historians can gain insight into the process that might be of value to policy makers, but will certainly help to advance our understanding of the past. A meaningful study requires that historians look beyond the bare bones of economics and investigate the cultural and social traditions of the people. Only then is it possible to understand why the same or similar kinds of economic pressures, problems, and opportunities often elicit quite different responses among different peoples.

Meyer Weinberg's massive documentary history provides some of the raw material needed for such an investigation. Through the documents the reader may see how Americans perceived the world in which they lived and learn something about how and why these perceptions changed over time. To appreciate these changing perceptions the reader must view the documents from the perspective of the time in which they were written. How did the authors of the documents view their world? What interpretation did they give to events and why did they respond as they did to the opportunities and problems the; faced? Modern readers, of course, have the benefit of hindsight; they know the future which the authors of the documents could not know. This provides insights into the direction thoughts and perceptions were moving, but it can also be misleading because it may suggest a reading which those who lived then could neither understand nor accept.

Although we know that the beginnings of the United States date from the early seventeenth century, we often forget the significance of this fact. Jamestown was named for King James I, the colony for the virgin queen Elizabeth I, who died in 1603. The early settlers therefore had grown up in late Elizabethan England; they were products of the English Renaissance. England was already undergoing massive social and economic changes associated with developing commerce, some industrialization, and the modernization of agriculture—all of which affected the outlook of portions of the population. Nevertheless, culture and politics remained medieval. The resulting tensions culminated in civil war in the mid-seventeenth century and in a bloodless "Glorious Revolution" in 1688-1689, which propelled England into the modern age. Those who embarked for the colonies during these years brought with them the experiences and the ideas associated with these events. Those who had arrived earlier closely followed changes in England, and these changes in the mother country therefore affected colonial ideology and institutions.

It is essential that the documents in Part I be read with this context in mind. It is also important to remember that the authors of the documents were responding to particular problems and opportunities they faced in the New World where traditional ways and the institutions that supported them had never been fully established and where change therefore faced less opposition and came easier.

The first document, an extract from John Winthrop's *Journal*, will illustrate my point. Note the explicit acceptance of the social hierarchy in Winthrop's description of the election of a committee to decide on the division of lands. He complains that the electors passed over the "chief men" and selected a majority of the "inferior sort." It is significant that this important decision was to be made by an elected committee which could include the inferior sort. This process could not have occurred in the England Winthrop and his fellow colonists has recently left because the distribution of land in England would require the expropriation of the land owners. Moreover, in England, the inferior sort had little voice in any major decisions, even those that might profoundly affect their lives and well-being.

Winthrop claims he was not personally offended by not being selected—which was probably not true—but, he says, other "chief men" were upset. The minister, John Cotton, seems to have convinced the people that it was God's will that the chief men not be bypassed, because Winthrop reports that after Cotton spoke to the people they agreed to a new election. Clearly the "inferior sort" were pressing for an increased voice in decisions, although their deference to older traditions led them to back down when pressed to do so. Winthrop explains the source of their concern: they feared "that the richer men would give the poorer sort no great proportions of land." Land was the major source of wealth and the basis for political power in England, and therefore it is not surprising that the inferior sort would seek to increase their landholdings and would fear that the elite might not support their efforts. Winthrop, whose views concerning social structure and the importance of the popular will seem very undemocratic, argues for a land distribution system that seems to be very democratic. He says that he and the other magistrates deemed it unwise to allow people to own more land than they could profitably use. Instead, vacant land should be held for distribution to later immigrants.

Placing the documents in the proper context so that they can be fully understood both for what they reveal about the outlook of their authors as well as about trends in economic and social change is difficult for those who are not experts in the periods and problems involved. But Weinberg provides invaluable aids for readers without that expertise. After each document he gives the source from which the document was extracted. In most cases the sources are published, and therefore interested readers may find the full document and others relating to it in any good library. In addition, the "Bibliography" provides at least one article or book, but usually several, for each of the 785 documents. These are scholarly books and articles by modern experts; they will lead readers into the issues being considered in the document, provide the necessary historical background, and in many cases, introduce some of the controversies among historians concerning the significance of the events and issues discussed.

I suspect that few readers will start at the beginning and read through this massive collection. Most will seek out certain problems or issues to pursue over time. Weinberg has organized his collection to facilitate this approach. He has divided each chronological part into sections containing documents relating to a particular sector of the economy or particular problems or social relations. This allows readers to skip from part to part in order to follow a specific matter over a long time span. For example, readers interested in the problem of the relationship between government and the economy may easily follow this matter through the documents printed in the appropriate sections of each of the four time periods in which the collection is divided. Many documents fit in more than one category and therefore some documents relevant to a particular problem may be found in other sections. Thus, documents concerning the conflict over the Second Bank of the United States are relevant both to government-business relations and to finance. Weinberg has chosen to place them in the section on finance. Readers will have no difficulties finding the documents they seek if they consult the detailed table of contents and the comprehensive index.

The documents concerning government-business relations, supplemented, when necessary, with items from the bibliography, will provide readers with valuable insights into the sources of that peculiar and often contradictory attitude Americans have towards government in a private enterprise economy. One conclusion will become immediately obvious. Despite all the talk about laissez-faire and despite all the complaints about government interference, government has played a significant part in the economy throughout our history. Where Western Europeans often distrusted and feared government, Americans usually looked to government to solve problems. An interesting and revealing manifestation of this difference is the contrasting meaning given to the word "liberal." In the United States, a liberal advocates increased government involvement in economic affairs, but in Western Europe a liberal is one who opposes government intervention in the economy. Liberalism arose in Europe in opposition to the remnants of mercantilism with its government sanctioned special privileges and monopolies; the liberal slogan was "laissez-faire."

Americans also opposed government-sanctioned special privileges (see, for example, documents 238, 239, and 241) but the opposition was not to government interference as such, but rather to monopoly which imposed unfair exactions on the common people. The bank, not the government, was the menace; indeed, the government in the capable hands of Andrew Jackson, could solve the problem. Later, reformers looked to the government to control big business, insure full employment, and in general keep the economy functioning. These views did not (and do not) prevent Americans from complaining about government interference. But the complaints, although often expressed in general terms condemning big government, are usually directed towards particular government actions that seem troublesome, expensive, or unneeded by particular groups.

I have presented only a few brief examples to illustrate how this collection, along with its splendid organizational and bibliographic aids, will be of value to general readers and students interested in American economic history. Teachers can send their students to particular documents or to particular themes in the documents to illustrate concepts covered in texts and lectures and to give students the experience of reading the evaluating contemporary documents. The collection provides endless subjects for term papers along with the bibliographic guides to help students get started.

But the collection can also help the advanced student researcher and even the professional historian. Of course, no collection of documents, even one as extensive as this one, can replace archival research for the serious historian. The documents Weinberg has chosen to reprint reflect his views about what is significant, and, although his views are well informed, others may not share them. Nevertheless, the historian embarking upon an investigation of an aspect of one of the many problems in American economic history and students of comparative economic development will find this collection with its bibliography and ample index a useful starting point for their investigations.

Meyer Weinberg is to be commended for his enormous effort in preparing this collection.

PREFACE

This work is a first-hand view of American economic history. The view is achieved by reproducing the texts of 785 significant primary historical sources. Virtually every source in the collection has met the following tests: (1) it is an eyewitness account; (2) it is recounted by an especially qualified contemporary observer, usually the actor himself; (3) it is representative of countless like events; (4) in the case of an invention, it is a statement by the inventor or by an early user of the invention; (5) in the case of government policy, it is a statement by a responsible official involved in that area of policy; and (6) it illuminates an important aspect of American economic history.

Broadly, the work is divided into two volumes. The first volume consists of three parts: I—Colonial history to 1815 (137 pages); II—1815 to 1860 (196 pages); and III—1860 to 1900 (230 pages). The second volume has one part: IV—Post 1900 (451 pages). Each source is introduced with a summary statement giving something of the historical setting of the source. Individuals mentioned in the source as well as the author of it are identified. Within each section, sources are arranged around nine different themes: Land, Agriculture, Commerce, Labor, Manufacturing, Foreign Trade, Government, Money and Banking, and Industrial Research. The applicability of these themes varies, of course, from period to period. Sub-themes are treated as parts of the major themes. Through explicit cross-references as well as entries in a detailed index, the reader's attention is called to related material appearing in more than one period.

The economic historian is heir to a superb series of sources simply because of the relative lack of division of labor in early American life. During the years 1789-1825, a man who was President or Vice-President or Secretary of State might also have been an operator of a nailery, or a tobacco planter, or a wholesale merchant, or a slave-owner—and if his name was Thomas Jefferson, he was all these. The sources are drawn from a wide variety of places. With respect to selected letters by George Washington, Benjamin Franklin, Thomas Jefferson, Alexander Hamilton, and James Madison, I have utilized microfilms of the originals in the Division of Manuscripts, Library of Congress. If, after inspection, I found the early or earliest printed version of the letter to be accurate, credit was given to the printed work. If, however, I found a significant discrepancy between the original and the printed version, a footnote reference is made to the manuscript collection only.

I have tried to present to the reader a broad sampling of various types of printed primary sources. For the colonial period, for example, extracts are reproduced from proceedings of Parliamentary committees and from Royal instructions to colonial governors. Letters are a rich source of knowledge about economic processes and events. Diaries and autobiographies reveal much. After 1865, transcripts of Congressional and other federal inquiries start to become valuable, though these come into their own only after 1900. Engineering and technical journals contain extensive contemporary materials.

Researchers in American economic history have become familiar with certain standard primary sources. Neither students nor general readers, however, consult these sources. I have reproduced extracts from a number both for their own value and as a guide for the interested reader. These include: the McLane Report on manufactures (1833); the Pujo investigation of high finance (1913); the Armstrong investigation of life insurance (1906); the Collom report on regulation of railroads (1885); the Ku Klux Klan hearings (1871-1872); the Industrial Commission hearings (1899-1901); the Industrial Relations Study (1914); the Public Lands Report (1880); the earliest dependable study of foreign investment in the United States (1853); and many more. I have also used the relevant correspondence and writings of several leading statesmen; these include John Quincy Adams (*Memoirs* and *Writings*), Sam Houston, Stephen F. Austin, John Calhoun, William Seward, Rufus King, and Henry Clay in addition to those mentioned earlier. Nowadays, when a certain degree of economic ignorance has become part of the qualification for high governmental office, the contemporary reader may be startled at the detailed knowledge of economic affairs demonstrated by these and other politicians of earlier years.

The class coloring of historical documentation has long been known. Written documents are the product of literate persons, yet, economic history is made by illiterate persons as well. I have been pleased to find authoritative narratives by slaves, shoemakers, dirt farmers, railroad brakemen, and sheep shearers. More numerous are accounts by organizers of small and large corporations, cotton and tobacco planters, factory managers, and importers.

I have tried to emphasize connections between economic and general history. This is done by placing the document in a broader setting so as to establish clearly its connection with larger trends and developments. Sometimes this has required a comment on the political context of the document or pointing out an interconnection between the industry at issue and other ones. Thus, the volumes contain materials relating to the history of corporate law, the politics of slavery, the economics of literature, and diplomacy of territorial expansion. I have treated technology as a fundamental dimension of economic history.

The bibliography, arranged by source number, lists from one to five secondary works for each of the 785 sources. In addition to book-length studies, a special effort was made to locate articles in leading research journals covering the fields of interest in this work.

The "old" economic history, which held forth until a generation ago, had little room for individuals. More an extension of the narrative style characteristic of political and social history, it stressed large-scale institutional change. Long-term trends in basic divisions of the subject occupied most of the space and some well-known leaders were cited occasionally to illustrate a generalization. The "new" economic history, heavily dependent on econometrics, was severely analytical and mined the past for its relevance to economic theory. It outstripped its predecessor in attending to long-term changes and often supplied theoretical explanations of the dynamic of these developments. But whatever its accomplishments, it was even less hospitable to the individual than the old economic history.

The present work presents the broad sweep of American economic history as delineated by individuals located along various axes of historical development. An account does not automatically become authoritative simply because its author was an eye-witness to an event, yet the historian's proverbial dependence on such accounts, properly sifted, remains well-taken. What, then, are the advantages of a first-hand view of American, or for that matter, any economic history?

First, an awareness of authenticity is heightened. An immediacy is created that few narratives can match. The reader shares with the first-hand source a common experience of an emotion that makes the subject matter far more than a past fact. Second, historical events can all the more readily be viewed in their human dimension. The result is not so much to reduce economic history to individual action as to place economic history in a human context. The play of motives, personal interest, prejudices, and personal insight sheds light on the historical character of the subject matter at hand. Third, first-hand accounts often are insightful. To be sure, while the inventor may well be the best authority on his or her creation, this does not always hold true. Nevertheless, it is especially enlightening to read the analysis of Eli Whitney of the cotton gin or of the Rust brothers of their mechanical cotton picker. Jefferson's directions to Lewis and Clark on the eve of their pioneering journey throw a unique light on the commerical situation of the United States at the outset of the nineteenth century. Simon Ramo's analysis of the contemporary corporate merger movement gains something special from his own background in high corporate affairs. Fourth, clashes of policies and interpretations are graphically present in the first-hand accounts. The present work is not designed as a debate handbook, nor has there been an effort to edit into the work a homogeneous viewpoint. A very wide variety of interpretations can be found herein. The first concern has been whether a given account presents a uniquely valuable view of its subject matter. Inevitably, different viewpoints are expressed.

During the past generation of the ascendancy of the new, econometric history, research in the primary sources of American economic history has suffered a set-back. Accordingly, another purpose of this work is to direct the attention of students and researchers to promising sources that may be unknown to them.

I wish to thank the Manuscript Division of the Library of Congress for its cooperation. The libraries of the University of Chicago and the University of Massachusetts, Amherst, opened their holdings to me without complaint or grimace. Betty Craker, my secretary, typed a long and complex manuscript with care and intelligence. During the summer of 1982, Josephine Ryan helped prepare the final manuscript for typing and assisted with permissions. An anonymous publisher's reader made many excellent suggestions, most of which were incorporated within the final draft. Aiding in the making of the index were Dan Weinberg, Ben Weinberg, Sue Simmons, David Spencer, Steve Gilson, and Maureen McAnnery. To all these persons I express my gratitude and relief.

PART IV

A MATURE ECONOMY, POST 1900

A.

RESOURCE USE AND
CONSERVATION

---

494. OVERCAPITALIZATION AND WASTE IN MINING (1904)

A candid analysis by a person familiar with the
technical and financial ends of mining. He was James
Douglas, a former president of the American Institute
of Mining Engineers; also, president of a copper-mining
company affiliated with Phelps-Dodge and Company.

Only some 60 per cent of the hundreds of millions which the
Comstock lode yielded was recovered at the time, and yet at first
those enormously rich tailings were not even collected--such was
the haste of the miner to empty that stupendous deposit, which
should have made Nevada prosperous for generations instead of
whirling the whole country into a mad dance of reckless speculation.
And at Anaconda there are said to be tailings by the millions of
tons which will run from 2 to 2 1/2 per cent of copper, made when
a large production rather than minute economies was the order of
the day. The values locked up in our Arizona slags, in the Comstock
slimes, in the Anaconda tailings, all represent a large waste and
heavy loss, even though they may be in part recovered by subsequent
treatment.

Who or what is responsible? Primarily the company system and
the heavy capitalization of our large mines, involving a large output at any expense, if the value of the shares is to be raised or
their price maintained at the financial centers. Overcapitalization
generally demands overproduction, and overproduction almost inevitably involves waste at some stage of the metal's progress from the
mine to the consumer.

The company system and the company managers may be greater
sinners than ourselves [engineers], for they set the pace, and we
must maintain it. At the same time the management at the eastern
end is generally composed of able and honest business men, whose
ignorance of technical details obliges them to rely upon their
technical advisers, and the more worthy the members of the technical
staff are, the more implicit will be the confidence imposed in them,
and, therefore, their influence. On us, therefore, ultimately rests
the responsibility in great measure of correcting the evils of waste
to which I have drawn your attention. For, depend upon it, if from
no higher motive, you will find the eastern management willing
enough to spend money in order to save money, and there is always
money saved in avoiding waste. But apart from this sordid view of
the subject, it will elevate your whole conception of the dignity
of your profession and your work, if you regard yourselves, which
indeed you should be, as the preservers of the gifts with which a
beneficent Providence has stored our world, for next to being a
creator, the highest function a man can attain to is being a saver--
a savior.

James Douglas, address at Michigan College School of Mines,
April 22, 1904, Untechnical Addresses on Technical Subjects,
(New York: Wiley, 1904), pp. 82-84.

495. IRON ORE ON THE GREAT LAKES (1907)

In 1890 the United States became the world's largest
iron producer. Development of Great Lakes transportation
was the key to this leadership. (For an earlier way of unloading iron ore at Cleveland, see Source No. 321.)

From the mines ore is hauled by rail to five Lake ports--
Duluth-Superior, Two Harbors, Ashland, Marquette, and Escanaba--the
rail distance varying from 12 to 90 miles. The nearest of these
shipping ports is about 550 miles by lake from Cleveland, one of
the principal centers of distribution to the furnaces, and the most
distant of them 300 miles farther away.
By reason of improved canal facilities, deepened channels, and
perfected mechanical devices for loading and unloading cargo, transportation cost has been reduced on these great waterways to a point
probably below that reached for a similar service in any other part
of the world. So completely has machinery replaced manual labor
that ore from some mines is practically never touched by the ordinary hand shovel until it reaches its destination. The ore is dug
and loaded into gondola cars by means of steam scoops, automatically
dumped into hopper-like containers, run into the holds of vessels,
and transported to the southern shores of lakes Erie and Michigan.

There the ore is unloaded from vessels by mechanical devices, for
use at Lake ports or for distribution by rail to inland furnaces.
This highly organized system of handling and transporting ore has
been an exceedingly important factor in influencing the growth of
Lake shipments. Its present state of efficiency seems the more
remarkable when compared with transportation methods of less than
sixty years ago. It is made possible by the enormous localized
supply, deep and open water routes, and a large concentrated demand.

Report of the Commissioner of Corporations on Transportation by
by Water in the United States, Part II, pp. 152-153.

496. PROFIT FROM STUMPAGE (1908)

Stumpage--i.e., timbered land--enjoyed the usual
advantages of real estate in a populating country.
That is, it rose continually in value. James Lacey,
who testifies, was a well-known "lumber baron." He had
bought and sold stumpage in every major timber area in
the country.

Mr. CLARK. It does not make any difference what happens, the
stumpage man either holds to what he has or gets more; the stumpage
always goes up?
Mr. LACEY. It will continue to go up.
Mr. CLARK. Nothing on earth makes them lose?
Mr. LACEY. No, sir.
Mr. CLARK. Everybody else may lose in the lumber business, but
the stumpage man makes his profit?
Mr. LACEY. Well, so far as the manufacturer of lumber is concerned, I do not think there is a lumber man in this room that can
show that he has ever made much profit on the strict manufacture of
lumber; he has made his money in buying low-priced stumpage and
holding until changed conditions of some kind advance it to a manufacturing profit.
. . . .
Mr. CLARK. Then, nothing in the world, no matter what happens
--earthquakes, or cyclones, or what--will keep them from making a
profit; they simply go on and make their profit?
Mr. LACEY. They make their profit up to a certain point, and
then it will stop, as cost of lumber approaches cost of brick,
cement, and iron construction.
Mr. CLARK. As a matter of fact, did they buy a million and a
half acres of land at about $6 an acre?
Mr. LACEY. I didn't know what the exact figures were. At the
time they were buying that at $6 an acre we were buying land on
the coast at about the same price.

Mr. CLARK. Was there not a great row about that whole thing being turned over to the Weyerhaeuser Company?

Mr. LACEY. I have never heard so.

Mr. CLARK. Did they not talk about investigating it, as a matter of fraud?

Mr. LACEY. About a million acres, I understand, belonged to the Northern Pacific, and they sold it to Weyerhaeuser.

Mr. CLARK. They got it at $6 or $7 an acre, did they not?

Mr. LACEY. Probably somewhere in that neighborhood; yes, sir; although I do not know exactly what they paid for it.

Mr. CLARK. Well, how much is that land worth now?

Mr. LACEY. It is worth probably an average of $50 an acre.

Mr. CLARK. That is a right steep profit in that length of time, is it not?

Mr. LACEY. Yes, sir.

Testimony, James D. Lacey, November 20, 1908, U.S. Congress, 60th, 2nd session, House of Representatives, Committee on Ways and Means, Document No. 1505, serial number 5551, Tariff Hearings, III, pp. 3023-3024.

497. THE BOSS TIMBER FALLER ON THE COLUMBIA (1910)

There really is not a great difference between the tall tales and the true stories of the lumber heroes. Oliver Hughson, who sold oil and paint to lumber camps on his route along the lower Columbia River, writes the following account.

No man in an early-day Columbia River logging crew was paid higher wages than the faller, for no other functionary could be any possibility waste or save more for his employer. The lay of the land, direction of wind, second growth available for buffers, all and much more were in the faller's trick bag....I had opportunity to see these skilled operators at their work. To fall a yellow fir seventy inches at the butt on rough ground and not break a log or two called for exceedingly highgrade skill.

. . . .

I went along with this giant [Tom Patton, Black] to see how he operated to gain and hold his proud title of the "Boss Faller of the Columbia." "Is it true," I asked him as we made our way into a forest of 250-foot firs, "that you can fall any one of those trees just as you wish?" As he laid his falling wedges, ax and seven-foot falling saw at the foot of a giant, he grinned and said: "When I get this tree lined up you lay your hat (I was wearing a new derby) where I tell you and we'll see how near I can come to hitting it." All suspicious of his great skill, I marched out and laid my

hat exactly as he directed. In an incredibly short while he had
undercut the tree with his keen saw and wedges and toppled it to a
crashing fall. I picked the shattered scraps of my beautiful derby
from among the topmost branches and made for the boat landing. I
can hear yet the echoes among those trees of his uproarious laughter
as bareheaded, I ducked out. I learned how he came by his reputation of Boss Faller, at the cost of a $4.00 derby. It lay in his
skill and selection of buffer or cushion trees against which he
threw the big one, and at the cost of whole trees, the logs from
which would look well on modern logging trucks, he with great
judgment, eased the fall.

Oliver S. Hughson, "When We Logged the Columbia," Oregon
Historical Quarterly, LX (June, 1959), pp. 191-192.

498. CONCENTRATION OF TIMBER OWNERSHIP (1913)

        Concentration of timber ownership characterized
        every timber frontier in our history.

        Three vast holdings alone, the greatest in the country, those
of the Southern Pacific Company, the Weyerhaeuser Timber Company,
and the Northern Pacific Railway Company (including their subsidiary
companies) together have 238 billion feet, or nearly 11 per cent of
all our privately owned timber. They have 14 per cent of that in
the "investigation area." With the five next largest they have
over 15 per cent of the total privately owned timber and over 19
per cent of that within the investigation area. Finally, nearly
one-half (48 per cent) of the private timber in that area is held
by only 195 great holders. The term "holder" covers any single
interest--individual, corporate, or group--which is so united as
to be under one control.
        The Pacific-Northwest.--Five-elevenths of the country's pri-
vately owned standing timber is in the Pacific-Northwest (California, Oregon, Washington, Idaho, and Montana), 1,013 billion feet.
One-half of this is now owned by 37 holders; many of these are
closely connected. The three largest holders (named above) alone
have nearly one-quarter. This section now furnishes only one-sixth
of the annual cut. Thus its timber is being largely held for the
future, and the large owners there will then be the dominating
influence in the industry.
        The Southern Pacific Company holding is the greatest in the
United States--106 billion feet. This is about 6 per cent of the
private timber in the investigation area, and 10 per cent of that
in the Pacific-Northwest. It is difficult to give an adequate idea
of its immensity. It stretches practically 680 miles along that
railroad between Portland and Sacramento. The fastest train over

this distance takes 31 hours. During all that time the traveler
thereon is passing through lands a large proportion of which for
30 miles on each side belongs to the railroad, and in almost the
entire strip this corporation is the dominating owner of both timber
and land.
     The second largest holder is the Weyerhaeuser Timber Company
(including its subsidiary companies), with 96 billion feet. This
does not include further very extensive timber interests of the
Weyerhaeuser family and close associates.
     These two holdings would supply the 46,584 sawmills in the
country for four and half years. They have one-eleventh of our
total private timber.
     The third largest, the Northern Pacific Railway Company, has
36 billion feet.
     These three holdings have enough standing timber to build an
ordinary five or six room frame house for each of the 16,000,000
families in the United States in 1900. If sawed into lumber and
placed in care, their timber would load a train about 100,000 miles
long.
     The holdings of the two railroad companies are Government
grants, and 80 per cent of the Weyerhaeuser Timber Company holding
was bought from the Northern Pacific grant. Many other holdings
(here and in other regions) were mainly pruchased from some land
grant.
     Southern Pine Region.--In the Southern Pine Region there are
634 billion feet of privately owned timber. Concentration in total
timber is much less than in the Pacific-Northwest. There is, however, a high concentration in the more valuable species, longleaf
yellow pine and cypress. Sixty-seven holders own 39 per cent
of the longleaf yellow pine, 29 per cent of the cypress, 19 per
cent of the shortleaf and loblolly pine, and 11 per cent of the
hardwoods.
     The Lake States.--In Minnesota, Wisconsin, and Michigan there
are 100 billion feet of privately owned timber. In Wisconsin 96
holders have three-fourths of all the timber. In Michigan 110
holders have 66 per cent. In Minnesota 6 holders have 54 per cent
of the very valuable white and Norway pine, 16 per cent of the
other conifers, and 2 per cent of the hardwoods. Taking all three
States, 215 holders have 65 per cent of all the timber.

     U.S. Department of Commerce and Labor, Bureau of Corporations,
The Lumber Industry, Part 1, (Washington, D.C.: Government Printing
Office, 1913), pp. xx-xxi.

     499. REGULATE SALMON FISHING ON THE COLUMBIA (1914)

     The salmon industry became important on the Columbia
soon after the Civil War. Packers first paid high prices
to the fishermen but after the first flush years, packers

were able to lower prices. (During 1959-1961, the
Washington canned salmon pack averaged 330,000 cases
per year. This was about one-tenth the Alaska pack.)
This is the testimony of H. M. Lorntsen, secretary of
both the Columbia Fishermen's Union and the Columbia
River Protection Union.

It is a fact that the Columbia River is the only stream that
the salmon protection is along the line of destruction. We have
passed laws and laws time and time again for the protection of
salmon. But there is never any protection at all. It is only protection for a few men so that they will be able to gobble up all
the fish. That ought to be regulated.

I know the Federal Government has done that in Alaska or
wherever they have any authority; they won't allow any fishing above
tidewater. In fact, fishing above tidewater and stationary fishing
appliances in the rivers has been abolished everywhere where they
are doing anything for salmon protection. But not so on the Columbia River, because there is a few men up there, who are getting rich
on the ruination of the industry, and are not going to give it up
as long as they can make money, regardless of the rest. There is
absolutely no reason why the Columbia River should not yield at
least 600,000 cases of first-class salmon. They do not yield
300,000 now. It is an inferior grade, something that the canneries
would not have looked at when I first came here on the river.

. . . .

I know this much, if we had the proper laws for the Columbia
River, the protection of the Columbia River salmon, there would be
no fishing above tide water; there would be no stationary fishing
appliances at all. If we got that it would be only five or six
years until the Columbia River would yield double the amount of
fish it is now. That is proven by the laws that was enacted for
the coast streams in 1901, and that shows conclusively what common
sense laws and regulations will do.

In 1901 the law was enacted to take away the stationary fishing
appliances and fishing above certain lines in the coast streams
of Oregon, and the Columbia River was included in that. But during
the juggling, and so on, the Columbia River was exempted after it
was passed.

In 1901 the total catch of coast stream salmon was less than
700,000, and less than 3,000,000 pounds silver sides. The law was
enacted in that session, and in February, in 1906, the salmon catch
in the coast streams increased to 3,019,000 pounds silver sides.
They couldn't say that this was the result of the hatcheries, although they are commencing the hatcheries too early to have the
result. It was simply common-sense laws, and the salmons had an
opportunity to go take care of themselves, and you can't beat
nature. I know that they have some bastard breeds of salmon in
the Columbia River now. They get in the hatchery and they mix them

up regardless of whether good or what. That is one reason that we
had such a poor salmon river last year, the poorest since I have
been on the river.

    Testimony, H. M. Lorntsen, August 21, 1914, U.S. Congress,
64th, 1st session, Senate, Document No. 415, Final Report and
Testimony Submitted to Congress by the Commission on Industrial
Relations, V, pp. 4641, 4642.

        500. TIMBER DEPLETION AND CONCENTRATION (1920)

        The first great wave of conservation sentiment had
    passed but the basic problem of depletion and concentra-
    tion remained untouched. The outstanding facts reported
    by the Forest Service are included here. E. T. Meredith,
    the Secretary of Agriculture, writes in a volume by the
    Assistant Forester, Earle H. Clapp.

        (1) That three fifths of the original timber of the United
States is gone and that we are using timber four times as fast as
we are growing it. The forests remaining are so localized as
greatly to reduce their national utility....
        (2) That the depletion of timber is not the sole cause of the
recent high prices of forest products, but it is an important contributing cause whose effects will increase steadily as depletion
continues.
        (3) That the fundamental problem is to increase the production
of timber by stopping forest devastation....
. . . .
    The concentration of timber ownership has not changed mater-
ially since the exhaustive report made upon this subject by the
Bureau of Corporations in 1910 [See Source No. 543]. One-half of
the privately owned timber in the United States is held by approximately 250 large owners, the ownership of the remaining timber
being very widely distributed. The tendency toward the acquisition
and speculative holding of timber beyond operating requirements has
been checked, and the present tendency is toward the manufacture
of large timber holdings. At the same time the lumber industry,
particularly in the Western States, is going through a partial
reorganization into larger operating and marketing groups. In this
there is a tendency for small mills to disappear and small timber
holdings to be blocked into larger ones adapted to extensive lumber
manufacture. Where there is still a large number of individual

timber owners and of sawmills operating as separate units, the
larger interests are acquiring a more dominant place in lumber
manufacture in the West.

E. T. Meredith, June 1, 1920, in Earle H. Clapp, Timber
Depletion, Lumber Prices, Lumber Exports, and Concentration of
Timber Ownership, (Washington, D.C.: Government Printing Office,
1920), pp. 3, 4.

501. A CAPSULE HISTORY OF THE IRON RANGE
COUNTRY (1912-1959)

In a capsule, it was a repetition of the descent
from boom town to ghost town. George Selke, Commissioner of the Minnesota State Department of Conservation,
explains.

My first general contact with the northeastern Minnesota and
particularly with the iron range country began in the spring of
1912. That is now nearly 50 years ago. Since that time I have
visited practically every community in the region that comprises
the so-called arrowhead country, which includes the Eighth Congressional District, the Vermillion, Mesabi, and Cuyuna iron ranges,
and the forested countries of northern Minnesota.

In 1912 the timber industry was just over its peak but still
flourishing; new iron mines were being put into operation, and new
villages and cities were springing into existence. Many also were
lured to the land, having been led to believe that only the clearing of the forest would be necessary to make the area an agricultural paradise. Northeastern Minnesota was a flourishing place with
abundant opportunities for employment. In the summers there were
the mines and the sawmills, and for those who wished to work for
themselves the development of tillable fields or forage producing
meadows, through the clearing of brush, trees, and, in too many
cases, available in the lumber camps. So great was the demand for
labor that people across the seas were encouraged to come to this
wonderful land that they believed promised hope for them and their
children. These folks represented the finest that their respective
countries had to give. They were men and women who were eager to
work and anxious to become citizens of this great democracy. Their
children went to schools because their parents wanted their sons
and daughters to learn the American way of life. It is worth
noting that for decades the highest rate of literacy has always
been found among the children of the American immigrants. The
situation on the range was one of optimism for the future.

A decade or two later the picture was less appealing. First,
the lumber of the extensive forests was gone. Ruthless unscientific

cutting and the even more destructive fires had closed that chapter
of lumber production, and charred stumps and cutover lands remained.
     In another decade people began to realize that there was no
speedy transition from lumbering to agriculture, and that farming
in northeastern Minnesota, in the main, would have to be different
from that in southern Minnesota, Iowa, and Illinois. Another decade
or so and the demand of two World Wars for material reduced the
available rich shipping ore. Exhausted mines meant population dis-
placements. Mechanization meant fewer jobs. The iron range had
become a single-industry area with but seasonal employment. This
condition, coupled with the fact that the iron ranges and the
surrounding and intervening region had never recovered from the
depression and the droughts of the thirties, created chronic unemployment problems. This condition undoubtedly will continue for
some years unless special plans for alleviation and improvement
are made.

Testimony, George Selke, November 20, 1959, U.S. Congress,
86th, 1st session, Senate, Special Committee on Unemployment
Problems, Unemployment Problems, IV, pp. 1552-1553.

502.   FROM PROGRESS TO POVERTY IN LETCHER COUNTY, KENTUCKY (1910, 1959)

     Five decades in the life cycle of a coal boom area.
The first testimony is made in 1910; that of Fess Whitaker,
former handyman, railroad worker and at the time of writing,
jailer of Letcher County, Kentucky. Nearly 50 years later
Thomas Gish testifies. He was editor of a newspaper,
The Mountain Eagle, published in Whitesburg, Kentucky, part
of Letcher County. In 1958, in an effort to focus national
attention on the plight of the County's people, Gish helped
lead a movement of several hundred people to "form a new
State or perhaps secede from the United States and apply
for foreign aid."

a.   [1910]

     Old Letcher stands first in wealth. If the whole united world
would shut down all of their coal mines Letcher County could furnish
the whole united world coal for thirty years. We have more timber
in Letcher County than in any other county in Kentucky. We have
twenty-six big mountains in Letcher County well covered with timber,
such mountains as the Black and Cumberland and others.

We have some of the richest corporations and companies in the
United States, such as the Consolidation Coal Company at Jenkins,
Kentucky and the Elkhorn Coal Company at Fleming, Ky. As to schools,
Letcher stands first.

. . . .

In 1910 [a company was organized] to begin work on the L. & N.
Railroad, which was a new construction from Jackson to McRoberts,
to the greatest coal fields in the world. The railroad right of
way had been surveyed many times, but the good old citizens never
thought it could be built, and finally they got a bunch of men to
get the right of way, which the biggest part of the citizens had
signed up for $50 per acre. So it was good for one year, and
finally the contract was let to build the road, and then here came
the people.

. . . .

There have been many changes in Letcher County since 1911.
It doesn't seem like the same country. So many new towns, people
and coal companies. We have about twenty through freights daily and
two locals and four passengers, except on Sundays, and since the
war we have only had two passenger trains, for the purpose of saving
coal.

. . . .

b. [1959]

In my county--with a potential labor force of some 12,000
persons, no more than 3,000 are gainfully employed. In other words,
for every one man who holds an adequate job, three others are walking the streets. Those are figures which don't show up in any unemployment statistics I have ever seen. But they are valid figures
and represent the best guesses of informed people in my county.
To put it another way, one-fourth of the population in my county is
gainfully employed--trying to carry the burden of the other three-
fourths.

Now it is obvious that one man can't even indirectly support
four families--and this shows up in every phase of life in eastern
Kentucky. All of eastern Kentucky's ills, it seems to me, can be
traced directly to this lack of employment. More jobs would, of
course, mean more money to spread around, and this would show up
in better schools, better medical facilities, more adequately
financed local governments, better food, better clothing, and so on.

. . . .

The capitalistic system which made America great has failed in
eastern Kentucky. And its failure should cause fear in the heart
of every American--because we can't ever really be sure of our
system until it is made to work everywhere, including eastern
Kentucky.

The failure is the fault of no one in particular, and yet is
the fault of everyone. Perhaps no area in the world has had a
greater abundance of natural resources than eastern Kentucky--and
with all of our natural wealth we should be wealthy people. But to

a degree that is shocking, eastern Kentucky was robbed by eastern
financial interests, and that robbery goes on today. Most of the
coal lands in this area were purchased some 50 years ago by sharp-
talking easterners who came in and purchased coal rights for $1 an
acre, even if the purchase had to be made at times at the point of
a gun.
    The result has been that whatever profit--and the profits often
have been fabulous--that has been made by coal operators in eastern
Kentucky has been drained away. In the county of Letcher--one of
the Nation's leading producers of coal--there is not a single major
coal operator or coal landowner who makes his home there. They make
their money and they move out--taking with them the wealth of the
county. Letcher County has built some fabulous homes in Louisville,
Lexington, Cincinnati, Pittsburgh, on the French Riviere, and in
Florida. But you won't find a single one in Letcher County.

    (a) Fess Whitaker, History of Corporal Fess Whitaker,
(Louisville, Kentucky: Standard Printing Company, 1918), pp. 88,
118-119, 120.
    (b) Testimony, Thomas E. Gish, December 11, 1959, U.S.
Congress, 86th, 1st session, Senate, Special Committee on Unemployment Problems, Unemployment Problems, V, pp. 1995-1996.

    503. SHORTAGE IN OIL EXPLORATION PERSONNEL (1969)

    In the 1950s, oil replaced coal as the principal
fuel in the United States. What is more, over four-
fifths of it came from domestic sources. Twenty years
later, only three-fifths came from American wells.
Between the two dates, there was a declining demand for
exploration personnel as U.S. firms bought into Middle
Eastern sources. Technical training institutions felt the
impact of diminished need for technical experts. Following is a statement of this recognition by Orlo Childs,
president of the Colorado School of Mines and of the
American Association of Petroleum Geologists.

    In 1950 to 1955 in Salt Lake City there were the exploration
offices of nine major oil companies. There is not one there today.
It is through this period that the exploration was done that found
Aneth, Ashley, Duchesne, Roosevelt, Red Rock, the whole bit.
    Every bit of oil and gas production in the State of Utah came
out of that period of exploration. There is no exploration, or very
sporadic exploration, going on there today. It is, therefore, obvious there was something in the economics of that period that saw
the greatest mounting of exploration effort in the United States,
and it stopped in 1957.

Between the period of 1957 and 1960, exploration fell through-out these United States, and there were 1,000 geologists fired by major companies and others during that period. There was a real cutback. This particular period really shows a tremendous readjust-ment. What has been going on since? There has never been the hir-ing of exploration expertise since that time. It has been on the decline. It has been in the status quo. Exploration people have been simply picked up to take positions of those who were retir-ing....

In the same dwindling there were three institutions in your state [Utah] that had splendid departments of geology, geophysics, the training of people for the petroleum business. There is not a course in petroleum engineering in your state today. There is only one institution--and please don't ask me which one--that really could provide the people.

This has become a national desert of training of exploration capability. We have drifted into this period over the last decade, and we are in serious problems....

In the United States in 1966 there were only 424 students en-rolled in geological engineering, 225 of these were in two institu-tions. There were only 16 institutions in the entire Nation offer-ing this course of study. Another vital subject is that of geo-physical engineering and this discipline was offered in only nine institutions. There were only 189 students majoring in the subject and 137 of those were in two institutions.

In 1966 there were only 26 institutions in the country where petroleum engineering could be studied. 1,149 students were enroll-ed as majors in this field. Half of these students were in only six institutions. Today we know of at least four institutions that have dropped the subject entirely.

It is apparent to me, with all that has been said about the need for exploration...that the challenges of finding the oil and gas that we are going to need are going to be met by only a handful of people and only a few of those will be specifically trained in their proper fields.

These were engineers. Geologists and geophysicists as scien-tists have also been used in the exploration area. But they, too, have seen a tremendous decline in the last decade.

Sir, we have let the emphasis on this aspect of our American economy dwindle to a point that it is no longer an attractive field for some of the brightest young people we could have. We are way too late in identifying this aspect of the inadequacies of the oil and gas for the future. We have to turn around. The time isn't over. I don't really mean to cry the blues too much. But we have to turn it around and make this an attractive area or we are never going to have the exploration techniques and capabilities to meet the tremendous problem of exploration and production that we face on the long-term solution of the natural gas problem.

Testimony, November 13, 1969, U.S. Congress, 91st, 1st session, Senate, Committee on Interior and Insular Affairs, Subcommittee on Minerals, Materials, and Fuels, Natural Gas Supply Study. Hearings. ..., (Washington, D.C.: Government Printing Office, 1969), pp. 186-187.

504. USING THE EARTH'S HEAT FOR POWER (1973)

In a search for new sources of power, attention
recently has been paid to naturally-occurring sources.
One of the most ancient of these is underground warm
water. How to tap it and bring it to the surface in a
form appropriate for helping generate electricity, for
example, is one of the problems. Following is a statement on geothermal resources by Bryce W. Johnson, an
associate of Science Applications of Palo Alto, California,
a firm with locations in 25 places in the country.

Geothermal energy appears to offer a number of significant
advantages over conventional fossil-fueled and nuclear powerplants
in that no off-site industry is required. It requires no mines for
coal or uranium, no oil wells, tank ships, or fuel processing
plants. Further, it has a distinct advantage over some other alternative power sources--controlled thermonuclear power, in particu-
lar--in that it can be developed without any great breakthrough in
technology.
Some of the apparent disadvantages of geothermal energy include
the following:
Geothermal sites are typically distant from load centers, requiring extensive transmission facilities. This feature is shared
with hydroelectric systems. The increasing installation of mine-
head coal burning plants may make this problem a typical one for
electric power systems.
Geothermal energy typically develops sizable volumes of potentially undesirable wastes--gases, liquids, and solids. Only nuclear
plants do not exhaust noxious gases and only gas- or oil-fired
plants do not have a solid waste problem.
The powerplants require considerable land area for the wells
and plants, themselves. However, when one considers the land required for oil wells, or for uranium mines and processing plants,
he recognizes the same disadvantage for conventional plants.
Removal of underground water or other fluids may cause land
subsidence. Subsidence has been noted in certain oil fields and
from water pumping in Mexico City and the Santa Clara Valley of
California. Similar problems may occur for conventional energy
sources. Shallow coal mines have collapsed, but with relatively
minor surface impact. However, a strip or an open pit mine can have
a disastrous effect on the surface.
Well blow out can occur in any operation involving drilling
into high-pressure fluids. It has occurred at The Geysers and in
the termal fields in Mexico. An analogous blow out of an oil well
in the Santa Barbara Channel illustrates vividly that this undesirable environmental effect is not unique to geothermal energy.
Heat rejection and disposal of waste heat is a problem with
any heat cycle. The lower the inlet temperature, the greater will
be the waste heat. Known geothermal sources indicate that the waste
heat from such a plant will be about twice that of a conventional
plant.

Experiments in Colorado indicate that some seismic activity may be simulated by injection of water deep underground. Withdrawal and reinjection of water at a geothermal site could possibly induce a similar effect. At this time this problem is still speculative but sufficiently credible to indicate the need for seismic monitoring.

For direct utilization of dry steam, noise pollution is a problem. This is particularly noticeable at The Geysers in California.

While this may not be a complete listing, it is representative, and it is adequate to demonstrate that the environmental impact of the several energy generation schemes is different largely in the degree of impact and usually not in the kind of impact. Efforts to solve the environmental problems of one energy system will apply in some measure to others, and in some cases will be directly applicable.

One environmental problem which is possibly unique to geothermal power is that of waste water disposal. In some cases this water may be consumed; for example, as makeup water for cooling towers, or it may be reinjected. However, even the turbine condensate at one field has been found to contain dissolved chemicals which preclude its discharge into local streams without added treatment. The mineral content is quite variable from field to field and in some cases from well to well in the same field. As an example, the water from the Cerro Prieto wells in Mexico contains about 2 1/2 percent dissolved solids. Ocean water averages about 3 1/2 percent. Some 50 miles north of Cerro Prieto in the Buttes region of the Imperial Valley, the average is 26 percent. The Cerro Prieto waste can be dumped in the ocean with little impact, but the Buttes brine cannot. Each field may require a solution unique to that field.

Testimony, August 10, 1973, U.S. Congress, 93rd, 1st session, Senate, Committee on Interior and Insular Affairs, Subcommittee on Water and Power Resources, Geothermal Resources. Hearings...., (Washington, D.C.: Government Printing Office, 1974), pp. 602-603.

505.   BURNING METALLURGICAL-GRADE COAL (1973)

A half-century ago, anthracite was the main source of heating homes on the East Coast of the United States. The rise of cheap oil not only replaced coal but it also destroyed a well-knit system of retail distribution. With the sharp increase in oil prices beginning in 1973-1974, East Coast homeowners seeking to buy lower-cost coal instead of oil came up against a shortage of anthracite as well as difficulties in finding retail outlets for it. Meanwhile, industrial users of anthracite were forced to compete for scarce supplies. E. P. Leach, vice-president for mining of the the Bethlehem Steel Corporation, explains the critical importance of the fuel for his industry.

My company is a major producer and consumer of metallurgical-grade coal. Within the general framework of market and production problems as already outlined, the role of metallurgical coal -- or steel industry coal -- is unique. Coal varies widely in its characteristics. Only a relatively small percentage has those special qualities that make it suitable for steelmaking.

First of all, the coal must be capable of being converted into coke; secondly, and still more important, this coke must be strong enough to support the burden of iron ore and limestone that goes with it in the blast furnace. This requires a proper combination of coals of low and high content of natural gas.

Finally, while many coals can make coke, the sulfur content of the coke must be low -- normally under one percent, for metallurgical reasons. Sulfur removal from the steel is so troublesome and expensive that a steel plant attempting to use coals with higher sulfur content cannot effectively compete with other producers using low sulfur coals. Since removal of sulfur from the coal itself is normally difficult or impossible with existing technology, it is necessary for the foreseeable future that the steel industry use low sulfur coals.

About five percent of the total U.S. energy is consumed by the steel industry and 75 percent of this is provided either by direct use or through by-products of metallurgical coal. In order to get the last "squeal from the pig", all the coke oven gas, tars, and blast furnace gas are used either in the generation of electricity for plant use or directly for process heat. None of the energy is surplus or allowed to escape and, since it is used in direct applications, efficiency is high.

Coking coal represents about 15 percent of all coal production in the U.S. The steel industry is by far the principal user of coking coal. The use of coke by other consumers, such as small foundries, is insignificant by comparison, but equally essential to those operations.

High quality coke is as essential to the steelmaking industry as iron ore. Coke provides both the reducing agent and all the energy required to convert iron ore to iron. There is no economic substitute for coal for this purpose and, specifically, that coal with special coking qualities.

Maintaining an adequate supply of metallurgical grade coal presents serious problems. I cannot overemphasize my earlier statement that of the total U.S. reserves of coal, only a relatively small part can now be classed as suitable for steel industry coke. Recent trends toward burning such coals in utility boilers in order to reduce sulfur in stack emissions will, if continued, have serious effects on the supply available to the steel industry. We question the wisdom of diverting a premium metallurgical coal to steam generation.

Testimony, June 8, 1973, U.S. Congress, 93rd, 1st session, Senate, Committee on Interior and Insular Affairs, Coal Policy Issues. Hearings.... Part 1, (Washington, D.C.: Government Printing Office, 1973), pp. 367-369.

506.   REFORESTATION IN MEDFORD, OREGON (1977)

So long as access, both legal and otherwise,
to the forested public domain was relatively un-
restricted, little thought was given to conservation.
Only when federal policy shifted, early in the present
century, from disposal to husbanding a permanent reserve did private lumber interests seriously begin to
practice conservation. When firms could no longer depend on seemingly endless supplies, it began to make
sense to conserve what one already had. Here is a
small example of commercial conservation as described
by Howard Mitchell, forest land manager of the Medford
Corporation, Medford, Oregon. Mitchell is a graduate
forester who left a job with the U.S. Bureau of Land
Management in 1960 for his present position.

Medford Corp. has an ownership of some 87,000 acres of forest
land. Our reforestation program was begun in 1962. It involves the
planting of approximately 300,000 seedlings each year on 800 to
1,000 acres each year.
The Medford area is characterized by a combination of factors
that have modified our silvicultural practice. It is an area of
excessive ground temperatures, long summer dry spells, areas of
excessive rodent and animal activity, and frost pockets.
Present management practices and harvest techniques are geared
to minimize these factors and foster a higher level of natural re-
generation as the reforestation program described above reclaims
the presently nonstocked acres.
Other measures which we will budget for are herbicide treatment projects designed to control unwanted grass and brush vegetation and restore tree dominance where a reasonable level of stocking
is present.
Speaking of the ownership, in general, remember that is 87,000
acres, somewhat more than that, about 40 percent of this acreage is
presently in good growth producing status, that is, it supports a
full stand of growth producing trees. Another 39 percent is in a
transition status, that is, it supports a stand of partially deca-
dent overmature timber with volume loss canceling growth, or the
stand is not fully stocked, or excessive disease is present. A
third category makes up 21 percent of the ownership, which is comprised of acres with severe vegetation problems--grass or brush--
rock outcrops, natural meadows, and roads. Some of these acres
can and will be brought back into production, but others will not
respond to management for timber production and will find their way
into other uses.
Examination of the company planting records for the past 10
years reveals the following statistics:
Average number of trees planted---------------------- 315,000
Average number of acres planted---------------------- 909
Average number of acres where site preparation was
        applied is------------------------------------- 642

```
Average site preparation cost------------------------- $8,120
Average cost of planting stock------------------------ $5,996
Average cost of planting labor----------------------- $21,628
```
These figures will tell you that about $40 per acre is the average cost of site prep and planting combined, but success is at about a 50-percent level; therefore, the cost of each successfully planted acre is approximately $60, plus the administrative costs. After this comes protection from fire, insects, disease, periodic spraying to sustain tree dominance--and growth--over brush and grass.

Our experience reveals that successful reforestation begins with commitment to a proven nursery for dependable production of growing stock from seed native to the area to be reforested. The decision to contract with a nursery for the growing of our seedlings is based on an examination of such details of their operation as: lifting, sorting, packaging, and storing of the growing stock; sowing rates and bed densities: ability to produce good stock of different ages, including transplants and even container stock.

Every measure possible must be employed to be sure we are planting live seedlings, and to this end, research has devised an electronic means for determining whether or not a given seedling is still alive.

Need is being shown more and more for seed orchards because being able to gather wild seed is too uncertain. Tree improvement is, of course, an integral part of seed orchards.

Testimony, July 8, 1977, U.S. Congress, 95th, 1st session, House of Representatives, Committee on Agriculture, Subcommittee on Forests, Reforestation Efforts in Western Oregon. Hearings...., (Washington, D.C.: Government Printing Office, 1977), pp. 131-132.

507. MINING AND ENVIRONMENT IN THE WEST (1977)

During the 1970s, especially after the OPEC-initiated price increases for petroleum, the return to coal accelerated. Domestic demand rose sharply as did overseas demand. Wyoming, which became the third largest coal producer, contained huge strip-mines which contracted over long periods to supply public utility companies. While the burning quality of the coal is somewhat inferior to the eastern variety, lower prices more than compensate. Farmers, ranchers, and others in the Far West frequently criticize the environmental effects of coal mining. In this case, Gerald W. Moravek, a rancher near Sheridan, Wyoming, and a member of the Powder River Basin Resource Council, describes some of the environmental problems created by coal. He is a native of the area, a graduate in animal science and agronomy, and a retired Lieutenant Colonel in the U.S. Army.

I don't own the mineral rights on my place. They belong to a charitable trust which also has other mineral rights in the locality. My deed gives the minerals owner "the right to enter on, explore for, develop and remove the minerals, specifying that the surface owner will receive reasonable compensation for the necessary surface disruption."

In 1973, the trust contracted with a local mining company to develop its resources. This mining firm decided its initial development would be on property which was 1 1/2 miles away from my property. In April of last year, the mining company requested a State mining permit. My review of the permit application showed the area to be on the valley floor immediately adjacent to the river. Additionally, I felt the company had not reviewed in sufficient detail the short- or long-range effects of the mine upon the normal high-water periods of the Tongue River, capability to return the area to its previous, highly productive condition, nor the effects upon the underground aquifers of the valley floor. Further, the company proposed moving the coal by 40-ton truck loads for 5.5 miles over a narrow secondary State highway constructed only for light vehicle traffic and used primarily as a farm-to-market road at a rate of one truck every 1 1/2 minutes.

This presented a safety hazard for my family and neighbors while at the same time requiring the public to maintain and reconstruct the road for their operation.

On the basis of these beliefs, I, in conjunction with the Powder River council, filed a protest to the mining operation. Immediately, we were termed in the local press obstructionists to progress and the public welfare. Under Wyoming law, a protested permit application requires a public hearing by our environmental quality council.

Well before the hearing date, the attorney for the trust advised myself and my family that they considered our protest to be a threat to their mineral rights and should we persist they would sue to recover the value of the denied coal. On the day of the prehearing conference, my wife and I were served with notice of a personal civil law suit which demanded title to our place and $14 million in damages to compensate them for loss of the coal reserves.

This was before the environmental quality council had even heard the merits of our protest, and I remind you that the proposed mine was 1 1/2 miles away from the boundaries of our surface ownership. No other individuals were named in the suit, however it stated that other John Does and John Doe, Inc. were involved, would be searched out and eventually would be named in the complaint.

After the suit was filed, my wife and I went to a lawyer and determined the following courses of action were open;

One: We could fight the suit and lose, thus guaranteeing the loss of our life's efforts to our opponents;

Two: We could fight and win and have the legal costs of the effort guarantee the same thing, or;

Three: We could drop our public protest and remain silent on all mining matters and have the suit dismissed. We chose the latter option and have remained silent since last August.

The Powder River resources council, because it is an incorporated, nonprofit organization, continued on with the protest and forced the mining application to be withdrawn, essentially proving the merits of our complaints.

Gentlemen, I think my personal experiences illustrate a number of things, primary among them the essential need for a strong Federal strip mine law. The strip mining industry is moving West whether we like it or not, and although some of the companies are different, the same tactics that have so long prevailed in Appalachia are coming to the northern Great Plains.

Gentlemen, without the strongest kinds of Federal guarantees for both personal rights and the environment, we will meet our energy needs at the expense of those principles that are the foundation of our Republic....

In the West, we have another situation, and that is with the irrigated valley floors that provide the bulk of our hay and crop production. The tremendous agricultural productivity of these areas, coupled with their hydrologic fragility, mandates special attention by the Congress. In my area, one can produce 4 tons of hay per irrigated acre, enough feed to winter two or three range cattle.

These same cattle require 40 to 80 acres of upland pasture for summer grazing. For each acre of bottom land that is stripped, the productivity of upland pasture is seriously reduced. I understand that there have been some problems with a definition of valley floors and I have heard industry representatives claim that alluvial valley floors cover the entire West. This is not true. In the Powder River Basin alluvial valleys comprise less than 3 percent of the surface if they are simply defined as those areas along a stream bed where gravity flow irrigation may be practiced or which are naturally subirrigated, including undeveloped range lands....

Valley floors, because of their delicate hydrology and tremendous productivity need protection. The potential for offsite impacts is great. The loss of farmland will affect much of the West. The hydrology is the single most important component of the ecosystem. Because of these items, and because reclamation has never been demonstrated on valley floors, I feel we should avoid these areas unless the coal is absolutely essential to national energy needs.

Testimony, January 12, 1977, U.S. Congress, 95th, 1st session. House of Representatives, Committee on Interior and Insular Affairs, Subcommittee on Energy and the Environment, Reclamation Practices and Environmental Problems of Surface Mining. Hearings...., Part 1, (Washington, D.C.: Government Printing Office, 1977), pp. 262-265.

508.   COSTS OF NUCLEAR POWER (1977)

In the late 1940s, speculation about peacetime uses
of nuclear energy centered on electric power production
and motive power for large ocean-going vessels. By 1970,
only about one percent of national electricity derived from
nuclear-powered reactors. Ten years later, however, one-
tenth was nuclear. Near the end of the 1970s, however, a
halt set in. Part of the reason was safety but another
was the rising cost of nuclear power. The two factors were
somewhat related inasmuch as safety features necessarily
added costs. Following is an argument in 1977 by Charles
Komanoff, an energy consultant in New York City, that
nuclear power had little future.

The economies of nuclear power are bad and getting worse. In
my judgment, no utility executive with an accurate perception of
the costs of nuclear power and a sincere desire to minimize customer
costs would propose ordering a new nuclear plant, with the possible
exception of utilities in New England. Nuclear plants cost too much
to build, relative to coal plants; are more unreliable and erratic
in performance than coal plants; and are available only in large
unit sizes unsuited to even the largest U.S. power grids.
    These problems more than cancel nuclear plants' fuel cost ad-
vantage over coal-fired facilities. On an overall lifecycle cost
basis, I believe that electricity from new nuclear plants will cost
22 percent more than electricity from new coal plants, averaged over
the seven regions of the country....
    Unfortunately, many people among the electric utilities, reac-
tor manufacturers, and federal energy agencies....are blinded by
the occasional reactor that meets its targeted capital cost or the
rare plant that operates at or close to its design capacity. They
fail to see that the golden age of nuclear economics--the period
from roughly 1968 to 1975, when reactors were cheap to buy, cheaper
still to run, and sometimes reliable to operate--is over.
    Comparing mid-1980's installation reactors with 1968 to 1975
installation reactors, capital costs and fuel costs have tripled--
in constant dollars--and reactor performance is likely to fall, as
large, unwieldy reactors replace the smaller, less complex units
which are easier to run. Coal costs have risen too, significantly,
but not nearly as much as nuclear....
    Overall, I agree with Lovins and others who point to conserva-
tion and cogeneration as more effective investments than new central
station powerplants, but if we are to have such plants, coal appears
to be the more economic choice.
    The figures in table 1 are not precise--they cannot be, in
view of the uncertainties in coal and especially nuclear costs--but
they are probably good guesses of average powerplant costs in particular regions. I offer them from the perspective of 3 years of
full-time study of nuclear and coal generating costs undertaken for
the Council on Economic Priorities and as a consultant to the U.S.

Congress and government agencies in seven States—New York, New Jersey, Connecticut, Wisconsin, Kentucky, New Mexico, and California.

I turn now to nuclear and coal cost variables.

First. Unit sizes: The nuclear plants in my cost analysis are 1,150-megawatt units. This and slightly larger units are virtually the only size reactors available from U.S. vendors. In contrast, the typical reactor installed in 1970 was 600 megawatt, and in 1974, 800 megawatt. Nuclear stations now under construction typically consist of two 1,150-megawatt units spaced a year or two apart, totaling 2,300 megawatts.

Coal plants are available in virtually any size, from 50 megawatt to over 1,000 megawatt. Bigger plants appear to cost somewhat less per kilowatt, but are less reliable. My analysis assumes 60-megawatt coal units, which can be installed with from one to four units at the same site.

Second. System reliability parity: Utility costs planners compare alternatives with equal amounts of megawatts. Thus, the alternative to 2,300 megawatts of nuclear capacity is considered to be 2,300 megawatts of coal capacity. This is fallacious. Expansions of a typical utility system by 1,800 megawatts of coal capacity—three 600-megawatt units—would achieve the same overall system reliability as would result from expansions by 2,300 megawatts of nuclear capacity—two 1,150-megawatt units.

This is the result of a precise calculation which takes into account the effect of the sizes and reliabilities of individual generating units on the required amount of reserve capacity. The amount of required reserve decreases when units are smaller, since the number of separate plant failures necessary to exhaust the available reserve increases as unit sizes decrease. Moreover, the smaller coal units are individually more reliable than the larger nuclear units. The result is that 1,800 megawatts installed in three coal units is the reliability equivalent of 2,300 megawatts of nuclear in two units. These are the stations compared in my analysis.

Third. Capital costs: The definitive Harvard-MIT study of powerplant construction costs found that nuclear costs, already higher than coal's in 1971, were increasing two to three times faster than coal costs for reactors completed and under construction during 1971 to 1981....

Nuclear plants not only require more material and labor than equivalent coal plants—they are subject to greater regulatory-mandated design changes, require more potentially scarce specialized labor, and consume more expensive engineering talent.

Reactor costs are still exceeding utilities upwardly revised estimates. A case in point is the Long Island Lighting Co's. Shoreham reactor. Shoreham received its AEC construction permit in early 1973, thus seeming to clear the way for speedy construction by 1978. Yet almost annually, Lilco pushes back the projected completion date and pushes up the cost. The next revision, due November 1 according to a recent article in Newsday, will increase last year's estimate of $969 million—for May 1979 completion—by 20 percent for a fall 1980 finish. The resulting $1,416 per installed kilowatt cost based on the plant's 821-megawatt capacity will make Shoreham the most expensive commercial powerplant ever built. For comparison, the last--and still current--AEC capital cost study projected $662 per kilowatt for plants of Shoreham's size--less than half the cost now projected.

Shoreham looks to be an extreme case,, but the cost overrun disease is real. In big round numbers, $1,200 per kilowatt for twin nuclear 1,150-megawatt units, and $950 per kilowatt for 600-megawatt coal units with scrubbers, look like reasonable national averages for 1985. Northeast plants would cost 5 percent more, South Atlantic and South Central plants 5 percent less, due to labor cost variation; California plants would cost 5 percent more due to stricter safety and environmental standards.

Fourth. Fixed charge rate: This refers to the cost of capital, local taxes and Federal taxes which determine the annual fixed charges the utility pays as a percentage of plant capital costs. Taxes are usually marginally less for nuclear than coal, due principally to accelerated depreciation permitted for nuclear, but nuclear marginal cost of capital may be considerably higher due to greater financing requirement and greater perceived risk. A reasonable assumption is 16-percent fixed charge rate, for both nuclear and coal--about 11-percent cost of capital plus 5-percent taxes.

Fifth. Capacity factor: A powerplant's actual kilowatt-hour production as a percentage of its maximum possible output, based on design capacity, is its capacity factor. A 75-percent capacity factor means a plant operating at full capacity 75 percent of the time--and shut down otherwise--or operating at 75 percent of capacity all of the time, or some combination. Utilities seek to maximize capacity factors of new nuclear and coal plants, especially nuclear, to minimize fixed costs per unit of output.

Utilities and the Nuclear Regulatory Commission staff facilely assume equal coal and nuclear capacity factors in their economic analyses, previously assuming 80 percent, now 75 percent or 70 percent, or, in a few cases, 65 percent. Yet plant reliability is a greater problem for nuclear units, especially with new ones sized twice as large as coal units. All powerplants, especially nuclear, suffer more frequent and longer breakdowns at larger sizes. Radiation and safety considerations often limit reactor output and complicate repairs. Through 1976, nuclear plants have averaged 64-percent capacity factor at units under 800 megawatts, but only 50 percent at units over 800 megawatts.

Capacity factors vary widely for existing plants, especially nuclear, and will likely do so for new units. I think 55 percent is a reasonable average capacity factor to project for 1,150-megawatt nuclear units, and 70 percent for 600-megawatt coal units with scrubbers.

These projections are based on my 2-year study of nuclear and coal powerplant capacity factors and reliability, the original data base of which was bought by the Federal Energy Administration. That study cut through utility and FEA/ERDA rhetoric to demonstrate that: Capacity factors fall as plant size rises, especially for nuclear; aging improves capacity factors for coal--up to age 10-- but for only one of the two U.S. nuclear plant designs; duplicate coal units have higher capacity factors, but duplicate nuclear units perform no better than other nuclear units; coal capacity factors rise as coal sulfur content falls, et cetera.

The correlations are richer than this summary suggests. Based on them, 1,150-megawatt nuclear units should have 50-percent capacity factors, but a 5-percent allowance for design and operating improvements seems reasonable, giving 55 percent. For coal, the correlations yield 70 percent for 600-megawatt units burning 2 percent sulfur--medium grade--coal with scrubbers. This source is also referenced in my notes.

No addition is made for this figure, despite potential improvements.

A nuclear plant with a 55-percent capacity factor makes electricity at a 22- to 29-percent higher cost than at the industry-assumed 70- to 75-percent capacity factor. Through 1976, only 6 of the 48 commercial U.S. reactors were averaging 70 percent or better capacity factor, as seen in capacity factor tables from reference 6, attached to testimony. Utility insistence that all nuclear plants will run at the high-capacity factors achieved by just a few units is a major factor in overstating the economics of nuclear power.

Sixth. Fuel costs: This is the area where nuclear has an edge over coal--outside of the Mountain States--but the advantage has been diminishing as an accurate appraisal emerges of the nuclear fuel cycle. Nucleonics Week reported recently that U.S. uranium sellers are not now accepting current high utility bids for as much as $45 per pound in 1977 dollars, for example, with escalation, versus $8 per pound only 3 years ago....

Uranium now accounts for over half of nuclear fuel cycle costs. Meanwhile, plutonium recycle is economically questionable and politically dead, and nuclear fuel produces significantly fewer kilowatt hours than utilities project for new plants, due to premature refueling forced by fuel failure and erratic plant performance, and to poorer than anticipated thermal performance. A 1985 nuclear fuel cost of 1.1 cents per kilowatt-hour is supported in the notes.

Coal mine and transportation costs are sensitive to mining region and plantsite. The nuclear fuel cost of 1.1 cents per kilowatt-hour projected for 1985 is equivalent to Eastern high-grade coal at $27.50 per ton, Midwest medium-grade coal at $25 per ton and Western low-grade coal at $19.50 per ton. Current coal prices are generally within the range of these figures--lower in the West-- but coal prices will of course rise between now and 1985.

For estimating 1985 coal prices in this analysis, I have taken average delivered coal costs by region for 1975--last year of FPC data available--increased this by 25 percent for a one-time increase attributable to new mine costs--50 percent in West North Central and 75 percent in Mountain States, due to anticipated State and Indian strip-mine severance taxes and royalties--and escalated by 6 percent per year through 1980 and 5 percent per year through 1985. California costs assume mining in Mountain States plus $13 per ton transportation in 1985--8,500 Btu per pound coal.

A life-cycle cost analysis should incorporate the effect of post-1985 fuel cost escalation. Equal escalation rates for nuclear and coal fuel would imply a widening of the 1985 nuclear fuel cost advantage--except in the Mountain States, where coal is projected cheaper. However, I believe nuclear fuel is likely to suffer greater escalation, due to the smaller size of uranium reserves--relative to coal--and the politicization of the nuclear fuel cycle, which increases uncertainty, adding to the market power of suppliers. Exclusion of post-1985 nuclear fuel cost escalation from this analysis, for simplicity, probably works to the advantage of nuclear costs, except in the Northeast where the 1985 nuclear fuel costs advantage is very large--1.6 cents per kilowatt-hour--and likely to widen slightly.

Seventh. Operating and maintenance costs: O. & M. costs include all nonfuel operating expenses; water treatment, ash and sludge disposal and limestone feed for coal scrubbers, nuclear radwaste treatment, maintenance and repair, spare parts inventory, et cetera. They typically account for only 5 percent of all annualized costs, though some analysts have attempted to attribute coal scrubbing O. & M. costs 3 to 4 times nuclear O. & M. Actual experience with coal scrubbers, such as at the Kansas City Power & Light La Cygne station, suggests only modestly greater per kilowatt O. & M. costs for coal, despite scrubbers, than for nuclear. My costs here use a detailed analysis by the New York power pool, and assume 55-percent capacity factor for nuclear, 69 to 73 percent for coal, depending on coal grade.

Eight. Costs excluded from the analysis: In brief, this analysis makes no provision for potentially expensive reactor decommissioning following useful life; assumes equal lives for nuclear and coal plants despite evidence of reactor performance deterioration in the few reactors older than age 10; and includes only a small allowance for nuclear waste disposal--about 15 cents per kilowatthour in 1985--which may substantially understate actual costs. These omissions, made because the ultimate costs are unknowable at present, improve the appearance of nuclear economics.

Testimony, September 7, 1977, U.S. Congress, 1st session, House of Representatives, Committee on Government Operations, Nuclear Power Costs (Part 2). Hearings...., (Washington, D.C.: Government Printing Office, 1977), pp. 1181-1185.

509. DRILLING FOR OIL AND GAS (1977)

In 1975, a serious shortage of natural gas was predicted. The Federal Power Commission, which joined the forecast, was accused by critics in Congress and elsewhere of accepting uncritically the data furnished by private power companies. It was charged that the industry, aiming at deregulation, was misrepresenting the level of supplies in an effort to promise relief once price bids were lifted. In the process of clarifying the conflict of views, Congress learned from one witness of some rarely-explained

technicalities of drilling for gas and oil. He was
James F. Justiss, Jr., president of the Justiss-Mears
Oil Company of Jena, Louisiana and of the International
Association of Drilling Contractors (IADC).

In 1976 we believe the entire U.S. land rig census was between
2,200 and 2,400 rotary units. Of these, about 24 rigs are owned by
operators--oil companies--and the remainder by drilling contractors.
    At this point it would be useful to point out that a rig is
just that. It is a composite of mechanical parts assembled for a
specific job out of components that might be assembled differently
by different contractors. In simplest terms, the rig employs a
derrick--the familiar tower so frequently shown as a symbol of oil
exploration--and a draw-work to raise and lower lengths of drill
pipe. Large motors transmit power through a "kelly" to translate
the driving forces into a rotary motion. The entire string of drill
pipe rotates to form a very long drive shaft. The bit at the bottom
of the drill string breaks up the formations underground.
    Drilling fluids called "mud" are pumped down the drill pipe
and circulate to cool and lubricate the bit and to wash away the
cuttings of rock. These cuttings are brought to the surface,
removed, and are carefully analyzed to provide valuable geological
information. The lengths of 30-foot pipe are joined together by
threading. When the bit must be replaced, the entire length of
drill pipe must be raised in 90-foot sections and disassembled.
This process of threading together the pipe and taking it apart
consumes much of the time of the crew.
    In order to prevent the well from caving in or from bursting
through weak geological formations, casing is placed in portions
of the well and cemented to the rock formations. Depending upon
the depth of the well, the type of underground pressures, and the
geological information available about the structure, appropriate
safety precautions are taken against unexpected blowouts.
    Drilling technology has improved greatly over the years but
the basic principles have remained unchanged. Even after hundreds
of millions of dollars of research on exotic methods, there is
little expectation that major innovative breakthroughs will occur
in the near future. Improved efficiency over the years has increased penetration rates by many times and has probably kept the
price of oil from going to as much as $40 per barrel.
    The contract drilling business is certainly one of the most
competitive in the world. Each contractor bidding on a job bets
on his ability to complete the assignment efficiently and without
delays. IADC stresses a strong safety and training program.
Contractors have come to know that accidents are costly and create
delays. Responsible contractors therefore avoid accidents stemming
from use of poorly trained crews, cutting safety corners, short-
cutting established industry procedures and use of improper equipment.
    Contracts are let either on a day rate or on a footage basis.
Sometimes the contractor will provide a "turn key" contract in
which he handles all the subcontracting such as for mud services,
roadbuilding and site preparation, cementing, catering and the

purchase of drill bits. In most instances, however, these attendant services are individually contracted by the operator; that is,
the owner of the lease.

During the last 15 years the industry has seen the population
of contractors go from 700 to half that number in 1972 and return
to about 500 today. The industry activity tends to follow by some
18 months geophysical contractors. The nature of the drilling
business has been cyclical due to weather conditions, tax considerations, constraints on oil and gas prices, availability of new
acreage, and limitations on production--such as provided by the
Texas Railroad Commission, et cetera.

The current statistics showing the large numbers of rigs working on land must be put into perspective. Much of this work is
development or exploration drilling in old known producing areas
where current economic conditions warrant the development of these
properties.

Drilling costs increase geometrically as depths increase. In
some areas a 20,000 foot well might cost 10 times as much as a
10,000 foot well. Payments to the drilling contractor represent
about 36 percent of the total cost which the lease holder pays for
the completed well. In 1975 the average cost of drilling--through
the stage of installing the Christmas tree--valve system--was
$262,008 for a U.S. gas well, $138,640 for a U.S. oil well. A U.S.
dry hole cost averaged about $177,500. A hole to 20,000 feet on-
shore can easily cost $5 million or more....

One of the most important questions facing the drilling contractor is investment in new equipment. Clearly the indications
point to ever-increasing depths for discovery of gas which requires
deeper rated equipment. At present we estimate a new 7,500-foot
capacity rig--one of the smallest which a rotary drilling contractor
would likely purchase--would cost about $1.5 million at today's
market. This type of unit would not be suitable for gas exploration in most areas because of its limited depth rating. A more
suitable rig for natural gas exploration would be in the $1.8
million to $3.5 million range for a land rig.

Testimony, March 25, 1977, U.S. Congress, 95th, 1st session,
House of Representatives, Committee on Interstate and Foreign
Commerce, Subcommittee on Energy and Power, Long-Term Natural Gas
Issues. Hearings...., (Washington, D.C.: Government Printing
Office, 1977), pp. 157-158.

B.

THE LANDED ECONOMY

510. MAKING MONEY BY CROPS IS TOO SLOW (1901)

       Once more, the old American theme: real estate
speculation as part of farming. (See Source Nos. 134,
142, 351, and 513.) This is the testimony of Brynjolf
Prom, a banker and farmer from Milton, North Dakota.
He owned a farm of seven quarter sections which he
rented out on shares.

       Q. Did the settlers maintain possession of their lands and
cultivate them, or did they preempt to sell?--A. They preempted
to sell mainly.
       Q. Into whose hands did these purchases go usually?--A. They
piled up mortgages on farms and took the money, and the lands went
to the loan companies. They have resold now.
       Q. Then the loan companies took the renting rates when they
sold them, didn't they, for income? They sold at renting rates so
as to get the money back with interest?--A. Yes.
       Q. (By Mr. A. L. HARRIS.) Have you many mortgaged farms?
A. Yes; the greatest number of farms in our country are mortgaged.
       Q. Are they heavily mortgaged?--A. No.
       Q. Are they being paid off?--A. Yes; but many that can pay
off will not pay off. They prefer to keep a mortgage on the farm
and keep the money to buy extra land.
       Q. What is the average rate of interest?--A. On farm mort-
gages, 8 per cent.
       Q. (By Mr. FARQUHAR.) Were not there a great many mortgages
made there to acquire more land?--A. Yes.
       Q. That is why the maintain them?--A. To a large extent.

Q. The 8 per cent interest they pay enables them to hold the land, and they are able to pay the interest?--A. Yes.

Q. And they make a little money on the crops they raise?--A. Yes.

Q. (My Mr. A. L. HARRIS.) Was that wise or unwise?--A. Wise.

Q. You do not look upon the fact that you have a great number of mortgages as being an argument in favor of adversity?--A. No, sir.

Q. Did it aid your country in developing?--A. Yes. There is no money produced out there except by crops; that is too slow.

Q. Could you have developed upon a cash basis?--A. No, we could not. Our country would not be settled to-day. Most of our farms are bought on a credit. We deem it wise to buy on credit. We can buy lands on crop payments, or we can buy for so many thousand bushels of wheat, and it is no hardship to the farmer. A man can buy a farm, for instance, on the crop payment. Say the price is $2,000, and he binds himself in the contract to pay one-half of the grain he raises every year. Now, an honest man will do that. All he has to do is to deliver his half and retain the other half for seed and expenses, and he can do it in that way. He can gradually pay for the farm. That he can do in connection with another farm he owns. A man can buy more land that way, and it is an excellent plan.

Q. When he gets out of debt in that way what does he do?--A. Buys more land. They are restless people up there; they can not lie still.

Testimony, Brynjolf Prom, February 7, 1901, U.S. Congress, 57th, 1st session, House of Representatives, Document No. 179, Report of the Industrial Commission on Agriculture and Agricultural Labor, X, pp. 789-790

511. DETERIORATION OF MARYLAND AND VIRGINIA LAND (1901)

Following is an outstandingly clear analysis of some non-physical aspects of soil deterioration. The author is Milton Whitney who was Chief, Division of Soils, U.S. Department of Agriculture. He had been a professor of soil physics in the Agricultural College of Maryland and was a native of that state.

The exhaustion of the soils, of which we have heard so much in Maryland, Virginia, and the Southern States, is due, unquestionably, to improper and injudicious methods of cultivation and cropping. It is also due to the decrease in value of farm crops, due in turn to the cheaper production in the West and to the reduced cost of transportation, as has been referred to in the case of the New England States; also to the increase and the development of special

industries in other localities--for example, in the production of
the White Burley tobacco in Ohio, which yields more per acre, is
grown at a less cost per pound, and can be sold at a cheaper price
than the Maryland leaf, and has largely taken the place of the
Maryland leaf in the foreign markets, particularly in the French
and Belgian markets. Furthermore, the changes in the social conditions due to the civil war, and the mortgages which are still outstanding against the lands have been a contributing cause to the
abandonment or to the deterioration of many of these areas. It has
been found possible in many portions of Maryland, with the prevailing crops and methods of cultivation, to obtain a fair interest on
the labor and expense of cultivation, but it has been impossible
to obtain a living from the land if at the same time the interest
on mortgages, which have been running since the war, has had to be
met. And I know of once prosperous communities in southern Maryland
where they could still be successful, where they could produce
sufficient to maintain families without stint and with a fair degree
of comfort, but where nearly all the farms are mortgaged as an in-
heritance of 30 years ago, and it is impossible to support the
families and to pay off the mortgages at the same time. Areas now
are being abandoned from that cause throughout Maryland and the
South.

One of the most important causes of deterioration, however, and
I think I should put this first of all, is the method and system of
agriculture that prevails throughout these States. In the first
place, I would state that the soils of southern Maryland are in no
way exhausted in the sense that that term is generally used--that
is, a chemical analysis shows that they have sufficient plant food
for innumerable crops and that there is apparently no lack of plant
food in the soil. Unquestionably, the soil has been abused, the
methods of cultivation and of cropping have been injudiciously selected, and the soils are not now as productive as they should be.
. . . .

The Maryland farm is seldom worked by the man who owns it.
There is, for some reason, an unfortunate prejudice which prevails
in many localities, at any rate in Maryland, for a man who actually
goes into the field and works his land. He usually has an overseer,
a man who is paid to look after and direct his interests instead of
doing this himself. Frequently he has not even so much control
over his interests, and lets his land out to a tenant farmer who
farms it in his own way, by his own methods, and for a portion of
the crop, and occasionally for a money consideration. The crops
grown are the ordinary staple crops of general agriculture. They
have corn, wheat, and tobacco. The competition from the West and
the low prices of wheat and corn make them scarcely profitable.
The competition with the Ohio tobacco and the general specialization which has taken place in the tobacco industry, and the necessity of producing something that is peculiarly adapted to a certain
market or to a certain demand, has lowered the price of the Maryland
tobacco. Now, after the Maryland farmer has raised these three
things he has done, as he thinks, the best he can, and he has nothing further to consider for his development. The corn is fed mainly
to his work stock, and it all goes to that and his own labor. The

wheat is sold and sent off the farm in exchange for flour, which he buys at a considerable increase in cost over what it would have cost him if he could have had it ground in his own neighborhood. The tobacco, of course, is sold and goes out in exchange for productions of all kinds for himself and his family. He buys his meat, he buys his groceries, and he frequently buys the vegetables that he should have raised in his garden.

There is no comparison with the conditions in a prosperous community like Lancaster County [Pennsylvania] and the improvident methods that prevail in some of our Maryland counties and Virginia communities. There is no comparison whatever in the economical methods that are employed: and it seems to me that one of the most important contributing causes to the abandonment and impoverishment of the lands in Maryland and Virginia and of many of the Southern States is due to this one fact, that they do not use the same thrifty methods that have marked the success in Lancaster County and in many other of the Northern States.

Testimony, Milton Whitney, March 12, 1901, U.S. Industrial Commission, Report...on Agriculture and Agricultural Labor, X, pp. 871-872.

512. LARGE AND SMALL LANDHOLDINGS (1904)

Along with increasing public attention to the growth of big business, the expanding conservation movement pointed up similar centralizing trends in the ownership of land and other national resources. The members of the Commission who wrote this report were W. A. Richards, F. H. Newell, and Gifford Pinchot.

Detailed study of the practical operation of the present land laws, particularly of the desert-land act and the commutation clause of the homestead act, shows that their tendency far too often is to bring about land monopoly rather than to multiply small holdings by actual settlers. The land laws, decisions, and practices have become so complicated that the settler is at a marked disadvantage in comparison with the shrewd business man who aims to acquire large properties. Not infrequently their effect is to put a premium on perjury and dishonest methods in the acquisition of land. It is apparent, in consequence, that in very many localities, and perhaps in general, a larger proportion of the public land is passing into the hands of speculators and corporations than into those of actual settlers who are making homes.

This is not due to the character of the land. In all parts of the United States known to your Commission where such large holdings are being acquired the genuine homesteader is prospering alongside

of them under precisely the same conditions. Wherever the laws have
been so enforced as to give the settler a reasonable chance he has
settled, prospered, built up the country, and brought about more
complete development and larger prosperity than where land monopoly
flourishes. Nearly everywhere the large landowner has succeeded in
monopolizing the best tracts, whether of timber or agricultural
land. There has been some outcry against this condition. Yet the
lack of greater protest is significant. It is to be explained by
the energy, shrewdness, and influence of the men to whom the continuation of the present condition is desirable.

Your Commission has had inquiries made as to how a number of
estates, selected haphazard, have been acquired. Almost without
exception collusion or evasion of the letter and spirit of the land
laws was involved. It is not necessarily to be inferred that the
present owners of these estates were dishonest, but the fact remains
that their holdings were acquired or consolidated by practices which
can not be defended.

The disastrous effect of this system upon the well-being of the
nation as a whole requires little comment. Under the present conditions, speaking broadly, the large estate usually remains in a
low condition of cultivation, whereas under actual settlement by
individual home makers the same land would have supported many
families in comfort and would have yielded far greater returns.
Agriculture is a pursuit of which it may be asserted absolutely
that it rarely reaches its best development under any concentrated
form of ownership.

There exists and is spreading in the West a tenant or hired-
labor system which not only represents a relatively low industrial
development, but whose further extension carries with it a most
serious threat. Politically, socially, and economically this system
is indefensible. Had the land laws been effective and effectually
enforced its growth would have been impossible.

It is often asserted in defense of large holdings that, through
the operation of enlightened selfishness, the land so held will
eventually be put to its best use. Whatever theoretical considerations may support this statement, in practice it is almost univer-
sally untrue. Hired labor on the farm can not compete with the
man who owns and works his land, and if it could the owners of large
tracts rarely have the capital to develop them effectively.

Although there is a tendency to subdivide large holdings in
the long run, yet the desire for such holdings is so strong and the
belief in their rapid increase in value so controlling and so widespread that the speculative motive governs, and men go to extremes
before they will subdivide lands which they themselves are not
able to utilize.

The fundamental fact that characterizes the present situation
is this: That the number of patents issued is increasing out of
all proportion to the number of new homes.

Second Partial Report of the Public Lands Commission, March 7,
1904, U.S. Congress, 58th, 3rd session, Senate, Document No. 189,
serial number 4766, Report of the Public Lands Commission, pp.
xxiii-xxiv.

513.   "EVERYBODY'S PLACE WAS FOR SALE" (ca. 1910)

This last great American farm frontier was no less
stricken by the real estate viewpoint than farmers on
earlier frontiers.

Anyone familiar with eastern agriculture and the farming of
the Middle West finds a sharp contrast in some of the practices
which prevail in California. If you chance to drop off at any
thriving village or "city"--as many modest towns are called out
here--you will discover that every second man you meet owns a
"ranch." In a few minutes' conversation you will discover also that
his holding consists of only two, five, ten or at most twenty acres
and that it is for sale or for trade, for cash or other equities.
When I first came to California it seemed to me that everybody's
place was for sale; which is merely to say that the Californian is
adventurous and ready always to move on to something new.

Roberts, Autobiography of a Farm Boy, pp. 303-304.

514.   STRUGGLE FOR LAND IN THE SOUTHWEST (1915)

Doctrines of socialism made noticeable headway in
various parts of the Southwest during these years. Deteriorating conditions for the tenant provided the basic
material for this spread. Charles Holman, a member of
the Commission on Industrial Relation's investigation
department, makes this statement.

He is subject--the tenant--to the supervision of the landlord.
He has no rights   unmolestment such as are implied for the tenant
in the laws of feudal origin. We may say, therefore, that the
tenant-laborer, or the "cropper," as he is known in the older sections of the South, is very closely akin to the casual laborer,
whose case you have heard during other hearings. The main difference between the casual laborer and the tenant farmer is that the
casual worker drifts by himself from place to place and may shift
over the whole of the continent, while the tenant farmer drifts from
farm to farm and carries his family with him by means of the covered
wagon.
A recent survey of the shifting farm population of the South
has been made by the Federal agricultural census, whose returns show
that over 50 per cent of the Southern tenants had lived on their
farms for less than a year from which they reported. In view of
this situation I submit that the relation of the so-called tenant
to the landowner is analogous to that of the wageworker to the
employer.

Conversely, the landlord has become the farmer by virtue of this new contractual relation, which is less than 50 years in origin. This is in marked contrast to the condition in some parts of America where the tenant is still the farmer and the landlord has a relation somewhat similar to that of the bondholder or the owner of stock in a corporation inasmuch as he has no supervision over the land and only draws an interest from it. But it should be noted that the same forces appear to be at work in those more prosperous sections that if uncurbed will tend to bring about the same evolution we are now studying in the Southwest.

. . . .

Forty years ago practically all of Texas farmers owned their land. To-day over half rent the land, and the trend toward concentration appears to be steady. In 82 counties of the State the percentage will run from 58 to 70 per cent in concentrated ownership.

In Oklahoma large blocks of land originally owned by Indians have been wrested from them by white men following the removal of restrictions. Yet the State also was generous to home seekers and to-day aids persons wishing to become home owners. Notwithstanding that, a larger percentage of tenancy exists in Oklahoma than in Texas, and the tendency toward concentration of land ownership proceeds unchecked.

To-day we have in this area a big change taking place that is akin to a struggle for the land. The active participants in this struggle are tenants and the landlords, small landowners, and large landowners, who have their own struggles as against each other, money lenders, banks, and merchants. Those directly or indirectly affected by this struggle constitute practically all of the population of the small towns in the area.

Aside from landlords who live in the country, the concentration of ownership is aided by farmers who moved to town, by town creditors, land speculators, Indian-lease speculators, etc., and a whole host of others.

The native white tenants are found throughout all of the southwestern area. The negro tenant is found mainly in east Texas, in the bottoms of the Red River, the Brazos and the Trinity Rivers, or what is known as the old plantation of the South, which starts and runs in a southwesterly direction from Texarkana. The Mexicans begin with the Rio Grande and form a large part of the labor supply throughout southern Texas. Foreign whites in small numbers have come into the Southwest in the last few years.

Testimony, Charles W. Holman, March 16, 1915, U.S. Congress, 64th, 1st session, Senate, Document No. 415, <u>Final Report and Testimony Submitted to Congress by the Commission on Industrial Relations</u>, IX, pp. 8952, 8953.

515. DEFENSE OF NATIONAL RANGE POLICY (1924)

The Federal Forest Service was recommending a new,
and increased, schedule of charges for use of the Western
ranges. Sheep and cattle men objected. Here are two of
their objections and the answers to them. C. E. Rachford,
U.S. Forester, was the author of the report.

Claim No. 2. The users of the national forest range contend
that the attempt of the Forest Service to put the new fees into
effect is a step to commercialize the forage, a policy not contemplated by law, Congress or precedent.
. . . .
Answer. In answer to this argument it seems unnecessary to
repeat what has been said elsewhere in this report relative to the
facts on which the principle of a fair and reasonable compensation
is based. That forage is a commercial commodity has not been questioned. The fact that it grows on Government land rather than on
land owned by individuals does not change its value to stockmen.
There is no clear reason, in justice to the entire stock industry
and the general public owning the land, why a fair price should not
be charged to the favored few who have grazing privileges on the
national forests. If following such a plan means the commercialization of the grazing resources on the national forests, then wise
public policy requires that these resources be commercialized to
that extent. An analysis of the information secured on many forests
would indicate that this question of commercialization is not so
abhorrent to stockmen if they themselves are permitted to do the
commercializing, as has repeatedly happened where sales have been
made and a cash bonus paid by the purchaser for grazing privileges
amounting in some instances to $3 per head for sheep and $5 per
head for cattle.
. . . .
Claim No. 8. It is said that the establishment of a commercial
value principle in the charging of grazing fees is "unjust, fallacious, and pernicious," because the Government is capitalizing the
pioneer efforts of a sturdy American citizenship. No one has greater reverence for the pioneers of the West than forest officers. No
one can sympathize to a greater extent with the hardships, the
trials, and tribulations the pioneer stockman has gone through.
It is difficult to separate national forest permittees, however,
from the large mass of pioneers who have contributed just as much
to the development of the West as these favored few. In other
words, the large number of pioneers who are now engaged in the
livestock business in the West and are not privileged to use the
national forest range are discriminated against. Here again if we
follow this principle of equal benefits it must be admitted that
these pioneers are as justly entitled to the use of the range as
those who by favored location are privileged in its use. No one,
of course, can determine from existing sources of information just
what percentage of those not privileged to use national forest range
have the use of public domain....As a matter of fact, a forest

permittee may be either a real pioneer who has used the range under most liberal terms for half a century, or he may be a newcomer from Iowa or Illinois who has recently purchased a western stock ranch and outfit, securing a waiver of the grazing privilege. Actually the real period of pioneering was past before the forest ranges were put under [government] administration, and during that period the pioneer collected the proper reward for his pioneer efforts in the form of stock raised without cost or restrictions on public lands. He got his pay as he went along.

. . . .

While approximately 85 per cent of the owners of cattle who use national forest ranges are small operators, they graze only 31 per cent of the number of stock on the forests. In other words, 69 per cent of the cattle grazed on national forests are owned by comparatively large operators. These men are in a commercial enterprise just the same as the lumber or power companies, and have no more relation to pioneering in the West than other commercial interests of Western States.

C. E. Rachford, Range Appraisal Report, November 5, 1924, U.S. Congress, 69th, 1st session, Senate, Committee on Public Lands and Surveys, National Forests and the Public Domain, I, pp. 33, 35.

C.

MECHANIZATION OF TRANSPORT

An evaluation of some operational advantages of motor trucks over horse-drawn vehicles is made here by Arthur Herschmann, an engineer with the Adams Express Company in Cincinnati, Ohio.

One of the necessities for the successful running of motor vehicles, for some time to come, will be a good road surface, and those responsible for the maintenance of public roads could well afford to encourage the new movement, seeing that by the use of motor wagons a considerable saving will be effected in the matter of street cleaning, let alone the improvements in the hygienic condition of the roads.

The matter of safety has often been doubted, and, while we will consider it later when studying the characteristics of different systems of motor wagons, it may here be said that statistics have already shown the new vehicle to be far safer from accidents than the horse-drawn vehicle.

At times the horse will stop of its own sweet will, and refuse to budge, but, in case of emergency, using his best efforts he could seldom pull up from full speed inside of less than thirty yards. It necessarily takes time to communicate the driver's will to the horse's brain, and from there to the horse's muscles. A motor wagon, on the other hand, can be quickly stopped, as powerful brakes are within easy reach of the driver, whose intelligence alone is challenged in case of emergency. In addition, the driver of the motor wagon will have a clear view of the road ahead without being perched high in the air. It is very difficult to avoid an accident

with a horse-driven wagon should the pole chain break, and it is
naturally most likely to break when it is most wanted, _i.e._, when
suddenly pulling up.

There is another important item which is strongly in favor of
the motor wagon as compared with the use of horses. Horses are dependent on the weather. Flies molest them in summer time, and the
driver is often led to believe they are sick or tired, and will
naturally slacken up for fear of straining them. Climbing a steep
hill, he will often get off the wagon to save his horses, and it is
evident that all this interferes with economical transportation.

We have briefly touched the matter of brakes, and this really
is the nucleus of the speed question. We need only consider the
speed of modern railway trains and ask ourselves whether such a
speed could be safely maintained without the use of air brakes, to
approach the speed question of motor wagons. It is an easy matter
to provide for powerful brakes on a motor wagon, and the propelling
motor lends itself in many cases as a very powerful second brake.
We have found that a load of three tons on a motor wagon, running
at a speed of eight miles, could be pulled up in eight yards, a performance which could never be obtained with horses. It may have
escaped the notice of the onlooker that when we speak of an 8-mile
gait with horses it should be asked, how long can they keep it
up, and then it should be considered that it would probably only
approximate a 5-mile gait of a motor wagon, which latter never gets
tired, runs evenly, and is ready to do work as long as we provide
fuel, and, further, is satisfied to remain where we leave it when
put out of commission. The latter consideration is an economic
advantage not to be overlooked in the operation of motor wagons.

Arthur Herschmann, "The Automobile Wagon for Heavy Duty,"
Transactions, American Society of Mechanical Engineers, XXI (1900),
pp. 846-847.

517. HORSE VS. TRUCK: COMPARATIVE EXPENSES (1900)

These figures are from a study extending over two years.

Comparison of Operating Expenses Taken for One of the Large American
Cities Covered by the Adams Express Company's Service

2-HORSE WAGON AND 3-TON STEAM WAGON

2 Horses capable of			3-Ton Wagon		
40 ton miles per day, 300 days.			120 ton miles net, 300 days.		
Cost of 2 horses ($130), $260.			25% interest and		
Life of horse, 6 years (then			depreciation.....	$625	35%
worth $30 each) (15%+5%)			Driver	800	40%
$30+13..............	$43	2 1/2%	Gross weight moved,		
Wagon cost, $300.			6 1/2 tons; fuel,		
Last 8 years (12%+5%).	51	3 1/2%	8 lbs. of coke per		
Wagon repairs mainten-			mile. Present mar-		
ance	96	6 1/2%	ket price, $2.70 per		
Stabling, maintaining,			caldron..........	100	7%
shoeing, rents, etc.,			Repairs, 10% of cost	250	15%
per horse and month			Stores.............	50	3%
($30)..............	720	46%	(The figures relat-		
Driver's pay per annum	600	40%	ing to "cost, depre-		
Cost of harness ($45),			ciation, and repairs"		
last 5 years, per			may seem to be high.		
annum, including			The author, however,		
repairs.............	18	1 1/2%	finds that they cannot		
			be much reduced, to		
			serve the purpose of		
			a safe, commercial cal-		
			culation. On the other		
			hand, cost of water and		
			expenses due to the		
			raising of steam have		
			been left out in the fi-		
			gures. In extreme cases		
			these items might add		
			another 5% to the expense.)		
Per annum........	$1,528	100%	Per annum.....	$1,825	100%

2 Horses		3-Ton Wagon
Miles per annum.....	6,000	12,000
Ton miles net.......	12,000	(net) 36,000 (gross) 78,000
Cost per mile.......	25.46 cents.	15.2 cents
Cost per net ton mile	12.73 cents.	5.06 cents. (gross) 2.34 cents.
4 trips daily, per trip		8 trips daily, each $0.76.
trip..............	$1.27	

Herschmann, "The Automobile Wagon for Heavy Duty," p. 859.

518. HAULING FARM PRODUCE TO MARKET (1900)

Overshadowed by the great achievement of railroads,
the problem of local haulage from farm to shipping points
persisted. John Crowell gives the testimony. He was an
"expert agent" of the Industrial Commission.

It has been shown, after careful inquiry, that the average haul
of the American farmer in getting his produce to market, or to the
nearest shipping station, is 12 miles. The average cost per ton for
hauling over the common country roads is 25 cents per ton per mile,
or $3 per ton for a 12-mile haul. Careful estimates, also, place
the total tons hauled at 300,000,000 per year and the average haul
at 12 miles, making the total cost of getting the surplus products
of the farm to the local market or railroad $900,000,000. This fi-
gure is greater than the operating expenses of all the railroads in
the United States, which for the year ending June, 1898, were only
$818,000,000. In other words, it cost $82,000,000 more to haul farm
products to the local points where they enter the distributive system
than it does to operate our entire railway system, comprising nearly
half the mileage of the world.
     Estimates have been gathered by some States to show how expenses
of hauling to local points compare with railway cost of carriage
thence to the principal markets. The returns of West Virginia are
given by counties in parallel columns, showing wagon and rail costs
of transportation. These returns show that the two elements of expense are about equal.
     The average cost of moving a ton of farm products to shipping
point in 55 counties in West Virginia is $3.40, while the average
expenses of shipping to the best markets by rail or water is $3.27.
These estimates are made by farmers and shippers, and are based on
actual experience in localities where costs of this kind do not vary
much for the year.
     A contrast such as this suggests that the defect in our system
of distribution is not so much in our railroads as it is in our wagon
roads.
     There are two policies which European and American experiences
suggest on this matter. One is that of a systematic improvement of
highways under joint cooperation of the central and local authorities
of each State; the other is that of utilizing light railways, as in
England, or trolley extensions to rural village points, as in some
parts of New England, for affording rural districts cheaper access
to market. A trolley system connecting rural villages with a central
town located on a railroad, thus affording a local market and a
shipping point for a wide productive area, would seem to be an outlet for investment and enterprise which must sooner or later command
the attention of city and country alike.
     The methods of reaching markets for the products of the farm
are in many parts of the country imperfect almost to the extent of
being primitive, if not prohibitive beyond certain distances. Our
public roads have not usually favored the farmer in the less

developed States. Even in New Jersey the farmer living farther than
6 or 10 miles from Trenton, for example, must use the railroad for
the purpose of marketing his products in larger markets. The use
of the public highway to reach market is limited by the capacity of
that market. In the most populous portion of the country the railroad is still the main agency for reaching markets.

In less populous States, such as West Virginia, it costs as much
per ton to get farm products from the farm to the railway station as
it does to freight it to the best market after it reaches the railroad. The minor farm products are less generally now, than formerly,
carried by express to large markets in the East. The rates by express are often twice those by freight. The use of refrigerating
freight cars has become so general that they now bring the greater
part of the milk to market. Butter and cream still come to market
quite largely from New England by express.

U.S. Congress, 56th, 2nd session, House of Representatives,
Document No. 494, John Franklin Crowell, Report of the Industrial
Commission on the Distribution of Farm Products, VI, pp. 446-447.

519. MOVING SURPLUS CEREALS (1900)

Following is a succinct statement of the larger
effects of the American transportation system on the
farm economy, again made by John Crowell.

Of primary importance in its economic bearing is the fact of
the organization of agencies for distribution of cereals in the
United States. In this respect these commonwealths are commercially
unique. These States have not only the natural outlets of the lakes
eastward and of the Mississippi and its tributaries southward, but
they have also the most fully equipped system of land transportation
known to the world in the railroads centering on the lakes and
rivers. These water routes and rail routes are complemental agencies
as well as competitive. By the railroads the surplus is concentrated
at the primary markets from the farms for future distribution; by
the lakes and rivers the movement of distribution to internal and
foreign centers of consumption is controlled; so that the water and
railway systems mutually complement and control each other in handling this surplus between productive areas and consuming centers.
This is a fundamental feature in the internal organization of the
cereal trade of this territory and of the United States generally.

The economic relation of these surplus States to the rest of
the United States is further noteworthy. Practically all other
States South and East rely upon these States for what is required
to supplement their own cereal needs in the course of the year. The
twenty-two deficit States are consuming States in relation to these
twelve surplus States, quite as much so as in Great Britain and the

Continent. This regularly available surplus affects the farm policy
of the Atlantic coast in quite the same way as it does that of
England and Ireland; that is, it obliges them to quit producing
cereals at a certain limit of diminishing return to labor and capital
and to substitute some other form of product less exposed to competition from this direction. Hence the very supremacy of these cereal
States in the American market has forced diversification in farm
industry upon widely different localities, both at home and abroad.
Where such diversification has not wholly abandoned grain farming
it has driven it from the extensive to the more intensive methods
of cereal culture, and so raised the yield per acre in the East to
a level of, if not above, that of the West New Jersey, for instance,
now produces "more wheat to the acre than any Western State."
No influence in our national commerce has so stimulated the
Southern and Eastern farmer to improvement in methods and organization of farm economy as this movement of surplus grain has. It is
not too much to say that this movement has revolutionized more than
one-half of our national agriculture.

U.S. Congress, 56th, 2nd session, House of Representatives,
Document No. 494, John Franklin Crowell, Report of the Industrial
Commission on the Distribution of Farm Products, VI, pp. 38-39.

520. THE AIRPLANE BECOMES A COMMODITY (1905)

The Wright brothers financed their early experiments
by earnings from their bicycle shop. When their plane
became operational, they sought to sell the use of it,
but under rather strict conditions. Here Wilbur Wright,
the younger of the two brothers, writes to Octave Chanute,
an air enthusiast, who had been encouraging and consulting
the Wright brothers from the earliest days of experimentation.

It seems that Capt. Ferber [of France] realized that it would
require a year or two for the French Government to act, and fearing
another nation would anticipate it, he went to some wealthy friends
and newspaper publishers and induced them to form a syndicate to
purchase our invention and present it to the nation as a gift for
war purposes. We have made an agreement by which the secret formulas
are communicated, not to the syndicate, but to the government direct.
We give a license to manufacture only for government use. The syndicate cannot exploit the invention commercially. The members are
not Aero-Club people, and have no wish to make the machine public.
Their idea seems to be to secure their return in the shape of army
promotions, or decorations of the "Legion of Honor," &c., &c. They
are to post a forfeit of 25,000 francs by Febr. 5th, of which sum
750,000 frs. is to become ours absolutely as soon as we have

delivered a machine to them, after a trial flight of 50 kilometers.
The balance is to become ours absolutely after an interval not
exceeding three months more, during which time we are to exercise
diligence in imparting instruction, &c.

We agree to furnish no machine or instruction to any other nation or individuals until a period of three months from the delivery
of the machine has expired. We reserve all rights to sell to other
governments after that time. They figure that it will take other
governments a year or two to act, and that France will accordingly
obtain much more than three months' start. M. Fordyce told us after
the contract had been signed that his instructions had been to waste
no words over the price but to make sure that the machine would do
what we claimed. He returned thoroughly convinced. All that his
associates were particular about was to avoid being "hoaxed."

. . . .

We make no concealment of our reasons for wishing to sell in
some other way than as a patented commercial invention. We prefer
to sell to governments because we can thus secure a sure return,
sufficient to satisfy us, without delay, and without burdening our
future with business responsibilities and the tedious lawsuits which
are always necessary to maintain a valuable invention by patent. We
wish to be as free as possible for further scientific explorations.

Letters, Wilbur Wright to Octave Chanute, January 2 and 19,
1906, Marvin W. McFarland (ed.), The Papers of Wilbur and
Orville Wright, II, (New York: McGraw-Hill, 1953), pp. 677-678,
686.

521. WATER TRANSPORT IS UNORGANIZED (1907)

The American water transport system was local in an
age of national markets and closely-held by its main compe-
titor--the railroads. Together, these conditions kept the
system of subsidiary importance in the economy. The
Commissioner of Corporations, Herbert Knox Smith, made
this report.

Specialization in vessels is not only with respect to the peculiar condition of the waterways, but it has gone further in adapting
them to the peculiar conditions of the different kinds of traffic.
This adaptation is especially conspicuous in what are known as bulk-
cargo vessels; that is, vessels which do not carry package freight,
or diversified freight, but which carry one or at most a few kinds
of articles in bulk, Thus on the Great Lakes bulk steam vessels for
ore or coal, and others for grain, are used to an enormous extent.
On the Atlantic and Gulf coasts there are bulk vessels for coal,
for oil, for fruit, etc. On the Pacific coast a type of steam

schooner has been developed, especially intended for hauling lumber
in bulk, and special lumber vessels are also used on the Great Lakes
and the Atlantic Ocean. On the Ohio and Mississippi bulk coal barges
are extensively used, and other bulk boats to some extent. The use
of rafts of logs on the Great Lakes, on the rivers, and on the Pacific coast is a special development of bulk transportation.

This development of the bulk water carrier is highly significant
of the peculiar demands of modern transportation. It has been most
successful in those cases where the products to be shipped are either
on or near the water. This is conspicuous, for example, in the case
of the coal carried on the Monongahela, Ohio, and Mississippi rivers,
most of which is produced at or very near the rivers. At the same
time, a large part of the traffic in bulk water carriers reaches
those carriers only by rail haul, and a considerable part is delivered by rail to the final destination. This occurs, as on the
Lakes, where there is a large uniform supply, a corresponding demand, and a proportionately long water haul connecting the two.

This specialization of types of vessels, as in the various
classes of bulk freighters, in the use of gasoline boats on the
Mississippi River, etc., indicates the struggle of a system to adapt
itself to its conditions. Probably had there been no rail competition, that adaptation would have gone much further and would have
approached something like a good operating system, even on the inferior waterways, such as rivers and canals. But in the keen
struggle with the railroad for existence, hand-to-mouth methods have
been necessary, except on the Great Lakes and the coast, and even
there it is to some extent hampered by rail competition. Could the
rail and water systems have cooperated instead of competing, it
seems probable that a reasonable share of traffic would have produced
a modern system of waterway transportation even on our smaller
rivers.

From these considerations as to the character of our waterways,
and of the vessels used upon them, it is obvious, as already stated,
that our inland waterways are far from constituting a unified system,
and that, save on the Great Lakes, and in the coal traffic on the
Ohio, they are very inferior in efficiency to railroads. In a later
part it will be shown that the traffic on rivers and canals of the
United States is insignificant in comparison with the rail traffic,
or with traffic on the Great Lakes and the coasts. Diversity in
channel and navigation conditions, diversity in vessel types, in
motive power, and in terminals, as well as in carriers' liability,
insurance, freight classification, and traffic contracts generally,
have resulted in extreme absence of organization of our water system
as a whole. It is thus helpless in competing for long-distance
traffic with a modern, unified, standardized system like that of the
railroads.

Report of the Commissioner of Corporations on Transportation
by Water in the United States, Part I, (Washington, D.C.: Government
Printing Office, 1909), pp. 10-11.

522. EARLY MOTOR TRUCK FIRMS (1910)

At the beginning of the century, use of motor trucks
for ordinary commerce was still exploratory (See Source
No. 517). Ten years later, it had become practical enough
to form the basis for financial rivalry. The writer of
the following is Edward Hewitt, grandson of Peter Cooper
and the son of Abram S. Hewitt. As of 1943 he was consulting engineer for the Mack Company.

About 1910, after many successes and failures, my automobile
business became too large for my small quarters in East Thirty-first
Street. My friend, Ambrose Monel, saw the possibility of making a
large business out of truck manufacture, so he proposed to me that
he refinance my company and put it in good shape to go ahead. He
did this by raising six hundred thousand dollars of new capital and
by interesting some of the most important businessmen of that time
in the company. He did the whole thing one day at lunch downtown,
walking about the room and seeing various men and writing down on an
envelope what each of them was willing to put into the company. When
he came back to my table he had been promised the six hundred thous-
and dollars that we sought. Monel wanted to have men of means in
the company, so that, when we needed more capital, we could enlarge
without going outside the original group of stockholders. He had in
view the building up of a large organization to take advantage of the
future growth of the truck industry.
I established the new factory at West Sixty-fourth Street and
Tenth Avenue, where I secured a large building with sufficient room
to develop new designs until we were ready to build a large plant
outside New York. I felt that the business was now started on a
sound and growing basis. Unfortunately for me, the Morgan interests,
at just that time, had financed the truck business developed by Joe
Mack, at Allentown, Pennsylvania, and had combined this with the
Saurer truck, which was of Swiss design. The Morgan people soon
found they had acquired an out-of-date truck design and that the
Saurer models were not suitable for manufacture and sale in this
country.
A majority of my stockholders were closely associated with the
Morgan interests, and they knew that my trucks and designs were
salable and suitable for cheap manufacture. They suggested a consolidation of the Mack Company and the Hewitt Motor Company, in order
to secure practical salable designs and good engineering ability.
I, of course, objected to any consolidation. But I was outvoted,
as I had no control of a majority of the stock of the Hewitt Motor
Company. So the combination took place. I knew that my company,
with its cash capital, which was sufficient for its present needs,
would be successful by itself. However, I was powerless. My five
hundred thousand dollars cash was at once used to pay dividends for
the new company which had not been earned--but that was the way
banking interests behaved in those days!

All the Mack and Saurer designs of trucks were soon abandoned, and only designs which I made were manufactured. The new company should have been called the Hewitt Motor Company. But my friend Monel begged me not to insist on this, because so much money had been spent in advertising the Mack name, he said, and all this capital would be wasted if I insisted on having my name carried on the company's product. I have always regretted that I consented to do this, as it was my work and that of the staff selected by me which made the Mack Company a success--a fact that ought to have received proper recognition.

Edward R. Hewitt, <u>Those Were the Days</u>, (New York: Duell, Sloan, and Pearce, 1943), pp. 220-221.

523.   EARLY AIR MAIL SERVICE (1926)

An intensely personal portrayal of the early years of commercial air flight written by Charles Lindbergh. He was chief pilot for the Robertson Aircraft Corporation and had been on the St. Louis-Chicago run for five months, ever since it was inaugurated.

We pilots, mechanics, postal clerks, and business executives, at St. Louis, Springfield, Peoria, Chicago, all felt that we were taking part in an event which pointed the way toward a new and marvelous era.

But after the first day's heavy load, swollen with letters of enthusiasts and collectors, interest declined. Men's minds turned back to routine business; the air mail saves a few hours at most; it's seldom really worth the extra cost per letter. Week after week, we've carried the limp and nearly empty sacks back and forth with a regularity in which we take great pride. Whether the mail compartment contains ten letters or ten thousand is beside the point. We have faith in the future. Some day we know the sacks will fill.
. . . .
Our contract calls for five round trips each week. It's our mission to land the St. Louis mail in Chicago in time to connect with planes coming in from California, Minnesota, Michigan, and Texas--a time calculated to put letters in New York City for the opening of the eastern business day.
. . . .
Lighting an airport is no great problem if you have money to pay for it. With resolving beacons, boundary markers, and floodlights, night flying isn't difficult. But our organization can't buy such luxuries. There's barely enough money to keep going from month to month.

The Robertson Aircraft Corporation is paid by the pounds of mail we carry, and often the sacks weigh more than the letters

inside. Our operating expenses are incredibly low; but our revenue
is lower still. The Corporation couldn't afford to buy new aircraft.
All our planes and engines were purchased from Army salvage, and rebuilt in our shops at Lambert Field. We call them DHs, because the
design originated with De Haviland, in England. They are biplanes,
with a single, twelve-cylinder, four-hundred-horse-power Liberty
engine in the nose. They were built during the war for bombing and
observation purposes, and improved types were put on production in
the United States. The military DH has two cockpits. In our planes
the mail compartment is where the front cockpit used to be, and we
mail pilots fly from the position where the wartime observer sat.

We've been unable to buy full night-flying equipment for these
planes, to say nothing of lights and beacons for the fields we land
on. It was only last week that red and green navigation lights were
installed on our DHs. Before that we carried nothing but one emergency flare and a pocket flashlight. When the dollars aren't there,
you can't draw checks to pay for equipment. But it's bad economy,
in the long run, to operate a mail route without proper lights. That
has already cost us one plane. I lost a DH just over a week ago
because I didn't have an extra flare, or wing lights, or a beacon
to go back to.

. . . .

But the cost--it would take ten or fifteen thousand dollars to
buy just one Wright-Bellanca. Who could afford to invest so much
money in a single airplane, to say nothing of the three that would
be needed for a mail route? Our Corporation has a hard enough time
to keep going with the DHs, and they cost only a few hundred dollars
apiece.

I grow conscious of the limits of my biplane, of the inefficiency of its wings, struts, and wires. They bind me to earth and to
the field ahead at Chicago. A Bellanca would cruise at least fifteen miles an hour faster, burn only half the amount of gasoline,
and carry double the pay load of a DH. What a future aviation has
when such planes can be built; yet how few people realize it! Businessmen think of aviation in terms of barnstorming, flying circuses,
crashes, and high costs per flying hour. Somehow they must be made
to understand the possibilities of flight. If they could see the
real picture, it wouldn't be difficult to finance an airline between
St. Louis and New York, even at the price of three Bellancas. Then
commercial pilots wouldn't have to fly old army warplanes or make
night landings with flares instead of flood-lights.

If only I had the Bellanca, I'd show St. Louis businessmen what
modern aircraft could do; I'd take them to New York in eight or nine
hours. They'd see how swiftly and safely passengers could fly.
There are all kinds of records I could break for demonstration--
distance, altitude with load, nonstop flights across the country.
In a Bellanca filled with fuel tanks I could fly on all night, like
the moon. How far could it go if it carried nothing but gasoline?
With the engine throttled down it could stay aloft for days. It's
fast, too. Judging from the accounts I've read, it's the most efficient plane ever built. It could break the world's endurance record,
and the transcontinental, and set a dozen marks for range and speed

and weight. Possibly--my mind is startled at its thought--I could
fly nonstop between New York and Paris.

        Charles A. Lindbergh, The Spirit of St. Louis, (New York:
Scribner's Sons, 1953), pp. 3-4, 13-14.

        524. THE RAILROADS WILL BE PUBLICLY OWNED (1934)

        Nationalization of the railroad industry was regarded
by some specialists as the ultimate solution to the chronic
ills of the industry. This is argued here by Joseph Eastman,
Federal Coordinator of Transportation.

        Theoretically and logically public ownership and operation
meets the known ills of the present situation better than any other
remedy. Public regulation of a privately owned and operated industry, reaching deeply into such matters as rates, service, capitalization, accounting, extensions and abandonments, mergers and consoli-
dations, is a hybrid arrangement. When an industry becomes so public
in character that such intimate regulation of its affairs becomes
necessary, in strict logic it would seem that it should cease to
masquerade as a private industry and the Government should assume
complete responsibility, financial and otherwise.
        While there are dangers incident to any governmental undertaking
ing, so there are to any private undertaking and to any private-
public undertaking. The history of the American railroads is proof
enough of this fact. There is reason to believe that many of the
dangers which are ordinarily seen in public ownership and operation
can be brought under control if suitable precautions are taken. I
incline to the belief that such ownership and operation will be the
ultimate solution of the railroad problem. However, if and when
that time arrives, the impelling motive will probably not be logic
or theory, but the practical one that private enterprise and capital
will not be able to carry on successfully. That has been the general
experience.
        Nevertheless, I am not now prepared to recommend resort to
public ownership and operation. This is for the principal reason
that the country is not now financially in a condition to stand the
strain of an acquisition of these great properties, imposing burdens
which cannot be definitely foreseen and might well, in present circumstances, be disproportionately severe. The danger would be enhanced by the fact that there would be a comparatively long period
before the new system could be got into smoothly running order, and
by the further fact that the railroad industry is now in a stage of
accelerated evolution. This is true, indeed, of the entire transportation industry, and it is at least questionable whether the
railroads alone could well be nationalized without including other

forms of transport to some considerable extent. The British Royal
Commission of 1930 was unanimously of the opinion that such inclu-
sion would be necessary.

Joseph B. Eastman, report to the Interstate Commerce Commission,
January, 1934, U.S. Congress, 73rd, 2nd session, Senate, Document
No. 119, serial number 9800, Regulation of Railroads, p. 30.

525. INNOVATING THE DIESEL LOCOMOTIVE (1930's)

How is a very small but imaginative firm attracted
to become part of a giant corporation? Why should the
latter concern itself with such a small firm? Here are
the elements of a case study in technological innovation
through large-scale organization. Harold Hamilton testifies here. He initiated formation of the original Electro-
Motive Company in 1922 and can be considered a pioneer
innovator of the Diesel locomotive. After his company
became a subsidiary of General Motors in 1930, Hamilton
became vice-president; at the time of testifying, he was
in retirement.

Mr. BURNS. At that time [ca. 1930] was General Motors making
any diesels of any type that you know of?
Mr. HAMILTON. No; they were not. General Motors at that
time, based on my conversations with Kettering--he had been thinking
seriously along the lines of the diesel cycle as per se, not an
engine or its application, but the diesel cycle per se, and that is
the subject of our conversations of great length, so they had been
thinking about it, talking about it among themselves, and I think
he had run some experimental phases on certain parts of the problem;
but there had been no manufacture of diesels. They did not have any
design even at that time.
. . . .
Mr. [Charles] Kettering...wanted to get right in the middle
of that one, right now, and I presume that his influence on General
Motors entered into their decision to put all these things together
and really get at this job, because up to that point he had been
thinking in terms of purely the scientific or technological problems
and the technical problems, unknown problems engineering-wise to
do to a diesel what had to have done with it.
That was the extent of his thinking. Here we come along and
here is the problem. We are waiting, we are stymied. All we need
now is an engine that will meet these specifications.
So the minute we fed him that it was just like ringing a bell
to a fire horse; he wanted to get into that act quick, and, of
course, that encouraged me, and there were further observations,

as I recall it, with the officer in General Motors that I carried my negotiations, in which all the things were laid out on paper, and we made it clear that we did not have any business.

He knew that. The records were there, he could see what was happening. Winton [a firm cooperating with Electromotive in experimentation] did not have any business, but none of us thought the country was coming to an end. We felt there was a future for us.

We knew we had an economic potential that was just opening up like a rose once we could get over some of these hurdles, and the hurdles were challenges to General Motors research people, and they were anxious to take hold of it, and I am sure Mr. Kettering assured the General Motors people there was no question but what we could do it.

It might take some time and dollars, but we could do it if we could get over this hurdle; but that is where it sat.

Mr. BURNS.   It appeared to you that Mr. Kettering was keenly interested in the scientific phases of developing and improving a diesel engine?

Mr. HAMILTON.   No question about it. We spent hour after hour and night after night talking about it.

Mr. BURNS.   And what you offered was this prospect of a specific application?

Mr. HAMILTON.   That is right.

Mr. BURNS.   And as you felt, a specific market in case you succeeded?

Mr. HAMILTON.   That is right. That is what we offered.

. . . .

Mr. BURNS.   And you were bringing to General Motors all that background and thinking which you had gone through.

Now, were there any others in your organization who, besides yourself, contributed to that development or were they all just working under your structure?

Mr. HAMILTON.   We had a staff of people. We had electrical engineers, a chief engineer, a man named Dillworth, and a book has been written about him. He was probably one of the leading engineers, particularly in this field, recognized in America. He was chief engineer of Electro-Motive. We had a substantial staff of people.

Mr. BURNS.   You had a substantial staff, and they were not purely mechanical. They helped to work on the development?

Mr. HAMILTON.   They were engineers; yes, sir; they were engineers.

. . . .

The problem was that the product that we knew how to make was inadequate, and to make a product which, in this case, was the engine, that would be adequate, was not considered in the cards at that time in the industry and, therefore, somebody had to supply the know-how and the energy and the capital to learn how to make the engine.

Once we learned how to design it, then problems took care of themselves. That was just ordinary manufacturing problems that could be met many ways.

So the barrier was really the fact that we had come to the end
of the road. We no longer had an engine or a prime mover that
would keep us in business, but we knew what would keep us in business, but we did not know how to design it.

. . . .

Mr. Codrington and I thrashed this problem over back and forth
between us probably for a year, how do we get out of this box we are
in, and ever possible phase of it was analyzed, and we analyzed the
mentality, if you will, of the people that we know in the industry,
those not only in the diesel industry and otherwise, but we did not
know any of them that we felt had the courage to take hold of that
thing in its nebulous stage, and start from scratch in view of the
fact that we were going clear out of the metallurgy we knew at that
time. We had to have crank-shaft bearing loadings that nobody had
ever used before, and that meant we had to go back and develop the
bearing material to make the thing work, and that gets us into new
metallurgy. We had to use piston temperatures that nobody had ever
used. We had to devise a machine to measure the temperature of a
piston clear across the crown. Nobody had ever done it before.
That was the nature of the problem, so you had to have courage to
step into that one.

Testimony, Harold L. Hamilton, November 10, 1955, U.S. Congress,
84th, 1st session, Senate, Committee on the Judiciary, Subcommittee
on Antitrust and Monopoly, A Study of the Antitrust Laws, VI,
General Motors, pp. 2432, 2433, 2434, 2435, 2437.

526.   THE STEAM LOCOMOTIVE IS HERE TO STAY (1935)

In 1935, when the remarks below were made, 97% of all
locomotives in service were steam-driven, and fewer than 1%
were diesel-powered. In 1957, 6% were steam-driven and 93%
were diesel-powered. The speaker is Robert Binkerd, vice-
president, Baldwin Locomotive Works, the country's largest
producer of steam locomotives.

Now it was only about 30 years ago that the railroads in the
United States were just about to be completely electrified. Yet
today, as we approach the completion of the greatest single electrification in the history of American railroads, I do not think I am
giving away any secret when I say that the expectations of our big
electrical companies with regard to future railroad electrification
are not very sanguine. Certainly I give up no secret when I say
that from a plain dollars and cents point of view the steam locomotive today is a more serious competitor with electrification than it
was 30 years ago.

Today we are having quite a ballyhoo about streamlined, light-
weight trains and diesel locomotives, and it is no wonder if the

public feels that the steam locomotive is about to lay down and play
dead. Yet over the years certain simple fundamental principles continue to operate. Some time in the future, when all this is reviewed, we will not find our railroads any more dieselized than they
are electrified, and in each case a substantial portion of those
operations will not be based upon what will produce the highest return on the investment, but on esthetic considerations or compulsion
of public bodies.

. . . .

Diesel motive power and high speeds in passenger service are
not synonymous. On the contrary, diesel power can attain high speeds
only by imposing rigid mechanical limitations on the loads to be
carried. These destroy interchangeability, deny the possibilities
of flexible service, and would practically destroy the existing investment in passenger equipment.

Steam power has demonstrated for generations its ability to furnish high-speed service provided the tractive force of the locomotive
is properly proportioned to the deadweight of the train.

The proponents of these dieselized, high-speed trains have
firmly grasped the principle of relating the deadweight of the trains
to their motive power. It is up to you men to do the same thing
with regard to steam.

The inherent nature of the diesel locomotive and its accompanying electrical equipment in the present state of development debar
it from high speed road service because of the physical characteristics of the power itself, its excessive capital cost, and its probable high maintenance cost.

Per contra, the outstanding advantage of the diesel is for work
at low speed in switching or hump-yard service.

Present fuel economies of the diesel locomotive are real, but
their continued repetition in the distant future is uncertain; and
it appears more likely that diesel oil will increase in price than
that coal will do so.

There is not ground in recorded experience for the claim that
diesel locomotives can be maintained at a lower cost than steam.
On the contrary, everything indicates that maintenance costs will
be higher, but how much higher no one can say with certainty.

When considering the possibility of diesel versus obsolete
steam operation, the first thing to aid good judgement is to set up
what modern steam power could do in the same operation.

If the internal-combustion locomotive still indicates substan-
ial economy, the diesel locomotive should be seriously considered,
provided that the savings on the diesel operation represent a return
on the capital investment at least equal to the return on the lesser
investment required for steam.

Robert S. Binkerd, April 25, 1935, Address to New York Railroad
Club, New York City, U.S. Congress, 84th, 1st session, Senate,
Committee on the Judiciary, Subcommittee on Antitrust and Monopoly,
A Study of the Antitrust Laws, VIII, General Motors, pp. 3965-3966.

527. BARRIERS TO INTERSTATE TRUCKING (1940)

Like China's warlords of old, who levied heavy local
tariffs and charges on goods travelling through their baili-
wicks, the modern States legislated burdens on interstate
motor truck transportation to suit their localistic interests. The testimony is given by Lee Conner, a truck driver
who travelled regularly a route from Akron, Ohio to Dallas,
Texas.

Mr. DONOHO. Through what States do you travel making your
trip?
Mr. CONNER. Ohio, Indiana, Illinois, Missouri, Kansas, Oklaho-
ma, and Texas.
Mr. DONOHO. Do you meet with what you consider trade barriers
in going through these States?
Mr. CONNER. I do.
Mr. DONOHO. Into what general types do these barriers fall,
Mr. Conner?
Mr. CONNER. License, for one, and length, weight laws, and
different permits that the various States have.
Acting Chairman PIKE. How often do you make this round trip?
Mr. CONNER. I make it twice a month.
Mr. DONOHO. Let's take your trip from Akron to Dallas, what
requirements must be met? What weight and size must you have, and
what license fees must you pay in Ohio?
Mr. CONNER. To start out of Ohio I have to have a license
plate and a P.U.C.O. card--that is, a Public Service Commission card
of Ohio.
Mr. DONOHO. How much does your license cost?
Mr. CONNER. The State license costs $150.
Mr. DONOHO. How much does the P.U.C.O. card cost?
Mr. CONNER. That is $45 per truck, and you must have this
P.U.C.O. card with you at all times. I can haul 25,000 pounds pay
load in the State of Ohio, but the other States----
Mr. DONOHO (Interposing). Now let's go to the other States.
When you go into Indiana what must you have with regard to license,
cards or permits?
Mr. CONNER. First, I don't have to have any license but I have
to have a permit, and the law doesn't require any definite place for
that to be painted on the side of your truck. Some officers will
tell you, "It wants to be on the side." Another officer will stop
you and say, "That ought to be on the bumper," and you have to erase
that, and the next one will stop you and say, "That has to be on the
back." You know, it is just continuous that way, most every trip
that you go through the State.
Acting Chairman PIKE. This permit is taken out once a year, or
for each trip?
Mr. CONNER. How is that?
Acting Chairman PIKE. The Indiana permit is taken out once
a year?

Mr. CONNER. That is right.

Acting Chairman PIKE. Except for changing it at the whims of the officers, that is good for the year?

Mr. CONNER. That is good for the year, that is right.

Mr. DONOHO. To continue with Indiana, what about the weight and size requirements?

Mr. CONNER. We have to cut our weight down there to 16,000 per axle, and your length law is 40 feet in Indiana.

Mr. DONOHO. What difficulties do you meet in Illinois?

Mr. CONNER. Nothing there in the way of license or permits, but speed of 20 miles an hour, and 35 feet length, and that is different.

Mr. DONOHO. Now what about Missouri?

Mr. CONNOR. That is the worst State we have....We have a card similar to this P.U.C.O. card. That costs us $500 per truck a year, and if you don't have that card, you have to have what they call a travel order, that is an emergency card that costs you $4.50 and you are limited to twenty-four hours in the State, and they tell you the time you enter the State and the time you must get out.

Testimony, Lee Conner, March 22, 1940, Verbatim Record of the Proceedings of the Temporary National Economic Committee, XII, (Washington, D.C.: The Bureau of National Affairs, Inc., 1940), p. 429.

528. WAR AND TRANSPORTATION FACILITIES (1942)

Urgencies of the war added to the normal shortcomings of a transportation system that had never been optimally organized. At this time Joseph Eastman, who gives the testimony, was Director, Office of Defense Transportation, and chairman, Interstate Commerce Commission.

Wholly in addition to this general growth of traffic are the diversions of water-borne freight which have come to the railroads, and those are very serious. As you know, the intercoastal ships are no longer operating through the [Panama] canal. All of the transcontinental traffic is being handled by the railroads and, of course, that is long-haul traffic. As you also know, the eastern seaboard, until very recently, was supplied with petroleum and petroleum products very largely by tanker vessels operating from the Gulf along the coast at very low cost. Due to the diversion of those ships and their stoppage for various reasons, the railroads have been called upon to handle the very greatly increased load of that traffic.

Back in December they were hauling about 70,000 barrels a day
in tank cars to the eastern seaboard. Last week it was just about
600,000 barrels. That, I may say, has consumed the attention and
time of 850 locomotives used in hauling that additional load to the
eastern seaboard.

. . . .

Now, in addition to that, we have the fact that owing to the
water situation along the coast, the efficiency of the colliers that
supply New England with a large part of its coal from Hampton Roads
has been diminished as much as 40 to 50 percent. That has already
thrown a heavy load on the railroads carrying coal from the Pennsylvania fields, and it promises to throw a still heavier load on them
in carrying coal over the long-haul routes from the West Virginia
fields into New England.

In addition to that, the ore carriers on the Great Lakes are
being called upon to carry about eighty-seven to eighty-eight million tons of iron ore this year as contrasted with 81,000,000 last
year, which was an all-time record. In order to enable those iron-
ore boats to carry that iron ore this year, it has become necessary
to divert as much coal as possible from the return hauls of these
boats where it involves an increase in the round-trip time. For
instance, when you move coal by lake to Chicago, that means that
the ore boat moves down Lake Michigan to Chicago and then back up
again and to the Lake Erie ports. If that coal movement to Chicago
can be cut out, the round-trip time of the ore boats is decreased.
We plan to have as much of that coal as possible shipped to Lake
Erie and Lake Huron and Lake Michigan ports by rail instead of by
water from the Lake Erie ports. That has already increased the load
on the railroads and will increase it still more.

Testimony, Jospeh B. Eastman, April 23, 1942, U.S. Congress,
77th, 1st session, Senate, Special Committee Investigating the
National Defense Program, Investigation of the National Defense
Program, XII, pp. 5200-5201.

529. PROGRESS IN EARTH-MOVING (1956)

Government-sponsored construction projects,
roads especially, greatly stimulated the earth-moving
industry. Since earth-moving constitutes about one-third
of the road contractor's costs, he is open to new means of
economizing that expenditure. (Contrast source No. 35).
Raymond Armington, general manager of Euclid Division,
General Motors Corporation, writes.

[Mr. ARMINGTON.] Within the memory of most of us here, earth
had to be moved with a horse-drawn shovel. A man with a horse and

scraper on a 1,500-foot haul could load and carry approximately 1 1/2 cubic yards of earth per hour, whereas, today the largest Euclid twin-engine, self-propelled scraper and pusher can haul over 250 cubic yards. Thus, 1 man and a machine can now do about the same amount of work that it used to take over 160 men and 160 horses. Today's mining operations from Labrador to the Tropics, our road-building programs, construction of airports and power dams and flood-control projects would not be possible without the earth-moving machinery industry which produces annually approximately $1 billion worth of machinery.

    Senator O'MAHONEY. May I interrupt you to confirm your statement by saying for the record that when I first went West, I found it to be the practice in several mining communities for the chamber of commerce to take a day or two off each month, and on these days the members of the chamber of commerce would get their shovels and go out and help the county to build its county roads to the mining area. That, of course, is a thing of the long-dead past.

    Mr. ARMINGTON. Well, then you really know the background of this industry, because that is where it started.

    Senator O'MAHONEY. Yes; I have lived through it.

Testimony, Raymond Q. Armington, November 17, 1955, U.S. Congress, 84th, 1st session, Senate, Committee on the Judiciary, Subcommittee on Antitrust and Monopoly, A Study of the Antitrust Laws, VI, General Motors, p. 2697.

530. TYPICAL MENUS FOR PIONEER VOYAGES (1492 and 1958)

    In 1958, the nuclear-powered submarine U.S.S. Skate travelled 2,405 miles in 31 days; it was submerged over the entire trip. Modern food technology made the trip possible.

	Nina, Pinta, Santa Maria	U.S.S. Skate
Milk group:	Cheese	Milk (fresh, dried, eva- porated) Cheese (canned) Butter Cream (dried, stabilized) Ice cream paste
Meat group:	Salt meat (beef and pork) Salt fish (barreled sardines and ancho- vies) (fishing tackle)	Pork cuts (frozen) Prefried bacon, pullman hams, brown-and-serve sausage (canned) Beef, boneless (fresh, frozen, canned, corned, dehydrated)

	Nina, Pinta, Santa Maria	U.S.S. Skate
Meat group, continued:		Veal, boneless (frozen) Liver, prefabricated (frozen) Luncheon meats (fresh, canned) Chile con carne (dehydrated) Poultry (chicken cuts, frozen; turkey logs, canned) Fish (frozen, canned, dehydrated) Eggs
Vegetable-fruit group:	Chickpeas Lentils Beans Rice Raisins Almonds Garlic	Potatoes (fresh, canned, dehydrated diced) Cabbage, string beans, peppers, onions (dehydrated) Peas (dehydrofrozen) Beans (dried) Other vegetables and fruit (fresh, frozen, canned, dried) Tomato juice, concentrated (canned) Orange, grapefruit juice (dehydrated crystals) Lemon, concentrated (frozen) Apples, pie style (dehydrated) Applesauce (instant) Soups: Potato, onion, vegetable (dehydrated) Soup bases Jellies, jams (canned) Sauces (canned) Peanut butter
Bread-cereal-wheat group:	Flour (salted at milling) Biscuit (well seasoned, good, not old)	Flour Flour mixes; bread, rolls, doughnut, cake, pancake Oatmeal Cornmeal Breakfast cereal, assorted Bread (fresh) Brown bread (canned) Cookies Macaroni, spaghetti, noodles Crackers

	Nina, Pinta, Santa Maria	U.S.S. Skate
Other foods:	Olive oil	Shortening, hydrogen-
	Honey	ated
	Wine	Salad oil
	Vinegar	Dessert powders
		Catsup, chili sauce
		Pickles, olives
		Vinegar
		Sugar, sirups
		Candies
		Spices, condiments
		Coffee (ground, in-
		stant)
		Tea
		Cocoa

U.S. Department of Agriculture, Power to Produce, (Washington, D.C.: Government Printing Office, 1960), p. 453.

531. PROBLEMS OF THE SMALL TRUCK-FLEET OPERATOR (1977)

In 1935, as a consequence of passage of the Motor Carrier Act, the Interstate Commerce Commission (ICC) began to regulate the trucking industry. Government had long been involved in some aspects of the industry. For example, between 1921 and 1974, federal, state, and local govern- ments spent some $400 billion on highways, much of it an indirect subsidy to the trucking industry. ICC regulated entry into the industry, rates, and countless other aspects of the business. Large firms tended to adapt to the regula- tion but many small firms shared only the leavings. William Myers, a small truck fleet owner from Orange, California, illustrates the meager nature of the rewards.

Having had 24 years of trucking experience and having been leased to five regulated carriers during that time, I feel qualified to discuss the problems of the small fleet operator.

Back in 1953, I started trucking with one unit and leased my equipment to a carrier that transported cars. Since then, I have either owned, leased, or managed a small number of trucks, and the number has varied depending upon whom I was leased to, or the commo- dity I have carried. Currently, I haul unregulated goods--fresh produce--eastward and try to obtain a return load back to the growing area.

At this point, it is interesting to note the intent of the Federal Government when it passed the Interstate Commerce Act [in 1887]. The Congress intended that fresh produce be left unregulated because of the need for rapid transportation to cities and towns around the country.

Congress believed that less interference by regulations would speed up the delivery. They were right. The unprocessed agricultural goods have always received good service by independent truckers, and for good reason.

The independent truckers and the small fleet operators have provided better service than the large carriers. A personal interest is involved in the transportation. My livelihood depends on the care and service I give to the shipper if I wish to continue to have his business. The large carrier driver is only interested in putting in his time and then forgetting about the job.

Let's take a look at transportation costs. In the exempt hauling business, there are no fixed rates. Rates do vary depending upon the availability of trucks and the volume of produce to be moved. With regulated freight, fixed guidelines are established. It is illegal to charge below the lowest published tariff rates when hauling regulated goods in interstate commerce. Remember that the big bulk of all transportation falls in the regulated category. Regulated goods generally are processed goods.

To be more specific, 10 years ago a load of fresh strawberries palletized for transportation paid the exempt hauler just about the same rates as we are getting today. However, frozen strawberries, falling under the classification of regulated commodities, have seen more than a doubling in the transportation costs. The same is true for most all the regulated traffic. The rate has doubled and sometimes tripled over the past 10 years. This has not been the case in the exempt field. Still, there are exempt truckers by the thousands who enter the field each year. Thousands make an exit each year, too.

On the surface, it appears easy to enter exempt trucking. But that is a flaw in the thinking of many would-be truckers who lack the experience needed to exist. A young man will think about the freedom of being on the highway, traveling across the country each week. He will save or borrow enough money for a down payment on a tractor and trailer. This is only the tip of the iceberg. A crooked product broker can vanish from sight without paying the trucker for the load. A serious mechanical breakdown can delay the trucker for several weeks, hence he may not have any income, and, therefore, he may lose his rig.

If the truck is not properly licensed and has no permits for the states he travels through, the trucker can be delayed and fined. Certain states require exempt authority for any truckers traveling through their boundaries, and without this, truckers won't be permitted to enter. A truck must meet the inspection requirements at weigh and inspection stations.

An inexperienced trucker will find out about these obstacles soon enough. Many do not make it through the so-called apprentice years. They vanish from the scene.

If we go back to the intention of the Congress when it passed the ICC Act, we find that Congress was not aware of the many problems that could easily put an exempt trucker out of business. Still, this

breed of man has survived over the past 41 [i.e., 90] years since
the the enactment of the ICC. It should be kept in mind that there
is a high mortality rate among newcomers to exempt hauling and that
only the experienced stand the best chances of remaining in business.
   In hauling exempt commodities, I have informed you that rates
have not increased proportionately to the costs of operation. Ten
years ago, a new tractor could be purchased for $25,000. Fuel was as
low as 15 cents per gallon. The total tractor-trailer and cargo
insurance averaged $2,200 per year. Today a new tractor will cost
$45,000 to $50,000. Fuel is now 55 to 60 cents per gallon, and a
complete insurance package will run approximately $6,000 per year.
Personally, I feel that the insurance cost is one of the biggest
rip-offs in trucking today. It is my suggestion that an investigation into truck insurance rates be initiated by Congress. Should
the rates be as high as they are? I question whether they should.
Should the exempt truck pay the insurance premium that high-tariff-
regulated trucks pay? You must remember that it is the trucks
carrying alcohol and tobacco that are often high-jacked, not the
trucks carrying lettuce.

   Testimony, April 15, 1977, U.S. Congress, 95th, 1st session,
House of Representatives, Committee on Small Business, Subcommittee
on Special Small Business Problems, Regulatory Problems of the
Independent Owner-Operator in the Nation's Trucking Industry (Part
2). Hearings...., (Washington, D.C.: Government Printing Office,
1977), pp. 204-205.

532. AGAINST DEREGULATION IN THE TRUCKING INDUSTRY (1979)

   The revenues of the trucking industry account for
about three-fourths of the income of all transportation
industries. First regulated in detail by a 1935 law,
during the 1970s a strong movement toward deregulation
took shape. In 1980, the Motor Carrier Act was passed
against the opposition of the Teamsters Union and the
organized truckers industry. Favoring the measure were
shippers, farm coops, and consumer groups. Prime goal
of the law was to foster competition and thus, hopefully,
to reduce prices and improve services. Entry into the
market would be greatly eased with the Interstate Commerce
Commission having greatly reduced powers to regulate the
advent of new competitors. While the trucking industry
included some 17,000 entities, about 1,000 or so grossed
over $3 million per year while the majority earned much
less. It was the smaller truckers who feared the worst
from the departure from regulation. Following is a statement voicing such fears by Paul Robert Newson, president
of Courier-Newsom Express, Columbus, Indiana.

My father started Newsom Trucking Co. in the early 1930's,
before there was regulation. He started with one truck, very little
money, hardly any insurance, and operated between Seymour, Columbus,
Franklin, and Indianapolis, Inc., for one customer, Noblitt Sparks,
a total of 43 miles.

When the Motor Carrier Act was passed, he applied for and got
operating authority for this service under the grandfather provisions.

Since that time, we have purchased either all or parts of eight
other truck lines, at a total expenditure of $1,800,000. We now
serve the areas of Rockford and Chicago, Ill.; Detroit, Mich., on
the north; Indiana and Louisville, Ky.; Asheville, N.C.; Knoxville,
Chattanooga, and Nashville, Tenn., on the south. We hold irregular
route authority, limited commodity, from Columbus, Inc., to 14
States.

We had a gross revenue of $25 million in 1978, operating 14
terminals in the areas mentioned. Our company has over 250 company-
owned power units and 600 trailers. We also employ 70 owner-opera-
tors in our special commodity division. In our freight division,
our company employs 600 drivers, dockmen, office personnel, salesmen,
mechanics, safety people, and operating personnel.

All of this expansion and growth has been done under the rules
and regulations of the Interstate Commerce Commission and the Motor
Carrier Act, with several of these years having operations in the
red or only being able to make 2 or 3 cents on the dollar after taxes
and interest. Yet, we are continually hearing and reading about how
much money the trucking industry makes and how many billions of
dollars can be saved if the trucking industry is deregulated.

My concern now is for the future, not only for our company and
its employees and customers, but for all the other carriers in
Indiana and their employees, who are like we are. Indiana carriers
are all middle-sized to small carriers. None of the large companies
are domiciled in Indiana, but they all serve Indiana and haul most
of the preferred traffic to the many thousands of points they make
direct. The local carriers must make their living off of short-
haul service and interline traffic, mainly to and from the small
towns and communities located outside the metropolitan areas.

Under deregulation, this is the area that will suffer. Small
shippers and stores located in small towns will be forced to pay
higher rates and will get poorer service, if they get service at
all. Large carriers dominated by a few will siphon off all the
traffic they want at low rates, and the rest will pay higher rates
to move their freight and will be placed in a noncompetitive position. Industries will have to move from the smaller towns to large
towns at a much higher operating cost in order to secure competitive
freight rates and service. It does not do an industry any good to
make a better mousetrap if he cannot get it to market at the same
cost as his competitor.

We are also feeling the effects of the ICC's unlimited policy
on entry. One carrier gained temporary operating authority on
August 27, and by September the 15, he had handled at least 15
loads from Detroit to Louisville, Ky . This was all traffic we had
handled for several years and created 15 empty movements for us. It
is impossible to replace that kind of traffic overnight.

Another example of lost traffic because of ridiculous granting
of authority is that for years our company has interlined, at Fort
Wayne, Ind., traffic between Indiana and Ohio. This summer, the
Ohio carrier we had interlined this traffic with, for no reason, was
granted temporary authority to serve all points in the State of
Indiana. They had only a small number of supporting shippers, of
which the majority were downtown shoe stores and hardware stores.
There is no way for this carrier to economically serve all points in
Indiana. At the many points we serve, this means they are delivering and we are delivering, and we are both running half-empty equipment to deliver the freight.
    The only way to replace this lost freight is to go out and take
it away from another carrier. To allow more carriers between two
points does not make more freight to haul; it just divides what
there is between more people.
    Indiana is blessed with motor carrier service. There are 65
common carriers who serve Indianapolis daily, and who knows how
many more. In Columbus, a town of 25,000, there are 26 carriers
with daily service to Chicago, 3 with direct service to the west
coast and 6 with direct service to the east coast. There is no town
in the United States and most of Canada that cannot be served on a
two-line basis, with through rates.
    Now, let us talk about more specifics: Ade, Ind. population,
50; Birdseye, Ind., population, 404; Chalmers, Ind. population,
544; Fort Wayne, 177,000; Indianapolis, 745,000; Wolcott, 894;
Yorktown, Ind., 1,673; and last but not least, Zionsville, Ind.,
with a population of 1,857....
    About 50 of these carriers have their home offices in this
state, and therefore, the subject of deregulation is not only important to me and my company, but also to these companies and the 5
million people in the 91 counties.
    Even though some of these towns located in Indiana are small
and the shipments are light and few and far between, service is
still provided on the same basis and cost as to the large metropolitan areas.
    In order to serve these small towns, a peddle operation is
used from a terminal location, in much the same manner as the old
huckster wagons of days gone by which traveled the highways peddling
their wares.
    Freight for a particular area which might include a dozen or so
small towns is loaded on a trailer and the driver will stop at each
small town en route and deliver what freight he has for the community. After making all the deliveries, he will reverse his direction
back through these same small towns, picking up any outbound freight
there might be. On a given day, one driver could travel as much as
200 miles picking up and delivering in small towns. It is certainly
a different operation than the one seen daily in the many large
industrial cities across the Nation. Yet, these people and communities are entitled to the same service and the same rate structure
as the shipper in the large areas, and today they have the same
service and costs.

One might think there would be a lack of carrier service to towns such as Ade, Birdseye and Chalmers with their small populations, but my routing guide shows 6 carriers serving Ade, 3 serving Birdseye, and 14 serving Zionsville. In addition, there are several irregular route and specialized commodity carriers who possess statewide authority.

At this point, you might begin to wonder what all this has to do with deregulation. The answer is very simple. The task force of the ICC has recommended the ICC institute proceedings aimed at total deregulation of motor carriers through master certification in 12 truckload commodity areas, including refrigerated, lumber and building materials, metals, bulk materials, heavy machinery, and oil field equipment.

In the case of Courier-Newsom, annually over 2,200 shipments, with a revenue in excess of $1 million, would fall in one of these 12 categories. Seventy-one percent of our revenue is derived from truckload traffic. While not all of this traffic is involved in these 12 commodities, it very well could be in the next 12 commodities, and definitely is being diverted at the present time because of all the new truckload authority granted during the last year on a wholesale basis.

This possible revenue loss, combined with the present decline contributed to the current recession, could be fatal. We are given the same prerogative as a couple taking their wedding vows--"for better or worse, 'til death do us part"--without the benefit of a courtship period to discern whether or not it will work.

Service to small communities is dependent on handling all traffic available. With fuel alone costing over 20 cents per mile, plus labor, depreciation, other overhead and a hoped-for provision for profit, there is no way these small places will continue to receive the services they are accustomed to presently for the same rates and charges.

If other carriers are allowed to come and select their traffic, a carrier will lose its most profitable traffic, and you can be sure, if master certification becomes a reality, the cream will once again be skimmed off, leaving the curds and whey for the scavengers to fight over.

Before the wholesale issuance of operating authorities by the ICC, who is presently receiving in excess of 2,000 applications for entry each month and granting about 98 percent, a carrier could use their certificate for collateral when borrowing money for purchasing operating authority, equipment or additional facilities. Today, that certificate is scarcely worth more than the paper it is printed on, and for $300, plus lawyer's fees, additional authority can be obtained.

Our company has delayed the building of a new terminal in Knoxville, Tenn., which we desperately need in order to serve this area in the most economical manner. The reason for this delay is because of the uncertainty of just what and how we are going to be forced to operate, if we are able to operate at all.

In March, we placed an order for 36 new fuel-efficient tractors to be put in service this fall. We secured a commitment from a major bank to finance this equipment, but last month, when the time came to finance the equipment, the bank reneged on its commitment,

because they too are uncertain about the value of operating certificates and about which way the ICC is going to go. Without the
asset of the operating certificate, for which we spent many thousands of dollars, companies such as ours will be unable to expand.
Private capital cannot be attracted to an industry which has a profit of less than 4 percent after taxes.

The only alternative we have is to operate our equipment
longer, facing more breakdowns on the highway, foregoing any attempt
to modernize our office equipment or programs, continue to operate
outdated fork trucks, dock equipment and garage facilities.

Instead of going through the cycle of preventive maintenance
and replacement of equipment, which is the most economical method,
carriers are being forced to operate with inadequate capital, or
repairing only when necessary, thereby eventually digging their own
graves. When these carriers go, along with them will go the every-
day personal service to the thousands of small communities across
the Nation--service that has been the backbone of the continued
economic growth of this country.

You can already see this in the airline industry, which has
now been deregulated for a year. Airlines have terminated service
to 103 cities, leaving 68 of these without any airline service at
all. Deregulation will be speeded up because, in December 1980, all
domestic routes will be deregulated. The Government will have to
subsidize the airlines to keep air service for hundreds of medium-
sized towns.

Air freight rates on minimum shipments have risen 89 percent;
freight rates on 100-pound shipments are up 21 percent; and on
5,000-pound shipments, the rates are up 75 percent. Insurance
costs, which the shipper has to pay for in the airline industry,
have gone up 3,900 percent. Air fares on passenger rates have
risen 23.3 percent.

At the present time, there are only two domestic airlines,
United and American, which are flying air freight planes. These
two companies readily admit they never made money on air freight
until they were deregulated and were allowed to raise their rates.
They must decide by 1985 whether or not to continue in the air
freight business on domestic routes due to the need to replace obsolete equipment.

Testimony, October 27, 1979, U.S. Congress, 96th, 1st session,
House of Representatives, Committee on Public Works and Transporta-
tion, Subcommittee on Surface Transportation, Examining Current
Conditions in the Trucking Industry and the Possible Necessity for
Change in the Manner and Scope of Its Regulations. Hearings....
Part 1, (Washington, D.C.: Government Printing Office, 1979),
pp. 939-943.

533. SMALL CARS ARE NOT NEW (1980)

In 1980, American automobile sales dropped to the
lowest in 19 years, and continued to fall during the
next two years. Part of the reason was foreign competition, especially from Japan and Europe, which accounted
for two-fifths of American car sales. Nearly three out of
five cars sold were "small," either compacts or subcompacts.
Why was the American industry so slow in responding to this
shift in American consumer demand? Understandably on the
defensive, a Ford executive points to early efforts to introduce small cars in the American market. Essentially, his
account fails to contradict the tardiness of American firms
to come abreast of consumer interest in such cars.

The statement that small cars in the past have not been profitable for the domestic producers, I can speak for Ford, that is true.
I was the product planning manager of Ford back in the late 1950's,
when we developed the Falcon and other small cars, and I can assure
you there was great opposition within the financial community in
Detroit to try to make a small car that would compete against imports being sold in this country, for the simple reason that our
costs were hundreds of dollars higher than the laid-down cost of
imported cars. This reflected currency differences, in large part.
    So that is a historical pattern. On that basis, the U.S.
industry--I'll speak for Ford--Ford reluctantly concluded in the
late 1950's and early 1960's that it would watch part of this market
go to the producers of small cars overseas who had enormous cost
advantages. Later, that could not be countenanced as the market
moved to small cars and, of course, today we face a situation where
the market for small cars is the big market, and is going to become
larger. And it is essential that the domestic producers be able to
proceed with their plans to redesign their products and convert
their facilities to meet this market.
    It is a changed world....
    Mr. SCOTT. Mr. Chairman, 18 months ago, we were operating our
V-8 engine plants on overtime, because we couldn't meet the demand
for large cars with V-8 engines. Since that time, the world has
turned completely around. In the years up to 1979, we found an
increasing public demand for cars of commodious capabilities.
Gasoline was not a particularly serious problem. In fact, the real
price of gasoline between 1965 and the embargo was declining, year
after year. The cost of gasoline became less a factor in a person's
deliberation as to his transportation requirements....
    Might I point out, sir, that ever since the late 1950's, there
has been a consistent and steady movement toward smaller cars in
this country, and it was not in the late 1950's so much as because
of gasoline costs or the costs of ownership. Back then we saw the
introduction of the VW in this country. We had a few Toyotas in
here. We bought the first three Toyotas that ever came into this
country and tore them apart.

We saw the movement toward small cars because people were
interested in lower prices, they were concerned about traffic con-
gestion, they were concerned about the lack of need to have two
large cars--when they had a second car, a wagon and a small car
made more sense for so many people. So there was a movement, and
we were on track doing something about that. Falcons came out in
1960, Mavericks and so forth followed. We tended to make these
cars a little bit bigger when we replaced them, because that's
what people wanted, because people would pay more for them, and
because our competitors were doing that to us, and taking our market
away.

But give and take the changes as they went along, there was
such a movement. What really happened with the 1973, 1974 situation
we had the shock, we ended up converting to make more small cars,
and 1 1/2 years later were paying $500 rebates to get them out of
the dealership. Our dealers were stuck with small cars.

Then came the Iran situation, and a very sudden change. What
really happened here is we have telescoped into a very brief period
what I think probably would have been a decade of change with which
we were dealing. We thought we were on the road to doing it right,
but we could not handle the abruptness with which the public changed
their buying habits. They can change their habits faster than we
can change our products, and that's where the problem lies....

There are almost no Japanese cars in Brazil. You can count
them on your left hand. I was down there a couple of months ago.
I didn't see one in 2 weeks.

The reason is that you have to make 95 percent of the car in
Brazil. We do that, we invest there, we hire Brazilians, we make
cars, we make profits.

In Europe, it's pretty much the same thing. The Common Market
has now pulled itself together in a way that's made itself the
second largest or maybe the third largest market for cars in the
world. We operate there, and in the several countries in which we
manufacture--Spain, Germany, England, Belgium, France--we are major
factors in the market.

Testimony, September 16, 1980, U.S. Congress, 96th, 2nd
session, House of Representatives, Committee on Foreign Affairs,
Subcommittees on Asian and Pacific Affairs and on International
Economic Policy and Trade, United States-Japan Economic Relations.
Hearings and Markup, (Washington, D.C.: Government Printing
Office, 1981), pp. 13, 15, 26.

534. AIRLINE DEREGULATION IS WORKING (1981)

In 1978, Congress passed the Airline Deregulation
Act, providing for a phased transition to non-regulated
status. By the close of 1981, the authority of the Civil

Aeronautics Board (CAB) over domestic routes was to end
as it was over domestic fares a year later. CAB itself
was to be abolished by January 1, 1985. Between 1938 and
1978, air transport had operated as a regulated public
utility. Now, it could make ordinary business decisions
without close regulation. Paul R. Ignatius, president
and chief executive officer of the Air Transport Association, representing all but a few of the country's scheduled
airlines, enthusiastically endorses the new status.

The purpose of the Airline Deregulation Act, overwhelmingly
approved by the Congress two and half years ago, is clear. It is
stated expressly in the Senate and House reports on S. 2493 and
H.R. 12611 of the 95th Congress, in the Conference Report accompanying the provisions worked out by Senate and House conferees, and in
the preamble to the final bill which became Public Law 95-504.
That purpose is to "...encourage, develop, and attain an air transportation system which relies on competitive market forces to determine the quality, variety, and price of air services." Senate
Report No. 95-631 aptly described that purpose as "...to return the
air transportation industry to our free enterprise economy."
    Essentially, the objective of the Airline Deregulation Act has
been met. Although a number of CAB regulatory functions scheduled
to be terminated or transferred under the Act still remain today,
the domestic air route system has been completely opened to new
entry and to carrier resource shifting that involves market exit
as well as entry. The growth in airline competition is evident,
as are the results of the many new competitive endeavors. Airline
route systems and service patterns are being adjusted to meet market
conditions. New markets have been entered, and new marketing
arrangements have been developed. New airlines have been organized,
and new air service products are being offered. The route patterns
of many airlines have expanded dramatically while those of others
have been reconfigured, in both cases as a consequence of business
judgments reached on a marketplace basis. And while airline pricing
remains under government control, the CAB has exercised its discretion to grant the industry significant pricing flexibility. A re-
markably increased degree of pricing innovation has, therefore,
been introduced and extensive competitive pricing now is a regular,
every day feature of airline marketing. These were the basic goals
of the Airline Deregulation Act.
    Deregulation has brought about a significant restructuring of
the airline system -- a restructuring which which was expected.
After 40 years of regulation, airline management has moved to a
fundamentally different way of doing business, with new challenges
and opportunities to be met entirely on the basis of free enterprise
considerations. The public, long accustomed to operations under the
former system, rather quickly saw extensive changes in airline
service patterns and practices -- largely beneficial changes from
the public point of view since they were the result of a new,
more vigorous competition in the air travel marketplace.

The public has generally responded favorably to the system
changes that have resulted. Some dissatisfaction has been expressed relating to changes in service to some areas as carriers
have shifted resources to gain efficiencies, and to the increased
cost of airline tickets. However, the increased price of airline
service and, to a lesser extent, the shifting service patterns, are
in fact more directly the product of the serious inflation affecting
all parts of our economy, including the airlines, than they are of
deregulation. At today's jet fuel prices, for example, it simply
makes no economic sense to operate large jet aircraft in some short
haul, minimum traffic demand markets. Airline costs, led by fuel
which added over $3 billion in expense last year alone, have risen
at almost twice the rate of general inflation in the economy. Basic
airline ticket prices simply track the sharply increased cost of
providing the service. These stark economic realities would have
to be met and surmounted whether or not the airlines were deregulated, but the Airline Deregulation Act enabled the airlines to more
effectively react and to better manage their resources in these
extremely difficult circumstances....

Since 1978:

. Airline costs have risen at an unusually high rate and
  yields have been forced to follow:
. Constant dollar yields today are still below levels
  of 5 or 10 years ago;
. Airline discount fare activity is at its highest level
  in history -- more reduction from full fare is being
  offered, and more passengers are using the reduced fares;
. There is a relatively close relationship between costs
  incurred and fares charged at all mileage distances,
  except for distances under 200 miles where unit costs
  sharply exceed average unit fare levels;
. Based on the latest available CAB data, scheduled carrier
  departures are up by 5,735 per week in April 1981 as
  compared with April 1978. While most of this increase
  occurred at the large and medium hubs, small hub departures also increased slightly, and departures from the non-
  hub communities declined by 1.5 percent; and
. In October 1978 there were 33 certificated scheduled carriers. Since that time 57 more have been certificated for
  scheduled service, bringing today's total to 90.

While there were understandable differences of view within the
airline industry in 1978 on the question of deregulation, there is
broad agreement today -- agreement: that deregulation is a fact of
life; that there can be no turning back to a tightly regulated
regime without completely disrupting public air service; that the
airline industry cannot and should not be expected to operate part
free and part regulated; that the economic problems facing the airline industry over the past two years would have been much more
severe in the absence of the management decision-making latitude
made possible by the Deregulation Act; and that the time has come
to complete the action taken by Congress in 1978 to free the airlines from unnecessary and burdensome economic regulation.

It is for these reasons that the airlines support the proposal to advance CAB sunset.

Testimony, July 9, 1981, U.S. Congress, 97th, 1st session, House of Representatives, Committee on Public Works and Transportation, Subcommittee on Aviation, Effects of Airline Deregulation; and Legislation to Advance the Date for Sunset of the Civil Aeronautics Board. Hearings...., (Washington, D.C.: Government Printing Office, 1981), pp. 187-190.

D.

COMMERCIAL SIGHT AND SOUND

535. "RADIO BEGAN TO RUN IN 1906"

The basic technical aspects of radio were mastered
between 1900 and 1918. Lee de Forest, whose autobiography
is called Father of Radio, writes the following.

Inventors were few in those earliest years of the century.
Invention was easy, the soil exceedingly fertile, and the Patent
Office not yet clogged with thousands of pending applications on
insignificant, or hardly distinguishable, details. Consequently
the incentive to strike out and pioneer on paths radically new,
and therefore wondrously attractive, was intense. In rapid succession followed the auto-detector (self-restoring, electrolytic,
and crystal types), the telephone receiver, the alternating-current
transmitter, the two-tuned circuits at sender and receiver, the
high-frequency spark, the quenched-spark gap, the Poulsen arc and
tikker, the direction finder, the series-selective circuits of
Stone, the heterodyne principle of Fessenden, the Audion as detector
and as radio-frequency generator, and the Audion oscillator (first
as regenerator for heterodyne reception, then as transmitter for
telegraph and telephone). All of these kaleidoscopic changes and
epochal achievements were accomplished in less than eighteen years--
from 1900 onward.
    And, excepting the more recent return to the short-wave trans-
mission of the very early days (such as the experiments of Hertz),
transmitter arrays of antennae and crystal frequency control, the
above list is, I believe, a truthful catalog of the really significant strides which made radio engineering what it was in 1940
(or until World War II ushered in the amazing miracles of radar and
ultra-high frequencies, and the generators thereof--the magnetron

and klystron). Everything else, though it may be important and
the result of years of careful research and study, may be classified nevertheless as improvement in detail, electrical, mechanical,
or chemical--as the case may be.

In truth this young giant Radio attained maturity with astonishing speed. We search in vain for a like development in all the
history of man. Radio began to run in 1906, ever quickening its
electronic stride. Thereafter it received a terrific impetus from
the relentless demands of World War I, only to find directly follow-
ing--instead of a breathing spell--a new incentive, alluringly
financial and sometimes esthetic, national radiobroadcasting, truly
the prelude to the Electronic Age.

Lee de Forest, Father of Radio. The Autobiography of Lee de
Forest, eds. Linton J. Keith and Arthur Brogue, (Chicago, Illinois:
Wilcox and Follett, 1950), pp. 249-250.

536. "RETROGRESSIVE AND TEMPORARY DIGRESSION" (1928)

The motion picture industry, while prosperous, was
suffering from a lack of growth. Box office receipts,
in a number of cases, had fallen. Sound movies--"talking
pictures"--were welcomed by industry executives as a stimulus to business. One prominent actor, Ronald Colman,
was asked to insert a clause into his contract in which
he agreed to work in sound movies. Colman, a Hollywood
star, writes here to Samuel Goldwyn, a leading Hollywood
producer.

With reference to the additional clause to the contract--I
would rather not sign this, at any rate just at present. Except as
a scientific achievement, I am not sympathetic to this "sound"
business. I feel, as so many do, that this is a mechanical resource, that it is a retrogressive and temporary digression in so
far as it affects the art of motion picture acting,--in short that
it does not properly belong to my particular work (of which naturally I must be the best judge).

That the public are for the time being demanding this novelty
is obvious, and that the producer is anxious to supply it is natural, and for the actor to dispute this situation or contend against
it would be foolish. After four years' experience with myself,
the firm should have no doubt as to my reasonable cooperation in
this matter--as in others.

For me to function conscientiously before the microphone is
one thing, but to sign a legally phrased document authorizing
this is a very different matter and would logically presuppose my
approval of this mechanical accessory to my work.

I hope I have made this clear, Sam. May I request that the
company will respect these convictions and leave the matter where
it is.

Letter, Ronald Colman to Samuel Goldwyn, August 5, 1928,
in Variety, January 4, 1961.

537. STATE OF ART OF TELEVISION (1939)

Note that television receivers were to be put on
sale as early as 1939. Philo Farnsworth reports on this.
He was a pioneer in the industry, and was vice-president
of Farnsworth Television, Inc.

The CHAIRMAN. Has the art of television been developed as
yet to that point where it would be possible to install a receiver
in your home which could receive various kinds of transmission?
Mr. FARNSWORTH. Yes, it has. It has been developed to
standards which are tentatively agreed on, which will make it
impossible for you to tell from which kind of transmitter the
signal originates.
The CHAIRMAN. What kind of pictures can be transmitted by the
present system of transmission and reception on one instrument?
Mr. FARNSWORTH. What kind of subject material?
The CHAIRMAN. I am talking now about the reception instrument.
What kinds of pictures, studio pictures or pictures in the field?
Mr. FARNSWORTH. Outdoor pictures of news events, scheduled
sport events, indoor studio pick-ups, stills for purposes of advertising, back projection and motion picture film, the whole scope
of television.
The CHAIRMAN. In other words, you can divide pictures which
are desirable to transmit into two types, broadly speaking, I would
say. One is the studio type where the scene is enacted before the
camera or the lens, and the other the outdoor type in which a
scene proceeds which is not rehearsed, which may go any way.
Mr. FARNSWORTH. The television is incidental to it.
The CHAIRMAN. Now either one of those may be transmitted
today?
Mr. FARNSWORTH. Either one of those may be transmitted by
Farnsworth today.
The CHAIRMAN. And you have a reception machine which can take
either one of those?
Mr. FARNSWORTH. And the signal sent out is not any different
in either case. One reception device gets them both.
The CHAIRMAN. Would a picture of a baseball game, let us say,
or the landing of a distinguished visitor at the dock in New York--
would that picture be clearly reflected upon the screen of the
reception instrument in the home?

Mr. FARNSWORTH. Yes. I will be glad to show you what the picture does look like. I have photographs of a girl on a bicycle. That will be clear there, a totally flickerless picture, a steady image, and I have heard it remarked many, many times that the picture could not be told from a motion picture if they hadn't known it was television.

The CHAIRMAN. In other words, a perfectly satisfactory image can be shown on the reception instrument.

Mr. FARNSWORTH. Yes.

The CHAIRMAN. Now then, if that is the case, why is it not on the market?

Mr. FARNSWORTH. Again we have the tremendous preparation necessary to get broadcasting under way and receiver production schedules. Receivers will be sold this year. We hope to go to the Federal Communications Commission as the R.M.A. [Radio Manufacturers' Association] Standards Committee and say "We have reached the standards and are ready to go ahead. Do you think it is ready for commercial use?" We hope their answer will be "Yes."

The CHAIRMAN. When you say "we" whom do you mean?

Mr. FARNSWORTH. I mean the engineering committee of the Radio Manufacturers Association.

The CHAIRMAN. Would you care to show those photographs now?

Mr. FARNSWORTH. Yes, I have those right here.

Mr. DIENNER. Mr. Farnsworth, might there not be some interference with present radio channels in placing television on the air?

Mr. FARNSWORTH. There is an enormous problem there of putting out these tremendously wide television bands, working them in an already over-crowded ether spectrum. The Commission has tentatively planned to give seven channels.

The CHAIRMAN. So there are interferences in the ether as well as in the Patent Office.

Mr. FARNSWORTH. There certainly are. There are problems of trying to find space for this new service with the short wave spectrum expanding so rapidly.

Testimony, Philo T. Farnsworth, January 19, 1939, Verbatim Record of the Proceedings of the Temporary National Economic Committee, I, p. 497.

538. A PARENT'S DISAPPOINTMENT (1922, 1946)

An inventor, Lee de Forest, judges the uses to which his invention has been put.

1922

In 1907, when the idea of radiobroadcasting first occurred to
me, and three years later when the music of the Metropolitan Opera
was launched upon the ether, and again in 1916 when for the first
time regular radio concerts were broadcast nightly, there dawned
before me a vision of the astonishing potentialities of radio.
I confess that in those early pioneer days my eager imagination
fell far short of picturing the astonishing hold with which during
the last eighteen months this idea has so suddenly gripped our
entire nation.
I predict that as an educational medium the radiotelephone
broadcast will in time prove second in importance only to the public
school.
When one seriously considers the human side of this broadcasting idea and its possibilities, one must admit that it possesses
potentialities for universal education--and for all the train of
good which results from universal education--which can be compared
only to that brought about during the past five centuries by the
art of printing. Only this new revolution will grow to maturity in
a decade, instead of 500 years--a graphic commentary on the
acceleration of man's present progress.
I have for a long time maintained that this educational value
of radiobroadcasting will prove by far its greatest worth--to the
people of our country--and later of all nations. No doubt just now
the entertainment feature is the most striking, the phase most
appealing to the popular desire, naturally enough. Unquestionably,
the fine programs which are now being given by the large broadcasting stations are accountable for the astonishing growth of radio
listening during the past eighteen months.

. . . .

1946

In the Palmer House [Chicago] is assembled the Convention of
the National Association of Broadcasters. There many words are
being spoken on behalf of a great industry which thrives chiefly on
spoken words.
One wonders if our simian ancestors had any conception that in
ages to come such monkey chatter as they originated would be transformed into the essentials of livelihood. Of such are the mysteries
of evolution. Today fabulous sums are paid for talk. Speech, not
silence, has proved golden; and the dispensers of such merchandise
to the millions are here foregathered to plan for more speech, for
more money.
Had I, who originated the idea and the means for broadcasting,
been invited to their council, I should say to them: "What have
you gentlemen done with my child? He was conceived as a potent
instrumentality for culture, fine music, the uplifting of America's
mass intelligence. You have debased this child, you have sent him
out in the streets in rags of ragtime, tatters of jive and boogie
woogie, to collect money from all and sundry, for hubba hubba and

audio jitterbug. You have made of him a laughing stock to the intelligence, surely a stench in the nostrils of the gods of the
ionosphere; you have cut time into tiny parcels called spots (more
rightly 'stains'), wherewith the occasional fine program is periodically smeared with impudent insistence to buy or try.

"Murder mysteries rule the waves by night and children are
rendered psychopathic by your bedtime stories. This child of mine,
now thirty years of age, has been resolutely kept to the average
intelligence of thirteen years, as though you and your sponsors
believe the majority of listeners have only moron minds. Nay, the
curse of your commercials has grown consistently more cursed, year
by year.

"But this British brother has had a different upbringing. Under
government sponsorship, radio appeals there to the higher intelligence, realizing its fine mission to elevate, and not degrade. This
is anathema to America's broadcasters--vastly enriched by their
freedom from all restraint. We prefer to pay the colossal bill in
gold, and in the debased coinage of the anesthetized intellect.
We might learn much from England.

"Yet, withal, I am still proud of my child. Here and there
from every station come each day some brief flashes worth the hearing, some symphony, some intelligent debate, some playlet worth the
wattage. The average mind is slowly broadening, and despite all
the debasement of most of radio's offerings, our music tastes are
slowly advancing.

"Some day the program director will attain the intelligent
skill of the engineers who erected his towers and built the marvel
which he now so ineptly uses."

de Forest, Father of Radio, pp. 441-442, 443-444. The 1946
statement was sent by de Forest as a letter to the editor of the
Chicago Tribune.

539. THE FUTURE OF SATELLITE COMMUNICATION (1963)

The first commercial satellite, Early Bird, was
launched in 1965. Between that year and six years later,
the investment cost per voice channel per year fell from
$23,000 to $618. Its earth station cost over $10 million
but by 1980 the cost was down to $100,000. Transoceanic
telephone calls made via satellite soon outstripped those
made by oceanic cable. Countries precluded from a thorough
telephone system by wiring soon sprouted satellites to
supply the needed communication media. Indeed, Bell
Telephone Laboratories early calculated that a small number
of satellites could readily replace the entire AT & T
long distance system. Transmission of television via

satellite became a matter-of-fact operation within a
decade or so after Early Bird. World-wide networks
became a possibility. David Sarnoff, chairman of the
Radio Corporation of America, speculated on some possible
effects of satellite development.

The technology of electronics is reaching today for summits of
national, global, and space communications beyond anything conceived
since the invention of movable type.

...The way is opened technically for the establishment over the
next few decades of a communications system by which governments,
organizations, or individuals may establish contact with anyone,
anywhere, at any time, by voice, sight, or document, separately or
in combination. In its most advanced form, such a system would be
based upon communication via satellite without intermediate routing
or wired connection.

...I see the development of satellite communications occurring
in three phases, whose timing will be determined as much by economics and social demand as by technology.

Phase 1, between 1965 and 1970, should see a global system of
low-power synchronous satellites....Positioned approximately 22,300
miles above the equator and completing an orbit in the same twenty-
four-hour period required for full rotation of the earth, they will,
in effect, hover constantly over a single point on the earth's
surface. At its high altitude, each of the satellites will be within direct line-of-sight range of about one-third of the globe.

Communications to and from these satellites will be handled
through high-power earth terminals whose antennas will be fixed permanently on one or more of the space relays. These stations, varying from simple installations to complex trunk types, will be linked
with landline and microwave networks crisscrossing the continents.
Most nations are likely to maintain their own terminal facilities,
in keeping with the present pattern of national systems.

With these facilities, communications could develop to the
point of direct telephone dialing between users anywhere in the
world. The system would accommodate television broadcasting and
closed-circuit television, although the latter would probably be
limited by economics to governmental use.

Phase 2, between 1970 and 1980, may mark the beginning of
international satellite communications between cities rather than
through centralized national terminal facilities.

Nuclear-powered synchronous satellites, weighing 3 tons or
more, would generate approximately 60 kilowatts of power....The
far greater output power of the satellite would permit substantial
reductions in the cost and complexity of the earth terminals, placing them within reasonable economic range for small nations and
users and permitting the design of mobile or stationary units that
could be simply assembled.

With such stations, the larger population centers could readily
undertake their own direct communications via satellite relay. For
example, a direct link could be maintained between New York and New
Delhi, employing simple base stations at or near each city and a

relay stage of microwave or even laser beams between the synchronous
satellites serving the respective regions.

The introduction of city-to-city communications can bring
immensely significant change to both commercial and private services. For nongovernmental organizations and business enterprises,
closed-circuit television on an international scale would be opened
by the ability of the high-powered satellites to transmit directly
to television receivers in the home.

Person-to-person voice communications could be provided through
fixed or mobile telephone and even pocket-radio links between individuals and the earth terminals of the satellite system. When this
happens, an individual moving within a city or its environs could
have wireless contact with any similarly positioned and equipped
individual on any continent.

Phase 3, beyond 1980, envisages on all-embracing satellite-
communication system: direct personal transmission of voice and
sight through satellites without intermediate routing.

Manned satellites, assembled in space, would range up to 100
feet in diameter and weigh some 100 to 150 tons. Nuclear energy in
the space station would provide up to 1 million watts of power,
equal to the output of twenty high-power present-day broadcasting
stations.

Each such satellite in a system of perhaps five to ten would
provide up to 500,000 voice and 500 television channels. Direction-
al antennas would link the satellite with individual cities through
narrow microwave "shafts" containing thousands of voice and hundreds of television channels. Equipped with a high-speed computing
system, the satellite would serve as a switchboard in space to route
calls from city to city, country to country, and continent to continent.

With this system would come the facility for direct two-way
contact through television receiver-transmitters installed in
private homes and offices. Beyond this, a new dimension in individual communications might be accomplished through parallel advances in miniaturization of electronic devices, circuits, and
power sources, together with continued progress in the development
of communications theory. This would lead to the incorporation of
television as well as sound in a two-way pocket-size device....

Even in the early stages of this process, the impact of satellite communications upon human society will be profound. There will,
for example, be an enormous hastening of economic development in
the vast regions which have yet to derive substantial benefit from
twentieth century science and technology. As the accessibility,
accuracy, and swiftness of intelligence are increased through the
coming global systems, commercial activities will be extended
through areas hitherto too remote for consideration. It will be a
two-pronged stimulus--from people demanding more goods and services
as they see and hear about them and from enterprises moving with
surer knowledge to meet the rising demand.

More and more, the full range of human, commercial, educational, and cultural activities will become international in scope,
encouraged by the ability to communicate across a span of continents with even greater facility than we communicate today within a

single country....Despite the pace of technological growth, it is
likely that the rate of progress toward the future global and
interplanetary communications systems will be determined as much by
political, social, and economic factors as by technical accomplish-
ment.

I feel, however, that the very existence of satellite communication will in large measure determine the solutions to the non-
technical problems that stand between the promise and its full
realization. For example, the day of the closed or remote society
is coming to an end. No barriers of time or distance or ideology
can long withstand the mounting flow of information and the vastly
improved access to information across the oceans and the continents.
The awareness of knowledge is the first step to its acquisition,
and the acquisition of knowledge is, in turn, fundamental to human
advance in every sphere....

David Sarnoff, "A Wireless World" in Saturday Review,
January 12, 1963.

540. SEX AND "ALL IN THE FAMILY" (1977)

Attracting a large television audience by the use of
titillating material may create a tension between commercial advantage and moral standard. Most feared by broadcasters is a viewer boycott of persons repelled by sexual
frankness. Here, Van Gordon Sauter, Vice-President of
Program Practices for the Columbia Broadcasting System,
testifies on the subject before a Congressional subcommittee.
Four years later, Sauter became President of CBS News.

Last year, CBS program practices editors read and screened more
than 1,500 scripts for series episodes, pilots, and special programs
for prime time. We read scripts and attended tapings or screenings
of more than 1,000 soap opera episodes. We reviewed more than 200
motion pictures. We carefully screened the content of our Saturday
morning schedule and other programs designed for children. The editors bring to their work backgrounds and expertise in different
areas of broadcasting, education, journalism, law. For instance,
the man responsible for program practices for our children's programs
has a Ph.D. in psychology from Harvard.

While we must be responsive to the sensitivities of our audience, at the same time we must not inhibit the creative process.
The most difficult job I know of is to sit behind a typewriter and
create material that will entertain people. Program practice editors are charged with the responsibility of assuring that our standards are met while trying not to diminish the legitimate creative

spirit and no doubt diminishing the quality of entertainment available for our audience.

At this moment, our two greatest concerns are the portrayal of violence and the representation of moral standards.

While a few organizations have thrust the question of violence into the news, there is no doubt in my mind that the vast majority of viewers have no basic difficulty with that issue, but are far more concerned about how television portrays personal relationships. . . .

I think the fundamental concern that most viewers have about television, if you would list their concerns in the sense of priorities, they are very concerned about how we portray sexual relationships, particularly sexual relationships that reflect the changing morality of our society. . . .

Let me deviate to tell you a story about "All In The Family," which is one of my favorite broadcasts.

It is for us a difficult broadcast but producer Norman Lear has been cooperative and we have been able to resolve our differences in an effective manner.

He recently had a script where Archie, to his astonishment learns that the girl to whom he lost his virginity in high school is coming to dinner with her husband and Archie is predictably confused and finds the whole thing unbearable and the dinner is the usual succession of very funny events and finally Edith begins to perceive what this is all about.

Finally, at the end of the meal Edith is in the kitchen with this girl and the script called for Edith to say, "Well, why didn't you tell me that years ago you and Archie had this thing," and the woman was supposed to answer, "But Edith it was just a day out of my life. It was 30 seconds out of my life."

And Edith was supposed to say, "That long?"

We would have had problems with that, quite frankly. Jean Stapleton who played Edith had greater problems with it and conveyed those, I think, to the writer. But whatever, that particular sequence disappeared entirely from the broadcast and it was not a problem for us but it is an indication of how the performers are frequently very beneficial in this and have as much concern as we do in the areas of taste.

Testimony, May 11, 1977, U.S. Congress, 95th, 1st session, Senate, Committee on Commerce, Science, and Transportation, Subcommittee on Communications, Television Broadcast Policies. Hearings...., (Washington, D.C.: Government Printing Office, 1978), pp. 212-218.

541. ECONOMICS OF THE LITERARY MARKET (1978)

Well into the 20th Century, book publishing was
said to be more an avocation than an industry. Relationships between entrepreneur and author were personal
and the scale of operation was typically small. By the
1960s and 1970s, however, a number of standard publishing
houses had grown in size and profitability to the point
where they became the object of conglomerate mergers.
Organized authors, who stood to lose in bargaining power
and who professed shock at the crassness of impending
mergers, protested. Following is the text of a letter
from officers of the Authors' Guild to the U.S. Department
of Justice and the Federal Trade Commission. (To most
authors, who earned marginal sums of royalties, the entire
matter was of little interest.)

                                            May 10, 1978

The Honorable Griffin B. Bell
Attorney General
Department of Justice
Washington, DC   20580

The Honorable Michael Pertschuk, Chairman
Federal Trade Commission
Pennsylvania Avenue at 6th Street
Washington, DC 20580

Dear Attorney General Bell and Chairman Pertschuk:

      The Authors Guild urges the Department of Justice of the Fed-
eral Trade Commission to investigate the possibility that the
Houghton Mifflin Company may be acquired by Western Pacific Industries, Inc. For the reasons discussed below, The Authors Guild
believes that if this acquisition were accomplished, it would violate Section 7 of the Clayton Act and do immeasurable damage to
the literary marketplace.
      The press reports that Western Pacific, a conglomerate, has
purchased 6.7% of the shares of Houghton Mifflin Company, one of
the few remaining major, independent publishers of textbooks and
trade books. The familiar pattern of conglomerate acquisitions has
caused concern on the part of several distinguished Houghton Mifflin
authors that this stock purchase may be the prelude to an attempted
takeover of this independent publishing company by the conglomerate
-- i.e., the acquisition of more Houghton Mifflin shares, then an
effort to win approval of a merger resolution. Apparently Western
Pacific has now acquired a total of 10.2% of Houghton Mifflin's
stock. Moreover, FORBES Magazine reports, in its May 15, 1978
issue, that Western Pacific Industries, Inc. plans to sell the
Western Pacific Railroad

"...along with its $100 million-plus in debt,
to a new company formed by its employees."   ***
"   What's in it for (Chairman of the Board) Newman
and WPI? Plenty. They wipe $100 million in debt
off their balance sheet. Better yet they generate
for WPI tens of millions of dollars in ordinary
losses for tax purposes."   ***
"   Since this holding company is selling rail assets
instead of the railroad's stock, it - not the railroad - gets to keep huge operating tax-loss carry-
forwards. Newman is already on the prowl for acquisitions whose earnings he can shelter. WPI has bought
sizable hunks of stock in Houghton Mifflin Co., the
Boston publisher, and Hazeltine Corp., a Long Island
manufacturer."
(emphasis ours) (At page 49; copy of article attached.)
     Western Pacific's acquisition of Houghton Mifflin would con-
tinue the trend to concentration that has destroyed the independence
of many major publishing companies acquired by conglomerates and
huge publishing complexes; a trend that already has exceeded the
limits of Section 7 of the Clayton Act. This elimination of independent publishing entities from the literary marketplace not only
violates a primary purpose of Sec. 7 -- it also endangers the uninhibited marketplace of ideas protected by the First Amendment. Consequently, even though Western Pacific may not own other publishing
subsidiaries, and even though the antitrust laws do not bar all conglomerate mergers, Western Pacific's acquisition of Houghton Mifflin
would, in our opinion, violate Sec. 7 of the Clayton Act for the
following reasons:
1. The takeover of Houghton Mifflin would eliminate another major
independently-owned publishing company from at least two relevant
lines of commerce.
     A primary purpose of Section 7 is to perpetuate and preserve,
for its own sake, the organization of an industry into many independent firms. (See Authors Guild June 7th State, pp. 6-9)
American book publishing was such an industry. But mergers and
takeovers have weakened that structure in most of its relevant lines
of commerce: e.g., in the mass paperback market; in the book club/
mail order publishing market; in the textbook market; and in the
trade book market. Many trade book and textbook publishers have
been absorbed by conglomerates. These include several of the medium
and large-sized independent firms that previously constituted the
backbone of both markets, made the most important economic and
social contributions, and accounted for much of the production and
competition in both lines of commerce.
     (a) Legislative history and the Supreme Court's opinions em-
phasize that Section 7 was intended to preserve the existence of
independently-owned companies such as Houghton Mifflin because of
the social interests they serve, as well as to safeguard competition. Nowhere in this purpose more important than in book publishing. For here, the elimination of independently-owned firms endangers the country's most important interest -- the diverse and
"uninhibited marketplace of ideas" which, said the Supreme Court,
"It is the purpose of the First Amendment to preserve ..."

The survival of numerous independent publishing entities is essential to preserve the uninhibited marketplace of ideas. Independent publishers, engaged only in publishing, are not vulnerable to outside pressures on their editorial policies and judgments. As conglomerate subsidiaries, publishers are vulnerable to outside pressures on their corporate masters, and also to the dictates of their owners' other interests and purposes.

Whether viewed separately or in the context of the continuing wave of publishing mergers, the acquisition of a major independent publisher by a conglomerate - in our opinion - violates the purposes of both Section 7 of the Clayton Act and the First Amendment.

(b) Book publishing is not "just another business." Its purpose is not merely to earn maximum profits for its stockholders. Thus, the Houghton Mifflin Company is a business enterprise of great social, educational and aesthetic value. For decades, it has contributed richly to American education, literature, and social thought. A primary reason for these contributions is its existence as in independently-owned enterprise; that independence has permitted its authors, its editors and its management to consistently maintain the highest professional standards of writing and publishing. The Authors Guild believes that a paramount purpose of Section 7 would be violated if a conglomerate is allowed to capture control of this publishing enterprise, and thus destroy the very independence which helped make possible its valuable service in the public interest.

2. The Authors Guild further submits that the takeover of Houghton-Mifflin might ultimately eliminate it as a competitor in one or more lines of publishing commerce. FORBES Magazine's analysis of Western Pacific's purchase of Houghton Mifflin stock indicates that a principal motive may be to "make acquisitions whose earnings (WPI) can shelter." It therefore is possible that the conglomerate might withdraw Houghton Mifflin from the trade book market since its trade book department is less profitable than its textbook operations. The elimination of still another major, independent trade publisher, does not serve the purposes of Section 7.

3. An independent Houghton Mifflin could continue to compete in the trade book market where it is surely needed. An independent Houghton Mifflin could continue to publish needed textbooks that do not yield high rates of return per dollar of investment -- as well as commercially successful textbooks. A conglomerate-owned Houghton-Mifflin, whose policies would tend sooner or later to be dictated by "bottom line" considerations of a conglomerate master could not continue to make such socially valuable business decisions. Section 7 of the Clayton Act preserves the independence of business enterprises so that they can thus serve the broader public interests.

The Authors Guild respectfully submits that this possibility that the independence of a major publishing company would be destroyed through a conglomerate acquisition warrants an inquiry by the Department of Justice or the Federal Trade Commission to determine whether, as The Authors Guild believes, the acquisition of Houghton Mifflin by Western Pacific Industries would violate Section 7 of the Clayton Act.

Sincerely,

The Authors Guild, Inc.

John Brooks, President   Roger Angell, Vice
                                          President

John Hersey, Chairman   Irwin Karp, Counsel
Contract Committee

Enc.: Page 49 FORBES Magazine, May 15, 1978

cc (w/enc.): Hon. Paul Rand Dixon   The Members of The
              Hon. Calvin J. Collier   Committee on The
              Hon. David A. Clanton   Judiciary, U.S.
              Federal Trade   Senate
              Commission   The Members of The
              Hon. John H. Shenefield   Committee on The
              Department of   Judiciary, U.S.
              Justice   House of Represen-
                                               tatives

Testimony, May 17, 1978, U.S. Congress, 95th, 2nd session, House of Representatives, Committee on Small Business, Subcommittee on Antitrust, Consumers and Employment, Future of Small Business in America, Part 2, Hearings...., (Washington, D.C.: Government Printing Office, 1978), pp. 41-43.

542. CONCENTRATION IN THE MASS MEDIA (1980)

The ownership of the mass media of communication has become increasingly concentrated. Diversity of viewpoints has narrowed accordingly. In the larger local markets, entry has become exceedingly costly. In radio, the proliferation of outlets has not led to meaningful departures from the standard fare. Here Ellen Berland Sachar, senior security analyst specializing in the media industries for Goldman, Sachs & Co., a large investment banking house, sketches the main outlines of concentration in the mass media.

At the present time, roughly 63 percent of daily newspapers and 73 percent of Sunday newspapers are under group ownership. This compares with 50 percent of dailies in 1970, 31 percent in 1960, and 17 percent in 1940.

In terms of circulation, about 74 percent of daily circulation and about 80 percent of Sunday circulation in the United States are now in group hands. Publicly held media companies now own about 17 percent of all the daily newspapers in this country and 25 percent of the Sunday papers. These account for about 27 percent of total daily circulation and 30 percent of total Sunday circulation.

Despite these numbers, no one publicly or privately owned newspaper group currently owns more than 5 percent of the total number of daily or 8 percent of the total number of Sunday papers in the United States, and none controls more than 6 percent of the daily or 8 percent of the Sunday circulation.

In fact, the average size of a newspaper group in the United States in 1978 was only 6.8 dailies, up from the 5.1 average in 1960, but still a small number.

On the broadcasting side, the FCC-imposed seven-station rule prohibits any one entity from owning more than seven AM, seven FM, and seven television stations--of which no more than five can be VHF.

A mere three firms currently have a full complement of radio stations, and only 36 firms control 10 or more radio stations. Only one company owns the maximum allotment of radio and television stations.

With 7,514 commercial radio stations on the air in 1978-- 4,513 AM's and 3,001 FM's--the degree of concentration of ownership possible in this area is, by definition, very limited.

In the television sector, however, each of the three networks, through its five owned-and-operated VHF stations, reaches roughly one-third of survey area households; that is, all households within a station's viewing range, including cable homes in distant markets, and about 22 percent of ADI households; that is, area of dominant influence households defined to avoid market overlaps.

Newspaper broadcast cross-ownership situation, long perceived as a potential threat to a true diversity of media opinions, are now down to 37 in number, 31 excluding the markets ordered to divest of one or the other interest by the FCC in 1975.

The threat of forced divestiture, rather than the action itself, seems to have produced the desired result.

And in the cable television area, roughly half the total number of basic and pay subscribers in the United States today are in the hands of the top 25 multiple system operators (MSO's), and about 75 percent of these MSO's are themselves or are part of publicly-held companies.

No one company, however, owns more than 7 percent of either the total number of pay or basic subs.

In terms of cross-ownership situations, as of September 1, 1978, the latest date for which these figures are available, 30.4 percent of the nearly 4,000 cable television systems were owned by broadcasters and 12.7 percent by newspapers....

Most discussions of media concentration until now have focused
on the inherent dangers in cross-ownership situations....

Most of these situations, and certainly the ones with the
greatest potential threat to diversity of opinion, have been de-
fused.

But a new form of concentration, vertical rather than horizontal, seems to be taking hold. Time, Inc., for example, is now not
only the second largest multiple system operator of cable television systems--likely soon to the largest, in fact--but also the
leading supplier of pay cable programing--covering over two-thirds
of this market--and a major supplier of films and television series
through its Time-Life film division.

The capital needs of these businesses being what they are,
such concentrations are inevitable and even desirable, if one wants
to see these businesses expand.

The policy questions raised are another matter.

Testimony, March 4, 1980, U.S. Congress, 96th, 2nd session,
Committee on Small Business, Subcommittee on General Oversight and
Minority Enterprise, Media Concentration (Part 2). Hearings....,
(Washington, D.C.: Government Printing Office, 1980), pp. 157-
158, 161.

543. "HOOK THE VIEWER" (1981)

Large-audience television has become identified
with the existence of three networks in the United States.
With the proliferation of cable television and other
new mass media of electronic communication, however, an
opportunity arises to define new kinds of audiences and
smaller units of business. Norman Lear, a highly successful producer for television and motion pictures, gives
Congressmen the benefit of his intimate knowledge of the
industry and the limitations of commercial thinking in
the area of programming. Among his programs were "All
in the Family," "Maude," and "Sanford and Son."

[I]t is axiomatic that in the proliferation of TV channels
to the home the aim of every channel, without exception, will be to
hook the viewer and secure him to the chair in front of that television set....

The history of network television teaches that the concentration of most of the resources of broadcasting in three companies
results in the kind of fierce competition which invites the kind of
homogeneous broadcasting that allows for too little diversity and
retards the development of new and competing technologies.

I would like to say I would never wish to take television out
of the context of all American business which seems to me to be
consumed by the need to perform according to the bottom line, and
television is just another victim of something that permeates our
society. I don't mean to take it out of the context of all of the
rest of American business. With the explosion of new technologies,
this history must not be repeated.

The opportunity for those in the creative end of the television
business never looked brighter. Narrow casting may finally become
a reality. Channels will exist to inform as well as entertain; to
inspire and improve the quality of life. These will be businesses,
but smaller businesses, without the need for profit margins that
broadcasting is accustomed to today. We will also see new and
experimental drama, allowing talents and pieces of our culture to
surface which have never had the opportunity before.

There will be new approaches to science and to the discussion
of issues for which commercial television, with its concentration
on ratings and instant success, has had no time. All of this and
more is possible so long as there is sufficient access to the
delivery systems for the small communications entrepreneur as well,
wherever he or she may be. If there are indeed going to be as many
as 100 or more channels to the home, then Tulsa and Orlando and
Perth Amboy and Cedar Rapids must have a crack at them, too....

Now, the networks are in the same business, and the way it
translates in network parlance is, How do I win Tuesday night at
8:30? So the name of the game for some users increasingly that way
has become, How do I beat two other networks at 8:30 or 9 o'clock
on any given evening?

When that is the concentration--and, of course, those ratings
translate to profits and profit statements. When the accent is on
ratings only, or ratings first, then it is logical that if your
network is at No. 2 and you want to succeed on a given evening and
you look at network No. 1 and you see that a show where there's a
lot of motorcycle riding is working well, another show with a
couple of young women in braless sweaters who move around a lot,
jump up and down excitedly when they hear what they are having for
dinner, run across the room as opposed to walking across the room,
you see that is working. Then you find a couple of lawyers on
another show that are also working, you might logically think if
ratings are your game why don't we put a couple of lawyers on motor-
cycles and have them have girl friends in braless sweaters?

So, 3 years ago when one network decided that Animal House,
the successful motion picture, was a good vehicle for carbon-copy-
ing, it turned out that all three networks did the same thing that
same season.

This happens quite a bit. I have to say again, because I have
great respect and affection for numbers of the men and women who
run network television, but it is a condition, and a condition
that permeates, I feel, our society. That is the name of the game
for them. They have no control over that. That's the way they must

function in order for them to make those ratings and those quarterly profit statements count, but that is how it occurs when there
are only three networks.

Testimony, September 23, 1981, U.S. Congress, 97th, 1st
session, House of Representatives, Committee on Energy and Commerce,
Subcommittee on Telecommunications, Consumer Protection, and
Finance, Diversity of Information. Hearings...., (Washington, D.C.:
Government Printing Office, 1981), pp. 85-86, 88-89.

544. CABLE TV IN RURAL AREAS (1981)

Traditionally, technological innovations lag on the
countryside. Electrification and telephones in rural
areas, for example, were tardily installed primarily
because relatively sparse population minimized the prospect of profit. Cable television, however, experienced
a very different course as explained by Thomas E. Wheeler,
president of the National Cable Television Association.
This group represented some 1,700 cable systems at the
time of Wheeler's testimony before a Congressional subcommittee.

It is ironic that the cable television industry is being
criticized by some for not wiring rural areas. Yet, to read the
newspapers, you might think that cable television is a new phenomenon, invented for lucrative big city franchises such as Dallas,
Chicago, Boston or Los Angeles--or for prosperous suburbs like
Arlington, Virginia, or Montgomery County, Maryland. In fact, major
cities are years behind rural communities in discovering cable
television. Unlike most industries, cable started in rural areas
long before urban ones.
Cable TV began 30 years ago as a community antenna service to
improve the reception of broadcast signals in communities too remote
to receive adequate over-the-air television. With the introduction
of microwave and then satellite technology, cable television systems
became the means for more and more rural communities to enjoy the
variety of programming available to urban areas over-the-air. The
introduction of a cheaper 3 meter satellite earth station made it
possible for additional cable systems to offer satellite-transmitted
programming. With an expanded market for satellite delivered services, programs where designed specifically for cable audiences and
rural subscribers were treated to programming options not available
to many urban populations.

A good example of this type of programming is the Appalachian
Community Service Network (ACSN). ACSN is a satellite delivered
programming service that provides adult continuing education classes
on many cable systems. Developed originally for residents in the
Appalachian mountains too far from any colleges or universities to
continue their education or brush up on professional requirements.
ACSN has spread to many rural communities, until now it has over
500,000 subscribers in rural as well as urban areas.

Mr. Chairman, one of cable's most important functions still
remains to even-out the disparity of television station availabiity
in the United States. While major cities have available a minimum
of 3 stations offering network signals, an independent station signal and an educational TV channel, almost one-third of all television markets (ADI's) do not receive all 3 networks' signals over-
the-air. Furthermore, nearly three-fourths (74%) of the TV markets
in the U.S., serving more than a third (35%) of the television
population, have no non-network TV stations. This is the result
of a governmental policy of deliberate scarcity in allocating
television station assignments, intended both to avoid signal interference between stations and to provide a safe economic base for
television stations.

Cable, which has no signal interference problems, and which
takes its economic base as it finds it, helps to even up the disparity by bringing television signals to places that otherwise would
have no non-network programming or substantially less programming
than is available in big cities.

Today, over 19 million American homes have cable TV. However
...fully 68 percent of all cable systems are located in predominant-
ly rural areas outside of major television markets. Of those systems, 28 percent serve markets below the top 100, but an even greater number, 40 percent, serve communities outside of all markets.
Cable is therefore even more available to rural Americans than it
is to urban.

Furthermore, there is no evidence that cable is ignoring rural
cable needs since cable has entered urban markets....Cable penetration in counties classified as "rural" (County Size D) have grown
steadily over the past decade. In 1973, Nielsen reported that
"rural" counties had an average penetration of 10.4 percent whereas
"urban" counties (County Size A) had an average penetration of only
3.8 percent. Today, the relationship remains unchanged. "Rural"
counties in 1980 had cable penetration of 23 percent versus "urban"
counties with cable penetration of 9 percent. The 23 percent penetration level in rural counties is only slightly below the national
average penetration level of 25 percent.

Thus, although cable TV is getting much publicity about its
entry into urban markets, the majority of cable systems still serve
smaller communities. Cable makes it possible for hundreds of
communities, like Higginsville, Missouri; Milford, New York;
Jackson, Alabama; Eloy, Arizona; and Sisseton, South Dakota, to
get decent television service and not be relegated to the status of
second-class citizens for their television service.

In fact, a good example of how committed cable operators are in providing rural service is the system in Nome, Alaska, where a cable operator dug through permafrost to rebuild his system for increased channel capacity.

Thus, the cable industry has an excellent record of service to rural communities. Our business began and has steadily developed there and we remain committed to equalizing television service for people who don't happen to live in big cities.

Testimony, June 22, 1981, U.S. Congress, 97th, 1st session, Senate, Committee on Commerce, Science, and Transportation, Subcommittee on Communications, Rural Telecommunications. Hearings...., (Washington, D.C.: Government Printing Office, 1981), pp. 31-32.

E.

AGRICULTURAL CHANGE AND CRISIS

545. PERSISTENCE OF THE COTTON FACTOR (1900)

The factor persisted because he continued to serve as a substitute for a bank, at least as far as the larger planters were concerned. F. M. Norfleet, who testifies, was a cotton factor in Memphis, Tennessee. He owned and operated cotton plantations in the Yazoo Basin and in Mississippi.

Q. Now, as a cotton factor, you buy directly from these farmers?--A. No, sir; we do not buy at all. We advance money and supplies to farmers--to the larger farmers and planters, you may call them--to make their crops.

Q. To white as well as black?--A. We advance to very few colored people, and then they, as a rule, do not come to a market like Memphis to get advances. The colored people trade in their locality.

Q. Is that the custom for years for the white farmer to come to the factor to get money to make crops?--A. Yes; for the last 50 years.

Q. What can you say as to that during the present spring?--A. There has been less demand for help this spring than for 15 years before.

Q. Why is that?--A. On account of the higher prices of cotton.

Q. They made money enough themselves to tide themselves over to make a new crop?--A. Yes.

Q. (By Mr. SMITH.) Better condition than formerly?--A. Very
much. I had a case on my books. I was down in Mississippi Saturday. My bookkeeper reported on my return that a gentleman had
called and seemed to be disappointed in not finding me present, and
stated that he was anxious to see me. I thought a good deal of his
business and was a little worried about it, and on Monday I wrote
him a letter that I was very sorry I was not at home, and wanted
him to let me know if there was anything I could do for him; I got
no answer to my letter. I felt a little bit put out from the way
the bookkeeper described his actions in the office on Saturday, so
I wrote a letter to a neighbor of his who is very friendly to me,
to see him in a day or two and find out if there was anything the
matter. I did not want him to slip out of our hands and go somewhere else. This gentleman called on him in his desire to help me
out if he could, and learned that he thought us the best people in
the world, and had nothing against us. After a few days I had our
bookkeeper make me out what I call a plantation ledger footing of
the accounts from our books showing debits and credits of various
parties doing business with us. I got along down to this party's
name, and to my surprise, I found about $3,500 dollars to his
credit. Now, I said, I understand what is the matter with that
fellow; he has not any more use for us. When he came up he said,
I had no particular need to answer your letter. That is just an
illustration of the condition of the country. He began by paying
perhaps $2,000 rent, and had commenced on a 3 years' option, and
had bought nearly all on credit; I was surprised to find the condition of his account.
Q. Landlord?--A. No, sir; renter.
Q. (By Senator KYLE.) Money in the bank to begin the new
year?--A. Money in the bank; yes.

Testimony, F. M. Norfleet, March 22, 1900, U.S. Congress,
57th, 1st session, House of Representatives, Document No. 179,
Report of the Industrial Commission on Agriculture and Agricultural
Labor, X, p, 488.

546. MECHANIZATION ON LOUISIANA PLANTATIONS (1900)

Sugar was the grand exception on Southern agriculture.
In connection with its cultivation and manufacture, one
found extensive wage labor, high degree of mechanization,
and control of the processing end. (For earlier references
to sugar, see Source Nos. 135 and 360.) William Carter
Stubbs reports here. Stubbs owned plantations in Virginia,
Alabama, and Louisiana. He was also director of the
Louisiana agricultural experiment stations as well as the
state's chemist, and he was currently serving as head of the
state's geological survey. He held an unspecified Ph.D.
degree.

The lower portion of Louisiana to-day is, perhaps, more intelligently cultivated, and there is more economy in methods, than is
any other portion of the world. This is due to the fact that in
south Louisiana all our estates are run with hired labor, by the
day, under intelligent supervision of managers, overseers, etc.
Our sugar interests have had to bring to their aid every single
implement and every single method or process that can best econo-
mize the production of sugar and rice, and they have done so. The
negroes are taught to use these improvements by the supervising
overseer or manager that accompanies them to the field and remains
with them all day long and comes out with them at night. They work
entirely under the eye or supervision of the manager. You will go
into a field and find a hundred 2-horse plows or cultivators with
a man on horseback riding from one to the other all day long pushing
and seeing that the work is done properly. These estates are under
experienced, educated managers and overseers, and their methods of
cultivation have improved enormously in the last 15 years. Culti-
vators--everything that can minimize labor--are now used where
formerly we used the plow and hoe. The hoe is largely dispensed
with to-day by the use of the improved cultivator. These laborers
living on the place are given house rent free--a house and garden
patch and all the fuel that is needed. The only condition of their
occupying these houses is that they are to work whenever called
upon, and they are usually called upon all the time. When they
refuse to work they have to vacate the house, and that is the chief
stimulus to make them work. In the southern portion of the State
they have no other place to go. There are no houses for rent off
the plantations, and hence they have to remain on some plantation,
and if they do so remain they have to work, of course, because the
houses are for the operatives of the estates.
     Q. (By Mr. A. L. HARRIS.) Does sugar plantation machinery
stop with the cultivation?--A. Oh, no; we have $100,000,000 in-
vested in sugarhouses, and these sugarhouses are up to date in
every respect. I speak advisedly, because during last summer I
had the pleasure of an official visit in the Hawaiian Islands; and
Hawaii to-day is leading the world in the production of sugar. We
have a large number of sugarhouses fully equal to any in the
world, and those sugarhouses have been reconstructed, I might say,
at the entire cost of all the profit made since the war. I believe
every dollar made in the sugar industry in Louisiana has gone into
the reconstruction of these sugarhouses, and they have been reconstructed with the object of increasing the capacity and diminishing
the expense. To illustrate: When I went to Louisiana 16 years ago
a sugarhouse that had a capacity of 200 tons of cane a day was considered a marvel of excellence; to-day we have several of them that
are taking up from 1,500 to 2,000 tons a day. It formerly required
40 or 50 hands to put the cane on the carrier. The wagon would
drive to the cane yard and drop its load, and then that cane was
transferred by hand labor to the carrier, about 40 to 50 hands being
required to keep the carrier going and feed a mill whose capacity
was 200 tons a day; to-day we have improved machinery that lifts up
the whole wagonload and puts it in cars that are run alongside the
carrier. The sides of the cars are lowered, and a machine very much

like an inverted hay loader puts that cane on the carrier, and 2 or
3 men will feed the carrier with 1,500 or 2,000 tons a day. That
is one of the economies.

We have also economized by increasing the capacity. The sugarhouse that will turn out 1,500 tons of cane, or the product of it,
to-day can, of course, produce sugar much more cheaply per pound
than one turning out 200 tons of cane, because the same amount of
intelligent labor is required in the 200-ton house as in the 2,000-
ton house. In other words, the vacuum pan discharging 300,000
pounds of sugar a day can be operated by 1 man just as easily as the
one in our sugarhouse at the experiment station of 2,500 pounds a
day. It takes just as much expert intelligence to run one as the
other. Now, the house that can turn out 300,000 pounds per day can
do it much cheaper than the small one of 5,000 pounds; hence improved machinery has saved our sugar industry.

Testimony, William Carter Stubbs, January 29, 1901, U.S.
Congress, 57th, 1st session, House of Representatives, Document
No. 179, Report of the Industrial Commission on Agriculture and
Agricultural Labor, X, pp. 770-771.

547. FINANCING THE MOVEMENT OF THE GRAIN CROP (1900)

The commercialization of agriculture is seen nowhere
so clearly as in the financial arrangements for moving
the crop. These are described by Will Payne, financial
editor of the Chicago Economist.

The banker in a western reserve city is now scarcely called
upon at all to supply capital with which to move the grain crops.
Broadly speaking, the country, meaning by that term the chief
grain-growing region, excluding the reserve cities, now has enough
capital of its own to move the cereals from first hands and to
start them well along in commercial channels. Whereas formerly the
country was a borrower to a large extent in the city, beginning with
the time the grain started moving from producers' hands and continuing until the bulk of that proportion of the crop which is
sold into commercial channels was out of first hands, recently--
especially in the last 2 years--the country has scarcely borrowed
a dollar in the city for this primary grain movement. This financial independence of the country is due first and principally to a
great accumulation of capital of late in the chief grain-growing
regions. A secondary cause is to be found in the improved machinery with which the crop movement is accomplished, this consisting
in great efficacy of transportation lines, notably lower freight
rates and a higher organization of the grain-handling interests, so
that now, in many instances, one single agency takes the grain from
first hands and carries it through to Europe or to the mill.

The financial side of the crop movement, in its simplest terms, is this: A is the "elevator man" or warehouse man at a country town. When wheat begins coming in from the farms after harvest he buys it and puts it in his warehouse, paying for it with his own capital. The moment the grain is in his warehouse it becomes a tiptop cash collateral on which he can borrow close up to the cost price from the country banker, giving the banker warehouse receipts on the grain as security. When a quantity of wheat has accumulated in the warehouse A begins shipping it to his commission man in Chicago, say. When a car is loaded A draws a sight draft on the commission house for an amount fairly well up to the cost of the grain, attaches the bill of lading, and deposits the draft in the country bank, receiving credit for it as a cash item.

The country banker treats the draft as a cash item, sending it through to his Chicago correspondent, who collects and gives him credit for it. The wheat goes into a warehouse in Chicago and is again available for a loan well up to the market price. If the Chicago factor sells it for export, his draft against the shipment, with bills of lading attached, is taken to his banker as cash at current rates of exchange, the rates, of course, including interest on the money until the draft is paid at Liverpool or Antwerp or wherever the grain is consigned. This is the elemental form of a transaction which is varied almost endlessly in details. The important fact is that the grain is a cash collateral in every position which will permit of its being insured and of its ownership being represented by some regular negotiable instrument, such as a warehouse receipt or bill of lading. Sometimes with a very small capital A will handle a very large amount of grain, shipping it out daily as fast as he takes it in and drawing against the shipments, his own capital representing simply the comparatively narrow margin between the cost price and the loan or credit price. The capital of A's banker also goes far when the grain is handled rapidly. A draws checks on the bank for the grain he buys. The banker cashes the checks for the grain during the day and at night remits A's sight drafts, as cash items for credit, to his correspondent at Omaha, St. Paul, or Chicago, and at the same time orders a consignment of currency shipped to him. But much of the money paid by A for grain is not withdrawn from the bank, or, if withdrawn, immediately returns. The farmer deposits the check or uses it to pay a note held by the bank or to pay bills due the town merchants, who in turn deposit at the bank. There is no break in the chain. The time when money begins to move from the city to the country to pay for grain is, as a matter of course, exactly the time when money begins to be more plentiful in the country, when bills and notes are paid and deposits begin to increase in the country bank, at least in so far as the movement of deposits is governed by the crop movement.

U.S. Congress, 56th, 2nd session, House of Representatives, Document No. 494, Will Payne, Report of the Industrial Commission on the Distribution of Farm Products, VI, p. 136.

548. "TOO MUCH GOOD AND CHEAP LABOR IN THE SOUTH" (1900)

J. H. Hale owned fruit farms in Fort Valley,
Georgia (2,160 acres) and in South Glastonbury,
Connecticut (300 acres). His experience in the two
sections of the country allowed him to more easily
see the significant contrasts between them.

On the question of labor and prices of labor in the South,
there is too much good and cheap labor in the South for its own
good. It results in overplanting, spreading out too far, to the
neglect of thorough agriculture, because labor is so cheap that it
does not matter much how it does, because it does not cost much
anyway. It is a temptation to overplant and skim over a great many
acres and get poor results. It is also a temptation to neglect
personal attention by the farmer or planter himself, because if the
labor is not intelligently worked out or supervised it does not
very much matter; it only costs 50 to 60 cents a day, and there is
a temptation to neglect the best methods of modern agriculture; and
therefore the abundance of cheap labor in the South is rather
against the success of agriculture. If agriculture was not so good
a business; if we could not get a living so easily, we would make
more money out of it. That may be a peculiar statement, but it
is warranted by the facts.

Testimony, J. H. Hale, January 13, 1900, U.S. Congress, 57th,
1st session, House of Representatives, Document No. 179, Report
of the Industrial Commission on Agriculture and Agricultural
Labor, X, p. 378.

549. AMERICAN FARM LABOR (1901)

The labor force of American agriculture was hardly
less varied than that of industry. So reports J. R. Dodge,
Statistician of the U.S. Department of Agriculture, and
an expert agent of the Industrial Commission.

The farms of the States of northern New England employ
labor to supplement the work of the farm done by the family of the
owner. Quite a large proportion employ no labor except in haying
time or casually in other harvest season by the day. The larger
farms, and those receiving more cultivation, require more help, and
on many of these, and on dairy farms, employment by the month, for
the season or year, is required. In the southern portions of New
England, where manufacturing industries control a very large part

of the labor supply, and farming is more in specialty lines--in
dairying, orcharding, small fruit and cranberry growing, and market
gardening--a very much larger part of the labor is hired; and everywhere the laborers are mainly native, the sons of neighboring farmers never employed in expectation of permanency, but as a temporary
expedient while awaiting other chances of employment or business
engagement, or in fewer cases the purchase of land for themselves,
for home making and the production of milk, fruit, and vegetables.

Foreign labor on the farm has been increasing for many years.
Irish immigrants were formerly the largest element, who generally
at first, and largely since, have sought industrial or municipal
labor in cities. Of those who accepted employment on farms a large
proportion have become land owners. For two or three decades the
volume of immigration has been large and continuous from Nova Scotia
and the Province of Quebec to the cotton mills, and in far less
degree to farms. They constitute the largest element of foreign
farm labor in New England.

. . . .

In the States of New York, Pennsylvania, and western Maryland
the work of small farms is done mainly by the families, and additional labor is obtained to a considerable extent from the native
population. In the larger operations of dairying, fruit growing,
and market gardening laborers are required in considerable numbers.
The skilled labor required in dairies, and most of the native labor
is probably quite as efficient as formerly, but the least skilled,
foreign and casual supply, can scarcely equal in efficiency the
native labor of a generation ago. Near the large cities the proportion of foreign labor is greatest.

In the fruit-growing belt, in the tide-water region from the
eastern shore of Maryland to the northern limit of Delaware, the
colored element largely predominates, and in the fruit and truck
growing districts in New Jersey it is considerable. There is a
large foreign element in the labor of New Jersey; including Swedes,
Germans, Hungarians, and Italians, many of them illiterate and
relatively unintelligent. The farms of western Maryland are largely
held by the descendants of Germans, industrious and thrifty, whose
influence modifies the character of farming in all that region,
and gives character to its labor as well.

. . . .

The productive labor of this section has three elements, small
farmers, white laborers, and colored laborers. The first, and a
very important constituent, is the small farmer in Virginia, the
more elevated parts of North and South Carolina, the mountains
of north Georgia, and the pine lands of the southern counties, the
hill lands of northern Alabama, eastern Tennessee, and scattered
throughout the cotton belt, wherever level plains or alluvial soil,
suited to extensive culture of cotton, are not found. Some of
these farmers may employ a little labor, but most of them produce
what is required for subsistence, with a few bales of cotton for
the purchase of clothing and food products not obtained from the
homestead acres. This is not technically the "farm labor" with
which we are dealing, but it represents a class of the population

which is the source of nearly all the white labor employed in the
South and working for wages or "on shares." It is in imitation of
the independence of this class that colored laborers, in a proportion so very large heretofore and now, elect to become, in a small
way, tenant farmers, or, if absolutely without capital, contract
for the cultivation of small areas on shares, as the nearest
approach to independent farming. The white farm labor class is a
small one relatively in the great cotton districts, and the positions requiring skill and intelligence are largely filled from it.
Where responsibility must be exercised, in the larger and in minor
details of management, many of the more capable of this class are
required. In the hilly and mountainous sections referred to, where
commercial agriculture gives place to provision for family wants,
with only a moderate surplus for cash markets, the labor is hired
only in limited amount, but it is in very large proportion white.
In some districts that surplus product is mostly cotton; in others
tobacco, peanuts, watermelons, peaches, small fruits, or vegetables.
     The colored race almost monopolizes the large cotton planta-
tions, which occupy really a small part of the area of the so-called
cotton States--a tenth part of North Carolina between tidewater and
the hill country, a similarly situated district in South Carolina,
a belt of considerable breadth in middle Georgia, the famous "Black
belt" of Alabama, the alluvial soils of Mississippi (including the
famous Mississippi bottoms between that river and the Yazoo), similar lands in northern Louisiana, and the central cotton lands of
Texas and the bottom lands of its great rivers. These cotton lands
are flat river bottoms, or more or less level plains, or rolling
lands, or rich soils not too rough and uneven for cultivation. Only
small areas in limited districts east of Texas were originally
prairies. Most of these lands were heavily wooded, requiring extensive clearing. The great plantations are mostly broken up, as
it is difficult to employ laborers, at wages payable in cash, few
accepting contracts for service controlling their time and movements, as they can not reconcile anything that recalls the ancient
regime with their ideas of freedom. They prefer renting, the rent
almost always payable in cotton, usually a prescribed share of
the product; but if they have no mule equipment or implements of
culture, they accept a certain share of the cotton produced, in
lieu of wages.
. . . .
     In the northern belt of this great central district, between
the Great Lakes and the Rocky Mountains, the laborers are in part
native Americans, ambitious to acquire homesteads, and largely
foreigners of the better class from northern Europe, Norwegians,
Swedes, and Danes, who are intelligent, industrious, and frugal,
soon establishing themselves in homes of their own. In the Ohio
Valley, a region with no waste land, and very little surface area
unoccupied by farms, settled by the citizens of the Atlantic Coast
States and by the more progressive of immigrants from European
countries, farm laborers are mostly allied by kindred of association
with the resident population constituting a body of farm laborers
unequalled, in intelligence and adaptability to environment and to
changing agricultural conditions, in any foreign country. A lower

class of laborers, for the simpler and least skillful kinds of
service, are foreigners and transients from the cities. The floating population seeks particularly the grain-growing sections, and
predominates in the harvest seasons of the northwest and central
belt beyond the Mississippi. That fertile and thrifty stock-raising
and grain-growing country, comprised in Iowa, Nebraska, Kansas,
and Missouri, is full of the latest improvements of agricultural
machinery, and farm operations are so facilitated and the cost of
production cheapened that the farmers do their own work with fewer
hands and are able to pay for the best.

This reliable help for the main operations of the farm, able
to manage machinery and care for farm animals is, therefore, better
than formerly, while a lower grade of service, in simpler and cruder
operations, can be and is undertaken by persons of less skill,
reliability, and permanence of employment. The advance of mechanical and scientific cultivation, led by trained experts in various
lines of rural industry, has its influence in elevating the average
efficiency, so that it must be admitted, on the whole, that labor
tends to a higher rate of efficiency than 30 years ago.

. . . .

The farm laborers of the States of the great mountain area,
the Rocky Mountain range, and the great Central Valley of Utah,
and the southern slopes of the Sierras, are as yet not a large
class. The settlers were first stock growers; later, irrigation
brought in alfalfa in connection with lamb feeding, the culture of
potatoes as a specialty for eastern and southern shipment, of fruit
growing in the western Colorado slope and the Utah Valley, and of
vegetables for the mining sections. All these operations were
undertaken by enterprising immigrants from the settled States,
who were able and willing to do most of the work required. Other
immigrants, without means for immediate home making or investments
in stock or lands, were willing to offer their services temporarily
as helpers. The cowboys, eager for adventure, were the laborers
of the ranches; as lands became restricted and fences general,
many of them have taken up ranches and become permanent residents.
It is claimed that the laborers of this section are of high efficiency, full of energy and ambition, demanding and obtaining high
wages, and as a rule thrifty and prosperous.

. . . .

Labor conditions on the Pacific coast are undergoing changes
probably more marked than at any former period. Wheat growing,
once the almost sole form of tillage, is now one of many. Stock
growing, to which nearly all open areas were formerly tributary,
has been circumscribed and limited and threatened with crowding
out of existence. Irrigation has made fruit growing steadily productive and profitable, and intensive agriculture possible and
actual. The new beet culture for sugar making was first to score
a success here, and has found in California one of its most favorable locations. Hop growing, especially in Oregon and Washington,
has attained such prominence as to overshadow the East in production, and dominate the hop-growing industry in the United States.
The coast has enjoyed a climatic advantage that has suggested monopoly in certain lines of production, and has seized the opportunity

to follow up its natural advantages with promptness and enterprise. It has thus produced more value per capita than the rural workers in any other section of the United States have been able to obtain, this opulence of production benefiting all its agricultural laborers as well as farm workers.

One of the changes most apparent is the gradual disappearance of Asiatic labor. The Chinese element is already relegated to a minor position, owing mainly to the exclusion act. Japanese laborers have in a limited degree taken the place of Chinese, but their increase is not feared. The beet-sugar farmers have brought in Italians and other immigrants from the south of Europe to cultivate their extensive holdings to avoid too great dependence on outside beet growers. The harvest hands are mainly transients, not all of the most desirable character of laborers. These are the less skillful, less reliable, less valuable elements of the labor of the coast. There are classes of much higher efficiency and greater skill, more valuable for labor and citizenship, in many lines of fruit growing, dairying, and general farming, which promise future improvement in the rural labor of the coast, and such labor is appreciated and in increasing demand.

J. R. Dodge, "American Farm Labor," U.S. Congress, 57th, 1st session, House of Representatives, Document No. 180, Report of the Industrial Commission on Agriculture and on Taxation in Various States, XI, pp. 87, 90, 91-92, 97, 104, and 107.

550.   DEPOPULATION OF FARM TOWNS IN MASSACHUSETTS (1901)

Following is a valuable insight into the decline of villages in the United States, written by J. W. Stockwell, who was Secretary of the Massachusetts State Board of Agriculture; he had been a farmer all his life. In 1879 and 1880, he was a member of the State senate.

It is unfortunate conditions that have depopulated our farming towns. Forty years ago the hill towns were engaged in various manufacturing enterprises. The land was well and regularly laid out in fine farms. Business of all kinds was prosperous. The farmer was making money, and, better than all, was bringing up children who were destined to spread abroad throughout the land, and whose influence, as I have said, is now felt throughout the Union. It was no sudden movement that reduced the population of these hill towns.

The general story of a great agricultural decline is, however, only half the story. The decline of manufacturing industries in the hill towns more than equals the decline of agricultural industries. The proportion of abandoned wagon shops, shoe shops,

sawmills, and other small mechanical businesses, which were once
the life of flourishing villages, has kept pace with, and indeed
far outstripped, the abandonment of farms; and much of the so-called
decadence of the hill towns is due to the changed methods of manufacturing industries, taking away the work that was scattered
through these towns and concentrating it in the larger plant and the
improved machinery of the stronger combination, and thus drawing
the workmen to the larger towns and railroad centers.

Testimony, J. W. Stockwell, February 19, 1901, U.S. Congress,
57th, 1st session, House of Representatives, Document No. 179,
Report of the Industrial Commission on Agriculture and Agricultural
Labor, X, p. 888.

551.   "REDUCED ACREAGE IS THE REMEDY" (1905)

A persistent remedy for low cotton prices was
reduced acreage. Several cotton organizations undertook
a campaign of agitation with sparse results. Even as the
campaign started, grave doubts were raised about means
of policing acreage reductions. Abraham Brittin, president
of the New Orleans Cotton Exchange, was addressing delegates
to the founding convention of the Southern Cotton Association, a producers' group.

Cotton is low in price by reason of one cause, and one cause
only. Remedy or remove that cause and values will go up with a
bound, irresistible to the combined short selling of all the "bears"
on earth. You have but to scan the records of the two years past
to abundantly prove this. No! Values of all earth's great products are regulated by the unchangeable law of supply and demand.
. . . .
Cotton, as all will admit, is doubtless below cost of production, and therefore unprofitable to the producer. You seek a
remedy, or rather, I should say, a preventive. There is but one
possible, and one only. It is supreme folly to seek any other.
As these low prices follow as the result of threatened oversupply,
it is hopeless to expect a restoration of values till a reduction
of such supply is made commensurate with the world's demand and
requirement. How is that to be done? You are here to give response
to that inquiry. Plant less cotton, reduce the acreage, say 25
per cent at least, and you have the remedy beyond question. Even
so, this will still leave land enough under cultivation, with a
fair season, to produce a supply quite sufficient with the great
surplus which promis s to be carried over from this crop for disposition the coming year to afford the world's mills enough for
consumptive requirements on a basis of fair and remunerative
prices.
. . . .

I warn you not to be misled, when planting time arrives, by any temporary advance which then or meanwhile may occur, and on such account fail to carry into rigid effect any agreement reached by you looking to acreage reduction. Do not be lured to ruin by any such false hope. As surely as lead sinks in the waters of the sea when dropped therein will prices sink to a still lower level than has yet been reached should it come to pass there is no substantial cotton acreage reduction.

Abraham Brittin, January, 1905, "Influence of Producers' Organizations on Prices of Cotton," Part V of Report of the Commissioner of Corporations on Cotton Exchanges, (Washington, D.C.: Government Printing Office, 1909), p. 331.

552. BOLL WEEVIL PANIC IN NATCHEZ (1909)

The boll weevil was scourging the cotton South. Two scholarly Mississippi planters, Alfred Stone and Julian Fort, surveyed the problem, finishing their study in December, 1910. Devastation, they concluded, was not inevitable--if certain measures were taken. These measures, they found, were rarely taken. Stone and Fort were owners and operators for 17 years of Dunleith Plantations, Dunleith, Washington County, Mississippi, in the Delta region. Apparently, Stone was the economic historian who published articles on various aspects of the Southern economy.

The appearance of the boll weevil [in Natchez] created the same panic and demoralization which we had investigated further West and South. But there was this radical difference: Not only was there no organized effort to allay fright, quiet labor, and instil confidence, but so far as we could learn, there was not one single planter or plantation to stand up and make a fight to demonstrate what might be done. Wherever we found the plantation system, with the single exception of the cane parishes of the Atchfalya and Red rivers, we invariably found individual instances of planters of means or credit who, from the very first appearance of the weevil down to the present time, had made cotton and had been able successfully to readjust their operations to the new conditions. These men created confidence in their neighbors, furnished object lessions of the folly of demoralization and marked out the way for the reestablishment of the business of cotton growing upon a sounder and more enduring basis than before.

Instead of this, there was in the Natchez district situation apparently but a single end and purpose. This was the saving by the advancing merchant of as much as possible for himself, out of what seems to have been considered from the very beginning an inevitable and hopeless economic wreck.

The merchant determined to realize what he could out of the meagre personal property which represented the only remaining asset of the negro tenant. The land owner, unaccustomed either to supplying his tenants or to handling his land himself, and wholly without confidence in the future, apparently made no effort to save the labor to the land by stepping in between his tenant and the advancing merchant. The merchant who combined landholding with an advancing business must necessarily have shared the general panic, just as his tenants shared the general demoralization of labor. It was at this juncture that the Delta planter appeared upon the scene, and added to the existing confusion by making possible an exodus for which the negro was already prepared, and which only needed financing to become an accomplished fact. We found no evidence that the planter from this section had ever stirred up the labor sitaution, or in any case persuaded a negro to leave. Nor do we see how any blame can be justly attached to his actions. The country roads leading into Natchez were filled with negroes, wagons and mules; the streets of the town were filled with puzzled negroes, upset, disturbed and bewildered. They knew nothing except that their merchants would carry them no longer, that they could not carry themselves, and that they had been called upon to pay what they owed or surrender what they had mortgaged. Every available pen in the city was filled with horses and mules. The planter from the Delta needed the labor, and the latter was ready to go. The planter paid the merchant an agreed price for the negro's account, loaded him and his family and household plunder on a boat or car, and brought the entire outfit home. Hundreds of negroes and carloads of live stock and personal property were thus removed from Adams and adjoining counties. Thousands of dollars of Delta money were put into circulation there in the process of exchange, but when the final account was closed, the net result to the counties was, on the one hand a group of fairly well satisfied city merchants, and on the other a disorganized country, stripped of labor, farming implements and stock, empty houses on tenantless land--a picture of desolation....

If any man imagines this description to be overdrawn, let him traverse that country and talk to its people today--even now after wasted fields have become a fixed feature of the landscape and the thought of dwindling crops a fixed habit of mind. In 1906, Adams county grew 23,836 bales of cotton; 20,455 in 1907; 14,155 in 1908; 1,700 in 1909; in 1910 conservative estimates place the crop at less than 900 bales. Under normal conditions there were 42 gins in operation. In 1909 there were sixteen. We are told that this year there were only eight.

Alfred H. Stone and Julian H. Fort, The Truth About the Boll Weevil, (Dunleith, Mississippi: Published by the First National Bank of Greenville, Mississippi, 1911), unnumbered leaves.

553.   PRODUCING WHEAT: HORSE OR TRACTOR (1911)

In 1911, only four thousand tractors were in use
in the entire United States. Four years later, however,
the number expanded to 25,000 while the number of horses
reached its all-time peak. L. W. Ellis, a Traction Plowing
Specialist with the M. Rumely Company, farm equipment manufacturer, writes here. The statistical table summarized
costs for conditions in easter North Dakota.

The lack of power for plowing and harvesting is the tremendous
obstacle to the sudden expansion into virgin field of our productive
area. The shallow plowing now generally practised consumes 60 per
cent of the total power expended to raising and harvesting the wheat
crop, even on old land. Deeper plowing to secure maximum yields
sharpens the necessity for power in the brief plowing season. The
slow process of animal reproduction cannot respond quickly enough,
and the price of horses has increased 143 per cent in ten years in
spite of a 50 per cent increase in the supply. Today in Canada,
where great added power is imperative, horses can be purchased only
in limited numbers. Even the United States Department of Agriculture cannot find an adequate supply of brood mares for the future
needs of the New South. Increased production cannot safely depend
on animal power.
     Nor is production the only consideration. Fifteen million work
animals, and the 10,000,000 more to keep up the supply, scarcely
develop sufficient power for present farm purposes. Their feed
alone costs $1,250,000,000 per year, equalling the total income of
2,000,000 average families. Thus the crops from one acre in five
are withheld from supplying human needs by the use of animals for
farm power.
     The farm tractor is the solution of the immediate problem.
It does not age nor deteriorate when idle and requires neither
fuel nor attendance when not at work. The time spent annually in
caring for a horse will keep the tractor in perfect working condition. It will endure heavy work 24 hours a day instead of 6 and
outlive the average animal in hours of service. It occupies less
floor space than two wagons, and with a year's fuel supply may be
sheltered in a building a tenth the size and cost required to house
and maintain horses of equal power. Efficient farm labor grows
increasingly scarce. The tractor concentrates in one man's hands
the power of 25 horses and the endurance of 100, and adds two-fold
to the acres he can cultivate.

. . . .

TABLE 4. COMPARATIVE COST OF PRODUCTION

Cost of Production per Acre of Wheat	With Horses	With Tractor
Land rental............................	$2.00	$2.00
Plowing...............................	1.35	0.76
Seed..................................	1.13	1.13
Pulverizing and seeding..............	0.63	0.17
Twine and cutting....................	0.75	0.39
Shocking.............................	0.22	0.22
Threshing............................	0.65	0.65
Machinery costs......................	0.62	0.67
Hauling..............................	1.00	0.26
Incidentals..........................	0.30	0.30
Total	$8.65	$6.55

L. W. Ellis, "The Economic Importance of the Farm Tractor,"
Transactions, American Society of Mechanical Engineers, XXXIII
(1911), pp. 109-110, 116.

554. COTTON-FARMING AND THE MERCHANT-BANKER (1915)

Once more the persistent problem of Southern agricul-
ture--how could the farmer gain the freedom to market his
crop without dictation by his sources of financing? (See
Source No. 17). W. B. Yeary was a cotton planter in
Farmersville, Collins County, Texas. He describes the
problem here. He rented out land, held some stock in a
bank, was agent for a silo-manufacturing company, and had
served as president of the Texas Cotton Growers' Association.

The farmer begins, as I say, 50 per cent of them, owe for last
year's debts. They begin on the first of the year to give mortgages securing their accounts for the year with the country merchant
and the country bank. By the time fall comes the merchants and
banks have all learned that there is not going to be cotton
enough to go around. They know they are not going to be able to
pay all the debts. And if John Smith in the dry-goods business
up there can jump in before John Jones in the grocery business can
jump in and get the cotton and buy it from him, he has made his
collection, and if anybody is going to get left it is the fellow
that did not buy the cotton. This applies to the farmer that is
not mortgaged. If the merchant or bank persuaded the farmer to hold

his cotton the other fellow is liable to get in and persuade him to
sell it and get it, then the other fellow is going to get left in
his collection. And so it goes. You can not blame the merchant
and the bank for not cooperating, especially when there is so much
uncertainty about it. If we are going to work and ask them to
cooperate together and hold their cotton, and we know that it is
not generally done over the South, the first thing we know some
section of the country will turn their cotton in with a whoop and
the market is broke and the fellow that we persuaded to hold his
cotton is going to take $5 or $10 a bale less than when he was
gathering, besides the expense. So the movement of marketing, selling, and holding the cotton, cooperation, has got to be spread
over the South and be taken up in a way by business people so that
they know that it is going to have effect before they can afford
to get behind it. You can not hope for them to do otherwise.

There is another class of banks and merchants who, beside
being as the above described, are financially interested in buying
cotton, seldom publicly, but often having stock with or partners
of some local cotton buying or exporting firm, or it may be that
the buyer pays for cotton through the bank or merchant and they thus
make their collections and secure deposits. To advocate holding or
organization would cause the buyer to boycott the bank or merchant,
thus depriving them of the opportunity of collections and deposits.

To this last class might be added the city banker, who finances
the exporters, who are often stockholders in the bank and sometimes
the bankers are stockholders with the exporters. All know that when
cotton is placed on a commercial or business system of sale that
the present system will readily be ended and the once most profitable business in the South will be no more. The same may be said
of the great exchanges. With these explanations it can be plainly
seen why the South does not act like business men should; the
farmers can not, a part of the others are afraid of losing collections and need all they can get, while others are financially benefited by not having any change made. Bankers, and business men,
including many of our best farmers feel that if any effective move
is made, not under Federal control, that there will be either mani-
pulations of the exchanges to reduce the price or destroy the movement, and for these reasons a great many have no faith and are dis-
heartened in anything being effective.

Testimony, W. B. Yeary, March 20, 1915, U.S. Congress, 64th,
1st session, Senate, Document No. 415, Final Report and Testimony
Submitted to Congress by the Commission on Industrial Relations,
X, p. 9172.

555.   VAGRANCY LAWS AND COTTON LABOR (1915)

Vagrancy laws had been a feature of southern labor
legislation in the earliest "black codes" of 1865 and
1866. The testimony here is by R. W. Getzendaner who
owned the Citizens National Bank in Waxahachie, Texas and
owned 3,500 acres of farmland in Ellis County where he
lived. He was also "interested" in 8,000 acres in Kaufman
County.

Chairman WALSH. What is the relation of the vagrancy law to
farm labor?
Mr. GETZENDANER. You asked me the question here, Why was the
vagrancy law enforced last September to force the negroes of
Waxahachie into the fields?
There were many idle negroes around town. Work was offered
and was plentiful, but they would not work. The farmers needed
labor badly.
Chairman WALSH. Is it not true that the negroes wanted 60
cents for cotton, the farmers could pay only 50 cents, and the
business men in town called upon the police officers to break this
strike of unorganized labor?
Mr. GETZENDANER. The negroes wanted 60 cents, and the farmers
regarded 50 cents as a fair price, considering the low price of
cotton. There was no concerted action among the business men, although there was a general feeling that the idle negroes should
go to work. The cotton grower of Ellis County pays more for what
he receives from labor than any other people. The negro willingly
works, generally speaking, for a reasonable compensation nine months
in the year, biding his harvest time--"cotton-picking season."
When such season arrives he or she quits the regular position for
the cotton patch. By a sort of mutual understanding they always
ask more than is offered, and usually get the price of picking
increased in that way as the season advances.
Chairman WALSH. Now, after the officers arrested these negroes
for vagrancy did they generally go to work for 50 cents instead of
60?
Mr. GETZENDANER. I don't think they arrested them.
. . . .
Of course, if the negroes are there and the farmer tries to
hire them and they won't work when work is offered and they are
living off of somebody, if you have a vagrancy law it should be
enforced, why, they ought to go to work.

Testimony, R. W. Getzendaner, March 17, 1915, U.S. Congress,
64th, 1st session, Senate, Document No. 415, Final Report and
Testimony Submitted to Congress by the Commission on Industrial
Relations, IX, pp. 9001-9002.

556. SHEEP SHEARING OUT WEST (1904-1948)

It should be recalled that the shearing was done not
with electric but hand shears. The blades were about 5
inches long. The sheep-shearer J. C. Lobato, who became
sheriff of Costilla County and whose account follows, was
surely the most meticulous bookkeeper in American economic
history. During 1904-1948, he states, he sheared 139,708
sheep! His annual minimum and maximum ran 900 and 5,700
head.

In 1904, I began sheep shearing with the hope that I would
make a fine shearer....Shearing sheep is not an easy job. You have
to be trained as in any other business. If a person is a good
lawyer he still cannot shear sheep without instructions....In 1906,
....we were paid 8¢ a head and board....The fastest man on the line
in 1911 was E. Santistwan from Huerfarro County, Colorado. Willie
Garcia could just about keep up with him. I saw those fellows shear
150 head of sheep in nine hours. There are a lot of sheep shearers
on the line who claim to be real shearers. Some of them, however,
are just "wool trompers." They shear sheep because they have a
grip, but they do not know how to fix the sheep shears....In those
days each fleece we sheared weighed about 11 pounds. My regular
tally ran from 115 to 120. My high tally was in 1909 at Holyoke,
Colorado, when I sheared 197 sheet in nine hours for the Standard
Sheep Company. They were small Merino sheep....A shearer's job is
not easy. It is hard work. A shearer needs a strong back.

J. C. Lobato, "My Forty-Two Years as a Sheep Shearer," Colorado
Magazine, XXVIII (July, 1951), pp. 215-218.

557. CONSERVING DUST IN DAKOTA (1936)

The New Deal soil conservation program aimed more
at conserving farmers than fertility. George Reeves
describes this.

Early in the summer of '36, when I was trailing to Elm Creek,
word went around that the Secretary [of Agriculture] would pay seven
dollars an acre for land returned to alfalfa. The land must be
plowed and seeded and the seed bills kept for proof of the seeding.
The land would then be measured and payment would eventually be
forthcoming.

But as the summer progressed, and Dakota soil was too dry to accept the point of a plow, let alone provide moisture to sprout the expensive seed, the Secretary yielded to the mood of the weather, and word went around that this handsome sum could be earned simply by a token discing of the land in question. Plowing and seeding could be omitted.

In mid-July I rattled and banged my disc over a suitable acreage. I never felt sillier in my life. The ground was so hard that the disc floated on its surface—a single team could have pulled it because it wasn't cutting any soil. But here I was with fifteen horsepower tracing aimless circles on farmland in midsummer and it was with the greatest difficulty that I could imagine anyone paying seven dollars an acre for these dim scratches on Dakota soil. I wished mightily for a ten-cent rain shower, so that I could leave some mark that might earn that money. But Dakota didn't give a damn whether I earned any money or not.

In the fall a committeeman came to appraise the extent of my "soil conserving" virtue. I led him to the fields which I had disced, and between us we managed to find some of the scratches that I made earlier in the summer. He stared unhappily at them. Then his eye sought out the sprawling patch of black where I had contoured my corn with a lister. The seed hadn't sprouted, the weeds hadn't grown, and the deep ditches still lay there, crossways of the slope. It looked like soil conserving to the committeeman.

"Let's look at that," he said. "I ain't got the heart to write this down as summer fallow."

We examined the cornfield, where the listed rows waited patiently for a rain to sprout the corn.

"Hell," he said, "that's the best piece of summer fallow I ever saw. How many acres of that have you got?"

I told him, and without further questioning he wrote the figure down.

"When do I get the dough?" I asked.

He shrugged.

"If the New Deal doesn't get tossed out on its ear," he said, "you may get it about planting time next year. But if Landon is elected they'll probably forget the whole thing. Personally I think you'll get it."

George S. Reeves, <u>A Man from South Dakota</u>, (New York: Dutton, 1950), pp. 180-182.

558. A FARMER'S HISTORY OF FARMING (1909-1937)

It is startling to observe how closely later general historical accounts resemble this contemporary one made by William Sitterly, a farmer from Fairfield County, Ohio.

I have observed, or rather farmed, during the period that we referred to so much, of 1909 to 1914; those were great days, because we farmers were receiving a fair share of the national income and things were going very well. I lived also as a farmer as many of the folks did here today when we started out in '14 on a rampage such as was never known in the history of agriculture; unprecedented expansion in our business took place in 1909 until 1919 and twenties.

We expanded it in very many ways. Our farms increased; doubled and trebled in price. We farmers bought expensive machinery. We had a lot of money. We began to live. We increased our equipment. We built dairy barns. We went into this thing on the thought of furnishing food and winning the war. It was partly patriotic and partly with the thought of making money, and we did produce and there wasn't a word said about surplus. We didn't have any.

The world took it all and they grabbed for it, and our exports increased nearly nine times from what it was when they started during that period. We plowed up 60 million acres of the best land in this country to continue producing. We expanded our farm land, corn land more, in order to produce corn and wheat; went into new territory. The war was over. The foreign countries didn't need our products. Something happened. There are many farms that have never been able to rise from the day the war closed with their barn lofts filled with high-priced feed and cattle and hogs and commodities, and it was a staggering blow. We were almost on the verge of a national crisis.

From then on until 1929 the financiers of this country rather than have a depression for both agriculture and industry, loaned to bankrupt Europe millions and billions of dollars to buy the products of the American farmer and of industry as well, and it did pick us up somewhat from the fall we had immediately following the war. We did go for several years without so much difficulty.

But finally the money played out and we didn't loan, and Europe was broke, and during those years she learned a lesson to produce for herself. She came to the conclusion that what America had produced that she needed she would go into the producing business herself, and no longer did we have a foreign market to take care of that immense production that we had.

The American farmer was the first person in this country in any line of business to feel that let-up of exports across the way. We had lost our market. It began in the West. Banks began to fail; the papers were filled with headline stuff of farm-relief meetings and an election was on in 1928 and the two political parties went before this country trying to outdo the other as to what they would do for the farmer.

. . . .
...We did live under the Farm Board [starting in 1929] and they did attempt to do something at that time to satisfy a cry for the fixing of prices and they did take a lot of money and they went on the Board and they did buy a lot of our commodities to peg the price of our commodities as would serve agriculture. They bought millions of bushels of wheat and they stored it in Government houses.

They bought thousands of bales of cotton and they stored it
and the price was maintained until they went off the market and our
commodities fell to the world price which was a tremendous drop.

Now the trouble with the Farm Board program that we farmers
had was that we had the wheat that was in the Government warehouses
to contend with for 4 long years. They wanted to sell Government
wheat every time the price was raised and we could expect a reasonable price for our wheat the Government had wheat to sell and it
depressed our price. And finally in desperation as our prices
began to climb, they wanted to give some of it to China or get
rid of it in some way to get it out of the Government warehouses.

Testimony, William Sitterly, October 30, 1937, U.S. Congress,
75th, 2nd session, Senate, Committee on Agriculture and Forestry,
General Farm Legislation, pp. 3958-3959, 3959-3960.

559.   SLOW CLIMB UP THE FARM LADDER (1937)

A plainspoken and realistic account of some difficulties in the way of farm-ownership is here made by L.
B. Eidman who farmed 214 acres in Mascoutah, Illinois.

I was born and raised on the farm that I now occupy. It was
owned by my father. I am almost 60 years old. I farmed this farm
from 1900 on, and in 1927 I took over the farm. I was not able to
pay for it and had some indebtedness on it, and in 1927, while we
talk about the depression coming on in 1929, the farmer felt the
depression in 1921, and I predicted then that the time would come
when industry would feel the depression as much as the farmer did,
but to my surprise they held on and held on until 1929, when the
crash came. We had felt the depression many years before that,
and I was trying to keep up the fertility of my soil by spreading
limestone. My father had retired in 1900 and did not pay much
attention to keeping up fertility. He thought as long as he lived
the land was producing pretty well, and some of those old men were
pretty hard to convince that they ought to add limestone and phos-
phate to the soil.

All the money I could accumulate as a tenant from 1900 to
1927 I put into improvements, because I believed my family was
entitled to just as modern conveniences on the farm as the people
in town were, and I knew I could not keep my boys and girls on the
farm unless I would give them some advantages over what we had when
we were at their age. So as I accumulated a little cash I applied
it to improving my home, with the consent of my father, or rather
the promise that he would fix his will so that I would sometime
be able to own that farm. If he had not done that, I would have
just taken a big chance on improving the farm as my home, and

probably lost it. But he lived up to his agreement and sold me the
farm before his death in 1927. Then my son wanted to get married,
and I needed him to help me on the farm, to run that farm. I could
not run it myself, and I said there was no better place for him, he
likes farming, and it would be best for us to stay together and farm
that farm, which we are doing today. He has been at it now for 10
years, and he said the other day: "I have worked here 10 years"--
I sold him a half interest in the livestock and machinery to begin
with. I owned the farm and operated it as the landlord and as a
part operator, he getting one-third of the crop and I getting two-
thirds of it, one third as a worker and one-third as a landlord,
and the livestock we divided 50-50. He said, "I have been working
here 10 years and haven't reduced my indebtedness but $200. What
is the chance of my ever owning this farm?" "Well," I said, "I
had a much harder time to pay for this farm than my father did,
and you will have a harder time to pay for it than I did." There
is not much future for a farmer unless we get things changed.

Testimony, L. B. Eidman, October 30, 1937, U.S. Congress,
75th, 2nd session, Senate, Committee on Agriculture and Forestry,
General Farm Legislation, pp. 4380-4381.

560. HOW TO DRY-FARM IN MONTANA (1937)

An insight into the speculative nature of dry-farming
of wheat. A farmer, Fred Roarn, of Liberty County, Montana,
who owned over 3,000 acres of wheat land, comments.

In Montana acreage doesn't mean much to us because we may have
30,000,000 bushels or we may have 3. Therefore, my success has been
based, I think mostly upon the fact that when conditions were good
I just spread out and put in all that I could, because as near as I
can find out, statistics show that when there is no moisture in the
ground in Montana and these northwestern States we have one chance
out of ten of making a paying crop and if that condition exists it
is up to us to cut our operations all that we possibly can because
we are just absolutely bucking against a stone wall to put in a big
acreage if the conditions are not right. So last winter it was too
dry to plant winter wheat. This spring it was awful dry. So I
double summer-fallowed over 200 acres, carried it over in order to
have it when the moisture does come; and it did come this fall and
consequently I have jumped from about 500 last year, and I didn't
seed any winter wheat last year, to about 1,000 this year because
as I said it is like playing "21". If you don't double when you
have got an ace in the hole, why, you are out of luck. [Laughter]

I found I had in 900 acres in 1932 because the conditions looked pretty good, and consequently I had 14,000 bushels. Then I dwindled down to 500 acres because the conditions were not so good, and in 1933 you see I did manage to make enough at 30-cent wheat to pay my bills and to carry over nearly 3,000 bushels for 1934; instead of taking 22 cents a bushel I took 85 cents a bushel in 1935.

. . . .

Senator ELLENDER. One question. How far ahead of the wheat planting can you tell whether there will be sufficient moisture to raise a crop? My information is that it can be determined, and if so, why should a farmer plant wheat when he knows in advance he will fail?

Mr. ROARN. I will tell you, that is just about like forecasting the weather. Whenever it rains all around you, and it has rained 5 or 6 inches, you are pretty sure to have got some moisture; and not before that.

Senator McGILL. In other words, when the time to plant comes you have to have the moisture then.

Mr. ROARN. You have got have it then.

Senator McGILL. You can't say a week or 2 weeks ahead of time.

Mr. ROARN. Not 24 hours.

Senator McGILL. The rainfall in this country, of course, is a thing that is uncertain and irregular?

Mr. ROARN. Absolutely.

Senator McGILL. Altogether different from some other parts?

Testimony, Fred Roarn, October 9, 1937, U.S. Congress, 75th, 2nd session, Senate, Committee on Agriculture and Forestry, General Farm Legislation, pp. 2111, 2113.

561. THE PACIFIC NORTHWEST WHEAT PROBLEM (1937)

In an age of world markets, the regional aspect of agriculture is often ignored. A. R. Shumway was a wheat grower and president of the North Pacific Grain Growers, a cooperative of nearly 8,000 members who marketed almost 30 million bushels of wheat. He writes here.

The Pacific Northwest is a section which has to export approximately half of its wheat. We are shut off from the balance of the country. We have to take our products that we sell in the eastern markets either through the Panama Canal or across the Rocky Mountains. If we go to Minneapolis we have to pay a freight rate of about 35 cents a bushel. I think it is 55 cents a hundred, which

makes 33 cents a bushel. If the balance of the country was prosperous and we had to take 33 cents a bushel less than other growers
in the eastern sections, we would become bankrupt. It is only
under exceptional circumstances and the low price of wheat here that
we can take advantage of those markets.

The best market which we have had since exports have been shut
off--I say by the Smoot-Hawley tariff, or by the tariff bill which
was passed in 1929. I believe it was the Smoot-Hawley, was it not?

Senator McGILL. That is right.

Mr. SHUMWAY. Tariff bill, we have been shut out of the foreign
markets for our wheat. We always had foreign markets up until
1929. Now we have to get rid of this surplus.

We have been distributing it in the Gulf States and the
Atlantic States in direct competition with soft red wheat in Ohio,
Indiana, and that part of the United States east of the Mississippi
River.

Every bushel of our wheat that goes there takes the place of
a bushel of soft red winter and makes the problem that much harder
there.

Testimony, A. R. Shumway, October 1, 1937, U.S. Congress,
75th, 2nd session, Senate, Committee on Agriculture and Forestry,
General Farm Legislation, pp. 1673.

562. CROP CONTROL AT THE EXPENSE OF TENANTS (1937)

In the farm hearings of 1937, which filled 20
volumes of farmer-testimony, the following witness,
J. R. Butler, was virtually the only one who testified
on behalf of poor tenants, sharecroppers, and farm
laborers. Butler was president of the Southern Tenant
Farmers' Union which claimed 40,000 members, mainly in
Texas, Arkansas, Oklahoma, Mississippi, North Carolina,
Tennessee, and Alabama.

The sharecroppers, tenants, and other farm laborers, of the
South have been the chief victims of the acreage-reduction programs
as administered by the A. A. A. and the Department of Agriculture.
As a result of the cotton crop-control plans of the past 4 years,
thousands of families have been driven off the land and the already
subliving standards of those remaining have been further reduced.
The small share of the benefits theoretically granted the sharecropper and tenant under the acreage limitation plans have in too
many cases failed to reach the people whose labor produces the
cotton.
. . . .

We submit that the program of limitation of cotton acreage has
failed, inasmuch as it has not maintained the price of cotton in
parity with the increased cost of living. Furthermore, the South
prior to the advent of the A. A. A. produced 60 percent of the
cotton sold in the world market. It is now selling 40 percent.
As we reduce our acreage, foreign nations increase theirs. If this
policy is to continue, it is only logical to assume that in a few
years the South will only have the domestic market left. The United
States consumes 8,000,000 bales yearly. In terms of labor engaged
in the production of cotton, the continuance of the present policy
will result in additional hundreds of thousands of sharecroppers and
tenant families being driven from the soil into the cities on the
relief rolls, and if there is no relief--and we cannot expect W.
P. A. and other relief agencies to continue indefinitely, and to
support increasing hundreds of thousands of people dispossessed and
driven from the land--into outright starvation or blind revolt
against such injustice.

. . . .

The base acreage as a means of determining the payments should
be discontinued. This method is entirely in the interests of the
large owners of land and penalizes the small farmer as well as the
sharecropper and tenant. Payment of such subsidies or bounties
should be determined by the share of interest in the crop. Thus,
a sharecropper working for half of the proceeds from the crop should
be paid one-half the bounty or subsidy. All such payments should
be made direct to the person for whom it is intended. The program
and rules and regulations should be simplified so that every person
could easily determine just what his share of the benefits would
amount to.

The successful operation of any program that may be adopted wil
will depend largely on its proper administration. Heretofore the
administration of the A. A. A. has been placed in the hands of
local committees and county agents as a rule constituting the most
prominent and largest owners of land in a county. These committees
serve their own interests and the interests of the class they represent. We submit that it is only fair that representatives of the
tenant and sharecropper class should also have adequate representation on local county and State committees.

. . . .

You have heard from everybody except the sharecroppers and the
usual run of tenants, and I want to tell you a little bit about
them. It is very regrettable that all the sharecroppers and tenants
could not be on the Oscar Johnston farm, according to the report
we had of his tenants; but is impossible for him to take care of
all of them himself. These tenants and sharecroppers are the
lowest-paid class of people in the world because they get only a
part of the crop that they make. Some of them make only $40 for
the year's work, for himself and his entire family. I know these
things are true. The crop-control program that does not give
consideration to these actual producers of the staple is not going

to be one that is going to benefit. Any time you reduce acreage
of the cotton crop in the South, these people are the ones that
suffer first.

Testimony, J. R. Butler , October 28, 1937, U.S. Congress,
75th, 2nd session, Senate, Committee on Agriculture and Forestry,
General Farm Legislation, pp. 1450-1452.

563. WE ARE NOT DEALING WITH AN EMERGENCY (1930's)

The farm crisis of the 'Thirties was part of an
older problem. This testimony is that of R. W. Hudgens,
Assistant Administrator of the Farm Security Administration. For thirteen years he had been the manager of the
stock and bond department of a South Carolina investment
firm. He had held other F.S.A. offices in Louisiana and
had served as regional director of South Carolina, Georgia,
Florida, and Alabama.

If I might, I will go back a little further in my own experience and say that my father was a tenant farmer. He died when I
was very young. One of my earliest recollections was our being
forced to move from wherever we were.
I did not realize the significance of that until later. My
mother married again and my stepfather was a furnish merchant, until
he went bankrupt in that business.
I clerked in his store. I knew the families who borrowed from
him and I knew something of the conditions out of which their
problems arose.
My point in mentioning that is that I saw a lot, and I am
afraid that others who have seen the same thing have misunderstood
the significance of what they saw.
Now, my main point is that we are dealing here [during the
depression of the 'thirties], not with an emergency, but with something that has been going on a long time before I ever sold a share
cropper a sack of flour and it is a process that has gradually
gotten worse.
The emergency simply gave us an opportunity to do something
about conditions that have been growing all of these years. Since
I have been old enough to realize that things happen to people,
these processes that we are coping with now have been grinding
down the people that I knew.
The average furnish merchant's interest rate through the
South is 35 percent on money for the time the loan is outstanding.
I can show you counties where I have good reason to believe
that the interest rate of a great many of our borrows was over 60
percent before the came on the [federal farm lending] program. It

may have some significance that in the counties where I made that study the hookworm rate was 60 percent.

Now, let me draw some conclusions based on the last two statements I made about my own background.

I have studied credit; I have studied agricultural credit. I have studied especially the causes of failure of agricultural credit.

Before depression hit the rest of the country, it hit the textile industry in the part of the South Carolina where I lived.

There were a lot of people on the breadlines, a lot of people who had been farmers were in the breadlines. I started, with some Red Cross money, what I believe was the first rehabilitation program in this country.

Now, it had nothing to do with what finally grew into Farm Security. I don't believe the people who started the rehabilitation program under the F.E.R.A. ever heard of me. We were dealing with the same essentials then in our little program that we are dealing with now in Farm Security.

And the thing I think we learned and which certainly I never will forget, is that something can be done with these people who have been written off.

Testimony, R. W. Hudgens, May 18, 1943, U.S. Congress, 78th, 1st session, House of Representatives, Select Committee to Investigate the Activities of the Farm Security Administration, Farm Security Administration, I, pp. 168-169.

564. "GIVE OUR LABOR BACK TO US" (1943)

By treaty with Mexico, the U.S. Government transported, at its expense, Mexicans who worked on Southwestern farms. Until mid-1943, the Farm Security Administration enforced relatively advanced work and pay standards. When the War Food Administration took over, in mid-1943, increased grower-influence was exercised and standards fell. H. S. Abbott who owned 5,500 acres of cotton land in Arizona, testifies. He was president of the Irrigated Cotton Growers which included growers in California, Arizona, New Mexico, and West Texas.

I would like to clarify the labor situation as it has existed here for the past 25 years. The Southwest has at all times had a large proportion of Mexican labor and during the last war [1914-1918] a great deal of labor was imported from Mexico. The claim was made by the Mexican Government because these people were not sent back that they were mistreated and there were cases of that, especially in the sugarbeet fields up north and in California. I know of none of these being here, in fact I never heard of it.

At the time of the depression in 1932 there was a large group of these nationals who had come in from the north and from this part of the country and migrated to Los Angeles. The relief problem there was very difficult and the American Government and the local authorities undertook to repatriate a lot of those people and they were sent back at Government expense. At the same time our own immigration authorities started scrutinizing the papers of all Mexican nationals in this part of the country and there were shipped out of the State of Arizona from 20,000 to 23,000 Mexican laborers, which was just about the number of laborers we required at all times to fill the present void. However, that void was filled by the migration, due to the dust-bowl conditions and to poverty of workers out of Arkansas, Oklahoma, Texas, and even Missouri, lots of Missourians, and those people in a measure filled the void until this war started and they were drawn off into war industry and into better jobs. Then the void reoccurred and being dependent primarily for the harvesting of our crops and today for the working of our crops on migratory labor, we of necessity, and quite naturally inasmuch as the Government took our labor away from us it is only natural that we ask the Government to give our labor back to us.

Testimony, H. S. Casey Abbott, November 22, 1943, U.S. Congress, 78th, 1st session, House of Representatives, Select Committee to Investigate the Activities of the Farm Security Administration, Farm Security Administration, IV, p. 1555.

565.   REVERSION TO HORSEPOWER ON FARMS (1943)

One little-noticed effect of the depressed thirties was an increase in the number of horses and mules. During the war, complications arose because of this heritage. The situation is described by Oscar W. Meier who was Chief, Agricultural Food and Textile Machinery Unit, Office of Civilian Supply, War Production Board. Earlier, he had worked in the Rural Electrification Administration, and as a county agent in Missouri.

Mr. MEIER. The full number of horses and mules, if I get your question correctly, which will disappear from farms, that is the reduction in total number at present is fewer than the number that disappeared from farms during most of the twenties and a good part of the thirties. During the depression years farmers, because they didn't have much cash, cut down materially on the purchase of tractors, and many of them started breeding the mares that they had so that we have actually had more colts foaled in the years since the depression than we had in the years immediately preceding the depression.

Mr. RUSSELL. How many would that loss be that you took into consideration?

Mr. MEIER. We estimated that the net loss of horses and mules would be somewhere between 300 and 350 thousand. But I would like to add here that the accelerated purchasing of tractors in 1940 and 1941 and 1942 left an unused surplus of horses on many farms which had transferred to tractor power, and those horses may not yet have been diverted to farms which are still depending upon horsepower.

Mr. RUSSELL. You have no knowledge whether they are or are not?

Mr. MEIER. The only knowledge that might be pertinent is the fact that several people who are quite familiar with the horse and mule auctions of this country have told me that the horse market is very "draggy", and they expressed surprise that that condition prevails.

Testimony, Oscar W. Meier, January 14, 1943, U.S. Congress, 78th, 1st session, Senate, Special Committee Investigating the National Defense Program, Investigation of the National Defense Program, XVII, p. 6770.

566. FINANCES OF THE MECHANICAL COTTON PICKER (1927-1952)

John Rust was the principal inventor of the first practicable American mechanical cotton-picker. He died in 1953, a year after the following account was published. He writes on the financial problems of developing a potentially revolutionary invention.

...I met a few men with little money and great faith in my undertaking. The first to extend financial assistance was an oil field worker of Texas who borrowed $500.00 from his brother in 1927 to enable me to get started building my first machine....In the fall of 1932 the machine was operated principally near Lake Providence, Louisiana. Financing a new corporation whose principal assests was a license on a new invention admittedly in the experimental stage, was most difficult during the depression of the thirties. So, when some of the leading planters of the community became interested and offered not only some financial backing, but a lease on a new metal building, we moved to Lake Providence....The machine rebuilt at Lake Providence made history in 1933. At the Delta Experiment Station Stoneville, Mississippi, it was the first machine in the world to pick five bales of cotton in a day....While the cotton picker gained much fame both nationally and internationally financing was never an easy question. When World War II came on the Rust Cotton Picker Company still had only a development shop with no facilities for producing machines in quantities.

Also the Company was caught in a precarious financial position.
For the first time since I started work on the first model of the
cotton picker, and for the first time since...1928, we were from
necessity forced to look for employment elsewhere....[my brother]
Mack [went to work] in Pittsburgh, and I as expediter on an Ordin-
ance project at Canton, Ohio....We were unable to obtain further
financing....Finally, the [Rust] company's charter was revoked by
the state of Tennessee because of its inability to pay its franchise
taxes....Then, in 1943, I set out to design the machine all over
again....While I was in Washington with my new drawings early in
1944 to file patents on the new improvements, I was approached by
Allis-Chalmers Manufacturing Company for a license to manufacture
and sell the Rust Cotton Picker....My wife and I were able to live
on my professional fee as consulting engineer with Allis-Chalmers,
so with the earnings from the machines I was able to continue
development of my new cotton picker....The year 1952 has seen the
culmination of many of my hopes and dreams. Not only have I produced the kind of cotton picking machine I set out to build, but
I have been able to fulfill all the financial commitments made to
those who supplied the funds necessary for a quarter of a century
of mechanical developments....The only remaining problem is getting
machines to the farmers at a low price so that eventually the cost
of production can be so lowered as to enable cotton to hold its own
against competing fibres.

John Rust, "The Origin and Development of the Cotton Picker,"
West Tennessee Historical Society Papers, VII (1953), pp. 46-47,
48, 50, 51-54.

567. CORPORATE FARMING IN CALIFORNIA (1960)

     Here is the application of large-scale business
organization to agriculture. The extract is from an
address by Mark Raney, Agricultural Manager, Kern County
Land Company, Bakersfield, California. The Company
farmed 11,000 acres and leased out 115,000 acres,
virtually all irrigated. It engaged in cattle, cotton,
water, and industrial operations. Its stock was listed
on the New York Stock Exchange.

As far as advantages and disadvantages are concerned, I suggest
these, starting with the disadvantages:
. . . .
Corporate and large scale farming are often discriminated
against by legislators and some of the general public. We are
considered undesirable because we are big, and often unfairly

become the whipping boy. Examples of this are the 160 acre limitation and the $50,000 limitation on government commodity loans.

. . . .

Our labor costs are generally higher than many other agricultural operators. We are, however, very proud of the fact that most
of our agricultural workers enjoy fringe benefits, including a profit sharing plan, pension plan, group insurance, vacation and sick
pay and so on.

. . . .

Our overhead costs may be bigger than an owner-operator
enterprise. Management and staff are expensive.

. . . .

As to advantages I suggest these:

. . . .

From a financing standpoint there may be an advantage, since
adequate funds are available when they are needed for capital,
operating and emergency needs if properly justified. One example
would be the failure of an irrigating well where an immediate
expenditure of $20,000 to $40,000 is required.

. . . .

We can take risks and try new crops on a commercial basis where
failure might be disastrous to a small operator.

. . . .

We can employ competent management or train people to handle
specific phases of our operation.

. . . .

Service functions can be established and exploited. I have
mentioned our Technical Services and Agricultural Marketing Divisions. Others include an Engineering and Personnel Department;
central shop facilities; people experienced in purchasing, insurance
and safety. Good legal advice is retained. Consultants can be
employed when needed.

. . . .

Professional accountants supported by modern accounting machinery can keep operators up to date with accurate cost accounting and
other frequent pertinent reports. This has been extremely helpful
to us. Just one example of this--we know what our potato harvesting and picking costs are each day by 10:00 A.M. the following
morning.

. . . .

Volume purchasing and selling can lead to lower costs and
higher returns. We fell that we have done a good job of selling
our cotton. We have an IBM card punched for each bale immediately
after it is ginned and classed. With these we can mechanically prepare a list of our offerings weekly. Cotton buyers find an adequate
volume to attract their attention and apparently like our list
presentation.

. . . .

We can put new machines and techniques to work quickly and
maintain an adequate equipment fleet. We have some indication
that we actually have a lesser investment per acre in tractors and
implements than smaller operators.

. . . .

I am sure there are other advantages and disadvantages which occur to you.

Mark Raney, June 14, 1960, address to a meeting of the American Society of Farm Managers and Rural Appraisers, Davis, California, Journal of the American Society of Farm Managers and Rural Appraisers, XXIV (October, 1960), pp. 23-24.

568. WE ARE THE ENVY OF THE WORLD (1978)

Traditionally, at least in the North and West, small commercial farms could be worked by family labor with an occasional hired hand. It was frequently believed that the owner typically had climbed an agricultural ladder-- beginning as family laborer, then a hired worker, then a renter, and -- finally -- as an owner. By the last quarter of the 20th Century, few owners could claim they had travelled the prescribed itinerary. Nevertheless, a number could, especially in the Midwest. Warren W. Carlson, a farmer from Winnebago, Illinois is an example, if not a typical one.

I first would like to give you a profile of a special American family farm, my own, because I am more familiar with this. My father started out as a renter on a farm; and after he had farmed many years, he was given an opportunity to buy the home and buy the farm that he was farming on . He was able to get that purchased before he passed away and by the time of retirement. So he then retired; and I, after farming with him in partners for 17 years, was able to be a tenant on my father's farm.

He then came to me later on and presented the most--how shall I say it--the greatest opportunity that I have had, when he came out and said, "Warren, would you like to buy the farm from mom and me?"

We did agree upon a contract that took a 12-year payoff, and after 12 years, by giving Dad half the milk check each year, I was owner of that farm.

By that time, my four children were then graduating from college. I have two sons and two daughters, and I now farm with my two sons and my son-in-law. The other daughter lives on one of the other farms. So we are all within a 1-mile area.

When Dad came out and said, "You can buy the farm from me," this gave me the opportunity when my son came home from college that I could say to Rich, when he told me he wanted to try farming rather going to other business--I then had to go to the banker and borrow some money to help Rich get involved with farming. This later developed also with my son-in-law and my youngest son.

The original farm was 180 acres. Dad and I farmed this together. It was a two-man operation. We had all kinds of livestock; dairy, chickens. We still have an expanded family farm, in
that we milk about 125 cows, we raise 15 hogs, we feed a couple
hundred head of steer, and we farm 1,000 acres.

We do it together; live together. My son-in-law, daughters-
in-law, are all involved in some responsibility. It makes a wonderful feeling for me, I suppose, that this was able to be accomplished. I don't know if probably anywhere in the world this can
be done and done as well as here.

We have in this country the greatest asset. The greatest
asset, next to our people, is bountiful American agriculture. We
are the envy of the world. We are the jolly green giant of the
world. We are now in prime time, and I guess we have got to look
at the alternatives to surplus. The alternative, as many of the
other countries have found, is deprivation. There aren't many
substitutes for food. We all like to eat.

I think the problem, one of the major problems that we have,
is the problem of distribution. We have many places in this world
that need what we have. I guess if you were a person that had an
excess of something and you wanted to get out in the excess, you
would get out and sell, sell, sell. And I think that is what we
ought to do. I think we ought to promote research and sell.

I think we have had other kinds of surpluses. And we certainly need to sell; we need the dollars in America, too, to pay
off some of the other fellows that are presenting us with bills.

I am a great champion of the free enterprise system and I
think our family farms exemplify this system. We compete with one
another right down the road. I compete with all my neighbors....

When we have a problem we cannot find the solution to and we
are all concerned, if we find the solution to the problem we probably go to our neighbor and tell him the solution, so that he can
beat us at our own game, really. You don't find this in many other
businesses. We do it as being good guys, I guess, and with the
idea of everybody succeeding.

I think one of the great things in American agriculture is
that we have had and been able to buy the necessary things that
would increase our efficiency. There are many places in the world
where there is good land, but they have a system that keeps their
farmers depressed. They do not have the money to purchase the tools
or the chemicals or whatever is necessary to be efficient.

We have had and are having that in this country. I know that
there are some problems now. We are into some temporary problems.
I think if you fellows in Washington and us guys out here can work
together to some of those problems, I'm convinced that we, too,
can climb the hill.

Testimony, May 13, 1978, U.S. Congress, 95th, 2nd session,
House of Representatives, Committee on Agriculture, Subcommittee
on Family Farms, Rural Development, and Special Studies, Problems
Facing Family Farms. Hearings...., (Washington, D.C.: Government
Printing Office, 1978), pp. 17-18.

569.   KEEP FARM CAPITAL HOME (1978)

During the late 1970s, a number of historic trends in American agriculture continued or were heightened, especially as a result of technological developments. The number of farms fell from nearly seven million in the 'thirties to 2.6 million in 1978 while the rate of decline eased during the seventies. The average size of farms in 1974 was 440 acres; in 1950 it had been less than half that. The farms going out of business were absorbed by remaining farms. Some 53 percent of total sales of farm products are supplied by only six percent of all farm producers, suggesting a high degree of concentration which has grown briskly. Farms of 1,000 acres or more accounted for 60 million acres in 1964; a decade later, 100 million were involved in these larger enterprises. Small farms -- i.e., with sales of less than $20,000 a year -- represent over two-thirds of all farms but account only for 11 percent of sales. Here, Gerald M. Boyle, a farmer from Dexter, Iowa, and a member of the American Agricultural Movement, describes some of the broader economic problems facing the farmers.

Up to this period of time in our recent history, farmland had not inflated. It was a fairly stable commodity, and even though there were farmers being absorbed into little larger units, there was nothing to prevent young farmers from acquiring land also. This was well within their means financially.

As the rest of the economy prospered, excess capital was generated beyond normal needs. As the tax advantages of cash accounting, and farm operations in general for persons with an outside source of income became apparent in the early sixties, investment capital in increasing amounts was diverted into the acquisition of agricultural land. This created a twofold problem, which I will deal with separately.

As the steadily increasing numbers of individuals with investment capital seeking tax shelters turned to farmland, an artificial upward pressure was imposed upon the price of an acre of land, one of the basic inputs into the cost of production. This virtually insured that young tenant farmers, with little or no equity, could never hope to own land, but rather must spend their productive lifetime farming under the guidelines of absentee owners.

As if this problem were not severe enough, it has been compounded by Government policy designed to continue the downward trend in parity prices for the theoretical benefit of consumers, at the real expense of producers. One might pose the question: "If the consumer is not benefiting, who is?" I feel that answer is readily apparent, but since that is not the intent of these hearings, I hope to be able to deal with that problem at a more appropriate time and place.

The point is, due to factors beyond his control, today's young farmer is caught in a price freeze.

In the form of a "coup de grace," Government tax policy is allowing outside investment money to sap the very lifeblood out of agriculture.

I'd like to make a brief explanatory remark for the purposes of the record. The means by which outside capital is doing this is simply greater dollar amount each deduction you take is worth to you; so a person with a high-level income, a deduction on a farming operation is worth much more to him than to an individual family farming at a low level of income; so you cannot compete.

The second part of the problem deals with rural communities. The effect of America's cheap food policy on "Small Town, U.S.A." has been nothing short of disastrous. How many small towns in Iowa have three businesses left, a grocery store, with high prices because of low volume, a grain elevator, and a tavern, because in a community that small and that poor, what other cultural activity is there?

We are constantly bombarded with statistics on rural poverty. The example of the small semideserted town, victim of the staggering outflow of equity and people from rural America, is occasionally flashed on our television screen and then conveniently forgotten. The solution to this problem is simple, and I will take exception to the remarks of the gentleman previously. There are simple solutions sometimes. Let agriculture retain its fair share of of the investment returns on its production. Keep the capital investment in land in its local area, so that income generated will be spent in the community. When outside investors own land in a community, that income leaves the area, only to come back as more investment capital to further deteriorate the economic base of rural America.

In summing up, foreign investment is only a symptom of a far greater problem, not the cause. If agriculture is a healthy, viable business, in balance with the rest of the economy, then it need have nothing to fear from foreign investment, nor from outside investment in general....

I'd like to ask you gentlemen a hard question. I'd like to ask each individually, and I'd like the answer to be as straightforward and to the point as the question is.

With this kind of testimony down through the years, why is it that whenever legislation is enacted, it is always in favor of the vested interests, the big capital interests in this country?

That is what is wrong with agriculture today, and why we have foreign investment problems.

Testimony, July 28, 1978, U.S. Congress, 95th, 2nd session, Committee on Agriculture, Subcommittee on Family Farms, Rural Development, and Special Studies, Impact of Foreign Investment in Farmland. Hearings...., (Washington, D.C.: Government Printing Office, 1978), pp. 410-411, 414.

570. GRAIN CAR SHORTAGES IN THE WEST (1978)

        The market price of grain and the weather affect
the capacity of railroads to carry the wheat crop. If
prices are low and lead to much storage, they may also
change rapidly and create a sudden demand for railroad
cars. Severe weather frequently interferes with the
operation of cars -- and, in the case of waterways, as
well. Railroad industry representatives stress the
succession of surplus and shortage in cars and cite
severe weather problems. They also maintain rates of
return are inadequate to finance the acquisition of sufficient freight cars. In opposition to these arguments is
the testimony of Vivian Thuesen, a wheat producer from
northern Montana and chairman of the National Association
of Wheat Growers.

The problem of grain car shortages in the western U.S. grain
producing territory is paramount. We have not seen a shortage this
severe for over a decade and the continuation of this shortage of
cars will deepen the already severe impact it is having on the
grain producer....
        The car shortages that have developed across the nation is a
most serious, short-term problem facing the producer. The railroads
are beginning to admit that they have been unable to make any appre-
ciable headway against the outstanding car orders and they are only
holding their own with respect to current orders. In other words,
the backlog of outstanding cars that has been created over the past
months is not being reduced. There are indications now that this
current shortage will remain with us through the next harvest and
probably through next winter. Producers have a responsibility to
read the signals of the marketplace and to respond to the regulatory
and congressional bodies with their concerns. Our chief concern is
that penalties are being assessed to the country elevators because
they are unable to deliver their grain to the markets due to the
lack of availability of cars. These penalties have been reported
to be as high as one-half cent per bushel per day. Of course, lack
of cars has inhibited the ability of the elevators to move grain
which, in turn, has limited their ability to purchase more grain
from the producers. One of the first things that occurs when grain
purchases are limited is that the premiums disappear. When commerce
is slowed the result is that profits are curtailed and the ultimate
bearer of these unfortunate circumstances is the one in the position
who is unable to pass reduced earnings on any further down the
chain. That person? In the grain car shortage, it is the grain
producer. He is the one who ultimately bears the cost of grain car
shortage.
        The causes of this present grain car shortage are legion with
no single cause under review taking a dominant position. The constant reoccurrence of these car shortages leads one to believe that
the current method of dealing with car shortages may be ineffective.

The midwestern and western railroads continue to tell us they
are increasing their covered hopper fleets and some figures bear
these claims out. Yet, when one looks at total grain carrying capacity, that is, boxcar and covered hopper capacities, one finds the
retirement of boxcar capacity occurring faster than the replenish-
ment in capacity of the additional covered hoppers. The result is
that the capacity of the roads is falling.

With the addition of the larger capacity covered hopper cars,
it is submitted that less carloads are required to move the grain
today than previously, but with a possible loss of flexibility by
the railroads. Of course, every elevator would much rather receive
and load hoppers than box cars because of the ease of loading, more
capacity, and less chance of loss or damage to the contents.

The overproduction of grain in the last few years has increased
the storage reserves of grain. However, demand for grain sales has
not been excessive and nowhere near the levels experienced during
the Russian grain sales when the last car shortage occurred.

There was the usual winter-related delays and this winter
happened to be particularly severe on the upper Great Plains States
during January and February. The major problems were blizzards,
drifting closed rail lines, and loss of power units due to the snow
getting into locomotives.

This car shortage, however, has some distinct characteristics
that have had the effect of tying up grain cars. The grain elevator
explosions on the gulf coast had caused shifts in origin-supply
points. The initiation and heavy utilization of multicar rates by
the railroads in the Great Plains have increased the turnaround
times by the time required to accumulate the required multicar size
or origin points. This extra time for consolidation at origins may
be lengthened considerably if one of the cars shows up as bad-
ordered upon inspection.

Service curtailments on some branchlines have also had the
effect of increasing times cars sit at origin points under load
awaiting the next service run.

Testimony, May 9, 1978, U.S. Congress, 95th, 2nd session,
Senate, Committee on Agriculture, Nutrition, and Foresty, Subcommittee on Agricultural Production, Marketing, and Stabilization
of Prices, Rural Transportation Problems. Hearings....,
(Washington, D.C.: Government Printing Office, 1978), pp. 41-42.

571.   CONSERVING SOIL IN BLACK HAWK COUNTY (1980)

While American agriculture may be the envy of the
world, the erosion of American soil is its greatest enemy.
Erosion is spurred by rainfall, snowmelt, and improper
irrigation. In Texas, wind erosion soil loss runs around
14.9 tons per acre; on other parts of the Great Plains it is

less. For tilled land in general, wrote Tom Barlow in
1979, "losses are higher per acre today than in the Dust
Bowl years of the thirties." Nearly two-fifths of the
country's rangeland are in need of conservation. Jim
Sage, a farmer from Waterloo, Iowa, describes how one
family farm cares for its soil.

"Live as though you are going to die tomorrow--farm as though
you are going to farm forever." I can be very thankful that this
motto, passed on to me by my father, has played a dominating role
in my life's work of producing food, not only for my family, but
for many people the past 23 years. In order to maintain and
increase food production from our land, we have learned that a
strong soil and water conservation program, established when my
great-grandfather first settled on part of our farm 123 years ago,
has been the guiding force in our farming operation.

With crop rotations, contour farming, minimum tillage, and a
livestock program, we have been able to live within the allowable
soil loss limits for our soil types of 5 tons per acre soil loss
per year, as established by the soil conservancy laws of Iowa. I
am especially proud to say that we have been able to accomplish this
without any financial assistance from any governmental agency. On
our 590-acre farm, we follow a crop rotation of 1-year oats, 1-year
hay or pasture, and 2 or 4 years of corn. Row crops are contoured
where needed and have been chisel plowing hay, pasture, and corn
ground since 1970. We feed approximately 180 head of cattle a year
and raise from farrow to finish 1,000 head of hogs mainly on a
summer pasture farrowing system.

From an economic standpoint, our farming operation has not
brought in the most dollars as could be gained by following a continuous row crop rotation, which would subsequently mine and ravage
the soil in our present generation. But we have been able to
expand our farm by purchasing additional acreage, of going through
the confiscatory process of over $160,000 in four estate settlements
of our parents since 1975 and raising a family, which will hopefully
have a dedication of producing food and maintaining the land in a
good productive state in the future.

I am sorry to say that I see this ravishment of the soil continuing at a faster and faster pace in the past 25 years throughout
the Midwest, because of the cheap food policy and extensive expor-
tation of our farm products that are being advocated by our national
leaders. These policies are really tragic, if you have studied
any history and read of other civilizations not following a policy
of maintaining their basic resource, soil. Also the misguided
efforts of consumer activists in changing the American consumer's
food purchases, from an animal and plant protein diet to an all-
plant protein diet, is very shortsighted. The soybean, from which
the majority of our plant protein comes from, is the most erosive
crop in American agriculture. We need to maintain a strong and
viable livestock economy, which does not necessitate so many of
our acres being placed in row crop production. Livestock manure
along with plant refuse are vital in maintaining a renewable

resource of nitrogen, phosphorus, and potassium. We are already
importing much of our potassium and within 20 years, at the present
rate of usage, most of our phosphorus. The soybean plant does not
have the ability to replenish the soil with these basic elements
as does a sound livestock program.

Instead of setting up broad extensive Government programs for
soil and water conservation, establish property, income, inheri-
tance, and estate tax reduction incentives, based upon each farming
operation living within the allowable soil loss limits for its
type of soil.

We would gain much more of each tax dollar for actual conservation practices, if it could be kept right here on the land
instead of filtering through a number of hands from here to Des
Moines or Washington and then back to the individual farm. It has
been my observation, when an individual places all of his own financial resources into the land, he will have a much more healthy
respect to see that the land is maintained in a productive state
for future generations.

Testimony, August 13, 1980, U.S. Congress, 96th, second
session, Senate, Committee on Agriculture, Nutrition, and Forestry,
Subcommittee on Environment, Soil Conservation, and Forestry,
Soil Conservation. Hearings...., (Washington, D.C.: Government
Printing Office, 1980), pp. 17-18.

572. DEVELOPING RURAL TELEPHONY (1981)

The telephone was preeminently an urban and commercial mechanism which was most useful economically where
rapid decisions needed to be communicated speedily and
over long distances. In the rural world of disparate farm
units, operated by small-scale business methods, and
attuned to slow natural processes, telephones could only
have been a luxury. In addition, the problem of high outlays for equipment that would be only sparsely used weighed
heavily against rural telephony. As A. Harold Peterson,
executive director of the National REA Telephone Association, recalls, telephones came to the countryside only
comparatively recently and only then by virtue of lobbying
successfully for federal aid.

Because there are so many new members of this committee who
may not be acquainted with the rural telephone program, who were
not here when the Rural Telephone Bank came into existence, I just
want to briefly recite the history of rural telephony.

The rural telephone amendment to the Rural Electrification
Act came into being in 1949 because of one significant economic
fact, and that was that there was no financing available in the

private market. The telephone systems that had been in operation
in this country, the old magneto and common battery systems, had
been operating for about 40 to 50 years and were in a state of dis-
repair and broken down. When these people decided that something
had to be done and went to the private market to get financial
help, there was none.

In that kind of an atmosphere, the rural telephone amendment
was passed.

I noticed, Mr. Chairman, that on the witness list today is
Mr. Robert Partridge of the National Rural Electric Cooperative
Association. Many people do not remember those days, as I do, and
I just want to say for the record that had it not been for the
National Rural Electric Cooperative Association in the late 1940's,
especially the work of its leader, Clyde Ellis, there would never
have been a rural telephone program as we know it today. The tremendous amount of work that Mr. Ellis and his organization performed
on behalf of rural telephone will always be appreciated by those of
us in the telephone business, and I wanted the record to reflect
that.

In the first days of the program, the interest rates charged
for loans to rural telephone borrowers was 2 percent. As the program progressed--and I might say, in a very successful manner--it
soon became apparent in the middle 1960's that the appropriations
that were made by the Congress were not keeping pace with the
actual financial needs of the systems.

I shall never forget a visit I had with the then Director of
the Office of Management and Budget in 1966, who, when we were discussing the plight of the telephone companies in this country, said
that the tremendous pressure on the Federal budget, that we had to
in some way figure out a better way for getting our job completed,
and that supplemental financing of some sort had to be devised.

We went to work, as the chairman and Mr. Fullarton will recall
very vividly, and developed what is now known as the Rural Telephone
Bank. It took us 5 years to get that legislation through. It was
passed in 1971. It is now 10 years old. In the original legislation, the bank was provided with $30 million of annual input or
infusion of funds from the Federal Government, to purchase class
stock with a 2 percent rate of return.

The purpose of this class A stock, which the $30 million pur-
chased, was to enable the Rural Telephone Bank to utilize that
money, together with the money which each borrower had to put into
the program by purchasing Class B stock in the amount of 5 percent
of the amount of the borrower's loan Class C stock involved voluntary purchases by the individual companies and other organizations
controlled by them.

The Rural Telephone Bank has been most successful. The rationale for the credition of this bank was to try to wean away borrowers
from the lower or insured type of loan to a higher interest type
loan, if the borrower was able to pay a higher rate of interest.
This endeavor has been most successful. We have now reached the
point where the 10 years is up and the $300 million of seed money
has been put in the bank.

The purpose of our appearance here today is to support passage of H. R. 1723, which will permit Government purchase of an additional $300 million for the purchase of class A stock to be put into the bank over the next 10 years.

It is as simple as that. What this amendment does is to reflect that type of change.

One of the benefits that comes of this kind of proposition is that actually the Federal Government's net borrowing cost is lower. How is that achieved? If the Rural Telephone Bank can take a number of borrowers out of the insured program--and let us assume for the sake of illustration that you could move $70 million worth of loans out of the insured loan program into the telephone bank--the net saving of that process of moving that amount of loans into the bank is going to innure to a savings of about $2 million a year to the Government in its financing cost.

Now, the reason I bring this up is that I am sure that the question is going to be raised, "Well, why are we doing this at such a time when the Government is trying to cut down on subsidies?"

The reason for bringing this to your attention is to indicate that you cannot consider the $30 million input by itself. You have to combine it with what the effect would be on the Government's borrowing cost in removing numbers of loans from the insured category into the Rural Telephone Bank.

Testimony, March 16, 1981, U.S. Congress, 97th, 1st session, House of Representatives, Committee on Agriculture, Subcommittee on Conservation, Credit, and Rural Development, General Farm Bill of 1981 (Conservation, Credit, Rural Development.) Hearings...., (Washington, D.C.: Government Printing Office, 1981), pp. 370-371.

F.

MASS PRODUCTION AND CONCENTRATION

573. "QUICKNESS, CONTINUITY, AND ECONOMY" (1900)

A striking insight into the spirit of the times, the era of modern machine industry. Charles Morgan, president of ASME, writes the extract.

No single aspect of modern manufacturing is more striking and pronounced than the drift towards continuity of operation. Not that of the continuous mill alone, although that mill has done its full share; but everywhere, in all lines of work, the search for economy and despatch has weeded out slow and needless intermediaries and unified functions before separate and distinct. Operations which heretofore hindered and delayed have now disappeared from the continuous mill, until it is a familiar sight to see a billet, one end still in the furnace--its length in all the reducing passes of the mill, and the other end coiled on the reel, a finished wire rod --a continuous and simultaneous performance of heating, rolling and reeling upon the same piece of metal without cut or separation of its parts. No less striking is the operation of rolling <u>larger</u> sections. The metal, a few moments ago a 6,000-pound ingot, and now a four by six-inch billet, is carried onward to the mill, a part of its length moving on the feed table, part moving faster through the passes of the mill, part being cut by the "flying shear," part caught up and carried away on the conveyor, and part being delivered on the car for transportation from the mill.
　Here again are parts of the same mass of steel being fed, rolled, cut, conveyed and delivered, continuously and simultaneous-ly. There is something a bit dramatic in the sight of a bar resting on the car ready for shipment, while the parent from which it sprung is still away back in the bite of the roughing rolls.

So it is everywhere. Be it the making of a newspaper or an
envelope, from roll to finished product--folding, cutting, printing,
stamping, and counting--it is continuous to the end. It is in the
very spirit of the times--quickness, continuity, and economy. In a
recent review of the astronomy of the century, Professor Dolbear,
of Tuft's College, drops a little sentence, "Creation is a
continuous process." If the scientist finds creative processes
continuous in his domain, no less so does the engineer find it in
his own. Creation of the raw materials upon this planet has been
a continuous process, and so is fast getting to be the creation
of the finished products from them.

Charles H. Morgan, "Some Landmarks in the History of the
Rolling Mill," Transactions, American Society of Mechanical
Engineers, XXII (1900-1901), p. 62.

574. THE MORSE HEAT GAGE (1900)

Improvements in machinery came rapidly in
these days. Morse's heat gage made possible a high
level of uniform quality. Note, however, that even
with the gage, the inspector still used his eyes.
Automatic quality controls were still in the
future.

A young man by the name of Morse, a graduate of Cornell
University, had invented and patented what was probably the first
electrically operated optical pyrometer. He called it the Morse
Heat Gage, and undertook to manufacture and sell it. This instrument consisted of a tube in which was mounted a small, closely
coiled, spiral filament very much like the hair-spring of a watch.
Through this filament was passed a carefully regulated electric
current which heated the filament to whatever temperature was
desired. By looking through the tube, one could compare the color
of the red hot filament with the color of a tool in the hardening
furnace. When the filament disappeared from view against the
background of the tool, because the colors were identical, the
temperatures were then identical also. By means of this device the
temperature of the tools in the hardening furnace could be accurately known and regulated to within two to five degress Fahrenheit.
This was an almost unbelievable advance over anything previously
known. Hitherto we had been compelled to rely on the judgment,
experience and skill of the hardener who, in turn, depended on the
constantly variable color sense of the unaided human eye.
When Mr. Morse demonstrated and explained his instrument, I
saw at once what a tremendous help it could be to us in attaining
uniform quality, and what an advantage we might gain over our

competitors if we could acquire exclusive rights to his invention.
We therefore promptly entered into negotiations with him and shortly
succeeded in acquiring the exclusive right to his invention for the
twist drill industry. On November 25, 1900, we installed the Morse
Heat Gage and soon had applied it to all the heat treating operations throughout the factory. I have always considered this to be
one of the most important steps we ever took towards the maintenance
of the utmost quality in our product. I believe it has been and
will continue to be, over the years, of the greatest advantage
to our company in its competitive struggle.

Cox, Building an American Industry, © The Cleveland Twist Drill
Company , pp. 172-173.

575. BRITISH MECHANICS FOOL AWAY THEIR TIME (1900)

A commentary on different styles of working
by Patrick McGarry who was owner of the Washington
Steam Boiler Works in Chicago, employing an average
of twenty workers. He had learned his trade in Liverpool, England which he left in 1875.

We have had many employers of labor before the commission,
here and elsewhere, and the testimony of these employers almost
invariably is that the American mechanic, hour for hour, will turn
out a greater product than the English mechanic or the mechanic of
the Continent. They say they are better housed; that they are
better fed; that they are better clothed; that they are better
educated; they live under better conditions generally, and those
are the reasons they give in accounting for their ability to turn
out a greater product than the English or Continental mechanics.
I should like to know what you would have to say on that point.--
A. I say the American mechanic will turn out more work in 2 days
than the Continental will in 3 in any branch of business. At the
same time I do not wish to make light of the English mechanic or
the Continental mechanic or European mechanic at any time. The
greatest mechanics that can be are in England. There are no
better. There are as good, but they can not be beaten; but they
fool their time away, which would not do in this country. There
is more energy; there is more "get up and get" in this country
than there is there, and, speaking from the practical point, as
soon as the English and Continental mechanic comes over here it is
contagious--the disease is contagious. They will do more work here
in 2 days than they will there in 3, and they will do it with
greater ease. Therefore I should wish to know why some of these
gentlemen who are objecting to giving 9 hours to machinists in this
city and 8 hours to boiler makers would not take their work to
England. It is all "bosh." They know they would lose every cent

they have got, and there is no danger of either England or any other
country cutting out the American mechanic.

Testimony, Patrick McGarry, March 29, 1900, U.S. Congress,
57th, 1st session, House of Representatives, Document No. 177,
Report of the Industrial Commission on the Chicago Labor Disputes
of 1900...., VIII, p. 310.

576. COMBINATION IN THE GLASS INDUSTRY (1900)

Here is a straightforward explanation of the
advantages of combination. (For a less concrete explanation, see Source No. 434). It is the testimony of Henry
Clay Fry, president of the National Glass Company,
who had been in the glass trade since 1858.

For 3 years before last July the works that I was president of
did not make a fair profit with 1,100 employees and $700,000 of
investment. It was such a state of affairs that led me to suggest
to a number of manufacturers scattered over various States that it
would be a better thing for us, and a just and proper thing to do,
if we could put our works under one management so far as the headquarters was concerned; allow the individual works to go on under
their present management, but do away with unnecessary expense,
such as unnecessary number of traveling agents going over the
country at an expense of about $10 a day; that fewer men of that
class and fewer resident agents could do the work, and we could do
away with unnecessary cutting of prices, and put prices back to
what we believed we were justly entitled to--a fair living margin.
For instance, we took that common tumbler, it was selling at 10
cents a dozen, and made it 16 cents a dozen, believing that we
ought to have from 1 to 2 cents a dozen profit on it. We took this
tumbler out of the market at 20 cents, and in some instances 18
cents a dozen, and we made it 25 cents a dozen, so we now get a
margin. I have 19 different works in this organization, which is
called the National Glass Company. Very few of them paid a dividend for several years before, and yet in 8 months since last
November, by using economy in all departments of the works, stopping
unnecessary expense, we advanced wages in all those plants 25 per
cent, so that the men are all happy and are taking care of their
families in much better shape than they could before; and a statement I made last month to the stockholders showed a profit on the
investment of 10 per cent. We did not take into consideration in
that 8 months wear and tear, because it was in the beginning of it,
although, perhaps, we ought to have taken off a margin of 3 or 4
per cent for that; but we feel that we fully made profit of 6 per
cent on the entire investment. That investment was not enlarged

by doubling the real value of the property, but we had a commission
appointed, consisting of half a dozen of the best and most experienced gentlemen that we could find, experts in each individual
line--2 on real estate, 2 of the best builders we could find, 2
who understood machinery thoroughly, and 2 more than understood the
peculiar work we use, furnaces, etc.--and they were sworn to visit
each works and carefully examine the property in every respect, and
put down on paper what they considered its real value, and that was
the value at which they should come into this organization. As many
as favored that plan--I tried to get them all in--but we got 19
factories that thought it was fair. Some thought they ought to
have double for factories, or three times the value, but we started
out to do a business on what we believed to be an equitable basis.
We thought we were entitled to a fair percentage of profit on the
real valuation, and we refused to take any factory into the National
Glass Company that was not willing to come in on what we believed
to be an honest basis. That represented real value when we say we
made a profit of 6 per cent on the real value of the money invested
in the business. We do not call ourselve a monopoly. We do not
absolutely control the prices, but, so far as these 19 factories
are concerned, the prices are all the same. We took 19 separate
organizations and let one head, or at least a small committee, make
the price for the entire number, and it has had a very beneficial
effect on the trade. There is more pleasure in doing business on
that kind of basis, and we believe the workmen employed are in
better condition.

Testimony, Henry Clay Fry, September 20, 1900, U.S. Congress,
56th, 2nd session, House of Representatives, Document No. 495,
Report of the Industrial Commission on the Relations and Conditions
of Capital and Labor...., VII, pp. 896-897.

577. COMMERCE VS. ART IN INDUSTRIAL DESIGN (1900)

Motor-driven mass production enabled manufacturers
to cut per-unit costs sharply. This posed the issue of
whether cost-cutting was compatible with quality considerations. It also raised the question of whether professionals in the employ of manufacturers or those training such
professionals could maintain the integrity of their science
or art. Engineers employed in large-scale industry were
already beginning to face up to such challenges. (See
Document No. 770). Thorstein Veblen, writing at this
time, also considered the impact of business -- as opposed
to industrial -- organization on standards of taste. In
the following material, Leslie W. Miller, who had been
principal of the Philadelphia School of Industrial Art for
20 years, explores how to give "industrial purpose" to art.

I am bound to say that I myself feel that a great deal of our
vaunted progress and so-called improvement is rather in the direction of cheapness than excellence. Improvements in methods of
dyeing or what are exploited as improvements, I am afraid, are too
often methods by which the cost can be saved rather than permanency
secured. While there is ability enough, in Philadelphia, undoubtedly, to make dyes at once brilliant and permanent, yet nearly always
the commercial consideration determines the choice of methods. I
feel that very strongly in a great many lines of production, and it
must be understood without any reflection on the ability of those
engaged in it or developing it to make the more excellent work if
they could be supported; but the commercial question comes in and
demands an amount of cheapness to an increasing degree which any
school is powerless to counteract.

Q. Do you make it a point of consideration and instruction in
your school to emphasize excellence and permanence in the matter of
coloring and dyes?--A. Why, of course; but we do not dodge the
other issue. We do not avoid or fail to face the problem of the
necessity of competing and of making things economically; and we
teach them the dyeing and the entire branch of textile work as if
in the presence of the commercial problem. Understand what I
mean--that things must be produced at a reasonable cost or they can
not compete in the open market; so we do not dodge that question,
but meet it very frankly, that things must be produced at as low
cost as is compatible with their merit.

Testimony, Leslie W. Miller, December 18, 1900, U.S. Congress,
57th, 1st session, House of Representatives, Document No. 183,
Report of the Industrial Commission on the Relations of Capital and
Labor Employed in Manufactures and General Business, XIV, p. 228.

578.   CREATING ORDER IN STEEL (1900)

The Carnegie Steel Company was the last obstacle
in the way of "creating order" in the steel industry
under J. P. Morgan's leadership. John Gates, chairman
of American Steel and Wire Company, later part of U.S.
Steel, testifies.

Mr. BEALL. Some time ago you said there was a fear that Mr.
Carnegie would demoralize the railroad business and the tube works
just as he had done the steel business, as I understood it.
Mr. GATES. That was Mr. Morgan's statement.
Mr. BEALL. That was Mr. Morgan's statement?
Mr. GATES. Yes.
Mr. BEALL. In what way had he demoralized the steel business
prior to this consolidation?

Mr. GATES. Well, in those days we used to have a few agreements.

The CHAIRMAN. A few what?

Mr. GATES. A few agreements; the boys would make them, and Andy would kick them over.

Mr. BEALL. Was Mr. Carnegie among those inclined to break these gentlemen's agreements?

Mr. GATES. I do not know anything about those gentlemen's agreements, but I know that if Frick and I would agree to one thing in the forenoon, as between our two companies, he might tell me in the afternoon that Carnegie would not stand for it. [Laughter.] In other words, no one in the Carnegie Steel Co., controlled Mr. Carnegie, but he controlled every other man in the corporation.

Mr. BEALL. Mr. Carnegie controlled all the operations of the Carnegie Steel Co.?

Mr. GATES. Yes.

Mr. BEALL. All these agreements and for their general object the regulation of prices, usually, did they not?

Mr. GATES. Well, I do not know that you could say that. My theory is that I would rather have an open market and be able to run full and not be hampered by any competitors saying: "You are selling goods too low," than to have a fictitious market, where I could only run 40 or 50 or 60 per cent. That has always been my idea.

Mr. BEALL. What is the agreement that you mentioned?

Mr. GATES. I never was in any agreement, and I do not know anything about that.

Mr. BEALL. Did it attempt to control the amount of the output of each mill?

Mr. GATES. What agreement are you alluding to?

Mr. BEALL. I am alluding to this agreement that you mentioned as being made when Carnegie was stirring up trouble.

Mr. GATES. I would like to tell you a story.

Mr. BEALL. All right; I would like to hear it.

Mr. GATES. Along about 1887 or 1888 a man by the name of Harry Smith was the purchasing agent of the Missouri, Kansas & Texas Railroad. The price of rails at that time, if I forget not, was about $35 a ton. Mr. Carnegie's concern at that time was a member of a rail pool, and the penalty for cutting the price was enormous. I think it was $20 or $25 a ton. Mr. Smith happened to meet a friend of mine, a hardware merchant at Sedalia, Mo., the agent of another company, and concluded he would buy his rails of him. He went to New York and happened to meet Andy Carnegie, whom he had known many years before, and Andrew cut the price very materially. Charges were preferred against the Carnegie Co. We questioned Mr. Carnegie and he denied everything in a general way. I knew the way he had cut the price. He had cut it by throwing in the track bolts, spikes, and angle bars, which amounted to about 15 per cent, or a cut of $5 a ton. I finally made an open charge, or Mr. Stirling made it, of our company-- the vice-president.

. . . .

He admitted all of the charge, but refused to pay any fine.
. . . .
    I can not state it any plainer than Mr. Morgan stated it to
Mr. Schwab and me--that if Mr. Carnegie should build this tube works
at Ashtabula and a railroad from Ashtabula to his works in the
Pittsburg district it would demoralize the whole situation.   That
was Mr. Morgan's statement and not mine.
    Mr. BARTLETT. And he created that belief upon the minds of
yourself and other gentlemen that, if he did do it, that would be
the result?
    Mr. GATES. That was Mr. Morgan's statement.
    Mr. BARTLETT. And you acted upon that statement?
    Mr. GATES. I did not act upon it. Mr. Morgan did.

    Testimony, John W. Gates, May 27, 1911, U.S. Congress, House
of Representatives, [Stanley] Committee on Investigation of United
States Steel Corporation, Hearings, (Washington, D.C.: Government
Printing Office, 1911), pp. 43-44, [44, 44].

                579. SELECTING U.S. STEEL DIRECTORS (1901)

        The U.S. Steel Corporation was rightly regarded
    a "Morgan firm," as per the following interchange.

    Mr. UNTERMYER. At the time of the organization of the United
States Steel Corporation [in 1901] did you name the entire board of
directors?
    Mr. MORGAN. No. I think I passed upon it.
    Mr. UNTERMYER. Did you not, as a matter of fact, name the
board and pass out a slip containing the names of the board?
    Mr. MORGAN. I can not say that no one else helped me in it.
    Mr. UNTERMYER. Do you not remember that it was your---
    Mr. MORGAN. I am willing to assume the final responsibility,
if that will answer your question.
    Mr. UNTERMYER. I want to know the fact, Mr. Morgan.
    Mr. MORGAN. I am trying to give the fact.
    Mr. UNTERMYER. Is it not a fact that you named the entire
board?
    Mr. MORGAN. I am endeavoring to give the fact.
    Mr. UNTERMYER. Yes; I understand that.
    Mr. MORGAN. But I say that whatever was done, if passing upon
it and approving it is equivalent to making it, I did it.
    Mr. UNTERMYER. Did you not only pass on it and approve it,
but did you not further select the board and determine who should
go on and who should stay off?
    Mr. MORGAN. No; I probably did the latter.

Mr. UNTERMYER. Yes; and having determined who should stay off, you necessarily determined who should go on?

Mr. MORGAN. I am quite willing to assume the whole responsibility of it, Mr. Counsel.

Mr. UNTERMYER. I only want the fact. We are not characterizing it or criticizing it at all.

Mr. MORGAN. I know you are not. I understand that, sir. But you must remember that it is 12 or 14 years ago that this thing took place.

Mr. UNTERMYER. Yes; it is 14 [11] years ago.

Mr. MORGAN. I can not recall all the conversation which led to it. I will say this, however, that whoever went on that board went with my approval.

Mr. UNTERMYER. And from time to time, as vacancies have occurred, or as the board has been changed, whoever has gone on has gone on with your approval, has he not?

Mr. MORGAN. Not always.

Mr. UNTERMYER. Has he gone on against your protest?

Mr. MORGAN. No, sir.

Mr. UNTERMYER. Nobody has gone on until he has been approved by you, has he?

Mr. MORGAN. Yes; because I have not always been here.

Mr. UNTERMYER. When you have not been here, then some representative of your firm has had that duty, has he not?

Mr. MORGAN. The question then comes up before the finance committee, first, for suggestions; but the election is made by the board.

Mr. UNTERMYER. Yes; I understand that; and the board is named by you and your associates?

Mr. MORGAN. No sir; not now.

Mr. UNTERMYER. Nobody is nominated for that board without your approval, is he?

Mr. MORGAN. Yes, sir.

Mr. UNTERMYER. Is anybody nominated for it against your protest?

Mr. MORGAN. Not against my protest.

Testimony, J. Pierpont Morgan, December 19, 1912, U.S. Congress, 62nd, 3rd session, House of Representatives, Committee on Banking and Currency, Money Trust Investigation, pp. 1025-1026.

580. ELECTRICITY IN MANUFACTURING (1901)

The economic advantages of electricity in manufacturing were increasingly obvious. During the decade 1900-1909, factories increased horsepower from inanimate prime movers by some 69 per cent. Except for the decade 1880-1890, this was an all-time record. (Figures do not include electric motors.) William Aldrich was an engineer from Champaign, Illinois who taught at the University of Illinois.

1. <u>Electric Transmission in Manufacturing Work is a Means
to an End</u>: Centralized power generation for light and manufacturing purposes; subdivision of the transmission system and the motive-
power equipment; execution of all classes of work, irrespective of
its location; maximum efficiency of workmen, machines, and labor
involved; intensified production at best speeds and at the power
limit of machines with improved quality, maximum output, and reduced
cost.

2. <u>Sanitary Considerations</u>: It is healthful, clean, and free
from dirt, dust, and dripping oil; it affords accommodations and
facilities for proper lighting and ventilation; it removes dangers
from overhead machinery shafting and belts; it reduces the sick list
to a minimum; it insures quietness from absence of much unncessary
noise with older systems, and develops cheerfulness among the workmen.

3. <u>Disciplinary Value</u>: It improves the <u>morale</u> and the
<u>personnel</u> of workmen; it conduces to shop order and discipline,
with the most economic use of the workman's time, quick handling of
material, and maximum efficiency of labor.

4. <u>Flexibility of the System</u>: Accessibility of all parts,
adaptability to various uses, and portability of tools are inherent
advantages.

5. <u>Reliability of Service</u>: It is free from any general breakdown, localizing casualties and stopping least machinery for repairs; no accident can affect the whole plant in any case of a
modern electrical installation properly designed, equipped, and
operated; it is more to be depended upon than any other system.

. . . .

If you wish, accept what it offers; adopt it, and get more out
of it per dollar invested, even as in the case of the piece-rate
system, than you have gotten heretofore by any other plan. In
other words, electricity enables you to do what you cannot do by any
other system. It gives the operator that control, facility, and
independence of action now absolutely essential from the standpoint
of the management of men and of workship ethics and economics. An
operator can rarely be persuaded to speed up his machine with the
belt system. Even if he could, the limit is soon reached. With an
electric drive he does not hesitate to turn the lever, speed up the
machine, and turn out more work per given expenditure of time and
labor than his next-door neighbor. Almost all manufacturers recognize the advantage of it. The analogy between electric driving and
the piece-rate system simply lies in a recognition, in dollars and
cents, of what a workman is able to do. It is a question of the
economy of production.

. . . .

This is the question coming to the front: What are you going
to do to increase the output? You cannot stand still, and yet there
is perhaps very limited floor space. As has been indicated in the
paper and in several of the discussions, it can be better solved by
the electric drive than in any other way. When it comes to establishing a new factory, you cannot afford to drive modern machine-
tools in the good old way, unless you wish to limit the output
instead of driving up to "the destructive limit" of the cutting
tool. Work cannot be gotten out of cutting tools by the belt system

that can be secured by using the electric drive. If the electric
system is installed, tools may be worked up to "the destructive
limit," as it has been termed, and therefore maximum output obtained under the most economical conditions, at the highest cutting
speeds allowed by tool steel of the best grades furnished by the
market.

William S. Aldrich, "Requirements of Electricity in Manufacturing Work," Transactions, American Society of Mechanical Engineers, XXII (1900-1901), pp. 1006-1007, 1038, 1039.

581. THE LIMITS OF CENTRALIZED MANAGEMENT (1901)

A promoter of industrial combinations, Charles
Flint, weighs the advantages and disadvantages of
centralized management.

Well, in general I think that a centralized management is the
most desirable if there are men of sufficient intellectual ability
to administer an extended business. It is difficult to find a man
of sufficient ability to run one large business, and there are not
a great many intellectual giants that have the ability to run ten
or more large businesses. In my judgement one of the dangers to
the success of industrials is that parties, without being intellectual giants, are liable to attempt to centralize too much. Taking
men as they are, I think that in businesses where high-class ability
is required at many places, and where the business if not of such a
character that its conduct can be reduced to rules, and where its
success depends on localability and local judgement, and where the
efficiency of the selling department is involved with long-time
personal relations, such a business it may be very dangerous to
suddenly centralize. It is far wiser, I think, in a case of that
kind, to sustain the independence and individuality of the separate
concerns. In that way you have the advantage of the organizations
that have created those concerns. At the same time your central
organization has the advantages of comparative accounting and comparative administration, and is able to hold the separate concerns
to a strict accountability, or, by appealing to their pride, to promote a healthy spirit of rivalry. In many cases it is my judgement
that this idea of centralization can be carried too far, and that
it is often much better to have these concerns run independently.
Now, it may be said that you do not get the full benefits of centralization. That is very true. But, on the other hand, I believe
you get a more efficient management than you would by centralization. Under that plan, through a system of comparative accounting,
you are enabled to measure the different managements, and you can
go a long way toward bringing the standard of all up to the standard

of the best, and in case of any great situation arising--for instance, like the one you have just brought up, where 40 important
customers suddenly united--it can be better handled. An individual
concern could not have dealt with that problem successfully.

       Testimony, Charles R. Flint, April 8, 1901, U.S. Congress,
57th, 1st session, House of Representatives, Document No. 182,
Report of the Industrial Commission on Trusts and Industrial
Combinations, XIII, p. 84.

              582. OPEN-HEARTH REPLACING BESSEMER (1905)

          By 1908, the output of open-hearth steel exceeded
       that of Bessemer steel. Open-hearth steel-making produced
       a more-closely controlled product and it could utilize
       scrap metal. H. B. Bope was general sales manager, first
       vice-president, and member of the board of directors of the
       Carnegie Steel Company, a subsidiary of the U.S. Steel
       Corporation. He testifies in the following.

       The tendency is steadily in the direction of open-hearth steel;
we are not able now to supply the Homestead-Bessemer with a full
schedule. The use of Bessemer is now practically confined to rails,
wire nails, and standard bars, and even in the bars, wherever we
supply steel to replace iron bars, we have to use soft non-Bessemer
steel. Some tonnage goes into tank work, but there is not a great
deal of this. The steel and wire company would prefer open hearth
if they did not have their own Bessemer production; and when they
get their Donora mill fairly in operation they will draw on our
open-hearth output at that plant. Taking the trade as a whole, I
do not see where there is going to be any considerable demand for
Bessemer in the future. At any rate, we have considerable Bessemer
production at other points.

       H. B. Bope, minutes of the board of directors of Carnegie
Steel Co., August 28, 1905, U.S. Congress, House of Representatives,
[Stanley] Committee on Investigation of United States Steel
Corporation, United States Steel Corporation, p. 4075.

583. BUICK MOVES TO FLINT, MICHIGAN (1905)

In 1905, the Buick Company moved from Jackson to
Flint. While Flint was a county seat where two railroads
crossed, it was not yet an industrial center.

Buick landed on the Hamilton farm in north Flint; one month
a cornfield, the next a factory.
. . . .
These newcomers from the orderly east to the then disorderly
north end of Flint were shocked at what they beheld in living conditions. Factories were being built and manned faster than houses
could be constructed and normal family life set going. People were
flocking into Flint from all quarters, especially lumberjacks from
the north woods, where work was scarce. Men lived in tents and
huts and plowed through quagmires; there were no pavements, no
sidewalks. Organizing a competent factory force took time, and
meanwhile the stress and strain in the shops was terrific. I recall
that the superintendents and foremen wore stiff derby hats at work,
the better to protect them from heavy bolts dropped from above by
not too friendly workmen. Of course, a good many steady old hands
from the carriage factories went over to automobiles, found better
jobs and kept on rising. Trouble came, not from them, but from
those who had never worked in factories before and resented the
necessary discipline to orderly planned production.

Arthur Pound, "General Motors' Old Home Town," Michigan
History, XL (1956), pp. 89-90.

584. IS "GOOD ENOUGH" BEST? (1906)

A frequent criticism but a rather theoretical one.
American factories contained, side by side, the very latest
and the most antiquated machinery. The writer here is
Frank Foster, an English engineer, who spent 12 months
in the United States as a worker in a power plant and a
factory. He visited 40 factories and 30 electricity
stations.

The claim is often made by Englishmen and accepted by Americans,
that as a rule English manufactures are of a more durable character
than those of America.
The American defence is that with the rapid changes in industry
taking place the useful life of a machine, say, is comparatively
short. At the end of a few years something better is on the market

which should be adopted if possible. They make their machines,
they claim, durable enough to last until something better is to be
had. If they made them too durable they would be too extensive
to scrap when something better came on the market.

Like many broad generalisations, this one has some strong
points in its favour, but it is liable to be abused if used indis-
criminately. Indeed, one thing which is noticeable in the States
is that there is a distinct tendency towards making machines and
other engineering work more durable. To a certain extent this may
be accounted for by the heavier duty required of engineering work
in these days.

In connection with American machine tools and machinery
generally, one finds a most extensive use of a soft grade of iron
which is easy to work, but materially shortens the life of the
machines where accuracy of adjustment is essential.

In the abstract this ideal of building for the useful life
only, is perfect. There can be no justification in putting valuable
labour and capital into a machine only to find that in a few years
it is a bar to further progress....

The directions in which American engineers attempt to reduce
the costliness of their designs—apart from methods of manufacture—
vary with the character of the work to be done, but a few may be
indicated.

So far as is practicable cheap materials are substituted for
the more expensive ones. Thus case-hardened bushes and pins in
locomotives are comparatively rare, the writer was given to understand. Iron pipes largely replace brass and copper in the smaller
engine connections; cast-steel replaces wrought-steel to a very
large extent, and the softer qualities of cast-iron are much used,
mainly in order to reduce the cost of machinery.

Less machining and polishing is given to machinery. On the
whole, bearings are properly machined and bedded, although the
writer saw some serious exceptions to this rule. Other parts which
in England would generally be polished, are merely rough-turned or
even left painted. There are two objections to this policy. In
the first place, machinery attendants, being human, like a nice-
looking thing, and will give more care and attention to a good
looking machine than to a shoddy article. Also machining discovers
and exposes hidden flaws, whilst painting and filling do just the
opposite....

As a rule Americans make their machinery—and most other
things—lighter than we do. They also very frequently pay less
attention to the details of construction so far as strength and
durability is concerned. Indeed American engineers take more
chances in their designs. Some of these risks are taken deliberately, it being held that the extra cost of the superior construction is too big an insurance premium for the risk involved.

Frank Foster, Engineering in the United States, (Manchester,
England: University of Manchester Press, 1906), pp. 8-11.

585. ON AMERICAN TOOLS (1906)

The following was written at a time when high-speed
tool steel was being very widely introduced into American
machine shops. (See Source No. 591).

As regards the tools used, one finds, of course, that they are
almost all of American make. Except in one or two special branches
of engineering--notably shipbuilding--it is seldom that one meets
with a British-made tool. American tools are well-known to English
engineers, indeed few British shops are without some. It is needless to give here a necessarily brief and incomplete description
of these well-known tools. Where they differ from most English
tools, is in the greater handiness of the small tools, and their
somewhat lighter build. The handiness of American tools is an
excellent feature which has of late years inspired our British
manufacturers to move along similar lines. The lack of strength
and wearing qualities in small American machine tools was badly
felt when high-speed tool steels became common. This defect is
being made good, or at least the stiffness is being increased, for
the writer is not convinced that American tools wear as well as
they ought; the iron is too soft and very easily rusts. Of course
it is open to question whether it is worth while to make a tool
exceedingly durable....Accuracy is one of the first requisites in
most tools, and in order to secure continual accuracy over a period
of years, good wearing qualities are desirable, and in many cases
absolutely necessary. On the other hand a tool may become antiquated even though healthy.

Foster, Engineering in the United States, p. 78.

586. THE "GARY DINNERS" (1907-1909)

Between November 20, 1907 and October 15, 1909,
Elbert H. Gary, chairman of the board of directors of
the U.S. Steel Corporation, conducted five meetings of
steel industry leaders. They eventuated in the formation
of the American Iron and Steel Institute. Here is an
account by a person who attended all five meetings.
He was Joseph Butler, a long-time Midwest steel man. He
was a large holder of stock in the Youngstown Sheet and
Tube Company, and served on its board of directors.

At the first dinner the principal address was made by Judge
Gary, in which he formulated the policy of conciliation and

cooperation among manufacturers. He said that probably no two of
the guests would agree as to the cause of the depression existing,
and that few could agree upon a remedy for it. We could all agree,
however, on a policy that would prevent further disaster and hasten
the return of prosperity, which policy he defined as a disposition
to help one another, instead of trying to get business at the expense of one another and at prices below actual cost. Judge Gary's
address was enthusiastically received. It was followed by numerous
others, all of which sounded the same note. Finally, a committee
was appointed to formulate some method of putting into practical
effect the sentiments of the gathering. This committee later
appointed others composed of representatives of the various lines
of manufacture. It was understood that they were to offer their
services to all manufacturers in the way of advice concerning
questions that might arise in the conduct of business and to urge
upon all of these manufacturers the policy of resisting temptation
to cut prices below the cost of manufacture in order to secure
business.

The second dinner was held at the same place on the evening of
January 30th, 1908. At this the committees appointed at the previous gathering reported progress. There was further discussion of
conditions and the best method of meeting them. Among the speeches
on this occasion was one by J. P. Morgan, whose firm had financed
the Steel Corporation. Mr. Morgan said that his principal reason
for becoming interested in the steel industry was his desire to see
if some way could not be found to stabilize it and prevent the violent fluctuations to which it had been subject, because these fluctuations invariably resulted in similar periods of inflation and
depression in all other lines of business and were therefore of
great harm to the country. I was among the speakers at this dinner,
and heard every word that was uttered there. Not a sentence could
be construed to even suggest any illegal method of restraining
production or maintaining prices at an exorbitant level. Nevertheless, so much discussion was provoked in the newspapers that Judge
Gary gave out a short statement concerning the purpose and proceedings at the dinner, in order to allay the suspicion that it had
been held to carry out an illegal and improper purpose.

The third dinner was held on May 21, 1908. By that time improvement in business conditions was marked. The public confidence
had been largely restored, and business was decidedly on the upturn.
Judge Gary congratulated the gathering on what had been accomplished
toward stabilizing business during the preceding depression, and
said that, as conditions were approaching normal, it would probably
not be necessary to hold a similar gathering for some time to come.
It was generally agreed that the effect of the meetings had been
eminently salutary, and that many companies had been saved by the
course encouraged at them. Willis L. King, of the Jones & Laughlin
Steel Company, voiced the sentiments of all present when he stated
that everyone interested in the industry, whether as a buyer or
seller, had been greatly benefited by the movement, and that it
had undoubtedly prevented the general demoralization of business,
with the serious results that would have followed that situation.
No one had made any profits during the period, but there had been

no losses compelling bankruptcy, and the whole industry was in a
position to enjoy a period of renewed activity which seemed to be
coming.

The fourth "Gary Dinner" was held at the Waldorf-Astoria in
New York on December 10, 1908, and the fifth, which was really only
a luncheon, with a comparatively small number of his more intimate
friends present, was held at Judge Gary's residence on February 18,
1909. After the guests had departed Judge Gary gave a statement to
the press covering the purpose of the preceding meetings quite
fully, and predicting that, although conditions had become such that
no future meetings of the kind would probably be held, it was believed that all steel manufacturers would be more inclined to cooperate with one another for the stabilizing of the industry, as well
as to associate more frequently with one another in a social way and
for the dissemination of information of value to the trade in
general.

The final dinner in this famous and much misrepresented series
was held at the Waldorf-Astoria Hotel in New York on October 15,
1909. It was a purely social affair, business being barred, and
the evening spent in celebrating the return of business prosperity
and the establishment of a genuine neighborliness in the steel
industry that had never been known in it until the Gary dinners
began. It was also meant to be a testimonial to Judge Gary for the
service he had rendered to the industry during the trying time preceding it.

Joseph G. Butler, Jr., Recollections of Men and Events. An
Autobiography, (New York: G. P. Putnam's Sons, 1927), pp. 153-
156.

587. COST ACCOUNTING NOT CRUCIAL (1909, 1911)

Cost accounting played a constructive role by pointing
up waste in industry. (See Source No. 376). What Taylor
regarded as "scientific management", however, incorporated
accounting into the very process of production and thus
cost-control was to be exercised daily and almost immediately. Taylor writes to Charles Conrad, a U.S. Navy paymaster.

Cost accounts, under the ordinary management, furnish the great
check which is needed upon the efficiency both of the superintendents, foremen, sub-foremen and workmen. Unfortunately, however,
it is impossible to get accurate costs within a month after the
work has been done. Fifteen to twenty years ago I looked upon a
correct cost system as one of the most important among the various
elements of management, and in fact devoted a large part of my time
to introducing systems of cost and of expense analysis in manufacturing establishments. Now, however, under the modern scientific

management, as far as they <u>influence</u> <u>cheapness</u> <u>of</u> <u>manufacture</u>, costs
and expense analysis become, comparatively speaking, elements of
lesser importance, and we generally leave them to the last in the
introduction of our system. Our time and money is spent upon <u>the</u>
<u>front</u> <u>end</u>, rather than at the rear end. We devote the energies both
of the superintending and of the clerical force to seeing that <u>the</u>
<u>workmen</u> <u>actually</u> <u>do</u> <u>the</u> <u>work</u> <u>fast,</u> <u>and</u> <u>do</u> <u>it</u> <u>right</u>, rather than to
the collection of cost data. The daily task which every workman
must perform renders cost analysis almost unnecessary, from the
standpoint of economical management.

I do not mean that the cost system should not be introduced.
Costs are needed, in many cases in order to regulate the selling
prices; also for the general education of the sales department, and
for deciding upon the future lines of progress for the business.
But under scientific management what was formerly their chief value,
namely, helping to get a low cost of manufacture, almost entirely
disappears. And, as I have said before, the time and money available for establishing a system of management should be spent, first,
where it will do the most good. It is utterly impossible to introduce all of the elements of good management at the same time;
therefore cost systems should wait until the last.

. . . .

[LETTER TO CONRAD]
My experience has led me to place less and less faith in
accounting as a road to economy. At the best, accounting constitutes merely a sign post which points, if it is of the right kind,
directly at the inefficient spot. It does not, however, in any
way tell how this inefficiency is to be remedied, because accounts
come, in nine cases out of ten, so long after the actual work has
been done that, unless an immense amount of digging up labor is
gone into, it is impossible, even where written records of every
act of every man exist, to place your hand upon the immediate cause
of the inefficiency.

As I told you, I think, when you were at the Tabor Company,
we have found for economy that the record which is made up early on
the morning of the day following the work, which shows how many men
in each department failed to earn their bonus, is the most helpful
record in promoting economy. It becomes possible then, the day
after bad work has been done by anybody, to chase it right home,
either to the foreman, the teachers, the tool department, planning
department, or to the workman himself, and prove right then and
there to the men or the department just what they have done that
is wrong.

This is perhaps the simplest possible account to keep, and yet
it results in a greater efficiency than all the balance of the cost
accounts put together.

. . . .

Our whole experience has been that the energy of those who
were engaged in recording facts should be put to obtaining records

which immediately follow the work, and therefore give immediate
valuable returns, right at the plant where the work is going on.

Frederick W. Taylor, extracts from his manuscript for a series
of lectures at Harvard University in 1909, and from his letter to
Charles Conrad, June 10, 1911, Copley, Taylor, I, pp. 367-368.

588. MATERIALS-HANDLING IN STEEL (1912)

Electricity reduced the element of manual pulling and
pushing on the job. But it also permitted the lengthening
of the workday in steel mills.

That is what made possible the 12-hour day. It was the dimin-
ution of the laboriousness of labor.
At the time of which Capt. Jones speaks [pre-1890], however,
8 hours was quite equivalent to 12 hours at the present day.
Mr. GARDNER. You mean that the 8-hour work was a great deal
more then than 8 hours work would be now in the blast furnaces?
It was a great deal more laborious?
Mr. ROBERTS. That refers to your steel works; to your finishing departments.
Mr. GARDNER. Yes; generally.
Mr. ROBERTS. The operations of the blast furnace 20 years ago,
where they had 12-hour turns, were far more laborious than the
operations of to-day. It was all hand labor. For instance, men
filled the cars with material, they were taken to the top of the
furnace on a hoist, men pushed them into the top of the furnace,
and the pig iron was tapped into the bed, and as soon as it was
cool, almost red-hot, men went into that bed and picked the red-hot
pigs up by hand, too, and carried them out and deposited them outside. All that work is now done by machinery. Your raw material
is handled electrically. No men are at the top of the furnace to
push it in. There are no men carrying red-hot pig iron, because
it is either run out in a liquid condition and put into the mixer,
or else it is put into a casting machine and mechanically carried
off and dumped on to cars.

Testimony, Percival Roberts, Jr., February 14, 1912, U.S.
Congress, House of Representatives, [Stanley] Committee on
Investigation of United States Steel Corporation, United States
Steel Corporation, p. 3274.

589. WHY INTEGRATE INTEGRATED OPERATIONS? (1912)

Perhaps the most frequently-proferred reason for
industrial mergers was efficiency. What savings, however,
could be gained from merging already-integrated operations?
Julian Kennedy was a mechanical engineer, experienced in
designing blast furnaces and rolling mills.

The CHAIRMAN. Mr. Kennedy, there has been considerable discussion here of the economy of integrating a steel plant, the saving
incident to the passing of the hot metal from the blast furnaces to
the open-hearth furances, or the Bessemer converters, and of using
the hot ingot--I am not well up as to the process.
Mr. REED. Ingots is right.
The CHAIRMAN. And producing a finished product without allowing your metal to cool, without the incident expense of reheating
or transporting the semifinished product.
I will ask you to give the committee your opinion of the extent to which that property should be integrated, if it does add to
the economy, and to what extent, and how?
Mr. KENNEDY. It is very desirable to have a plant which will
take the ore, coke, and limestone, transform it into rails, billets,
or sheet bars, in the same plant. There is a considerable saving
in keeping the metal hot all the time, and especially between the
blast furnace and the converter or open-hearth plant, as the case
may be. There is a saving in using liquid metal of $1 to $1.25,
as compared with casting the metal and remelting it.
The CHAIRMAN. You mean a dollar to a dollar and a quarter
a ton?
Mr. KENNEDY. A dollar to a dollar and a quarter a ton, as
compared to casting the metal and remelting it.
Also there would be a saving of any cost of transfer, in case
the metal were moved, so that the blast furnace which casts this
metal into pig and allows it to cool and ships this off to another
plant, is at a disadvantage of not less than a dollar plus the
cost of haulage.
There is also some collateral advantage in the way of utilizing
power from the gases in case the blast furnace is connected with a
steel plant. After the material reaches the form of sheet bar, or
small billet, the advantage of having the remainder of the plant
running in connection with it is not so great. There would, however, still be the saving of haulage on the material.
The CHAIRMAN. The sheet bars are not run hot from the mill in
which they are rolled to the tin-plate factory, and the like of
that.
Mr. KENNEDY. No. Sheet bars are allowed to cool, in any
event, so that the only saving at this point would be the cost of
transfer.
The CHAIRMAN. Was this Carnegie Co. perfectly integrated
or approximately so?

Mr. KENNEDY. Very largely so. They had some furnaces, such
as the Lucy furnaces in Pittsburgh, which were detached; but the
majority of their plants were arranged for taking the material
through without losing the heat and without unnecessary haulage.

The CHAIRMAN. Was the Federal Steel Co. an integrated company?

Mr. KENNEDY. To a large extent; yes.

The CHAIRMAN. Where you have two or more perfectly integrated
plants, is there any economy from the point of cheapness of produc-
tion--leaving out this question of competition entirely or of fixing prices; just simply from the point of cheapness of production--
is there any economy in combining two or more distant and integrated plants in the one concern?

Mr. REED. By integrated plants you mean the steel works
combined--the blast furnace and steel works?

The CHAIRMAN. Yes.

Mr. REED. Which will produce billets or sheet bars from the
ore and limestone and coke?

The CHAIRMAN. I mean a company having its ore supply and its
various apparatus for the making of semifinished products adjacent
from the blast furnace to the billet.

Mr. REED. I simply wanted to get your conception of the term
"integration."

The CHAIRMAN. That is what I mean.

Mr. KENNEDY. There would be no advantage as far as the actual
production of the work is concerned. But if you take into account
the delivery to the market, and assume that to be part of the cost,
there would be a saving, as, for example, complete works at Chicago
and complete works at Pittsburgh, if run in unison, could distribute
their material to the consumer to better advantage than if each
were working independently, and the Pittsburgh plant shipping some
of its material to the vicinity of Chicago and the Chicago plant
shipping the other way. As far as the actual production at the
works is concerned there would be no advantage in working them
together.

Testimony, Julian Kennedy, March 27, 1912, U.S. Congress,
House of Representatives, [Stanley] Committee on Investigation of
United States Steel Corporation, United States Steel Corporation,
pp. 5100-5101.

590. DELAY IN ADOPTING MASS PRODUCTION (1908-1913)

Auto mass production did not spring into existence
immediately it was conceived. Personal factors, problems
of factory design, resistance to new investment, and other
factors delayed the movement until the end of 1913.
Charles Sorensen, who writes here, became chief engineer
at the Ford Company. Ed Martin, of whom he speaks in the

extract, was plant superintendent at Ford and Sorenson
was his assistant at this time; Clarence Avery, a teacher,
became Sorenson's assistant in program planning in 1912.

If it was proved in 1908 that an auto could be put together
while moving a chassis past a sequence of waiting parts, why did
five years elapse before this technique was adopted? Why so long
between conception and birth?

First, remember that while Mr. Ford encouraged the experiment
he did not necessarily accept it. Second, recall the layout and
manufacturing operations of the Piquette plant. Parts were elevated
from the ground and second floors to assembly on the third floor.
Once a car was put together, it descended by the same route that
its component parts had come up.

This, of course, was an unthinking rejection of the aid of the
long-accepted principle of gravitation. But to reverse the procedure would have turned Model N production literally upside down
during the last few weeks of its life. Moreover, the time needed
to accomplish that reversal would have indefinitely delayed Model
T production and the realization of Mr. Ford's long-cherished ambition which he had maintained against all opposition.

Although Model T was announced in the spring, it was not shown
until October. Production did not start until December, and first
delivery of cars was made in February, 1909, eleven months after
the first announcement. Nevertheless, the advance orders pouring
in indicated that Piquette Avenue, the last word in auto plants
from years before, was too small to meet the demand.

. . . .

Naturally, the biggest of all developments leading up to Ford
mass production was building and equipping the Highland Park plant.
Decision to erect that plant was made...in 1908 while...Ed Martin
and I were rearranging the Piquette Avenue layout for production
of Model T. The Highland Park tract was a former racetrack along
Woodward Avenue and comprised some sixty acres, all of which by
1914 was covered by Ford Motor Company buildings. In other words,
the entire plant had to be functioning before the Ford mass production and assembly system could be completely worked out into one
great synchronized operation from one end of the place to the other.

It was that complete synchronization which accounted for the
difference between an ordinary assembly line and a mass production
one. Meanwhile, Highland Park was laid out for progressive but not
fully integrated operation. Wills, who headed all Ford production
and machinery procurement after Flanders resigned, left most of the
new plant layout in my hands. A room was set aside for my assistants. We set up layout boards on which we worked out the production lines and placements of machines to scale. Numbered brass
plates were attached to all machines in the Piquette plant with
corresponding tags on the layout boards so that every machine
would be set up in its assigned place when the move to Highland
Park was made. Edward Gray, the company's construction engineer,
whipped these layouts into floor plans and building dimensions.
Supplied with this material, Architect Albert Kahn then made

detailed plans and specifications. When Kahn finished, his main
building was of striking, revolutionary design. Four stories high,
nearly three hundred yards long, it was one of the first industrial
structures with glass, saw-tooth roof allowing for an unusual amount
of light and air. Machine shop, gas-engine plant, foundry, and
office building were soon to follow.

. . . .

With firsthand familiarity with each step in each parts department, Avery worked out the timing schedules necessary before installation of conveyer assembly systems to motors, fenders, magne-
tos, and transmissions. One by one these operations were revamped
and continuously moving conveyers delivered the assembled parts to
the final assembly floor. Savings in labor time were enormous;
some parts were put together six times as fast.

By August, 1913, all links in the chain of moving assembly
lines were complete except the last and most spectacular one--the
one we had first experimented with one Sunday morning just five
years before. Again a towrope was hitched to a chassis, this time
pulled by a capstan. Each part was attached to the moving chassis
in order, from axles at the beginning to bodies at the end of the
line. Some parts took longer to attach than others; so, to keep
an even pull on the towrope, there must be differently spaced intervals between delivery of the parts along the line. This called
for patient timing and rearrangement until the flow of parts and
the speed and intervals along the assembly line meshed into a
perfectly, synchronized operation throughout all stages of production. Before the end of the year a power-driven assembly line was
in operation, and New Year's saw three more installed. Ford mass
production and a new era in industrial history had begun.

Today historians describe the part the Ford car played in
the development of that era and in transforming American life.
We see that now. But we didn't see it then; we weren't as smart
as we have been credited with being. All that we were trying to do
was to develop the Ford car.

Charles Sorensen with Samuel T. Williamson, My Forty Years
With Ford, (New York: Norton, 1956), pp. 118-119, 125-126,
130-131.

591. HIGH-SPEED STEEL REVOLUTIONIZED THE SHOP (1914)

In 1900, Frederick W. Taylor and Maunsel White
tried to patent a new steel that was capable of being
made into high-speed metal-cutting tools. Here is a
sketch of the impact the new steel had on one firm.
Ultimately, the patent was not granted on the ground
that the supposed innovation was in common use throughout
industry. James Dodge, who testifies, was chairman of
the board of directors of the Link Belt Company which had

plants in Indianapolis, Chicago, and Philadelphia, and
manufactured elevating, conveying, and power-transmitting
machinery.

The Taylor-White steel, when used as a tool in a lathe, or on
a planer, would do variously from 5 times to 20 times as much work
as any of the then existing steels. I heard of this and went up to
Bethlehem and saw it and bargained with the Bethlehem Steel Co. for
the use of the Taylor-White steel. We were the first people that
ever made a bargain with them at all.

We then got some of the steel, brought it to Philadelphia, and
tried to use it on cast iron, and it was a failure. The steel that
would cut almost the hardest known steel, like armor plate, would
not cut cast iron. The reason was that the peculiar principle of
Taylor-White steel, or high-speed steel, is its enormous strength
when it is hot, and a tool made of that steel would take a peeling
off of a piece of steel that was turning in the lathe the same as
you would take a peeling off of an orange. Your fingers do not go
into the place where the peel and the orange are united and cut them
loose from each other, but they pry the outside layer off. That
attribute of the Taylor-White steel, doing this wonderful work,
would lead a person, naturally, to suppose that it would cut cast
iron the same as it would a piece of cheese; but it appears that in
cutting cast iron the tool has to go right in there and work on
the particles of iron with its cutting edge.

I made some tools in Philadelphia for turning off big pieces
of steel. One of them had four little steel balls in the end instead of a cutting edge, and the other had a little roller, and as
long as we could keep those things lubricated it kept taking off a
layer of steel on the outside. But it was a very difficult thing
to keep it lubricated, and as soon as you failed to keep it lubricated it was ruined. That shows the wonderful difference between
cutting cast iron and a piece of steel. We started then a series
of experiments, with the aid of Mr. Taylor, and a steel was developed that would do equally good work on cast iron. That cost a
great deal of money and took a number of years. Just as soon as we
saw that a lathe would do twice or three times as much work with
the Taylor steel as it had done before, we realized that our old
piece rates, our old methods of management, were not in harmony
with this new development.

We found that the tools themselves--the lathes and the planers
and everything we had--were too weak to properly use this high-
speed steel. We rebuilt the tools that we could, and eventually
we ordered new tools properly made for use. At that time, if we
were going to buy a lathe, the salesman would come in and want to
sell us lathes, and we would say, "How much power does your lathe
take?" and if it was 5 horsepower, we would say, "How much does this
other take?" That would be 4 horsepower, and we would buy the 4-
horsepower lathe, because that was cheaper to run.

After Mr. Taylor, Mr. Barth, and Mr. Gantt began with their
practical work, then when a man came in to sell us a lathe, we
would say, "How much power can we safely transmit through your

lathe to the cutting tool?" and the man that said the most, up to
50 or 60 horsepower, he was the man that we dealt with.

Now, there was a revolution in the tools of the trade. It was
no revolution in the workmen; it was no revolution in the boss; it
was simply a fact, the same as Maximite is better for some things
than gunpowder. It required an adjustment of everything. So, then,
we felt and knew that we would have to have management, accounting,
and everything that goes with it, in our business, commensurate
with this wonderful discovery.

Mr. Taylor had been working on this shop management--he called
it the "art of management"--for a great many years; some 35 or 30
years ago he started, and about 15 years ago or so--12 or 15 years
ago--he published a paper on the subject. We had known Mr. Taylor,
and we knew the manner of man he was, and we immediately made up
our minds that if we were going to have a shop that was thoroughly
abreast of the times, we must have not only high-speed steel and
the best tools and the best electric driving, which we were pioneers in putting in, in a sense, but we would have to have a commensurate management. So we asked Mr. Taylor what he could do for
us.

. . . .

Mr. THOMPSON. What was the effect of the introduction of the
system on the quantity of product?

Mr. DODGE. The product was very largely increased.

Mr. THOMPSON. To what extent? What percentage?

Mr. DODGE. Oh, I would not dare say that. In individual cases
the product might be increased tenfold. In other cases it would be
increased twofold. I suppose it would be safe to say that if we
could have held all the conditions exactly alike, which is impossible, of course, we certainly would have turned out twice as much
work as we did before; but we have no data on that, because there
was no use in keeping records under a system that had been in vogue
since the Pyramids had been built. Questions were never asked.

Mr. THOMPSON. You think it has paid, though, from the standpoint of production, well?

Mr. DODGE. Oh, absolutely paid; yes, sir.

Testimony, James Mapes Dodge, April 14, 1914, U.S. Congress,
64th, 1st session, Senate, Document No. 415, Final Report and
Testimony Submitted by the Commission on Industrial Relations, I,
pp. 862-863, 864.

592. A WAR BOOM IS LIKE ANY BOOM (1915-1918)

Historically, the American financial system has
not proved an effective stabilizer of economic tendencies.
The short-term perspective of the system is exemplified in
the following interchange.

Senator VANDENBERG. On page 2, Mr. Morgan, in the black-face type, you are emphasizing the fact that this loan [1915] is essential to the encouragement of this new export trade which had been developed in the course of the war, and you are making the point that this makes the loan a pro-American affair because it is in favor of American business.

Mr. MORGAN. Yes.

Senator VANDENBERG. Mr. Morgan, is it a healthy thing for a country to have an export trade booming on the basis of war orders that necessarily must be temporary. Is it not a direct invitation to inflation, which must be followed by a disastrous deflation?

Mr. MORGAN. I do not think that you can look ahead that way at the time and say that.

Senator VANDENBERG. Let us admit that you cannot look ahead at the time; let us just look at it abstractedly, because, after all, that is the function of the inquiry, as I see it. Would you not now say that when you are encouraging a war export trade of this nature you are encouraging an inflationary trade which must come to an end and which, therefore, must be followed by a very disastrous deflation?

Mr. MORGAN. I should say that to the extent that you have real exports and are paid real money for them, or advanced real money on them--it is the same thing--that you do not have an inflationary situation at all.

Senator VANDENBERG. But have you not induced a vast industrial activity which has to be demobilized at any moment when the war stops?

Mr. MORGAN. That is the case in any case of times of prosperity. There are times when your production exceeds your needs. That comes afterward.

Senator VANDENBERG. Precisely; but if you build industrial expansion to fit a trade and appetite which is definely known to have a terminus, is not that an invitation to industrial inflation that is bound to have a deflationary postcript subsequently?

Mr. MORGAN. I should not say that that was so; no.

Senator VANDENBERG. You think necessarily war trade is healthy?

Mr. MORGAN. I think the increase of exports helped this country....

A man will not decline an order that he is able to fill because later on he may have difficulty in selling all his products. He will take what he can get at the time, inevitably.

Senator VANDENBERG. Precisely, but is he a wise manager if he stupendously expands his production if the knows that these new orders have to stop next year or the year after?

Mr. MORGAN. Yes; I think he is.

Testimony, J. P. Morgan, January 13, 1936, U.S. Congress, 74th, 2nd session, Senate, Special Committee Investigating the Munitions Industry, Munitions Industry, XXVII, p. 8157.

593.   LIST OF AMERICAN MILLIONAIRES (1915-1920)

Following is a list of 181 millionaires. Each one
earned a minimum of $1 million net taxable income, after
all deductions and losses, at least once during the years
1915-1920.

Ahnelt, William P., Deal, New Jersey
Andrus, J. E., Yonkers, New York
Arbuckle, Christina, New York City, N.Y.
Armstrong, W. M., and wife, Los Angeles, California
Astor, John Jacob, New York City, N.Y.
Astor, Vincent, New York City, N.Y.
Astor, Waldorf, New York City, N.Y.
Baker, George F., New York City, N.Y.
Bauernschmidt, Fred, Baltimore, Maryland
Beebe, Junius, Wakefield, Massachusetts
Beebe, Marcus, Boston, Massachusetts
Benedum, M. L., Pittsburgh, Pennsylvania
Berwind, Edward J., New York City, N.Y.
Bingham, Harry Payne, New York City, N.Y.
Bingham, William 2nd, Cleveland, Ohio
Blossom, Elizabeth B., Cleveland, Ohio
Blum, Herbert J., Chicago, Illinois
Blunt, Cecil Charles, Paris, France
Bolton, Frances P., Cleveland, Ohio
Bostwick, Helen C., New York City, N.Y.
Bourne, Frederick G., New York City, N.Y.
Brady, James C., Albany, New York
Brown, W. Harry, Pittsburgh, Pennsylvania
Candler, Asa G., Albany, New York
Cannon, James W., Concord, North Carolina
Carnegie, Andrew, Hoboken, New Jersey
Chapman, James A., Tulsa, Oklahoma
Chapman, P. A., Waxahachie, Texas
Ciotti, Andrew, Baltimore, Maryland
Clark, William A., New York City, N.Y.
Cochran, Alex Smith, New York, N.Y.
Converse, Edmund C., Greenwich, Connecticut
Couzens, James, Detroit, Mich
Cowles, Russel A., New York, N.Y.
Crane, R. T., Jr., Chicago, Illinois
Curran, Maurice J., Andover, Massachusetts
Curtis, Cyrus H. K., Wyncote, Pennsylvania
Cutten, Arthur W., Chicago, Ill
Davison, Henry P., New York, N.Y.
Dearborn, George S., New York City, N.Y.
DeLamar, Joseph R., New York City, N.Y.
Dodge, Cleveland H., New York, N.Y.
Dodge, Horace E., Grosse Point, Michigan
Dodge, John F., Detroit, Michigan

Dodge, Mary M. H. (Miss), New York, N.Y.
Douglas, James, New York, N.Y.
Duisberg, Carl, Leverkusen, Germany
Duke, James B., Somerville, New Jersey
Du Pont, Alfred I., Wilmington, Delaware
Du Pont, Mr. Francis G. (Elsie W.), Wilmington, Delaware
Du Pont, Henry F., Winterthur, Delaware
Du Pont, Pierre S., Wilmington, Delaware
Du Pont, Thomas Coleman, Wilmington, Delaware
Du Pont, William, Wilmington, Delaware
Durant, William C., Deal, New Jersey
Eastman, George, Rochester, New York
Ehret, George, Sr., New York, N.Y.
Elkins, George W., Philadelphia, Pennsylvania
Endicott, Henry B., Dedham, Massachusetts
Epstein, Jacob, Baltimore, Maryland
Ford, Edsel Bryant, Detroit, Michigan
Ford, Henry, Dearborn, Michigan
Forstmann, Julius, Passaic, New Jersey
Frelinghuysen, Adaline H., New York, N.Y.
Frick, Henry C., Pittsburgh, Pennsylvania
Friedenhit, Isaac, New York, N.Y.
Gates, Dellora R., New York, N.Y.
Goelet, Robert Walton, New York, N.Y.
Grace, Eugene G., Bethlehem, Pennsylvania
Gray, David, Grosse Pointe Farms, Michigan
Gray, Paul R., Detroit, Michigan
Gray, Philip H., Detroit, Michigan
Green, Edward H. R., Terrell, Texas
Grundy, Joseph R., Bristol, Pennsylvania
Hanna, H. Melville, New York, N.Y.
Harkness, Anna M., New York, N.Y.
Harkness, Edward S., New York, N.Y.
Harkness, Wm. L., New York, N.Y.
Harriman, Mary W., Arden, Orange Co., New York
Havemeyer, Horace, New York, N.Y.
Hayden, Charles, New York, N.Y.
Hildrup, William T., Jr., Harrisburg, Pennsylvania
Houser, M.H., Portland, Oregon
Howard, Charles S., San Francisco, California
Howard, Fannie May, San Francisco, California
Huntington, Arabella D., New York, N.Y.
James, Arthur Curtiss, New York, N.Y.
Jamison, Mrs. Catherine, New York, N.Y.
Jamison, William A., New York, N.Y.
Johnson, Eldridge R., Moorestown, New Jersey
Johnson, George F., Endicott, New York
Julliard, A. D., New York, N.Y.
Kales, Alice G., Detroit, Michigan
Kirkland, J. L., Wheeling, West Virginia
Lamborn, Arthur H., Upper Montclair, New Jersey
Lamont, Thomas W., New York City, N.Y.
Lantz, J. B., Arkansas City, Kansas
Lapham, Lewis H., New York, N.Y.

Leggett, David G., New York, N.Y.
Lewis, Arthur R., New York, N.Y.
Livermore, J. L., New York, N.Y.
Marland, E. W., Ponca City, Oklahoma
Mather, Samuel, Cleveland, Ohio
Matthiessen, Frederick W., Chicago, Ill
McFadden, George, Philadelphia, Pennsylvania
McFarlin, R. M., San Antonio, Texas
McLean, James, New York, N.Y.
McLean, William L., Philadelphia, Pennsylvania
McNeely, George H., Haverford, Pennsylvania
Mellon, A. W., Pittsburgh, Pennsylvania
Metcalf, Manton B., New York, N.Y.
Metz, Herman A., New York, N.Y.
Mills, Ogden, New York, N.Y.
Monell, Ambrose, Tuxedo Park, New York
Moore, William H., New York, N.Y.
Morgan, J. P., New York, N.Y.
Morgan, William A., Buffalo, New York
Morrell, A., Tuxedo Park, New York
McVoy, Eugene J., Chicago, Illinois
Nichols, William H., New York, N.Y.
Oliver, Edith A., Pittsburgh, Pennsylvania
Osborn, Alice D., New York, N.Y.
Palmer, Edgar, New York, N.Y.
Palmer, Zilph Hayes, New York, N.Y.
Parriott, F. B., Pittsburgh, Pennsylvania
Patten, James A., Evanston, Illinois
Plant, Morton F., New York, N.Y.
Price, Michael G., Philadelphia, Pennsylvania
Prentiss, Francis F., Cleveland, Ohio
Rackham, Horace H., Detroit, Michigan
Rainey, Paul J., New York, N.Y.
Rainey, Roy Alvin, New York, N.Y.
Rea, Edith Oliver (Mrs.), Pittsburgh, Pennsylvania
Reid, Mrs. Elizabeth Mills, Purchase, N.Y.
Rice, Eleanore Elkins, Newport, Rhode Island
Robinson, Lucius W., Punxsutawney, Pennsylvania
Rockefeller, John D., New York, N.Y.
Rockefeller, John D., Jr., New York, N.Y.
Rockefeller, William, New York, N.Y.
Roebling, Charles G., New York, N.Y.
Roebling, Washington A., Trenton, New Jersey
Rogers, Mrs. Grace Rainey, New York, N.Y.
Rosenbloom, Sol, Pittsburgh, Pennsylvania
Rosenwald, Julius, Chicago, Illinois
Ryan, Thomas F., New York, N.Y.
Sayles, Frank A., Pawtucket, Rhode Island
Schiff, Jacob H., New York, N.Y.
Severance, John L., Cleveland, Ohio
Shaffer, Charles B., Chicago, Illinois
Sinclair, H. F., New York, N.Y.
Smathers, Elmer E., New York, N.Y.

Snyder, W. P., Pittsburgh, Pennsylvania
Starkey, W. P., Harrisburg, Pennsylvania
Steel, Charles, New York, N.Y.
Stillman, James, New York, N.Y.
Stone, Galen L., Brookline, Massachusetts
Stotesbury, Edward T., Philadelphia, Pennsylvania
Straight, Mrs. Dorothy Whitney, New York, N.Y.
Strong, Henry A., Rochester, New York
Taylor, Henry A. C., New York, N.Y.
Tracy, David E., Harrisburg, Pennsylvania
Twombley, Florence A. V., New York, N.Y.
Ulman, J. Stevens, New York, N.Y.
Vanderbilt, Frederick W., New York, N.Y.
Valderbilt, William K., New York, N.Y.
Vincenti, Charles, Baltimore, Maryland
Walters, Henry
Webb, Charles J., Philadelphia, Pennsylvania
Webb, Electra H., New York, N.Y.
Wellington, William H., Boston, Massachusetts
Whelan, George J., New York, N.Y.
Whitman, William, Brookline, Massachusetts
Whitney, Harry Payne, New York, N.Y.
Whitney, Payne, New York, N.Y.
Widener, Joseph E., Elkins Park, Pennsylvania
Wilks, H. Sylvia A.H.G., New York, N.Y.
Willys, John N., Toledo, Ohio
Winthrop, Kate W., New York, N.Y.
Wood, William M., Andover, Massachusetts
Woolworth, F. W., New York, N.Y.
Wrigley, William, Jr., Chicago, Illinois

Statistical exhibit No. 1112, prepared under direction of
Edward White, chief of the Statistical Section of the Income Tax
Unit of the Bureau of Internal Revenue, U.S. Congress, 73rd,
Senate, Special Committee Investigating the Munitions Industry,
Munitions Industry, XIII, pp. 2987-2989.

594.   THE DANGERS OF INVENTORY ACCUMULATION (1920)

The following is a graphic account of rapidly descend-
ing inventory values, a descent that led to the bankruptcy
of a large corporation.

In order to make our plans for the coming year we had organized
a Board of Control to make a continuous study of customer requirements, and make up an estimate each fall as to how many tires we
would have to build. Once this forecast had been approved by

Seiberling, I would start in buying materials, ordering equipment, hiring men, doing whatever else was needed to meet the schedule. A bonanza year seemed to be ahead in 1920.

With sales in the spring running at the rate of a million dollars a day, our manufacturer customers warned us again and again that they were depending upon us for deliveries. We were using eight million pounds of rubber a month and we normally had to have four times that amount in our inventory or on order. Now the way things were going we had to figure five or six months' supply to be safe. Rubber was my special responsibility. I had started early to build up the inventory, and as the price moved up from thirty-eight cents a pound to fifty-seven cents I quit buying, feeling that our supply was in good shape, and rather congratulating myself that our inventory, with commitments, was worth twenty million dollars more than we had paid for it.

In the case of fabric, we were using three million pounds a month and again had to figure a four-month supply because of the length of time required to convert cotton bales into rolls of fabric. The fabric mills were running at capacity, the owners were building new plants as fast as they could, but eventually the industry found itself making contracts for cotton not yet planted, and for fabric made in mills not even built. Dunlop, the big English company, wanted to get into the American market, but found the mills and machinery men committed for two years ahead. The boom was on and the end seemed nowhere in sight....

Business began to fall off however in the early summer of 1920, gradually at first, but quickly gathering momentum. We began retrenching as soon as the danger signals became serious, cut our working force back in line with the shrinking volume of business, stopped all new projects like Plant III and the engineering building.

But there was nothing we could do to prevent our inventories and commitments from shrinking in value. Ours dropped fast and far. A company with good reserves can absorb inventory losses of 10 per cent or more, but our inventory values shrank 40 per cent. We did not have the financial reserves for losses of that magnitude.

Once the thing started it built up like a snowball rolling downhill, carrying everything with it. Cotton dropped to seven cents a pound, and the rubber which was worth twenty million dollars more than we paid for it in May, was worth thirty million dollars less than we paid for it in November.

Moreover our customers could cancel their orders to us, but we could not cancel the orders we had given to the suppliers of rubber fabric, compounds, machinery, and equipment. Car-manufacturer contracts were drawn up not on a fixed number of tires, but enough tires for their needs, whatever those were. We could not ask anyone to take any more tires than he needed.

One thing we got out of that grim era was the policy that we would not make any long-term commitments at a fixed price. We would endeavor to set things up so as to pay the market price, whatever that was, at the time of delivery.

Our sales for March 1920 were twenty million dollars. By
November they were down to four and a half million.

P. W. Litchfield, Industrial Voyage, My Life as an Industrial
Lieutenant, (Garden City, N.Y.: Doubleday and Co., 1954), pp.
192-194.

595. STEEL PRODUCTION AND CONSUMPTION (1939)

During the previous decade, steel production--in
million long tons--had reached as low as 13.7 and 28.3
in 1932 and 1938, and as high as 56.4 and 50.6, in 1929
and 1937. This testimony was given by Eugene G. Grace.
Grace was president of the Bethlehem Steel Company, the
industry's second largest firm. Questioners were: Leon
Henderson, member of the Securities and Exchange
Commission, and John V. W. Reynders, Consultant to the
Secretary of Commerce.

Mr. GRACE. The business is not being best conducted when we
as a basic industry are producing products that are not going
reasonably into consumption. As those products start in accumulation, we are robbing tomorrow.
Mr. HENDERSON. That is the kind of a situation that happened
in late 1936, for example, where it was well known that not only
was there to be the prospect of a December price increase, but
probably it would be followed by a higher posting in the following
period.
Mr. GRACE. You combine a bit of a panic, let's say, in the
buyer's mind with a little element of speculation in it, and the
first thing you know, we get an entirely out-of-line demand and we
will see our properties required to run 100 per cent in order to
satisfy that demand, and in a few months time, bang! we come down
through the processes you speak of, we take off these very important units, expensive to put into operation, expensive to take
off.
There isn't any industry I know of that has anything like the
requirements of investment in units in order to produce its product
that the steel industry has.
Mr. HENDERSON. Or another element which is in relation to
your assets, of the turnover that you get--that is another important element, is it not?
Mr. GRACE. Right.
Mr. HENDERSON. Did most of that backlog you spoke of as continuing through 1937 get put on your books in late 1937?
Mr. GRACE. In late 1936 and early 1937, and now, wouldn't it
have been a great deal better if at the beginning of '36 we had had

a reasonable demand, if possible. A basic industry is definitely
in the hands of the purchasing public, just definitely there. We
are at the mercy of their whim. We can't help it.

Mr. HENDERSON. Isn't there anything you can do when your
customers get to a position like that about assuring them? Take
the condition that we have been in with the change that has taken
place, do you have any positive selling policy with relation to
your customers tending to smooth out this curve?

Mr. GRACE. We definitely say to our trade, yes, and everybody
is saying it now over this period when things have become sort of
excitable, people feeling that they weren't going to get the service
maybe because of war conditions or other conditions, because all
inventories were down to bone, there just wasn't anything in
Mother Hubbard's cupboard in many cases.

It was ridiculous in a way, but a large number of our customers, large consumers of steel, were working on too low an amount of
inventory. A lot of them didn't have any inventory and they got
caught because they didn't have; they were just working from hand
to mouth.

They saw the possibility that maybe with a repetition of war
conditions, they were going to have difficulty being serviced.

We have said to our customers, "You are going to get all the
service we can give you. Please don't get stampeded. We are not
going to take any opportune business that would replace the service
that we are indebted to you to give. Now just don't get foolish
and inflate your ideas for protection purposes. Sure, you have
been running too low in inventories, you always should have normal
working inventories." We believe it is bad business not to have.

Mr. REYNDERS. Mr. Grace, may I ask this question? Isn't
this matter of inventories frequently overemphasized? There are
a great many lines of steel where I don't see how inventories can
be accumulated. Now there are some, but take the matter of rolled
structural sections that is out entirely.

Mr. GRACE. That is right, but Mr. Reynders, I was thinking
along the line of the definite user of steel for this line of
product, his established line of product. He got entirely too
low in his normal supplies to take care of himself. He was
depending on getting service from the steel mills overnight.

Well now, that is not the best business--that is not the
best business tactics if we are going to get a reasonably ironed-
out operation.

Mr. REYNDERS. In the matter of volume it couldn't represent
a tremendous lot. Go through your various products and you don't
accumulate inventories in rails, you can't accumulate inventories
in those sheet products that go into automobiles, because the
models may change overnight.

Mr. GRACE. Your point is a good one. We cannot as a basic
industry the way we operate and the tonnage we operate, accumulate
any important inventories to take care of the peaks and the
valleys, no, certainly we cannot do it.

Mr. REYNDERS. I think it will add to our correct understanding
of that problem if we analyzed these products, because I do think
the question of inventory, to my mind, is rather misunderstood as

far as the steel industry is concerned. There are a few items on
which you can accumulate inventory, but by and large, I hardly think
that is always true.
    Mr. GRACE. But at the same time, I am not going to let some
of our trade, some of the purchasers of steel commodities, for their
ordinary standard production of their commodity, get away from the
thought that in my estimation they were running entirely too low
for normal inventory purposes.

    Testimony, Eugene G. Grace, November 9, 1939, <u>Verbatim Record</u>
<u>of the Proceedings of the Temporary National Economic Committee</u>,
IX, pp. 293-294.

596. "IT IS A WAR BOOM" (1939)

    In the same month the following industrial leader
spoke, American production reached its depression high
and equalled the 1929 level. But, "the boom was a war
boom." Ernest T. Weir was chairman of the National
Steel Company and president of the American Iron and Steel
Institute; he was addressing the annual meeting of the
American Institute of Steel Construction in New York.

    Three months ago we were still in a depression frame of mind.
Subnormal business, agricultural surpluses, relief, unemployment,
taxation--these were paramount subjects of interest and concern as
they had been in each of the previous months of this decade. Then,
overnight as it were, came the change in spirit, outlook and actual
conditions that is remarkable even in a time which, as I said,
takes change for granted. Action of the stock market became
strongly reminiscent of pre-October, 1929. Buyers began bidding
against each other for commodities. In industry--notably the steel
industry--worry about getting orders was replaced with worry about
filling orders. Workmen on part time or layoff came back to full
schedules. Increased retail trade quickly showed that expanded
production was having its effect on consumption--that the upward
spiral was starting.
    Now I would be the happiest of men if I could believe that this
activity was sound. Nothing would please me more than the ability
to say at this moment that I am convinced we have entered that genuine economic revival so long awaited, that the broken threads
of progress have at last been tied together, that America has resumed the continuous march to higher and better living standards
that characterized our country in most of the years since its birth.
But I do not believe and cannot say this. We may as well face
facts. It is true that the course of business has been upward
since 1938, but without sound fundamentals mere increase in volume

cannot be sound. And however pleasant it may be as a respite from depression, the present greatly increased business activity does not have its base on an economic foundation which can support sustained and genuine prosperity. It is a war boom. Despite the fact that the great bulk of activity to date has been exclusively domestic activity, it owes its existence of war in Europe.

The point does not need to be labored. The real jump in the business curve coincided with the declaration of war [September 1, 1939]. On the commodity and stock markets the greatest activity was in the commodities and in the stocks of companies most likely to be affected by the initial demands of war. The activity of non-war business can be ascribed partly to increased consumer purchasing as the result of increased employment, but mostly to the rush to protect inventories against material shortages and higher prices prices. Wall Street gives a clue to the slenderness of the reed which supports this boom every time it goes up on war news and goes down on peace news. And if a real peace were declared tomorrow, do any of you think we would not be right back where we were two months ago; that orders now piling on top of one another would not be cancelled; that inventories would not go back to their previous subnormal levels?

At this moment, I do not believe that any in this group or very many in the general public are deceived as to the elements supporting the present increased activity. And so long as its impermanent and unsubstantial nature is recognized, the so-called recovery holds little avoidable danger. But if war continues and if under war's stimulation business activity continues and grows greater, there is serious danger. Memory can be very short. A year or so of good employment, good wages and good business in general could lull us into the belief that war prosperity had solved depression problems for us. Even those with clearer heads and longer memories, those who kept in mind the fact that another depression waited at the end of the boom, would equivocate by saying to themselves, "Let's cross that bridge when we come to it."

Address, Ernest T. Weir, October 17, 1939, reprinted in Verbatim Record of the Proceedings of the Temporary National Economic Committee, IX, p. 322.

597. BARGAINING ON STEEL PRICES (1939)

An interesting view of the "poker-playing game" of bargaining on prices between large industries. The speakers involved were Harold Vance, chairman of the board of directors of the Studebaker Corporation, and Joseph J. O'Connell, Jr., who was special assistant to the general counsel, representing the Treasury Department.

Mr. O'CONNELL. To be quite precise, I should think, from what
you had indicated about the volume of purchasing and the way you
purchase, that in dealing with the steel industry in buying cold
rolled sheets you would probably be in a better bargaining position
today as you were a few months ago than would the individual purchaser of some fabricated material, an office building or something
of that sort. In other words, you are such a substantial purchaser
that you may be better able to deal with commodity increases in
this country, I mean, as distinguished with foreign materials.
Mr. VANCE. That is a very difficult question to answer precisely, for this reason: That steel prices are published, as you
know, from quarter to quarter, and that the attitude of steel companies is, of course, that those are prices for everybody, and that
they have not other prices.
Mr. HENDERSON. Now that is exactly different; what the steel
industry contended was that that published price merely meant
nothing, that they very seldom got it except from the Government
and all the rest of you sharp bargainers got a lower price. They
did admit, however, that as volume started to go up they tended
to come closer to that price.
Mr. VANCE. I said, Mr. Henderson, that that was their attitude. Their attitude was that these were published prices and
those were prices for everybody. Now there have been times when it
has been possible to buy steel at more favorable prices than the
current published lists. There have been other times when it has
been much more difficult. It depends to a great extent upon the
supply and demand situation in the steel industry at a given time.
Mr. O'CONNELL. Let me ask you this. Preliminary to the posting of steel prices for cold rolled sheets, say for any given quarter, is there or is there not a period of negotiation between the
steel people and the automobile people? I mean are you helpless
or do you just wait for the posting of the price of cold rolled
sheets?
Mr. VANCE. Sometimes we do and sometimes we don't. What is
much more effective in the purchase of steel by us that this poker-
playing game which you describe, negotiations so to speak, between
the purchasing agent and the agent of the steel company at the
moment that the purchasing agent wants to buy--what is much more
potent with respect to the steel prices that we ultimately pay is
that we watch the steel market and try to make up our mind when it
is the time to buy. Those of you who are familiar with steel prices
of course know--I am telling you nothing when I say that there was
a period late last spring when the steel prices were very unstable.
Mr. HENDERSON. You mean very competitive, don't you?
Mr. VANCE. Yes. There are degrees of stability in prices,
as you know. There was a time late last spring when steel operations were at a low level and when prices were very unstable, and
for a purchaser of steel that was the time to buy steel in substantial quantities for future deliveries, and that is what the automobile industry did.

Testimony, Harold S. Vance, December 6, 1939, Verbatim Record
of the Proceedings of the Temporary National Economic Committee,
IX, p. 513.

598.   SUBCONTRACTING IN AIRPLANE MANUFACTURE (1941)

The unprecedentedly large output of military aircraft depended upon the innovation of subcontracting which,
in turn, depended upon the existence of a broad base of
smaller shops with skilled labor fairly available. The
speaker is William S. Knudsen who was director-general of
the Office of Production Management. Formerly, he had been
president of General Motors Corporation.

You see, a job like an airplane, you can talk about 100 airplanes a day and 500 a day, and all that sort of thing, but you
have to cut the thing into sections. You have to make many pieces
out of the airplane, and then have these pieces made in as many
places as possible, and be sure when you get them they go together
and make one airplane. That is the only way you will get quantities on airplane production.
    If you have to build the whole thing up like a boat you could
get airplanes, but you can't get enough of them. So we immediately
started the plane up into sections. The first one was a bombing
plane made by North American, that we laid out in 32 sections. We
had something to start from then, and first we recommended that they
themselves go out and find people to make sections. That was the
beginning of the subcontracting business in airplanes. Previous
to that the airplane manufacturer bought the standard parts, bolts,
nuts, rivets, and so forth; but he did everything else himself;
and, of course, we felt that we were going into higher production
in airplanes in a very short time, and if he had to build for this
sole-purpose factory, we would have millions of square feet of
factories; whereas, if we could split it up, we thought that was
the answer to it.

Testimony, William S. Knudsen, April 17, 1941, U.S. Congress,
77th, 1st session, Senate, Special Committee Investigating the
National Defense Program, Investigation of the National Defense
Program, I, p. 101.

599.   "THE REAL NEWS OF THE WAR" (1943)

The war called for imaginative use of tried
industrial techniques. Charles Wilson, president of
General Motors Corporation, describes what occurred.

Mr. WILSON. Well, I have said several times, and I would like
to say it again, that the real news of the war is not that we have

learned a lot of things in the war that we can use in our peacetime
products; the real news is that our American methods of production,
our knowhow about the business, could be applied to the mass production of all these war things, many of which a good many of our
people, not only in General Motors, but in other places, had never
even seen before. Anybody who really understood the essentials of
progressive manufacture, accurate interchangeability of parts, and
mass production, could take the blueprints of anything and, if the
blueprints were right, he could make it in quantity effectively and
efficiently. That is the real news, and that is the one factor
that I think our Axis enemies overlooked. They didn't think we
could get together in this country and do that job.
     The CHAIRMAN. We fooled them.
     Mr. WILSON. I think we fooled them. It was a little close,
though.

     Testimony, Charles E. Wilson, November 24, 1943, U.S. Congress,
78th, 1st and 2nd sessions, Senate, Special Committee Investigating
the National Defense Program, <u>Investigation of the National Defense</u>
<u>Program</u>, XXI, pp. 8630-8631.

          600. PER UNIT COSTS IN AUTO MANUFACTURING (1956)

          Here is a very rare statement on the matter from
     inside the industry. George Romney, president of American
     Motors Corporation and of the Automobile Manufacturers
     Association, is the speaker. From 1941 to 1948, he was
     head of the Detroit office and managing director of the
     association. During the period 1948-1954 he occupied var-
     ious positions in the Nash-Kelvinator Company (American
     Motors was created by a merger of the latter firm with
     Hudson Motor Car Company).

     Mr. ROMNEY. Yes, sir, but that break-even point depends on a
number of things, and I will be very happy to discuss to the extent
the committee wants to what the hard-core facts are with respect to
break-even points and the hard-core point at which manufacturing
expense and tooling expense get improved with volume and the extent
to which the improvement becomes negligible.
     Senator KEFAUVER. Do you want to do it right now? This would
be a very good time.
     Mr. ROMNEY. Well, all right. Let me go on here because I
cover it to some extent here and then let me add to the comment.
     Our present sales "travel rate" is in the neighborhood of
160,000 cars a year and we expect it to go higher.
     Now this figure of 120,000 cars is a pretty small percentage
of even 5-million-car year, which should be a good indication

that you do not have to have the volume of the Big Three manufacturers to be efficient.

Our studies, based on our own experience and that of our competitors, is that optimum manufacturing conditions are achieved with
a production rate of 62.5 cars per hour per assembly line.

To absorb the desired machine-line and press-line rate, two
final assembly lines would be required.

Of course your press line and your machine line are the principle lines on which you depend for work leading up to subassemblies
and the ultimate production of the car itself on the assembly line.

This would result in production of 1,000 cars per shift.

A company that can build between 180,000 and 220,000 cars a
year on a 1-shift basis can make a very good profit and not take a
back seat to anyone in the industry in production efficiency. On a
2-shift basis, annual production of 360,000 to 440,000 cars will
achieve additional small economies but beyond that volume only
theoretical and insignificant reductions in manufacturing costs are
possible. It is possible to be one of the best without being the
biggest.

I would like to remind committee members that the testimony I
am giving is not at variance basically with what Mr. Curtice
[president of General Motors] has stated previously in hearings
held here in Washington.

Before the O'Mahoney committee in the fall of 1955 Mr. Curtice
indicated that you can have a very efficient operation with 30 cars
an hour.

Well, I think 30 cars an hour is a little low. I think 62--it
used to be 30. Pre-World War II you could do it with 30. You cannot do it with 30 today because cost factors have increased so it
is about double where it used to be. But my point is that his figure was lower than the figure I am using, and also my point is that
when you get up to 180,000 to 200,000 cars a year, the cost reduction flattens out, from a manufacturing cost standpoint, and from
360,000 to 400,000 on up it is a negligible thing.

Now the thing you have to keep in mind is that the 1 1/2 million Chevrolets or Fords that are produced a year, they are not all
produced in 1 plant. They are produced at plants scattered all over
the United States, from an assembly standpoint and a good deal of
the other processes are scattered.

Now to the extent they are not scattered, if they do centralize
something, then they have got terrific material handling costs and
freight costs that an integrated operation in one spot does not get
into.

Their assembly plants and other operations are keyed in with
these basic figures that I am talking about. They do not assemble
the rates substantially in excess of these at any one point. They
do not assemble in excess of the ton figure given at any one point.

Senator WILEY. You have exploded one idea right there that I
think has brought some light into the picture because everyone always thinks that every time you increase your volume, you decrease
the rate per unit cost.

Mr. ROMNEY. Which is not so.

Senator WILEY. Which is not so.

Mr. ROMNEY. And Senator, they [the Big Three] beat us in certain elements of cost and we beat them in certain elements of cost.

. . . .

Now I have been discussing the manufacturing cost aspects of the automobile business in relationship to volume. There are other aspects of it, but I think I have said enough to indicate that the huge volumes that the Big Three have are not necessary to get efficient and minimum manufacturing costs.

Now let's take tooling. There are all sorts of tooling, and when you provide tooling for high volume, you provide more expensive tooling and it costs more, and beyond these areas I am talking about you get into duplications, and if you take the most modern tooling on a 440,000 basis or 360,000 basis, which is that required for most highly efficient manufacturing results, then you have got about double the cost for that tooling as compared to tooling for 180,000 to 220,000 units, and if you will take the 2 sets of costs and divide them by volume per unit, it happens that the cost per unit comes out right on the button.

So all this talk about the disadvantages of lack of volume in relationship to tooling costs is grossly exaggerated. What I am saying is that if you have got 180,000 to 220,000 volume a year, you can compete effectively and efficiently in the automotive industry as we are demonstrating, because we are currently running at about 160,000 cars a year and the thing we are trying to do is to get our production up to a point where the manufacturing cost benefits begin to level off; namely 180,000 to 220,000 cars a year, and compared to where we were, 2 or 3 years ago, we are pretty well along.

Senator KEFAUVER. Mr. Romney, did I understand you to say you thought about 360,000 a year was the most efficient and economical production?

Mr. ROMNEY. I said, yes, Senator, from 360,000 to 440,000. I mean in that area, because in that area you reach the point where further reductions in manufacturing costs are highly theoretical and depend on factors other than just the manufacturing factors, and you get into complications in other areas that begin to eliminate the benefits of increased volume.

Senator KEFAUVER. That is 2 shifts on 1 line, is that correct?

Mr. ROMNEY. That is correct, 2 shifts, Senator, on 1 line in press shops and machining, and 2 lines in final assembly.

Now the other thing I discussed was tooling and the two are separate matters.

Testimony, George Romney, February 7, 1958, U.S. Congress, 85th, 2nd session, Senate, Committee on the Judiciary, Subcommittee on Antitrust and Monopoly, Administered Prices, VI, Automobiles, pp. 2851-2852, 2852-2853.

601. SHORTCOMINGS OF MANAGEMENT THINKING (1981)

Twice during American history -- 1898-1902 and during
the late 1960s -- numerous industrial corporations merged.
At the very end of the 1970s, a third comparable movement
was underway. From 1979 to 1982, $170 billion was spent
on corporate acquisitions of other corporations; in 1981
alone, nearly $83 billion was spent. To finance these
transactions, banks extended $47 billion in lines of credit
during the latter half of 1981. Very likely, the extension
and later utilization of the major part of such enormous
sums added to existing upward pressures on interest rates,
thus worsening inflation. Commenting below on the "merger
mania" is Simon Ramo, retired principal officer and co-
founder of TRW, Inc., of which he is a director.

On the first matter, the short-term thinking of the management
of American industry--I think you are absolutely right. You very
succinctly stated a bad and growing characteristic of American management. The inflationary environment has made it worse. Whenever
there is economic instability, whenever there is a concern about how
the government is going to try to handle inflation, and indefiniteness about the economic results of government action, the fear that
the government may make it even worse in trying to cure it--this
tends to drive business managers toward short-term policies. We
must remember that many companies have accumulated, as a result of
their poor past performance, very bad debt-equity ratios. Some have
to pay better attention to the short term, because otherwise they
may not be in business in 4 or 5 years.
     Now, this tendency toward purely short-term thinking is even-
tually very penalizing to the nation. We need statesmanship; we
need long-range thinking for the nation, whether it be political
leadership or business leadership. I can only hope this will improve because of the increasing focus on this problem, the fact that
it's being articulated now. There is now much analysis about it
and emphasis on it. There probably will be growing statistical
examination, probably not perfect but showing that companies that
have been short ranged in these management decisions have not fared
well, 5, 10, 15 years later. This will, I hope, create pressure
from the top. A typical head of a division will be told:
          Look, your bonus, your position in the company,
     the way you are regarded, your chances of promotion,
     have all been hampered by positive evidence that your
     thinking is too short-range. You're worrying so much
     about looking good for a year or two or three that
     you are looking bad to your bosses as to the longer
     picture. I want you to know this. If you don't straighten
     out somebody else will be in your job!
     This problem may be lessened as it becomes known and clear,
the inflationary situation meanwhile improves. Then the two improvements will be put together and longer range and successful management will become the rule not the exception....

Just expressing one person's opinion, my hunch is that more
than half of the mergers we read about taking place are not based
on sound benefits to either the shareholders or the public. This
is not because they constitute a violation of the spirit of the law
about competition and antitrust--nothing like that. Rather, they
are the result only of top management's looking for larger empires
to operate or for a possibility they think they see that in larger
size alone, they will increase their chances of success. They can
spread thinner some of the fixed costs of doing business. They
often hope for benefits that are, however, only weakly in evidence.
I think this merger mania also goes to the matter of short- versus
long-range thinking. If a company leader puts together a group of
dogs with the idea of making a lion, and it turns out some years
later that what he has is still a bunch of dogs, and not a lion,
the result will be quite clear to everybody. Maybe, this situation
will right itself eventually. Later if the company management proposes to the board a merger where there isn't a real rationale, not
a good case, the board will turn down the idea because of bad previous experience.
There are of course, some sensible mergers. It can be the case
that a company with lack of technology or imagination or long-range
ideas, but with large cash flow owing to a strong position in a
mature field, can provide financial backing for an acquired entity
that is loaded with ideas that ought to be pushed, but doesn't have
the cash or the position to raise the investment funds. It can be
true that a company with strong research and development, but poor
manufacturing and marketing can join up with a company that is
strong in manufacturing and marketing. Then they're just right for
each other. There can be other good reasons for a merger.

Testimony, July 16, 1981, U.S. Congress, 97th, 1st session,
House of Representatives, Committee on Banking, Finance and Urban
Affairs, Subcommittee on Economic Stabilization, Revitalization and
the U.S. Economy. Hearings...., (Washington, D.C.: Government
Printing Office, 1981), pp. 474-476.

602. ROBOTS ARE A MANAGEMENT PROBLEM (1981)

The use of robots is an effort to automate the labor
force rather than the production process. While novelists,
dramatists, and science fiction writers long ago visualized
the use of robots, only during the 1970s did robots start
to become a practical innovation. The following material
is taken from testimony by Joseph F. Engelberger, founder
and president of Unimation, Inc. as well as founder and
chairman of Consolidated Controls Corporation. He is a
leader in the field of industrial robotics.

The Japanese are not ahead of us technically, no question about
it. Their technology is on a par, at best. The main thing I discovered is that the Japanese are fabulous implementers. They can
pick up an idea and go with it. We agonize over it.

I will just give you an example. I was in Japan on my last
trip, and our licensee asked me, what was the largest order you ever
had for robots? I said, well, it was 128 machines, from Fiat in
Italy. He said, we just got an order for 720. An order from whom?
Toyota. Kawasaki took me to Toyota, and I talked to Takahashi, the
car body-building manager. I said, "What are you going to do with
the 720 robots?" He got up to about 250 and stopped, I said, "What
about the rest?" He said he didn't know. We're going to get 25 a
month, and when they arrive, our engineers will use them.

This is the message I am bringing to our automotive industry.
The Japanese see this technology. They are putting it to work. And
they have no technical edge at all....

The managers of U.S. companies often say "Well, it's a union
problem, isn't it?" I say absolutely not. It is not labor; it is
management. The managers sit in a plush office and whisper "robot"
to each other. If you go out to the UAW, the International Association of Machinists, and you show them this equipment, by and large
they are likely to say, "Well, whatever it is, I am smarter than
that." The next thing is they will say, "What trade takes care of
them?"

So I have never seen a union barrier to robotics--I put the
blame on management.

Another thing responsible for slowness is that nobody needs a
robot. You can always get a human being to do any job, and do it
better than a robot can. The only distinction is economics. If
nobody else has robots, then there isn't any economic pressure to
even have your first robot.

So robotics is one of those things that needs a critical mass
to get going. Today I can say that in this country there is a
definite change. I am invited to speak with the heads of the largest companies who want to send the word down, because they finally
believe. For who has them? The Japanese are the ones that have
them. That is where the competitive pressure is coming from....

The question as to the percentage of the factory workforce
that could perform tasks of humans is a poor question because this
must be time related. It is also related to how much is done to
rationalize the workplace through complementary technologies in
order to make factory work compatible with the capabilities of
robots. Presuming all of it comes together by the end of the
eighties, then a program that could match the program of productivity gain in agriculture would not only be justified but be essential,
and it is my opinion as much could be accomplished in manufacturing
over a 50 year period as we accomplished in 100 years in agriculture....

Actually robots are not the technology of choice in very high
volume activities. For very high volume activities one selects
"hard automation." That is, automation which is purpose-built to
make products in very high volume for long production runs. The
robot comes into its own when product life is short, when there are

many different models to be coped with and when there is no reasonable hard automation manufacturing solution.

The major purchasers of robots today certainly have been large concerns because the major purchasers of robots have been automotive companies around the world. On the other hand there is no barrier to the use of robotics for smaller concerns. Indeed, die casters who have made great use of robots are generally smaller companies as are companies with small machine shops, companies who do injection molding or investment casting. The issue is whether or not a job can be roboticized with the current technology. The size of the company is not germane.

One caveat however and that is robots are sophisticated equipment that require sophisticated staff to keep them functioning properly. A smaller business should never be advised to hire a robot unless the plant involved has a potential for at least five robots....

In a technical world that is changing rapidly, virtually no activity is absolutely secure for a normal human work life. So I cannot guarantee that a robotics serviceman has a cradle-to-the-grave sinecure but for someone entering the workforce today or retreading him or herself in the workforce, the robotics game has got to be one of the best opportunities. If these individuals go further and recognize that once in the game, their training and their education is a never-ending activity, they will have something pretty close to ultimate security if they remain able to cope with the current level of technology as it evolves.

Testimony, July 16, 1981, U.S. Congress, 97th, 1st session, House of Representatives, Committee on Banking, Finance and Urban Affairs, Subcommittee on Economic Stabilization, Revitalization and the U.S. Economy. Hearings...., (Washington, D.C.: Government Printing Office, 1981), pp. 459-460, 489, 495-496.

603. INFORMATION INDUSTRY DEVELOPMENT (1981)

Into the 1950s, manufacturing workers made up the single largest group of workers but since then "information workers" have succeeded them in the distinction. The U.S. market for electronic products -- largely informational -- was estimated by the U.S. Department of Commerce as some $75 billion in 1979. Some of the constituents of this total include the following sales of services during recent periods: overseas telephone service ($252 million in 1970 to $976 million in 1978); overseas telex service, same years ($63 million and $267 million); total exports of information merchandise ($19.3 billion in 1979 and $24.3 billion in 1980); total electronic employment (350,000 workers in 1950 and 1.5 million in 1979). A

commentary on the industry follows, as given by
Dean Gillette, executive director, corporate
studies division, Bell Telephone Laboratories.

U.S. industry leads the world in the technologies fundamental
to future information systems: solid state electronics, computing,
optical fiber systems and communication satellites. Industry depends on NASA, of course, for development of launch vehicles, but
in all other areas is capable and eager to continue its programs
of research in the sciences and technologies of information systems.
In this time of rapidly advancing technology, the edge in applicable
science and fundamental technology provides the basis for continued
leadership through earliest introduction of the newest equipments
and services. Mr. Chairman, I believe that the U.S. has that leadership in its research institutions in government, academia and,
especially, industry.

The information industries are also aggressive in bringing new
technologies into widespread use. Just a few examples illustrate
this leadership:

- The U.S. telephone system is of unsurpassed equality
  and service is available to virtually everyone.
- U.S. researchers can use remote terminals to access
  over 600 computerized data bases covering subjects from
  accounting to water.
- U.S. industry leads in introducing such new communications technologies as digital transmission and switching,
  packet data systems, optical fibers, sophisticated customer premises switching systems, and applications of
  communications to energy conservation and control.
- U.S. industry leads in introducing computing hardware
  and software over the full range of computing capability.

We should not be complacent in making these observations, however. As Congressman Brown has noted, other nations throughout the
world have developed great competence in these fields and hope to
penetrate U.S. markets in computing and network communications as
they have so successfully penetrated U.S. markets in consumer electronics. In some instances, other nations have brought information
services into commercial use before they have been brought in by the
U.S. This fact is particularly ironic because the fundamental technologies upon which these systems are based originated in the U.S.

Thus, I believe that it is only in the final stages of the innovation process in information systems and services that other nations
are beginning to lead the U.S. That final stage is introduction of
systems into the economy -- introduction of new techniques for
increased productivity and introduction of services for use by the
public. What we need from government is encouragement in completing
the innovation process, in bringing these new information technologies which we have pioneered into widespread national service....

One need is for government recognition of the rapid obsolescence
of manufacturing equipment in high technology industries. The semiconductor industry provides one example of the need to change manufacturing processes quickly so as to remain at the forefront of
technology.

The number of components on a single "chip" of silicon has been doubling every year since 1960. To accomplish this feat, manufacturing processes, hence the equipment on the factory floor, must be replaced every two or three years. For example, to move into more advanced forms of integrated circuits, the semiconductor industry is now replacing its projection printers with new equipment having a five-fold higher cost than the brand new machines of a few years ago, and within another few years we may want to replace today's newest machines with x-ray lithography to move into what is referred to as submicron technology.

The semiconductor industry is not unique in using manufacturing technology that can be obsolete in a very few years. The point was made clear at the April, 1980, National Technological Cooperation Conference in which experts and leaders from government, academia and industry met to examine ways of expediting the movement of new technology through the U.S. manufacturing industry. The Conference Coordinating Committee, of which I was a member, intended to focus on the processes of transfer of technology from the research community to the factory floor. It turned out, though, that we could not ignore economics. There are two conclusions from the conference. As stated by John S. Foster, Jr., Conference Chairman, they were:

. "Despite all our attempts to avoid the consideration of economic incentives, it seems we must emphasize that economic incentives make or break businesses. Currently, many of our businesses are in trouble. The removal of disincentives and the institution of new economic incentives are necessary. However, it is unreasonable to expect that economic incentives by themselves will be sufficient."

. "Another necessary element is the assurance of an adequate technology diffusion system."

...The Federal government does recognize the need for industry incentives, for example, in tax measures currently before Congress. Aggressive Congressional action can help all of U.S. industry take advantage of advances in information science and technology.

Technology transfer was also a point of concern to some representatives of smaller manufacturing companies at the National Technological Cooperation Conference, but it is less so in major elements of the information industry. IBM, Texas Instruments and the Bell System, for example, are all leaders in creating the technology underlying the most advanced information systems. They are also "vertically integrated," including within one enterprise the functions of research, engineering, product design manufacturing and introduction into the market. Within each, the technology transfer process is thoroughly developed and managed. There are no questions of the relevance of research, or of the processes of selecting promising research results and applying them through engineering, design and manufacturing.

As I came to understand the difficulties of small manufacturers in getting access to research and in developing technology applicable to their mission, I came to appreciate even more the reasons why our vertically integrated enterprises in the U.S. information

industry have been so successful in putting the U.S. in its current
leading position, and why vertically integrated enterprises have
been leading the rapid progress in other nations. The increased
appreciation also further underscored the dangers to our national
position of destroying such productive vertical integration, as
some have advocated.

Testimony, June 9, 1981, U.S. Congress, 97th, 1st session,
House of Representatives, Committee on Science and Technology,
Subcommittee on Science, Research and Technology, The Information
Science and Technology Act. Hearings...., pp. 271-276.

604. RISE OF THE INFORMATION SERVICES INDUSTRY (1981)

The electronic data processing (EDP) industry has
become a significant economic factor within the past 30
years. Its total revenues in 1979 were about $46 billion.
Seven large firms produce mainframe computers while three
others manufacture minicomputers. International business
is pretty well concentrated among these large firms.
Microcomputers are made by numerous firms, many of them
new. Auxiliary equipment to extend the power of existing
computers amounts to seven billion dollars in sales, most
of it going to major companies. Data communication, dealing
with transmittal of data between computers, requires
specialized hardware and services and is a growing field.
Special applications of microprocessors -- from games to
word processors -- are potentially as pervasive as the
present electric motor. Thomas J. O'Rourke, president,
chairman of the board, and founder of Tymshare, Inc. of
Cupertino, California, gives an overview of one sector of
the data processing industry.

The information services industry provides a great variety of
products and services which make the computer more accessible, more
usable, and less expensive for users.
Some companies sell time on their own computers, others provide
custom programing and related training and consulting or facilities
management to clients who own their own systems. Still others sell
prepackaged software programs or provide access to those programs
via their processing services.
When our industry began in services, applications were limited
to simple payrolls, inventories, and sales analyses. Today the list
of applications is endless. Our customers utilize our services to
operate steel mills and petroleum refineries, to control production,
and to perform any or all of their accounting functions.
Many Fortune Five Hundred industrial customers, in spite of the
fact that they have extensive in-house computers, use our interactive

services to perform market and statistical analyses and financial
modeling on line from terminals.

Engineers use our services to design bridges, buildings, and
atomic reactors. Banks have teller terminals connected to our computer centers to provide all types of financial services.

The use of our services by customers to maintain data bases for
inquiry is limitless. Educators utilize our services for computer
based education systems. Federal, State, and local governments perform all types of statistical, accounting, and engineering applications by means of our services.

In summary, almost any business, educational institution or
government entity, large or small, is in some way being provided information services by our industry.

Although it is impossible to trace the exact birth of this
industry, computer services first received judicial recognition and
definition in a 1956 consent decree whereby IBM was required to
transfer "all its contracts for service bureau business" to a maxi-
mally separated corporate subsidiary.

In addition, 1956 was also the year the U.S. Department of
Justice and A.T. & T. agreed to a consent decree in a similar antitrust case.

At that time, A.T. & T. promised to keep its business within
the regulated areas of communications and those "incidental to communications," and stay out of unregulated, competitive industries
such as data processing.

From these decrees, the information services industry began to
emerge as a distinct business sector. Growth came slowly back then,
since there were relatively few computers--only about 100 in the
entire world and those carried an average price of $3 million.

During the early 1960's some of the innovators in our industry
began offering remote processing computer time sharing services at
a fraction of the cost of purchasing or leasing a main frame computer and developing the necessary software.

Another major development in the late sixties was the decision
by IBM to "unbundle" its software from its hardware. From that time
on, the information services industry really began to boom. For
example, in 1966...700 companies were involved in commercial computer services; annual revenues amounted to $534 million.

Five years later, in 1971, the number of participants had more
than doubled, and the industry's revenues had more than quadrupled.

This short introduction to the information services industry
leads me to the first of four key points I would like to make about
our industry:

First, the information services industry is highly competitive.
This is an intensely competitive industry, born of vigorous entre-
preneurial activity. Just 25 years ago the information services industry was a $15 million business. Now it is a $12.5 billion industry in the United States alone, with over 11,000 firms engaged in
offering the public an ever-increasing number of products and
services.

The revenues of the industry have grown at an average of 25
percent per year compounded and financial analysts expect the same
pace of growth to continue over the next several years.

Processing services is the oldest and largest segment of the industry, supplied by over 4,000 firms generating around $7.3 billion in revenue, or about 60 percent of the entire information services industry's revenues....

Market share by participants in this industry is very small, with no one firm having any significant part of the market. Most leading firms have less than 1 percent of the major segments of the industry.

Second, the information services industry is composed of mostly small firms. As noted in the previous point, the growth of the information services industry is not attributable to the expansion of one or two dominant firms. To the contrary, this industry is a highly diversified one with literally thousands of small firms. In fact, the industry has grown and flourished in the absence of one dominant company.

Today, fewer than 50 industry participants--one-half of 1 percent of all firms--have annual revenues in excess of $25 million. Almost 95 percent of the companies generate less than $2 million in revenues using 1979 figures.

While there is no solid information on barriers to entry, it appears not to be a significant problem for the information services industry as a whole when one considers the large numbers of companies with less than $250,000 in revenues.

Third, the information services industry offers a great diversity of products and services with constant innovations. Due to the high level of competition within our industry, great emphasis has always been placed on technological innovations.

This competitive drive led to considerable time and effort being devoted to reducing our equipment and telecommunications costs, by more efficient use of computer power and communications facilities. These cost savings resulted from technological breakthroughs.

Improvements in data processing and data communications equipment, software and services have, in turn, increased the speed and quality of data processing and remote access information processing.

This diversity of products is necessary to reflect the needs of an ever-increasing number of consumers, since no one package or service could be developed to fit all of a customer's requirements. In short, this range of services and products directly benefit the consumer by keeping competition intense, prices low, and innovations frequent.

The last and most important point is:

Fourth, the information services industry is characterized by a major dependence on telecommunications services. As I mentioned earlier, the largest segment of the information services industry is processing, which comprises $7.3 billion, or just over one-half of the $12.5 billion total revenue.

The major portion of this revenue involves remote batch processing, data base management systems and inquiry systems which are totally dependent on the availability of the high quality, cost efficient basic telecommunications facilities controlled by A.T. & T.

The largest purchased cost items in this type of processing are equipment and telecommunications. Over the past decade, the price of computer equipment has drastically declined, but the cost of telecommunications services is rapidly increasing.

Our processing industry itself has had to come forward with numerous innovations for the use of basic telecommunications services such as private line and local distribution services in order to keep telecommunications costs under control.

For instance, techniques such as packet switching protocols to maximize the amount of data which can be transmitted over a private line were developed and in use by our industry long before these services were offered as communications devices.

Because of our absolute dependence upon A.T. & T. as a supplier, we feel very strongly and perhaps just a little apprehensive about some of the current changes that are being contemplated in that particular segment of our world.

For example, we are looking very carefully at the decision by the FCC in the computer inquiry to allow A.T. & T., the principal and really the only supplier of our life blood, to compete directly against us in information services....

I would like to reiterate that the information services industry is a collection of successful, highly competitive, mostly small firms. Because information is the key element in today's society, our industry has grown from its modest beginnings to become larger than TV broadcasting, larger than the semiconductor manufacturing, and larger than the entire periodical publishing industry. This growth has been spurred by the almost insatiable demand for information services, not only within the United States, but worldwide. This industry can continue to survive and prosper only with the continuation of this free, fair, and open competitive environment. ...

We think that we are in an exciting growth industry. We think we grew rapidly and are prosperous because our principal supplier, A.T. & T. was able to furnish us with effective and efficient communications services.

Testimony, May 20, 1981, U.S. Congress, 97th, 1st session, House of Representatives, Committee on Energy and Commerce, Subcommittee on Telecommunications, Consumer Protection, and Finance, Status of Competition and Deregulation in the Telecommunications Industry. Hearings...., (Washington, D.C.: Government Printing Office, 1981), pp. 314-317.

G.

A MODERN LABOR FORCE

605. "WHY ARE AMERICAN BOYS NOT LEARNING TRADES?" (1900)

The answer, if there was only a single one, must
have been: Because there are too many more socially
attractive ways of succeeding. Recall that these were
the heydays of the Horatio Alger heritage. The writer,
M. P. Higgins, was an engineer from Worcester,
Massachusetts.

The fact that so very few of our best American boys are learning
trades, with a loving intention of working at them, is of the most
important significance. If our larger machine shops are visited,
it will be seen that where apprentices are found, nearly all the
places are filled by boys of foreign parents. I have made inquiries
in several large cities, and I find that only a few shops are able
to offer good opportunities for learning the machinist's trade, and
that there are constantly a large number on the waiting lists. And
that not over one-third or one-quarter of the acceptable apprentices
are American boys. Also, that the American boys are the most unsatisfactory. By following up this surprising statement, I found that
while the American boy has the natural mechanical ability, he lacks
that reliability and vigor which comes from a less delicate home
life. For example, the American mother would offer for the excuse
of her son's tardiness or absence, the fact that Charlie was obliged
to be out late attending to some social obligation, most unobjection-
able in itself, and that he was so sleepy and tired that she had not
the heart to call him to breakfast.
I mention this phase of our American life to show one reason
why more of our boys are not learning trades and becoming leaders in

a very promising field. It seems that the real solid inducements
for learning a trade are being overshadowed by a few imaginary objections. Do not our boys feel that a mechanic must be deprived of
too much time for social enjoyment and leisure, that some of the
refinements of life must be given up, that the garb of a machinist
and his surroundings are not to be desired, and possibly that his
associates will be inferior and undesirable? Add to these the objection of being unable to dress in "purple and fine linen" and keep
the hands clean, and I think we have the principle reasons why
American mechanics are growing proportionately fewer every year.

M. P. Higgins, "Education of Machinists, Foremen, and
Mechanical Engineers," Transactions, American Society of Mechanical
Engineers, XXI (1900), pp. 1119-1120.

606.   SOURCE OF WHITE MILL LABOR (1900)

Of what social class were the Southern whites who
entered cotton mills as laborers? Here is one contemporary answer made by Harry Hammond, who lived on Beach
Island, South Carolina; he was a retired cotton planter
who had written extensively on cotton culture and commerce.
He had been a State supervisor for the Tenth Census.

Q. Does the establishment of these cotton mills take out of
the labor field a great deal of the white labor that used to compete with the black?--A. No; it does not.
Q. Is not the labor of your mills exclusively white?--A. It
is.
Q. What occupation did the white laborers have before they
went into the mills?--A. It is hard to say what occupation they
had. They were managers of little places. The white people were
not doing much actual labor themselves. There is perhaps as much
planting and hoeing and plowing done by white people now since the
mills started, but these other people were owners or overseers or
planters, hiring a little piece of land and tilling it by themselves. I do not think the factories have taken away any of the
owners. They have taken away the overseers and the like of them.

Testimony, Harry Hammond, February 13, 1901, U.S. Congress,
57th, 1st session, House of Representatives, Document No. 179,
Report of the Industrial Commission on Agriculture and Agricultural
Labor, X, p. 833.

607. MILL LABOR RETAINS TIES WITH FARM (1900)

Being a factory hand was still not a life-time
commitment for the surplus farm people in western North
Carolina. This testimony is that of William Graham, a
tobacco and cotton farmer in Machpelah, North Carolina.
He had been a land sales agent for twenty years, had
served in the State Senate, and was currently president of
the North Carolina Farmers' Alliance.

Thirty years ago, almost, I think a larger per cent of the
young men of this section as they grew up emigrated--went South or
West about 1873; from that [time] on, they ceased, and consequently
our country has been filled up with laborers, so there is a much
larger number engaged in agriculture than were formerly. Now it is
very seldom you see a man emigrating.   When the Georgia lands
(Cherokee Indian) were opened, and after that Mississippi and
Louisiana, a great many people of this section of western North
Carolina sold their lands and went to these places, and then we
had a large number of old fields, abandoned lands.
    Q. The cotton mills have drawn very largely on agricultural
labor, have they not?--A. They have.
    Q. So if he is not satisfied with the present conditions, he
has the cotton mills to fall back on?--A. Yes; he not only does
that, but a man will buy a piece of land, contract for it, and rent
that land to some other man, and he will go to the cotton factory
and make the money to pay for it. I know of instances right among
my own people. It is not that they prefer factory labor, but it is
the long credit on farms, sir. That is where it is; wait until the
crop is made before you get anything, while in the factory every
Saturday night you get cash pay.
    Q. And that is the practice?--A. Yes; that is one reason.
    Q. In other words, it is a rather new thing in Southern life
to receive cash payments from week to week?--A. Yes; but the poor
returns from the farm and the large families helped to induce moving
to factories. A family of 10 to 14 is no unusual thing in this
Piedmont section. Where they are only getting from 3 to 5 cents
for cotton, it did not yield enough for his board; and such a man
would take his family and go to the cotton mills.

Testimony, William A. Graham, March 13, 1900, U.S. Congress,
57th, 1st session, House of Representatives, Document No. 179,
Report of the Industrial Commission on Agriculture and Agricultural
Labor, X, p. 435.

608. PATERNALISTIC VIEW OF INDUSTRIALIZATION (ca. 1900)

The following letter was written by one textile
manufacturer, H. R. Fitzgerald, to a second one who had
requested help in opposing the work of the Southern
Industrial Conference, formed in 1927 to expose poor
working conditions and low pay in Southern industries.
Fitzgerald was president of the Dan River Mills; he writes
to W. D. Anderson, who was associated with the Bibb
Manufacturing Company of Georgia.

We built additional mills at intervals of a few years apart
until the Riverside group of seven mills was completed....We then
conceived the idea of developing a water power higher up the river
and of starting the Dan River plant, of which the first mill was
erected about 1902. It so happened that at that time other developments were going forward thruout the South very rapidly and instead
of a large surplus of help we had about digested the supply in our
immediate community, so that it became necessary to develop the
village of Schoolfield. We had to draw upon the mountain districts
of the Piedmont section. I would not now attempt to describe the
conditions that existed among virtually all of these families in
their state of run-down poverty and ignorance, and eking out a precarious existence on mountain farms. Some of the worst cases of
disease and a long chain of evils and vices that had grown into the
their methods of living, were enough to shock the sensibilities of
anyone who loves humanity.
     While it had been our custom to promote educational work among
our cooperatives in the city and to assist in their churches and
social affiliations, we soon recognized that it was a question of
business necessity to begin at the very bottom with day nurseries,
kindergardens, primary departments, as well as district nursing
and medical department, if we were ever to develop a nucleus of
capable and efficient workers. For anyone to have seen their methods of living, cooking and sanitary surroundings they would have
wondered how anyone could live under those circumstances, and it
is true that the death rate was high and the health rate extremely
low.
     Furthermore, they were proud as well as ignorant, and any
attempt to get at them in other than a very practical way would have
been an utter failure. It required several years in which to make
any real progress in this direction, but having laid the foundation
we kept persistently at it and did not hesitate to gradually broaden
and enlarge the scope of our work as fast as circumstances justified....
     After a few years we could begin to see some of the results of
this work, and I may say that after ten or fifteen years we had
virtually succeeded in transforming the entire community and, inci-
dentally, in developing a corps of operatives of intelligence and
efficiency which, in our opinion, has more than repaid all that it
cost, to say nothing of the infinite satisfaction of having had some

small share in the transformation of so many lives and in bringing
happiness and reasonable prosperity to thousands of people who other
otherwise would never have had it.

. . . .

As to the criticism of the mill village and the suggestion
that it represents a system of serfdom, etc., the idea is so ridiculous as to show on its face that the author of the suggestion know
knows nothing about it. I do not suppose there is a more independent or self-asserting class of people anywhere, who know better
what they want or who represent a more genuine type of Democracy
than will be found among the mill villages of the South.

In the first place it would not be possible to meet the housing
situation in any other way, but even if this could be done experience shows that the character of houses that could be rented from
outside parties or that the people would build for themselves are
so much below the standard maintained by the mills that it would
constitute a grave difference in the facilities for homelife.
Furthermore, it would have been impossible to have made the progress
along educational, moral and sanitary lines if the people had been
scattered thruout the city. We find, however, as the years go on
that more and more of our people are disposed to buy small farms
or plots of ground and build homes for themselves, which with their
improved resources and experience after having worked in the mills
for some years enables them to live on a higher basis than they
previously did and we think that this is healthy growth....

Letter, H. R. Fitzgerald to W. D. Anderson, April 13, 1928,
in Robert S. Smith, Mill on the Dan. A History of the Dan River
Mills, 1882-1950, (Durham, North Carolina: Duke University Press,
1960), pp. 242-243, 243-244.

609. THE BLACK A RESERVE AGAINST STRIKES (1900)

Negro labor was demeaned in its choice of jobs and
degraded in its social role. J. P. Coffin, who writes,
was vice-president of the Southern Industrial Convention.
He described himself as having been a newspaperman and "a
large employer of labor in different lines of industry."

Q. What is the real meaning of the expression in your paper
there, of having in the negro of the South a reserve force in case
of strikes and labor troubles and combinations against capital in
the South?--A. The real meaning that I intended to convey was that
he would be a buffer against injustice: that the negro is absolutely loyal to his employer: he is not given to strikes: he does his
work faithfully, and can be depended on. Now, while I do not
believe it is going--in the near future--to be necessary to use this

buffer, in my opinion it is a thing that will keep out much of the
agitation of labor in the South, because the Southern people and
manufacturers of the South will, before they submit to unjust domination by unions, negroize their industries. They will not want
to do this, and they will not do it if labor is at all reasonable.
They do not desire it. Many of them to-day do not think they would
do it under any circumstances, but you bring them to the test, and
it will be done. If labor is reasonable, if labor will work for
anything within reason, white labor will dominate the South forever;
but they will not submit to such outrages as have been frequently
committed by organized labor.

Q. (By Mr. KENNEDY.) That would bring negro domination in
industry then, would it not?--A. It will bring negro domination
of the labor market if labor is unjust.

Q. And the white man will dominate the social and political
conditions of the South, and the negro will dominate the labor market of the South?--A. The negro will never dominate the labor
market of the South, and when I said negro domination, I only had
reference to it as far as negro labor was concerned. In other
words, he would dominate the labor that he did, but would never
dominate the market. The white employer would simply put him in
place of unjust white, probably foreign, labor.

. . . .

You say the negro is the great reserve force, and that the
employers, rather than submit to what you have in mind as an unjust
demand, would negroize their institutions, their factories, etc.
You spoke of them as a reserve force for this purpose. Is he not
really, then, to be held up as a menace over the white labor to make
them understand that they must not make unjust demands, but that
they must submit to the will of the employers in all things?--A.
You could make the same remark about nonunion labor. In other
words, the employer must have something to hold over union organizations, or just turn his business over to the union and let them run
it. Now, I do not say that the manufacturers of the South, if put
to a vote to-day, would say that they would do it, I believe they
would turn me down; but I know the sentiment that they feel and the
sentiment of the people of the South. The people of the South are
not fighting the negro as a negro. They will employ a white man
before they will employ a negro if they can do it; but they do feel
toward the negro that they will put him in if an injustice is done,
and the sentiment of the South will carry that out in the future if
it comes. I hope the day will never come, and I do not think it
will, when the negro will be put in place of the white labor, and
very likely it would be only temporary if he was put in, because
his forte is in the lower grades of labor. I am speaking of the
race as a race, and he has not the mechanical ability that the white
race has.

Testimony, John P. Coffin, June 14, 1900, U.S. Congress, 56th,
2nd session, House of Representatives, Document No. 495, Report
of the Industrial Commission on the Relations and Conditions of
Capital and Labor...., VII, pp. 790-791.

610.   STEEL LABOR POLICY IN THE MAKING (1901)

The Amalgamated Association of Iron, Steel and Tin
Workers was about to present its new wage and recognition
demands. The board of directors of the newly-formed U.S.
Steel Corporation discusses strategy here.

Mr. Converse feels that public opinion would be with us inasmuch as we had not attempted to crush unions but had simply accepted
the various situations as they were; that we had left the management
at the individual plants just as heretofore and advised the local
officers to use their judgement. He pointed out that we are assured
by certain presidents that they can run everything in their nonunion
plants. He firmly believes that the association would never attempt
to call out their men at the plants; that if such were the case he
would be in favor of running all we can and feels certain that the
final result would be entirely in our favor.
    In brief, the position of Mr. Roberts is that if the represen-
tatives come to this corporation they shall be referred to the local
company; that the presidents should not arbitrarily decide, but
rather state that the matter would be considered and an answer given
later; that then it could be taken up by the local board and considered. Mr. Roberts does not believe in establishing a hard and
fast rule until we know what the association wants. When the matter
is actually presented they can then come to a decision. We can then
be positive as to just what is fair and what ought to be done. In
other words, Mr. Roberts does not approve of instructing the presidents to do something before they reach the bridge.
    The president informs the committee that there is in the air a
well defined feeling that the corporation is indifferent as to
fighting the extension of the labor unions.
    On a vote being asked, on the question of whether or not the
members of the committee would approve of fighting the thing out
if a general strike were ordered, of the members the majority voted
affirmatively, one did not vote, another voted in the negative.
Another member stated in reply that he would vote in favor of not
recognizing labor unions anywhere but feels that if 50 per cent of
the works were union it would be rather inconsistent not to recognize them in the other 50 per cent.
    After some further discussion Mr. Converse put this proposi-
tion:
    That as a matter of fact it is not a question of finessing the
situation except up to a certain point; that the very worst the
association can do is with about 33 1/3 per cent and he believes
it will not do it with that low percentage; that if our president
says to the presidents that they will please understand that the
United States Steel Corporation did not exist, they will be very
careful not to get into trouble.
    This met the unqualified approval of the president, Mr. Steele,
and Mr. Reid.

Mr. Roberts objects to the situation being thrust upon us that fast. Before the association comes forward, we should make a positive announcement as to what we would do or not do. The following suggestion brought forth by Mr. Steele was finally voted upon and the president instructed to convey it to the president:

That we are unalterably opposed to any extension of union labor and advise subsidiary companies to take firm position when these questions come up and say that they are not going to recognize it, that is, any extension of unions in mills where they do not now exist; that great care should be used to prevent trouble and that they promptly report and confer with this corporation.

Minutes, meeting of the executive committee of the U.S. Steel Corporation, June 17, 1901, U.S. Congress, House of Representatives, [Stanley] Committee on Investigation of United States Steel Corporation, <u>United States Steel Corporation</u>, pp. 3830-3831.

611. "HEY, BIG SHOT, NO MORE SPEAK HUNGARIAN?" (1904)

A constructive and gayer aspect of the immigrant worker written by Charles Eisler who later organized the Eisler Engineering Company of Newark, New Jersey. Between 1916 and 1958, he patented fifty-seven inventions useful in the production of tubes and light bulbs.

When the train pulled into East Pittsburgh there were about eight boys and girls from Budapest waiting for me; we spent the next hour recounting experiences. Then I was taken to Sandor's house, where his mother gave me breakfast. A room had been prepared for me. After some more visiting, I got my first instructions on how to look for work. I would have to purchase a thirty-dollar tool kit, which I could pay out at a dollar a week. I was told that it would not be necessary to learn English since all foremen were either Hungarian or German and I spoke both languages.

Early the next morning I went to the Westinghouse employment office. I saw about nine hundred people waiting to be called and I said to myself, "What are my chances here with so many people standing in line looking for work? I'm still a greenhorn and the old-timers will come first, <u>if</u> there is any work." Suddenly the employment man opened the office door and yelled out, "Are there any toolmakers here?" I raised my hand; my heart was pounding so I could not talk. When I was called into the office I was so excited that what little English I had learned was forgotten. He questioned me in German, asking what I did in Hungary, if I had any toolmaking experience and if I could make working drawings, etc. I was given an examination, which I passed, and then I was told to report the next day for work at 7 A.M.

. . . .

Apparently all the factory workers came from Europe; I saw no Americans in the plant. German, Hungarian, Polish were the languages spoken, with little or no English. We all got along well together, since every one was happy to be working at all,

. . . .

Of course, the skilled toolmaker was at a premium. Just the word toolmaker or tool draftsman got you a job in almost any factory in the country with no difficulty. It was the beginning of the tooling age, so to speak.

A knowledge of English was unimportant, since all the tool-makers were foreigners or sons of foreigners--Germans, Poles, etc. In fact, if you did speak some English in the factory, your fellow greenhorns would be quick to spot you: "Hey, big shot, no more can speak Hungarian? What's the matter, ashamed to talk your mother tongue?"

The Europeans dominated the field of good mechanics because of the European apprentice system, in which every boy participated from an early age and thus received a very thorough training.

Charles Eisler, The Million-Dollar Bend. The Autobiography of the Benefactor of the Radio Tube and Lamp Industry, (New York: The William-Frederick Press, 1960), pp. 58-59.

612. NATIONALITIES, LANGUAGES, AND UNIONS (1904)

Nationality and language differences have often been designated as important reasons for the slow growth of American unions. It would be interesting to measure the extent to which such differences were nur-tured by interested parties, as in the following example reported by John Commons, an economist, with a special interest in labor.

I visited the employment office of Swift and Company. I saw, seated on benches around the office, a sturdy group of blond-haired Nordics. I asked the employment agent, How come it you are employ-ing only Swedes? He answered, Well, you see, it is only for this week. Last week we employed Slovaks. We change about among differ-ent nationalities and languages. It prevents them from getting to-gether. We have the thing systematized. We have a luncheon each week of the employment managers of the large firms of the Chicago district. There we discuss our problems and exchange information. We have a number of men in the field, some of them officers of labor organizations. They keep us informed about what is going on. If agitators are coming in or expected, and there is considerable un-rest among the labor population, we raise the wages around 10 per

cent. It is wonderful to watch the effect. The unrest stops and
the agitators leave. Then when things quiet down we reduce the
wages to where they were.

        John R. Commons, "Introduction" to Don D. Lescohier and
Elizabeth Brandeis, History of Labor in the United States, 1896-
1932, (New York: The Macmillan Company, 1935), p. XXV.

        613. CONTRIBUTORY NEGLIGENCE ON THE JOB (1904)

        After countless examples like the following one,
an organized movement arose to change the old common-
law conception of contributory negligence. Starting
with Wisconsin, by 1917 only eight states lacked a
workmen's compensation act levying financial accountability upon the employer. At the time, Ching, who writes,
worked for the Boston Elevated. Much later, he was in
charge of labor relations for the U.S. Rubber Company
and after that, Director of the Federal Mediation and
Conciliation Service.

        In 1904, four years after I came to Boston, I had advanced from
motorman to the position of trouble-shooter in the repair of electric railway equipment. This job was twelve hours a day, seven days
a week, and the pay was $18.50 per week.
        One warm day in August, the height of the afternoon rush-hour
found me working rather hurriedly to fix a loose shoe fuse on a
stalled train. Standing on a dry board, I gripped a wire carrying
5,000 amperes and began to twist it off--a clear case of contributory negligence or recklessness. My clothes were wet with sweat,
and while leaning over, my rump touched the damp wall of the tunnel.
The initial shock threw me off balance, I slipped and grabbed a
steel truss rod with my free hand. Then, the full power of the
voltage flashed through my body, enveloping me in blue flame. It
blew the circuit-breakers in the powerhouse and stopped the entire
subway and elevated system.
        When the police arrived, they found all my hair and my clothes
burned off. My body was charred. They wrapped me in blankets and
carried me to the nearest hospital in a horse-drawn ambulance.
        Six days later I regained consciousness--in the DT ward. The
doctors, not expecting me to live, had put me there to get me out
of the way. They now gave me a chance to live, although they
thought I would be permanently blinded. Actually, I was completely
recovered in about four months. A rugged constitution plus kind
attention of nurses and doctors worked miracles. My body still
bears scars of the near electrocution, and the memory of it is
still as vivid with me as though it happened yesterday.

As it turned out, that terrible experience did more to chart my career than anything else that ever happened. Some friends inquired and came to see me while I was recovering, in the hospital, but as far as I know, no one from the company ever called. From the minute the news of the accident came into company headquarters I was off the payroll. It was simple, and the truth, for them to say my negligence caused the accident. Although not very humanitarian, it was the practice of the times. I not only lost over four months' pay, but I had to foot the doctor bills. There was no recourse for me under the laws of those days.

Cyrus S. Ching, <u>Review and Reflection, A Half-Century of Labor Relations</u>, (New York: B. C. Forbes, 1953), pp. 9-10.

614. COLLECTIVE BARGAINING, 1905 STYLE

At this time, Chicago was perhaps the most unionized large city in the country.

Can a man buy clothing for himself and his family, school books for the children and pay doctor's bills on 3 cents a day? The Chicago representative of the Standard Oil Company, the richest, and most powerful monopoly in the world, said yesterday that was a problem for the 3-cent-a-day man to work out for himself.

The views of the Standard Oil representative came to light when a committee acting for seventy teamsters stood before him and pleaded for an increase in wages which would enable them to meet the necessities of life. The rule of supply and demand stood in their way and they were turned away, with the resort to a strike as the only hope of obtaining a single concession.

The committee was sent by the Oil Wagon Drivers' Union, and the employer was the Standard Oil Company. Holding in his hand a table showing the daily cost of living for an oil wagon driver and his family, James Duffy, business agent for the union and spokesman of the committee, explained to Manager Hurd of the company and his assistant, J. C. Cleverton, who gave them a hearing, that after the bare means of existence are paid for there remained but 3 cents a day for shoes, clothing and other necessities for a family.

"Our drivers are only getting $2 a day, which is entirely insufficient. We are asking for a minimum scale of $75 a month, and I am sure we are entitled to it." He then handed Manager Hurd the following table, showing the cost of living for an average family as computed from reports made by members of the union:

```
Rent..............................50 cents
Food..............................75 cents
Fuel..............................30 cents
Light............................. 7 cents
Car fare..........................10 cents
Extra meal for driver.............25 cents
                Total          $1.97
```

"I want to ask you if you think you could support a family on the wages our drivers are getting?" said Duffy to Manager Hurd.

"I must confess that I don't believe I could," replied the latter, looking up from the table which he had been scanning.

"Our figures show that after paying expenses that must be met there remains but 3 cents a day for doctor's bills, children's school books, gloves, clothing and other necessities. You should remember that the oil wagon driver has to pay 25 cents a day for an extra meal and 10 cents for car fare, leaving but $1.65 for the daily support of himself and family."

"Many teamsters pay but 15 cents for their extra meals," said Manager Hurd. "As for granting a wage increase I want to say we can get plenty of drivers at $2 a day, and under the circumstances we will be compelled to refuse your demand."

Chicago Record Herald, November 21, 1905.

615. A PIONEER IN INDUSTRIAL MEDICINE (1910)

Alice Hamilton, a twentieth-century pioneer in a branch of applied science, whose whole life was continual exploration, wrote the following extract.

Thirty-two years ago, in 1910, I went as a pioneer into a new, unexplored field of American medicine, the field of industrial disease.

. . . .

American medical authorities had never taken industrial diseases seriously, the American Medical Associations had never held a meeting on the subject, and while European journals were full of articles on industrial poisoning, the number published in American medical journals up to 1910 could be counted on one's fingers.

. . . .

As I look back, some striking pictures come to me of that anarchic period. One is the picture of the works manager of a big white-lead plant, a gentleman of breeding and something of a philanthropist. He is looking at me indignantly and exclaiming, "Why, that sounds as if you think that when a man gets lead poisoning in my plant I ought to be held responsible!" Another is that of a

Hungarian woman at Hull-House, telling me of a terrible accident in
a steel mill on the South Shore in which her husband had been injured. He and the other victims were being held incommunicado in
the company hospital. No one was allowed to see them, she knew
nothing except that her husband was not dead. It took a formal protest from the Austro-Hungarian Consul to the State Department to
change that system.

It was not that employers were brutal. They really did not
know what was happening in their plants, for there was no system of
workmen's compensation to open their eyes to the hazards and to
force safety measures. The workman might sue for damages, and that
fact led to the sort of secrecy the steel industry and other big
concerns practised. But even if he was seriously injured, it was
hard for him to get past the strong defenses erected by law for the
employer: the "assumption of risk," which meant that he had deliberately chosen to run the risk inherent in the job; or the "negligence of a fellow workman," which meant that he, not the employer,
was responsible for the carelessness of the other employees. When
we wonder why the workers did not rebel, we must remember that big
industry employed almost exclusively immigrant labor at that time.
In the heavy industries especially, the rule was to work the men as
hard as possible--the seven-day week and twelve-hour day continued
in steel until 1922--pay them as low wages as possible, and then,
to put it down with force, discharge and blacklist the trouble-
makers, and start afresh with a new lot of immigrants. In this, it
must be added, the heavy industries were greatly helped by the
courts of law and by the state constabulary forces.

Many times in those early days I met men who employed foreign-
born labor because it was cheap and submissive, and then washed the
their hands of all responsibility for accidents and sickness in the
plant, because, as they would say: "What can you do with a lot of
ignorant Dagoes, Wops, Hunkies, Greasers? You couldn't make them
wash if you took a shotgun to them." They deliberately chose such
men because it meant no protest against low wages and wretched
housing and dangerous work, no trouble with union agents; but
rather a surplus of eager, undemanding labor. They wanted to have
men whom they could deal with as if they were children, but in that
case they should have treated them with the protective care and
patient guidance that children are entitled to. They had all the
advantages of the system; they took, for the most part, none of the
responsibilities that it entailed.

Exploring the Dangerous Trades. The Autobiography of Alice
Hamilton, M.D., (Boston, Massachusetts: Little, Brown & Co., 1943),
pp. 3, 4-5.

616. IMMIGRANTS GET THE LEAST DESIRABLE JOBS (1910)

Between 1900 and 1910, over 9 million gainful
workers were added to the work force. During the same
period, more than 3.1 million foreign-born persons were
added to those already here. These changes in the labor
market powered a steady, patterned structure of employment,
as the following illustrates. There was very little of
a churning-up process at work.

In the first place, a larger proportion of native Americans and
older immigrant employees from Great Britain and northern Europe
have left certain industries, such as bituminous and anthracite coal
mining and iron and steel manufacturing. In the second place, a
part of the earlier employees, as already pointed out, who remained
in the industries in which they were employed before the advent of
the southern and eastern European have been able, because of the
demand growing out of the general industrial expansion, to attain
to the more skilled and responsible technical and executive positions which required employees of training and experience. In the
larger number of cases, where the older employees remained in a
certain industry after the pressure of the competition of the recent
immigrant had begun to be felt, they relinquished their former occupations and segregated themselves in certain occupations. This tendency is best illustrated by the distribution of employees according
to race in the bituminous coal mines. In this industry all the so-
called "company" occupations, which are paid on the basis of a
daily, weekly, or monthly rate, are occupied by native Americans or
older immigrants and their children, while the southern and eastern
Europeans are confined to pick mining and to the unskilled and
common labor. The same situation exists in iron and steel and glass
manufacturing, the textile manufacturing industries, and in all
divisions of manufacturing enterprise. It is largely due to the
stigma which has become attached to the fact of working in the same
occupations as the southern and eastern Europeans that in some cases, as in the bituminous coal-mining industry, has led to the segre-
gation of the older class of employees in occupations, which, from
the standpoint of compensation, are less desirable than those
occupied by recent immigrants. In most industries the native
Americans and older immigrant workmen who have remained in the same
occupations as those in which the recent immigrants are predominant
are made up of the thriftless, unprogressive elements of the original operating forces. The third striking feature resulting from
the competition of southern and eastern Europeans is seen in the
fact that in the case of most industries, such as iron and steel,
textile, and glass manufacturing and the different forms of mining,
the children of native Americans and older immigrants from Great
Britain and nothern Europe are not entering the industries in which
their fathers have been employed. All kinds of manufacturers claim
that they are unable to secure a sufficient number of native-born
employees to insure the development of the necessary number of

workmen to fill the positions of skill and responsibility in their
establishments. This condition of affairs is attributable to three
factors: (1) General or technical education has enabled a considerable number of the children of the industrial workers of the
passing generation to command business, professional, or technical
occupations more desirable than those of their fathers; (2) the
conditions of work which the employment of recent immigrants have
largely made possible has rendered certain industrial occupations
unattractive to the prospective wage-earner of native birth; and
(3) occupations other than those in which southern and eastern
Europeans are engaged are sought for the reason that popular opinion
attaches to them a more satisfactory social status and a higher
degree of respectability.

U.S. Congress, 61st, 2nd session, Senate, Document No. 633,
Reports of the Immigration Commission, Part 23, Summary Report on
Immigrants in Manufacturing and Mining, I, pp. 49-50.

617. CONVICT LABOR IN ALABAMA MINES (1911)

In Alabama, convicts were contracted out to the
highest bidder. In 1911, the Tennessee Coal and Iron
Co., part of the U.S. Steel Corporation, paid the
county or state from $10.50 to $46.00 per month per man.
When not working, the men lived in a company-owned prison.
One reliable observer estimated the value of the daily
food ration for the miner-convicts at 15 cents. This is
the testimony of Shelby Harrison, a writer for Survey
Magazine, who had investigated the treatment of convicts
in Alabama during May and June, 1911.

The CHAIRMAN. What is the advantage--I wish you would explain
it--from an industrial standpoint of working these inexperienced
and unfortunate creatures, instead of using experienced miners?
That is a business requiring some experience and skill, is it not?
    Mr. HARRISON. Mining does not require the same skill not that
it used to, because machine workers come in thoroughly; but there
are several advantages. One is that in the case of the State convicts they are obtained for at least the same price as free labor,
and in some cases slightly less.
    In the case of the county convicts, they are obtained for from
8 to 10 per cent less than the current free-labor rate in the
district. In the course of a year that saving amounts to something.
    Another reason is that the convict labor is very regular.
    In the Birmingham district a great deal of the common labor
is done by negroes, and most of the large companies have to keep
from 50 to 75 per cent larger number of negroes on the pay roll than

they expect to be working from day to day, in order to keep the regular equipment on hand.

In the case of the convict labor, 300 men, for instance, go to sleep at night, and 300 men get up the next day and are ready for work, and are ready for work the next day and the next day throughout the year of 310 days. It is regular. I was told by a number of employers that that was one of the greatest things they liked about it.

The third reason is that it is a block toward the growth of labor unions in the district. I was told by a number of employers that is hindered the labor unions, because men in the convict mines could not strike. If they quit work they could be beaten for it.

Mr. YOUNG. That is, the convicts?

Mr. HARRISON. Yes. When free labor has a grievance which it wishes to make emphatic by some kind of united front in the district, the convict camps grind out their regular quota from day to day, and they take the edge off of the protest that free labor makes. In other words, they furnish a nucleus of coal for operating during labor troubles.

The CHAIRMAN. Did you ever discuss this with any of the officers of the steel corporations who also operate steel plants as well as coal mines for the same of merchantable coal?

Mr. HARRISON. I did.

The CHAIRMAN. What did they say about it?

Mr. HARRISON. The president of the Tennessee Co. told me frankly that he thought that the employing of convict labor in the district was a block toward unionism. He was fair-minded enough, however, to say that he thought that they ought not to have that leverage over the unions.

The CHAIRMAN. Do you know anything about whether this character of labor was so employed during the strike of 1908?

Mr. HARRISON. It was employed, and a number of men in the district told me that they believed that that was one of the factors in driving out unionism from the coal mines of Alabama in 1908.

Testimony, Shelby M. Harrison, February 7, 1912, U.S. Congress, House of Representatives, [Stanley] Committee on Investigation of United States Steel Corporation, United States Steel Corporation, p. 2982.

618. DISCIPLINING CONVICT COAL MINERS (1911)

This is testimony on the degraded character of labor relations under prison conditions.

Mr. HARRISON. There are three methods of keeping the men up to their tasks:

If he fails to get out his required task and does not have a sufficient excuse, he can be strapped, flogged.

If he persistently fails, and that kind of treatment does not correct his failures, he can be put in solitary confinement for 30 days on a bread-and-water diet, providing that after the third day the State physician examines him and decides that his physical condition would permit of that kind of treatment.

The third method is of course the better one of the three. A bonus is offered, or a payment to the convicts for coal mined above their required task.

In the camps of State convicts the bonus is approximately the free-labor rate. In the camps of the county convicts it is about half the free-labor rate.

Mr. STERLING. Do some of them make money out of that?

Mr. HARRISON. And some of them, by reason of that method, draw something for their extra work.

The CHAIRMAN. What sort of a delicate instrument do they use for the flogging--a peach-tree switch, or something like that?

Mr. HARRISON. I saw one strap which was made out of leather about 5 feet long, three-ply leather, and had a wooden handle on it.

The CHAIRMAN. Three-ply? Three different thicknesses of leather? That is what would make a good tug for a wagon harness?

Mr. HARRISON. It much resembles a tug.

. . . .

Mr. DANFORTH. I understand you to state the State has its wardens and guards there, who have charge of these men, or supervision of the State prisoners?

Mr. HARRISON. Of the State prisoners; yes, sir.

Mr. DANFORTH. And the same with the county prisoners? Do they have their own county officials?

Mr. HARRISON. The wardens and guards of the county convicts are employees of the company, but approved by the State Board of Convict Inspectors.

The CHAIRMAN. So that the Tennessee Coal & Iron Co. whips its own convicts whenever it is necessary?

Mr. HARRISON. As I say, the warden who does the whipping is an employee of the company.

Testimony, Shelby M. Harrison, February 7, 1912, U.S. Congress, House of Representatives, [Stanley] Committee on Investigation of United States Steel Corporation, United States Steel Corporation, pp. 2969-2970, 2971.

619. A DEFENSE OF SOLDIERING ON THE JOB (1912)

As mass-production techniques spread throughout industry, production potentials rose swiftly. In order for employers to realize the fullest advantage from such plenty,

systems of piece-work were introduced. As
productivity rose, pay rates per unit of output
fell. The workers resorted to soldiering. (See
Source No. 629).

Now, gentlemen, I have no sympathy whatever with the black-
guarding that workmen are receiving from a good deal of the community; there are a great many people who look upon them as greedy,
selfish, grasping, and even worse, but I don't sympathize with this
view in the least. They are not different in the least from any
other class in the community; they are no more grasping and selfish,
nor are they less so than other classes of people. It may be a
debatable question as to whether they are or are not more grasping
than other people. There is one thing, however, we can be perfectly sure of and that is, whatever else they are or they are not, they
are not fools. And let me tell you that a workman, after having received one cut of that sort in his wages as a reward for turning
out a larger day's work, is a very extraordinary man if he doesn't
adopt soldiering and deliberately going slow instead of fast as a
permanent policy so as to keep his employer from speeding him up and
then cutting his piecework price. I soldiered when I was a workman,
and I believe that even many of the most sensible workmen, understanding the conditions as I have outlined them, will inevitably
adopt the policy of going slow. Under those conditions it would
take an exceedingly broadminded man to do anything else than adopt
soldiering as his permanent policy. I will not say that this
soldiering is the best policy for the workman to adopt, even for
his own best interest in the long run, but I do say that I do not
blame him for doing it. In spite of the miserable policy of cutting
piecework prices when men increase their output, I believe that
those workmen who do not adopt the policy of restraining output
and going slow, i.e., soldiering, will in the end be far better off
than those who soldier. Certainly, this whole situation is no fault
of theirs; they didn't introduce the system which makes soldiering
seem to be necessary, and if blame rests anywhere it certainly does
not rest with the working people, but somewhere else.

Testimony, Frederick W. Taylor, January 25, 1912, U.S.
Congress, Special Committee to Investigate the Taylor and Other
Systems of Shop Management, The Taylor and other Systems of Shop
Management, III, (Washington, D.C.: Government Printing Office,
1912), p. 1386.

620. THE TWELVE HOUR WORKDAY IN STEEL (1912)

In 1914, ninety-five percent of all manufacturing
workers labored 60 or fewer hours in a normal week. In
the steel industry, however, the normal work day was 12

hours and the week, six to seven days. Two factors
conditioning this anomaly were: (1) the extraordinarily
high degree of immigrants in the steel plants, and (2) the
weakness or absence of unionism in the industry. Percival
Roberts testifies. Roberts had been in the iron business
since 1876; had been president of the American Bridge
Company, and was currently a member of the board of directors and finance committee of the U.S. Steel Corporation.

When I first entered the iron business, steel was practically
unknown, except for purposes of railroad rails and tools. The blast
furnace was operated 7 days a week, 12 hours a turn. The unit of
activity in rolling mills was then the puddling furnace. Those men
operated on the night shift, 5 nights a week, 21 hours; and on the
the day turn they operated 6 days a week, 12 hours; the finishing
departments did the same. They were all 12-hour turns.

The introduction of steel extended the continued processes
beyond the blast furnace, in making iron. The blast furnace made
cold pig-iron, which was transported, possibly, many miles to the
puddling mills and finishing mills.

There was no dependence of one upon the other. By the use of
steel a continuous process was formed from the melting of the
pig-iron until the finished article was produced. Hence all these
subsequent processes became more or less dependent upon the running
of the blast furnace and continuity of their operations was necessarily increased.

So that we find that, prior to 1900, many of the mills operated
not only six days of the week, but the six nights of the week, ex-
cepting Saturday night. They would commence Sunday night, and end
their work Saturday, at 6 o'clock in the afternoon.

Such was the situation upon the formation of the Steel
Corporation.
. . . .
I think that one man in a certain occupation can work 12 hours
alongside of another man who is working 10 hours. My experience
is that I have seen no ill effects from that 12-hour labor. I must
confess I see no worse effects on the part of the 12-hour men than
I have seen among the 10-hour men.

In other words, those men that work 10 hours a day I do not
think have any brighter, happier homes than the men who work 12
hours a day; not a particle.

You may take extreme instances in both cases and you may present very sad results, undoubtedly, but then, you can find just the
contrary. Human nature varies very much in that respect.
. . . .
The CHAIRMAN. The 12-hour day is not a natural law, is it?
The 12-hour day, seven days in the week; do you think that is a
natural law, ordained by God or nature?

Mr. ROBERTS. It is a law of nature that men must subsist.
What brings these men to this country is that they expect to find
better conditions than those under which they have existed in the

countries they are leaving. I see no reason for this immense immigration we are having unless conditions in this country are better than those which they leave at home.

Testimony, Percival Roberts, Jr., February 14, 1912, U.S. Congress, House of Representatives, [Stanley] Committee on Investigation of United States Steel Corporation, United States Steel Corporation, pp. 3260, 3264, 3265.

621. VOLUNTARY WAGE CUTS SLOW MECHANIZATION (1914)

Fifteen years earlier, the same union official had testified about mechanization in his trade. (See Source No. 397). The Union hoped now, as then, to save the mere job, let alone the wage-standards, of its members. The speaker, Denis A. Hayes, had been president of the Glass Bottle Blowers' Association for eighteen years.

Mr. HAYES. You see your trade going from you. You see men set out in the street. You see a machine that can make bottles 50 per cent cheaper than the blower. You see them putting up million-dollar plants, and going to market and selling their ware $1 cheaper than the blown article. And then you see that you have not got very long to live as trade unions, and you have got to act quickly. Now, the only practical thing under the circumstances that we could see to do is...reduce the difference in the cost between the hand-made bottle and the automatic machine made bottle; to bring the cost closer. And if you could bring this cost closer you would be prolonging the life of the blown ware manufacturer and give the blower a longer period to work at his trade, and as time will go on some change or circumstances would happen that would give you an opportunity to still keep the blowers employed. So we took a 20 per cent reduction in 1909. Two years ago we took another reduction of 20 per cent, which figured up amounts to 38 per cent (36 per cent). That is pretty hard. Our men made good wages before the reductions. The glass blowers made from $6 to $18 and $20 a day. Of course they were only the exception--the $18 and $20 men. That was for carboys and demijohns. But $8 and $10 were about the average wages for a glass-bottle blower. So by reducing it this difference in cost, there has been a check put to the installation of automatic machinery. Other manufacturers have come into the trade with other means that will employ blowers that are cheaper in construction and which do not require specially built plants. And notwithstanding that those machines will make 14 pint beer bottles in a minute and make 29 pint flasks in a minute, and make 400 gross of 1-ounce bottles in 24 hours, we have 7,000 men at work to-day and they are averaging from $4.50 to $5 a day.

It is hard medicine to swallow about this reduction in wages, but it was either do that or go out of the business.

Commissioner LENNON. You mean $4.50 for the days they work?

Mr. HAYES. Four dollars and fifty cents to $5 a day for the days they work.

Testimony, Denis A. Hayes, June 27, 1914, U.S. Congress, 64th, 1st session, Senate, Document No. 214, Final Report and Testimony Submitted to Congress by the Commission on Industrial Relations, III, p. 3016.

622. INSIDE CONTRACTING AT BALDWIN'S (1914)

Inside contracting was, in some industries, a transitional step towards direct wage-employment by a capitalist employer. Special circumstances seem to have been the primary explanation of the system. It is improbable that the system was in general use. The testimony is that of Alba B. Johnson who was president of the Baldwin Locomotive Works, and employing some 18,000 workers in Philadelphia; and John M. Tobin, an international vice-president of the International Brotherhood of Blacksmiths and Helpers. He had worked as a blacksmith for twelve years in the Baldwin plant.

Mr. JOHNSON. As I said, we have two classes of pieceworkers. Such operations as can be handled best be a group of men collectively, as joint pieceworkers, that we call a contract. There are other men who will take a contract or a particular piece of work individually. Those are pieceworkers. Some operations, for instance, would require at least 200 men or more on a contract. There we would have contractors employ their men, subject to our supervision; that is, we employ the men and they are applied or assigned to their contract.

Mr. BUSIEK. You employ the men and they work for these various contractors?

Mr. JOHNSON. They work for these various contractors and have their share in the proceeds of the contract.

Mr. BUSIEK. Have they any accounting committee? The contractor is paid--is he paid a flat price for the contract?

Mr. JOHNSON. They all receive a rate per hour--the contractor as well as his workmen. When the work is completed and the volume of work turned out is known, then the contractor is credited with whatever surplus there may be, and he divides that according to his own arrangements with the men who are joined with him.

Mr. BUSIEK. Where does this surplus come from, if there is any?

Mr. JOHNSON. It comes from the piecework rate being higher than the hour rate.

Mr. BUSIEK. And the contractor himself makes a private or individual agreement, then, with the men under him?

Mr. JOHNSON. Subject to the approval of his foremen.

Mr. BUSIEK. Subject to the approval of his foreman; and the contractor--how much money can he make out of it? Is he just an ordinary workman, or---

Mr. JOHNSON. Well, the contractors, as a rule, are ordinary workmen. They are highly skilled workmen who, by reason of their experience and proficiency, are better able to organize the work and get out quantity than a less intelligent workman would be. Therefore, by reason of their organizing ability they become, in effect, supervisors of their fellow workmen, and they share in the profits of the contract. Their share is naturally larger than that of the subordinate workmen.

Mr. BUSIEK. For instance, if a contractor can get men under him to agree to work at the hour rate, and they can turn out goods at the piecework rate far in excess of the hour rate, if it is possible for him to make such an arrangement with the men, would he get all the profit over the hour rate?

Mr. JOHNSON. Theoretically, yes; but, practically, no. Theoretically, he would--whether it has ever been done or not, I can not answer, because I am not sufficiently familiar with the working out of it. Practically, the workmen share with the contractors.

. . . .

Mr. BUSIEK. In this system of contract employment about what percentage of your employed worked under the contract system?

Mr. JOHNSON. As principals or as parts of contractors, I should guess roughly about 75 per cent. The great majority of our men are associated in contracts.

Mr. BUSIEK. Do any of the contractors account to the company for any excess profits over a certain amount that they may make?

Mr. JOHNSON. None whatever; everything that they make belongs to them.

Mr. BUSIEK. Are the contractors all skilled men in their lines?

Mr. JOHNSON. They are the most skilled men.

Mr. BUSIEK. They are the most skilled men?

Mr. JOHNSON. Yes.

Mr. BUSIEK. Is there any opportunity for any person who is not an expert mechanic in a line in which the men under him are working to become a contractor under your plan?

Mr. JOHNSON. Well, in the first place, we select the contractors because of their knowledge of the business; and, in the second place, because of their organizing ability.

Mr. BUSIEK. Are they all selected from among the workers?

Mr. JOHNSON. Yes; all from among the workmen. Any workman who has the qualifications can become a contractor.

. . . .

Mr. TOBIN. As to the contract system there, I had better illustrate. It is like I buy you a set of tools and equip you with

some machinery and put a roof over them and give you the tools and
supply you with all the work you can do and tell you to go ahead
and do it. That is your contract. And I come along and hire with
you and you put me to work and give me just what you think you can
give to keep me on that job; and if I insisted on piecework, you
wouldn't want to give me piecework but you would give me the most
unprofitable work to do; but if you gave me piecework you would put
the price on it yourself. You would be working in conjunction with
the foreman.

And I want to say that the foreman, in many instances, is
under obligations to the contractor, and many times the contractor
is the foreman's relative, as, for instance, in one shop, there is
a machinist--or in one part of the machine shop there is a foreman
there who brings in his cousin or some relation that is a baker
and makes him a contractor in the machine shop.

Mr. BUSIEK. What department?

Mr. TOBIN. Another one is a butcher, and he puts him in
there as a foreman.

Mr. BUSIEK. What departments were those?

Mr. TOBIN. Well, that is in the machine shop.

Mr. BUSIEK. How long ago was that?

Mr. TOBIN. Well, that is within the last two or three years--
three years, and in the blacksmith shop the contractor brings his
son in and then presumes that his work is too heavy for him to do
and he needs a partner in it, and his son is made a partner in the
contract with him.

Mr. BUSIEK. We are talking too much about contracts without
understanding particularly what that system is.

Mr. TOBIN. Just as I told you, buying a man a lot of tools and
machinery and putting him to work and telling him that is yours,
make what you can of it. Just that.

Mr. BUSIEK. Well, supposing you are working in the Baldwin
plant as a blacksmith?

Mr. TOBIN. Yes.

Mr. BUSIEK. You say the plant furnishes you with your tools?

Mr. TOBIN. Yes; if I am the right fellow.

Mr. BUSIEK. If you are the right fellow?

Mr. TOBIN. Yes.

Mr. BUSIEK. And they give you a certain stunt to do--that
is, a certain amount of work to do, for which you receive a certain
price?

Mr. TOBIN. No. As Mr. Johnson said yesterday, there is an
evolution taking place every year in locomotives, and I am doing a
certain kind of work--I have got the contract in the blacksmith shop
of the radius bars, the crossties, the slays, and valve yokes and
things like that. I employ men to do it, and I pay those men just
what I can get them for to do it.

Mr. BUSIEK. What you can get them for? Why, doesn't the
Baldwin Locomotive Works make the arrangement with the man as to
how much they are to be paid?

Mr. TOBIN. No. We ask them to put even the price on the back
of the sketch. They agree to it, but the foremen later on say
that one man would know what the other man was getting for the work,

and the foremen later on eliminated that because it left everybody
know what the price was in each contract; it was too fair. The
proposition is that one man gets a price on a job and another man
gets less, and you lose your job if you tell the other fellow what
you got.

Mr. BUSIEK. You make an individual agreement then with the----
Mr. TOBIN. With the contractor--that is, if you will stand
for it.

. . . .

Mr. TOBIN. No, sir; he gives me a job to do; he says, "Tobin,
here is an order for 25 sets of radius bars to make. You make 25
sets. They are $7 a piece." Now, I get $7 a piece for every one of
them I make. It is none of my business what he makes. If he gets
$10 a piece for it, that is his business; I get none of that. If
I am working on such work and he says, "I will pay you $4 a day,"
he pays me $4 a day, irrespective of what he makes; if he made
$1,000 a day he would not give me more than $4 a day.

Commissioner O'CONNELL. There is no printed schedule or anything published or posted as to the prices paid in the Baldwin
establishment?

Mr. TOBIN. No, sir.

Commissioner O'CONNELL. Nobody knows, prior to the time a
contract is given him, what the price is going to be or what it was
formerly for a similar contract?

Mr. TOBIN. Unless you did the business yourself.

. . . .

Commissioner LENNON. Now, in regard to this surplus, if there
is any, under that contract, do you deny that that is divided among
the men under the contract?

Mr. TOBIN. Yes, sir.

Testimony, Alba B. Johnson, June 24, 1914, and John M. Tobin,
June 25, 1914, U.S. Congress, 64th, 1st session, Senate, Document
No. 415, Final Report and Testimony Submitted to Congress by the
Commission on Industrial Relations, III, pp. 2822, 2823, 2838-2839,
2845, and 2847.

623. ON THE DOCKS IN LIVERPOOL AND NEW YORK (1914)

The "shape-up" in New York and the "hiring-hall"
in Liverpool, is here described by Timothy Carroll, a
25 year old longshoreman who had started work in Liverpool
at 16, and had come to America at 22.

Mr. BARNES. Now, tell us something about the way the longshoremen are hired in Liverpool.
Mr. CARROLL. Well---

Mr. BARNES (interrupting).   Compare it with here.   Do you go down in front of the pier?

Mr. CARROLL.   We go down in front of the pier at the present moment: I am speaking of the present moment now.

Mr. BARNES.   Yes.

Mr. CARROLL.   You go down in front of the pier at 7 o'clock, and you shape.   Well, if you don't catch on, if you don't cop, as the saying is, you go to what they call a "clay house."   You have got to be at that "clay house" at a quarter of 8, and if the stevedore is short of men, he has got to go to that clearing house and get the men.

Mr. BARNES.   Wait one minute.   When you shape at 7 o'clock in front of the pier, all the men the foreman thinks necessary are taken.   Is that so?

Mr. CARROLL.   They are taken on at that time.

Mr. BARNES.   Then you go to the clearing house?

Mr. CARROLL.   Then you go to the clearing houses, and if there are any stevedores short, and the men who have already shaped off, if he is short men or sends a stevedore, or comes to the clearing house himself, and he orders the men he wants in the clearing house.

Mr. BARNES.   Do I understand that the clearing house is a labor exchange?

Mr. CARROLL.   On the same scale.

Mr. BARNES.   The men all leave the water front, do they?

Mr. CARROLL.   All leave the water front and go to this clearing house.

Mr. BARNES.   Do men hang around the water front in Liverpool the same as they do here?

Mr. CARROLL.   Positively no.

Mr. BARNES.   Positively not?

Mr. CARROLL.   No.   Once 7 o'clock goes, they all get off the water front.

Mr. BARNES.   They all get off the water front after 7 o'clock?

Mr. CARROLL.   Yes; the delegate won't allow them to be around the water front.

Mr. BARNES.   You say they go to this clearing house, or station, and if the foreman has made a miscalculation and needs more men, he goes out and gets the men?

Mr. CARROLL.   Yes.

Mr. BARNES.   Does he pay the same to that man, or those men, the same as he pays to the men he took on at 7 o'clock?

Mr. CARROLL.   Absolutely.

Mr. BARNES.   They get the half day?

Mr. CARROLL.   Five hours' pay.

Mr. BARNES.   Then what is the next hiring?

Mr. CARROLL.   One o'clock.

Mr. BARNES.   The same conditions obtain again?

Mr. CARROLL.   The same conditions, but you work four hours; you work from 1 o'clock until 5 o'clock.

Mr. BARNES.   You don't work a 10-hour day in Liverpool?

Mr. CARROLL.   No, sir; 9 hours.   I think that is enough, too.

Mr. BARNES.   Then, I want to state this, and correct me if I am wrong.

Mr. CARROLL. Yes.

Mr. BARNES. The conditions in Liverpool are such that the men shape in the morning at 7 o'clock and as many are taken on as foreman thinks necessary?

Mr. CARROLL. Yes, sir.

Mr. BARNES. If he has made a mistake in any way, or an emergency arises, he goes to the clearing house or labor exchange and gets his other men, or sends some other man to get them?

Mr. CARROLL. Yes, sir.

Mr. BARNES. But all men are paid for a half day?

Mr. CARROLL. For a half day.

. . . .

Chairman WALSH. Now, you were talking about your treatment here. You don't mean that the foreman strikes a man?

Mr. CARROLL. But he will go a good way to it if you don't look out for him.

Chairman WALSH. Well, does the abuse consist of abusive language? Does he curse or swear at you?

Mr. CARROLL. Certainly.

Chairman WALSH. That is the sort of abuse you refer to here?

Mr. CARROLL. Yes, sir.

Chairman WALSH. He curses them to make them go faster?

Mr. CARROLL. That is what he does.

Commissioner O'CONNELL. The success of the boss is largely his ability to swear and get results?

Mr. CARROLL. That is his success; yes.

Commissioner O'CONNELL. The man who can swear the most and drive the men fastest is the best man?

Mr. CARROLL. He gets the most work and the most pay. That is from my point of view. I don't know what anybody else's.

Testimony, Timothy Carroll, June 8, 1914, U.S. Congress, 64th, 1st session, Senate, Document No. 415, <u>Final Report and Testimony Submitted to Congress by the Commission on Industrial Relations</u>, III, pp. 2103-2104.

624. THE LOGGING CAMP AT GRAYS HARBOR (1914)

In the last great timbered area of the country, logging camps were still logging camps. Such is clear from the testimony of J. G. Brown, president of the International Union of Timber Workers, which claimed 8,000 members and was organized mostly around Puget Sound.

In the logging camps the wages are a little better, because there is a higher per cent of skill required than there is in the sawmills. However, for common labor I don't think the wages are

very much higher, perhaps 25 cents a day higher, than they are in
the sawmills. One of the biggest logging camps on Grays Harbor pays
$2 a day for common labor. They charge $5.25 a week for board at
that mill, and deduct the hospital dues from each month or a fraction of a month that the man works there. The worst thing I find
that the men in the logging camps have to contend with is the bad
conditions. There is one logging camp on Grays Harbor where they
have a bunk house with room in the bunk house for about 50 persons.
Those men sleep in wooden bunks; those bunks are double tiers running clear around the building. Those bunk houses have only one
window in one end of them. A man would have to light a lamp to read
in the middle of the day. They have a big stove in the center of
that, and the only other comfort is a bench that runs around on a
level with the lower bunk. A man can sit on those benches, or
perhaps have a box or something of that sort to sit on if they want
to sit around the table and play cards or something of that character. They have stoves, and in the periods of the year when it is
raining the stoves are hung all about with wet clothing. That is
their only method that these loggers and woodmen have of drying
their clothes. The men naturally in the bunks have to inhale the
steam that comes off of these drying clothes. In the wintertime
or fall of the year the men keep the door open in order that they
can be more comfortable from the heat of the stoves. When the fire
dies out that makes a sudden change in the temperature. They are
victims of colds and other diseases that come from that--rheumatism
and the like of that. They work these men in the fall and winter
all of the daylight there is. In the summer time they work them
about 12 hours a day. They start out from the bunk house at 6 o'
clock, presumably; frequently it is 20 minutes to 6. They walk anywhere from 20 rods to a mile and a half to their work. They reach
their work and leave at 6 o'clock at night and have to go that
distance back home on their own time. They theoretically walk one
way on the company's time and the other way on their own time. It
frequently happens that what is theoretically 10 hours is stretched
into a 12-hour day, sometimes even longer than that. Those long
hours of employment, the uncertainty of it, and the bad conditions
under which they live are the main complaints that the loggers have.
They resent very bitterly this compulsory payment of hospital fees.
But speaking further about the insanitary conditions: It usually
happens that 25 or 30 feet from the bunk house is the cookhouse,
and the cookhouses usually have a habit of throwing all their gar-
bage and empty cans and everything right out of the window. In the
hot time of the summer that not only makes a bad odor but attracts
swarms of flies, and presumably the idea is they convey disease to
a greater or less extent. Of course, the work in the logging camps
is in the open and healthful, and that, perhaps, is one reason why
they are not the victims of diseases that they otherwise would be.

Testimony, J. G. Brown, August 12, 1914, U.S. Congress, 64th,
1st session, Senate, Document No. 415, Final Report and Testimony
Submitted to Congress by the Commission of Industrial Relations,
V, p. 4211.

625.   THE ANNUAL MODEL-LAYOFF (1933)

The annual layoff added a regular element of job
insecurity which came to be accepted as inevitable.
Clayton Fountain worked in the Chevrolet gear and axle
plant in Detroit on a rotary resistance welder and a
punch press. He describes the process.

The annual layoff during the model change was always a menace
to the security of the workers. Along about June or July it started. The bosses would pick the men off a few at a time, telling
them to stay home until they were notified to come back. There
was no rhyme or reason in the selection of the fortunate ones
chosen to continue working. The foreman had the say. If he
happened to like you, or if you sucked around him and did him fav-
ors--or if you were one of the bastards who worked like hell and
turned out more than production--you might be picked to work a few
weeks longer than the next guy. Some few lucky fellows were transferred to the maintenance or materials departments, which meant
that they worked right through the period of the inventory layoff
and model change. But most of the men were laid off outright, and
there was no unemployment compensation to tide them over until
they were rehired.
   It was customary for auto workers to go broke during this
layoff. Sometimes you could get a job in another plant, maybe a
feeder plant, where they made parts. These plants were busy during
the layoff in the big shops, building up an inventory of parts for
the new model.
   One summer I tried my hand at selling vacuum cleaners during
the layoff. A high-powered and glib gent representing the vacuum
cleaner company rushed a gang of us through a class designed to
make us into super-salesmen. Each morning we opened the class
with songs--parodies of popular tunes--extolling the virtues of
our cleaner. We were taught a number of sly tricks used to be-
little the products of competitors. As a last resort, to crack
the resistance of dubious housewives, we were taught the stunt of
emptying the contents of a vacuum clearner dust bag on the floor
and threatening to drop the baby into it. When the outraged mother
protested, we were supposed to say: "But madam, I took all this
dirt out of your rug; your baby has been playing in it for days."
For all this schooling in the wiles of free-enterprise marketing,
I flopped as a salesman. In three weeks of ringing doorbells and
giving housewives the song and dance, I managed to sell only one
machine.
   General Motors in those days operated a kind of private welfare system that many workers had to depend on to get groceries
enough to get by during the layoffs. It worked like this: when
you were broke and still unable to get back into the plant, you
went to the personnel office and applied for help. If you proved
your need, the company gave you a book of coupons that could be
exchanged for groceries at a chain store. These coupons were a

kind of scrip, in denominations running from a dollar down to a
dime. The company charged these against your name on its books;
and when you went back to work, they deducted five or ten dollars
a week from your pay until they had it all back.

Any way you looked at it the layoffs were tough. In 1935 I
had to sell my 1931 Ford in order to keep on paying the rent, while
selling my groceries with the Chevrolet coupons. The year before
that, I had my electricity turned off because I couldn't pay the
Edison bill.

In October and November we began to trickle back into the
plants. Again, the bosses had the full say as to who was rehired
first. Years of service with the company meant nothing. Every day
the lunchroom upstairs over the front end of Plant Two at Chevrolet
Gear and Axle was crowded with workers for an hour before the
shift started. The foreman would come upstairs and walk down the
aisles picking out those they wanted on the job. Apple-polishers,
suckers, and job-killers got the nod first in most instances. I
must note here that all the foremen were not given to practicing
this system of favoritism. There were some who felt that years of
service were important, and who tried to work out a kind of un-
official seniority system in their departments. But, generally
speaking, the laid-off worker had no assurance of any kind that
he would be called back at any specific time. He had to be there
when he was wanted, in most instances, or someone else got the nod.
Sometimes, when the job was hot, workers were notified by mail to
report for work.

Clayton W. Fountain, _Union Guy_, (New York: Viking Press,
1949), pp. 41-42.

626. INDUSTRIAL UNIONISM MUST COME (1935)

The moving personality behind the effort to
develop industrial union organization tries to convince his conservative colleagues in the labor movement.

I do not speak without some background and some knowledge of
this subject acquired in the field of actual experience. I have
not gained that knowledge through delving into academic treatises
or in sitting in a swivel chair pondering upon the manner in which
those upon the firing line should meet their daily problems....I
served an apprenticeship of five and one-half years as a general
organizer for the A.F.L. before I became an officer of the United
Mine Workers of America. During that period...I worked in the
steel industry, the rubber industry, the glass industry, the lumber
industry, the copper industry, and other industries in most of the
states of this Union.

Then, as now, the A.F.L. offered to the workers in these industries a plan of organization into Federal Labor unions or local
trade unions with the understanding that when organized they would
be segregated into the various organizations of their respective
crafts. Then, as now, practically every attempt to organize those
workers broke upon the same rock that it breaks upon today--the
rock of utter futility, the lack of reasonableness in a policy that
failed to take into consideration the dreams and requirements of
the workers themselves, and failing to take into consideration the
recognized power of the adversaries of labor to destroy these
feeble organizations in the great modern industries set up in the
form of Federal labor unions or craft organizations functioning in
a limited sphere....a record of twenty-five years of constant,
unbroken failure should be convincing to those who actually have a
desire to increase the prestige of our great labor movement by expanding its membership to permit it to occupy its natural place in
the sun....This convention floor is teeming with delegates from
those industries where those local unions have been established and
where they are now dying like the grass withering before the Autumn
sun, who are ready to tell this convention of the need for that
change in policy....it is an absolute fact that America's great
modern industries cannot be successfully organized and those
organizations maintained against the power of the adversaries of
labor in this country under the policy which has been followed for
the last quarter of a century in dealing with that subject.

There has been a change in industry, a constant daily
change in its processes, a constant change in its employment conditions, a great concentration of opposition to the extension and
the logical expansion of the trade union movement. Great combinations of capital have assembed great industrial plants, and they
are strung across the borders of our several states from the north
to the south and from the east to the west in such a manner that
they have assembled to themselves tremendous power and influence,
and they are almost 100 per cent effective in opposing organization of the workers under the policies of the A.F.L.

What are we going to do about it?...Why do we hesitate? We
hesitate, perhaps, because there are men here representing great
organizations that have rendered a splendid service to the membership formed, on craft lines, who fear that such a policy would
jeopardize the interests of their members and jeopardize the
interests of their own positions. Their unions are already jeopardized and their membership is already jeopardized because unless
the A.F.L. may be successful in organizing these unorganized
workers, it is extremely doubtful whether many of these organizations now so perfect, now so efficient, will long be permitted
to endure and to function in a manner that is conducive to the
well-being of their membership.

There are great influences abroad in the land, and the minds
of men in all walks of life are disturbed. We are all disturbed
by reason of the changes and the hazards in our economic situation
and as regards our own political security. There are forces at
work in this country that would wipe out, if they could, the labor
movement of America, just as it was wiped out in Germany or just

as it was wiped out in Italy. There are those of us who believe
that the best security against that menace and against that trend
and against that tendency is a more comprehensive and more powerful
labor movement....

John L. Lewis, October 16, 1935, Report of Proceedings of the
Fifty-Fifth Annual Convention of the American Federation of Labor,
1935, (Washington, D.C.: Judd and Detweiler, [1935]) pp. 534-
536.

627. INDUSTRIAL UNIONISM IS UNDESIRABLE (1935)

During the early 1930s, a movement arose in the
mass-production industries -- autos, steel, rubber, and
others -- to unionize in industrial unions, i.e., without
respect to specialized skill (craft). The United Mine
Workers of America (UMWA) was one of the oldest industrial
unions in the country but the American Federation of Labor,
to which it was affiliated, fought against the spread of
industrial unionism. Industrial workers, however, conducted large-scale strikes, including at times, the occupation
of factories (sit-ins). Here is a statement by John Frey,
head of the AFL's Metal Trades Department, who found it
difficult to understand the changed conditions that were
outdating traditional organizing techniques.

I will confess that in all of my years of experience I have
never known exactly what was meant when any one used the words
'craft union' or 'industrial union.' All I know about the term
'industrial union' is that it was not applied by trade unionists
to any form of organization; it was an exotic importation from
groups who do not believe in the A.F.L, who for years endeavored
to prevail upon us to change our policy, and they used the term
which our trade union movement has taken up and used as its own.
There are a number of delegations in this convention who claim
to represent industrial unions -- at least their international
unions are always called industrial unions. I don't intend to refer
to any organization by name, but if this convention, representing
a large number of men in organizations that have been called industrial, are more narrowly craft unions in their policies, in their
methods of conducting their organizations than a number of the so-
called craft unions.
I am speaking particularly now of three organizations in one
industry. The same material, or practically the same, is used
in all three; the same type of machinery is used in all three to
produce the finished article, and if these three international
unions were to amalgamate tomorrow they would still be, in spite
of that amalgamation, more narrowly craft unions than any of the

international unions that compose the metal trades department.   If
we are to discuss this question we should go into it with our minds
open and not be misled by terms.
     There are in this country a few unions which are thoroughly
industrial, or thoroughly vertical, if you want that term.   There
are some unions in Europe that are thoroughly industrial, that is,
all the members employed in the industry are members of one union.
The only thoroughly industrial unions I know of in this country
are company unions, organized by the employers, who compel the
office workers and manual workers to belong to the organization
they form.
. . . .
     There is a very laudable desire on the part of those employed
in portions of the radio industry to have an industrial union.
And for what they have done to organize I have nothing but praise.
With the enthusiasm these young men have, their willingness to work
for organization, I have nothing but commendation; but they present
one of the problems that is involved in this whole question.   They
want to organize the radio industry.   What is the radio industry?
There are some manufacturers who manufacture all of the parts of
the radio, who manufacture the cabinets, who assemble it, so that
inside of that plant all of the material necessary is fabricated,
assembled and the complete radio is put on the market.
     However, it happens that some radio manufacturers do not do
their own cabinet work and they buy their cabinets from those who
manufacture woodwork, and so if this radio industry is to have
complete control over those who want an international charter feel
that they must have jurisdiction over the woodworking plant which
makes the cabinets...how about other organizations organized along
industrial lines that use some of the material made in that woodworking plant?   Should they be given to the radio workers or to
some other organization?....Many non-union men are of the opinion
that unless this convention adopts a program such as has been advocated that there is to be another Federation of Labor organized
which will include nothing but the industrial unions.   I feel
deeply on the question....Never before have I been called upon in
this convention to discuss a question which was accompanied by a
threat, where the public statement has been made that unless we
do what somebody wants us to do, there might be secession and the
organization of another Federation of Labor....If we should for
a moment yield to those who come into our convention with the
threat of secession, if they fail to secure their purpose, if we
yield, we surrender every drop of independent blood that ever
flowed through our veins.

     John P. Frey, October 16, 1935, Report of Proceedings of the
Fifty-Fifth Annual Convention of the American Federation of Labor,
1935, (Washington, D.C.: Judd and Detweiler, [1935] pp. 553,
554-555, 558-559.

628. WHAT A SPEED-UP IS NOT (1937)

Rather blandly, a production official dissolves the
issue of speed-up. The speaker is Herman Weckler, vice-
president and general manager of DeSoto Motor Corporation,
Chrysler Corporation.

There are all sorts of claims of speed-up. Some have occurred
in the assembly operations, and others occur in manufacturing operations, and there is a change in the speed in various departments,
which is perfectly natural.
It is quite evident to anyone who is familiar with an operation
that at the beginning of a model, when the model which has been for
a month or 6 weeks is all out and new models come in, and if radical
changes have been made in method of attachment or the design of the
parts themselves, all of the skill which the men have obtained during the previous years' work is gone, and they have to adjust themselves to this new form of work, and it is natural then that at the
beginning of the model the work does not flow as easily over the
production lines as it would later during the same production year.
Of course, in some cases that is called an indication of speed-up.
At the beginning of the model the line may be running, for the first
week, 10 or 15 jobs an hour, the second week 30, the fourth week it
might be going to 50. It might be 4 or 5 weeks before the line
attains the same speed it attained the year previous.

Testimony, Herman L. Weckler, January 26, 1937, U.S. Congress,
75th, 1st session, Senate, Committee on Education and Labor,
Violations of Free Speech and Rights of Labor, IV, pp. 1200-1201.

629. WHAT A SPEED-UP IS (1937)

Resentment at the speed-up was perhaps the deepest-
felt sentiment in the auto plants. James Mangold, an
assembly worker in the Chevrolet plant in Flint, Michigan,
gives the testimony.

Mr. MANGOLD. Well, the speed-up, the way it is effected, the
man power is cut down every year, as I have told you before, they
take off so many men every year and install modern machinery to
speed the job up, to get more units per hour with less man-hours on
the job. In our case, on this cab-top line, that is the biggest job
in the Chevrolet, and we were run up this year from 10 to 15, we
had to get 15 units against 10 last year, and we had 10 men last
year and we had 6 men this year to get the same jobs out.

Senator THOMAS. Fifteen units in how much time?

Mr. MANGOLD. In 1 hour. That is the whole cab top, you know, that covers the cab, a steel top.

Senator LA FOLLETTE. Well, now, when this so-called speed-up takes place and a fewer number of men turn out more units per hour do the men that are working on the job and getting out more material usually get an increase in pay?

Mr. MANGOLD. They do not. They never get an increase in pay.

Senator LA FOLLETTE. Do you know of any instances where they slacken speed?

Mr. MANGOLD. Well, I have never known of the speed-up cut down on the job after it was timed up there.

Senator LA FOLLETTE. What is the effect of the speed-up and the reduction of men on the quality of the work?

Mr. MANGOLD. Well, it turns out a poorer quality of work, the work is not as efficient as it was before. They just try to cover up the things, what they have done the year before, where they finish it the year before, they will just cover those over so they will get by inspection and will not be noticed.

Senator LA FOLLETTE. Have you ever had an instruction to help accomplish speed-up regardless of its effect on quality?

Mr. MANGOLD. Yes, I have.

Senator LA FOLLETEE. Tell us about that.

Mr. MANGOLD. Well, I have been told to not be particular with anything, to push it on through, that they had to get them out, they had a rush order on and they wanted to get it out. They would put their fastest men that they had at the start on the job, pick out one man that would be scared of the foreman, let the forman stand over him. Some fellows, when the foreman gets close to them, they get nervous, they work as fast as they can possibly work, because they are afraid the foreman will say something to them. That is the kind of men they put at the head of the line, and the rest of them have got to keep up or else they are taken off of the line, they are either taken off of that job and put on another one or else they are taken off of the job altogether and put on outside. That is the way the speed-up is started.

Senator LA FOLLETTE. What is the effect on the men?

Mr. MANGOLD. Well, the men are overtaxed physically and mentally as the result of the speed-up.

Senator THOMAS. Do they reduce the number of foremen?

Mr. MANGOLD. They never do; they increase the number of foremen every year.

Senator THOMAS. That is, you have more foremen in the speed-up and you have fewer workers?

Mr. MANGOLD. More foremen; yes.

Senator THOMAS. And his aim seems to be speed all the time?

Mr. MANGOLD. Nothing but speed. It is not the quality, it is only speed.

Senator THOMAS. Have you ever heard of a foreman suggesting that it is easy to slip over something?

Mr. MANGOLD. Oh, yes.

Senator THOMAS. They tell you the idea is speed all the time, do they?

Mr. MANGOLD. I have had them come and tell me, when I have
been doing the job--I am a metal finisher, that is my trade--when
I would be finishing out this thing so it would get by the inspector
he would tell me, "Don't do that; let it go through. If he don't
see it that is his hard luck."
Senator THOMAS. So the foreman is worked up just as much as
the men, is he?
Mr. MANGOLD. Yes.

Testimony, James H. Mangold, February 19, 1937, U.S. Congress,
75th, 1st session, Senate, Committee on Education and Labor,
Violations of Free Speech and Rights of Labor, VI, pp. 2118-2119.

630. UNIONISM IN THE SOUTH (1930's)

  This account by a Southern black touches upon a
number of special problems of unionism in the South.
Oscar Thomas was a steel worker in Memphis, Tennessee.
He became the first black staff member of the CIO steelworkers employed in the South.

  I worked in the Orgill Brothers Hardware plant. My job was
order clerk. I filled the orders as they came in. It was a wholesale house, handling hardware and furniture. I did my work and was
frank in my dealings and always got along with the fellows I worked
with. I worked there twenty-two years.
  One of the fellows from our plant got a job at Pidgeon Thomas
and he came back and told us about the union and what it was getting
for the people over there. Then some of the fellows in Orgill went
to a union meeting of Pidgeon employees. They came back and told
other people at Orgill's and that started organizing in our plant.
  The men had this organization well underway before they mentioned it to me, because I had been employed by the company so long
they were skeptical about me. They invited me to come to a meeting
and I accepted their invitation and went and listened to the information given by Steel Representatives Will Watts and Bill Henderson.
  After weighing this information carefully, I decided that the
labor movement would not only help me, but help the other fellows
working around me, who needed it more than I.
  For many evenings I had heard one of the foremen tell the
men not to come back if they could not do more work than they had
done that day. At that time they had started a speed-up system of
piece work by giving contracts to the men to unload cars by the
job. After checking this high rate of speed in unloading, the
company wanted to hold the men to the speed-up system.
  At the expiration of the NRA [in 1935] all colored employees
were carried to the basement. There they were told about the

discontinuing of the NRA and the new rules of the company which said
we would no longer work forty hours a week, but would have to make
forty-six hours.

Overtime rates after that were less than the regular hourly
rate of pay. For instance, men who worked for thirty-seven cents
as a regular daily hour's pay would get only twenty-five cents an
hour for overtime. Sometimes they worked the men overtime with no
pay for the extra time except fifty cents to buy supper.

At the conclusion of the meeting in the basement we were told
that if anyone did not like it he should speak then--for if there
were any rotten apples in the barrel they wanted to get rid of them
there.

The company meeting in the basement answered a long question in
my mind, because it showed the attitude of the superintendent toward
the colored employees who had been with the company a long time. I
saw why we needed a union and what it could do for us.

There were many other things the company did that were not fair
to the colored. The company had a practice that gave the colored
a one-week vacation and the white two weeks. They also gave a bonus
twice a year, the colored receiving one-half the amount the whites
received. They gave picnics, parties, and dances to the white employees and none for the colored.

All these practices were equalized when the United Steelworkers
came into the plants. From that time on, I took an active part in
the union.

In Memphis as a whole, in most all locals the white and colored
worked jointly in the same union. Sometimes these mixed unions had
some colored officers, including the president. The first meeting
I went to I was elected financial secretary. Later on they wanted
to elect me as president. I objected, for this reason: To elect
me president in place of the man who was holding that office, would
make us lose him. In other words, he would quit the union. If he
remained as president he would still have to abide by the decisions
of the body, and I felt I was just as influential with the group as
he was. So I remained as financial secretary until I felt ready to
join the staff of the Steelworkers.

I want to speak about a spirit of religious devotion that is in
these unions. Most of the local unions have ministers among their
members, who work in the plant. One of these ministers will serve
as chaplain to the local, and open and close the meetings with
prayer. Religion is part of the life of the union.

I came into the labor movement in the Steel Union under the
leadership of Mr. Henderson and Mr. Watts. But our rapid progress
came after Mr. Earl A. Crowder took over the Memphis area for the
Steelworkers. Mr. Crowder got the steel locals to move their meeting
place down town, and also to affiliate with the Memphis CIO Industrial Union Council.

In April, 1944, I went on the staff of the Steelworkers' Union.
I was then moved to Chattanooga and since then I have traveled all
over District 35, of which Mr. W. H. Crawford is director.

Since being on the staff, I have found that CIO has the most
to offer the low-paid workers, especially in the South. This gives
me double courage in trying to reach the colored brothers wherever

I am assigned to work, for I know that the workers have all to
gain and nothing to lose in voting themselves into the CIO.
       For the union is the only salvation of the working man, and
the CIO is the only organization in the South that advocates, and
has, joint meetings of both races in any section they enter.

       Oscar Reese Thomas, in Lucy Randolph Mason, To Win These
Rights. A Personal Story of the CIO in the South, (New York:
Harper and Bros., 1952), pp. 171-173.

       631. MECHANIZATION AND STEEL UNIONIZATION (1940)

              Technological advance in a period of sagging indus-
       trial output meant the technologically unemployed could
       not find jobs in other parts of the economy. Note the
       tendency of wage standards to sag in technologically sta-
       tionary segments of the industry. (For an engineer's early
       celebration of the principle of continuous strip milling,
       see Source No. 573. For earlier examples of worker ad-
       justment to technological change, see Source Nos. 436 and
       642). This account is that of Philip Murray, president of
       the Steel Workers Organizing Committee--C.I.O.

       The [automatic] strip mills are not through with the killing.
Fourteen plants or departments of integrated steel producers are on
the industry's death list. These old-style hand-mills are scheduled
to be abandoned permanently. Some of them have worked irregularly
in recent years, and some are completely idle at present. Twenty-
two thousand nine hundred fifty workers are employed in these
plants, soon to be thrown into the streets, to be made idle through
no fault of their own, and no longer wanted by the steel industry
or by private industry generally.
. . . .
       These companies are doomed, because their obsolete mills de-
pend, in the main, upon manual power; while the automatic strip
mills derive their power primarily from electricity. The difference
in the cost of production is fatal to the smaller companies. Men
cannot compete against electricity. This is plainly demonstrated
by a comparison of the cost of producing a gross ton of tinplate,
for example, on the hand-mills with the automatic strip mills.
. . . .
       The hand-mill desires, of course, to live, it wants to live,
it fights to live; it knows that life to it is a question of the
survival of the fittest in the great competitive field. It cannot
compete and pay the same wage that is paid at the low cost, high
producing, more efficiently managed, better machine facilities of
the big mill. The employer in a state of desperation who owns the
small hand-mill comes to the organization and says, "Give me a

chance to live, won't you? Help me along. Won't you agree to a
cut in our wage rates here so that we can live for another two or
three months?"

Now there is an economic repercussion that runs through this
distorted competitive picture in the steel industry today that the
workers employed in the industry are constantly confronted with,
reducing their standards, to meet these newer conditions created
by the production of these large continuous mills.

Testimony, Philip Murray, April 12, 1940, Verbatim Record of
the Proceedings of the Temporary National Economic Committee, XIII,
pp. 151, 152, 153.

632. THE DIAL TELEPHONE IS AN ANTI-SOCIAL DEVICE (1940)

Until the late 1930's, when you picked up the telephone receiver to place a call, an operator asked, "Number,
please?" You told her. Introduction of the dial was directed, among other things, at reducing the direct labor cost
of placing calls. Rose Sullivan, general organizer for
A.F.L., had organized telephone operators into a union.
She had worked as an operator for five years. Here she
comments on the dial telephone.

Nobody likes the dial, nobody wants it. It gives inferior
service at a very greatly higher price. It is an inconvenient abom-
ination. It is useless in a personal emergency. It cracks up completely in a community emergency. It is nothing that a telephone
ought to be and everything that it shouldn't be.

It is inanimate, unresponsive, stupid, when telephone service
ought to be vital, animate and intelligent. It does none of the
things which machinery is supposed to do in industry. It does not
reduce human labor, it merely transfers labor from the operator, who
gets wages, to the subscriber who doesn't. It does not cheapen the
product, it costs more. It is not more efficient, it is far less
useful than the manually operated service. It destroys jobs and
closes off an entire employment field, with no compensation to
society.

. . . .

The dial telephone is the perfect example of a wasteful,
expensive, inefficient, clumsy, anti-social device, being substituted for satisfactory, competent, human labor which received wages
for work now performed at exactly the same expenditure of human
effort without the compensation wages.

. . . .

The personnel problem in the American Telephone and Telegraph
Company is becoming a very vital one. There was unionization in
New England. It was small but very competent and very militant.

The keeping up of the company union is an expensive project for any corporation, and the Telephone Company undoubtedly saw that this personnel problem would one day be a factor in regulating conditions and hours and wages, and therefore went hog-wild on this dial installation, which unquestionably is expensive but which they felt in the long pull--no one knowing how long the pull may be--will reduce their personnel.

Testimony, Rose S. Sullivan, April 17, 1940, Verbatim Record of the Proceedings of the Temporary National Economic Committee, XIII, pp. 294-295.

633.   COAL STRIKE AS BUSINESS CONFLICT (1941)

On April 2, 1941, a coal strike started. Northern coal operators and the United Mine Workers agreed on a raise of $1 a day for northern miners and $1.40 a day for southern miners. This arrangement would abolish the differential of 40 cents a day in wages between northern and southern miners. Southern operators refused to give up the differential, and the strike continued. L. T. Putman, spokesman for the southern coal-mine operators, reports.

Now, in 1941, on March 11, prior to that, I may say, there was general agreement, as I understood it and as I still understand it, between the operators in the South, first, and later in the North, in a joint meeting of northern and southern operators in the Biltmore Hotel, in New York, that the question of differentials, as far as the operators were concerned, would not be pursued in the coming conference. When the conference convened, we had Mr. [John L.] Lewis' demands, many in number, but among them was the perennial demand of the elimination of all inequitable differentials. We didn't take it seriously; neither, I think, did the northern operators, and we didn't think that the mine workers took it seriously, because it was always there. We subbed down to a committee of four on a side shortly after starting our negotiations, and nothing was said for some time about differentials. We didn't make a lot of progress, I thought, however. Finally, the Ways and Means Committee of the House saw fit to conduct some investigations preliminary to the reenactment of the Guffey law, and that was so far as I could see, as a member of that small committee, the bomb which blew open the whole proposition of differentials. It was indicated, as I understand it--and I am not too familiar with those investigations--that it might be in the interest of the general good to divide price area No. 1 into two sections, the southern and the northern section, putting Pennsylvania in a section of its own.

At any rate, that seemed to be the thing which tore open the question of differentials, because it was asserted that if that were
done, it would make the sale price in the northern districts
higher and allow the southern districts to sell at lower prices,
thus acting to let the South in on markets which it couldn't then
get in on.

The CHAIRMAN. Then this is a controversy not between labor
and operators, but between operators, and that is all that is holding up the production of coal. Is that right?

Mr. PUTMAN. It appears to be pretty largely, so far as they
are concerned, Senator, a question of an argument between operators.

Testimony, L. T. Putman, April 28, 1941, U.S. Congress, 77th,
1st session, Senate, Special Committee Investigating the National
Defense Program, Investigation of the National Defense Program, II,
pp. 418-419.

634. NORTHERNERS RUNNING SOUTHERNERS IN COAL (1941)

Northern investment in Southern resources had become
extremely widespread in 1941. The phenomenon threw doubt
on the meaning of geographical expressions like "north" and
"south." This is the testimony of John L. Lewis, president
of the United Mine Workers of America.

Why, who is conducting this strike down in the South, this
lock-out? It is mostly northern coal operators and northern money.
The Koppers Coal Co., which mines some 13,000,000 tons of coal, more
or less, and consumes six or seven million of it in their own
Koppers ovens, is northern-owned, by the Mellon interests in
Pittsburgh, who own the Pittsburgh Coal Co. They are closing their
ovens in Massachusetts today, shutting down at Carnegie, New Jersey,
and in Philadelphia and elsewhere because that company has locked
out its employees and as a result can't render service to their
customers and the community and the Nation in the North. But whenever the Mellon interests or the Koppers Coal Co. find out they are
not going to be able to starve these people into subjection from
the South or evict any from their homes, or run the country with
gunmen, the Koppers Coal Co. will sign this agreement and they will
sign on the dotted line. They mine that coal in the North for
their northern ovens, and the people in the North pay the price and
the people in the North have a right to believe that those men in
the South who mine that coal are getting the same wages as they
have to pay in the communities where they live in the North.

If the Consolidation Coal Co., Rockefeller money, accepts this
agreement in Maryland and in northern West Virginia it must also
accept this agreement in Kentucky, where their mines operate.

The Berwind-White Coal Co.--we all know who the Berwinds are.
In Pennsylvania they accept this agreement: they refuse to accept
it in the New River field of West Virginia. The New River Coal Co.,
Mr. L. E. Gaines, who sits here, is the president of it, sometimes
purporting to represent this group. Northern capital, Boston money,
and the C. & O. Railroad; Mr. Putman, who sits here representing
Illinois capital. There are plenty of companies down there who are
following a Dr. Jekyll and Mr. Hyde policy here. They are willing
to make an agreement in the North, but at the behest of certain
people in the South, who urge them not to compromise their position,
they go along on the southern policy of "fighting this out along
this line if it takes all summer."

Testimony, John L. Lewis, April 28, 1941, U.S. Congress, 77th,
1st session, Senate, Special Committee Investigating the National
Defense Program, Investigation of the National Defense Program, II,
p. 435.

635. IS WELDING A CRAFT? (1941)

Specialization and technological advance were making
a general mechanical technique of what had once been a
strict craft specialty. General vice-president of the
International Association of Machinists, Eric Peterson,
speaks here.

We know that employers are specializing even when it comes to
welding. We know that there are operators in mass-production industries who do spot welding and flash welding, where they operate huge
machines that weld bodies, automobile bodies, at one throw of an
electric switch. We know that there is welding in the jewelry industry where girls use the acetylene torch in welding processes on
jewelry. We know that in contract shops welders are also qualified
craftsmen. They are capable of doing machinists' work when it comes
to operating machine tools or erecting machinery or assembling
machinery, and also welding.
We know that in some industries they have men who use nothing
but the electric-arc process. They are not familiar with acetylene
welding and possibly could not qualify when it comes to welding
alloys. We know there are men that specialize in what we call high-
pressure welding, welding of tanks and containers that have to
withstand pressures running up as high as 3,000 pounds to the square
inch. We know there are men who are confined to just building up
processes, where they build up worn parts. In other words, employers have specialized even the welding field until we find that there
are a very limited number of welders who can be said to be general
all-around welders, men who can qualify where they have to pass

examinations and do what is called X-ray work, so, in our opinion, the welding problem isn't as complicated as it has been presented here....

I gathered the impression here that representatives of the welders were more concerned in establishing an independent organization than they were in improving conditions and establishing better wage rates for those who follow the welding work. In that connection I might point out that in the railroad industry, again using that as an example, we have established a differential for men who do welding. That differential is 5 cents an hour over the rate set for journeymen of various crafts. A man may weld for 1 hour during the day or 2 or 3 hours or more, and he gets 5 cents an hour above the rate for journeymen in the various crafts while he is on that work.

Testimony, Eric Peterson, December 4, 1941, U.S. Congress, 77th, 1st session, Senate, Special Committee Investigating the National Defense Program, Investigation of the National Defense Program, X, pp. 3751-3752.

636. "CONSUMERS MADE IN THE GOOD OLD-FASHIONED WAY" (1958)

Even as this striking statement was being made, it was outdated by in vitro fertilization, a partial automatizing of human reproduction. Walter Reuther is the speaker. Reuther was president of the United Automobile, Aircraft, and Agricultural Implement Workers of America, AFL-CIO. Before he became a union official, he had been a tool and die maker.

Senator LANGER. You say these 3 corporations put $7,200 million into automotive machinery, whatever it may be.

How many men did that put out of work?

Mr. REUTHER. Well, it is hard to give you an exact figure. They are some of the things we would like to know more about. We do know that we have felt the impact of automation. The first time I went to work in the automotive industry, was back in 1927, in February. They were making the last of the model T Fords, Senator Langer, and you know all about a model T because up in your country they were very handy back in the days when the roads were not very good.

Senator LANGER. Very handy in politics, driving.

Mr. REUTHER. I would not be surprised that they were.

Senator KEFAUVER. I think Senator Langer still campaigns in a Model T.

Mr. REUTHER. Anyway, when I went to work at Ford in 1927, before we had automation, it took thousands and thousands of workers

on individual machines to make a Model T engine, which is a relatively simple mechanism.

They bored each cylinder separately and did all the other
things in separate operations.

In 1951, the Ford Motor Co. opened up a new engine plant in
Cleveland, Ohio, adjacent to the municipal airport. It was the
first fully automated engine plant. They take a rough casting of a
V-8 engine, which is a very complex piece of engine compared to a
Model T engine block. They bring it from the foundry and feed it
into the automated feeding line, completely automatic, and without
a worker's hand touching that engine block, 14 6/10 minutes later
it is fully machined.

I went through that plant many years back and the people who
were showing me around said to me--I could hardly see the workers
because there were just a few here and a few there, watching electric panels, red and green lights, going on to show where the machine was operating to standard.

When all the green lights were on, it meant every tool in a
battery of machines was up to performance, meeting the precise
tolerances of the machining operation.

When an amber light came on, the machine was still operating
but there was a signal that the tool in station No. 82 was becoming
fatigued. The worker got a replacement tool, walked over in front
of 82. When the red light went on, the machine stopped, he put the
new tool in, the green light came on, and the operation went on.

Without a worker's hand touching it, 14 6/10 minutes later the
engine block was fully machined.

So they said to me, "Aren't you worried about how you are going
to collect union dues from all of these machines?"

I said, "the thought never occurred to me. The thought that
occurred to me was how are you going to sell cars to these machines?
You know you can make automobiles, but consumers are still made in
the good old-fashioned way." [Laughter.]

Testimony, Walter P. Reuther, January 28, 1958, U.S. Congress,
85th, 2nd session, Senate, Committee on the Judiciary, Subcommittee
on Antitrust and Monopoly, Administered Prices, VI, Automobiles,
pp. 2206-2207.

637. "PEACE WITH POVERTY" (1959)

Between 1953 and 1960, over 8,000 jobs--22 percent
of the total--in Lynn, Massachusetts plants of General
Electric were moved to plants in other cities. Remaining,
was a concentration of defense-related work. This outcome
symbolized a larger problem of the American economy. The
speaker is Albin Hartnett, Secretary-Treasurer, International Union of Electrical, Radio, and Machine Workers,
AFL-CIO.

Now there is the problem in the electrical industry, an industry in which I have spent all of my adult career. The electrical workers of Lynn and New England I assure you are just as efficient, if not more so, as workers in other areas. They have great skills. They are devoted to their jobs. They have pride in this industry. They share our pleasure at the great technical advances which have been brought about in the American electrical manufacturing and electronics industries.

Yet what is their reward here in Lynn?

Employment in the River Works plant has gone steadily down as jobs have been moved to other areas. The effect on the greater Lynn area thus becomes cumulative. Families move out at the first good opportunity. Young people migrate elsewhere in search of jobs. A deteriorating downward spiral begins to affect a local economy under these circumstances. Furthermore, the type of work that has been left here in Lynn has been so concentrated in defense activity that we face a fantastic paradox. So far as the people employed at GE in Lynn are concerned, peace in the world--which we would all cherish as an expression of true Christianity in international relations--would be calamitous to the workers employed in GE here in Lynn.

A situation that produces this sort of result is morally wrong. A situation has been brought about where Lynn must face "peace with poverty"--because General Electric has put all of Lynn's big economic eggs in one defense basket.

For instance; General Electric manufactures thousands of products--15,000 different ones, I am responsibly informed. Certainly, out of that vast array of production there must be some which could be produced here in Lynn efficiently and economically, and which would give greater balance to the employment picture in this city.

Mr. Chairman, here is a picture of the truck entrance of the GE plant with the sign above it which shows the products manufactured in this plant, Aircraft Accessories Turbine Department, Lynn Computers FPLD, Small Aircraft Engine Department, Flight propulsion Laboratory Department, Medium Steam Turbine Generating Department, all of which is defense and other Government work.

Now if we have peace, which everybody in the world seems to be striving for vigorously, this kind of work may be drastically cut back, indeed, may be completely terminated, and the people here in Lynn would suffer because of the fact that we have peace with the poverty that would follow, and this isn't, I assure you, a pleasant prospect for the people here in Lynn.

Surely we have a right to expect better economic planning than this. Surely we Americans have a right to hope that the dawn of world peace and a future and of the cold war, would provide a "peace with prosperity" for the people of Lynn. Peace without poverty would be possible in Lynn if there were substantial amounts of civilian work--work on consumer goods or peacetime industrial goods--in the General Electric plant here. But this type of work has been moved out, presumably to the lower wage areas; and Lynn is left with its overconcentration of defense work. That sort of work can blow up in the city's face when peace descends on the world.

This prospect of peace with poverty is an unnecessary prospect
for Lynn.

Testimony, Albin F. Hartnett, January 11, 1960, U.S. Congress,
86th, 2nd session, Senate, Special Committee on Unemployment
Problems, Unemployment Problems, IX, p. 4029.

638. EXPORT OF JOBS IN THE ELECTRONICS INDUSTRY (1970)

During 1969-1973, employment in American manufacturing fell by nearly two percent while the economy was
booming. Part of the reason for the decline was an
increasing tendency of multinational firms to export
jobs. For example, in 1972 there were 46,000 workers
in 350 plants on the Mexican border; two years later,
the figures were 83,000 and 527. All but a few of the
plants were American-owned. In Taiwan, plants producing
for U.S. electronics manufacturers began with single components but in time put out complete units. Between 1969
and 1973, electrical apparatus imports from developing
countries rose from $339 million to $1.7 billion. Partial
relief was afforded by passage of the Trade Expansion
Act of 1962 which offers workers adjustment assistance
as well as relocation allowances if increased imports were
the cause of the unemployment. Paul Jennings, president
of the International Union of Electrical, Radio, and Machine
Workers, explores the impact of job export on the members
of his union.

In my own industry, and in industries closely related, we have
seen plant after plant shut down in recent years, their production
discontinued, products, technology and jobs exported to offshore
manufacturing facilities of the same multinational firms.
Zenith, Admiral, Ford-Philco, RCA and others, for example, have
recently shifted monochrome and color TV set production to Taiwan.
Last year, Westinghouse closed its Edison, N.J. TV plant and transferred production to one of its Canadian facilities as well as to
Japanese firms. It imports sets now for distribution under its own
label.
Emerson Radio and Phono Division of National Union Electric
also discontinued production of TV sets, closing down its Jersey
City, N.J. plant, and transferring production to Admiral, which,
in turn, transferred production of major TV product lines to Taiwan.
Warwick Electronics transferred production from its Arkansas and
Illinois plants to its Mexican facility. The rush to relocate outside the United States is on. At this time, practically all radio
sets, tape recorders, and cassettes sold in this country are produced abroad, and before long the same may be true of black and

white and color TV sets. Currently, about half the black and white
sets and about 20-25 percent of the color sets sold here are
produced abroad. Some growth products, such as home video tape
recorders, will not even be produced in this country because patents
held by Ampex Corp. have been licensed to Japanese firms.

About a year ago, General Instrument Corp. transferred TV
tuner and other component production to its Taiwan and Portuguese
plants, shutting down two New England plants and most of a third.
Between 3,000 and 4,000 workers were permanently laid off. General
Instrument increased its employment in Taiwan from 7,200 to over
12,000. General Instrument is that nation's largest employer, with
more workers there than in all its U.S. operations combined.

A few months ago, Motorola shut down its picture plant,
selling its machinery and equipment to a General Telephone and
Electronics subsidiary in Hong Kong. A second picture tube firm
commenced operations in Mexico, taking advantage of item 807 of
the Tariff Schedules. Friden, a subdivision of Singer Corp., and
Burroughs, both discontinued production of electronic desk calculators. Their desk calculators are now being made for them in Japan
by Hitachi and other former manufacturers under the latter's label.
So, here we have another growth industry that U.S. based multinational firms have abandoned as producers--becoming importers of
the products they once made....

Several hundred U.S. firms, it is estimated, have set up plants
in Mexico, below the border under the program advertised as a "Twin
Plant" concept. Under this concept, plants on the Mexican side of
the border assemble parts and components shipped to them by their
U.S. parent, and then return them for final processing to a twin
plant somewhere in the United States. Duty is paid only on value
added.

In actual practice, work and jobs are transferred from the
United States to Mexico in order to take advantage of the cheap
labor available at 30-40 cents an hour. In transferring production
of TV lines from Warwick Electronic's Illinois and Arkansas plants,
approximately 2,000 U.S. jobs have disappeared. Advance Ross Electronics transferred 250 jobs to Juarez, Mexico, from El Paso, then
set up a U.S. facility with about 15 employees. Transitron has
1,500 workers in its Laredo, Mexico, plant and only management personnel in Laredo, Texas....

The electrical-electronics industries have spawned and nourished a very considerable number of our multinational giants and
conglomerates. The growth of the industry, particularly its electronics segment, has been spurred by heavy government support. More
than half of this year's $25 billion in sales of electronics instru-
ments, devices and equipment is to the federal government's Defense
Department, NASA and FAA. Government contracts have likewise sustained the computer industry. This year's total awards to this
industry have been reported as over $2 billion.

The federal government has been a substantial and generous
customer down through the years. Additionally, it has contributed
very significantly to the industries' technological growth through
initiation and support of the industries' research and development
programs. More than two-thirds of the $22-$23 billion R. & D.
outlays in electronics and communications equipment between 1957

and 1965 were federal funds--that is, taxpayers' money. Annual
R. & D. outlays have since increased but the federal government's
portion has not declined.

The technological lead of American electronic firms was made
possible only through government support. As the OECD Directorate
for Scientific Affairs points out, "Semiconductors, numerical
control, electronic computers, * * * as well as a host of other less
significant innovations owe their development to federal support."
A great many of these basic, government-subsidized, privately
patented inventions have been licensed to foreign, especially
Japanese, competitors. The latter pay royalties to the U.S. multinational firms holding these patents.

General Electric, for example, has licensed Japanese companies
to produce parallel phase detector circuit for TV receiving sets;
optical gunsights; transistors and semiconductor elements; lamps,
including mercury and infrared lamps; television receiver converter
circuitry, color photographic camera systems; steam turbine electric
generators, et cetera.

RCA has licensed Japanese firms in the following components,
products, and processes, among others: magnetic memory cores;
electron microscopes; electrostatic cameras; color picture tubes;
monolithic integrated circuits; et cetera.

Other multinational U.S.-based corporations that have licensed
Japanese firms include: Westinghouse, IBM, Sperry-Rand, CBS,
Bendix, Zenith Radio, Fairchild Camera and Instrument, Allis
Chalmers, Singer Co., Texas Instrument, et cetera. Licensing
agreements cover color picture tubes, video tape recorders, computer
data processing devices, navigational instruments, planer semiconductors including integrated circuitry, microelectronic equipment, et cetera, et cetera....

Multinational firms are constantly adding to and improving
their mobility, transferring operations, technology and resources
in accordance with corporate profit objectives. Workers may improve
their productivity and skills, but they cannot overcome their basic
"disadvantage"--their high wages and benefits, compared with those
prevailing in other parts of the world.

A recent survey of 167 IUE shops showed 55 had a minimum plant
wage of less than $2 an hour. Two dollars an hour is just over
$4,000 a year. The administration, in its welfare legislation,
puts the poverty line at $3,920 for a family of four persons a year.

But even if we were to reduce wages to $1.60 an hour, the legal
minimum, American workers cannot compete with wages of 10 to 30
cents an hour paid to Far Eastern and Mexican workers. Nor could
American workers become competitive by increasing their man-hour
productivity. In my industry, annual increases in man-hour productivity during the sixties approximated 4 percent. Wage and fringe
benefit gains from 1960 to 1969 averaged 2.8 percent a year at
General Electric and 2.6 percent a year at Westinghouse....

The electric-electronics industry as a whole, depending on
how it is measured, remains a trade surplus industry, but, while
the ratio of exports to imports was 3.8 to 1 in 1960, it declined
to 1.4 to 1 in 1969. If we were to eliminate government-financed
exports, the current ratio would show an even steeper drop.

Employment, of course, has been affected. In the electronics
segment, we estimate a drop in employment since 1966 of over 60,000
jobs for workers. What is perhaps of equal importance is that the
labor force will increase substantially during the next 5 years.

Testimony, July 27, 1970, U.S. Congress, 91st, 2nd session,
Joint Economic Committee, Subcommittee on Foreign Economic Policy,
A Foreign Economic Policy for the 1970s. Hearings...., (Washington,
D.C.: Government Printing Office, 1970), pp. 813, 815-820.

639. WALKING BACKWARDS (1970)

In 1935, a researcher first suggested a causal
connection between lung cancer and asbestos work.
During the next 25 years or more, no research project
investigated the matter. Meanwhile, some 50,000 new
workers were hired into the industry. During the 1960s,
for the first time, research was undertaken by the
scientist whose testimony follows. He is Dr. Irving
J. Selikoff, professor of medicine and of environmental
medicine, and director, Environmental Sciences Laboratory,
Mount Sinai School of Medicine, City University of New
York.

In 1924, almost 50 years ago, Dr. Crooke, in England, described
a case of severe lung scarring in a woman who had spent 20 years
weaving asbestos into cloth. He termed this new type of lung scarring which had not been previously described, asbestosis.
Our own Public Health Service in 1934 investigated the asbestos textile industry in this country and found many such cases of
severe lung scarring. They urged in their report, which was published in 1938, that appropriate precautions be taken and that urgent measures were necessary to eliminate these hazardous exposures.
I will repeat that in the thirties, 40 years ago, we understood
well, we had definitive information, we had documented well, the
severe risks of asbestosis.
It is depressing to report, then, in 1970, that the disease
that we knew well 40 years ago is still with us just as if nothing
was ever known.
It is an unhappy reflection on all of us, on Government, public
health authorities, the medical profession, on labor, on industry,
that at this time in the United States, in the 1960's and 1970's,
8 percent of all deaths among insulation workers in this country are
due to a completely preventable cause.
It may be of interest to outline the studies which have demonstrated this continuing problem.

On January 1, 1943, two locals, Local 12 in New York and Local 32 in Newark, N.J., of the International Association of Heat and Frost Insulators and Asbestos Workers, had 632 members. We have followed each one of these men from that day to the present. During these years, 32 men have died of asbestosis, of a total of 405 deaths.

Since there is no other cause of pulmonary asbestosis but the inhalation of asbestos fibers, these deaths have been unwarranted and unnecessary.

Moreover, many of the men who have not been so badly affected as to die of the disease, have been and are disabled to a greater or lesser extent.

Thus, of almost 400 insulation workers examined by me with more than 20 years from the onset of their work, more than half have the abnormal X-rays of asbestosis and almost one-third have shortness of breath of some degree.

I might add we have evaluated our data through 1967. Among the 632 men who were members of the union in 1942, there should have been 251 deaths, had their experience been the same as all other U.S. males. Instead, 349 men died.

When we looked into the cause for the extra 98 deaths, we found several very disturbing facts. First of all, 32 men died of asbestosis, scarred lungs. Since there is no other cause for asbestosis than the inhalation of asbestos, these were absolutely unnecessary deaths.

I have treated these men. In addition to my research, I have also seen them clinically. I can tell you, it is a terrible way to die....

In my clinical contact with these people, there has been much tragedy. Mr. [Albert] Hutchinson [President, Asbestos Workers Union] and I were talking this morning of one of the men in his union, who, before he died, used to walk backwards. I had never seen this before until I began to care for asbestos workers.

You may wonder why asbestos workers walk backwards. They don't always walk backwards. It is only going upstairs. They are so short of breath that after two steps they have to sit down. It is easier to go up a flight of stairs backwards than walking up. It is a terrible way to die.

U.S. Congress, 91st, 1st and 2nd sessions, Senate, Committee on Labor and Public Welfare, Subcommittee on Labor, Occupational Safety and Health Act, 1970. Hearings...., Part 2, (Washington, D.C.: Government Printing Office, 1970), pp. 1073-1074.

640. MONOTONY ON THE JOB (1972)

An unscheduled product of the assemblyline is
alienation, an absence of meaningful relationship
between the worker and the productive process of which
he is a small part. In such a context, endurance is
the sole triumph. Shop discipline and work rules establish the outer limits of the worker's narrow world. Here
is an example in the person of Dan Clark, an assembler in
the Lordstown, Ohio Chevrolet plant. A year earlier,
the workers had struck against what they scored as the
inhuman routine in the plant.

I have been there now about 5 years, which is a year and a half
short of the highest seniority there.
The problems that face the workers are monotony of the job,
repetition, and boredom. We are constantly doing the same job over
and over again. Where you have problems of hours, like right now--
I am on sick leave, just had an operation, but before I left, 4
days ago, we were working 10 1/2 to 11 hours, which you have no
excuse to leave.
Eight hours, a working day, which it should be 8 hours, you
cannot leave in 8 hours unless you have an excuse to go to the
doctor's, hospital, or emergency call of one of your kids are sick.
That is the only way you are going to leave.
You stay in that plant for 10 1/2 to 11 hours of their choos-
ing, and it may be maybe 95 degrees outside, but inside you can
almost bet in the body shop it is a good 110. But that is not the
warmest place in the whole plant. The warmest place in the whole
plant is the paint shop. That is on the second level.
When it is 95 outside, it is 120 or so in that paint shop, and
your ventilation system, the air you are getting blown in on you,
is supposed to be so cooled down--that is that 95 degree temperature outside that is coming on. You have no ventilation really at
all. They are situated in such a place, they are not on the job
anyhow. Your job may be off to the lefthand side and the ventilation is on the righthand side.
They say there is nothing we can do about it, that is the way
it was designed, and that is the way it is. There is nothing we
can do.
There is the noise level in the plant. The body shop is worse.
One man says, he is a supervisor there, has taken under his control,
he says noise level, I know there are problems there, it is above
the noise level that it is supposed to be. He says I will take
care of it. That is a year and a half now which has gone by and
nothing has been done yet. There has been nothing provided unless
you want to provide it yourself.
I know I put cotton in my ears, because I cannot take it too
much longer. There is pollution in the plant.
In the body shop that consists of, where you are welding, you
are assembling the car together, and you are welding. You will

have fumes like smoke or something that come on over, and dust and fumes and smoke coming out, and they do not have anything for that either. You put on your safety glasses and grin and bear it. That is about it.

You are going to find men today, who are younger--most of the men there are my age. I am 25 years old, and most of us agree that we do not want to spend all of our life in this plant working under these conditions.

In the 1930's our fathers or forefathers, whatever you want to say, they revolted. They wanted the rights for a union.

In 1970 we revolted and all we want to do is improve on things. That is all we want. Why should we be criticized for something like that? All we want is improvement in working conditions.

Testimony, July 25, 1972, U.S. Congress, 92nd, 2nd session, Senate, Commitee on Labor and Public Welfare, Subcommittee on Employment, Manpower, and Poverty, Worker Alienation, 1972. Hearings...., (Washington, D.C.: Government Printing Office, 1972), pp. 12-13.

641.   ORGANIZING IN A FIBERGLASS PLANT (1980)

The South has always been the least unionized section of the country. Industry in that area has traditionally depended upon low wages, plentiful labor, and benevolent local and state governments. Manipulation of racial animosities has also played an important part in management strategies against unions. Only seldom has any national administration undertaken to help unions overcome such obstacles. Alice Wilcox, a fiberglass worker in a PPG plant in Lexington, North Carolina for over 12 years, tells about the travails of organizing in the plant.

I first signed my union card in May 1978 and joined the in-plant organizing committee in June. I have been an active union supporter ever since.

I work in the fabrication department, which is more than 80 percent women, and that is where the company has been putting on most all the pressure, not in the forming department, which is about 90 percent men....

When they asked me to come up here and testify, I was scared to death. All I could think was that I was supposed to have gone on the same trip with Sonny to Pittsburgh and it could have been me out the front door. I sat down and talked with my mother and my children to see what their feelings were.

My mother said, "I'm for whatever will help the situation
down there." I just made up my mind to stand up and fight for
something I believed in. I'm still scared to death that I might be
fired when I get back to Lexington. I haven't slept a night since
last Friday, when I decided to testify.

The reason I am so scared is that I'm the only support for my
family and I have seen what the company has done to other union
supporters and how they can't find jobs anywhere after they are
fired.

One of PPG's favorite ways to frame us is by secretly writing
us up. Before the union campaign started, we were told about our
writeups and they were discussed with us. Since the union campaign
started, however, every week we hear of new cases where union
supporters find out about secret writeups on their jobs that they
never knew anything about. Many of the secret writeups are over a
year old. They use these secret writeups to eventually fire us.

At his unemployment hearing, Sonny found out he had 17 pages
of writeups, most of which he had never seen. They wouldn't even
let him look at them to see if they were true. Just last month my
friend found out that she had been written up in March 1979 for
doing what company supporters do all the time.

Since the first of the year, the company had been doing lots
of new things to put on more pressure. They have split us up into
smaller groups for our daily preshift meetings so we don't get to
talk to or see our friends any more. They have a new rule that we
can't stay on the parking lot after shift changes. Lots of us use
that time to get together and talk for a few minutes or pass out
union handbills. They are even showing antiunion movies to all
new hirees before they start working.

Since PPG started all their delaying tactics at the Labor
Board, the pressure in the plant has become unbearable. The union
supporters especially are under a lot of pressure. Supervisors and
company supporters laugh at us all the time at how much harder we
have to work just to keep our jobs.

We don't feel like we can be ourselves. We don't even feel
free to talk. We never know when we are being bugged, but we do
know that we are constantly being watched. Supervisors have even
admitted this to us. They now have three to four times more supervisors than before the election who just seem to sit around all
the shift and watch us.

My former boss man admitted to me that he could not treat
union supporters the same as he had before the campaign started.
That is pretty much true about all the boss men. You would never
know they were the same people. Lots of our nerves are bad. I
even had to start taking nerve pills and I know lots of others
that have as well.

I would like to thank you for letting me tell my story. It
seems that the Labor Board doesn't seem to have enough authority
to make companies like PPG obey the law. If you have any power to

pass some new laws that would make PPG have to sit down and negotiate a contract and be fair to us, we and others like us in the
South would be very grateful....

Testimony, February 27, 1980, U.S. Congress, 96th, 1st and
2nd sessions, House of Representatives, Committee on Education and
Labor, Subcommittee on Labor-Management Relations, Pressures in
Today's Workplace. Oversight Hearings...., Vol. III, (Washington,
D.C.: Government Printing Office, 1980), pp. 227-228.

642. BLACK LUNGS IN THE COAL MINES (1977)

Pneumoconiosis, or impaired capacity of the lungs
to transfer oxygen to the blood, may be caused by the
deposit of coal dust particles in the lungs. In 1969,
some 100,000 active and retired coal miners suffered from
"black lungs" as the illness is commonly known. That
year, pressed by the United Mine Workers of America
(UMWA), Congress passed the Federal Coal Mine Health and
Safety Act which for the first time provided for benefits
to be paid afflicted miners. In 1972, the Black Lung
Benefits Act was passed and it amended the earlier
measure. Two separate measures were passed in 1977: the
Black Lung Benefits Reform Act and the Black Lung Benefits
Revenue Act. The former levied a tax on every ton of coal
mined; the receipts were earmarked for black lung benefits.
Unfortunately, by 1981, the benefits fund showed a deficit
of more than one billion dollars and Congress considered
changes in the laws. Here is part of the testimony of Dr.
Lorin E. Kerr, director of the department of occupational
health of the UMWA.

When the Social Security Administration ceased operation of the
black lung program on July 1, 1973 nearly 600,000 applications had
been filed. Of this number about 225,000 totally disabled miners
and 140,000 widows were approved for federal black lung benefits.
Since the inception of the SSA program seven years ago on December
30, 1969 nearly 60,000 of these disabled miners have died. It is
likely that half of these deaths can be directly attributed to the
chronic pulmonary diseases occurring among coal miners. This means
more than eleven men every day wheeze away their lives as the penalty for mining coal to earn a living. Were the 77 deaths a week
to occur all on the same day in the same place--remember the
Farmington disaster and its 78 victims--the nation would undoubtedly
demand immediate and universal compliance with mandated standards.
In fact the standards would be made stricter.

The current federal expenditures of somewhat less than $1 billion a year for black lung benefits is scant recognition of the long years of neglect the miners have endured. The payments to the living survivors of decades of uncontrolled coal mine dust exposure can never equal worker's compensation payments which should have been initiated at least as long as 1943 when Britain first provided such coverage. The federal costs will decrease with the gradual demise of the widows and the totally disabled miners.

The 1969 Act as amended in 1972 advanced the date the Department of Labor (DOL) would assume responsibility for the black lung benefits program from July 1, 1972 to July 1, 1973. However, there was no change in the initial stipulation in P. L. 91-173 that the DOL program is worker's compensation with the attendant adversary relationship between the miner and the coal mine operator. This program is now worker's compensation with an adversary vengeance rarely encountered.

In nearly four years DOL has received more than 106,700 black lung claims of which about 53,500 have been disallowed and 49,200 are pending. About 4,000 claims have been approved. Of these approximately 60 percent (2,400) are receiving federal black lung benefits because DOL has been unable to locate the last employer. The last employer has been located for the remaining 40 percent (1,600) and DOL has authorized federal payment of benefits for all of them except the 138 who are being paid by the employer. For various reasons the responsible operators are contesting their payment of the other 1,462 claims. Finally, no state worker's compensation legislation has yet been improved to comply with the federal standards specified in the 1969 coal mine act as amended. It is doubtful that such action ever will occur—certainly not in the absence of a compelling reason, such as the loss of specific federal funds.

Equally lamentable is the fact that about 13 percent of the underground miners and approximately 2.5 percent of the surface miners exhibit x-ray evidence of coal worker's pneumoconiosis. These figures are a conservative indication of the overall effect since prevalence studies cannot take into account sick miners who have left mining. Moreover, chronic obstructive airways disease which is detected by lung function tests has been found in 30 percent of underground miners and 19 percent of surface miners.

Alarming as all the black lung statistics are, it is important to realize that every one of the thousands listed in some report or study is a human being whose lungs have been diseased and disabled as the penalty for mining the nation's vitally needed coal for a living. It is small consolation for a miner with black lung to know that he is "only" one out of a group of five or ten who are so afflicted. Every figure represents a coal miner who is paying a dreadful price for his long years of service in the mines.

A further need to lower dust levels appears in a soon to be published NIOSH report entitled "Mortality Among Coal Miners Covered by UMWA Health and Retirement Funds." The report indicates that contrary to earlier studies lung cancer is killing coal miners at a greater rate than occurs among the rest of the population.

The report also indicates the same is true for cancer of the stomach. In both instances coal mine dust is highly suspect.

There is also grave concern about the unknown hazards of diesels underground. There seems to be a two-fold danger--the neurological distress produced by emissions and the possible synergistic action of the particulates and the coal mine dust hastening the development of coal workers' pneumoconiosis and possibly lung cancer. A recent report issued by the Bureau of Mines states the particulates could make it difficult to meet the 2 mg. dust standard. The Bureau recommends that the emission of particulates should be minimized or diesels should be located in underground coal mines where miners would not be exposed. Until these matters are clarified the coal miners refuse to permit themselves to be exposed to another unknown hazard. The miners reinforced this position with the unanimous passage of a resolution at the UMWA 1976 Cincinnati Convention calling for the removal of all diesels now in underground mines and the prohibition of any additional diesel equipment being introduced into the mines.

Finally, there is the travail surrounding implementation of the Congressionally mandated transfer option in P. L. 91-173. As you know, this provides the miners with an opportunity to transfer to a less dusty--1 mg. of respirable dust--area of work when the specified chest x-ray indicates the advisability of such action. While 5,830 miners have received notice that they may exercize this option, only 1,190 have elected to do so and only 400 of them continue to be protected by the transfer.

We are convinced that the vast majority of miners do not exercize their transfer option because of the economic penalty inflicted by the present requirement in P. L. 91-173. Realistically this means that miners are now deprived of wage increases to which they are entitled when they elect to transfer to protect their health-- their only asset. I seriously doubt that this Subcommittee in 1969 foresaw this as the discriminatory barrier which now plagues the miners.

Closely associated is the need for P. L. 91-173 to provide all miners with x-ray evidence of coal workers' pneumoconiosis with the option to transfer to a less dusty area. It is impossible to predict with any accuracy which miner with category 1, simple pneumonoconiosis will eventually progress to category 2 and beyond. In the absence of such medical capability the only action which can be taken is to specify that the transfer option include all miners with x-ray evidence of CWP.

The UMWA recommends that P. L. 91-173 specify that all miners with x-ray evidence of CWP be provided the option to transfer to a less dusty area with no loss in the rate or amount of pay they would continue to receive prior to transfer.

The Union also recommends that P. L. 91-173 prohibits the use of potentially hazardous or toxic practices such as the use of

diesels in underground coal mines until such time as the non-
existence of hazard or toxicity has been adequately validated.

Testimony, June 9, 1977, U.S. Congress, 95th, 1st session,
House of Representatives, Committee on Education and Labor,
Subcommittee on Labor Standards, Oversight Hearings on the Coal
Mine Health and Safety Act of 1969 (Excluding Title IV).
Hearings...., (Washington, D.C.: Government Printing Office, 1977),
pp. 395-399.

643. CORRUPTION ON THE NEW YORK CITY WATERFRONT (1981)

Corruption by some labor union officials has been
a persistent, if minor, theme in American economic history.
It often takes the form of betraying the economic interests
of union members in exchange for a monetary advantage for
the leaders offered by employers. Familiar corrupt practices are secret concessions to employers on wage demands
and failure to enforce contract rights of members.
Corrupt leaders are sometimes used by businessmen to help
sell services or direct business to the corrupting employer.
Leaders of few unions have been found guilty so frequently
as in the International Longshoremen's Association (ILA).
Following is an account of corruption in New York City.
It is by Robert Fiske, who, as U.S. Attorney in that city
between March 1966 and March 1980, led an investigation
into the corrupt activities of certain ILA officers.

The investigation and the indictments and convictions resulting
from it disclosed a pervasive pattern of corruption and payoffs in
both labor and management in the waterfront industry. On the labor
side the investigation disclosed payoffs to labor leaders to facilitate the performance of work called for by collective bargaining
agreements like the loading and unloading of vessels, payoffs to
reduce workmen's compensation claims, and payoffs to obtain the
respective labor union leader's assistance in obtaining or maintaining business.
On the management side, along with management's payoffs of
labor leaders, the investigation disclosed a pervasive pattern of
kickbacks among middle management throughout the industry that
recognized members and associates of organized crime have played
a significant role in controlling and influencing business activities on the waterfront.
At this point in time, the waterfront investigation conducted
by the southern district of New York has had a very impressive track
record. More than 20 separate companies or their respective executives were convicted of crimes relating to payoff or commercial
fraud schemes.

More than 10 elected officials of the International Longshoremen's Association were convicted after trial of racketeering
offenses relating to payoff schemes. Included among those ILA
officials are the presidents from five separate ILA locals in the
New York metropolitan area. Moreover, the investigation in New
York has also led to successful investigations in the ports of
Norfolk and Philadelphia, as well as contributed evidence to
successful prosecutions in the Southern ports, about which you
heard testimony last week.

Before turning to the specifics of a few of these cases, I
want to touch briefly on two historical facts which apply to the
entire investigation. First, I cannot overemphasize the pervasive
nature of the corruption and payoff schemes discovered in the investigation. Not only have nearly all ILA locals, through their
leaders, been involved in these schemes, but companies from all
aspects of the waterfront industry in one way or another have
participated in these plots.

Moreover, the evidence disclosed that payoffs are not a new
phenomenon to the waterfront industry. One witness testified at
the Scotto trial that payoffs on the waterfront was a "way of life"
and many businessmen testified in court, and told us in interviews,
that the payoff scheme of which they were a part was simply a
pattern of business which they continued for many, many years,
having inherited it from their predecessor.

Second, the investigation and the trials have disclosed that
business on the waterfront is controlled by organized crime. Tape-
recorded conversations obtained from electronic surveillance confirmed that organized crime controls the selection of important
ILA officials and the disposition of waterfront business in ports
in the New York area....

I would like to turn briefly to a description of another subject which you have requested that I cover, which is the prosecution of Anthony M. Scotto and Anthony Anastasia, which I conducted
together with Mr. Levine and in which Agent Barrett testified as
a witness.

On November 15, 1979, a jury sitting in the U.S. District
Court for the southern district of New York returned guilty ver-
dicts against Scotto and Anastasia on 43 counts, including a con-
viction for participating in a pattern of racketeering activity
against Scotto, conspiring to participate in a pattern of racketeering activity against Scotto and Anastasia and numerous violations of the Taft-Hartley Act against both defendants for receiving
illegal labor payoffs....

During the period 1975 through 1979, Scotto was president of
ILA Local 1814 in Brooklyn and vice president for legislative
affairs for the ILA nationally. From 1975 through 1978, Anastasia
was secretary-treasurer of a companion Brooklyn ILA local.

In April 1979, he became executive vice president of local
1814. In addition, he was employed as an organizer of the ILA
nationally. Local 1814 is the largest ILA local in the country.

The evidence at trial demonstrated that throughout the period
1975 through 1979 Scotto and Anastasia corruptly used these positions as high-ranking ILA officials both in Brooklyn and on a

national level to demand illegal labor payoffs exceeding $300,000 from at least six separate waterfront businesses employing ILA labor in the New York area. Through the testimony of three separate witnesses, each of whom were employers of ILA labor and through taperecorded conversations of Scotto and Anastasia obtained pursuant to court-authorized electronic surveillances, as well as other evidence, the Government proved the receipt by the defendants of a total of more than 40 separate cash payments--some as high as $15,000--paid on a quarterly basis, as kickbacks or commissions on business, or as "extra" Christmas bonuses.

Briefly summarized, the proof established that Walter D. O'Hearn, the chief executive of John W. McGrath Corp., a Brooklyn stevedore company, paid Scotto $65,000 per year in cash payable $15,000 each quarter and $5,000 at Christmas--to obtain Scotto's assistance as an ILA official in reducing fraudulent and exaggerated workmen's compensation claims filed by members of Scotto's ILA local.

The proof also established at trial that William "Sonny" Montella, the general manager of Quin Marine Services, Inc., of Brooklyn, paid Scotto $25,000 per year--$5,000 per quarter and $5,000 each Christmas for 3 years for the purpose of obtaining Scotto's assistance in obtaining new business and keeping the business he had from shipping and stevedoring companies with which Scotto dealt as a labor leader and generally for what he described as "peace."

Pursuant to an ongoing arrangement in which Scotto was also involved, Nicholas Seregos, of Jackson Engineering Co., Inc., an ILA-affiliated marine engineering company, paid Anastasia a 10-percent "commission" for business he received with Scotto and Anastasia's assistance from two shipping lines which employed ILA labor.

In addition, three other waterfront employers of ILA labor--Marine Repair Services, Joseph Vinal, Ship Maintenance Co., and C. C. Lumber Co.--made payments of $5,000 or $3,000. None of these cash payments, which, as I indicated earlier, total over $300,000, was reported by Scotto or by Anastasia, on their personal income tax returns.

Testimony, February 25, 1981, U.S. Congress, 97th, 1st session, Senate, Committee on Governmental Affairs, Permanent Subcommittee on Investigations, Waterfront Corruption. Hearings...., (Washington, D.C.: Government Printing Office, 1981), pp. 220-223.

644. HAPPY ENDING IN SILVER CITY (1981)

The intensification of foreign competition, obsolescence of machinery, and changes in consumer taste led many American plants to close down during the 1970s. Some moved to low-wage areas here and overseas while others

simply disappeared. Here and there union workers and
community supporters organized to save jobs by creating
non-profit entities to operate the factories and mills.
In most cases, however, the decision to move proved
irrevocable. Here, however, is a case to the contrary.
The speaker is Jerry Newmin, president of the International
Silver Co., a subsidiary of INSILCO which is a Fortune 500
company.

It is no accident that the community where we are located,
Meriden, Conn., is called the Silver City. Our company's roots
go back to the 1700's in this community, and we have employees whose
ancestors began work with us over a century ago. This is significant, because we have long been the largest employer in the community, and our concern for our people reaches far beyond just providing them with a job.

For more than 100 years, a natural thing for a local young man
or woman to do was to aspire to a job at the silver company. And
fortunately, we were able to provide jobs for them as the silver
company grew and prospered.

The company was the mainstay of the community until our stainless steel flatware business came under severe and devastating
attack from low-priced imports of foreign goods during the 1960's
and 1970's. Over these two decades, the Government's answer to
growing unemployment in our industry was to impose tariff-rate quotas. In fact, tariff-rate quotas were in effect for most of this
period. With the benefit of hindsight, however, we were able to
see that these solutions were both ineffective as well as costly
to the American consumer.

At the same time that consumers were paying tens of millions
of dollars to reimburse importers' duty expenses, imports increased
to more than 80 percent of total domestic consumption and employment in the industry dropped sharply. Our own flatware employment,
for example, dropped from 1,750 people in 1970 to about 250 people
today....

In 1968, when the flatware facility which we call factory C
was constructed at a cost of $18 million, it was the largest, most
modern facility of its type in the world, designed specifically for
the manufacture of flatware.

Despite these advantages, the company's efforts to compete in
the stainless steel flatware business were unsuccessful, and market
share declined from over 40 percent to almost zero by the end of
the 1970's.

As losses in the flatware operation mounted, the easy decision
would have been to close the factory and sell the equipment and
the real estate. There were three important reasons, however,
why the company chose not to do so.

First, recovery of our investment in machinery and equipment
would have been difficult because the processes and operations
involved in the making of flatware are peculiar to the product and
could not easily be transferred from one industry to another.

Second, the mobility of our employees was severely limited.
By the mid-1970's, the average age of the flatware work force passed
50 years, and average length of service exceeded 20 years. Today,
as a matter of interest, the average age in our flatware factory
is 56, and they have 26 years of service on the average.

In addition, like the equipment itself, the work force possessed unique skills indigenous to the flatware business. For these
reasons, the employees were "locked" to our industry, our company,
and the community, and they looked to the company and the union for
help.

And third, for each worker employed in our facilities today,
we support two retired employees and their families who reside in
the community. The company's moral commitment to this group was
paramount.

Despite declining sales, we continued to manufacture stainless
steel flatware in this facility until 1979. By that time, it was
clear that the domestic stainless steel flatware business was doomed
and that the company could no longer survive the tremendous financial drain it was incurring.

During 1979, the decision was made to discontinue the remaining
domestic production of stainless steel flatware. A three-phase program was outlined which provided for the foreign production of all
stainless steel flatware, the consolidation of the remaining silver-
plated flatware business into approximately one-third of this facility, and the redirection of the other two-thirds of the facility
to new businesses.

To be successful, this diversification program would require
a smooth transition of our flatware work force to newly created
jobs and the development of entirely new technologies.

In seeking new business opportunities, management outlined
the following set of criteria to guide its diversification efforts.

First, due to the relatively high fixed cost of this facility,
we would look for businesses which had low selling distribution and
administrative costs so that we could compete on a total cost basis.

Second, because the flatware business is seasonal in nature
and is hit hard during recessionary periods, we would seek products
which were anticyclical and recession insulated.

Third, since stainless steel flatware had become a commodity
business with little value added in the manufacturing process, we
would seek products with high technology and high value-added components.

Fourth, since our employees possessed unique skills such as
hand-buffing, plating and metal-forming, we would attempt to utilize these skills wherever possible.

And fifth, rather than competing in shrinking markets such as
flatware, we would seek expanding markets where competition would
be less keen and a new venture would have a greater probability
of success.

After extensive market research and a careful analysis of our
existing skills, we concluded that the aerospace industry and the
U.S. automotive retooling markets provided excellent opportunities
for us.

The first market identified was fuel and lubricant transfer lines for turbine aircraft engines. These products are made primarily of stainless steel and required plating which would enable us to use some of the skills of our flatware employees. Further, we would be answering the need of a nearby Connecticut aerospace company, the Pratt & Whitney division of United Technologies, who was seeking new subcontractors.

The company proposed to Pratt & Whitney that we would equip and staff a facility capable of complete fabrication of tubing from raw tube stock to finished pieces on a competitive basis. Pratt & Whitney management was receptive to our proposal and we became a qualified vendor to them by September of 1979.

Today, International Silver is an established supplier of tubing to Pratt & Whitney for the TF-30 U.S. Phantom Navy carrier jet and the JT9D engine, which powers the Boeing 747. During 1980, we have received an "excellent" rating on quality from Pratt & Whitney for our performance. This is the highest rating a vendor can receive.

In the near future, the company will be supplying tubing to other aerospace companies, including Sikorsky Aircraft, for its helicopter engines.

The training program for this new department was entirely on-the-job and was developed by us with the assistance of Pratt & Whitney and financed by the company with no outside help.

In training our tubing employees in new skills, we were successful in 80 percent of the individual cases with a 20-percent dropout rate. All of these employees are former flatware workers who would have been laid off were it not for this program. It should be kept in mind that the average age of employees who went through this 1-year training program was 53 and that they had never made tubing assemblies previously.

In addition, the company invested in automated equipment to shorten the learning period for employees as well as to reduce costs. This program currently employs 30 direct labor employees plus related support personnel. We are optimistic that this department will employ at least 60 workers by the end of next year.

As the tubing program progressed, an opportunity to enter into the related precision machining components business also developed. A special machining area to support the tubing operation was established which generated additional employment for 20 direct labor personnel, broadened the skills of our employees and added significantly to our new capabilities.

The objective of the precision machining department is the employment of 40 direct labor employees plus the usual peripheral jobs. This department also services the same market as the tubing operation, and the training program was developed and financed by the company.

Lastly, it was determined that the company possessed a reservoir of skilled toolmakers and mechanical maintenance personnel who for years had designed and manufactured tooling and equipment to support the flatware business.

The existence of these basic worker's skills enabled us to enter the business of designing and rebuilding of tooling equipment under contract for other companies.

However, the machinery and equipment we were going to design and build for new markets would require more advanced skills on the part of existing toolmakers as well as the training of additional skilled personnel.

A training program for existing flatware employees was developed which would require 4 years of classroom and shop apprenticeship instruction. This program was endorsed by the United Steelworkers of America, AFL-CIO, whose local 7700 represents our employees of Meriden through subdistrict director John Santori.

The union assured the company of their complete cooperation and has given their active support to this program. In addition, the union and the company went jointly to the Connecticut State Department of Labor for necessary financial assistance, since this program would represent a substantial investment of time and money.

International Silver applied for and received a grant in the amount of $164,000 from the U.S. Department of Labor's Trade Adjustment Assistance program which assists workers who lose their jobs because of imports. This grant was administered through the Connecticut State Department of Labor and covered instructor costs, partial wage reimbursement, supplies and 75 percent of the used machinery needed to set up the vestibule training....

On January 1, 1970, the company employed 1,750 people in its flatware operation. Today, 250 workers are employed in flatware, and 140 are employed in the new ventures just described. The balance, 700, have retired, of which 400 voluntarily retired on an early basis at company expense, and 660 have been displaced.

The number of people displaced during the seventies is certainly disturbing. But today, in 1980, our recall list has been exhausted, and the International Silver Co. hiring office is open for the first time in 20 years. Further, the 140 new direct labor jobs are supported by 46 new salaried positions. These numbers will grow in the future as these new ventures prosper.

The success of this diversification effort can, however, be measured in more than numbers. We are no longer reeling from the impact of imports. We have saved Factory C which in all probability would have been closed without this program. The morale of our people has been substantially restored. We are upgrading the skills and earning power of our employees and their productivity is increasing. We are saving the jobs and the personal dignity of our older employees.

And finally, our efforts have been rewarded with improved earnings, and our confidence in the future has been restored.

Testimony, September 18, 1980, U.S. Congress, 96th, 2nd session, Senate, Committee on Labor and Human Resources, Workers and the Evolving Economy of the Eighties. Hearings...., (Washington, D.C.: Government Printing Office, 1981), pp. 314-319.

645. UNEMPLOYED IN ATLANTA (1981)

Late in 1981, unemployment in the United States
reached nine percent while the economy as a whole
remained mired in an unprecedented combination of inflation and stagnation. J. R. Jones, an unemployed auto
worker in Atlanta, Georgia, tells a Congressional committee
of some human costs of unemployment

I was also employed by the Ford Motor Co. I have 14 years of
service and am laid off. I have three kids and a wife. My wife
does not work. I am the only source of bread that comes in that
house.

I am not the only one that is laid off from that plant with 13
or 14 years of service. You take a man that is the head of a house.
Even you would not let your children starve, you would not let them
go hungry. You would do something. This is what the people is
asking for: Give us a job.

I had a pretty good attendance record when I was working. I
think I was out something maybe like 3 or 4 days a year, maybe 5
days a year. The average working American would work every day
if he could get a job and work. You go to the employment office.
I was down at the unemployment office Monday. You go in the employment office and from wall to wall, people are standing up, three
abreast, waiting to try to file unemployment insurance.

You exhaust all of your unemployment insurance. Your medical,
your insurance, all that stuff lapses. What do you do? When your
kids have to go to the doctor, these bills still have to be paid.
We were drawing TRA. You go in one day, they say well, Mr. Jones,
as of today, you do not draw any more TRA. You get a $90 check,
whatever, however you are going to do it. What do you do? You have
three kids, a wife, you have to buy groceries. You got to pay gas
bills, to buy gas. If you do not, you freeze to death.

You do not--like the other brother said, you do not have any
form of recreation. You just go and do the best that you can, try
to survive. You know it is easy. I thought well, a layoff would
not be too bad. Take a layoff, it would not be too bad. But you
get out there for a little while, 1, 2, or 3 years and you wonder
what is going on.

I think the average person that is laid off from Ford Motor
Co., General Motors, Chrysler today--not only Ford Motor Co. I
picked up a guy yesterday coming from the unemployment office. He
had been with the steel company 26 years; laid off. What do you
tell your kids? They say daddy, why are you not working today?
You sit and look at them and one of your kids, 10 years old says
well, I hope you can go to work tomorrow, this, or that.

What do you just--I mean what do you tell them?....This is
our livelihood. I got a daughter that is 14 years old. These
other brothers and sisters have daughters 11, 12 years old. We are
not working. When they get 11, 12--I mean 18, 19 years old, where
are they going to go to work?

I have been in the automobile industry about 15, 16 years
of my life. My only source of--I guess--I can say longer than
that, because my dad worked for 25 years. This was a means of eat-
ing for me. When you sit down, look all over the country, and see
plants closing, jobs gone, people just sitting, no food stamps,
no nothing, you just--I mean I do not think the average worker in
America wants a handout, but we want a job.

Testimony, December 4, 1981, U.S. Congress, 97th, 1st session,
House of Representatives, Committee on Banking, Finance, and Urban
Affairs, Grassroots Hearings on the Economy. Hearings...., Part 3,
(Washington, D.C.: Government Printing Office, 1981), pp. 166-
168.

H.

ADVERTISING AND MERCHANDISING

646. SCHLITZ BEER IS PURE (ca. 1900)

        Make your article _seem_ better, even if it isn't.
This was the heart of Hopkins' advice. In an age of
differentiated products, this seemed good business advice.
Claude Hopkins became president and then chairman of the
board of Lord & Thomas, the nation's largest advertising
agency. He writes the following.

        Schlitz Beer was another advertising campaign which I handled
for J. L. Stack. Schlitz was then in fifth place. All brewers
at that time were crying "Pure." They put the word "Pure" in large
letters. Then they took double pages to put it in larger letters.
The claim made about as much impression on people as water makes on
a duck.
        I went to a brewing school to learn the science of brewing,
but that helped me not at all. Then I went through the brewery.
I saw plate-glass rooms where beer was dripping over pipes, and I
asked the reason for them. They told me those rooms were filled
with filtered air, so the beer could be cooled in purity. I saw
great filters filled with white-wood pulp. They explained how that
filtered the beer. They showed how they cleaned every pump and
pipe, twice daily, to avoid contaminations. How every bottle was
cleaned four times by machinery. They showed me artesian wells,
where they went 4,000 feet deep for pure water, though their
brewery was on Lake Michigan. They showed me the vats where beer
was aged for six months before it went out to the user.

They took me to their laboratory and showed me their original
mother yeast cell. It had been developed by 1,200 experiments to
bring out the utmost in flavor. All of the yeast used in making
Schlitz beer was developed from that original cell.

I came back to the office amazed. I said: "Why don't you
tell people these things? Why do you merely try to cry louder
than others that your beer is pure? Why don't you tell the reasons?"

"Why," they said, "the processes we use are just the same as
others use. No one can make good beer without them."

"But," I replied, "others have never told this story. It
amazes everyone who goes through your brewery. It will startle
everyone in print."

So I pictured in print those plate-glass rooms and every other
factor in purity. I told a story common to all good brewers, but
a story which had never been told. I gave purity a meaning.
Schlitz jumped from fifth place to neck-and-neck with first place
in a very few months. That campaign remains to this day one of
my greatest accomplishments. But it also gave me the basis for
many another campaign. Again and again I have told simple facts,
common to all makers in the line—too common to be told. But they
have given the article first allied with them an exclusive and
lasting prestige.

That situation occurs in many, many lines. The maker is too
close to his product. He sees in his methods only the ordinary.
He does not realize that the world at large might marvel at those
methods, and that facts which seem commonplace to him might give
him vast distinction.

That is a situation which occurs in most advertising problems.
The article is not unique. It embodies no great advantages. Perhaps countless people can make similar products. But tell the
pains you take to excel. Tell factors and features which others
deem too commonplace to claim. Your product will come to typify
those excellencies. If others claim them afterward, it will only
serve to advertise you. There are few advertised products which
cannot be imitated. Few who dominate a field have any exclusive
advantage. They were simply the first to tell certain convincing
facts.

Claude C. Hopkins, My Life in Advertising, (New York: Harper,
1927), pp. 79-82.

647. U.S. STEEL CONSIDERS ADVERTISING (1901-1911)

The U.S. Steel Corporation was organized in
1901. The next year, the corporation's general sales
managers formed a committee on advertising. Its role
was minimal. In 1911, there first appears in the

corporation's printed record mention of an advertising
expenditure thought necessary to meet competition.

[EXECUTIVE COMMITTEE]
    In a general way the president and Mr. Converse expressed
themselves as not in favor of advertising.
                                            [April 9, 1901.]
. . . .
    On the subject of advertising Mr. Edenborn stated that he
does not approve of general advertising. It was the general
opinion of the members of this committee that except in certain
technical and trade papers, or where some special thing was
required to be brought before the public, no advertising should be
done. It was voted that the president convey this suggestion to
the presidents of the subsidiary companies.
                                            [May 23, 1901.]

. . . .
    Since the last meeting of your association additional state-
ments of the advertising expenditures have been received from the
tin plate, Carnegie, and steel hoop companies, which at that date
had not reported. These statements enable us to make a complete
summary of the expenditures for publication advertising only as
follows:

American Tin Plate Co.............................$27,663.03
American Steel & Wire Co.......................... 27,016.05
American Sheet Steel Co........................... 11,394.13
American Bridge Co. of New York................... 9,854.15
National Tube Co.................................. 7,320.77
H.C. Frick Coke Co............................... 2,495.00
Carnegie Steel Co................................ 1,890.00
Shelby Steel Tube Co............................. 1,850.00
American Steel Hoop Co........................... 1,765.00
Lorain Steel Co.................................. 2,479.00
                            Total.......... 93,727.38

    Illinois Steel Co., none.
    National Steel Co., none.
    This statement covers the advertising in 130 publications,
with a total of 172 advertisements, which are generally on a continuous contract basis from year to year and, with a few exceptions, may be classed as trade journals; also 64 publications
utilized by the tin plate company in advertising its M.F. roofing
tin, which are also on a yearly contract basis; and 162 publications used by the American Steel & Wire Co. for brief periods in
advertising its woven-wire fencing, making a total of 356 mediums
in which one or more of the companies have advertising at the
present time.
    To the sum of $93,727.38, expended for advertising in trade
and agricultural journals, should be added at least $10,000 for
special advertising not included in the reports received. No
estimate of the cost of book and pamphlet advertising of the cost
of (plates) illustrations has been made, but $15,000 will probably
cover this item, so that the expenditures chargeable to advertising

now approximates $125,000 per annum, exclusive of the cost of
advertising managers' services.

[May 2, 1902.]

. . . .

    Inquiry by the president developed that approximately $140,000
per year is being expended by the various companies in direct advertising as follows:

Steel and Wire.....................................$75,000
Sheet and tin plate............................... 20,000
Carnegie.. 10,000
Tube.. 15,000
Lorain.. 3,000
Bridge.. 15,000

    A very full discussion of the matter developed that a majority
of the members are of the opinion that much better results would
be accomplished by a consolidation of this expenditure and the
establishment of an advertising bureau, the head of which eventually
could be made the spokesman of the corporation, if thought desirable, in matters pertaining to general policy or such other subjects
as the corporation might think it wise to make public.

    The chairman was requested to lay the matter before the cor-
poration for consideration, at the same time stating that Mr.
Farrell and Mr. Davis dissented from the opinion of the remainder
of the members.

[August 21, 1901.]

. . . .

    It was the sentiment of the meeting that while advertising
brings practically no returns, except perhaps in the case of
specialties, it would be policy to continue as we have been doing
and it was thought wise to handle this matter through this body
as suggested, but appointment of the committee was deferred until
the next meeting.

[June 17, 1909.]

. . . .

    Mr. Andrews advised that a number of their principal sheet
competitors have been carrying on a very expensive advertising
campaign for a year or more, and in order to meet this they have
practically been forced to place advertisements recently in Good
Roads, American Metal Market, the Hardware Reporter, and the
Engineering News, at a cost of $2,405. These expenditures were
approved.

[September 20, 1911.]

    Extracts from minutes of meetings of the executive committee
and meetings of general sales managers of U.S. Steel Corporation,
U.S. Congress, House of Representatives, [Stanley] Committee on
Investigation of United States Steel Corporation, United States
Steel Corporation, pp. 3778, 3786, 3934, 3959-3960, 3967, and
3973.

648.   CHAIN DRUG STORES ARE A THREAT (1912)

This representative of a small-business trade
association attacked the Sherman Act for its failure
to prevent chain stores from arising, and he called for
a fair-trade law as protection against chains. Frank
Freericks, a lawyer and registered pharmacist from
Cincinnati, Ohio, was a member of the legislative committee of the National Association of Retail Druggists.
The following is his comment.

We have today in this country 46,000 retail druggists. Their
average investment in business is about $3,000. Of the total num-
ber, fully 50 per cent have an income not to exceed $3 per day of
from 15 to 16 hours' work. Of the remaining 50 percent, it is
safe to say that not more than 5 per cent have an annual income exceeding $3,000. At the same time the Sherman Act became a law the
so-called "chain drug store" was practically an unknown thing. Today chain drug stores are found from one end of the country to the
other. By way of illustration, there is now operating in the
Eastern and New England States, including New Jersey and New York,
a $15,000,000 corporation, engaged in the retail drug business,
which operates from 70 to 80 stores--very large stores as a rule--
throughout those States. It seems to be a combination of a number
of such chain store corporations. Having in mind that the average
investment in a retail drug store is $3,000, which investment is
used by the retail druggist for the needs of the average retailer's
business, including manufacture on a small scale, and then comparing
it with this corporation employing a capital of $15,000,000 in the
same line of business, it will be seen that said corporation is
practically replacing to-day 5,000 retail druggists who otherwise
would be conducting an independent though small business on their
own account. The Hegeman & Riker and Riker-Jaynes Corporations,
which are here referred to, as well as some other similar chain
stores, are, as already stated, gradually extending their business
and influence over larger territory, and are thus constantly reducing the opportunity for independent small business in other
sections as they already have successfully done on a large scale
in New York and in the New England States. One of these chain
drug store corporations, it has been freely asserted, is at least
in part capitalized by some of the same people who have capitalized
the National Cigar Stores Co., and its tactics are said to not
be greatly different from those of the Tobacco Trust.
    Again, by way of illustration, and this is true of every city
of any size in the country, in the city of Cincinnati, my home, in
the early nineties, we had something over 180 retail druggists.
To-day, with an increase in population of nearly 150,000 people, we
have some in the 160 retail druggists. In the early nineties all
but 4 or 5 of the retail druggists in Cincinnati were employing
registered clerks, to-day fully 50 per cent are without registered
clerks and reduced to the necessity of confining themselves to
their stores for from 15 to 16 hours per day in an effort to

survive. These illustrations are cited to show a condition existing in one line of retail trade, but which will be found in all
lines of retail trade to a more or less extent, in the face of a
law, which we believe to have been expressly enacted for the
purpose of preserving equal opportunity and in aid of the smaller
interests.

Testimony, Frank H. Freericks, March 27, 1912, U.S. Congress,
62nd, Senate, Committee on Interstate Commerce, Control of Corporations, Persons, and Firms Engaged in Interstate Commerce, II, pp.
2709-2710.

649. CHANGES IN MERCANTILE CREDIT (1913)

Should the projected Federal Reserve System permit
member banks to borrow from Federal Reserve on the basis
of unsecured, one-name notes signed by merchants? James
Cannon, president of the Fifth National Bank, New York
City, gives a view of the question.

[Mr. CANNON.] The mercantile business of the country is done
on single-name paper; it is not done upon security. The merchant
who buys goods does not give an indorsed note, as he used to in the
old-fashioned days. It is done on a single-name basis. He buys
goods, and, on the 10th of October, for instance, which is the
settlement day for the dry-goods people, he comes to us and says,
"I would like to borrow $200,000 or $300,000." He has nothing to
give except his own plain note, without a dollar of collateral behind it. We have to take the risk. We take the risk of loaning
this merchant $200,000 or $300,000 on his own promise to pay. It
is his own note, payable to our order, with nothing behind it.
    Senator HITCHCOCK. Can you do that now, in national banks?
    Mr. CANNON. Oh, yes; it is done very largely. The whole
business of the country is done on single-name commercial paper.
    Of course in the States--I am not speaking outside of the
national bank--it may be different. The large mercantile interests
insist upon borrowing on single-name commercial paper, and we are
obliged to assume that risk. We have got to look to the merchant's
responsibility, business capacity, and the nature of his business;
and we take, in the banking business, a very large risk in handling
single-name commercial paper.
. . . .
    That is the old-fashioned way, where the merchant came down
to New York and went to the dry-goods district, or to the hardware
district, or somewhere else and bought a bill of goods for $10,000
and turned around and gave his note, and then the dry-goods man

indorsed the note and put it in his bank. That is not the method
now. All good men have credit, and use their credit, and they
will borrow from the banks and pay their bills until they make
their collections.

Testimony, James G. Cannon, October 10, 1913, U.S. Congress,
63rd, 1st session, Senate, Committee on Banking and Currency,
Hearings....on S. 2639, part 27, pp. 2124-2125, 2156.

650. FINANCING THROUGH A BILL OF LADING (1913)

A very ordinary form of bank financing of merchandise whereby the bank extends credit to the seller and
holds claim to the goods as security for the credit.
James Coxey, from Massillon, Ohio, had led the famous
"Coxey's Army" in 1894. He appeared before a Senate
committee to testify on the pending Federal Reserve Bill.

I quarry stone and grind it into sand. I supply some of the
principal steel works of the country, and have been supplying the
steel works of the country for 32 years. When I ship out a carload
of sand to-day we get the railroad weight to-morrow, and we make an
invoice against the party to whom we have shipped the sand. We
attach a draft and bill of lading to the invoice, take it into the
bank, and the banker takes his rake-off of 8 per cent and credits
me with the balance. I make that draft due and payable on the
20th of the month following the month of shipment. If it is shipped
to-day, that account will be due on the 20th of next month, and I
make that draft for that number of days and they discount it and
place the balance, after deducting the discount to my credit.
When they remit for this--they may remit direct to the bank
or they may remit to me, but in every case that remittance is taken
in and the draft taken out. If it is not paid on the day that it
is due, it runs on and the interest is charged up to me. That is
one system.
Under that system the banks are furnishing the means to exchange the products; they are furnishing in this case the working
capital--the money with which to do business--because we have first
the money for the investment in the enterprise which is necessary.
In a case of this kind the bank furnishes the working capital, but
they get their interest in Ohio of 8 per cent for doing it.

Testimony, Jacob S. Coxey, October 23, 1913, U.S. Congress,
63rd, 1st session, Senate, Committee on Banking and Currency,
Hearings...on S. 2639, p. 2952.

651. THE WESTERN BUSINESS (1959)

The commercialization of our western heritage
may by now have yielded as much income as the discovery of gold. The following is an extract from an
interview with Roy B. Huggins. Huggins, a summa cum
laude graduate of the University of California at
Los Angeles and former graduate student in political
philosophy, entered the motion picture industry after
World War II as a writer, producer, and director. In
1955, he became a television producer. During the
late 1950's, he wrote and produced "Maverick." Shanley
was television and radio editor of the New York Times.

After producing more than fifty installments of "Maverick,"
Roy Huggins is convinced that the Western will last as long as
there is television.
    This statement, which is bound to cause depression or resent-
ment in some quarters, was among a series of unequivocal assertions
made by Mr. Huggins the other day during a visit to New York from
the West Coast. He is an energetic man, approaching middle age.
He talks volubly and seldom has to pause for an idea.
    His show, seen on the American Broadcasting Company network
on Sunday nights, would tend to corroborate his confidence in the
durability of Westerns. In its two seasons on the air "Maverick"
has consistently won greater audiences than its competition,
according to the rating services. Last Sunday night, for example,
it was credited with having enticed more viewers than either the
first half of Mary Martin's one-hour special Easter telecast or
Ed Sullivan's weekly variety show.
    Mr. Huggins qualified his statement about the future of
Westerns by saying, "they will have their cycles just as they have
had their cycles in the movies." But he added:
    "I think the Western will last because it combines two of the
most deep and persistent desires of mankind--freedom and security.
I know they are usually incompatible, but in a Western you get
both."
    Mr. Huggins paused and then said:
    "The hero rides into town, ties up his horse, enters a saloon
and orders a drink. Instantly you get the feeling that he's free.
He doesn't have to carry an identification card, Social Security
card or a letter of recommendation. He's utterly without restraint.
When he pays for his drink there's never a question about where he
gets the money. Everything is wonderfully secure.
    "You never ask what these people do for a living, because if
you did, the whole thing would go to pieces. As it is, the Western
gives the audience a sense of well-being, an escape from
reality."
    For many years a successful motion-picture and TV writer,
Mr. Huggins has carefully supervised each of the scripts for
"Maverick" and has written some of them himself. His conception

of the program was one in which he would try to violate all of the
rules and stock situations that had prevailed previously in Western
programs.

When he prepared a pilot film for exhibition before potential
buyers from networks and agencies, however, he built it along
rather conventional Western lines. "It would have been too risky
to break the rules right away," he commented.

But when he presented an episode called "The Jail at Junction
Flats," his ambition was fulfilled.

"It ended with the hero abandoned and all tied up in the middle
of the desert, with the 'heavy' riding off into the sun," he said.
"We really got letters after that one. The writers protested,
"There are some things you can't do' and 'We'll never watch your
show again.' But I never had a single protest from the agency,
network or sponsors."

Using writers such as Marion Hargrove, "Maverick" has offered
its viewers other departures from the conventional. Among them
were "Gunshy," (a satire on "Gunsmoke") and a Western based on
Sheridan's "The Rivals."

Mr. Huggins' wife, an attractive actress named Adele Mara,
appears in the show occasionally. Once, clad in a rather diaphanous
gown, she portrayed a dancer who performed on a bar in a frontier
saloon. The producer later received a strongly worded protest
against this sequence from a mother who objected to the "half-naked
woman." Mr. Huggins wrote a reply in which he informed the com-
plainant, "That was no half-naked woman; that was my wife."

He continues to be surprised, however, by some of the things
that can be said in a Western without causing objections from
audiences. He gave the following example:

"Once Bret Maverick, the hero, said that his father had told
him, 'You're shifty, self-centered and you know the value of a
dollar. You'll die wealthy and honored.'

"If this doesn't oppose the American idea, I don't know what
does," Mr. Huggins said. "But I invented Pappy, Maverick's father,
to put a buffer between what the hero has to say and his audience.
Whenever Maverick has something cynical or inconoclastic to say
he quotes Pappy. It seems to work."

Interview with Roy B. Huggins by John P. Shanley, New York
Times, April 5, 1959.

652. FRANCHISING WITH KENTUCKY FRIED CHICKEN (1970)

During the decade of the 70s, according to the
Department of Commerce, the share of Gross National
Product accounted for by franchising rose from ten
to 15 percent. In 1980, franchising made up one-third
of the total retail market. Most prominent in
franchised businesses were food specialties, restaurants,

real estate, business services, and convenience stores.
Fast-food restaurants were a product of the late 1960s
and early 1970s. During the 1970s, large conglomerate
corporations began buying up the more profitable franchises. In 1979, nearly 20,000 American franchised outlets operated in foreign countries, a one-eighth increase
in a single year. Over 3,700 outlets operated by 42
franchises failed during 1980 while more than 1,238
franchised were not renewed in 1979. The total value of
retail sales in all franchised units was $295 billion in
1980. A devotee of franchising is Leon W. Harman, a
franchisee of Kentucky Fried Chicken in San Francisco.

I was a high school dropout and only an average restauranteur
before joining Kentucky Fried Chicken.

When I went into business for myself over 30 years ago, my wife
and I borrowed $700 on time to buy a hamburger place in Utah. Our
first day of business grossed $14, and the second day we had a
decline of 9 percent and brought in only $12.74. We struggled for
about 10 years to keep things going.

My wife ran the business herself while I was in the Army for
2 years. By 1952 we had built our business from $14 a day to a
yearly gross of $165,000, and were making a fair living. At that
time, we met Colonel Sanders and put his first franchise in our
restaurant.

The chicken sold so well that soon we were able to build another restaurant. Then other restauranteurs became interested in
the colonel's recipe, and from there his franchises began to grow.

Because of the foresight of the franchise company and their
careful planning, Kentucky Fried Chicken grew vigorously. The
franchise company not only offers a good recipe for food, they also
offer knowhow. They teach franchises how to market their product
as well as provide field service representatives to visit the stores
on a regular basis to help the franchises.

They have seminars at least twice a year for our people to get
together and exchange ideas and learn new methods. They sponsor
an annual convention, as well as supplying technical bulletins as
learning aids.

They also teach us how to organize ourselves for effective
advertising, and, by so doing, we have created a national image
for our product. For 4 years, the franchise company has contributed
over $250,000 a year to the national co-op advertising fund which
has tended to furnish real leadership in advertising.

In 1970 the franchise company will budget $2 million to the
national co-op advertising fund. The total cooperative effort by
the national franchise company and the franchisees will be $24
million this year.

They are constantly conducting research to improve the
company and its products in every way possible to best serve the
franchises and the public. Out of our 277 franchisees, not one has
failed and in the history of the franchise company there has been
only one minor lawsuit.

Some of the basic things our franchise company does to help its franchisees are:

(1) Gives the franchisee a chance to operate a business with widespread public acceptance of the product.

(2) Helps the franchisee in establishing equipment layout, site locations, decor, and so forth, which are all scientifically tested.

(3) They assist in advertising.

(4) Set up a field service system to help franchisees.

(5) Provide training seminars and technical bulletins.

(6) Provide manuals containing clear-cut objectives, sound policies and practicable methods and procedures.

(7) They provide a tested and proven merchandising program.

As a result of these efforts, I grew from a one-restaurant operator to a franchisee operating a $25 million retail business with 100 locations, consisting of 85 Kentucky Fried Chicken stores and 15 H. Salt, Esq., Fish & Chips shops.

One important thing the franchise company does is to always listen to the franchisees for important needs and improvements. As a franchisee, I am still on their board of directors and have a voice in decisionmaking. This has been important in keeping the franchisees' point of view before the management company.

The gentleman before me mentioned a lot of turnover in franchises in the oil industry. I don't know of many franchisees who have actually been dissatisfied and had a franchise canceled. Most of them that have sold out have actually joined the company as executives in it, in the administration.

Through national expansion, all Kentucky Fried Chicken franchisees have been protected in their franchise area rights. Franchisees were given more area as fast as they could grow. When our franchise company went public, 10 percent of the total stock, worth $30 million, was offered to the franchisees.

Every franchisee had a stock option equivalent to 388 shares per unit at a cost of $3 a share. The stock is presently selling for $34 a share.

Because of the opportunity given people, Kentucky Fried Chicken has made millionaires out of over 132 people, most of them franchisees. A lot of these people were individuals who had a less than average chance to succeed in business according to all traditional standards. I myself was a high school dropout.

With the help of my loyal people, we were able to become successful, and because of this we wanted to see others succeed. That is why each of my stores is a coventure with an operating partner, which is usually a man and wife team. Every manager owns 40 percent of the store he operates, and is tied into the profits of that store.

Therefore, his success is proportionate to the efforts he puts into his store. Managers average $30,000 in salary and equity a year.

I don't believe in absentee ownership. An owner needs to work in his store to see that business is taken care of. It is impossible to be a productive owner and be away from the store for a long period of time. Because each of my managers is also a 40-percent owner of the business, our stores are well taken care of.

The goal of our Kentucky Fried Chicken franchise is to build people. A large percent of our proceeds go toward the development of people. We want to make them feel that they belong.

We sponsor bimonthly management dinner meetings for sharing of ideas and successes, management seminars and many individual training sessions for employees as well as managers.

We have many more things which help develop our people and add to their success. For the building of our middle management, we always promote from within. All of our middle managers have been store owner-managers at one time. I have learned from experience that if we take care of our people, the profits take care of themselves.

Our company has appreciated the efforts of our franchise company in what they have done and are still doing to keep us number one in the food business. They have shown many small businessmen how to be successful in the food industry and how to improve their business with this top quality product and nationally known image.

Rather than being an independent, we are associated with the leader in the food business, and, as a result, we are somebody.

Testimony, March 30, 1970. U.S. Congress, 91st, 2nd session, Senate, Select Committee on Small Business, Subcommittee on Urban and Rural Economic Development, The Impact of Franchising on Small Business. Hearings ...., Part 2., (Washington, D.C.: Government Printing Office, 1970), pp. 67-672.

653. THE PLIGHT OF THE SERVICE STATION OPERATOR (1973)

Unlike many other retail businesses, the sale of gasoline still occurs on a single-brand basis in small-sized establishments which are leased from very large oil companies. Price competition is virtually unknown as emphasis is placed upon brand-loyalty. On a regional basis, various brands became market leaders in setting and maintaining prices. During the 1920s, and 1930s, when oil companies were establishing the outlines of the present system, the automobile market was already a mass one and marketing gasoline had to be highly decentralized. But the companies went to extremes in compelling service station operators to sell only one brand. Here is a statement of dealer grievances against oil companies by Charles Binsted, president of the National Congress of Petroleum Retailers.

There is a major change taking place in the marketing of gasoline which will further tighten the noose around the neck of the independent branded dealer and raise the price of gasoline to the consumer.

With refineries now running at capacity, and a shortage of
gasoline--either real or contrived--facing the country for the next
decade, the "majors" will be seeking new sources of profit. In the
past, they have focused on production and refining. Now, the major
suppliers are looking downstream to retailing as an additional source
of profit.

Their monopoly control of refining with its attendant noncompetitive behavior, such as identical lock-step pricing at even higher
levels, will be extended to retailing. The signs are everywhere.
We have heard from other witnesses what is happening to the independent dealer in Utah. But Utah is only a part of a pattern which
is emerging nationally.

First, the majors are shortening their marketing lines by
pulling out of some States and concentrating on others. They are,
in fact, dividing up the country among themselves and increasing
their share of already concentrated markets. For instance, 2 years
ago, three companies sold approximately 4.5 percent of all the gasoline purchased in Utah. These percentages, of course, can be expected to and are on the rise. What is emerging are more highly
concentrated local markets in which the nonflexibility and upward
pricing patterns at the refinery level are transferred to retail
sales.

Second, the majors are moving more rapidly toward the taking
over of their most profitable branded stations. An independent
dealer is allowed to develop the station until, by dint of hard
work and good reputation, he builds up his gallonage. The major
then refuses to renew his lease and operates the station itself.
By operating their own branded stations in selected areas, the
majors, with the help of short-term dealer leases, are able to control the price at which their remaining independent dealers sell
gasoline.

In the past, the short-term dealer lease has been the basic
source of supplier control. Major petroleum companies operate a
system in which the dealer must lease his station from the supplier.
In most cases, the leases are for a year or less. The dealer is
allowed to purchase his supplies from no one except his lessor.
Because of the coercion and intimidation inherent in the short-term
lease, the supplier is able to direct, to a large extent, the operation of the independent dealer station, including the price at
which gasoline is sold. By this additional device of taking over
the management of selected high volume stations in a highly concentrated market, the major is able to effectively control the price
at which all branded gasoline will be sold in that particular area.

Third, the major suppliers are moving increasingly into
secondary brands, including self-service stations. The price differential between what they charge themselves and the inflated dealer
tank wagon price they charge their own dealers, gives the supplier-
retailer additional leverage over pricing of branded dealers. More
important, perhaps, it provides the major with the necessary device
to control and dominate the prices of the independent retailers
selling non-branded products.

In the past, the only effective competition in petroleum has
been at the retail level. The new moves by the major suppliers

mean that the independent branded dealer will lose what little independence he has left and consumers will pay higher and higher prices
for gasoline. The takeover by the majors of all aspects of the retailing of gasoline will be the last step by which a handful of
giant energy conglomerates, acting in lockstep, will determine the
price every motorist will have to pay for his gasoline.

Competitive retail markets of gasoline are approaching death
and the independent branded dealer will soon be a relic. As usual,
when competition disappears and is replaced by a monopoly, the consumer is the biggest loser of all. Competition, of course, requires
a sufficient number of truly independent retailers competing with
each other, subject not to the command of the suppliers, but only
to the command of the marketplace.

It is still possible to resurrect a competitive marketplace
as the arbitrator of gasoline prices. However, this would require
liberating the dealers from the death grip of their suppliers and
forcing the suppliers out of the retailing function.

Solutions, such as dealer day-in-court legislation, divestiture
and divorcement, could be effective. Hopefully, this is an area
this subcommittee can explore in more detail so that realistic solutions can be devised before it is too late and another of our major
markets if foreclosed forever to the benefits of competition.

I heard you ask the question of several other witnesses of
what causes price wars.

Now, I'm not going to attempt to answer that question, because
I don't think any of us probably are able to effect an absolute
answer, but I did want to make some observations on it. I believe
that you'll find that, here in Salt Lake City, you have a price
war, as such, or at least I believe that's what I have observed
here, just in the few hours I've been here.

The fact that we have a price war, and, supposedly, in short
supply, indicates to me, or proves to me, that gasoline pricing
does not respond to the market. It does not answer the supply and
demand. Rather, these price wars are a tool to discipline the
markets, and that's what they're used for.

Now, there was a time when we blamed the increment in production for it. You had production operating at 85 or 90 percent
capacity, and so you had excess gasoline on the market.

Something had to be done about it. But with the unrealistic
tank wagon prices that branded dealers had to pay there is enough
fattening for the major suppliers to engage in price-war activities
in the market to discipline the market, while they're charging the
full price in another market and recovering that money which is lost
in the market where the price war happens to be.

I wanted to make one other observation concerning the advertising budget of the major oil companies. The question was raised as
to how much money they spend. I think it's interesting to note
that they do spend many millions of dollars in branded advertising.
Then, the company blames the higher branded price on that fact.

This is one of the factors, at least; their cost of advertising
the brand.

Testimony, March 17, 1973, U.S. Congress, 93rd, 1st session,
Senate, Committee on Interior and Insular Affairs, Market Performance and Competition in the Petroleum Industry, Hearings....,
Part 1, (Washington, D.C.: Government Printing Office, 1974),
pp. 55-56.

654.   COMPETITION IN FOOD RETAILING (1977)

Before the 1920s, retail food stores sold one type
of product: dry groceries, meat, or bakery products.
Service was personal and credit was often extended.
During the 1920s, however, cash-and-carry merchandising
grew as stores began also to offer self-service. Large-
volume sales required greater space while minimal furnish-
ings became the norm in the modern supermarket. Chain
stores, which operated small stores, began in the 1930s to
close them down in favor of supermarkets. By 1966, supermarkets made up about one seventh of all grocery stores
but did seven-tenths of the business. Automobile transportation made it feasible for large numbers of customers
to travel relatively far to trade in supermarkets while
the advent of improved home refrigeration enabled consumers to stock reserves of meat, also purchased at omnibus
supermarkets. Here, Robert O. Aders, president of the
Food Marketing Institute, contends that competition remains
vital in food retailing.

Food retailing is widely recognized as one of the most competitive industries in the nation.
From the national standpoint, food chains (classfied by government as firms operating eleven or more stores) represent less than
50 percent of total U.S. food store sales: independent retailers
including those affiliated with cooperative and voluntary groups
account for more than half of food retail industry volume. Independents, particularly those affiliated with voluntaries and co-ops,
are the fastest growing segment of food retailing, reflecting largely the dramatic and constant growth of small 4-10 store operators.
The dynamics of the industry are further illustrated by the success
of new forms of competitive rivalry, such as convenience stores,
whose sales increased more than 16.5 percent in 1975. For independent stores, the increase was 9.4 percent and for chains, 9.0 percent. The national share of food store sales of the largest firms
in the industry has remained relatively stable during the
period 1967-1972.

In another study, the U.S. Department of Agriculture traced
trends in market shares by type of business for the period of 1963
to 1972. The USDA found the share of market held by independents
up 8.5 percent, the share held by local or regional chains up
3 percent, and the market share held by the top chains down 20
percent.

I might add that the argument that this lack of growth of the
larger chains has been attributable to the problems faced by A&P
is irrelevant. In fact, A&P's performance problems, rather than
being an aberration, are characteristic of the turbulence always
present in the food retailing business. The problems of A&P during
the recent part were similar to problems borne by other chains in
other periods--for example, Safeway in the mid-50's. To eliminate
the typical competitive problems of particular food retailers as
atypical--which the Research Group Report does--is to ignore the
basic characteristics of the industry. And to discount the years
1970-1974 as a period of "unusual" circumstances producing abnormally low profits is equally inappropriate.

The impact of food retail competition is even more direct at
the local market level. We do not adcept the theory that a mere
counting of firms active in a market is any indication of the competitive nature of local markets. Even if we accepted the notion
that local market concentration is somehow relevant...there has
been no significant increase in concentration in the 200 largest
metropolitan areas since 1958....

Mr. Chairman, by every accepted measure, food retailing in
this country meets the criteria for an extremely competitive business. Basically, those criteria are that:

1. Entry into the market is relatively easy.

2. Upward mobility is possible for the small seller. The
relative market positions of sellers will change over time.

3. Industry earns normal profits over a long run--that is,
no more profit than is necessary to cover the opportunity costs of
capital and the entrepreneur's time and to offset business risks.

4. Products and services offered by competitors are essentially similar so consumers can and do change their loyalties on
the basis of price and how their needs are serviced.

I ask that these tests be put to the food retailing industry.

First, ease of entry into food retailing is widely understood;
this condition has been noted by the Federal Trade Commission in
its only contested merger decision involving the industry. Moreover, even the Research Group Report is cognizant of the ability of
small firms to enter and thrive through association with cooperative
and voluntary groups. A striking illustration of this aspect of
industry competition appears in a 1972 tabulation prepared by Chain
Store Age, which lists more than 300 firms then operating four or
more stores which were "unknown" as of 1962. Even in the unlikely
event that the 300 figure represents a complete inventory, it
would mean that nearly 25 percent of all firms operating four or
more stores in 1972 were either not in existence or did not operate
as many as two stores 10 years earlier.

Second, upward mobility is common in this business. Consider
this fact: The 10th largest food retailing company in the nation
today wasn't even among the top 50 companies 50 years ago....The

top companies today often aren't the same companies that held the
largest market shares even five years earlier. In 17 of the 20
largest markets, different firms held the top four positions in
1972 than in 1967....

Third, profits historically have averaged less than a penny on
a dollar after taxes as a percentage of sales. As return on a
shareowner's equity, according to the latest Forbes Magazine study,
food retailing profits rank 27th out of 30 major industries.
Surely, numbers like these show no evidence of more than normal
profitability. On the contrary, the profitability of our industry
has been relatively low.

A fourth characteristic of competition--the ability of consumers to change loyalties on the basis of price and service--is easily
demonstrated by the food retailing business. We are fully aware of
how carefully our customers watch prices.

Economists, I understand, usually cite price advertising as
one of the most useful sources of information to consumers and a
major characteristic of a competitive industry. I don't think any
business uses more price specific advertising than the food retailing business. Food shoppers see the competitiveness of the food
retailing business every week in the advertisements that competing
firms place in local newspapers. The competitive climate is so
intensive that food retailers fear loss of customers if there are
even minor variations from the lowest price charged to key items
in a market area.

Testimony, April 5, 1977, U.S. Congress, 95th, 1st session,
Joint Economic Committee, Prices and Profits of Leading Retail
Food Chains, 1970-74. Hearings....., (Washington, D.C.: Government
Printing Office, 1977), pp. 171-172.

655. SQUEEZING THE SMALL RETAILER (1981)

During the adverse economic conditions of late 1981,
small businesses especially bore the brunt of short
supplies and shrinking sales. Bankruptcy rates for businesses and individuals soared. High interest rates prevented access to credit which in turn, led to restriction
of customer credit, especially by small businesses. An
example is Michael Stoller of Massachusetts, a small
retailer in New England.

We used to have seven stores in Rhode Island, and now it is
one in Rhode Island and one in Massachusetts. My name is Michael
Stoller. I reside in Massachusetts. My place of business is in
Pawtucket, R.I., with a branch store in Attleboro, Mass. I have
been asked to give my analysis of the present economic conditions.

That is a two-fold question, because we have the haves and we have
the have-nots.

Let's talk about the haves for a minute, big business, important people, the IBM's the Du Ponts, Levi Strauss, the banking
industries. They have no problems. In fact, everything that is
coming out of Washington today seems to be helping them. When I
read in the paper that IBM has purchased umpteen million dollars of
tax writeoffs from Ford Motor, IBM doesn't need it, but the small
businessman does.

Let's go to the have-nots, small businesses and the average
workers. The small businessman today is being squeezed from both
sides. One, the supply side. I happen to be in the apparel business, and I will relate to you incidents that we are having problems
with.

The United States is no longer capable of clothing the population of the United States. We have to look offshore for merchandise. This is a sad state of affairs, but nevertheless it is a
fact of life. We run into what is called the embargo.

Right now I would say that 60 percent of all shirts being sold
in the United States are not made in this country, but we have to
do this. Why? Because the workers, the people, the shoppers come
in and say, "Hey, I can't pay $16 for a shirt. I want a shirt for
$11. I don't care whether it is made in the United States or not.
I can only afford $11."

That is one thing. The embargoers come on, and what has happened here, a manufacturer today signs a contract overseas to produce, we will say, for example, 1,000 cases of men's shirts.
Because of the embargo, he only receives 500 cases. Now, who do
you think gets the 500 cases, a small store like Saltzman's or a
big store like Jordan Marsh or what have you?

Credit, here is another incident where the small store is
squeezed on both sides. If small stores are a little late in payment, he has a late penalty charge. If not, some of the big manufacturers will cut him off completely. Now go to the other side.
The small store in order to survive today has to have credit. At
one time when interest rates were manageable, they were sufficient
enough to pay the cost of carrying credit and the cost of writeoffs.

With double-digit interest rates, this is no longer the case.
Our writeoffs have doubled over the last 3 years. It is getting to
the point where we are refusing credit to most customers that walk
into our store today.

The workers, the have-not workers in which I put my own employees, they will not receive raises equal to the cost of inflation. There is no way that we can afford it. The have workers--
and I will tell you a little incident that happened to me last week.
We had a broken window. The glass company sent down four men who
worked 3 hours. The labor bill came to $528. That is 12 hours at
$44 per hour. You have no choice. You need a plumber, you have
no choice. He says $20, you pay him $20. He says $30, you pay
him $30.

The administration today has talked about the filter-down
process, where it is going to be a panacea for the American people.
I conversely say, how about the filter-up process? People today
cannot spend money.

They don't have the money. That will affect the merchants.
The merchants, if they don't sell, will not buy. That will affect
the manufacturers. The taxes that are going to be paid will shrink
instead of increase. The tax law was a laugh, because all it did
was help the haves, not the have-nots.

In my own case, last year my company paid Federal taxes $6,000.
This year if projections come through, Uncle Sam will pay me $2,000.
That is a spread of $8,000. If you multiply that by hundreds of
thousands of small businesses throughout the country, well, you
will come up with a pretty good figure.

Testimony, December 7, 1981, U.S. Congress, 97th, 1st session,
House of Representatives, Committee on Banking, Finance, and Urban
Affairs, Grassroots Hearings on the Economy. Hearings...., Part
3, (Washington, D.C.: Government Printing Office, 1981), pp.
252-253.

656. WHAT'S THE WORTH OF A HUMAN LIFE? (1981)

Consumerism as a mass movement first arose in the
1960s and is closely identified with the person of
Ralph Nader, a lawyer and activist leader. Many demands
of the movement were cast in the form of calls upon the
federal government for new legislation and re-invigorated
administrative action by agencies such as the Consumer
Product Safety Commission and the Federal Trade Commission. Courts have come to play a far more significant
role in consumer protection: between 1960 and 1974, for
example, the number of product liability claims rose from
35,000 to 600,000. In the statement below, Ralph Nader
raises a central if seldom-mentioned problem--what is the
worth of a human life and how much protective regulation
does it merit?

What does the economy really exist for? It does not exist for
the auto companies to produce a lot of cars. It exists for a motorist to have a good surface transportation system which is safe and
efficient and gets people around on the ground. The economy does
not exist for the drug industry just to produce more drugs. It
exists for consumers to have the benefit of competitively priced
pharmaceuticals which advance their health.

The economy, in short, has as its rationale for existence the
well-being of the consumer. That is what it is ultimately for.
And yet, the measures of economic progress...are often exclusively
kept to the selling side of the economy, to sales figures and production figures, instead of to the well-being of the consumer as a
result of these production and sales performances.

So let's start by simply saying that the economic health, safety and well-being of millions of consumers are the ways to judge our economy. It is not judged by production. There are many drugs produced which are unsafe, ineffective, monopolistically priced, and all told, gouge people's pocketbooks and do not advance health in the United States as they would under safer and more competitive conditions....

Now, traditionally, consumer protection and corporate battles go through cycles, and one cycle is a cycle of factual interaction. Whenever there is a cycle of factual interaction, consumer protection improves. That was true, for example, in the middle and late 1960's and early 1970's here in Congress. Whenever the consumer issue is monopolized by ideological slogans and principles, the consumer's progress tends to recede. We are now in this latter period....

I think it is also important to comment on how little regulation there really has been, contrary to the protestations of the American Enterprise Institute and other trade associations. It is a documented fact that regulations have been few and far between. They have been weak, to the extent that they have been issued at all; and to the extent that they have taken up a lot of pages in the Code of Federal Regulations, that is, a reflection of both the complexity of the matter and exceptions, inclusions and other provisions demanded by companies and trade groups to further their sense of equity.

In the auto safety area there has not been a single--I repeat, a single significant auto safety standard issued in the last 11 years, period. Not a single significant auto safety standard. The passive restraint standard was to be the first, and that is not to be issued. The tire standard, Senator, has not been updated since 1968. So that illustrates how much baseless sound and fury there is about overregulation.

In addition, I think it is important to note that the cost-benefit debate of recent years has not been entirely candid by the antiregulatory position. You cannot have a cost-benefit analysis unless you put a dollar figure on an American life. I have yet to see a corporate lobbyist with a dollar figure on an American life. If there was a bill here in Congress to say all cost-benefit analyses of the Federal executive branch shall be premised on the value that each American life to be saved will be valued at $3 million, I doubt whether any Senator or Representative would vote against that bill. And yet, the implicit values are running around $200,000 and $300,000 per life, in order to rig lower the benefit part of that equation....

What are the benefits in dollar terms of clear air, for example? It is pretty hard to determine; although we know there are many benefits, it is pretty hard to monetarize.

But if they are going to be monetarized, then Congress should give a statutory evaluation of life worth for the regulatory agencies to measure by.

Testimony, June 24, 1981, U.S. Congress, 97th, 1st session, Senate, Committee on Commerce, Science, and Transportation, Subcommittee for Consumers, Consumerism in the 1980's. Hearings...., (Washington, D.C.: Government Printing Office, 1981), pp. 66-67, 69, and 72.

I.

THE WORLD ECONOMY

657. AMERICAN BRANCH FACTORIES ABROAD (1900)

Wage and market considerations were prominent
in determining whether an American firm would establish
foreign branches. As of this time, the movement to establish branch factories was on the eve of a period of
great expansion. (See Source No. 681). Here is testimony by W. J. Chalmers and Enos Barton. Chalmers was
president of Fraser and Chalmers, manufacturer of mining
and other machinery; Barton was president of the Western
Electric Company which manufactured electrical machinery.
The main plants of both firms were located in Chicago
where Fraser and Chalmers employed 1,500 men and Western
Electric 5,200 men.

[Mr. CHALMERS.] We operate in Kent, England, a shop employing
the same number of men on an average the year round that we employ
in Chicago, and our wage per week in England is 40 per cent less
than it is in Chicago.
    Q. Is that the actual wage?--A. That is the actual wage paid
to the workmen. If we have, for instance, a thousand men on our
pay roll here and a thousand men on the English pay roll, our work
here is 40 per cent higher in wages for that thousand men than where
we are working on identically the same models, the same type of
work. It is true there may be more of this particular class to do
there than there is here, but averaging it by the year it is pretty
fair supposition to say our output on all the different lines is
the same.

Q. Is the output per man and machine about the same?--A.
Much less. There is no country in the world where an individual
man turns out so much work as an American. Just what causes that
I am not prepared to say. We feed our men better here; we house
them better, and they are able and capable of doing more work.
Now, I am speaking more particularly of the English workman. The
German workman is well housed, and so is the Belgian workman; but
the English and Scotch workmen are not nearly as well housed or as
well fed; for instance, get meat about once a week.

Q. (By Mr. A. L. HARRIS.) Are our men more intelligent and
energetic?--A. And less drunk--I think the three things combined.
They have a very bad practice in England of going to work before
breakfast, and then shutting down for breakfast. We do not do it
in our shop; but in many factories they shut down at 9 o'clock
and go out for breakfast, and it is almost a certainty that every
man before he comes back has had one or two drinks in him. I do
not consider that they can do as well as our men who have a hearty
breakfast.

. . . .

Q. (Mr. Mr. KENNEDY.) What advantage is there in having a
branch in England?--A. The Englishman, wherever he goes, is very
true to his country. He is prejudiced; and we found, after the
African trade had developed into being a very large trade--we
having shipped as much as 8,700 tons of machinery there in a
single year--that our patterns were being copied and models were
being made by English shops, notably Sandycroft, and Roby, of
Lincoln. It occurred to us that it would be a very good thing to
become an English concern ourselves, inasmuch as the building of
works in England would make us such; and, our seniors being
Scotchmen, we claimed a little nationality. We built these works,
and we now do a very large foreign business there, which of course
would come here if it had not been built there. To a certain extent they look upon it now as English machinery.

Q. Can you go out and get markets that you could not get as
Americans?--A. In America, yes; although the fact is, we can ship
from Chicago 1,000 miles to New York, and thence on the Transvaal,
for one shilling a ton, never more than that, against English
competition.

. . . .

[Mr. BARTON.] Q. Where in Europe is your shop or work?--A.
Our largest establishment is in the city of Antwerp, in Belgium.
We have also a factory of considerable importance in Paris, and
one in Berlin, and one in London.

Q. Do you produce there substantially the same kind of
machinery that you produce here?--A. Quite similar, and in some
cases almost identically the same.

Q. How do the wages and hours of labor compare in those
countries, in your works, with those in this country?--A. In
Europe the hours are longer than they are here; the wages are much
less. The wages for common labor--you could almost say that it
is as francs to dollars.

Q. About one-fifth as much as here?--A. Yes. I may say in
that connection, and it will perhaps interest your committee, that
notwithstanding that difference in wages the economy of production
is not the motive that leads us to do manufacturing in Europe; but
it is rather having factories nearer to the market, where we can
exactly meet the demands of our customers, and to some extent meet
the requirements in the local governments that the work furnished
shall be of home manufacture.
Q. Do you export?--A. We still export very largely, notwithstanding that fact that we have factories under our own management,
yes; very largely. We send our products from Chicago to Japan
and Australia and various countries in Europe.
Q. Do you export to those European countries where you have
works?--A. To some extent, but our factories in Paris and Berlin
are there for the reason that our customers, being the governments,
require articles that they buy to be made in their own countries.
Q. Is the most of your work produced in Europe sold to
European governments?--A. None of it comes to this country. It is
mostly sold to European governments.
Q. Because those governments are operating electricity in one
way and another?--A. Because those governments are operating the
telegraph and telephone systems. The telegraph and telephone
systems of the country are under governmental control.

Testimony, W. J. Chalmers, March 20, 1900, and Enos M. Barton,
March 29, 1900, U.S. Congress, 57th, 1st session, House of
Representatives, Document No. 177, Report of the Industrial
Commission on the Chicago Labor Disputes of 1900...., VIII,
pp. 11-12, 17, 298.

658. AMERICAN SILVER MINING IN MEXICO (1902)

At this time, ownership of mining enterprises
was the principal form of American foreign direct
investment. Foreign firms owned the dominant part of
Mexican silver mines. This account is that of Grant
Shepherd who wrote The Silver Magnet. Fifty Years in a
Mexican Silver Mine.

It was not all beer and skittles during the thirty-odd years
of mining the precious metal in Batopilas. Silver went 'way down
in price; there was a heavy floating debt and the overdraft allowed
by the Banco Minero in Chihuahua was overreached. But before
matters hit the absolutely fatal spot at any one time, we would
run into a bonanza of greater or less extent, and sometimes in the
very last two weeks of the month, at the end of which the bullion
would leave for Chihuahua, we would knock out anywhere from fifty

to a hundred thousand dollars. One month we took out four hundred
and fifty thousand dollars worth of silver. At various times we
had run into debt with the bank for around eight hundred thousand
dollars and paid it back all from a few months' production.

After my father died, we had been going through a trying
financial time. Our credit was not as good as his had been; we
were the younger generation and had not proved that we could move
mountains as he had done.

My much-beloved brother-in-law Ned Quintard had died suddenly
in Washington while we were on the road with my father's remains.
Alex had been made general manager of the mines. On a certain
afternoon instructions were sent me to report to him at the Main
Office. When I got there I found Conness also at the Hacienda
San Miguel, and we were informed that the Banco Minero now refused
to permit us the overdraft of sixty thousand dollars which had been
agreed on, unless we would send them that much as well as a pretty
large additional amount in bullion at the end of the month.

Dios es grande! It chanced that the previous night I had
showed up in a small working some signs of native silver. This
ground ought to prove productive. I personally was satisfied in
my mind that it would do so. We decided that we could telegraph
the bank that we would meet their demands.

We met them.

By the end of the month we sent out a little over one hundred
thousand dollars worth of silver bullion. This was the beginning
of the bonanza which paid off all the floating debt and more besides
during the next twelve months. If I am not mistaken, and I believe
that I am not, the debt was eight hundred thousand dollars or
thereabouts. This example is cited to demonstrate the richness
of the ores of Batopilas and also that we worked plenty hard to
get them out.

Grant Shepherd, The Silver Magnet. Fifty Years in a Mexican
Silver Mine, (New York: E. P. Dutton and Company, 1938), pp. 254-
255.

659. MORGAN PUTS IN A GOOD WORD FOR ENGLAND (ca. 1903)

        Mr. Morgan could be imperious even with his
country's Secretary of the Treasury. Lyman J. Gage,
former Secretary of the Treasury, testifies to this.

While yet in the Treasury Department, I was one day visited
by him [J. P. Morgan] which led to a talk, here substantially
reported:

"Are you aware, Mr. Secretary, that the financial situation
in Europe is very grave?"

"Yes, I have observed the reports."

"The situation in London is especially trying. If the crisis there is not alleviated, its evil effects will be reflected in our own business affairs. I suggest a course of action which, if you will adopt it, will go far to restore the disturbed equilibrium abroad and so protect our own threatened domestic finances."

"What is the suggestion you have to offer?"

"Our Government Treasury is overflowing with money. You have large sums on deposit with our national banks. Transfer by cables to the Bank of England, twenty millions for your credit there. Of the strength of the Bank of England and the safety of the proposed deposit, there can be no doubt, or if you are fearful, the house of Morgan will guarantee the deposit."

"No doubt such a re-enforcement to the reserve of the Bank of England would be very helpful to it, but it is impossible for me to act on your suggestion. The laws of Congress control and limit the powers of the Secretary, and to transfer funds from the public treasury to a foreign bank would be an impeachable offense. Besides, were I to issue such an order on the Treasurer, he would not obey it, for he too is subject to the law."

"Well, that may be so," he admitted, "but cannot it be managed indirectly? Is there not a large appropriation for the use of the War Department?"

"Yes," I replied, "more than one hundred and forty millions of dollars."

"Why then cannot Secretary Root withdraw twenty millions in one sum, deposit it as I suggest and disburse it from there?"

"Unfortunately perhaps, the law is again in your way. The Secretary of War cannot make direct withdrawals. He can only approve requisitions made from time to time by the several branches of the service for the support of which Congress has authorized the Treasury to make payments."

This, of course, was final, but the imperious man seemed to regard my position as perverse and unreasonable.

Memoirs of Lyman J. Gage, pp. 155-156.

660. WE NOW HAVE A SURPLUS OF CAPITAL (1906)

Early in the nineteenth century, the U.S. had regarded itself as a carrier of foreign-manufactures to South America. Later in the century, emphasis shifted to supplying the goods from U.S. sources. Now a new function emerged--the export of capital. The following is part of an address by Elihu Root, the Secretary of State.

Since the first election of President McKinley [1896] the
people of the United States have for the first time accumulated a
surplus of capital beyond the requirements of internal development.
That surplus is increasing with extraordinary rapidity. We have
paid our debts to Europe and have become a creditor instead of a
debtor nation; we have faced about; we have left the ranks of the
borrowing nations and have entered the ranks of the investing
nations. Our surplus energy is beginning to look beyond our own
borders, throughout the world, to find opportunity for the profitable use of our surplus capital, foreign markets for our manufactures, foreign mines to be developed, foreign bridges and railroads
and public works to be built, foreign rivers to be turned into
electric power and light. As in their several ways England and
France and Germany have stood, so we in our own way are beginning
to stand and must continue to stand toward the industrial enterprise of the world.
. . . .
This is only the beginning; the coffee and rubber of Brazil,
the wheat and beef and hides of Argentina and Uruguay, the copper
and nitrates of Chile, the copper and tin of Bolivia, the silver
and gold and cotton and sugar of Peru, are but samples of what the
soil and mines of that wonderful continent are capable of yielding.
Ninety-seven per cent of the territory of South America is occupied
by ten independent Republics living under constitutions substantially copied or adapted from our own. Under the new conditions of
tranquillity and security which prevail in most of them their eager
invitation to immigrants from the Old World will not long pass
unheeded. The pressure of population abroad will inevitably turn
its streams of life and labor toward those fertile fields and
valleys. The streams have already begun to flow; more than two
hundred thousand immigrants entered the Argentine Republic last
year; they are coming this year at the rate of over three hundred
thousand. Many thousands of Germans have already settled in southern Brazil. They are most welcome in Brazil; they are good and
useful citizens there, as they are here; I hope that many more will
come to Brazil and every other South American country, and add
their vigorous industry and good citizenship to the upbuilding
of their adopted home.
With the increase of population in such a field, under free
institutions, with the fruits of labor and the rewards of enterprise secure, the production of wealth and the increase of purchasing power will afford a market for the commerce of the world worthy
to rank even with the markets of the Orient as the goal of business
enterprise. The material resources of South America are in some
important respects complementary to our own; that continent is
weakest where North America is strongest as a field for manufactures; it has comparatively little coal and iron.
. . . .
The investment of American capital in South America under the
direction of American experts should be promoted not merely upon
simple investment grounds, but as a means of creating and enlarging
trade. For simple investment purposes the opportunities are

innumerable. Good business judgement and good business management
will be necessary there, of course, as they are necessary here; but,
given these, I believe that there is a vast number of enterprises
awaiting capital in the more advanced countries of South America,
capable of yielding great profits, and in which the property and
the profits will be as safe as in the United States or Canada. A
good many such enterprises are already begun. I have found a
graduate of the Massachusetts Institute of Technology, a graduate
of the Columbia School of Mines, and a graduate of Colonel Roosevelt's Rough Riders smelting copper close under the snow line of
the Andes; I have ridden in an American car upon an American electric road, built by a New York engineer, in the heart of the coffee
region of Brazil, and I have seen the waters of that river along
which Pizarro established his line of communication in the conquest
of Peru harnessed to American machinery to make light and power
for the city of Lima. Every such point is the nucleus of American
trade--the course of orders for American goods.

Elihu Root, Address to Trans-Mississippi Commercial Congress
in Kansas City, Missouri, November 20, 1906, U.S. Congress, 59th,
2nd session, Senate Document No. 211, serial number 5071, pp. 2,
3, and 7.

661. GROWTH OF COTTON-TRADING RULES (1911)

Business ethics arise first in the relations between
businessmen and are aimed at facilitating a business purpose. The writer of the extract below was Lamar Fleming,
chairman of the board of directors of Anderson, Clayton
and Co., the world's largest private trader in cotton.

When I went to work as a cotton clerk 45 years ago, the rules
and ethics of the American cotton trade were still in the formula-
tive stage. The tales of chicanery that we used to hear were fabulous. One warehouseman accommodated his customer by cutting the
bales in half, so that the value of two bales could be borrowed
against the weight of one. Other warehousemen issued warehouse
receipts against bales that did not exist. Two merchant firms got
the railroad agent to sign through bills of lading to Europe in
blank, filled them in, drew drafts on England and France and Germany
against them, and then used the proceeds to buy the cotton. Everything might have been fine if the market had gone down, but it went
up; the money wouldn't buy enough cotton to match the bills of
lading, and a number of foreign buyers were ruined.

This last incident brought on an international conference on
rules for bills of lading; and the ocean bills of lading which we

use today are called Conference Bills of Lading and refer to the
Liverpool Bill of Lading Conference of 1907.

For our cotton trading rules, we used to rely largely upon rule
books borrowed from the older markets, for instance the Liverpool
Cotton Association rules. As our trade matured, we set up local
cotton exchanges, State and regional cotton associations, and a
national association. These bodies have elaborated standard contract forms and rules; and they provide facilities for arbitration
of differences and distribution of information and quotations, as
well as meeting places for the trade. The old wrangles and
chicaneries have been eliminated in very large degree.

Testimony, Lamar Fleming, Jr., March 6, 1956, U.S. Congress,
84th, 2nd session, House of Representatives, Committee on Ways
and Means, Organization for Trade Cooperation, pp. 268-269.

662. SELLING FARM MACHINES IN SIBERIA (1908)

The federal government was becoming very active
in facilitating the export of American manufactures.
The writer here was Roland Dennis, a special agent of
the Department of Commerce and Labor. He had visited
Europe and Siberia the previous year.

If the Russian Government succeeds in carrying out its very
extensive migration schemes, the population of Siberia will be
increased by many hundred thousands within the next few years. As
most of these migrators arrive with few, if any, agricultural
implements, an immense demand for all classes of labor-saving tools
must be the natural result. American manufacturers are doing comparatively nothing to secure a share of this trade. With the exception of the mower, reaper, and binder manufacturers, who are
to be found wherever grass or grain grows, and one or two plow
factories, I have failed to discover one single well-considered
persistent effort to create a market for American-made implements
in the East. It is true there is at Blagoveshtchensk, for instance,
a great assortment of implements imported from the United States,
but all, or nearly all, had been brought in by foreigners who had
ordered them from catalogues.
. . . .
With the exception of the manufacturers mentioned I failed
to hear of any representatives of American implement factories
that had visited this part of the world endeavoring to develop
a demand for their goods.
. . . .

I met wide-awake young Americans selling flour, files,
wood screws, and meat.

Roland R. Dennis, American Agricultural Implements in Europe,
Asia, and Africa, (Washington, D.C.: Government Printing Office,
1909), pp. 73-74.

663.   AMERICAN HARVESTER SALES IN SIBERIA (1912)

Siberia alone is almost 1 1/2 times the size of
the United States. The Russian market was by far the
largest of all International Harvester foreign markets.
Out of 173 wholesale distributors of International
Harvester products overseas, forty-two were located in
Russia. In all of Africa, the next largest outlet, the
number was only 17. This statement is that of Charles
Haney who was manager of foreign sales, International
Harvester Company. The company's Siberian foreign houses
were located in Novo-Nikolaievsk, Omsk, and Vladivostok.
A "foreign house" had its own manager, and travelling,
sales, and mechanical departments.

The economic conditions in Europe and Siberia in 1902, which
promised well for the development of the harvesting business
abroad, were the great fields of grain then being cut by hand almost entirely, or with crude machines; while the peasants, the
laborers, were emigrating to America and leaving a deficiency of
labor in some countries. In others, the development of manufacture
was taking labor from the country, making it necessary for the
farmer to supply that deficiency by machinery.
     In addition, year by year wages were increasing, and from the
economic standpoint, the farmer could buy machines to harvest crops
because he could do it more quickly, satisfactorily and cheaper.
     Siberia commenced taking harvesting machinery about 1900 in
small quantities. The field was very great--a great expanse of
country, larger than the United States, almost entirely undeveloped,
inhabited by nomadic tribes which drove their stock back and forth
over the prairies to feed. About that time the Russian Government
built the Trans-Siberian Railway and commenced assisting the peasants in European Russia to emigrate to Siberia. The peasant was
placed on the land and had to cultivate it himself, with the assistance of his family. There was no labor he could call upon to
help him. His only assistance, then, must be machinery, just as
it was in the western part of the United States and Canada.
     As to climatic conditions in Siberia and their effect upon
the demand for harvesting machinery; the larger portion of the
grain-growing sections, as at present cultivated, lies far to the

north. Winters are very long and severe and summers very short.
They must sow and harvest it within a very limited period,--probably
ninety to one hundred days between seeding and harvesting, sometimes a little longer. The need for doing the work quickly is
absolutely imperative.

. . . .

In Siberia there were very few local merchants. There are
few towns; the people live in villages, with no stores other than
little shops to supply groceries or kerosene, or something of that
sort. I started our local retail "skads," or local retail warehouse. To conduct these retails stores we were, of necessity,
forced to buy plows and various other mahchines not manufactured
by the I.H. Co., in order to have a complete stock of implements,
such as the farmer in that locality demanded. As we were able to
find someone to take this retail business off our hands and establish himself there as a local merchant and buy goods from us, we
turned the business over to him.

In changing the business from jobbing to the branch house basis, it was impossible to find men in Europe with knowledge and
experience in harvesting machinery business, qualifying them as
managers. It was necessary to get men trained from America--men
of experience, knowledge and ability and put them in charge. We
got these men from the International organization--men from the
McCormick, the Champion, Deering, Plano and Osborne Companies.
Knowledge of the business is more important than of the language
of the country. We try, naturally, to find men who speak the
language; but knowledge and experience are the first qualifications,
even if he spoke only English.

In 1912, the Omsk branch of the I.H. Co., in Central Siberia,
did the largest business:--$3,184,325.63. Vladivostok at the
extreme eastern end of the Trans-Siberian Railway on the Pacific
side, did a business of $569,278.09 last year.

Testimony, Charles H. Haney, The United States of America vs.
International Harvester Company, No. 624, In the District Court
of the United States for the District of Minnesota, Appendix to
Defendants' Brief, (Chicago, Illinois: The Gunthorp-Warren Printing
Co., 1913), pp. 4-5, 151-152.

664. AMERICAN CAPITAL IN CENTRAL AMERICA (1911)

The problem was: How deeply should the American
government involve itself in the collection of Central
American debts due American firms? Philander Knox,
Secretary of State, discusses the question.

The development and peace of all Central America must result
in a direct and very substantial benefit to the southern ports of
the United States--Galveston, New Orleans, Mobile, etc.--as they
will all have more frequent intercourse and be able to cultivate
a more extensive market for their products, while the Central
American Republics, with their production increased, will find a
ready market in these gateways of the United States. Railways
leading to them must carry this freight for distribution throughout the Southern States.

For the fiscal year 1908-9 the total imports of the Republic
of Honduras amounted to $2,581, 553, of which the United States
alone furnished $1,769,876, or over 68 per cent.

The amount of the export trade of Honduras for the same
period was $1,990,601, of which the United States alone took
$1,834,565, or more than 92 per cent.

As stated above, most of this trade is carried on with
Honduras from the Gulf ports of the United States.

The principle involved, therefore, in this convention, which
will enable the maintenance of peace in Central America, is in
reality most important from a material standpoint to the South.
In short, the matter may be summed up as follows:

Shall the Government of the United States make American
capital an instrumentality to secure financial stability, and hence
prosperity and peace, to the more backward Republics in the neighborhood of the Panama Canal? And in order to give that measure of
security which alone would induce capital to be such instrumentality without imposing too great a burden upon the countries concerned, shall this Government assume toward the customs collections
a relationship only great enough for this purpose--a relationship,
however, the moral effect and potentialities of which result in
preventing the customs revenues of such Republic from being seized
as the means of carrying on devastating and unprincipled revolu-
tions?

Statement, Philander C. Knox, May 24, 1911, Foreign Relations
of the United States, 1912, reprinted in James W. Gantenbein (ed.),
The Evolution of our Latin-American Policy. A Documentary Record
(1950), p. 80.

665. AN INTERNATIONAL COFFEE LOAN (1906)

The Brazilian state of San Paulo borrowed £3,000,000
from a London-New York banking combine, using 2 million
bags of coffee as security. As the price of coffee fell,
San Paulo was obliged to--and did--supply more margin.
Note the novelty of a coffee loan to the very large National
City Bank. Hermann Sielcken, a member of the import firm
of Crossman and Sielcken, the country's largest importer
of green coffee, testifies in the following.

I was active in procuring the loan of £3,000,000 for the San Paulo Government. San Paulo did not only not get any more than the market value [of the coffee] but they were obliged to pay us a margin as the market went down. We greated the San Paulo Government exactly the same as we would treat any other speculator or any other merchant. They had to keep good their margin of 80 per cent; and that was done not only once, but was continually referred to. The merchants called upon the Government for margins. The market price for coffee going down from 7 cents to 6 cents and from 6 cents to 5 cents, the Government had to put up further margins.

At that time, knowing that the Government needed money, and that the credit of the Government was good and always had been good, that they could borrow money, could raise a loan without security, I was instrumental in negotiating the loan of £3,000,000, of which £1,000,000 was done with the City Bank in New York and £2,000,000 in London. The National City Bank in New York was not at all willing. They were afraid and it was a business to which they were not accustomed. They only accepted it, first, because of my saying, "My firm will take 25 per cent of that loan, and if you do this business you will do a great act for commerce in the United States. In case Brazil needs money, and can only find it in Europe, the commerce of Brazil will go to Europe." We said to the City Bank of New York, "This will be the entering wedge for the future, larger business between the United States and Brazil. If you go into this, it is safe, you will get a surtax, it will pay you, and you can pay the loan."

These were the conditions of that loan, and the inducements I held out to the City Bank were particularly the larger and better business in future with Brazil, not only for the City Bank but for the country at large.

. . . .

Mr. UNTERMYER. I understood you to say that the National City Bank had been induced by you to go into this business not for profit, but as a great act to promote the commerce of the United States; is that right?

Mr. SIELCKEN. I do say so. I repeat it.

Mr. UNTERMYER. Yes; what inducements did the Schroeders, who were their partners also, have for going into it--to assist the commerce of the United States?

Mr. SIELCKEN. Schroeders had been bankers of San Paulo for many years.

Mr. UNTERMYER. Then their purpose in being partners with the City Bank was what?

Mr. SIELCKEN. Partners with the City Bank? They were never partners. In all the loans that Schroeders have brought out in the State of San Paulo they had no partners. In this particular loan they desired the City Bank, because generally the American influence is recognized in politics in South America, and they said, "We would like to see the American flag covering this loan."

Mr. UNTERMYER. You mean the Schroeders would like to see the American flag?

Mr. SIELCKEN. Yes.

Mr. UNTERMYER. That is the reason they joined with the City
Bank, is it?
Mr. SIELCKEN. They were induced more than if anybody else
had joined it but the Americans.

Testimony, Hermann Sielcken, May 16, 1912, U.S. Congress,
62nd, 3rd session, House of Representatives, Committee on Banking
and Currency, Money Trust Investigation, pp. 52, 61.

666. AMERICA IS BECOMING A LENDER (1913)

The Federal Reserve Bill was being considered
by Congress. The following witness, John Johnston,
rightly apprehended the increasingly evident fact that
the world financial role of the United States was
changing, and that this required a new banking system.
Johnston was president of the National Reserve Bank of
Kansas City, Missouri.

We all know it; every banker knows it. There has been almost
a quiet panic going on throughout the world; and that is the basal
causal reason that the bankers of America are working for immediate
action on this bill.
Do you understand that this bill [National Banking Act], which
was established in 1863, this bill under which we are working, was
established to meet a war exigency, and it was for the purpose of
putting those 700,000,000 bonds out--those 2 per cent bonds--to
raise this money for this war bill? That was the main feature of
the bill then; but, gentlemen, look at the elastic feature. And
why has it worked all these 51 years?...I will tell you one reason.
It is because we have had a place for our expansion. We have had
the wealth of 1,000 years accumulating in England and Germany and
France and continental Europe; and when we have got hard up here,
until seven or eight years ago, we got all we needed right over
in London, until the war came up--that is, the African war--and
they began to build great battleships to protect themselves against
possible war with Germany, and various other things came up, and,
finally, four years ago, they quit taking our money. Four and a
quarter was a big rate, and we could always get it there. Then
they kind of stopped. Then, until two years ago, we got all we
wanted in Germany at 3 1/2 or 3 1/4, or 4 1/4. Germany, with her
industrial development, largely, and with her commercial enterprise,
has spent a vast amount in building the second greatest navy,
next to England, to compete with England. Then she shut up, and
now Germany is wanting money from us and offering us 6 1/4 and 7
per cent; and money in Hamburg and Berlin is to-day selling for 7
and 8 per cent.

Then we had France and even until a year ago she was the
natural outlet. We could get it; we could always find it there; but
a year ago they took over $100,000,000 Frisco bonds at a rate of
about 4.60 per cent; but now, since the war scare arose, these
French citizens, women as well as men, are taking their money out
of the bank; taking the gold, too, and to-day France is not only
wanting securities, but she is really getting to the point where
she wants money from us.

Six hundred million of stocks and bonds have been cashed from
Europe in the past nine months, and because of our commerce here
in this country, our great development of this vast territory, so
many things have gone on that we have, in the last decade, gone up.
We have increased four billions in our debt outlet and have increased two hundred millions in real money, gold or its equivalent.

So, now, every country on this earth--Japan, China, Russia,
The Balkans, England, France, all the countries, are not only cash-
ing on the stocks they have been taking from us, of which they have
taken $5,000,000,000 worth in the last 20 years, four billions of
that being railroad stocks and the other billion in various industries, but they are knocking at our doors for money.

Therefore we need immediate action on this bill, because as
perfect a bill as possible is needed on account of the world-wide
conditions demanding it, and to put it off shows a lack of courage
or brains to face the issue and work it out as wisely as possible.

Testimony, John T. M. Johnston, September 3, 1913, U.S.
Congress, 63rd, 1st session, Seante, Committee on Banking and
Currency, Banking and Currency, pp. 115-116.

667. STIMULATE OVERSEAS EXPANSION IN BANKS (1913)

A Senator favors permitting American banks to
open branches overseas but stresses that these banks
must be large enough to afford the action. The
speaker is John Weeks, a Senator from Massachusetts and
formerly a Boston banker.

It seems to me that in order to develop our foreign trade,
especially in the newer countries, it is absolutely essential that
we have banking facilities as well as transportation facilities and
other means of doing so. Take South America, for instance.
European countries engaged in trade with South America have not
only transportation lines, but they have banking facilities there,
so that every inducement is offered for those people to buy goods
of the European countries. Now, we have no transportation lines
sufficient, and we have no banks whatever, and we ought to establish
them.

It seems to me we ought very specifically in this bill to provide that sufficient capital be furnished for such purposes, and
that such regulations be imposed in connection with the management
of those branches that there could be no reasonable possibility or
probability of failure, because the failure of an American bank
would endanger trade materially. I do not think we ought to leave
it open to loose management, and I think we ought to insist that
sufficient capital be furnished to compete successfully with the
European banks of that character.

Now, this bill proposes that a bank with a capital of
$1,000,000 or more may set aside a part of its capital for that
purpose. It does not seem to me that a bank with a $1,000,000 cap-
ital can afford to set aside sufficient of its capital to warrant
its going into any such business as establishing foreign branches.

Senator John W. Weeks, October 1, 1913, U.S. Congress, 63rd,
1st session, Senate, Committee on Banking and Currency, Banking
and Currency, p. 1511.

668. FOREIGN INVESTMENT AND THE MONROE DOCTRINE (1914)

A clear description of some political aspects of
foreign investment in Latin America, which were part
of a memorandum to the Secretary of State by Robert
Lansing, then Counselor for the State Department.

Within the past quarter of a century the rapid increase of
wealth in the United States and the great nations of Europe has
caused their people, in constantly increasing numbers, to seek
investments in foreign lands. No richer field has been presented
than the vast undeveloped resources of the republics south of the
United States. Hundreds of millions of dollars have been expended
in these lands by the capitalists of this country, Great Britain,
France, Germany, and other European nations in the construction
of railways, the establishment of steamship lines, the development
of mines, the cultivation of cotton, fruits, and other agricultural
products, and the operation of various industrial enterprises.

In the opening up of these countries and the development of
their resources their governments require financial aid, or seize
the natural riches of these regions and the possibilities of reward
to those who obtain the right to exploit them, lend their money
readily in exchange for special privileges, concessions and large
rates of interest.

The governments of many of these republics, impoverished and
improvident and frequently in the hands of unscrupulous and
greedy men, careless of the future and heedless of their country's

welfare, borrow beyond the limit of their capacity to repay, hypo-
thecating every possible source of national revenue for years to
come. As a result some of the smaller American republics, ruled by
military dictators or oligarchies, who have enriched themselves at
the expense of their countries, have become hopelessly bankrupt.
In some cases the United States, in others a European power, is the
chief creditor, to whose favor the insolvent nation must look for
the means to continue its political existence.

With the present industrial activity, the scramble for markets,
and the incessant search for new opportunities to produce wealth,
commercial expansion and success are closely interwoven with political domination over the territory which is being exploited.

The European power, whose subjects supply the capital to install and operate the principal industries of a small American republic and furnish the funds upon which its government is dependent, may, if it so wishes, dominate the political action of the
American government. To state it in another way, a European power
whose subjects own the public debt of an American state and have
invested there large amounts of capital, may control the government
of the state as completely as if it had acquired sovereign rights
over the territory through occupation, conquest, or cession.

Memorandum to the Secretary of State by Robert Lansing,
June 11, 1914, Papers Relating to the Foreign Relations of the
United States. The Lansing Papers 1914-1920, II, (Washington,
D.C.: Government Printing Office, 1940), pp. 462-463.

669. "GOLD IS TRUMPS" (1914)

In 1914, the United States exported (net) $165.2
million in gold. War orders changed the direction of
gold flow. In 1915, the United States imported (net)
$420.5 million. Virtually all of this was shipped here
to pay for vastly increased merchandise exports to Europe.
Frank Vanderlip, president of the National City Bank of
New York, writes the following comment.

"Gold is trumps," James Stillman cautioned me as he sailed for
Europe in September, 1914. He was never more right. London very
much wanted about $98,000,000 due on a New York City bond issue;
it was wanted in gold. Everything in America that was owned in
Europe seemed to be for sale as the war began. Those who sold
wanted gold. That was the most cogent of the reasons for keeping
the New York Stock Exchange closed month after month. There simply
was not enough gold to buy back all our bonds and stocks that were
owned abroad and if the attempt to do so had not been effectively
hampered it would have been as apparent in 1914 as it is in 1934

that the gold standard is something that ceases to work when everybody is suddenly eager to possess gold. With the Stock Exchange
closed and stock and bond trading reduced to a small volume of
illicit transactions, we managed to ride the storm.

Even if there had been no war we would have had a tough time
in 1914; indeed, the war saved the Wilson Administration from the
blame for a serious domestic situation. Along with other factors,
the Democratic tariff had increased unemployment to an alarming
degree; millions were out of work and the number was increasing.
However, it was soon apparent to most business men that the war was
going to create a fabulous market for American goods, for American
labor and for American capital. I had been made chairman of a
committee that raised a pool of $100,000,000 in gold to ship abroad
to preserve American credit. Just as soon as it was known overseas
that we had that gold and would ship it on demand, the demand eased.
None of that $100,000,000 of gold was exported. What began to come
over then were orders for goods and requests for credits.

Frank A. Vanderlip, From Farm Boy to Financier, (New York:
D. Appleton-Century, 1935), pp. 242-243.

670. "MONEY IS THE WORST OF ALL CONTRABANDS" (1914)

Here is the statement of outright opposition to
any loan being extended to a belligerent nation. It
was written by William Jennings Bryan, the Secretary of
State. Lansing, who is mentioned, was Counselor of the
State Department.

I beg to communicate to you an important matter which has come
before the Department. Morgan Company of New York have asked
whether there would be any objection to their making a loan to the
French Government. I have conferred with Mr. Lansing and he knows
of no legal objection to financing this loan, but I have suggested
to him the advisability of presenting to you an aspect of the case
which is not legal but I believe to be consistent with our attitude
in international matters. It is whether it would be advisable for
this Government to take the position that it will not approve of any
loan to a belligerent nation. The reason that I would give in
support of this proposition are:

First: Money is the worst of all contrabands because it
commands everything else. The question of making loans contraband
by international agreement has been discussed, but no action has
been taken. I know of nothing that would do more to prevent war
than an international agreement that neutral nations would not
loan to belligerents. While such an agreement would be of great
advantage, could we not by our example hasten the reaching of such

an agreement? We are the one great nation which is not involved
and our refusal to loan to any belligerent would naturally tend to
hasten a conclusion of the war. We are responsible for the use of
our influence through example and as we cannot tell what we can do
until we try the only way of testing our influence is to set the
example and observe its effect. This is the fundamental reason in
support of the suggestion submitted.

Second: There is a special and local reason, it seems to me,
why this course would be advisable. Mr. Lansing observed in the
discussion of the subject that a loan would be taken by those in
sympathy with the country in whose behalf the loan was negotiated.
If we approved of a loan to France we could not, of course, object
to a loan to Great Britain, Germany, Russia, Austria or to any
other country, and if loans were made to these countries our citizens would be divided into groups, each group loaning money to the
country which it favors and this money could not be furnished without expressions of sympathy. These expressions of sympathy are
disturbing enough when they do not rest upon pecuniary interests--
they would be still more disturbing if each group was pecuniarily
interested in the success of the nation to whom its members had
loaned money.

Third: The powerful financial interests which would be
connected with these loans would be tempted to use their influence
through the newspapers to support the interests of the Government
to which they had loaned because the value of the security would
be directly affected by the result of the war. We would thus find
our newspapers violently arrayed on one side or the other, each
paper supporting a financial group and pecuniary interest. All of
this influence would make it all the more difficult for us to
maintain neutrality as our action on various questions that would
arise would affect one side or the other and powerful financial
interests would be thrown into the balance.

I am to talk over the telephone with Mr. Davidson of the Morgan
Company at one o'clock, but I will have him delay final action until
you have time to consider.

It grieves me to be compelled to intrude any question upon you
at this time, but I am sure you will pardon me for submitting a
matter of such great importance.

With assurances of high respect, I am, my dear Mr. President,
     Yours very truly,

                                   W. J. Bryan.

P.S.--Mr. Lansing calls attention to the fact that an American
citizen who goes abroad and voluntarily enlists in the army of a
belligerent nation loses the protection of his citizenship while
so engaged, and asks why dollars, going abroad and enlisting in
war, should be more protected. As we cannot prevent American citizens going abroad at their own risk, so we cannot prevent dollars
going abroad at the risk of the owners, but the influence of the
Government is used to prevent American citizens from doing this.
Would the Government not be justified in using its influence against
the enlistment of the nation's dollars in a foreign war? The

Morgans say that the money would be spent here but the floating of
these loans would absorb the loanable funds and might affect our
ability to borrow.

   Letter, William Jennings Bryan to President Woodrow Wilson,
August 10, 1914, U.S. Congress, 74th, 2nd session, Senate, Special
Committee Investigating the Munitions Industry, Munitions Industry,
XXXVI, pp. 7665-7666.

671.   TRADE PAYMENTS ARE NOT CONTRABAND (1914)

     Eleven weeks after the preceding letter was sent to
the President, American policy came to distinguish between
loans and commercial credits. The former were means of
financing war, while the latter were means of financing
legitimate trade. This comment is by Robert Lansing.

     From my conversation with the President I gathered the
following impressions as to his views concerning bank credits of
belligerent governments in contradistinction to a public loan
floated in this country.
     There is a decided difference between an issue of government
bonds, which are sold in open market to investors, and an arrangement for easy exchange in meeting debts incurred in trade between
a government and American merchants.
     The sale of bonds draws gold from the American people. The
purchasers of bonds are loaning their savings to the belligerent
government, and are, in fact, financing the war.
     The acceptance of Treasury notes or other evidences of debt in
payment for articles purchased in this country is merely a means of
facilitating trade by a system of credits which will avoid the
clumsy and impractical method of cash payments. As trade with
belligerents is legitimate and proper it is desirable that obstacles, such as interference with an arrangement of credits or easy
method of exchange, should be removed.
     The question of an arrangement of this sort ought not to be
submitted to this Government for its opinion, since it has given
its views on loans in general, although an arrangement as to
credits has to do with a commercial debt rather than with a loan
of money.
     The above are my individual impressions of the conversation
with the President who authorized me to give them to such persons
as were entitled to hear them, upon the express understanding that

they were my own impressions and that I had no authority to speak
for the President or the Government.

Memorandum by Robert Lansing on a conversation with President
Wilson, 8:30 p.m., October 23, 1914, U.S. Congress, 74th, 2nd
session, Senate, Special Committee Investigating the Munitions
Industry, Munitions Industry, XXV, p. 7666.

672. WE MUST EXTEND LOANS (1915)

Ten months after the preceding memorandum was
written, war orders from Europe had dispelled the
recession of 1914-1915. Also, Robert Lansing, pro-
ponent of loans to belligerent countries, had replaced William Jennings Bryan as Secretary of State.
Pressure increased on President Wilson to adopt a
pro-loan policy. The following is from a letter to
President Wilson by William McAdoo, Secretary of the
Treasury and the President's son-in-law.

Great prosperity is coming. It is, in large measure, here
already. It will be tremendously increased if we can extend reasonable credits to our customers. The balance of trade is so largely
in our favor and will grow even larger if trade continues, that we
cannot demand payments in gold alone, without eventually exhausting
the gold reserves of our best customers, which would ruin their
credit and stop their trade with us. They must begin to cut their
purchases from us to the lowest limit, unless we extend to them
reasonable credit. Our prosperity is dependent on our continued
and enlarged foreign trade. To preserve that we must do everything
we can to assist our customers to buy.
We have repeatedly declared that it is lawful for our citizens
to manufacture and sell to belligerents munitions of war. It is
lawful commerce and being lawful is entitled to the same treatment
at the hands of our bankers, in financing it, as our other part of
our lawful to commerce. Acceptances [i.e., negotiable paper secured
by a bank's endorsement] based upon such exportations of goods are
just as properly the subject of legitimate bank transactions as if
based on noncontraband. We have reaffirmed our position about
munitions in our recent note to Austria--clearly and conclusively.
If our national banks are permitted to purchase such acceptances freely it will greatly relieve the situation. They can do so
without any danger of rendering "non-liquid" even a small part of
our present extraordinarily large credit resources. But national
banks will not buy such acceptances freely unless they know that
they are eligible for rediscount at Federal Reserve banks.
. . . .

It is imperative for England to establish a large credit in this country. She will need at least $500,000,000. She can't get this in anyway, at the moment, that seems feasible, except by sale of short-time Government notes. Here she encounters the obstacle presented by Mr. Bryan's letter of June 20, 1915, to Senator Stone in which it is stated that "war loans in this country were disapproved because inconsistent with the spirit of neutrality" etc., and "this Government has not been advised that any general loans have been made by foreign governments in this country since the President expressed his wish that loans of this character should not be made." The understood part is the hardest hurdle of the entire letter. Large banking houses here which have the ability to finance a large loan, will not do so or even attempt to do so, in the face of this declaration. We have tied our hands so that we cannot help ourselves or help our best customers. France and Russia are in the same boat. Each, especially France, needs a large credit here.

The declaration seems to me most illogical and inconsistent. We approve and encourage sales of supplies to England and others but we disapprove the creation by them of credit balances here to finance their lawful and welcome purchases. We must find some way to give them needed credits but there is no way, I fear, unless this declaration can be modified.

Letter, William G. McAdoo to President Wilson, August 21, 1915, U.S. Congress, 74th, 2nd session, Senate, Special Committee Investigating the Munitions Industry, Munitions Industry, XXVI, pp. 8123, 8124-8125.

673.   PROSPERITY REQUIRES FOREIGN LOANS (1915)

Some two weeks after Secretary McAdoo's letter, above, Secretary Lansing repeated essentially the same argument to President Wilson. The President responded orally, and shortly thereafter a large American loan to England was made.

It is estimated that the European banks have about 3 1/2 billions of dollars in gold in their vaults. To withdraw any considerable amount would disastrously affect the credit of the European nations and the consequence would be a general state of bankruptcy.

If the European countries cannot find means to pay for the excess of goods sold to them over those purchased from them, they will have to stop buying and our present export trade will shrink proportionately. The result would be restriction of outputs,

industrial depression, idle capital and idle labor, numerous failures, financial demoralization and general unrest and suffering
among laboring classes.

. . . .

Manifestly, the Government has committed itself to the policy
of discouragement of general loans to belligerent governments. The
practical reasons for the policy at the time we adopted it were
sound, but basing it on the ground that loans are "inconsistent
with the true spirit of neutrality" is now a source of embarrass-
ment. This latter ground is as strong today as it was a year ago,
while the practical reasons for discouraging loans have largely
disappeared. We have more money than we can use. Popular sympathy
has become crystallized in favor of one or another of the belligerents to such an extent that the purchase of bonds would in no way
increase the bitterness of partisanship or cause a possibly serious
situation.

Now, on the other hand, we are face to face with what appears
to be a critical economic situation, which can only be relieved
apparently by the investment of American capital in foreign loans
to be used in liquidating the enormous balance of trade in favor
of the United States.

Can we afford to let a declaration as to our conception of
the "true spirit of neutrality" made in the first days of the war
stand in the way of our national interests which seem to be seriously
threatened?

If we cannot afford to do this, how are we to explain away the
declaration and maintain a semblance of consistence?

My opinion is that we ought to allow the loans to be made for
our own good, and I have been seeking some means of harmonizing
our policy, so unconditionally announced with the flotation of
general loans. As yet I have found no solution to the problem.

Letter, Robert Lansing to President Wilson, September 6, 1915,
U.S. Congress, 74th, 2nd session, Senate, Special Committee Investigating the Munitions Industry, Munitions Industry, XXVI, pp. 7882,
7883.

674. BUYING INTO THE BRITISH COMMERCIAL EMPIRE (1917)

It would be far too much to say that the British
commercial empire was dismantled by American purchases
of British securities during World War I. For one thing,
as the following testimony by J. P. Morgan and George
Whitney explains, such wholesale transfers might be
unwise from a managerial viewpoint.

[Mr. RAUSHENBUSH.] Here I am sure Mr. Morgan is going to agree.
Surely, if the American financiers saw the opportunity to take at a

reasonable price what the British had spent a couple of hundred years building up, a commercial empire in the Argentine, the oil fields, and so forth, they would, as shrewd businessmen, have been glad to take that opportunity.

Mr. MORGAN.   I am not at all certain that you are right about that, Mr. Raushenbush.   They did not want the responsibility of managing them.   If they took over the control of a thing they would have to manage it, and the management of a thing five or six thousand miles away is not so easy to the American mind as it is to the English mind, because they have had less experience at it.

It would have taken a long time to persuade a good many gentlemen whom I used to know quite well, who were willing to buy things-- if they thought they had a strong British group with them who managed it, they were perfectly willing to take a part and sell back the shares to the British group later on if that relieved them at all for the moment.   But to buy the whole of a company, they were not out for creating a commercial empire all over the world.

Do you see what I mean there?

Mr. RAUSHENBUSH.   I defer to your judgement on the American investing habits.

Mr. MORGAN.   The theory of management is that troubles are very great if you have to deal with a thing six or seven thousand miles away from you.

Mr. RAUSHENBUSH.   Surely.   Do you not think they would even have been willing, if this thing was dumped in their laps, at pretty much a reasonable price, to have taken a considerable share of those things?   Those were good things.

Mr. MORGAN.   They might have done it.   That is what we hoped they would, if they were properly coached.

Mr. WHITNEY.   Do you not think that they thought the opportunities in this country were even greater than abroad?

Mr. RAUSHENBUSH.   I do not know.

Mr. BROWN.   If I may break in on that, the fact remains, it seems to me, that the suggestion was made in pretty definite form in this cable.

> * * *   while I understand the exceedlingly disagreeable character of our suggestion our advice is definite as it has been before, that we see no other way of accomplishing the raising of the necessary sums on this side.

Mr. WHITNEY.   That is what I said.

Mr. BROWN.   I judge from Mr. Morgan's remarks that while the American market might not have been particularly glad to have these, that being a debate we have no way of settling because they never came, at this point the commercial fabric of the British Empire was being endangered by its American needs.

Mr. MORGAN.   I think you figure the thing would go to an amount that is far in excess of anything that we could possibly have managed.   The British commercial empire does not rest on 5 or 10

securities. There are hundreds and hundreds of them, and closely
held, at that.

Testimony, J. P. Morgan and George Whitney, January 16, 1936,
U.S. Congress, 74th, 2nd session, Special Committee Investigating
the Munitions Industry, Munitions Industry, XXVIII, pp. 8615-8616.

675. GOVERNMENT APPROVES FIXING EXPORT PRICES (1919)

Prior to 1918, American exporters were restrained
by the Sherman Anti-Trust Law from combining to control
export prices by concerted action. On April 10, 1918,
the Webb-Pomerene Act was passed and thereafter it became
permissible for exporters to fix export prices. All this
was done under supervision of the Federal Trade Commission.
The following is an extract from a letter by John Ryan,
president of the Copper Export Assocaition, Inc.

During the war, while the copper production of this country
was being distributed under Government direction, there was no need
for taking advantage of the Webb Act. With the falling off of the
war requirements, however, the need has returned for combined action
in export trade by the copper producers of the country.
After conference among a number of producers, a plan has been
agreed upon, resulting in the formation, under the laws of Delaware,
of a corporation known as COPPER EXPORT ASSOCIATION, INC., which
will act as exclusive agent for the sale of export copper for such
producers or operators who sell or control the sale of export copper
at prices named by the Association, to allot such orders among the
members pro rata according to the amount of copper each member has
available for export, to average the prices monthly to each member
so that each member will secure for his export copper every month
the same price as every other member and at the same time to leave
each member free to sell, ship, and bill his export copper direct
to the foreign purchaser and to maintain, if he so desires, his own
selling representatives abroad, subject always, to the foregoing
provisions in respect of apportioning orders and averaging prices.
For greater certainty, reference is hereby made to the Agency
Agreement herewith enclosed. The plan adopted has been approved
by counsel.

Letter, John D. Ryan, January 13, 1919, Verbatim Record of
the Proceedings of the Temporary National Economic Committee,
XI, p. 112.

676. LONG-TERM GOVERNMENT FINANCING OF EXPORTS (1919)

The Wilson administration facilitated the new
role of American industry as a major exporter to a war-
torn world. Where the American banking system was backward, the federal government stepped in to fill the breach.
(See also Source No. 667). Louis Whele, who served as
general counsel to the War Finance Corporation from
1919 to 1921, writes here.

The American pre-war credit system for financing exports was
useless for revising them because it was not geared for long-term
loans to the exporter. In the normal course of business the American exporter's needs had generally been satisfied by loans from his
own bank covered by his thirty- to ninety-day notes, which were secured by his foreign customer's note or acceptance for a similar
period.

But now the foreign manufacturer-buyer needed a much longer
time to pay for raw materials or machinery. Payments were not
flowing to him at intervals from past transactions to start his
business or keep it going. In the case of raw materials, he needed
credits long enough to span the entire prospective cycle for processing them, selling the product, and collecting payment from his
own wholesaler-customer. But the wholesaler, too, was starting
from scratch. He had to have a long credit for paying up, because
the retailer-customer in turn would need credit until he could convert his stock into cash.

The pre-war banking customs of Britain and the Continent were
normally geared to meet the new need for such an over-all cycle of
credits. Commercial obligations with years to run might be acceptable. Europe's trade, intra-European and with the Middle and Far
East and Latin America, was built up largely on credits that American banks would reject as "frozen." Indeed, one may say that our
export trade grew in spite of our credit policy. The United States'
advantages in natural resources and large-scale production could
normally offset the disadvantage of that policy.

But after the Armistice the Federal Reserve System's ninety-
day restriction on rediscounting commercial paper for a commercial
bank conclusively shut out the American exporter from selling
abroad. Why? In most cases he was not strong enough to hold long-
term paper; and because he could not borrow on it from his bank he
was unable to make the sale. The three-month credit limit kept the
American exporter and his pre-war customer as isolated as though
they were on different planets.

. . . .

The Treasury Department had at hand a sword that it now turned
into a plowshare. In April, 1918, Congress had created the War
Finance Corporation (W.F.C.), with an authorized capital stock of
$500 million to be held by the Treasury Department. W.F.C. had
authority to use its half-million working capital as a revolving
fund. It also had power to raise $3 billion more by selling its
tax-free bonds. Congress originally organized W.F.C. to lend money
for war. Because in the war's first year many concerns, large and

small, old and new, of second- or third-class financial standing,
had expanded their operations more rapidly than was consistent with
their getting sound banking assistance, the Government had offered
to finance them. Under the statute the W.F.C. could make loans to
such concerns or to the banks that would make new loans to them or
extend loans previously made to them.

The W.F.C. had, during the war, lent funds to electric-power
plants and public utilities, to coal mines, chemical concerns,
cattle raisers, railroads, to banks that had loans outstanding to
war industries, and to other enterprises. Congress now transformed
it into a peace finance corporation, with power to make loans to
exporters for up to five years secured by their pledge of long-term
foreign obligations, or to lend money for up to five years to banks
that had discounted such long-term foreign obligations for exporters.

Louis B. Wehle, Hidden Threads of History. Wilson Through
Roosevelt, (New York: Macmillan Co., 1953), pp. 70-71, 71-72.

677. CHEMICAL COMPETITION AND PUBLIC OPINION (1921)

The post-war American chemical industry feared a
revival of German competition and so employed publicity
men to go overseas and plant anti-German articles in
American newspapers. It was hoped that American public
opinion would thus come to favor legislation on behalf
of the American industry. Ben Raleigh, who writes here,
was head of the Du Pont public relations office in Paris
and was European representative of the Whaley-Eaton News
Service; he writes to Charles Weston, head of the Du Pont
publicity office in Wilmington, Delaware.

The A. P. carried a cable on the substance of an interview I
had with Professor Blondell, professor of economics and political
science of the College of France, and I suppose you noted it in the
cable despatches. The [Philadelphia] Public Ledger syndicate and
the Chicago Tribune syndicate papers are to be supplied with a
story I have arranged which will point out that the French Government, upon confidential information from its investigators in Germany regarding a coming great German dump of goods, will further
increase its coefficient tariff rates on dyestuffs, chemicals, etc.
The stories will point out that France will increase the coeffi-
cients not only to safeguard French industry but also to prevent
further unemployment due to French production being stopped by a
great stream of German goods. This will checkmate the German plans
as far as France is concerned but will have the effect of concentrating Germany's attention on the United States, which alone of
all the great countries has not acted to safeguard its dye industry. This story should bring out some editorials in the American

press, and it might be possible to have it suggested to some of the newspapers that editorial treatment of the cable would be of public service.

Dr. Jacoby, who is Dr. Chapin's associate, showed me yesterday a clipping from one of the Ledger syndicate newspapers. It was a cable dated January 7, and was the article you supplied. The clip had been sent him from America, and the last paragraph had been heavily blue-penciled as a mark of approval.

I sent you a cable yesterday notifying you of the coming appearance of the stories for the P. L. syndicate and C. Tribune papers. I hope to get some more material over the A. P. wires shortly.

I have made arrangements with Dr. Chapin and Captain Norris, who is a good fellow, to be tipped off promptly if Karl von Weinberg arrives in Paris. He would get in touch with either of these two men upon his arrival. I shall then attempt in an interview to get him to boast a little and to have three or four of the other correspondents with me at the interview.

Dr. Chapin says confidentially that he sent some information to a friend of yours, who, I believe, is Mr. Poucher, and that his action was objected to in the office here when it became known. He gives this as an illustration of how careful he has to be, although in full accord and entire sympathy with our purposes. Dr. Chapin went over all his difficulties thoroughly when we had luncheon together yesterday.

By the way, I suppose that an occasional luncheon, etc., in furtherance of the project would not be objected to, but I should like authorization. In this case Dr. Chapin paid for the lunch, but I want to be in a position to come back at him and the other people who we want to cultivate, including such men as Williams, of the P. L. Roberts, of the A. P., Descheil, who is a good plugger, etc. Floyd Gibbons, of the Tribune, should be cultivated more closely, and you know how much can be done over a bite to eat and a drink.

Carl Ackerman, who dropped into the Ledger Bureau while I was there, over on a short visit from London, requested me to remember him to you.

I shall have a new office next week, right at the Place de la Concorde. The address will be 8 rue Saint-Florentin, Paris (1er), off the Rue de Rivoli at the Place de la Concorde, just over the bridge from the Chambre des Deputies and the French Foreign Office, and right up against all the hotels, etc. I am very much pleased with it.

Letter, Ben K. Raleigh to Charles K. Weston, January 25, 1921, U.S. Congress, 73rd, Senate, Special Committee Investigating the Munitions Industry, Munitions Industry, IX, p. 2580.

678. CUBAN BENEFITS FROM AMERICAN SUPERVISION (1924)

An old "Cuba Hand", Edwin Atkins, regards the island's affairs from a commercial and investing perspective.

Cuba has benefited in many ways by the supervision of the
United States since the Spanish-American War. Through the efforts
of the United States Sanitary Commission, yellow fever, malaria,
and other tropical diseases have been practically eliminated from
the Island. The ever-present threat of military intervention in
case of disturbances has made it possible for foreigners, not only
to live in Cuba, but also to invest millions of dollars in Cuban
industries with comparative safety. The tariff differential on
sugars given Cuba by the United States has greatly stimulated the
sugar industry and encouraged the investment of American capital.
Even before the Spanish-American War, Cuba felt the influence of
the United States. Following carefully the rise and fall of sugar
production in Cuba for sixty years, it will be seen that the in-
surrections coincide with the changes in the economic conditions
brought about largely by tariff legislation in the United States
and the former bounty system, now fortunately abolished.
. . . .
The population of Cuba is now estimated as but little over
3,000,000, and her sugar production has now exceeded 4,000,000
tons. The wealth of the Island is very largely in the hands of
foreigners, including Spaniards. This class of the population has
no vote or voice in the Government, and as upon these foreigners
Cuba must largely depend for her taxes, it is becoming a question
of taxation without representation.
These people look to the United States for protection of their
investments under the terms of the Reciprocity Treaty and the stipulation in regard to loans, and such protection will probably be
afforded, but it should be remembered that the Reciprocity Treaty
is not a permanent agreement, and may be cancelled upon due notice.
The danger will not come from Cuba, but rather from the domestic
sugar producers in the United States.
The changes in methods of manufacture and business through
which Cuba is passing and the heavy investment of capital required
to develop new sugar enterprises are to a great extent eliminating
private [individual] ownership; while many individual or family
interests still remain, they are gradually being absorbed by corporate ownership. The old-time planter is disappearing, and with
him many of the interesting customs connected with the earlier
history of the Island under Spanish rule.

Atkins, Sixty Years in Cuba, pp. 345, 346-347.

679. AMERICA IN THE WORLD FINANCIAL COMMUNITY (1920's)

In a decade, American finance had become the
stabilizer of European economic affairs.

In 1923, no outcome from the hopeless situation seemed possible; in a less degree, the paper currencies even of England and
France were heavily depreciated. But American finance seemed equal
to the task. On Wall Street everyone was talking, in the early
twenties, of the huge foreign "dollar loans"--sometimes put out by
the lately belligerent European governments, sometimes by other
states, in sums often ranging from $100,000,000 to $250,000,000,
which were offered by our important banking syndicates and were
instantly subscribed by American investors. Our Federal Reserve
banks were applying their abundant surplus to helping Europe reconstruct its disordered currencies. That work seemed altogether
logical, economically, when the United States was visibly the
world's money centre, when nearly half of the whole world's gold
had been lodged in America, yet when our surplus of merchandise
exports over imports continued unprecedentedly great. I frequently
met in those days, at the New York Federal Reserve Bank or at the
dinner table of its governor, the late Benjamin Strong, responsible
chiefs of the great European central banks who, contrary to all
precedent, were visiting New York periodically to shape a cooperative programme. So intimate was this affiliation that Strong, who
was in many ways an original, used across the dinner table to
address Montagu Norman, governor of the Bank of England, as
"Monty"; once in a while even addressing Hjalmar Schacht of the
Reichsbank as "Greeley"--a middle name discarded by the German
banker, but which his father, once a resident of America and a
warm admirer of the older-time Tribune editor, had actually conferred upon him. Those were the days when England resumed gold
payments, when the Latin nations returned to the gold standard,
when the Dawes Commission set Germany's currency on its feet--all
with the cordial assistance of financial America.
Perhaps it was not surprising that even conservative financiers should have come to believe that, thanks to the good offices
of the America which had emerged from war apparently impregnable
economically, further baleful consequences of Europe's four-year
struggle would be averted.

Alexander D. Noyes, The Market Place, pp. 296-297.

680. EXPANDING U.S. DIRECT FOREIGN INVESTMENTS (1920's)

Tariff and the market as influences stimulating
establishment of foreign plants are described here by

P. W. Litchfield, a man involved in U.S. business
at that time.

Australia was the first to move, in 1926, when it imposed heavy
duties on all imports, 50 per cent in the case of tires. Australia
had been an excellent market for years. But we could not build tires
in the United States or Canada, ship them halfway around the world,
pay a 50 per cent duty, and still sell them in competition with
tires made locally. We were out of business there.

The step I had decided on in case this happened was to go in
behind the tariff walls and build factories in those countries--if
they were willing. Our salespeople had already sounded them out.
The Australian Government would welcome the investment of American
capital.

I will always feel it was a compliment to our standing as a
business house that leading business and banking people there cooperated fully, offered to buy stock in the company if we wanted
them to. Vice-President Stillman, one of the Wilmer men, who had
had considerable corporation experience, hurried out to Sydney to
set up the arrangements. We furnished the major part of the capital. The stock offered locally was oversubscribed even before it
was even put on the market.

Stillman was just completing these arrangements when the second
blow fell. England renounced free trade, passed the McKenna Act,
which in the case of tires slapped on a 33.3 per cent duty. England
was our biggest foreign market. Our engineers started work on the
factory at Sydney, and Stillman headed for London. His reception
there was almost identical to that in Australia. We had to move
fast, did not have time to build a new factory, found an enamelware
plant which could be changed over. The two factories got into production about the same time.

I encountered no little criticism for investing American capital in other countries and paying wages to foreigners which should
have gone to American workmen. I had already thought that over.

We were not taking jobs away from American workmen. We had no
alternative. Those jobs were lost when the tariffs were set up.

Also it was unlikely that business would be bad everywhere at
the same time, and good business in one part of the world might offset bad times elsewhere. That proved out. There were periods later
on when export took up all the slack of bad times in America--in
fact when a good part of the company's profit for the year came
from abroad.

Argentina came next.

Our neighboring countries to the south have always held great
interest for me because they raised things we needed and could not
ourselves produce, which made for a natural basis of trade. Language
and cultural ties had long inclined them toward Europe. Wealthy
South Americans used to send their sons to Paris to be educated.
English and German capital had gone in, into banks, railroads, power
plants, hotels. Economic forces however were bringing Latin America
closer to the United States. The Panama Canal helped, by making the
west coast more accessible, and two world wars brought huge demand
for its raw materials, gave great stimulus to trade. American packing houses built plants in Argentina. General Motors, Ford, and

Chrysler put in assembly plants there and in other cities.

We have been selling goods in South America for forty years, starting with Argentina and Brazil, and I like to think that the tires we sold down there for cars and trucks, and later tractors and airplanes, as well as hose and conveyor belting to bring their great mineral resources to the surface, helped in the development of those countries. Now however Latin America was feeling the same nationalistic influences as England and Australia. Argentina was the first to act, set up tariff duties in 1928. We did not debate the matter long. We had three quarters of the tire business of the country. The government proved cordial to our going in there with a factory. I made my second trip to South America in 1929 to look over the site.

P. W. Litchfield, Industrial Voyage, My Life as an Industrial Lieutenant, (Garden City, New York: Doubleday and Co., 1954), pp. 232-233.

681. AMERICAN BRANCH FACTORIES ABROAD (1930)

American industrial expansion abroad waited upon the establishment of a mature industrial structure here at home. By 1900, such a structure started to give rise to significant numbers of overseas branches. By 1929, American-owned plants in Canada and Europe produced large amounts of electrical and telephone equipment as well as automobiles and machinery. R. P. Lamont, Secretary of Commerce, is the author of the following.

Although it is quite true that since the war [1918] the tendency toward the establishment of branch manufacturing plants and operation of public utilities has been more pronounced than toward the exploitation of natural resources in under-developed parts of the world, we can not ignore the fact that the movement of American industry to Canada had reached a considerable development before the outbreak of the war, and that some important American industries had started to branch out in Europe. In the case of Canada it may be stated that the tariff obstacle against the movement of goods across the border, on the one hand, and the strong pull of proximity, similarity of taste, standard of living, and of language, on the other, have served to hasten the expansion of American industry beyond the national frontiers.

In considering the postwar period, it is found that a considerable share of our investment capital is still going into the exploitation of the natural resources of foreign countries, as exemplified by the developments in petroleum, copper, water power, etc. It is quite clear, therefore, that there is no sharp line of demarcation between the two periods. The utmost that can be

claimed is that before the war the bulk of our foreign industrial
investments went into the exploitation of natural resources, while
since the war the emphasis has been placed on the extension of
markets for American products through the establishment of branch
plants.

The pre-war phase began at a time when the natural resources
of the United States were still being exploited to a marked extent
with the aid of foreign capital--in other words, when the United
States was still largely a capital-importing country. As outstanding examples of our foreign industrial investments during this
period might be mentioned the mining enterprises in Canada and
Latin America, the branching out of the American packing industry
in South America, the Central American banana enterprises, the
sugar plantations in Cuba, etc. Although it is true that in many
of these cases the application of American industrial methods was
an important element in the success of such enterprises, it probably
was not the chief factor, as a rule. There were also established
branches of manufacturing plants in Canada and to some extent in
Europe, but they represented a minor share in our total industrial
investments abroad.

Since the armistice a constantly increasing proportion of our
foreign investments has gone into branch plants, established primarily to exploit foreign markets and to overcome certain sales obstacles like tariffs, transportation, lack of service facilities,
national sentiment, and patent provisions.

. . . .

It is hardly necessary to emphasize the fact that the bulk of
our foreign branch plants represent industries that are in practical control of the domestic market; in other words, industries with
an actual or potential surplus production. It is also quite evident that those industries, in the majority of cases, have an
initial advantage in the way of industrial methods, patent rights,
financial reserves, and experience which enables them to overcome
many of the obstacles connected with the migration of industry.
Many of those industries are also in the mass-production stage
based on the purchasing capacity of broad classes of population,
and therefore most concerned in bringing their products within
the purchasing capacity of their foreign consumers. Under the
circumstances it might be said that the branch factory, by and
large, is merely a more intensive method of selling an American
product in foreign markets; the branch factory, theoretically at
least, takes up the work where the ordinary sales methods stop,
even if the factory is established long before such sales methods
have reached their full capacity. The branch factory, which represents a long-view policy, is better adapted in most cases to form
a basis for the application of the typical American sales technique,
with its emphasis on service and intensive cultivation of a market.
In many lines, the sales opportunities for the American product at
a price increased by the charges incidental to getting it to the
foreign consumer, would be so restricted as to make the business
of slight value to the American producer. No comprehensive campaign
for the introduction of the American specialty could be justified

on a basis that would imply a much higher price for the foreign
consumer, with his low purchasing power, than for the American
consumer.

R. P. Lamont, January 20, 1931, U.S. Congress, 71st, 3rd
session, Senate Document No. 258, serial number 9346, American
Branch Factories Abroad, pp. 3-4, 5.

682.   PRESSURES FOR NEW LATIN AMERICAN POLICY (1933)

Usually overlooked in this regard was American
business pressure for a new policy. These remarks are
those of Lawrence Duggan, Chief, Division of the American
Republics, Department of State.

First of all it had become apparent that the antagonisms fired
by our past activities [in Latin America] had resulted in the erec-
tion of a barrier of distrust more efficacious in its insulating
quality than any physical barrier of distance or topography. At
international gatherings the United States delegations instead of
being welcomed as friends and associates were eyed askance and with
misgivings. This suspicion extended beyond the confines of the
Government to include our citizens, regardless of walk of life.
They were distinctly handicapped because they discovered that outside the confines of the United States they were considered to
possess to a greater or lesser degree the same qualities that their
country was considered to have exhibited in its international
dealings. They found that the influence of the United States was
related directly to that flowing from the might of material
strength. They came to realize that the United States had few real
friends on this hemisphere, friends who shared a similar outlook,
friends whose sympathy and aid could be counted upon in case of
need. And as storm clouds arose in other parts of the world, and
the depression deepened, our people wondered whether this was a
healthy situation.
Moreover, the antagonisms were adversely affecting our commer-
cail interests. During the period of the second intervention in
Nicaragua (1926-1933) and of the acute period of our intervention
in Haiti (1920-1930), groups in many countries boycotted United
States goods. While for a variety of reasons the trade statistics
are poor indices of the force of those boycotts, our businessmen
were well aware of the business actually lost because of the ill
feeling toward the United States. Their concern was not alleviated
by the passage of the Smoot-Hawley tariff of 1930, which, because
of its very substantial increases on many important export products
of the other American countries, caused deep resentment. Retalia-
tory tariffs were erected, and the new far-reaching trade controls

instituted during the depression were sometimes availed of to our
disadvantage. Some of the more enlightened and far-sighted American
businessmen even took steps of their own to endeavor to correct
some of the misconceptions regarding the United States—for there
were many of these. For instance the International American
Committee, composed of several of the important business interests,
took several useful steps in the early thirties along this line.
Finally, considering that the other American countries have known
us by our interventions and dollars, it was not surprising that the
United States should have been regarded as a great culture desert,
void of art, music, literature—in short, of a soul. Oases here
and there were admitted, but they were not considered typical and
were generally believed to be nourished by subterranean foreign
springs. Of course there were persons in every one of the American
countries who knew that the United States was not a cultural vacuum.
They have stood out like lighthouses. To them, this country owes
a deep debt of gratitude for their efforts to interest their coun-
trymen in the cultural activity of the United States. If they have
not been successful, the fault is not theirs. It lies with the
antagonisms created by our past policies, and with the indifference
of our scholars and scientists and foundations to the almost un-
charted sea of cultural cooperation in the Americas. With a stead-
fastness reminiscent of the captain's daughter lashed to the mast
of the Hesperus, they have kept their attentions and activities
riveted on the Old World.

Address, Lawrence Duggan, April 2, 1938, Department of State
Press Releases, April 2, 1938, reprinted in James W. Gantenbein
(ed.), The Evolution of our Latin-American Policy (1950), pp.
190-191.

683. FINANCING EXPORTS (1939)

The Roosevelt Administration strengthened existing
federal programs for stimulating private American exports.
(See Source No. 677). Jesse Jones was head of the
Reconstruction Finance Corporation, and chairman of the
board of the Export-Import Bank. He writes the following
with Edward Angly.

The [Export-Import] Bank's first aid went to the American
manufacturer and the American workman whose job often depended
upon whether a plant's front office was successful in bidding for
overseas orders. The foreign buyer of durable goods, such as
locomotives, railway cars, and heavy machinery of all sorts,
seldom pays spot cash. Heavy machinery must help pay for itself—
and this takes time. What we did was to provide medium-or-long-

term loans to permit the exporting manufacturers to fill orders on long-term credit.

Sometimes an exporter would come to tell us of an order on which he wanted to bid, and we would agree to advance him money if his bid were successful. Usually we tried to cooperate with his banker in arranging the necessary financing.

An alternative method involved the appointment of the applicant's commercial bank as our agent to carry out all the details of a particular transaction. The bank was accorded the privilege of being reimbursed by us for its outlays, upon demand. Thus, while taking the risks unto itself, the Export-Import Bank encouraged commercial banks to supply the funds and the supervisory personnel to as great an extent as we could persuade them to go. By prompting commercial banks to service these loans we were able to handle all the Export-Import Bank's affairs with a staff of less than sixty.

On the other end of the line--in the countries to which the shipment of exports or the advances were made--we usually tried to get the purchaser's obligation guaranteed by substantial local banks in his country. Though in this way we dealt with several state-owned or state-controlled banks, we rarely did business with a foreign government itself. Banks cannot repudiate their obligations and continue in business. A state can. My feeling was that we should not lend money that we did not expect to get back. However, in some of the smaller and less prosperous countries we made a few small loans which I termed "soft"; but they worked out all right.

Examples of how foreign banks were brought into the picture were the credits of more than $12,000,000 arranged between 1937 and the war's beginning in 1939 for some one hundred different American cotton shippers who held orders from Italian spinners. We arranged to have the credits for the purchasers guaranteed, in varying amounts, by more than a dozen of the strongest banks in Italy.

Jesse Jones, with Edward Angly, Fifty Billion Dollars. My Thirteen Years with the RFC (1932-1945), (New York: Macmillan, 1951), pp. 220-221.

684. THE DOLLAR, NOT THE MARK, RULED SOUTH AMERICA (1930's)

Nazi political and economic penetration of the western hemisphere was a frequent topic of U.S. governmental concern during the 1930's. The following is from the testimony of Hermann Göring, deputy head of state under Hitler and who also served as commander-in-chief of the German air force.

Dr. HORN: American war propaganda consistently spoke of
Germany's aggressive intentions toward the Western Hemisphere.
What do you know about this?
GÖRING: The Western Hemisphere?   Do you mean America?
Dr. HORN: Yes.
GÖRING: Even if Germany had completely dominated the nations
of Europe, between Germany and the American continent there are,
as far as I still recall from my geographic knowledge, about 6,000
kilometers of water, I believe.   In view of the smallness of the
German fleet and the regrettable lack of bombers to cover this
distance...there was never any question of a threat against the
American continent; on the contrary, we were always afraid of that
danger in reverse, and we would have been very glad if it had not
been necessary to consider this at all.
As far as South America is concerned, I know that we were
always accused, by propaganda at least, of economic penetration
and attempted domination there.   If one considers the financial and
commercial possibilities which Germany had before and during the
war, and if one compares them with those of Great Britain or
America, one can see the untenability of such a statement.   With
the very little foreign exchange and the tremendous export difficulties which we had, we could never constitute a real danger or
be in competition.   If that had been the case, the attitude of the
South American countries would presumably have been a different
one.   Not the mark, but only the dollar ruled there.

Testimony, Hermann Göring, March 18, 1946, International
Military Tribunal, Trial of the Major War Criminals, (Nuremberg,
Germany: Allied Control Authority for Germany, 1947), IX, p. 402.

685. THE POLYBUTENE CARTEL (1941)

World distribution of a basic material for synthetic
rubber was controlled by agreement of an American and a
German firm.   The following letter was written sixteen
months after World War II began.   It was written by H. W.
Fisher, manager of the commercial department of the Standard
Oil Development Company.   He writes to L. B. Turner who was
employed in the company's Esso Laboratories in Linden, New
Jersey.   "I. G." refers to the I. G. Farbenindustrie
Aktiengesellschaft, the largest firm in the German chemical
industry.

In answering your questions, it is necessary to distinguish
between Polybutene used in the petroleum industry, for example in
the form of Paratone and Paratac, and Polybutene used outside the
petroleum industry.

With respect to the former, we have not reached a final settlement with the I. G., but meanwhile are following the arrangement
originally in existence whereby we sold Polybutene in the petroleum
industry throughout the World except Germany. On Polybutene for
use outside the petroleum industry, we have reached an agreement
with the I. G. whereby patent rights are divided between us on an
exclusive geographical basis. Under this arrangement, our territory comprises the United States and its territorial possessions,
the British Empire and the French Empire. The I. G.'s territory
is the rest of the world.

If we sell for export to some South American country, for
example, or to Japan, we cannot convey to the customer any license
whatever to use the Polybutene in these areas; furthermore, by so
doing, we are presumably not only violating our agreement with the
I. G., but may be partially liable for our customer's violation of
the I. G.'s patent rights. It is apparent, therefore, that we
cannot knowingly sell to an exporter who is going to move Polybutene
into some part of the world where the I. G.'s patent rights obtain.

Naturally, under the present war conditions, it is physically
impossible for us to reach some markets that properly belong to
us, for example, occupied France, and conversely, it is impossible
for the I. G. to reach certain other markets. Therefore, there
always exists the possibility of making some temporary arrangement
with the I. G. if it is to our mutual advantage to do so. About a
year ago, we had customers in Norway, Sweden, and the Netherlands
who wished to purchase Polybutene and could not obtain it from the
I. G. We asked the I. G. for permission to supply them and they
refused to give us this permission for a period. It should be
noted that we cannot presume inability of the I. G. to deliver. It
is therefore necessary to refer South America and Japanese customers to the I. G. for permission to supply them. I shall be glad
to request this permission from the I. G. In any case where you
have gone through the necessary preliminary steps herein outlined.

Letter, H. W. Fisher to L. B. Turner, January 20, 1941, U.S.
Congress, 77th, 1st session, Senate, Special Committee Investigating
the National Defense Program, Investigation of the National Defense
Program, XI, p. 4661.

686.   LIQUIDATING BRITISH INVESTMENT IN THE
UNITED STATES (1941)

In March, 1941, the British-owned American Viscose
Corporation was sold to a syndicate of Wall Street bankers
in order to raise funds to pay for British war orders
here. One group of American officials headed by Jesse
Jones wanted to help England by lending the money and
thus stave off sale of the Corporation. Another group
headed by Treasury Secretary Henry Morgenthau opposed

a loan and pressed for a sale; this group won out. Here
Jesse Jones writes to President Roosevelt.

If the British are required to sell their United States investments on a forced sale basis, they will probably not be able to
realize their fair value, and the fact that these investments are
hanging over the market will have a depressing effect on the entire
market, and in that way adversely affect investments of our own
citizens.

Furthermore, the British have made a point of the fact that
many of their investments in this country are an important factor
in their economic affairs. The income from them is being used to
buy our products, and otherwise to provide them with dollar
exchange.

I think we all feel that the British should pay as long as
they can, and should use their foreign investments to fight the
war and buy war supplies. But it may not leave a very good feeling
with them if they are forced to sell investments that are vital to
their existence.

I suggest that we arrange to lend on these investments at
approximately the cost of money to us, and for a period--not too
long--that will enable them to sell in an orderly way, and probably
save some of these investments by applying the earnings toward
interest and in liquidation of the debt.

In the case of the Viscose, as I understand the deal, it was
hurried and forced, the bankers advancing $40,000,000, and agreeing
to account to the British for 90% of the sale price over the
$40,000,000 advance, and their fees of $2,700,000, and expenses
estimated at $150,000.

In other words, from the total sale price, after paying the
advance and the bankers' fees and expenses, aggregating approximately $43,000,000, the bankers take 10% of any excess.

The Company is in excellent shape with almost $40,000,000 cash
on hand and a substantial amount of other liquid assets. Its earnings for the past two years have been approximately $9,700,000 a
year. This may have been before income taxes, but even allowing
for taxes, the net earnings would be more than $7,000,000 a year.
This may have been before income taxes, but even allowing for
taxes, the net earnings would be more than $7,000,000 a year.

If the bankers should sell the property at, say, $75,000,000,
which would not be a big price, the bankers' total fees will be in
the neighborhood of $6,000,000, or a net to the British of approxi-
mately $68,000,000. The British will be justified in feeling that
this is a very big price to pay the bankers, particularly since
they are selling their choicest United States investments.

If we had loaned $68,000,000 against the property at 3%,
the earnings would have paid the interest on the loan, and amor-
tized the entire debt in approximately ten years, based upon the
last two years' earnings.

Letter, Jesse Jones to President Franklin D. Roosevelt,
March 20, 1941, Jones, Fifty Billion Dollars, pp. 473-474.

687. SUBSIDIZING THE KING OF SAUDI ARABIA (1941)

In 1941, King Ibn S'aud of Arabia pressed American
oil concessionaires for a $30 million subsidy over the
next five years. The concessionaires asked the U.S.
Government to make the payments. President Roosevelt,
Navy Secretary Frank Knox, presidential adviser Harry
Hopkins, and presidential press secretary Steve Early
were contacted by an oil representative. On October 9,
1941, the issue was resolved in accordance with the
following letter. Jesse Jones, who was Federal Loan
Administrator and chairman of the Reconstruction Finance
Corporation, writes to James Moffett. Moffett was
chairman of the boards of directors of Bahrein Petroleum
Co., Ltd., and of California-Texas Oil Co., Ltd. From
1924 to 1933, Moffett had been senior vice-president in
charge of foreign and domestic sales for the Standard
Oil Company of New Jersey.

With further reference to your request that aid be provided
by our Government for King Ibn Saud, through an advance of several
million dollars, beg to advise I am informed that funds cannot be
advanced to the King under the Lend-Lease Act, and no Government
agency has the authority to provide the King with funds.
  I discussed the matter with the President and the Secretary
of State. They were both sympathetic with the King's needs and
regretted that our Government was not in a position to make him a
loan, or an advance on oil royalties that may accrue to him through
leases held by your company at some future date.
  At the instance of the President and the Secretary I suggested
to the British Ambassador that Britain consider providing King Ibn
Saud with such funds as in its opinion were necessary to meet
his requirements.

The oil companies interested might, if they wanted to do so,
work out some arrangement between the British Government and the
King.

Letter, Jesse H. Jones to James A. Moffett, October 9, 1941,
U.S. Congress, 80th, 1st session, Senate, Special Committee
Investigating the National Defense Program, Investigation of the
National Defense Program, XLI, p. 24745.

688.   ANGLO-AMERICAN OIL POLITICS (1943)

The British were paying King Ibn S'aud his special
subsidy. American oil interests feared the possible
consequences of British payments. As a result of the
events described below, on February 18, 1943 President
Roosevelt certified that "the defense of Saudi Arabia
is vital to the defense of the United States." American
Lend-Lease payments replaced the British payments and
thus presumably protected American oil leases in Saudi
Arabia from British competition. W. S. S. Rodgers, who
testifies here, was chairman of the board of directors of
the Texas Company, and was part owner of the Arabian-
American Oil Company (ARAMCO) which was the successor-
company to the concessions mentioned in the preceding
source.

Mr. RODGERS. When lend-lease was passed, Senator Ferguson, I
thought the British were going to put up all the money necessary
to keep that country going, as they were doing in Iran, Iraq, and
so forth. But I thought in doing that, over these war years, they
were going to gain the ascendency, and this country of Saudi Arabia
would fall in the sterling bloc or in the zone of influence of the
British; which we didn't naturally want.
     Senator FERGUSON. But under this agreement, did you not have
all the concessions in Arabia, all oil lands?
     Mr. RODGERS. No, not all of them; probably a very substantial
part of them, however.
     The CHAIRMAN. You said a little while ago that you were afraid
of a division. I think that was the word you used. You indicated
you were afraid of a division of the country which would adversely
affect you. Did you mean that with relation to the possible development of concessions?
     Mr. RODGERS. I meant a division of the concession.
     The CHAIRMAN. Yes. So that if you did not satisfy the King,
he might allow someone else to take over part of it.
     Mr. RODGERS. If we fell in the British zone of influence.
     The CHAIRMAN. And I suppose it applies over there, as it
does here, that the fellow who pays the piper is the one who calls
the tune.

Mr. RODGERS. I think you have the answer.

The CHAIRMAN. And Ibn-Saud, if he got the money from Winston Churchill, was naturally apt to think that Winston was the one that was in charge, is that right?

Mr. RODGERS. That is correct.

The CHAIRMAN. And even though the King himself knew that this money essentially came from the United States, what he really knew was that he got it through the British; is that right?

. . . .

[Mr. RODGERS.] We realized that he had to have the money, but we didn't like the British Government making these advances. And to offset their influence, we made these advances here, in 1941 and 1942, that I mentioned.

And then, at the beginning of 1943, it go so bad that we came down here and called on many people, trying to get the matter straightened out.

The CHAIRMAN. Now, you say "got so bad."

Mr. RODGERS. Well, the inroads that the British were making. I am sure that you, Senator, have heard of that famous locust party.

The CHAIRMAN. I have, but I am not sure that the others here have. I would like to have you tell us about that.

Mr. RODGERS. I can't give you the details of those things. Mr. Duce can do that. But the British moved this locust party in there. Now, whether it was bona fide or not, I don't know; but many Government people were going over there, State Department, Army, Navy. They were awfully suspicious about it. It may have been entirely bona fide.

I remember that some of them thought they were geologists in that [locust] party, and they thought it was just a scheme to get in and get their hands on the concession. We people in Aramco didn't feel as strongly about it.

The CHAIRMAN. Well, that was a rather formidable British expedition; and pretty well equipped, was it not, for covering that?

Mr. RODGERS. That is as I understand it, yes.

The CHAIRMAN. And presumably in search of a locust that was reaping havoc in the crops?

Mr. RODGERS. That is correct.

The CHAIRMAN. And with quite a military complement; and, as you say, with suspicions as to geologists that were possibly looking around for oil indications. Or what did you call them?

Mr. RODGERS. Possible oil areas. You understand, I was not particularly concerned about it. But it was the gentleman here in Washington, representing the armed services, and State, and other departments that were coming back, and they really got excited about it.

Testimony, W. S. S. Rodgers, October 29, 1947, U.S. Congress, 80th, 1st session, Senate, Special Committee Investigating the National Defense Program, Investigation of the National Defense Program, XLI, pp. 24814-24815, and 24829-24830.

689. "A LOPSIDED INDUSTRIAL ECONOMY" (1945)

The memory of unemployed resources was still
strong during the last days of World War II. American
policy-makers regarded the foreign market as a critical
step towards keeping the expanded American industrial
capacity occupied. Note the realistic reference to
credits. William Clayton was Assistant Secretary of
State for Economic Affairs. He testifies in the following.
Clayton had been principal factor in Anderson, Clayton
and Co., the cotton firm.

It is true that prior to the war we produced in the United
States a large surplus of industrial products over and above the
consumptive capacity of this country, but that situation has been
greatly intensified since the war.
At the end of this war we will have what I call a lopsided
industrial economy. We will have a great surplus capacity of production of certain types of goods--capital and producers goods,
machine tools, equipment of all kinds, and, of course, technical
know-how.
For example, in the machine tool industry we have increased
our capacity of production by 12 to 15 times during this war over
what it was before the war. If you take some other lines of business the increase is even much greater. For example, in the light
metals industry like magnesium, we increased about 100 times during
the war, and aluminum we increased 6 times during the war.
Now, if we are going to arrive within any reasonable time after
the end of the war at a condition of satisfactory employment in
this country, we are going to have to find the markets for some of
this surplus production. Obviously, we cannot find markets for all
of it. In some cases either the plants will have to close down, or
they will have to be converted to something else, but we can find
in the world very large markets for a great deal of this surplus
production, for several reasons.
At the end of the war some of the great industrial nations,
nations which formerly produced equipment of this kind, will be
rendered industrially impotent for several reasons--Japan and
Germany, of course--so that the United States will have a great
majority of the producing facilities for this kind of product. But
more important perhaps than that, the rest of the world will be
greatly in need of goods of that kind, not only because of the de-
vastated countries, the destruction that has been wrought by war
and the necessity to reconstruct, but there are other countries
that have not suffered devastation by the war that are anxious to
develop and they want to buy capital and producers' goods; countries
that because of war have had their economy and their imagination
quickened and expanded, and they are looking for goods of that
kind.
Now, we will have a great market for that kind of goods. We
will have the productive capacity for it, the plants, the capital,

the labor to make the goods, but we cannot sell these goods unless
the people who need them have the means with which to purchase
them. Obviously, in the end they can only purchase them by paying
us with their goods or services.

For several years after the war it is believed that these
countries will not even have the ability to pay us in that way because they will not have their productive facilities reconstructed
so as to produce goods surplus to their own wants because many
of these countries will have a big job to satisfy their own domestic requirements in the beginning. So, perhaps for several years
after the war they will not be in a position to pay us with goods
and services. Therefore, it is contemplated that perhaps 5 years
after the war the United States may have an excess of exports over
imports in the order of perhaps $15,000,000,000 to $20,000,000,000.
Obviously, that will have to be financed by credit.

Testimony, William L. Clayton, April 18, 1945, U.S. Congress,
79th, 1st session, House of Representatives, Committee on Ways
and Means, 1945 Extension of Reciprocal Trade Agreements Act, I,
pp. 23-24.

690.   DEMOCRACY AND LATIN AMERICAN TRADE (1945)

Following is an early example of the obvious
embarassments that could ensue from the intrusion
of political philosophy into the area of foreign-
economic policy. Nelson A. Rockefeller was Assistant
Secretary of State in charge of relations with Latin
American States; he was being questioned by Representative Carl T. Curtis of Nebraska.

Mr. CURTIS. How many of the 15 South American countries with
which we have trade agreements are ruled by so-called dictators?

Mr. ROCKEFELLER. Well, I would like to have your definition
of what a dictator is, sir.

Mr. CURTIS. I am afraid I might be impeached for my
language.

Mr. ROCKEFELLER. Let me say this----

Mr. CURTIS. A dictatorship in general would be a rule by men
and not by law, and where the people are not generally self-
governing, where the provisions of their constitution, if they have
one, have been overridden, where a man has continued on in power.
Those are just some of the factors.

Mr. ROCKEFELLER. Well, it is a little difficult in wartime to
determine because those powers have been delegated by the Congress
to the chief executives in all the countries including our own.

Mr. CURTIS. Well, how many of them would come in what is generally accepted as a dictator category?

Mr. ROCKEFELLER. I would like to be very frank and state that I do not think that the discussion which we are entering into here is one which is to the interests of our country or to our relations with other countries.

Mr. CURTIS. Yes; but just right there. I beg your pardon, but I did not start the discussion. It was testified here between you and Mr. Robertson and between Mr. Clayton and Mr. Robertson that you had carried on these trade agreements with people whose concept of government was the same as ours and were democracies.

Mr. ROCKEFELLER. That was not in my testimony, sir.

Let me say we pledged ourselves to a policy of nonintervention in the internal affairs of the other countries in this hemisphere in 1933 at the Montevideo Conference and again in 1936 and we have followed that policy.

Mr. CURTIS. Well then, the general platitudes that have been put out, that this is a promotion of trade between people who have the same concept of government as we do, is not correct; is that not true?

Mr. ROCKEFELLER. I am not familiar with the point of view which you were expressing. But I should like to say that the development of the economics of these countries is one of the strong contributing factors to the growth of democracy, because you cannot have democracy in a country which does not have economic develop-ment and educated people. In areas where you have illiteracy up to 60 or 70 or 80 percent, it is impossible to have a democracy in a country of that character.

Mr. CURTIS. What is a democracy?

Mr. ROCKEFELLER. A democracy is where the government is se-lected by the people, where the people participate in the voting.

Mr. CURTIS. All right. How many of these 15 countries are democracies?

Mr. ROCKEFELLER. I am not in a position to say, sir.

Mr. CURTIS. You do not know?

Mr. ROCKEFELLER. I do not think this is a fruitful discussion from the point of view of our relations with these other countries.

Mr. CURTIS. It is a matter of public record, is it not, what kind of governments they have?

Mr. ROCKEFELLER. No question about that.

Testimony, Nelson A. Rockefeller, April 19, 1945, U.S. Congress, 79th, 1st session, House of Representatives, Committee on Ways and Means, 1945 Extension of Reciprocal Trade Agreements Act, I, pp. 425-426.

691. DOLLAR CONTROL IN THE STERLING AREA (1945)

Less than a week after the Nazi armies surrendered unconditionally, attention to postwar economic policy with England became urgent. Trading advantage overshadowed military cooperation as a principal motivation. Charles Taft, Director, Office of Transport and Communication Policy, Department of State, described the situation at the time.

The operation of the dollar-pool regulations has necessarily reduced the supply of dollars available to businessmen in certain sterling area countries for purchases in the United States of goods deemed nonessential, and has reduced the sales which American exporters might otherwise have made in those particular places. It has of course increased the sales to other places in the sterling area. An illustration will explain the operation.

India happens to be one of the [sterling] area countries which contributes an excess of dollars to the pool. Let us say that an Indian merchant sells a shipment of jute to a concern in the United States. Payment is made by dollar draft on a New York bank. The Indian merchant turns the dollar over to his bank in India which in turn has to turn the dollar over to the British treasury. That is the way the dollar gets into the pool. Now if another Indian merchant wants to buy a bill of goods from the United States he must apply to the exchange control for a license to buy the dollars to make payment, and to the import control, which backs up the exchange control, for a license to import goods. Neither license will be granted unless the goods are essential to the war, and even if they are essential neither will be granted if they can be bought at somewhere near the American price from some other source which does not require payment in dollars. That sort of an experience, repeated many times, is the wartime situation that has faced American exporters.

The Government of the United States--and on this I can speak officially--regards the general form and purpose of these regulations as appropriate and necessary to the successful prosecution of the war. Dollars in the sterling area are scarce, and they have had to be allocated to war uses like any other scarce commodity. That allocation has undoubtedly prevented waste, and reduced the total drain of lend-lease on the Treasury of the United States. But it is very easy to see why particular American exporters who have lost sales do not like the regulations or the system. Their complaints against it have been numerous and strong.

Testimony, Charles P. Taft, May 12, 1945, U.S. Congress, 79th, 1st session, House of Representatives, Committee on Ways and Means, 1945 Extension of Reciprocal Trade Agreements Act, II, pp. 2686-2687.

692.   IT IS MUCH MORE THAN A LOAN (1946)

On December 6, 1945 the United States and the
United Kingdom signed a financial agreement in which
the United States set up a line of credit for England
of $3.75 billion. American negotiators traded this low-
interest loan for British concessions to American export
interests. Fred Vinson, Secretary of the Treasury,
speaks here.

For any goods or services purchased in the United States,
England will pay in dollars or, if payment is made, in pounds,
American exporters will be able to convert the sterling into
dollars. That goes for American movies as well as American machinery. And it applies to income from American investments in England.
No American firm need hesitate to do business with England for fear
that its earnings cannot be transferred. American businessmen will
be just as sure of payment in dollars from England as they were
before the war.

Within a year, unless we agree to a temporary extension,
England will remove all the restrictions on the convertibility of
sterling for ordinary current transactions. In practice, this will
mean that the money that England pays to Canada, Australia, and
India for her imports will be converted by England into dollars
and can be used by these countries to pay for goods they purchase
in the United States.

Within a year, unless we agree to a temporary extension,
England will dissolve the sterling area dollar pool. Each country
in the sterling area will be completely free to use any dollars
it earns to buy goods anywhere. India, for example, could use all
the dollars it gets for its exports to the United States and Latin
America without turning over any part of them to England.

A settlement will be made by England with the countries holding
blocked sterling balances. England has agreed that any payment in
liquidation of these blocked balances can be used to buy goods in
any country, including the United States. Instead of being forced
to spend the blocked sterling balances in England, the holders of
these balances, like India and Egypt, will be free to buy goods
wherever they prefer. American exporters will have a fair chance
to export in these markets.

. . . .
Naturally, the interest rate is less than Britain would have
to pay on a strictly commercial loan obtained from bankers. The
financial agreement, however, is much more than a loan. It is an
agreement on the major aspects of financial and commercial policy.
When we take into consideration the commitments we receive from
England on her currency and trade policies, it becomes clear that
the agreement would amply repay the American people even if no
interest were paid. And some would say we would have made a good
investment if the whole sum were a gift.

. . . .

But basically, we want to have the markets of the world opened
to our goods without discrimination. We want the restrictions that
Britain agrees to remove, removed. We are trying to look forward a
few years to when our surpluses need to be sold in the world markets.
Even I saw with some clarity the effect of the piling up of surpluses
which could not move into the world markets. That had a direct
effect upon the domestic market during the thirties. We want to
avoid that if we can. And we, in good faith, feel that this financial agreement will help avoid that economic catastrophe.

Testimony, Fred M. Vinson, May 14, 1946, U.S. Congress, 79th,
2nd session, House of Representatives, Committee on Banking and
Currency, Anglo-American Financial Agreement, pp. 7-8, 8-9, and 145.

693.   POLICING THE ANGLO-AMERICAN LOAN (1946)

On September 17, 1946, an Anglo-Argentine trade
treaty was signed. American officials quickly noticed
what they regarded as a clause potentially in conflict
with the Anglo-American loan agreement of December 5,
1945. John Snyder, American Secretary of the Treasury,
writes to Hugh Dalton, British Chancellor of the Exchequer.

In examining the agreement signed by representatives of the
Governments of the United Kingdom and Argentina on September 17,
1946, I have noted that Section B (6) of Article I provides as
follows:
> "If in any year the balance of payments with the
> sterling area be unfavorable to Argentina, Argentina
> may furthermore dispose freely within the said area
> of its sterling balances for an amount equivalent to
> the deficit."

This provision, which appears to have the effect of making the
amounts so released available for expenditure solely within the
sterling area, seems to be inconsistent with Section 10 (ii) of the
United States-United Kingdom Financial Agreement of December 6,
1945, which provides as follows:
> "(ii) In consideration of the fact that an important
> purpose of the present line of credit is to promote
> the development of multilateral trade and facilitate
> its early resumption on a non-discriminatory basis,
> the Government of the United Kingdom agrees that any
> sterling balances released or otherwise available for
> current payments will, not later than one year after
> the effective date of this Agreement, unless in special
> cases a later date is agreed upon after consultation,
> be freely available for current transactions in any
> currency area without discrimination."

You will recall that Section 10 (ii) was considered by both of
our Governments to be a very significant provision, and that it was
only after considerable discussion that agreement was reached as to
its formulation. It seems clear from the discussions before your
Parliament and the documentation relative to the Agreement that the
meaning of this section and the importance attached to it by the
United States were fully appreciated by your Government. In the
light of these facts, I am sure you can understand the concern of
this Government upon learning that the Government of the United
Kingdom had entered into a subsequent agreement containing a provision apparently in conflict with Section 10 (ii).

While I have not completed my consideration of the other provisions of the Anglo-Argentine agreement, the importance of the
apparent conflict explained above impels me to invite your attention
to it without delay. I hope it will be possible for you to consider
this matter and communicate with me in respect to it at an early
date.

Letter, John W. Snyder to Hugh Dalton, October 31, 1946, U.S.
Congress, 80th, 1st session, Senate, Committee on Finance,
International Trade Organization, II, p. 1261.

694. STATUS OF U.S. INVESTMENTS IN GERMANY (1946)

In 1940, private American direct investments in
Western Europe totalled $1.4 billion which represented
a fifth of all U.S. direct investment overseas. American
ownership rights in Western European investments were
protected during wartime, in some cases, by intricate
ad hoc arrangements with Swiss banks and companies.
General Lucius Clay, Deputy Governor, American Military
Government, Germany, is the speaker in the following.

Senator BREWSTER. What is the policy about acquisition of
interests in German industries?
General CLAY. That is not permitted.
Senator BREWSTER. There is no way any American concern could
acquire interests in German industry?
General CLAY. There are ways to do it, but it is absolutely
illegal and if it would be proven, it would be worthless.
Senator FERGUSON. Do you know of anybody who has done it?
General CLAY. We know of several people who tried. We had a
case in Berlin recently of an officer that was charged with attempting to invest in a German trucking corporation. He was just recently
court-martialed and he received a year and a dishonorable discharge.

Senator BREWSTER. What about the investments of Americans in Germany preceding the war? How are those treated?

General CLAY. At the present moment, wherever we have been able to locate them, they have been placed in blocked accounts under our trusteeship and we are trying to preserve them the best we can. You actually have the remaining problem which we have not solved, American partial ownership of firms that are listed for reparations. We are trying to obtain quadripartite approval to an agreement in principle that those firms, if the American ownership is substan- tial--if Allied ownership is substantial--would only be taken in reparations as a last resort and then under the principle of compen- sation by the German Government. We have not yet gotten an Allied quadripartite agreement on that principle.

. . . .

Senator FERGUSON. We will say that General Motors had a con- trolling interest in Opel.

General CLAY. Yes, sir.

Senator FERGUSON. Is that taken over by the Federal Government and held by our National Government?

General CLAY. It is taken over by our civilian administration, our military government, and we are now endeavoring to let the American management take it over again.

Senator FERGUSON. Well, has that been accomplished? That is not considered as trading with the enemy, for an American corpora- tion to operate that plant?

General CLAY. It would be if they came in and operated it themselves, but we can permit them to designate the German manage- ment.

Senator FERGUSON. Are you doing that?

General CLAY. Yes, sir.

Senator FERGUSON. So, today an American citizen or corporation, owning an interest in an industry in Germany, really has no rights in that industry.

General CLAY. He can designate the German management.

Senator FERGUSON. You are holding it for him.

General CLAY. We are holding it for him until the Trading with the Enemy Act is modified or abrogated. Until that time we are protecting his rights and we are permitting him to designate the German management.

Testimony, General Lucius D. Clay, November 18, 1946, U.S. Congress, 80th, 1st session, Senate, Special Committee Investigating the National Defense Program, <u>Investigation of the National Defense Program</u>, XLII, pp. 25869, 25870.

695.   PRIVATE CAPITAL SHOULD DEVELOP LATIN AMERICA (1948)

Emphasis upon private capital as a means of economic
development was characteristic of official American thinking at this time. George Marshall, then Secretary of
State, gives this view here.

The United States is qualified. I submit, by its own historical
experience to respond understandingly to the purpose of other American republics to improve their economic status. We understand the
wish to achieve balanced economies through development of industries,
mechanization of agriculture, and modernization of transportation.

My Government is prepared to increase the scale of assistance
it has been giving to the economic development of the American
republics. But it is beyond the capacity of the United States
Government itself to finance more than a small portion of the vast
development needed. The capital required through the years must
come from private sources, both domestic and foreign.

As the experience of the United States has shown, progress can
be achieved best through individual effort and the use of private
resources. Encouragement should therefore be given to the increase
of investment capital from internal as well as external sources. It
is obvious that foreign capital will naturally gravitate most readily
to countries where it is accorded fair and equitable treatment.

For its part, the United States fully supports the promotion of
economic development in the American republics. We advocate the
prompt preparation of sound development programs, which will set
specific and realistic goals to be accomplished in the next few
years.

The United States supports the International Bank of Reconstruction and Development as an important source of long-term capital for
developing the ecnomies of the American republics. My Government
confidently expects the role of this institution to be one of increasing usefulness. The President of the United States is submitting to Congress a request for an increase in the lending authority of the Export-Import Bank which will be available for sound projects in the American republics. These Government funds will be in
addition to the private financing which will be needed for a much
greater number of development projects.

The United States has studied the proposals regarding the taxation of foreign investments, with a view to avoiding double taxation
and to encouraging the flow of private capital into other countries
desiring it. I am glad to report that the President has under consideration measures to liberalize taxes on capital invested in foreign countries. These measures are designed to encourage not only
initial investment but also the rentention and reinvestment abroad
of earnings derived from such capital. These measures also would

liberalize the tax treatment of United States citizens residing abroad, and should therefore encourage technical experts to accept employment in other countries.

Address, George C. Marshall, April 1, 1948, <u>Department of State Bulletin</u>, April 11, 1948, reprinted in James W. Gantenbein (ed.), <u>The Evolution of our Latin-American Policy</u> (1950), pp. 280-281.

696. I.T.T. AND CHILEAN ELECTIONS (1970)

During the 1960s, Chilean governments tried to modernize the country's economy by, in part, increasing governmental ownership of foreign-owned enterprises, especially in copper, the main export which was owned principally by American firms. A secondary American owner of Chile's telephone system was International Telephone and Telegraph Co. (I.T.T.). This firm as well as American firms in the copper industry feared nationalization. When, in 1970, Salvador Allende, socialist candidate of the Popular Unity coalition, ran for president, American firms such as I.T.T. attempted to mobilize opposition. In the following colloquy, Senator Frank Church, Chairman of the Senate Intelligence Committee, is questioning William V. Broe, who in 1970 was in charge of Clandestine Services for the Western Hemisphere in the Central Intelligence Agency (CIA). Reference in this statement is made to Richard Helms, then-director of the CIA, and to John McClone, former director of the CIA and a member of the board of I.T.T. Harold Geneen was president of I.T.T. William R. Merriam was head of the Washington office of I.T.T.

Senator CHURCH. Did Mr. Helms advise you that Mr. John McCone, former Director of the CIA, had called him and suggested that some-one on Mr. Helm's staff meet with Mr. Geneen?

Mr. BROE. Yes, sir.

Senator CHURCH. Did Mr. Helms advise you that Mr. Geneen would be in Washington on July 16 and that you should get in touch with him and arrange a meeting with him?

Mr. BROE. Yes, sir.

Senator CHURCH. So you went to the hotel that evening at the direction of and with the authority of Mr. Helms?

Mr. BROE. That is right.

Senator CHURCH. Did you call Mr. Geneen to arrange the meet-ing?

Mr. BROE. No; no, I was supposed to contact Mr. Geneen, but I was contacted by Mr. Merriam and advised Mr. Geneen had an appoint-ment in the early evening, and he desired to see me after the appointment but late in the evening.

Senator CHURCH. So the arrangement you made was through Mr. Merriam?

Mr. BROE. That is right, sir.

Senator CHURCH. When you met with Mr. Geneen, did Mr. Geneen ask you for a detailed briefing on the political and economic situation in Chile?

Mr. BROE. Mr. Geneen requested information on the electoral situation, such as the status and potential of the candidates and their parties and the campaign as of that date. That is what we talked about.

Senator CHURCH. You talked about the political situation?

Mr. BROE. That is right. How the campaigns were going, who the campaigners were.

Senator CHURCH. What their prospects were?

Mr. BROE. That is right, sir.

Senator CHURCH. You then gave him such a briefing on the political----

Mr. BROE. Yes.

Senator CHURCH [continuing]. Situation in Chile?

Mr. BROE. Yes, sir.

Senator CHURCH. Did Mr. Geneen say to you that he was willing to assemble an election fund for one of the Chilean Presidential candidates, Mr. Jorge E. Alessandri?

Mr. BROE. Yes; he did.

Senator CHURCH. Did he say that the amount of the fund would be substantial?

Mr. BROE. He indicated he was considering a substantial fund.

Senator CHURCH. Did he mention a specific figure?

Mr. BROE. No; he did not.

Senator CHURCH. Did he say to you that he wanted the fund controlled and channeled through the CIA?

Mr. BROE. Yes; he did.

Senator CHURCH. Did you agree to accept the fund offered by Mr. Geneen?

Mr. BROE. No; I did not.

Senator CHURCH. Did you explain to Mr. Geneen why the CIA could not accept such a fund?

Mr. BROE. Well, I told him we could not absorb the funds and serve as a funding channel. I also told him that the U.S. Government was not supporting any candidate in the Chilean election.

Senator CHURCH. I think you have already testified that no one else other than yourself and Mr. Geneen were present at the time this discussion took place?

Mr. BROE. That is right.

Senator CHURCH. During the discussion did Mr. Geneen at any time indicate what the fund that he stood ready to contribute was to be for, or was intended for, constructive use, technical assistance to agriculture, the building of houses or anything of that character?

Mr. BROE. It was to support Jorge Alessandri.

Senator CHURCH. It was to support Jorge E. Alessandri, one
of the Presidential candidates?
   Mr. BROE. Yes, sir.

Testimony, March 27, 1973, U.S. Congress, 93rd, Senate,
Committee on Foreign Relations, Subcommittee on Multinational
Corporations, Multinational Corporations and United States Foreign
Policy. Hearings...., Part 1, (Washington, D.C.: Government
Printing Office, 1973), pp. 245-246.

697. PENETRATING JAPANESE AND EUROPEAN MARKETS (1973)

During the first fifteen years after World War II,
America dominated the world economy. Foreign aid and
military weapons flowed overseas in huge amounts.
American industry, unscathed by war's ravages, found new
markets in older industrial countries while also expanding
direct investment in the same places. Most spectacular
were the advances registered by innovative science-
sensitive industries which included preeminently, electronic
products but also cars and other mass consumer goods. By
the 1960s, however, recovery from the war was complete and
the economic burden of rearmament scant in Europe and Japan.
As the United States became mired down in Vietnam, during
the 1960s and early 1970s, its position in the world
economy changed significantly. Peter G. Peterson, formerly
chairman of the board of Bell & Howell Camera Company
and Secretary of Commerce, had just returned from a world
tour on behalf of expanding American foreign trade and
here shares his insights on the subject. Several years
later he became Chairman of the Board, Lehman Brothers,
Kuhn & Loeb, an investment banking house.

For example, in Japan, I think we could understand the following
reactions which some expressed to me on this trip. I remember one
rather prominent figure saying, "Well, Mr. Ambassador, I want to
be sure that we understand what the point of view of your government
is. You certainly haven't forgotten that in the 1950's and 1960's
it was you who told us not to spend money on defense and to invest
it in our economy; it is you who told us we should develop our management skills and indeed set up all kinds of programs for accelerat-
ing that. In essence, what you seem to be telling us now is that
we are doing too well what you told us to do."
   In Europe I heard people say it was you as a country that in
the 1950's and the 1960's talked about an expanded Europe and how it
was the cornerstone of our political relationship and that the
more successful the European Community was, the better. Now, you

are telling us you are bothered by these preferential arrangements and the extending throughout the world some of our other policies to unify Europe....

Most expectations are that the Japanese economy by 1980 will grow to a level that will begin to approach a trillion dollars. They will have a population somewhere in the range of 115 to 120 million people. Their GNP per capita will most likely be at least as large and probably larger than ours.

Now, translated, what that means--because now foreign products have a very small share of that market as we all know--is that it is appropriate to state as a strategy for the 1970's that America get a large share of what is going to be one of the greatest markets of the world by any definition. Therefore, our trade negotiations, might well focus on trying to prevent what happened in the 1950's and 1960's, when the Japanese were able to dominate their own markets in a protective situation, getting a very large and competitive production base which then could be used to go throughout the world.

Now, this means, for example, that as they lift their investment restrictions--and there are some important changes taking place in Japan as they cut back on their trade barriers--we ask ourselves what are the main restrictions and the opportunities that will exist over the next 10 years that will inhibit future U.S. penetration of the Japanese market, and start taking steps now in our negotiations to reduce them.

For example, we are good at computer products and information products. It is already evident that Japan is embarking on an extraordinary large program in both research and other areas to expand its position in the information industry and, indeed, in the advanced field of cybernetics. They are spending large amounts of money. If this is a field in which America wants to be very important, and I trust it does, it becomes a matter of high negotiating priority to remove restrictions in those fields where we have a real opportunity to capture a large share of the market. Also, there is still a lot more than can be done in opening up the distribution structure to American products.

Let's start thinking of Japan, not in the ways we did 5 and 10 years ago, when we were inclined, with justice to complain about lack of access to investment and trade, and ask ourselves where we want to be in 5 to 10 years and be sure that American products play a full role there.

In Europe, a similar set of problems will be emerging 5 or 10 years from now, and I think it is important you look at them.

For example, I hear discussions in Europe about something called a common industrial policy, and if you have not looked into this, I think it is probably worth some of your time.

The concept of the common industrial policy as articulated to me in Europe is to approach the entire European market as one market and to cooperate to increase the European position of self-sufficiency in several fields, sometimes through problem procurement policies that will clearly import U.S. products.

Now, I don't think it is an accident that the three fields that they seem to have picked are aircraft, nuclear reactors, and computers. I have no need to elaborate on that.

It is also no accident that these are fields in which the
United States has a very important interest. I think while these
kinds of policies are in their formative stages, it is very important that, as we think through our negotiating priorities, we ask
ourselves what are the problems 5 years from now that could be
important problems if we don't anticipate them.

They are planning to spend large amounts of money on something
called common regional development policies, and I think it is
important to ask ourselves what new problems they might create.
For example, very large subsidies could result in actions that
could encourage such practices as dumping and other things.

So I think the third point I would make is that bodies such
as yours and bodies outside of the Government should ask themselves where might we be 5 or 10 years from today and what can we
do today to minimize those problems....

I talked to quite a number of parliamentarians when I was
there and I would have to say that by and large our legislators
are substantially less sophisticated about international economics
than are the parliamentarians of other countries.

For example, it is interesting for me to hear Congressmen who
are not as sophisticated as they might be--which is to say none of
you, obviously--talk about the fact that the American market is the
dominant market to Europe. I have heard this all over. All we
need to do in this country it is said is block off our markets and
the European community, you know, would not survive.

I wonder how many of these people know what percent of
Europe's exports now, not 10 years ago, but now, go to the United
States?

I have some of the numbers here. For example, in the case of
France, only 5 percent of their exports go to the United States,
you see. When you turn it around and say what percentage of our
exports are to Europe, something close to a quarter of our exports
are to Europe.

Now, I think if you spend more time abroad we will begin to
rid ourselves of some of these impressions that are about 10
years behind the time. That is something I think we can do.

Testimony, May 3, 1973, U.S. Congress, 93rd, 1st session,
House of Representatives, Committee on Banking and Currency,
Subcommittee on International Trade. Annual Report of the Council
on International Economic Policy. Hearings...., (Washington,
D.C.: Government Printing Office, 1973), pp. 139-140, 145.

698. WAIVING ANTI-TRUST PRECAUTIONS (1974)

American firms may cooperate among themselves to
fix prices on goods for export without violating the
Sherman Anti-Trust Act of 1890 provided no effort is

made to do the same in the U.S. domestic market for
the goods. At the same time, any American firm or group
of firms may ask the U.S. Department of Justice to decide
whether a contemplated business action is likely to invite
prosecution under the Sherman Act. After investigation,
the Department may conclude that the action will not set
off a criminal federal proceeding. This conclusion is
stated in a Business Review Letter and is customarily
published as guidance for other business firms. Ordinarily, the Letter reserves the right of the Department
to file civil proceedings later on. Following is an
authoritative account by John J. McCloy, counsel for
Exxon Co. and former president of the World Bank, U.S.
Military Governor and High Commissioner for Germany, and
chairman of the board of Chase Manhattan Bank. (Note
that the Review Letter in this case was not restricted
to criminal proceedings).

As a background, I think I should say that President Kennedy
sought on a number of occasions or some occasions, at least, to
learn my views on a subject which he felt that I had some experience in. I don't mean to presume that I was a constant adviser
of his at all. It was on particular subjects. Usually it was on
matters related to arms control, security, defense, and Germany.
   On one of these occasions, one of the subjects he also talked
to me about was the situation in the Middle East. He had received
recently--then recently--quite a shock after his talk with Mr.
Krushchev in Vienna, as you know, and he expressed concern about
the possibility of a political confrontation that could arise in
the Middle East. He was well aware, of course, of the oil reserves
in that area which added to their strategic and economic importance
as a whole.
   In speaking of oil, I referred to the formation of OPEC, which
was public news at that point, and I suggested then that it might
be necessary at some point in order to offset the pressures by joint
action on the part of OPEC countries to obtain some sort of authority for concerted action, collective bargaining, whatever you will,
on the part of the companies having interests there. I said that
if at that time any action seemed to be necessary, I thought it
would be desirable to talk to the Department of Justice about it.
He asked me if I had talked to them about it, and I said no, I
hadn't.
   To the best of my recollection, he right then and there made
an arrangement for me to see Mr. Robert Kennedy, and I did talk
with him....
   Mr. Robert Kennedy said he was aware of his brother's concern
about the Mediterranean and the Middle East, and if I had something
in mind which I thought could be helpful, to let him know, or
something to that effect.

I repeated then at some point I felt that maybe some joint action on the part of the companies to meet the combined pressure of the oil-producing countries might be necessary, and that some consultation with the Department of Justice might be advisable beforehand.

He replied, and this is quite clear in my mind, that he would be prepared to give the Department's attitude toward any such contemplated action if it was desired. I told him that I knew of no contemplated action at the time so we didn't get down to the point of discussing what sort of procedure might be followed....

I think at that time I was thinking in terms of an opinion of the Attorney General rather than a Business Review Letter. But we didn't talk about procedures. The point is that the option to come to the Department for an expression of view was very clearly extended. He asked me to inform Mr. Byron White, who then, I believe, was the Deputy Attorney General, or an attorney--I guess Deputy Attorney General at that time--and I did see Mr. White on one or two occasions in which the same subject was discussed and the same result arrived at.

I later had some conversations with Mr. Katzenbach, before and after he became Attorney General, along the same line. Again there was no commitment and no specifications of any form that the attitude of the Department might be expressed in. But the invitations for such a determination of the Department's attitude were confirmed....

Mr. Robert Kennedy, as I recall it, was a little more forthcoming....Some of the others were, "Well, we can't say that we will express an opinion but at least come and see us about it." Mr. Kennedy was saying, "We will tell you what we can do about it." And, "We will tell you what we will do about it." Then I made it a point to call on each succeeding Attorney General just for the idea of keeping the thing fresh in his mind because any moment I was afraid we would have to do something.

Also, as was pointed out, the turnover is so great in the Department of Justice....

So I called on Mr. Ramsey Clark when he became Attorney General, and I had the same commitment--no commitment but invitation to consult, understanding, with him....

I also called on Mr. Mitchell. I have had an opportunity to read his deposition and I think it is accurate, as far as my recollection is concerned. I called on him first on the same routine basis that I called on the others, without any specific conduct in mind. Then, at the end of 1970 or the beginning of 1971 I called on him again to tell him that now I thought the time had come for some form of collective bargaining on the part of the oil companies with OPEC and with the producing governments....

I wanted to bring in Mr. McLaren because Mr. Mitchell asked Mr. McLaren to come in at that point. There, Mr. McLaren, for the first time, broached the question of the matter of the business review letter. I didn't know much about what a business review letter was at that time. I know that sounds strange. I rather argued for a more affirmative type of opinion from the Attorney General which, in days past, in years past, I had obtained in

connection with private transactions. But he said this was the
procedure they were now operating on. They weren't moving under
the old opinion basis anymore.

Since this was well recognized, he thought that they had best
follow that then well-recognized procedure and I had no objection
....

[On January 13, 1971, Richard W. McLaren, Assistant Attorney
General for the Anti-Trust Division, wrote a letter to Mr. McCloy,
saying, among other things:

We have reviewed the attached proposed message to OPEC and
this is to inform you that the department does not presently intend
to institute any proceedings under the antitrust laws with respect
to this proposed message or the discussions called for thereby.

In accordance with established policy, we reserve the right
to take action in the future if warranted by receipt of additional
information or by subsequent developments as set forth in the
above cited regulations.]

It is an enforcement intention letter. It was pretty left
handed, but I don't believe Mr. McLaren would have ever given us
that if he had the feeling that it was a violation of the
antitrust laws....

So, he couldn't give us a waiver; he couldn't give us an
exemption. I didn't ask for it and didn't want it. All I wanted
to know is, "What is your view at this point so that we can get
some guidance?"

He said, "I will give you this letter," which is the common
procedure that they adopted. In the past, they used to give you
Attorney General opinions. They didn't do it recently. They have
abandoned that procedure, as I understand it....

I felt, so clear in my own mind about the nonviolative aspects
that I was satisfied with that even though it was a rather restricted sort of form in which it was expressed.

Testimony, February 6, 1974, U.S. Congress, 93rd, 1st and
2nd sessions, Senate, Committee on Foreign Relations, Subcommittee
on Multinational Corporations, Multinational Corporations and
United States Foreign Policy. Hearings...., Part 5, (Washington,
D.C.: Government Printing Office, 1974), pp. 255-258, 260-261.

699. THE WORLD URANIUM CARTEL (1977)

As recently as 1940, there was no market for
uranium since it had no significant economic usefull-
ness. With the advent of nuclear energy, the situation
changed suddenly. Since uranium is concentrated in a few
places on earth, the setting was favorable for concerted
price control by a few producers. In 1972 a cartel
was formed to tailor world production to estimated demand.

The results were highly successful. In five years, the
price of uranium rose eight-fold, from five to 40 dollars
a pound. One participant in the cartel was the Gulf
Minerals Resources Co., a wholly-owned Canadian affiliate
of the Gulf Oil Corp. Since the Sherman Anti-Trust Act
of 1890 made participation of an American firm such as Gulf
illegal, it is no wonder the following internal memorandum,
dated July 20, 1972, was marked "specially confidential."
The writer was Roy D. Jackson, Jr., a lawyer who had been
employed by Gulf. The persons mentioned at the opening of
the memorandum were high officials of Gulf or its Canadian
affiliate.

SPECIALLY   July 20, 1972
CONFIDENTIAL   <u>Uranium</u>

Frank O'Hara and I met yesterday in Toronto with Messrs.
Allen, Ediger, Estey, Gregg, Ramsey, and Zagnoli.

Although the factual situation is still somewhat fluid, the
basic pattern now seems sufficiently stabilized to permit preparation of the legal opinion discussed with Jack Howrey. Frank and
I will work on this, collaberating with Irwin and Roger.

On the basis of yesterday's session, I advised Mr. Zagnoli
that the basic antitrust viewpoints and conclusions reached at the
last Pittsburgh meeting in your office remained valid.

The antitrust evaluation boils down to this: (a) the economic
impact study being prepared by Wen Ramsey will necessarily be less
precise; but (b) in my judgment, the basic fact of Canadian Government direction is even clearer than before. The latter fact
is of predominant and overriding importance in again concluding
that the degree of antitrust risk involved is acceptable.

At the Paris meeting in April, you will recall that tentative
agreement was reached in the context of a January 1, 1972 through
1977 period. Term was one of the main points considered in our
antitrust evaluation. At Johannesburg, the Australian group insisted upon extending the international marketing arrangement
through 1980. Further, the Operating Committee ground rules adopted
at Johannesburg indicate a probable extension of some aspects of the
arrangement even beyond 1980. This really gets too far down the
road for meaningful impact analysis, especially since the supply
and demand curves are estimated to cross somewhere around 1978 or
1979; at which time the economic reason for the international marketing arrangement disappears. Accordingly, I suggested to Wen that
there was really no valid purpose to be served in attempting an impact projection beyond 1980; and his final impact statement, which
will constitute part of the definitive legal opinion, will deal
only with the announced period of the marketing arrangement; that
is, 1972 through 1980.

Extension of the time line also generated a new line of thinking on the part of the Canadian Government, which should prove
helpful to us since their plans, which are now in the process of implementation, will more clearly evidence what has been the

actual fact from the inception, namely, that Gulf has no viable
alternative: it must either submit to effective Canadian Government
direction or get out of Canada (insofar as uranium is concerned).

Without getting into too much detail, the Canadian Government
has decided the following: Acting under relevant sections of the
legislation controlling the functioning of the Canadian Atomic Energy
Board, the Minister of Energy and Resources has issued a <u>Directive</u>
to the Board. Pursuant to this unpublished Directive (which may or
may not be made public at a later date), the Board has prepared the
equivalent of <u>Regulations</u> for Cabinet approval. Under these Regulations, the end result is that the Canadian Government will only permit the granting of licenses to Canadian producers for the export of
uranium when the Board approves both the amount and price. Effectively, the Board's standard for approval will be compliance with the
international marketing arrangement worked out in Paris and
Johannesburg. This arrangement constitutes an actual, but informal,
intergovernmental agreement. The Canadian Government, for policy
reasons of its own, has avoided any treaty or other formal arrangement, and, according to Mr. Estey, will probably continue to do so.
Quantities and prices set by the Board will not be made public.

We probably will secure a copy of the Regulations as soon as
the Cabinet has given its formal approval and released the same for
publication. The Regulations (prepared in mid-July for Cabinet
approval) will be published concurrently with a <u>Public Policy</u>
<u>Statement</u> by the Minister (probably in August). The Minister's
Statement, which is the practical equivalent of a general directive
or instruction, will likely be made in the Commons. Thus, the explicit Canadian Government direction will be evidenced by (1) the
general background material we already have, including public policy declarations of certain Canadian Government officials; (2) the
Ministerial Directive; (3) the Board's Regulations as concurred on
by the Canadian Cabinet; and (4) a Public Policy Statement by the
Canadian Minister of Mines and Energy.

Gulf Minerals Canada Limited (GMCL) is not presently represented on the Operating Committee set up to implement the international
marketing agreement, working through a Secretariat located at CEA's
offices in Paris; however, GMCL is in contact with the Canadian
representative on the Operating Committee; his alternate; relevant
Canadian Government officials, as required; and, initially at least,
will receive club material directly from the Secretary out of the
Secretariat's Paris office.

GMCL will be participating (in a non-control capacity) in a
continuing variety of market allocation and pricing arrangements
under the overall plan adopted by the Canadian Government. Although
it is not possible to delineate precisely the probable scope of these
arrangements, it appears to be the fact that the Canadian Government
will continue to maintain effective control of what they have directed all the Canadian producers to do and Gulf's actions, therefore,
must necessarily be the result of and remain within the area of such
governmental direction. Nevertheless, it will be advisable that
Frank be kept adequately and currently informed of significant developments which might affect Gulf's overall antitrust posture.

Messrs. O'Hara, Ramsey, and I did not participate in subsequent detailed discussions concerning GMCL problems with their German partners concerning interpretation and implementation of the Rabbit Lake joint venture documentation. It seems probable, however, on the basis of those facts known to us that a substantial restructuring of the joint venture arrangement might well be required. This fact, coupled with open-ended Canadian Government control of production and prices of all exports of Rabbit Lake production, make economic forecasting of the venture far more speculative than before.

As mentioned to you, I will continue to collaborate with Messrs. Coleman, O'Hara, Allen and others until we have a reasonably definitive work product in hand.

Roy D. Jackson, Jr.

RDJJr:ps

cc R. K. Allen, Denver
    I. W. Coleman, Pittsburgh
    W. Z. Estey, Q.C., Toronto
    N. M. Ediger, Toronto
    F. R. O'Hara

Testimony, August 15, 1977, U.S. Congress, 1st session, House of Representatives, Committee on Interstate and Foreign Commerce, Subcommittee on Oversight and Investigations, International Uranium Cartel. Hearings...., Vol. 1, (Washington, D.C.: Government Printing Office, 1977), pp. 567-569.

700. JAPANESE-AMERICAN COMPETITION IN SEMICONDUCTORS (1981)

The American semiconductor industry, from 1960 to 1977, increased shipments from $571 million to nearly $5 billion, an annual increase of 13 percent. This extraordinary expansion came at a time of sharply falling unit prices. In 1962, for example, the price of a transistor averaged $4.39; ten years later it cost 27 cents. At the same time, the technical complexity of individual products grew. Large-scale integrated circuits in the mid-60s had fewer than 100 elements; by 1978, they contained over 10,000 transistors and other devices. The four largest producers of semiconductors accounted for 51 percent of all the industry output in 1957 and 50 percent in 1972, a high degree of concentration. Principal markets for semiconductors in 1975 were computers (33%), industrial (29.9%), consumers (23%), and government, including military and space (15%). Following is a detailed

account of an important aspect of the industry's affairs
by George Scalise, senior vice-president, administration,
Advanced Micro Devices, Sunnyvale, California.

During the 1950's and 1960's, the U.S. vacuum tube producers,
such as G.E., Sylvania, and Philco-Ford, yielded leadership in the
semiconductor industry to a second generation of high technology
companies, principally Texas Instruments, Motorola and Fairchild,
which in turn spawned a third generation of innovative growth firms,
including Intel, Advanced Micro Devices, and Mostek. The American
companies produced wave after wave of innovations and energetically
marketed the resultant products throughout the world. The American
firms not only facilitated the take-off of the new computer industry
in the U.S., but also played a key role in creating the high technology sector in the European Economic Community with exports and
direct investments in Great Britain, West Germany, France and Italy.
    The American companies also sought entry into the Japanese mar-
ket, stationing the labor intensive assembly processes in Southeast
Asian plants to assure labor cost competitiveness, and applying to
the Government of Japan to obtain import licenses and permits to establish marketing subsidiaries and manufacturing subsidiaries in
Japan, so as to help play a part in getting the nascent semiconduct-
or industry off the ground in that country as well.
    Japan's market, although only half the size of the U.S. market,
was already visible as the second or third largest market for the
future.
    But these overtures were countered by Japanese law and the
policies of the Ministry of International Trade and Industry.
Instead of allowing the U.S. companies to bring their comparative
advantage to bear in Japan, through the medium of direct investments, the authorities chose instead to "take the package apart"--
to patiently negotiate patents on American semiconductor products
and processes over a period of many years and allocate them among
the major Japanese companies to preserve the domestic competitive
balance for firms such as Nippon Electric, Hitachi, Toshiba,
Mitsubishi, and Fujitsu.
    In a familiar pattern to that experienced by many other Ameri-
can industries, the Japanese firms adopted the American semiconductor technology and where possible introduced manufacturing refinements.
    During this period, Japan was operating under the Foreign
Exchange and Foreign Trade Control Law adopted in 1949 after World
War II, enabling Japan to rebuild its industries and financial base
free of external influences. This law remained fully in effect for
many years until reforms made in the last several years and, con-
ceptually, provided that all external economic transactions were
"prohibited in principle," so that foreign trade was permissible
only as exceptions to the law.

While Japan remained essentially closed, the United States adopted an internationalized world trade posture. However, U.S. companies were able to export only sporadically into Japan. Moreover, with the dramatic exception of Texas Instruments, which obtained permission to manufacture integrated circuits in Japan by applying leverage based on patent rights, no American company was allowed to invest in a semiconductor plant in Japan. In 1960, IBM was permitted to engage in computer production in Japan in exchange for entering into licensing agreements with 13 Japanese companies.

As a consequence, the American based companies were able to achieve only approximately 10 percent of the Japanese market--primarily through sales of integrated circuits which the local firms were not yet capable of producing. By contrast, with substantial protection applied (including a 17 percent tariff), the U.S. industry obtained a 65 percent share in Western Europe.

Early in the 1970's Japan began liberalizing restrictions on imports of, and investment in, computer equipment. Computer duties began to be reduced. Then in 1971, Japan took the significant step which was to lead to their industry's challenge to U.S. leadership in the world semiconductor and computer markets. Realizing the vast potential in many industries of this knowledge-intensive industry, the Japanese government sponsored the promotion of computers through selected Japanese companies which were to develop high-performance computers and peripheral equipment (and later software) to support Japan's entry into worldwide competition. Direct subsidies in the order of $200 million were granted for this effort, but more significant were the cooperative laboratories, carefully orchestrated by the Ministry of International Trade (MIT) and the quasi-government monopoly, Nippon Telegraph and Telephone (NTT).

Significant tax incentives were afforded integrated circuit and computer operations under the government development program:

In addition to normal depreciation, facilities and equipment were allowed to be depreciated in the first year by an amount equal to one-third of the initial book value.

The Government also provided tax incentives to Japanese end-users to promote the purchase of computers.

Research and development tax credits were furnished participating firms for incremental expenditures over a base year.

An important element of this initial government-industry research program was the Very Large Scale Integration (VLSI) program whose mission was to develop processes to manufacture the most advanced integrated circuits by the mid-to-late 1970's. As part of this effort, the latest American process equipment was purchased for detailed evaluation and refinement. The VLSI program terminated in early 1980, having achieved a very significant result: through systematic adaptation of American state-of-the-art products and processes, the Japanese companies closed the technology gap with the American companies for the manufacture of the 16K RAM, a high volume memory chip used in computer systems.

Using their newly obtained innovative parity, the Japanese companies began to increase their exports to the United States in the late 1970's of the 16K RAM's and, taking advantage of temporary imbalances in demand in the U.S. market and operating from a protected home market, used, successively, very low pricing and then, when the threat of antidumping action became apparent, switched to a strategy of supplying product which exceeded specifications to take a 40 percent market share position in the U.S. market in this state-of-the-art commodity product. The U.S. industry "blew the whistle" on two tier Japanese pricing in 1979 and it ceased. The U.S. industry has vigorously focused on quality measures and expended the requisite management energy and scarce capital to neutralize the Japanese companies' temporary advantage in this area by early 1981.

During the 1970's, the American semiconductor companies continued aggressive attempts to penetrate the Japanese market. Under its program of progressive liberalization of the computer and integrated circuit sector, the Japanese Government removed import license controls in 1974 and relaxed the prohibition of foreign direct investments in integrated circuits in 1976.

Nevertheless, the American companies made little headway in their export drive and two post-liberalization attempts at integrated circuit manufacturing joint ventures with Japanese firms--Motorola with Alps, and Fairchild with TDK--were dissolved before the commencement of production.

Traditional commercial trading patterns in integrated circuits in Japan...have been typical of oligopolistic competition. A few major Japanese firms dominate the market (they are also the chosen participants in the government development program). These individual vertically integrated firms specialize in integrated circuit products most suited to their final systems; they sell their products to other Japanese producers while procuring the bulk of their other integrated circuit needs from other Japanese producers.

Under this strategy, each of the major integrated circuit producers has been able to reach scale volumes sufficient for international competition with a protected production base. Procurement by the Japanese integrated circuit firms of American integrated circuits traditionally has been limited to state-of-the-art circuits for which no Japanese source exists or sporadic procurement of products for which there is a temporary capacity shortage. One would infer that this controlled procurement environment reflects a deeply ingrained "Buy Japan" attitude carrying over from the pre-liberalization era as a conscious Japanese trade strategy.

An examination of the U.S. Department of Commerce import/export data for the period 1975-1980 shows clearly the efforts of Japan's new-found technological parity in advanced memory products and the continued difficulty of the American companies in expanding their exports to Japan.

According to U.S. Commerce data, Japanese exports of integrated circuits to the United States from 1975-1980 were:

```
                                                      In thousands of
                                                         U.S. dollars
1975----------------------------------------------------------  25,650
1976----------------------------------------------------------  19,100
1977----------------------------------------------------------  39,888
1978----------------------------------------------------------  82,753
1979---------------------------------------------------------- 176,090
1980---------------------------------------------------------- 296,040
```
Conversely, U.S. exports of integrated circuits to Japan were:
```
                                                      In thousands of
                                                         U.S. dollars
1975----------------------------------------------------------  51,780
1976----------------------------------------------------------  64,944
1977----------------------------------------------------------  53,715
1978----------------------------------------------------------  79,081
1979---------------------------------------------------------- 138,290
1980---------------------------------------------------------- 113,080
```
As a consequence, the U.S. industry shifted from a bilateral surplus in integrated circuit trade to a deficit in 1978 which has grown sharply.

To sustain and strengthen its position in the U.S. market, the major Japanese companies--NEC, Toshiba, Funitsu, and Hitachi--have invested or committed $200-225 million of direct integrated circuit manufacturing investment in the United States, including a fully integrated VLSI manufacturing plant which NEC plans to bring on stream by 1983.

Through its government's past policy of preventing foreign investment, as opposed to the complete openness of the American economy, the Japanese industry has gotten the jump on the American integrated circuit manufacturers on investment in their respective markets with the exception of Texas Instruments, although Motorola, and my company, Advanced Micro Devices, plan to initiate manufacturing ventures in Japan. Fairchild and Intel are also reportedly contemplating Japanese operation.

Testimony, July 9, 1981, U.S. Congress, 97th, 1st session, Joint Economic Committee, U.S.-Japanese Economic Relations. Hearings...., (Washington, D.C.: Government Printing Office, 1981), pp. 92-94.

J.

FINANCIAL CENTRALIZATION AND EXPANSION

701. "BANKERS. . .ARE VERY GOOD NEIGHBORS" (1901)

At the turn of the century, the great banking
interests constituted an informal but definite community of interest which had evolved since the Civil War.
(For an earlier lack of solidarity among New York
bankers, see Source No. 456). Jacob Schiff, a senior
banking partner in Kuhn, Loeb & Co., investment bankers
specializing in railroads, is being questioned here.

Q. (By Mr. KENNEDY.) I would like to ask you if there is any
probability or danger of this community of interest in railroads
running into industrial combinations, such, for instance, as the
United States Steel Corporation, and that company or corporation
receiving favors on account of this community of interest which
would be detrimental to the independent iron and steel manufacturers?--A. Personally I have no experience in industrial finances.
My firm has not occupied itself with them, and I can give you
very little information.
Q. (By Mr. RIPLEY.) Did not your firm underwrite a part of
the securities issued for the United States Steel Corporation, for
the American Bridge Company, the National Tube Company, and others?
--A. Community of interest exists among bankers too. Bankers as a
rule are very good neighbors, and we meet each other and combine
capital when we have large financial transactions--larger than our
resources can handle; we ask others to unite their resources with
ours to handle a given concern under our management. That is what
is generally termed a syndicate, and such exist very generally.
Now, while my firm, as I said before, as a rule does not occupy
itself with industrial undertakings, when the financing is managed

by others. Your question is perfectly well understood. If large
bankers who financed the undertakings which you have named invited
our firm, we no doubt to a very moderate amount accepted the invitation, but we had nothing to do with the details or the management.

Testimony, Jacob H. Schiff, May 22, 1901, U.S. Congress, 57th,
1st session, House of Representatives, Document No. 178, Report
of the Industrial Commission on Transportation, IX, p. 775.

702. RULES FOR FINANCIAL WRITERS (1902)

A prominent financial editor, Alexander Dana Noyes,
experienced in the excitements of the stock exchange,
states some rules in the following extract. (Not repre-
duced here, but in the primary source, is an enlightening
discussion of the financial temptations of financial
writers).

Describe the existing state of business fairly. Emphasize
its good points, even when the stock market is "over-discounting"
it, but state the potential offsets, notably those created by excessive demand on credit. Be cautious when indulging in prediction, unless as regards the necessary longer result of visible tendencies. Lay an unsparing hand on illusions which, at times of
overdone speculation, beset the mind both of professional operators
and of the speculative public. Under prevalent conditions, this
formula opened up the opportunity, not always presented in financial
writing, for infusion of humor. This, however, even when exposing
popular fallacies to ridicule, should always be good-natured, basing
itself rather on weaknesses of human nature than on individual motives. Under the circumstances then prevalent, the financial article would frequently have to take the opposite side from the general
public. Everyone realizes, nowadays, that illusion is as widespread
and positive during the depths of business depression as it is at
the height of speculative mania. It is essential for useful financial criticism to dispute the extravagant ideas which an excited
Wall Street boom invariably creates,--whether in 1901 or 1929,--but
it is equally essential for such criticism to do its part, in the
subsequent period of reaction, towards dispelling exaggerated de-
spondency regarding the financial future.

Noyes, The Market Place, p. 219.

703.   "I AM BUT [CLAY] IN THE HANDS OF THE POTTER" (1905)

Several large New York banks dominated the investment policies of the greatest insurance companies. When
the companies tried to buy securities directly from the
issuing corporations, these latter feared to grant the
privilege. (See, however, the following, Source No. 704).
Mutual Life Insurance Company had over $440 million in
assets at this time. Frederic Cromwell, treasurer and
member of the finance committee of the Mutual Life Insurance
Company, is being questioned here. He had been with
that firm since 1880.

I went to my personal friend, Mr. Stuyvesant Fish. We had at
that time four of their directors on our board. I said to Mr. Fish,
"See here, this thing cannot go along any further, it is time for
us to buy our bonds of you directly----"
Q. You are talking now of the Illinois Central? A. Yes, the
Illinois Central, and he said he could not afford to sell the Mutual
Life bonds, and I could see the justice of his remarks when he explained it, that it was a necessity for his railroad to do their
business through banks in block, it could not afford to take them
to single buyers, and he must keep up his associations with the
bank.
Q. So the railroads must keep in with the banks in order to
float their bonds? A. They have to, yes, sir.
Q. And the insurance companies must keep in with the banks
in order to get the investments they want at low prices? A. Yes.
Q. So the banks control the situation? A. There is no
question about it.
. . . .
Q. Do you think they would be so successful in carrying these
enterprises through if they did not have the assistance of the insurance companies? A. Yes, sir.
Q. How could they? A. They sell more bonds in Europe in a
week than we buy in a month. This is a very big world, if you will
pardon me for saying so, and if the Insurance companies undertook
to control the situation they could not do it. You have to meet
the situation as it is. You cannot do that. You have to fall in
and get as good securities as as favorable a rate as you can.
Q. If I gather the import of your remarks, it is despite the
great volume of your assets and the immense business of the large
insurance companies, when it comes to investing your money you have
really got the poorer end of the negotiations? A. No, we have to
take our proper and proportionate value in the transaction. You
must remember, as Mr. Baker says, when it comes to an investment--
take this very Cuba issue of $35,000,000, and this Pennsylvania
issue and so on--we must be participants, only to a moderate degree.
I do not know how much we had in this system, but we can only invest to a limited amount. We cannot exaggerate our importance,
we are only worth so much to these people.

Q. Relatively, you occupy the poorer position in the negotiations. They can get along without you and you cannot get along
without them? A. They can get along without us, if we were not
wise enough to get in on the ground floor, certainly.
. . . .
You cannot blame the bankers, of course. In this world all are
doing the best they can for themselves. I am but in the hands of
the potter, but the Finance Committee controls this thing, and they
do the best they can in the getting of them.

Testimony, Frederic Cromwell, September 14, 1905, Testimony
Taken Before the [Armstrong] Joint Committee of the Senate and
Assembly of the State of New York to Investigate and Examine Into
the Business and Affairs of Life Insurance Companies Doing Business
in the State of New York, I, (Albany, New York: Brandow Printing
Co., 1905), pp. 627-628, 628-629, 629-630.

704. INSURANCE COMPANIES WILL SOMEDAY DEAL DIRECT (1905)

Would insurance companies some day by-pass the banks
and buy securities direct? Yes, answered one authority.
But such direct buying would not be in competition but in
cooperation with the rest of the financial community,
including the banks. George Perkins was vice-president
of the New York Life Insurance Company; a partner in the
firm of J. P. Morgan & Company; and chairman of the finance
committee of the U.S. Steel Corporation. He is testifying
in the following. Committee counsel questioning Perkins
was Charles Evans Hughes.

Mr. Hughes made a point with some witness, a friend of mine,
on that the other day--why don't these insurance companies deal
direct. J. P. Morgan & Company, since I have been in the firm, a
matter of four years and a half, have marketed more bonds in the
time we are talking about than the New York Life and the Mutual and
the Equitable have accumulated in 60 years. Now, you are accustomed
to talking about the size of these insurance companies. What about
that? We have marketed more bonds in that office [i.e., J. P.
Morgan & Company] in four and a half short years than these three
companies have been sixty years in accumulating.
. . . .
I want to say I appreciate the delicacy of my situation, but
I believed in it and believed that I was working to get ultimately
to a condition where my company, the New York Life, could get
nearer to being the original purchaser, and this is a great step
from where we were 10 years ago. But Mr. Hughes brought out a
question a day or two ago, why shouldn't we deal direct? Why, the

New York Life, the Equitable and Mutual couldn't go to a railroad
company that has a fifty million bond issue and say we will take
that bond issue and market a part of it, because we would assume
the moral validity and legal validity and all that in that bond to
other people. Now, these banking houses go into that, they put
their guarantee on those bonds, which to a reputable house means
very much more than the money which is in it, and they take the
situation and create it and make it possible for the Life Insurance
Companies to go into it. When I was a boy the life insurance companies had to buy them at the second, third or fourth hand. We
have gradually moved up closer and closer, and the ultimate situation will be that these life insurance companies will get to the
point where they will, between them, come more directly to the
financial situation. The old idea that we were raised under, that
competition is the life of trade, is exploded. Competition is no
longer the life of trade, it is co-operation, and whether it is cooperation between you gentlemen in re-framing these laws which need
it, or whether it is co-operation between the policy holders of the
New York Life for their own benefit, and they, by the way, are the
biggest syndicate in the world, because whether it is Mr. Vanderbilt
who carries a million dollars of insurance or one of these gentlemen
here or anywhere who carries a thousand dollars, the money all goes
into one great treasury and is handled for the mutual advantage of
everybody. That is a syndicate. And these are tremendous questions
and will involve all the people of our country and every other
country.

Testimony, George Walbridge Perkins, September 15, 1905,
Testimony Taken Before the [Armstrong] Joint Committee, I, pp.
773, 774-775.

705.   MR. RYAN BUYS EQUITABLE LIFE (1905)

In 1905, Equitable Life owned over $412 million
in assets and its controlling stock was up for sale. In
a battle between the Harriman and Ryan financial groups,
the latter won control. (See, however, Source No. 709).
This extract is from a letter written by Thomas Ryan, a
large owner of Northern urban lighting utilities and
transportation facilities; he was also a significant
owner in American Tobacco Company and various brokerage
houses.

You may be aware that a bitter controversy exists regarding the
management of the Equitable Life Assurance Society and that public
confidence has been shaken in the safety of the funds under the
control of a single block of stock left by the late Henry B. Hyde.

This loss of confidence affects a great public trust of more than
four hundred million dollars representing the earnings of over
600,000 policyholders, and the present condition amounts to a
public misfortune.

In the hope of putting an end to this condition and in connection with a change in the executive management of the Society, I
have, together with other policyholders, purchased this block of
stock and propose to put it in the hands of a Board of Trustees
having no connection with Wall Street, with power to vote it for
the election of Directors--as to twenty-eight of the fifty-two
directors in accordance with the instructions of the policyholders
of the Society, and as to the remaining twenty-four directors in
accordance with the uncontrolled judgement of the trustees. This
division of twenty-eight and twenty-four is in accordance with a
plan of giving substantial control to policyholders already approved
by the Superintendent of Insurance.

I beg you to act as one of this Board with other gentlemen who
shall be of a character entirely satisfactory to you.

I should not venture to ask this of you on any personal
grounds; but to restore this great trust, affecting so many people
of slender means, to soundness and public confidence would certainly
be a great public service, and this view emboldens me to make the
request.

The duties of the trust would be very light as, in the nature
of things, when a satisfactory board is once constituted, there
are few changes and all the clerical and formal work would be done
by the office force of the company.

I have written similarly to Justice Morgan J. O'Brien, Presid-
ing Justice of the Appellate Division of our Supreme Court, and to
Mr. George Westinghouse of Pittsburgh, two of the largest policyholders in the Society.

Letter, Thomas Fortune Ryan to Grover Cleveland, June 9, 1905,
Exhibits in Connection with Testimony Taken Before the [Armstrong]
Joint Committee, I, pp. 991-992.

706.   OPERATION OF SECURITIES SYNDICATES (1906)

The primary objection to the participation of insurance companies in securities syndicates was that the companies thereby became brokers and, in any case, too deeply
involved in the affairs of other corporations. They might
be tempted to take great chances with premium-money that
should be invested conservatively.

Most syndicates are merely partnerships formed for a single
transaction. They are gotten up to carry through an operation that

is a larger one than is feasible for a single bank or banking house
or individual. The ordinary type of syndicate agreement and that
in which these [insurance] companies have usually been participants,
is for placing upon the market a large output of corporate securities. Often the interests of the makers of the security demand the
immediate use of a large amount of money. And, in order to realize
promptly such large amount, the makers are inclined to sell the
entire output at a price considerably below that which can be
realized at a gradual sale. The securities are therefore offered
in lump to some bank or banking house at a lower price and are forth-
with purchased in lump. In connection with this purchase the party
taking the securities, who is known as the syndicate manager, invites a considerable number of associates to agree to take a certain
portion of the securities at the original price within a certain
time, if called upon to do so. The securities are then put upon
the market for gradual sale at a higher price. If the public take
them at the proffered price no call is made upon the participants
or underwriters, except, perhaps, for certain expenses or temporary
advances. In consideration of the participant's contingent obligation to take up his share if called upon, he is given a proportionate share of the profits from the sale to the public. Sometimes
the participant is permitted to withdraw for investment securities
to an amount equivalent to his subscription, relinquishing his
interest in the profits on the public offering. In a great many
cases persons undertaking these financial operations find considerable difficulty in procuring partners in the enterprise. Very many
of the syndicates are hazardous and many have entailed serious losses upon the participants. In many instances, however, the securities are of such a character that a considerable profit is practically certain. The reason for putting out the securities in such
a way is merely because the makers of them have not the facilities
or the time for themselve making direct sale to the public. In
this class of cases the "giving" of participation by the original
purchaser is in the nature of a favor bestowed. The syndicates in
which the life insurance companies and their officers have participated have usually been of the last-named description. It is
quite obvious that in cases of this kind, where participation is
offered to a life insurance company the dominant motive is to secure the good will and the favor of the company as a purchaser of
securities rather than to get the protection of the company as an
underwriter. And those who, as officers and members of finance
committees [of life insurance companies], have determined the course
of the company in its participations and purchases have frequently
been in a position to profit by their action on behalf of the
company.

Report of the [Armstrong] Joint Committee of the Senate and
Assembly of the State of New York Appointed to Investigate the
Affairs of Life Insurance Companies, (Albany, New York: Brandow
Printing Company, State Printers, 1906), pp. 386-387.

707. SEASONS OF CREDIT (1906)

On the eve of the Panic of 1907, bankers criticized
the inflexibility of American currency. John Claflin was
chairman of the Special Currency Committee of the Chamber;
other members were: Frank A. Vanderlip, Isidor Straus,
Dumont Clarke, Charles A. Conant, and Joseph F. Johnson.

This harvest demand for currency and capital is first felt in
July by the reserve cities of the southwest, as the winter wheat of
that region ripens. At that time the country banks of Oklahoma and
Kansas and the banks of the reserve cities in that region, especially
those of Kansas City and St. Louis, are pressed for loans by the
buyers of grain, and for currency in small denominations for the
payment of harvest hands. Their surplus stock of currency being
soon exhausted, these banks draw upon their balances in Chicago,
New York, and other eastern cities. Then, as the season progresses
and crops in various sections of the country are harvested, a flow
of currency from the east to the south, to the west and to the
northwest sets in and does not cease until the cotton, corn and
wheat of the country are all marketed and the farmers' work for the
season is over.
No statistics are available showing the total of this periodical movement of currency. The increase in the demand for loans on
account of the crop movement cannot even be conjectured, but the
shipments of currency from the banks of the cities into agricultural
regions might easily reach $150,000,000. The amount passing through
six Chicago banks last year reached $92,000,000. This currency goes
in the form of gold certificates, silver certificates, United States
notes and National bank notes. All these except the bank notes,
which form only a small proportion of the whole, are "lawful money,"
and their shipment, therefore, causes a corresponding reduction of
bank reserves.
Since experience has proved that a dollar in a bank reserve
is adequate protection for an indebtedness of four dollars due to
bank depositors, it is evident that the withdrawal of $100,000,000
from the banking reserves of the country might lead to a contraction
of bank loans and deposits by an amount four times that sum, namely,
$400,000,000, such contraction being the result of the efforts of
banks to increase their reserves by calling loans. Thus at a time
when the legitimate demand for loans is increasing in order that
the great agricultural yield of this country may be brought to
market, the lending power of our banks is actually curtailed by
several hundred million dollars. As a result, borrowers of all
classes are forced to pay unsecure customary accommodations from
banks, and the prices of many articles of commerce suffer, the
buying demand having weakened.
Unfortunately these evils are not the only ones that result
from the defective character of our monetary system. During the
winter and spring there is a return flow of lawful money from the
country to the cities, and the surplus reserves of the banks in

financial centers are increased as rapidly as they have been diminished in the fall. As the city banks pay interest on this money,
they cannot suffer it to lie idle in their vaults; hence the rate
of interest is lowered, and speculation is thus unduly encouraged.
Bankers are aware that the country will again call for this money
in the fall and are careful not to lock it up in long-time paper.
Most of it, therefore, is put out on call, and so finds its way into
the hands of men whose interests are largely speculative. Here we
have the secret of our so-called "spring boom" in speculation. It
is the product of inflation, just as our autumnal stringency is the
product of contraction. So long as reserve money to the extent of
$150,000,000 is being shipped about the country, now lying for a
few months in the vaults of banks, now circulating among the farmers
and the planters of the west and the south, these alternate periods
of excessive speculation and depression are inevitable.

John Claflin et al., The Currency, (New York: Chamber of
Commerce of the State of New York, 1906), pp. 4-6.

708. WHAT THE CURRENCY QUESTION REALLY IS (1907)

The reasoning in the following is of the type that
led to formulation of the Federal Reserve System six
years later. Victor Morawetz is the writer. Morawetz
was a director of the National Bank of Commerce in New
York, and was chairman of the executive committee of the
Atchison, Topeka, and Santa Fe Railroad Company, in charge
of financial affairs.

A stringency of the money market, whether throughout the whole
country or only in some section of the country, may result from
several causes, viz.:   (1) the banks may be unable to grant further
credits, or may be compelled to reduce the amount of their credits,
because their reserves have been reduced by unusual withdrawals of
lawful money, as may happen when a large amount of money is used to
pay duties and other taxes and is locked up by the Government, or
when a large amount of currency is withdrawn for use as a circulating medium in the West and South to "move the crops," or to be
hoarded by panic-stricken depositors, or when a large amount of
gold is drawn for export; or (2) the banks may be unable to grant
additional credits, because the aggregate amount of the credits
desired has been increased through extraordinary activity in business to the limit permitted by their reserves of lawful money; or
(3) those persons who desire credit may be unable to furnish satisfactory assurance or security to those banks whose ability to
grant credits is not exhausted.

It is obvious, therefore, that the currency question is really
a question of bank credits and bank reserves. The problem is to
find a way, while preventing any unsafe expansion of credits or the
issue of any unsafe currency, (1) to avoid a depletion of bank reserves and the consequent large reduction of bank credits when lawful money is withdrawn to pay taxes and is locked up by the Government, or when a large amount of lawful money is withdrawn for use
as a circulating medium; or to be hoarded, or when gold is withdrawn
for export; and (2) to enable the banks to expand their deposit liabilities and their loans and discounts in times of great business
activity and at the same time to increase proportionately their
reserves of lawful money.

Victor Morawetz, The Currency Question, 2nd edition, November,
1907, pp. 10-11.

709. MR. MORGAN BUYS EQUITABLE LIFE (1910)

In 1905, Thomas Fortune Ryan bought out Equitable
Life. Somewhat later, he sold some of the stock to
Edward H. Harriman. In 1910, J. P. Morgan decided to
buy control of Equitable. While in the following interchange, Morgan is unable to present a specific reason
for the purchase, it is clear that control of Equitable's
half-billion in assets was the principal motive. (See
Source Nos. 706-707).

Mr. UNTERMYER. You may explain, if you care to, Mr. Morgan,
why you bought from Messrs. Ryan and Harriman $51,000 par value of
stock that paid only $3,710 a year, for approximately $3,000,000,
that could yield you only one-eighth or one-ninth of 1 per cent.
Mr. MORGAN. Because I thought it was a desirable thing for
the situation to do that.
Mr. UNTERMYER. That is very general, Mr. Morgan, when you
speak of the situation. Was not that stock safe enough in Mr.
Ryan's hands?
Mr. MORGAN. I suppose it was. I thought it was greatly improved by being in the hands of myself and these two gentlemen,
provided I asked them to do so.
Mr. UNTERMYER. How would that improve the situation over the
situation that existed when Mr. Ryan and Mr. Harriman held the
stock?
Mr. MORGAN. Mr. Ryan did not have it alone.
Mr. UNTERMYER. Yes; but do you now know that Mr. Ryan originally bought it alone, and Mr. Harriman insisted on having him
give him half?

Mr. MORGAN. I thought if he could pay for it at that price
I could. I thought that was a fair price.

Mr. UNTERMYER. You thought it was good business, did you?

Mr. MORGAN. Yes.

Mr. UNTERMYER. You thought it was good business to buy a stock
that paid only one-ninth or one-tenth of 1 per cent a year?

Mr. MORGAN. I thought so.

Mr. UNTERMYER. The normal rate of interest that you can earn
on money is about 5 per cent, is it not?

Mr. MORGAN. Not always; no.

Mr. UNTERMYER. I say, ordinarily.

Mr. MORGAN. I am not talking about it as a question of money.

Mr. UNTERMYER. The normal rate of interest would be from 4
to 5 per cent, ordinarily, would it not?

Mr. MORGAN. Well?

Mr. UNTERMYER. Where is the good business, then, in buying a
security that only pays one-ninth of 1 per cent?

Mr. MORGAN. Because I thought it was better there than it was
where it was. That is all.

Mr. UNTERMYER. Was anything the matter with it in the hands
of Mr. Ryan?

Mr. MORGAN. Nothing.

Mr. UNTERMYER. In what respect would it be better where it
is than with him?

Mr. MORGAN. That is the way it struck me.

Mr. UNTERMYER. Is that all you have to say about it?

Mr. MORGAN. That is all I have to say about it.

Mr. UNTERMYER. You care to make no other explanation about
it?

Mr. MORGAN. No.

Mr. UNTERMYER. The assets of the Equitable Life are a little
over $500,000,000, are they not?

Mr. MORGAN. I do not know what they are.

Mr. UNTERMYER. According to the charts and papers in evidence,
on December 31, 1911, they were $504,465,802.01.

Testimony, J. Pierpont Morgan, December 19, 1912, U.S. Congress,
62nd, 3rd session, House of Representatives, Committee on Banking
and Currency, Money Trust Investigation, pp. 1068-1069.

710. "FINANCIERS HAVE NO PRIDE OF MANUFACTURE" (1911)

Edison, Taylor, T. A. Watson--men with the machine
shop in their bones--regarded the bankers as unproductive
and irrelevant to the real work of the industry. Thorsten
Veblen also followed this approach in his writings.

Personally my experience has been so unsatisfactory with financiers that I never want to work for any of them. If there is a
manufacturer at the head of any enterprise, such as shipbuilding
or construction work of any kind, and he is a large-minded man,
that is the man whom I want to be under. As a rule, financiers are
looking merely for a turn over. They want to get in and out of
their business quickly, and they have absolutely no pride of manufacture. It is all a question of making money quickly, and whether
the company is built up so as to be the finest of its kind and permanently successful is a matter of complete indifference to almost
all of them.
    A good example of the utter lack of "proper pride" of the manu-
facturer is to be seen in the present managers of --------. They
are among the leading financiers in Philadelphia and New York, and
absolutely refuse to spend a cent for much needed physical improvements or for improvements in management. All that they are looking
for is the chance to unload on some one else and get out whole.

Frederick W. Taylor, 1911, in Copley, Taylor, I, p. 388.

711. HOW TO IMPROVE THE FINANCIAL SYSTEM (1912)

    The financial community was in broad agreement on
the desirability of these three changes in the money
and banking system. In one form or another, they found
their way into the following year's Federal Reserve Act.
This is the testimony of A. Barton Hepburn, chairman of
the board of directors of the Chase National Bank.

    There are three things that, in my judgment, are indispensable
to be done in order to improve our banking and currency system, and
we should undertake to do those. In the first place, the reserve
of the country ought to be under a central altruistic control that
could use it for the benefit of the whole country and where it was
needed. Instead, where we have a money stringency now, each one
of the 26,000 banks in the country begins competing for cash reserves, locking it up in their vaults, and they aggravate the condition instead of relieving it. The central reserve, properly
administered, would obviate that.
    Then there should be a flexibility to our currency which we
have not and never can have in a bond-secured currency where you
must invest more money in your bond than you can get currency in
return. And then there should be a market for commercial paper,
and this would provide such a market for paper, running less than
30 days, of an acceptable character. It may be discounted by
this association, and the proceeds, if need be, paid over in

currency, thereby preventing anything like a currency famine.

Testimony, A. Barton Hepburn, June 11, 1912, U.S. Congress,
62nd, 3rd session, House of Representatives, Committee on Banking
and Currency, Money Trust Investigation, p. 313.

712.   SELL SHORT DURING A PANIC (1912)

Short-selling was a subject still tinged with a
moral tone. (For an early denunciation of short-
selling as immoral, see Source No. 243). Frank
Sturgis, who testifies here, was a banker and a member
of the brokerage firm of Strong, Sturgis & Company. He
had been a member of the New York Stock Exchange since
1869, a member of its governing committee since 1876,
and had served as the president of the Exchange from
1892 to 1894.

Mr. UNTERMYER. Under what circumstances would you regard
that sort of short-selling as legitimate and proper?
Mr. STURGIS. I would regard it so if there was a panic raging
over the country and it was desirable to protect interests which
could not be sold. I think it would be a perfectly legitimate
thing to do.
Mr. UNTERMYER. Let us see about that. If there was a panic
raging over the country and a man sold stocks short, would not
that simply add to the panic?
Mr. STURGIS. It might. Self-preservation is the first law
of nature.
Mr. UNTERMYER. Hold on--self preservation?
Mr. TURGIS. Yes.
Mr. UNTERMYER. But, as I understand it, if there is a panic
raging over the country, you think it is defensible for a man to
depress stocks by selling stocks he has not got, with the idea of
adding to the panic?
Mr. STURGIS. Mr. Untermyer, if a person has property which
is absolutely unsalable, and he can, so to speak, protect his
position by selling something for which there is a broad market----
Mr. UNTERMYER. That he has not got?
Mr. STURGIS. (continuing). I do not consider it wrong.
Mr. UNTERMYER. Mr. Sturgis, let us just analyze that, because I do not think I understand you. You do not want to be misunderstood, do you?
Mr. STURGIS. It is not my wish.
Mr. UNTERMYER. And I do not want you to be misunderstood.
Do you mean to say that if there is a panic raging it is a defen-
sible thing for a man, under any circumstances, to sell stock

that he has not got, with the idea of getting it back cheaper?

Mr. STURGIS. I do think it is defensible. I certainly
think it is defensible.

Mr. UNTERMYER. For what purposes does he do that except to
try to make money?

Mr. STURGIS. To try to save his credit, perhaps.

Mr. UNTERMYER. How does he save his credit in a panic by
selling stocks that he has not got, with the idea of adding to the
panic and getting them cheaper?

Mr. STURGIS. Because if he can make a profit on that sale
it may repair the losses that he has made on stocks he can not sell.

Mr. UNTERMYER. I see. You know that would simply accentuate
the fierceness of the panic, do you not?

Mr. STURGIS. It could not be otherwise.

Mr. UNTERMYER. Certainly. And his only purpose in doing a
thing of that kind in time of panic would be to make money, would
it not?

Mr. STURGIS. To protect himself.

Mr. UNTERMYER. It would be to make money, would it not?

Mr. STURGIS. Yes; and that would protect him.

Mr. UNTERMYER. Of course it always protects a man to make
money, no matter how he makes it, does it not?

Mr. STURGIS. Yes, sir.

Mr. UNTERMYER. And that, you think, is justifiable?

Mr. STURGIS. I think under those circumstances it is.

Mr. UNTERMYER. You do not want to make any further explanation of that proposition, do you?

Mr. STURGIS. I do not.

Mr. UNTERMYER. Is it any more justifiable for a man to sell
short in a panic than in a normal market?

Mr. STURGIS. It depends very much upon his financial necessities.

Mr. UNTERMYER. Do you regard it as justifiable in a normal
market for a man to sell a thing he has not got, with the idea
of depressing prices in order to buy in the stock at a lower level?

Mr. STURGIS. I think it is a question between a man and his
own conscience, Mr. Untermyer.

Testimony, Frank Knight Sturgis, December 13, 1912, U.S.
Congress, 62nd, 3rd session, House of Representatives, Committee
on Banking and Currency, Money Trust Investigation, pp. 831-832.

713. MINORITY CONTROL IS THE RULE (1913)

The new giant corporations had been created primarily by merger within the past eighteen years. Already,
however, majority control was something unheard-of in
such corporations. George Baker is being questioned in
the following. Baker was chairman of the board of directors

of the First National Bank of New York, a Morgan firm.
He also had owned a controlling block of shares in
Chase National Bank but disposed of it very soon before
his appearance to testify at these hearings.

Mr. UNTERMYER. Is it or not the fact, Mr. Baker, that in
these great companies, like railroad companies and large industrials where the ownership of stocks is scattered, a very small minority is an actual control as a rule?
    Mr. BAKER. Yes.
    Mr. UNTERMYER. Would you say----
    Mr. BAKER. If it is owned by active, enterprising men; yes,
sir; who take an interest in the concern.
    Mr. UNTERMYER. Well, have you ever seen the men in charge
turned out of a big railroad property by the stockholders?
    Mr. BAKER. Not when it is properly managed.
    Mr. UNTERMYER. Whether properly or improperly managed? Is
there a single instance in the history of your business career
where the stockholders, widely scattered, in a big railroad or
industrial corporation, ever got together and turned out the management, no matter what it was.
    Mr. BAKER. I do not recall any.
    Mr. UNTERMYER. No. Is it or not then true, that ordinarily
in a railroad company where the stock has been held for many years
and is widely scattered, that a holding inside the board of directors of 5 or 10 per cent has always assured continuity of management and control?
    Mr. BAKER. I do not think it generally makes much difference
about the holdings.
    Mr. UNTERMYER. The question is who is in the saddle, is it
not?
    Mr. BAKER. Yes, sir; and how satisfactorily to the stock-
holders they are handling the property.
    Mr. UNTERMYER. How has that ever had anything to do with it
in your experience, since you say that none of them ever has been
turned out?
    Mr. BAKER. I can not recall at the moment any.
    Mr. UNTERMYER. Until a management is turned out is it not
rather difficult to find out what they have been doing in practical
operation?
    Mr. BAKER. I never tried. I do not know how difficult it
is.
    Mr. UNTERMYER. Have you ever known anybody to try in any of
the corporations in which you have been identified?
    Mr. BAKER. Not that I remember.

Testimony, George F. Baker, January 10, 1913, U.S. Congress,
62nd, 3rd session, House of Representatives, Committee on Banking
and currency, Money Trust Investigation, pp. 1499-1500.

714. NATIONAL WEALTH AND CURRENCY RESERVES (1913)

The example of Germany was studied for its financial
lessons for the projected Federal Reserve System. Charles
Conant, who had been treasurer of the Morton Trust Company
from 1901 to 1906, makes this statement. He had been
Washington correspondent for some business papers and
had written two books on banking.

There has been credit inflation, and such a locking up of
capital in fixed form is chief precursor of trouble because of the
reduced supply of capital available for current commercial or productive purposes. The trouble with Germany has been all the time
the ambition of the Government and of German merchants and financiers to extend trade and to obtain commercial or diplomatic advantage all over the world, and they have strained their capital
resources. But the currency factor has been a subordinate factor.
. . . .
Of course, if a country can afford to set aside 65 or 100
per cent of gold against its currency it may be a good investment;
but even so far as 50 per cent is concerned, it is a dead investment, unless it is necessary to secure it. A country should make
a considerable sacrifice of income to secure a sound credit currency. If 75 per cent reserve were effective it would pay the
country to make that investment, even though it involved a large
loss of income.
Nations like Germany, with less accumulated riches than
France, can not afford to make that investment. They can not
afford an investment of 65 per cent, permanently, in their reserves.
They need to invest capital in great productive and commercial enterprises. What has occurred in Germany has been that the people
of Germany, stimulated by the Government as well as by the commercial bodies, have tried to do more business than their capital
justified. But the volume of currency constitutes a very small
factor in the matter. Theoretically, if the currency had been very
much more restricted, it might have put a little more of a curb
upon speculation, but not much, because speculation does not have
to be made through currency--it is made through banking transactions and credit. But the trouble in Germany, as it was in this
country prior to the panic of 1907, has been the conversion of the
productive capital of the country, the annual product, into fixed
forms, to such an extent that the liquid capital has been reduced
to an almost inadequate point.
Now, the German banking system is designed, as far as practicable, to facilitate transactions, to turn corners, because in
Germany, you know, there are the quarterly settlements, which are
occasions when there is a great demand for currency. But that
demand closes in a week or 10 days, and they can afford a certain
currency inflation for that one week. So that the last amendment
to the law in 1911 permitted the Imperial Bank to issue 200,000,000
marks (about $50,000,000) in the week ending each quarter, which

is considerably more than they can issue in ordinary times. This
does not relate to the amount that can be issued on deposits of
gold. You can issue any amount, if you deposit gold, mark for mark.
Above that you must pay a 5 per cent tax.

I do not think the monetary experience of Germany can be used
to illustrate the evils of currency inflation. It might be used to
illustrate the evils of credit inflation. The German law makes no
requirement for reserves against deposits, and that the great joint
stock banks have gone on locking up capital, engaging in great enterprises, and holding no reserves or very small cash reserves,
relying upon the Imperial Bank to supply them with currency when
they needed it.

Testimony, Charles A. Conant, October 1, 1913, U.S. Congress,
63rd, 1st session, Senate, Committee on Banking and Currency,
Banking and Currency, pp. 1494, 1495-1496.

715. "NEW YORK TROUBLE IS BIG TROUBLE" (1913)

The Federal Reserve Bill aimed largely at avoiding
such "big trouble." F. E. Marshall was a retired banker.
In previous years he had been a bank examiner, vice
president of the National Bank of Commerce of Kansas City
and the National Bank of St. Louis, and president of the
Continental National Bank of St. Louis and the Phoenix
National Bank of New York. The following is from testimony before the Senate.

I think that really down at the bottom of the bill that probably the experiences that we went through [the Panic of] 1907,
which brought us facing the fact that we must do something that
would put us on a more stable basis in times of stress and that
we can not simply go on in times of stress and shut down and say
"No," that that was what 1907 did for us.

When New York gets in trouble, it is big trouble, and there
is no place for that city's banks to go for help, and therefore
the reserves of the country are locked up and are not available
and I assume that the purpose of this bill is, first, to get the
reserves back into the country, where they are needed and belong,
and at the same time establish a bank or banks that is a safe depository and a surer source of supply in times of stress. Whether
this meets it I can not say any more than you can. Unless the
banks come in and work with you, of course, it will not be worth
much. It all depends upon the banks coming in.

Testimony, F. E. Marshall, September 16, 1913, U.S. Congress,
63rd, 1st session, Senate, Committee on Banking and Currency,
Banking and Currency, p. 457.

716. MORGAN-SPONSORED CORPORATIONS (1897-1913)

The forty-two corporations listed below were either
organized or their securities were underwritten, in whole
or part, by J. P. Morgan and Company.

American Bridge Co.
American Telephone & Telegraph Co.
Associated Merchants Co.
Atchison, Topeka & Sante Fe
Atlantic Coast Line
Atlas Portland Cement Co.
Boomer Coal & Coke Co.
Central of Georgia R.R. Co.
Chesapeake & Ohio
Chicago & Western Indiana R.R. Co.
Chicago, Burlington & Quincy
Chicago Great Western
Chicago, Indianapolis & Louisville R.R. Co.
Elgin, Joliet & Eastern Ry. Co.
Erie Railroad System
Federal Steel Co.
Florida East Coast Ry.
General Electric Co.
Hartford Carpet Corporation
Hocking Valley Ry. System
Inspiration Consolidated Copper Co.
International Harvester Co.
International Mercantile Marine
J. I. Case Threshing Machine Co.
Lehigh Valley R.R. Co.
Louisville & Nashville
National Tube Co.
New York Central System
New York, New Haven & Hartford System
New York, Ontario & Western R.R. Co.
Northern Pacific Ry. System
Pennsylvania
Pere Marquette R.R. Co.
Reading
St. Louis & San Francisco R.R. Co.
Southern Ry.
Terminal R.R. Association of St. Louis
United Dry Goods Cos.

United States Motor Co.
United States Rubber Co.
United States Steel Corporation
Virginia-Carolina Chemical Co.

Exhibits 238 and 238A, February 25, 1913, U.S. Congress, 62nd,
3rd session, House of Representatives, Committee on Banking and
Currency, Money Trust Investigation, p. 2149. (The page numbers
were very badly garbled by the printer; 2149 appears twice,
separated by sixteen other pages. The above listing is from the
second page 2149.)

717. USURY IN RURAL OKLAHOMA (1915)

Oklahoma law set maximum interest rates at 6 percent
without a contract and 10 percent with a contract.
E. J. Giddings, general counsel of the Farmers'
Protective Association of Oklahoma, an organization of
tenant farmers, gives his report.

The interest rate on chattel mortgages in Oklahoma to-day
ranges from 20 per cent up to 200 per cent. In the cities I had
[knowledge of] usurious contracts for laborers there that went as
high as 230 per cent per annum.
On farm loans the interest charges are not so great, so far
as the realty is concerned. Conservatively speaking, the farmers
of Oklahoma owe to the banks and other money lenders at least
$60,000,000 and $40,000,000 of that is out at a usurious rate of
interest.
The farmer goes to the bank and he makes his note covered
by a mortgage payable ordinarily the 1st of October. If he borrows
$100 he pays $20 in the spring for it. You can always detect the
usurious note by virtue of the fact that it bears interest after
maturity. The trouble with fighting the usurious banks is that it
is a poor man's fight, and he can not fight against the machina-
tions and combinations of that character.
. . . .
The farmer who borrows money from a bank can not fight a
usury charge ordinarily, because immediately he does so he is boycotted by the banks, and the coming year he can not borrow any
money. The banks have a sort, I suppose, of telepathic communication one with the other on that score. If you borrow money from
the First National Bank in a certain town and they charge 40 or 50
or 60 per cent, as some of the banks have done, if you contest that
usury charge, when you come the next year to apply for money you
are boycotted by every bank in that community and in all the

surrounding communities. I suggested a remedy with regard to that,
making it an offense for banks to boycott those who make a defense
to usury charges.

Testimony, E. J. Giddings, March 18, 1915, U.S. Congress,
64th, 1st session, Senate, Final Report and Testimony Submitted
to Congress by the Commission on Industrial Relations, X, pp. 9096,
9097.

718. MR. MORGAN WILL DECIDE (1916)

Three years after the death of the elder J. P.
Morgan, the younger Morgan re-formulated the conditions
of the partnership. While his control was unquestioned,
it was not unlimited. Perhaps this was the principal
difference between the two Morgans.

Sixth. In case of a difference or dispute between members of
the partnership, the same shall be submitted to the decision of
Mr. John Pierpont Morgan, which shall be final.
Seventh. The partnership may be dissolved at any time by
Mr. John Pierpont Morgan, subject to the liquidation thereof; provided that partners representing a majority in the interests in
the profits of the partnership shall consent to such dissolution.
Eighth. Any partner may withdraw from the partnership upon
giving 3 months' written notice of his intention so to do. In
that event, the remaining partners may continue the business and
the shares of the profits or losses of the withdrawing partner,
or partners shall be divided thereafter among the remaining partners, or otherwise disposed of, according to the decision of Mr.
John Pierpont Morgan, who shall fix the valuation of the assets,
determine what portion of the assets, if any, shall be appropriated
as an offset to liabilities, and also be the judge of the amount
due such withdrawing partner or partners on account of capital
undivided profits and credit balances.
. . . .
Ninth. It is further agreed that Mr. Morgan may, at any
time, compel any partner at once to withdraw and retire from the
partnership, upon giving him written notice to that effect, and
in that event, the amount due such retiring partner shall be dealt
with in the same manner as above provided for in the case of a
voluntary withdrawal by such partner.

Articles of Copartnership of J. P. Morgan & Company, March
31, 1916, U.S. Congress, 73rd, 1st session, Senate, Committee on
Banking and Currency, Stock Exchange Practices, II, p. 522.

719. WAR AND THE STOCK MARKET (1914-1917)

Readers of the following graphic account should
keep in mind that the actors described therein comprised
a small if spectacular element in the economy. (See
Source No. 720). John Moody, from whose autobiography
this is taken, was the publisher of investment service
manuals.

Even as late as October, 1914, Wall Street had only partially
adjusted itself to the fact of war. The Stock Exchange had been
closed since the first of August, and would remain closed many weeks
more before the scions of finance would have the courage to reopen
it. The crash in security values at the opening of the war had
been catastrophic, as a flood of sales had poured in from all Europe
which had completely swamped the New York market; and it was feared
that this liquidation would again start on a large scale if the
Exchange were reopened. There were still held in Europe several
billions of dollars of American corporation securities.
. . . .
But along in November the dollar commenced to rise in the
London exchange market, and the exchange rate soon turned definitely
in our favor; sterling lost its premium in New York and gold
commenced to flow to us in ever-increasing volume. What did this
mean? It meant that the Allies were placing immense orders in
America for war supplies, and establishing heavy credits here. It
was the forerunner of the war boom that was to follow. The stock
market was opened to unlimited trading in December, and by February
of 1915 a wild, speculative bull movement was in full swing.
The upward rush of prices persisted without serious interrup-
tion for many months, and there was a golden harvest for the speculator. And in the big-business fields vast prosperity began to
prevail. Europe did liquidate the bulk of her remaining American
securities in the New York market during that year and in 1916, but
we drew her gold from her with equal or greater rapidity, and then
commenced to pile up that great mountain of the yellow metal which
has by no means melted away at this writing.
. . . .
Wall Street, of course, was the center of all this stupendous
war financing and dealing. The boiling market of 1915 soon inspired
the hope of a long war; just the reverse of what the Street had been
hoping for a few months earlier. A long war, with America not in,
became the creed of every speculator. When the Lusitania was sunk
and it was momentarily feared that this colossal crime might draw
us in, the stock market suddenly slumped; only to wildly recover
when President Wilson hinted that we might be too proud to fight.
This is not to say that there were not a large number of men
in the financial world who deprecated the war and were appalled by
its horrors. But the preoccupation of the mass was certainly money-
making above all else. Every one who could afford it (and many who
could not) seemed to be playing the "war babies"; brokers' offices

were everywhere crowded, the wire houses extended their lines and
opened branch offices all over the country. And women, for the
first time in large numbers, commenced to flock into Wall Street to
gamble in these "war babies," many of which were really worthless,
having been conceived in sin and brought forth in iniquity.
. . . .
Few in the financial world expected that the United States
would really get into the war; more than two years' preoccupation
with war profits had distorted our perspective. The reelection of
Wilson in 1916 had been accepted as a practical guaranty that we
would keep out, and the stock market had strengthened. But in
December of the same year, when Secretary Lansing sounded the alarm
that we were "rapidly drifting into the war," a stock-market smash
immediately ensued. And in February, 1917, when the President gave
Bernstorff his walking papers, the markets crashed again; and from
that time on prices continued downward until after war actually
had been declared by Congress.

John Moody, The Long Road Home. An Autobiography,
(New York: The Macmillan Company, 1933), pp. 182-183, 183-184,
185, 186.

720. THE SECURITIES MARKET (1915)

It is rather surprising to see how recently the
securities business became a large-scale enterprise.
George Whitney and Thomas Lamont, who testify in the
following, were partners in J. P. Morgan and Company.

Mr. WHITNEY. Mr. Brown, you know today it is supposed that
according to the studies made by the Securities & Exchange Commission, there are something like 10,000 firms engaged in the distribution of securities.
At that time [1915], according to our best guess, there were
about 175. I am leaving out of that, of course, members of the
stock exchanges, who at that time did nothing but pure brokerage
business.
Also we must remember that until the Liberty Loans, or until
the war, really, this country was a debtor Nation, and the question
of buying bonds was an almost unknown business.
At that time, if you go back to study the records, you will
find that the savings among the people generally went to the savings
banks and to some form or other of insurance. It was only with the
introduction of the Liberty Loan and all the very intensive work
that was then done that it became the customary thing for the
ordinary individual to buy securities.

Of course, with that development there grew up in the post-war period a very large and active organization for distributing bonds to private investors. Prior to the war practically the only buyers of securities individually were savings banks, insurance companies, and certain people of substantial means, who knew about it and who understood it.

There were not many salesmen. They say there are 300,000 salesmen in this country now. At one time back there, in 1916, we figured it out and there were about 2,000 salesmen of bonds and at that time about 250 bond houses.

So, obviously, when you say the distributing people were loaded up, I think the records will show the people who were engaged in the actual distribution of bonds were rather few and were not particularly loaded up because they were not of any substantial capital. That was long before the days of so-called "bank affiliates", and there were about five or six what you call national bond distributing houses. It was a long, slow, and difficult process in the first place to educate the distributing houses themselves, and then, in the second place, to distribute to the salesmen they had and ultimately through them to the public.

It is just like any other merchandising proposition.

. . . .

Mr. LAMONT. There were some figures on that. You said, "Increased during the Liberty Loan financing." I think they are of great interest, and I will give them from memory.

We figure that the total number of investors in Allied loans in the United States was not over 400,000, possibly 500,000 investors in all the United States.

The first Liberty Loan campaign resulted in 4,000,000 applications for that one loan. There is a jump from 400,000 to 4,000,000; 400,000 for all the Allied loans to 4,000,000 for the first Liberty Loan.

Testimony, George Whitney and Thomas W. Lamont, January 13, 1936, U.S. Congress, 74th, 2nd session, Senate, Special Committee Investigating the Munitions Industry, Munitions Industry, XXVII, pp. 8166, 8168.

721. REORGANIZING THE SEIBERLING COMPANY (1921)

Here is a first-hand account of a hard-driven bargain.

Seiberling was able to arrange with Goldman Sachs, New York banking house, in November for a revolving loan of $25,000,000 (the highest amount actually loaned was $18,835,000), with our materials and finished goods as security, and for several weeks our stockroom doors carried the sign, "Property of Dauphinot and Cummings," who were the trustees. I think it was around Christmas Day that the bankers recommended that other arrangements of a permanent nature would have to be made. That sounded like a receivership.

That was the last thing we ever wanted to see happen, and fortunately other people now became concerned. If we went to the wall we might drag down banks and industries to whom we owed money. Even the J. P. Morgan Company became interested, and under the leadership of Paul D. Cravath, New York attorney, a concerted effort was started to set up new securities which banking and merchandising creditors would accept in place of cash. Dillon, Read and Company, a relatively new investment house, undertook to sponsor the reorganization, providing all creditors would agree on a program which would pay off the bills and provide ample working capital for a fresh start. It was not until May that the plan was worked out.

If I had had not too much occasion earlier in my life to study finance I took a practical course in the subject during those difficult weeks.

...We got only 90 cents to the dollar on the new money (or credit) received and would have to pay it back at $1.20 or $1.10 to the dollar--and pay 8 per cent interest. Boiled down, we were in effect borrowing eighty-seven million dollars at 14 per cent interest.

The Goodyear reorganization, one of the largest in the country up to that time, was criticized then and afterward as driving a hard bargain with a company in difficulties, and later led to a notable lawsuit instigated by common stockholders, which mitigated some of the terms but did not change the basic settlement.

The defense of the settlement was that the terms were the best that the committees could get, that you had to offer an incentive to get creditors to take the risk involved in accepting securities, which might prove of little value, instead of cash. Those securities would be worth something only if the company was basically so sound and the extension of credit would give it time to get back on its feet.

This would call for expert financial management, and in view of this, one item in the plan set up ten thousand dollars in management stock to be given to three trustees, who were to control the company, select its officers, and run things until the bonds were paid off. The trustees selected were Dillon, representing the bondholders; John Sherwin, Cleveland banker, representing the holders of the debentures; and Owen D. Young of General Electric, representing the merchandise creditors. The program became effective May 21, 1921, the Seiberlings and Treasurer Palmer resigned, and a new organization, headed by Edward G. Wilmer as president, took over.

The company had been saved, but at quite a price. All the new securities ranked ahead of the old Goodyear stock. Goodyear common was listed on the stock market at five dollars a share, but its book value at that time was approximately forty-four dollars less than zero.

This last statement may sound strange to people unfamiliar with stock values. In this case our debt together with senior

securities amounted to more than the assets of the company, and with
the arrearages on our preferred stock, the common was without value,
in effect a minus figure amounting to forty-four dollars per share.

Most of my holdings of course were in common stock rather than
in the more conservative preferred, since I believed in the earning
capacity of the company, and preferred's share in earnings was fixed.
I was not back where I started. It was worse than that. I was
liable for three hundred thousand dollars, which I saw no way of
paying, and I might even be looking for another job.

In those seven months my hair turned from a chestnut brown to
almost as white as it is today.

P. W. Litchfield, Industrial Voyage. My Life as an Industrial
Lieutenant, (Garden City, New York: Doubleday and Company, 1954),
pp. 195-197.

722.   FEDERAL RESERVE'S EASY MONEY POLICY (1927)

An attempt to explain the factors conditioning the
Reserve decision of 1927 to reduce the rediscount rate
is here written by Alexander Noyes.

Three or four years later it became the fashion to assign, as
the primary cause for the monstrous speculative upheaval of 1928
and 1929, the Reserve system's insistence in 1927 on a very low interest rate. Considered in retrospect and in the light of what
happened afterward, that policy was wrong. But it was adopted im-
pulsively or by inexperienced officials. Discussing it with me in
1927, Governor Strong of the New York Reserve Bank, with whom my
personal acquaintance was close, emphasized the necessity for easy
money: first, to encourage the agricultural West, which in his
view was only recovering gradually from its setback of 1922; next,
to reduce our own market's abnormally large requisition on gold,
which Europe urgently needed at home to safeguard British and
Continental currency rehabilitation. Nor was the easy-money policy
introduced during a trade boom. In the autumn of 1927 employment,
building construction, railway freight loadings and average prices
of commodities were all at the lowest in two years. The Reserve
Board's monthly "production index" went below the 1923-1925 average
for the first time since 1924. It is quite true, there had occurred
in 1925 a wild and insensate real-estate speculation, in which
"Florida lots" were bought at fancy prices by an army of speculators
who knew nothing of land values and many of whom, as I learned
from personal knowledge of participants, had never seen Florida.
But that boom had broken down very suddenly; it was short-lived; in
1927 it was referred to, usually, as a warning against such ventures by the ignorant.

But in 1927 there was another side. Some things were visibly
happening of which present-day remembrance makes it seem as if even
experienced watchers of the scene were blinded by the utterly abnormal post-war situation. This country's "merchandise export surplus,"
though much less than in wartime, had amounted to $2,700,000,000 in
four years. No four-year period before 1914 had approached that
figure. Before the war, "excess of exports" was usually considered
to be payment for interest on our own indebtedness to Europe; the
war had changed all that. The Commerce Department's "Balance of
International Payments" bulletin estimated that the country received
in 1927, for interest on money loaned abroad by our government and
citizens, during and after wartime, very nearly $1,000,000,000.
Partly to balance the resultant very lopsided international account,
partly because of their own necessities, and largely, doubtless,
because of the unusual opportunity for getting money, foreign countries were offering new loans on our market.

Noyes, The Market Place, pp. 315-316.

723. FEDERAL RESERVE INADEQUACY IN 1928-1929

The following analysis blamed Federal Reserve weakness in the crisis in part to the tardiness of the System's
changes and in larger part to the influence of outside investors. (Gold export, it was hoped, would lessen the
basis for credit, in effect reduce the supply of money,
and thus weaken the upward tendency of prices). George
Harrison, who testifies, was governor of the Federal
Reserve Bank of New York.

[Governor HARRISON.] Of course, there was speculation in New
York; there was speculation all over the country and all over the
world. It was a matter of the greatest concern, not only to you
but to all of us in the Federal reserve system. We exercised our
imagination and ingenuity, I think, to the limit to do what was
proper to control it.
    Beginning in 1928 we raised our discount rate three times. We
sold over four hundred millions of Government securities. We lost
$500,000,000 in gold. Had anybody said two years before that it
was possible to raise the discount rate three times and sell
$400,000,000 of Government securities and export $500,000,000 of
gold without checking inflation, it would have been thought impossible; but that is just what happened.
    The CHAIRMAN. Did your rediscount rate for 1928 stop specula-
tion?
    Governor HARRISON. No; it did not.

The CHAIRMAN. That question is important because I understand
it is your view that the raising of the commercial rediscount rate
has a tendency to put a stop to speculation.
    Governor HARRISON. I think it has.
    The CHAIRMAN. Did it do so in 1928?
    Governor HARRISON. No; it did not. I think, in looking back,
in retrospect, we made mistakes and probably will again in years
to come. We want, however, to minimize the number of those errors
in the future and to decrease their effect. I hope we are learning
as we go on. This inquiry of yours will be most helpful to us.
When I look back on 1928, I feel that we made two particular mistakes—first, we raised our rate the first time too late, and
second, we did not raise it enough. I mean that had we had at that
time the light of the experience we have since had, it would have
been better perhaps to have raised the rate 1 per cent in December
of 1927. I do not think except once in our history we have ever
raised our rate more than 1 per cent. Instead of that we waited
until January, after the turn of the year, when we raised it only
one-half of 1 per cent. I think that more prompt, vigorous rate
action at that time would have been more helpful. The difficulty
with Federal reserve control, through rate action, over excessive
use of credits for speculation, such as we experienced in 1928 and
1929, was very much enhanced by the fact that we developed in this
country what individuals seeing the opportunity to get higher returns on readily available funds, started loaning first in moderate
amounts and then rapidly growing amounts, to brokers and dealers
in stocks on stock-exchange collateral. In other words, loans that
have been reported as "loans for others." At one time over half
the total volume of money borrowed by brokers and dealers was money
advanced in that fashion. It was money that was wholly outside of
the control of the banking system; it was money loaned by lenders
who had no responsibility to the money market or to the banking
system. It was loaned without any responsibility on their part to
maintain reserves of any character.
    So what happened was this: When we raised our rate and put
pressure upon the bank reserves, instead of putting a grind, as
we call it, on the judgment and the freedom of the lending officers
of a member bank, instead of putting a pressure upon them to contract in a way which might be effective in reducing loans, the
higher rates resulted importantly in attracting other lenders quite
outside of the banking system to come in and lend their funds to
speculators.

    Testimony, George L. Harrison, January 22, 1931, U.S. Congress,
71st, 3rd session, Senate, Committee on Banking, Operation of the
National and Federal Reserve Banking Systems, pp. 65-66.

724.   CORPORATE CAUTION ABOUT CALL MARKET (1928)

A prominent industrialist, Owen Young, explains
why he and his colleagues regarded investment in the
call market as too risky. Young was chairman of the
board of directors, General Electric Company.

While it may not be possible to control individuals from loaning direct to the call market, it does seem to me that corporations
not engaged in the banking business might be so controlled. After
all, the business corporations who perhaps produced a very large
part of these funds are not purveyors of credit and they have, I
feel, no responsibility about the money market.
. . . .
All I can say about that, and the only company for which I
can speak with knowledge and a sense of responsibility, is the
General Electric Co., which at that time had very large cash
balances and which decided not to put its funds into the call
market. That represented substantially less income than might
have been gained had it put those funds in the call market.
. . . .
We decided not to do it because we felt that the loans by
others, if they were going in the market uncontrolled, would inevitably lead that speculative market to a break with its inevitable
repercussion on business.
. . . .
We felt that perhaps if we were to be one of several to set
that example, all corporations would follow. I think it was the
practice of the Steel Corporation. My recollection is that similar
practices were adopted by the Telephone Co. Of course, we were
getting only the rate then yielded by Government bonds instead of
10, 12, or 15 per cent, which the call market would have paid.
Now, corporations engaged or authorized to do business in a certain
field, having large liquid funds at their disposal I think should
be limited in the matter of making loans to activities which would
contribute to their business and that loans to the market entirely
unrelated to their business should either be penalized or prohibited. I am not willing to concede. . .that you can not control
that outside market. I think some way can be found and should be
found to do so.

Testimony, Owen D. Young, February 4, 1931, U.S. Congress,
71st. 3rd session, Senate, Committee on Banking, Operation of the
National and Federal Reserve Banking Systems, pp. 358-359.

725.   RAID ON THE GUARDIAN TRUST (1920's)

This story of avarice, chicanery, official
negligence, and gullibility made a forceful impact
on public opinion during the early 1930's and helped
bring about reforms. The report was made by Walter
Seymour, senior examiner of the Committee on Banking
and Currency.

The closing of the Guardian Trust Co., like that of the Union
Trust, was not the result of the "Michigan bank holiday" nor the
"National bank holiday", but was the result of unsound practices
and mismanagement.
. . . .
 . . .the Guardian Trust Co., through the medium of its
accounting methods, has never issued a statement of condition which
has shown the true facts. These 25 subsidiaries were used by the
bank management to cover up those activities of the Trust Co. other
than of the banking business.
. . . .
From a summary of the activities of these subsidiaries we find
that the Guardian Trust Co., besides being a bank, was actually
engaged in the following businesses:
1.   The operation of an office building.
2.   The operation of a chain of hotels.
3.   The operation of a coal mine.
4.   The ownership of a produce market house.
5.   The operation of residential, apartment, and business
     property.
6.   The holding of vacant allotment property.
7.   Speculation in stocks and bonds.
. . . .
The affairs of the Guardian Trust Co. were dictated and managed almost wholly by J. Arthur House, president, and Mr. H. C.
Robinson, executive vice-president. Associated with these 2 were
4 or 5 of the other senior officers; however, all important questions and final decisions were left to the Messrs. House and
Robinson.
The Guardian Trust Co. has never issued a report to stockholders which showed the earnings for any period. The stockholders
were apprised of the company's earnings through the medium of a
report read at the annual meeting of stockholders. None of the
published annual reports or statements of the bank disclosed the
earnings.
. . . .
Earnings were reported greatly in excess of their actual
amount, as a result of which excessive dividends and bonuses were
paid. The entire method of reporting earnings and the condition
of the bank was misleading and contrary to sound principles of
accounting.
. . . .

The profits of the Guardian Trust Co. were exaggerated in the annual report, due to the fact that in preparing the consolidated statement, only the operations of certain subsidiaries were included, these being companies that were making money, while losing companies were completely ignored.

. . . .

One of the chief reasons for the widespread confidence in the Guardian Trust Co. prior to the closing of that institution in February 1933 was undoubtedly the belief by depositors that their savings, often those of a lifetime, were adequately protected through the medium of frequent examinations as to the condition of the bank by National, State, and local bodies.

Sections 710-1 to 710-36 of the Ohio Banking laws provide that the superintendent of banks must examine each bank "at least once each year." Section 9281 of the Federal Code provides that examinations should be made by the Federal examiners "at least twice each year", except that examinations by State authorities may be accepted in the case of State banks.

(Report re: Examinations)

There have been only six examinations of the Guardian Trust Co. conducted in the period from 1922 to the time of the bank's closing as follows:

1922:   December 8, Federal Reserve examiners assisting.
1924:   October 11, Federal Reserve examiners assisting.
1926:   February 26, Federal Reserve examiners assisting.
1928:   January 27, Federal Reserve examiners assisting.
1929:   November 15, State department examiners only.
1932:   February 29, Federal Reserve examiners assisting.

In our report regarding the examinations of the Guardian Trust Co. we have severely criticized the number and the methods of these examinations. Also, we have condemned the "examinations" made by the directors' examining committee.

. . . .

A group of officers and directors of the bank formed a syndicate known as the "Directors' Syndicate" to trade in the Guardian Trust Co. stock. The syndicate was predicated on the plan that each director and officer of the bank was to subscribe to a certain number of shares in the syndicate, and the syndicate was to acquire the stock from the outside matter.

Mr. H. C. Force, vice president, acting as agent for the syndicate, borrowed from the retirement fund to make the stock purchases for the syndicate.

The syndicate was never completed, and was left with 287 shares of Guardian bank stock on hand. Thereupon, these 287 shares were sold by Mr. Force, after approval had been arranged by Mr. House, to the employees' retirement fund at $265.23 per share, notwithstanding the fact that the retirement fund had purchased only the day before 49 shares in the open market at $69.72 a share.

Report, Walter H. Seymour, May 3, 1934, U.S. Congress, 73rd, 2nd session, Senate, Committee on Banking and Currency, Stock Exchange Practices, XVIII, pp. 7978, 7979, 7980, 7983, 7985-7986.

726.   COUNTRY BANKS IN THE "FARM-LAND" GAME (1930's)

As had happened often before in American economic history, banks became adjuncts to a real estate or other business. (See Source No. 256). Elmer Adams, president of the First National Bank of Fergus Falls, Minnesota, a town of 7,000 which was the county seat of Otter Tail County, discusses the situation.

In the past eight years nine [state] banks have failed in our county. No national bank has failed. While the failure of these nine banks was due in part to unwise loans during the land-boom period, there was dishonesty in nearly every one, and 10 officials of the banks which failed in the Fergus Falls area were sent to the pentitentiary.

It may be interesting to know that 85 bank officials and employees were sentenced to the penitentiary during the incumbency of superintendent A. J. Veigel, who has just retired as commissioner of banks after 10 years of service. Practically every one of these little banks which failed was in the farm-land game. For their profits they took second and third mortgages, and these second and third mortgages drifted into the bank, and when they once had this paper on their hands they thought it was necessary to make advances to help the occupants of the land carry on. Sometimes additional machinery or twine with which to bind their grain, and the banks, in trying to save what they already had loaned, followed up. A crop failure or an improper diversion of the proceeds of the crops soon put loans of this character into the frozen class.

These small banks not only borrowed when they ought not have done so, but they had no secondary reserve of any kind which could be cashed when people wanted their deposits. If their stockholders had been substantial men of the community who had had any funds with which to engage in the banking business, there would have been some chance of relief, but about the first intimation the director and stockholders had of the condition of their bank was when they were called upon to mortgage their own property and raise funds in hopes that the bank might be saved.

I do not believe it is any exaggeration to say that in 90 per cent of the country banks the directors have no knowledge of the condition of their banks. Recently there have been many lawsuits in which directors have been sued, not only for receiving funds in their institutions after they were insolvent, but for their failure to use proper diligence in guarding the funds which were attached to the institution through their good names.

Testimony, Elmer E. Adams, March 2, 1931, U.S. Congress, 71st, 3rd session, Senate, Committee on Banking, Operation of the National and Federal Reserve Banking Systems, pp. 599-600.

727. THE TELEPHONE GROUP OF INVESTMENT BANKS (1939)

The traditional lines of connection between business
firm and banking house were still maintained. Charles
Mitchell was chairman of Blyth & Company, Inc., and had
been chairman of the National City Bank of New York.
Peter R. Nehemkis, Jr. was special counsel from the
investment banking section of the Securities and Exchange
Commission. The following is their testimony.

Mr. NEHEMKIS. And now will you tell me which of those six or
seven [investment banking] houses are regarded as being members
of the Telephone group?
Mr. MITCHELL. I would say that for a long period of years--
and I give that from recollection--the business has been headed by
J. P. Morgan and latterly, by Morgan Stanley & Company. And there
have always been in that group, always according to my recollection, Kuhn Loeb & Company, Kidder Peabody & Company, Lee Higginson
& Company, and latterly, Lee Higginson Corporation.
Since Morgan Stanley & Company have handled this financing,
those names have headed the list. There have also followed them
in all of the issues, The First Boston Corporation, Brown Harriman
& Company, and Edward B. Smith & Company, and those names, by and
large, have been the names that have appeared in the public advertising.
Mr. NEHEMKIS. And it was that list of names and those underwriting houses which you have just enumerated that you regard as
being the group?
Mr. MITCHELL. Those names have appeared so often with the
head of the group, with the head of the underwriting syndicate,
that I would say that they were regarded as the principal names
in the telephone business. I would say that in certain issues,
that list has been materially enlarged.
. . . .
For instance, in the issue of December 2, there was
$140,000,000, there were---
Mr. NEHEMKIS (interposing). That is the American Telephone
& Telegraph Co. issue?
Mr. MITCHELL. Yes. There were 97 names in these issues.
The unusual feature appears of the manager of the account guaranteeing to the issuer the responsibility of the underwriters. You
will bear in mind that over a long period of years, the underwriting house first bought the issue outright, then formed a
separate banking group that might be followed by a purchase group
and a selling group. The underwriter, the principal underwriter,
took the sole responsibility.
Since we had the Security Act, it will be borne in mind that
the responsibility of the underwriters is severed.
Now, when one finds a list of 97 names scattered all over the
country, we meet immediately the problem of due diligence on the
part of all of these underwriters and the work of the underwriting

manager, the work of the lawyers, becomes doubled and redoubled. In fact, I will say that one of the principal difficulties in the long underwriting list today is to really satisfy the requirements of the law on the subject of due diligence by underwriters.

I am making that point in passing, Mr. Chairman, as a point of particular interest, and I mention it because in this telephone financing we find something that is rather unusual. The obligation is severed, ordinarily, but in these telephone issues, Morgan Stanley guaranteed to the issuer the responsibility of their entire underwriting list.

Testimony, Charles E. Mitchell, December 14, 1939, <u>Verbatim</u> <u>Record of the Proceedings of the Temporary National Economic</u> <u>Committee</u>, X, p. 91.

728. "I HEAR YOU WANT A TOOTH PULLED" (1940)

Once more illustrating the Kuhn, Loeb dictum that bankers are very good neighbors (see Source No. 703). John Schiff, partner in Kuhn, Loeb and Co., an investment banking house, testifies.

Mr. NEHEMKIS. Now in view of the fact that the Armstrong Cork account had been a former account of the Guaranty Company and in view of the fact that you and your associates recognized that E. B. Smith & Company had certain relationships to that account were you not somewhat reluctant to discuss this matter with Mr. Freeman? [of Armstrong Cork]?

Mr. SCHIFF. Well, I think we told Mr. Freeman that after all, any company could pick its own bankers, it was entirely up to the company----

Mr. NEHEMKIS. But---

Mr. SCHIFF. May I go on with that--that if the company wanted to leave the people who had done their banking in the past, for some legitimate reason, naturally we should be glad to receive them provided they were the type of company that came up to the standards, but on the other hand if it was a perfectly happy relationship and they had been successful in taking care of their needs and had done it properly, we had no desire to try to take that away from them.

Mr. NEHEMKES. Mr. Schiff, according to the professional code of the street, would it not have been distinctly unethical for you to discuss this business with Mr. Freeman without first contacting E. B. Smith & Company, or unless you were quite certain that the company was coming to you of their own free will?

Mr. SCHIFF. I think it would have been bad business.

Mr. NEHEMKIS. But not unethical?

Mr. SCHIFF. Well, unethical and bad business, but after all you have a certain code of ethics, which I agree with, but you are also guided by what is good business and what is bad business.

Mr. NEHEMKIS. But you do think that it would have been distinctly unethical to have discussed this with an official of the Armstrong Cork Company without first having been in contact, let us say, with Mr. Swan's house?

Mr. SCHIFF. I think it would have been unethical and bad business, just as if some dentist called me on the telephone and said, "I hear you want a tooth pulled," and tried to get the trade away from my usual dentist who had been doing a satisfactory job.

Mr. NEHEMKES. So you feel that under similar circumstances it would be necessary, if one were adhering to the code of ethics of the Street, first to be clear of the other banking firm.

Mr. SCHIFF. But I want to point out one thing. It is not only the code of ethics; it is what is good business, what is good business and bad business for the continuation of your future business with your clients.

Mr. HENDERSON. With your clients and with other members of the fraternity, too?

Mr. SCHIFF. I suppose there, but I mean basically with the corporations with which you deal.

Testimony, John M. Schiff, January 10, 1940, <u>Verbatim Record</u> <u>of the Proceedings of the Temporary National Economic Committee</u>, X, p. 547.

..

729. THE BUSINESS OF ECONOMIC KNOWLEDGE (1955)

The following stock market operator defined the speculator as "one who observes the future and acts before it occurs." Both financial foreknowledge and economic knowledge were helpful. But the speculator, despite himself, tended to judge knowledge by its usefulness to his purpose.

[Mr. BARUCH.] I think economists as rule. . .take for granted they know a lot of things. If they really knew so much, they would have all the money and we would have none.

. . . .

[The CHAIRMAN.] Is it true you do not think very highly of any of them [i.e., economists]?

Mr. BARUCH. No. I will tell you, Senator, why I think economists came into popularity. After 1929, these businessmen and everybody said, "What is the matter with me? Where did I go wrong?" So they had to go to a doctor. The only economic doctor is an economist and they go to him and say, "Professor, what about

so and so?" And these men can take facts and figures and bring
them together, but their predictions are not worth any more than
ours. If they were, they would have all the money and we would
not have anything.

The CHAIRMAN. Do you think the only criterion, valid criterion, of knowledge is how much money you have?

Mr. BARUCH. Oh, no; oh, no. I do not think so, sir. But
the economists deal with money.

The CHAIRMAN. They deal with ideas, do they not?

Mr. BARUCH. Sir?

The CHAIRMAN. I thought they dealt with ideas rather than
money.

Mr. BARUCH. They may have ideas like philosophers, but if
economists could predict what was going to happen in the future,
I rather suspect--I do not know, but I rather suspect--that they
all would speculate if they knew, and they could make a lot of
money. But I do not want to discuss any particular branch of
livelihood. They all have difficulties. I think there are some
very fine men in that field. I differ with many of them, but they
are of the Keynes School.

. . . .

The CHAIRMAN. Since you mentioned Dr. Keynes, I have been
told that the late Dr. Keynes was extremely successful as a speculator. Have you not heard that?

Mr. BARUCH. Yes, I have heard that. He made a lot of money
at it. But he did not follow the views that he publicly advised.

I had many contacts with Mr. Keynes on the Treaty of
Versailles. He was a very smart fellow, though I did not agree
with him.

The CHAIRMAN. I thought that would have enhanced your
respect for Mr. Keynes, if he made a great deal of money. You seem
to have very little for Mr. [John K.] Galbraith because he has not
made any money.

Mr. BARUCH. No, I am not against Mr. Galbraith at all. And
I am not for any fellow that runs any of the great rackets because
he has made a lot of money. I do not mean to compare them. Money-
making is not all there is. The fellow with the most money is
not the man we ought to look up to. No, I am certainly not making
any disparaging remarks about Mr. Galbraith. I only made a general
observation about economists.

Testimony, Bernard Baruch, March 23, 1955, U.S. Congress,
84th, 1st session, Senate, Committee on Banking and Currency,
Stock Market Study, pp. 1001, 1002, 1003.

730.   FEDERAL RESERVE--INDEPENDENT OF WHOM? (1958)

An imprecise definition of a slippery concept--i.e.,
"independence." Being questioned is M. S. Szymczak, a
member of the Board of Governors of the Federal Reserve
System since June, 1933.

The CHAIRMAN. Now, I want to ask you about the independence
of the Federal Reserve.
Whom do you consider you are independent from?
Mr. SZYMCZAK. Independent of any influence on the part of
any particular party in power in the administration; independent
of any particular departments of Government; independent of the
banks; independent of the insurance companies and other private
financial groups, but not independent of Government as a whole,
and not independent of the people of the economy.
The CHAIRMAN. You are not independent from the President,
from the executive branch?
Me. SZYMCZAK. We are not?
The CHAIRMAN. Are you?
Mr. SZYMCZAK. Well, under the law we are not reporting to
the President. We report to the Congress of the United States.
The CHAIRMAN. That is right, but you are not independent
of Congress. You are a servant of Congress.
Mr. SZYMCZAK. Oh, no, we are not independent of Congress.
The CHAIRMAN. How do you reconcile your statement with the
Constitution of the United States, Article II, Section III, which
says that the president shall see that the laws are faithfully
executed?
The Federal Reserve Act being a law, how do you say that you
are independent from the Executive, who is charged with the constitutional duty of seeing that the laws, including the Federal
Reserve Act, are faithfully executed?
Mr. SZYMCZAK. Well, the President of the United States is
many Departments of Government. It is not an individual, so
therefore, you come to the Treasury, quite naturally.
The Treasury would have to tell us whether we are conforming
or not conforming. We don't construe the congressional action
on the Federal Reserve System to mean that we have to take orders
from the Secretary of the Treasury.
The CHAIRMAN. Well, I didn't say "take orders." But I am
talking about the President of the United States. I would like
to know how you reconcile your statement about independence with
the constitutional duty of the President under Article II, Section
III of the Constitution which requires him to see that the laws
are faithfully executed.
Now, does that include the Federal Reserve banks, too?
Mr. SZYMCZAK. I presume it would----
The CHAIRMAN. Well, his is charged with the duty, then----
Mr. SZYMCZAK. But the President cannot see that each and
every Agency or Government does what the Congress has asked it

to do. Therefore, he has people who are called secretaries and
head of independent agencies that follow through for him.
     The CHAIRMAN. Including Cabinet officers, of course.
     Mr. SZYMCZAK. That is right.
     The CHAIRMAN. I shall not pursue that any further. I think
the Board has gone a little far with independence. I think you
have left the impression with the country that we have four branches of Government in this country, the Legislative, Judiciary,
and Executive, and the Federal Reserve System. You don't want
to leave that impression, do you?
     Mr. SZYMCZAK. Not at all.
     The CHAIRMAN. You are just subject to the laws under the
jurisdiction of the President which the Constitution conferred
upon him.
     Mr. MULTER. May I interrupt?
     The CHAIRMAN. Yes.
     Mr. MULTER. On that very subject, Governor, during your time
of service as a member of the Board of Governors, has any President
of the United States exercised or attempted to exercise any
jurisdiction over the activities of the Federal Reserve Board?
     Mr. SZYMCZAK. No; we are constantly in touch with any
President and his Cabinet, particularly the Secretary of the
Treasury, and also the Comptroller of the Currency, and also the
F.D.I.C., because of our various responsibilities. So therefore,
we are constantly in touch with them and they with us, because we
can't operate in a vacuum, as indicated by the Chairman. We have
to know what the other Agencies of Government are doing.
     Mr. MULTER. You exchange information back and forth and try
to cooperate as much as possible without letting any other agency
dictate to you your course of action.
     Mr. SZYMCZAK. The essence of monetary policy, and Congress
wisely decided this long ago, is that it cannot be subject to the
whims of any particular individual, because if the whims of any
individual, whether a private interest, banking, or somebody
else, are to be respected, then you would be up here today and
down there tomorrow, and then the third day you would be out the
window. So Congress wisely said we have to have a continuing
policy and know where to place the blame and the responsibility.

     Testimony, M. S. Szymczak, April 16, 1958, U.S. Congress,
85th, 2nd session, House of Representatives, Select Committee on
Small Business, Problems of Small-Business Financing, II, pp. 427-
428.

          731. FEDERAL FINANCING OF SMALL BUSINESS (1958)

          Under discussion was the advisability of Congressional
     action to create a new federal agency to finance small
     business beyond the ability of the Small Business

Administration. Reference was made to an earlier bill
that had set up a committee consisting of the Treasury
Secretary, the Commerce Secretary, and the Administrator
of S.B.A. James Vardaman is the speaker; he had been
a member of the Board of Governors of the Federal Reserve
System since April, 1946. Prior to that he had been
counsel and officer for a number of banks and insurance
companies in the St. Louis area.

[Mr. VARDAMAN.] I have had the privilege of knowing every
Secretary of the Treasury since I was a child, beginning with
William G. McAdoo [1913-1918]. I have never known a Secretary
of the Treasury but one who had a basic understanding of the
responsibilities, the problems, the heart-breaking experience of
little business. We do not select under our system of Government
that type of man to be Secretary of the Treasury.

I have never known any Secretary of Commerce who had ever
experienced, except probably during his early childhood, in a log
cabin, as most of them come from, that sort of experience. It
is not criticism of them. It is simply that they have not been
down and gone through the mill.

. . . .

Mr. EVINS. And that its [i.e., the Reconstruction Finance
Corporation] greatest contribution was to big business of the
Nation.

Mr. VARDAMAN. Oh, yes, percentagewise, there is no question
about that, and I would say--well, I do not like to mention dates,
because they indicate people, but at the last, we will say, it
became almost solely the vehicle of big business. But I would
hope that if this organization, this small business effort is to
be made by the Congress, that you would create a board and keep
your hands on them, and see that it does not degenerate into a
creature of big business, because even though the Federal Reserve
statistical report is not yet ready (you have five volumes of it).
I suppose all of you have read them, having nothing else to do.
There is sufficient indication there to show quite clearly that
there is a rather troublesome gap in the national financial structure.

There is a real necessity for somebody to push aggressively
the organization and perpetuation of small business enterprises.

. . . .

But unless you make them aggressively responsible, or rather
responsible for an aggressive campaign, to seek out and encourage
the organization of small business, I do not think you need to
start the thing. But it will be a futile effort if you make it
the stepchild of any department. How many small-bussness men are
on the Business Advisory Council of the Secretary of Commerce?
It is no reflection on the Secretary or the Council. This small
business is Greek to the average big-business man, and unless he
has come up the hard way, as I happen to have been fortunate
enough to do, and some of you have been fortunate enough to do,
it is just awfully hard for him to conceive of a business being

worth while because it only employed 4 people and only wants to
borrow $7,000 a year. That is peanuts in this day and time, but
it fails to be peanuts if you happen to be in a small town and
are sitting down there waiting for reasonable credit.
. . . .
     I read the last bill presented, 1 in the House and 1 in the
Senate, and those bills, the highlight in it which I just cannot
recommend, is the fact that it creates a policy board consisting
of the ex-officio, the Secretary of the Treasury and the Secretary
of Commerce, and I believe the Director of the Small Business
Administration. My objection, to repeat, is you don't mind, sir,
to that, Congressmen, is that it makes immediately a stepchild out
of this Small Business effort. It gives the final authority, the
first authority and final authority, to---
     Mr. MULTER. I am in complete agreement with you, sir.
     Mr. VARDAMAN. --to a group of men who, in most cases, have
neither had the experience nor are they in sympathy, because they
have no concept of the problems of the little-bitty businessmen.
When you talk about small businesses, most of these people think
a quarter of a million or half a million dollars.
     I am talking about loans that run from 20 thousand, 25
thousand down. That is where we have got to create purchasing
power, and there is where your fatalities, your mortality rate
in these small businesses is the highest.

     Testimony, James K. Vardaman, Jr., April 28, 1958, U.S.
Congress, 85th, 2nd session, House of Representatives, Select
Committee on Small Business, Problems of Small-Business Financing,
II, pp. 489, 493, 495, 496.

     732. THE SECURITIES INDUSTRY HAS MODERNIZED (1973)

     Between 1952 and 1970 the number of shareholders
in the country rose from 6.5 to 30.9 million. Trading
volume rose from over one billion in 1961 to more than
2.5 billion in 1967. Daily turnover grew from three to
over 20 million shares. By the late 60s, the New York
Stock Exchange was simply unable to keep up with this
cascading volume of transactions. Following is an account
by Robert M. Gardiner, president of Reynolds Securities,
Inc. and an official in the Securities Industry Association, outlining the steps taken by the securities Industry
to meet the challenge of modernization.

The causes of the securities transaction processing problem
in the late 1960's were twofold: Paper and the segmentation of
the securities processing industry itself.

On the paper side, the documents and procedures in use during
the 1960's were too old fashioned, too slow and too complex. They
did not permit the prompt, efficient handling of the enormous
upsurge in volume experienced during the bull market of the 1960's.
Since the late 1960's, when the problem was first identified, the
brokerage community has made significant strides forward in its
capacity to process securities. Let me list just some of these
improvements for you.

(1) Securities firms have upgraded significantly the caliber
and capabilities of the operations work force. Between 1966 and
1971, stock exchange firms added 2.3 operations and administrative-
support personnel for each new salesman. The percentage increases
were 52 percent in the operational and support area versus a 37-
percent gain for the sales force. Training of supervisory and
clerical personnel has been upgraded markedly. Clerical turnover
has been reduced from 55 percent per year and more in the 1968-70
period to under 40 percent in mid-1972.

(2) Firms have modernized operating systems through major
investments in automation. A survey of seven large firms last
year revealed that their computer capacity has increased by 80
percent over the level that existed in 1968. The number of pro-
gramers employed by these firms, a sign of the quality of such
effort, has more than doubled in the same period. Joint industry
activities, such as the New York Stock Exchange's clearing facilities, the Midwest Service Bureau, and the Pacific Coast Clearing
Corp. has provided expanded operational capacity for smaller firms.

(3) The industry has created a series of new centralized
facilities and procedures designed to simplify the settlement of
securities transactions and to immobilize stock certificates.

Under that broad heading:

(a) The Depository Trust Co., formerly Central Certificate
Service of the New York Stock Exchange, has reduced the physical
handling of securities in transactions between brokers and is on
the way to doing the same in the settlement of transactions with
banks.

(b) The National Clearing Corporation, NCC, created by the
NASD, is producing needed improvements in processing of over-the-
counter securities.

(c) The New York and American Stock Exchanges have merged
their stock clearing operations into the Securities Industry
Automation Corp., SIAC, to eliminate duplication and standaridze
industry clearing efforts.

(d) The SLA Securities Processing Committee, made up of representatives of both national and regional firms, is at work on
the goal of a single, cost effective clearing and settlement system.

(e) The SIA, the National Coordinating Group for Comprehensive Securities Depositories and the New York Clearing House
Association have officially endorsed the concept of funds-valued-
tomorrow as the national standard for the payment of all securities
transactions throughout the entire securities industry.

(4)   Reporting and internal control systems have been upgraded materially throughout the industry, so that management
can be made quickly aware of potential problems in the operational
area.

(5)   Interrelationships between banks and brokers in the processing of securities transactions have been enhanced through a
number of improved EDP procedures in the receipt and delivery of
securities, transfers and dividends. The CUSIP numbering system
with its standard identification for securities is operative.
BASIC, which has completed its work, contributed a number of
studies and recommendations that materially aided this cooperative
effort.

(6)   In the area of rulemaking, the SEC, the exchanges, and
the NASD, have made important changes in the interest or safe-
guarding customers' securities, as well as to streamline operational activities.

Under that broad heading, four points:

(a)   The net capital rule of the New York Stock Exchange was
modified last year to reduce the maximum capital ratio from 20 to
1 to 15 to 1, and to provide an early warning system when a firm's
ratio reaches 10 to 1. Also, securities differences and aged dividend receivables produce a mandatory charge against capital, whereas previously there was discretion in treating such items.

(b)   Rules require monthly reports to be submitted to the
exchanges and the NASD on operational performance, capital
strength, and profitability.

(d)   In the over-the-counter area, the NASD has effected
rules on mandatory buyins of OTC securities and introduced new
standards through its National Clearing Corp.....

A great deal has been done to upgrade operational facilities
and to assure that the difficulties which occurred in 1967 and 1968
will not be repeated. Our industry today is able to handle with
facility much higher volumes than it could in 1968. Last year
in my appearance before this subcommittee, I expressed the view
that securities firms were capable of handling without an operational jam daily trading volume in a magnitude well above 20
million shares on the New York Stock Exchange, 10 million on the
AMEX and 15 million in NASDAQ securities. This would be nearly
twice the volume that caused the industry to operate on a 4-day
trading week and under shortened hours in the late 1960's. We
believe that this estimate continues today to be a reasonable
assessment of the capacity of the operations side of our industry.

Testimony, September 14, 1973, U.S. Congress, 93rd, 1st
session, House of Representatives, Committee on Interstate and
Foreign Commerce, Subcommittee on Commerce and Finance,
Securities Exchange Act Amendments of 1973. Hearings....,
Part 5, (Washington, D.C.: Government Printing Office, 1973),
pp. 1944-1945.

733.   THE SALES FORCE OF SECURITIES (1973)

The employment of a large sales force by securities
firms was based on a market composed almost wholly of
individual buyers and sellers. Personal contact was
crucial. During the years 1969-1974, however, as the
stock market slumped, the securities sales force shrank
by some 20,000. By 1980, however, as individual investors began returning to the market, brokerage employment
started to rise. Merrill J. Chapman, president of the
Association of Investment Brokers, sketches the development of this sales force over the years.

Around the turn of this century, New York Stock Exchange (NYSE)
stockbrokers, no longer able to handle all their customers personally, took unto themselves assistants. The assistants were assigned
to service certain customers designated by their employers. As customers would call or come in to do business, they would ask for
their assigned "man." And, so, the customers' man came into existence. A simple registration procedure was inaugurated in the
1920's and in the normal course of events these quasi-stockbrokers
began to develop a following, a clientele as it were, of public
investors.
    Their numbers mounted, in the late 1930's and 1940's to 10,000
at the half-century mark; spurted to 25,000 in the late 1950's; more
than doubled in the decade of the 1960's. We estimate that today
there are somewhat over 50,000 registrants of the New York Stock
Exchange, down a few thousand from the peak of recent years. Along
the way, an examination became a requirement together with a 6-month
training period. The constitution and rules of the NYSE were amended and modified to provide for this vast body of registered representatives as they were dubbed by the NYSE. This, very briefly, is
the history of what has become the largest people-unit in the securities industry working directly with public investors.
    However, to further explain this group, we call to the sub-
committee's attention the fact that there are a large number of
registered persons who service institutions only, such as pension
funds, banks, and insurance companies, for their firm. There is
another large number of such registered persons who, while registered, function primarily as secretaries, order clerks, analysts,
et cetera, and may or may not have a limited clientele as well.
Thus, we estimate that perhaps 30,000 registered persons with the
NYSE are full-time retail-oriented stockbrokers who have built up
a clientele and their incomes and careers are dependent on nurtur-
ing and building that clientele. As an aside at this point, we do
not address ourselves to the estimated 100,000 additional full- and
part-time NASD registrants with broker-dealer firms nor to another
estimated 100,000 NASD registrants who are with insurance companies

and whose registration has accomplished solely to sell mutual funds
provided by these entities.

Testimony, July 20, 1973, U.S. Congress, 93rd, 1st session,
House of Representatives, Committee on Interstate and Foreign
Commerce, Subcommittee on Commerce and Finance, Securities Exchange
Act Amendments of 1973, Part 4. Hearings...., (Washington, D.C.:
Government Printing Office, 1973), pp. 1355-1356.

734. DETERIORATING LIQUIDITY ON THE STOCK MARKET (1973)

      Normally, charges on the securities market are
regulated by a fee-system, established and maintained
by the securities industry. Fundamental to enforcement
of the system is the prevalence of individual transactions. With the advent of institutional investors --
such as pension funds, banks, and money managers -- it
becomes possible to negotiate fees to fit the circumstances of each large transaction. Brokers as a whole
were critical of such a development since it diminished
their bargaining ability. By the beginning of the 1980s,
negotiated sales of large blocks of stock made up nearly
one third of all sales. M. James Arachtingi, chairman
of the board and president of Auerbach, Pollak & Richardson,
Inc., an institutional research brokerage house, states
some of the fears of brokers.

We share the concern of others--financial institutions, stock
brokers, and the public corporations--that the hub of the U.S.
capital system, the auction marketplace, is rapidly disintegrating.
Meanwhile, an array of well-intentioned repairmen argue over some
of the less important parts of its structure, such as the system.
Should the auction market system become further disrupted, this
drive wheel, which provides the growth momentum for our free enterprise system, may never again function smoothly....
    The key problems facing this country's capital system, on our
opinion, relate to concentration of ownership and lack of liquidity,
not fixed versus negotiated rates.
    Because of these problems the experience to date with negotiat-
ed rates has shown that neither the institutions nor brokers have
reacted in coping with negotiated rates as those favoring the end
of fixed rates expected they would. We present both factual and
empirical evidence showing the severity and lack of success to date
of the negotiated-rate experiment.
    The effect of negotiated rates has broader significance than
the revenue and profit losses now threatening the economic viability
of the securities industry.

The current environment of negotiations has not increased either market or capital liquidity. There is, in fact, growing evidence that the opposite has occurred.

Negotiated rates appear to be having a negative effect on the capital formation and commitment process.

Because of fear of fiduciary liability to always procure the lowest net-cost transaction, including the brokerage fee, institutions still seek net trade in the nonauction, nonpublic third and fourth markets. This fragmentation of the marketplace has been a contributing cause in the increasing inability of the public auction-market system to provide depth and liquidity. It is in the best interests of all investors that all traders who would make markets must compete fairly and under the same regulations, with full public exposure.

We strongly suggest no further action be taken in the rate area until the fundamental inconsistency between the Congress' desire to create a free-market environment and the unnatural impediment to that environment—the requirement of the lowest net cost—be realistically assessed and corrected in H.R. 5050.

We respectfully submit legislative recommendations dealing with the need to create free competitive market environment that is essential if negotiated rates are to become economically feasible and the bulwark of the American capitalist system—the auction marketplace—is to survive.

Less than a dozen years ago institutions accounted for less than 30 percent of New York Stock Exchange activity and owned an even smaller percentage of the total value of its equities. Today, it is generally believed, institutions own directly, or as fiduciaries, approximately 45 percent of all NYSE equity values and account for 70 percent of the public volume. We have rapidly evolved from a market whose activity was affected by hundreds of thousands of stock buyers and sellers to a market of several hundred traders and investors. Some would even argue that the bulk of activity on today's markets is generated by only a few score of very large and influential buyers and sellers in a few store of listed issues.

What is the impact of this concentration of the country's wealth on the free flow of capital?

There are several important responses that could be made to this question. But the one that cries out with increasing urgency, whose significance is materially altering the free flow of capital can be summed up in two words—Deteriorating Liquidity.

Testimony, July 20, 1973, U.S. Congress, 93rd, 1st session, House of Representatives, Committee on Interstate and Foreign Commerce and Finance, Securities Exchange Act Amendments of 1973, Part 4. Hearings...., (Washington, D.C.: Government Printing Office, 1973), pp. 1377-1379.

735. INSIDER ABUSE IN COMMERCIAL BANKS (1977)

Many of the earliest commercial banks in the United
States were organized in order to lend money to the organizers of the same banks. The possibility of thus gaining
an advantage became an incentive to formation and operation
of banks. In time, such practices were outlawed. Yet,
being on the inside of a bank continues to constitute a
potential advantage. How insiders use the advantage is
explained by George A. LeMaistre, chairman of the Federal
Deposit Insurance Corporation, an official body charged
with policing such practices.

It is important to note that the problem of insider abuse is a
general one not limited to overdrafts or compensating balances or
extension of credit on preferential terms. For example, over the
years the FDIC has uncovered and responded to insider overreaching
involving exorbitant management fees, excessive legal fees, preferential treatment in the purchase and sale of assets, favorable lease
arrangements, misuse of bank assets, and other devices whereby insiders use their institutions for their personal advantage.

The question of what constitutes abuse is, of course, one which
generates some disagreement. My own view, and the predominant view
at the FDIC, is that insider conduct is abusive and constitutes an
unsafe and unsound banking practice when an insider obtains a benefit which is not available to a noninsider otherwise similarly situated and when the result of the insider's obtaining that benefit is
detrimental to the bank. While such a standard is easy to apply in
many cases, in other instances the question is a complex and difficult one....

As you know, the most glaring example of the abuse of an insider relationship is the failure of U.S. National Bank in San Diego,
a failure which was caused by what has been termed "a riot of self-
dealing." This failure led the FDIC to reassess the effectiveness
of its policy and procedures in dealing with insider abuse. The
result of this appraisal was the adoption of a regulation dealing
with insider transactions which became effective on May 1, 1976.
The Corporation's reasons for adopting this regulation are stated
further in the preamble to the regulation and in the notice published in the Federal Register which announced its adoption. This
notice stated:

> This action is based on the experience of the Corpora-
> tion which indicates that many banks have suffered loan
> losses, loss of revenue, excessive costs and other sub-
> stantial economic detriment as a result of ill-
> considered transactions with insiders. The need for
> more rigorous supervision of such transactions by
> boards of directors and bank supervisory agencies is
> indicated by the fact that abusive self-dealing has
> been the primary cause or a significant contributing

cause in more than half of all bank failures
since 1960, including the failure of 30 non-
member insured banks. The most dramatic example
of the harm which can result from abusive self-
dealing is the 1973 failure of the United States
National Bank, San Diego, California, for which
the Corporation has had to establish a reserve of
$150 million for loss to the deposit insurance
fund. Review of existing and past "problem" bank
cases also reveals insider overreaching as a significant source of serious difficulty. Moreover,
an insider transaction that is not effected on
an "arm's length" basis will lead to a diminution
of earnings and an erosion of capital, even where
the immediate result is not the bank's failure or
its designation of a "problem" institution. It
follows, therefore, that insider transactions
whose terms and conditions cannot be justified
when viewed in light of all the circumstances
surrounding the transaction, increase the risk of
loss to depositors and ultimately to the deposit
insurance fund. In addition, insider transactions
whose terms and conditions cannot be justified
constitute a diversion to insiders of resources
that properly belong to all shareholders on a pro
rata basis, as well as a misallocation of a
community's deposited funds....

Most importantly, the regulation itself makes clear that formal
compliance with the board of director review and approval requirements does not relieve the bank of its duty to conduct its operations in a "safe and sound" manner. Nor does it prevent the Corporation from taking whatever supervisory action is deemed necessary
and appropriate. And, we have made it clear that the FDIC board
views any significant insider overreaching as an unsafe or unsound
banking practice, and, as such, will not be tolerated.

That this is the case is reflected in the Corporation's record
in bringing 51 cease and desist orders since January 1, 1978. As
discussion below reflects, 35 out of the 51 cease and desist actions
brought during this period were aimed at least in part at correcting
some insider abuse.

Particularly notable are 8(b) actions brought this summer
against five related banks in which former and present officers
and directors were charged with abuse of their authority by causing
the banks to pay excessive expenses to companies owned by insiders.
These cases represent a significant innovation in that recovery
was sought from the individuals for the first time in the history
of the use of the Section 8(b) power -- bringing what is tantamount

to a derivative action. By consent, the offending insiders agreed
to reimburse the banks in an amount agreeable to the FDIC and the
state supervisor.

Testimony, September 28, 1977, U.S. Congress, 95th, 1st session,
House of Representatives, Committee on Banking, Finance and Urban
Affairs, Subcommittee on Financial Institutions Supervision,
Regulation and Insurance, The Safe Banking Act of 1977. Hearings.
..., (Washington, D.C.: Government Printing Office, 1977), pp.
2377-2379, 2342.

736. DATA SOURCES FOR MULTINATIONAL BANKING (1981)

Since World War II American banks have become multinational but only since the advent of computers can the
banks command almost instantaneous contact with the principal money markets of the world. Factors favoring this
expansion include the need to finance operations of U.S.-
based multinational industrial and service corporations,
the growing stream of foreign investments in American
enterprises, and the rapid growth of private American
lending to foreign governments. Explaining one aspect of
these operations is the following account by Robert E. L.
Walker, vice-president and associate corporate counsel of
the Continental Illinois National Bank and Trust Company,
Chicago, Illinois.

As an international bank, our business is entirely dependent
upon the free flow of instantaneous communications. In the course
of our banking business, we need to have minute-by-minute intelligence from the money markets across the world. In addition, we need
to be able to provide fund-transfer services to our customers who
move large amounts of funds on a day-to-day basis from one country
to another. These same customers require immediate information
about their account balances in different parts of the world, the
state of the world foreign exchange, the interest-arbitrage markets
in the major world money centers, and so on.
For our own part, Continental Bank's management philosophy on
information and data processing is that it should be centralized
as fully as possible to allow management of the bank to have financial information which will allow them to monitor and to manage
credit exposures which the bank has by customer, country, and foreign currency. We perceive that this will enhance our customer
relationship in international banking and allow us to quickly recognize and meet the needs of our multinational customers for banking and financial services.

At present, Continental has either installed or plans to install computer capabilities throughout the world which will enable us to centrally process all of our account information, credit facilities, and general bank books in Chicago. So far we have implemented this approach in all of our European units, and I think a brief description of how we are processing data from Europe will best illustrate how we perceive our plans worldwide.

In Europe, our branches enter all of their transactions into intelligence data terminals which transmit this information over leased lines to Continental Bank's communications centers in Brussels, Belgium. The data, after being assembled and verified, is cued for high-speed data transmission to the central processing center in Chicago over international leased lines. The information is processed in Chicago; customer accounts and the bank's general ledgers are updated; management reports are created, customers' statements are produced; and the processed information is then sent back to Europe for use by those units the following business day.

By utilizing the centralized processing approach, we can have available to our account officers, on a worldwide basis, all of the banking activities transacted with the customer for whom they are responsible. We have found that this information is invaluable for providing services to our customers in making decisions concerning the proper management of the bank's assets and liabilities and insuring that we have prudent management of our worldwide loan portfolio.

It is planned to extend this system approach to other units throughout the world as soon as we have refined and completed our systems development in the European market. The full value of a system of this nature can be realized only when all of the units worldwide are included. Any inhibition or restriction in any way of data flow from unit to our head office would compromise and degrade the whole concept of this centralized processing system.

This global approach not only meets our own internal needs but also provides financial services which customers require to manage their international affairs. Customers may use our international deposits and clearing of checks in their accounts in our international branches and, importantly, to know the status of collected and uncollected funds which may be available for their use in managing their business.

Today, a customer may dial directly into our central computer and obtain this type of detailed information, not only on a specified account in an individual office of Continental, but also what activity has occurred in our total system relating to that company.

As an overview, this is how Continental Bank has used multinational data to manage its credit facilities worldwide, to provide bookkeeping and management reports to our banking system, to monitor foreign exchange and market facilities, and to provide financial ancillary services--the international cash management--to our domestic and international customers.

From that we have experienced, and from our perception of the transborder data flow issues, we are seriously concerned that we may be hampered in running our international banking business with efficiency, efficacy, and immediacy, which we believe are essential in the competitive international environments in which we operate.

From those issues, let me quickly highlight some potential threats and problems we see today in the transborder data flow developments.

One: We feel that there is a strong possibility that information flows could actually be blocked by restrictive legislation in foreign countries. If this occurs, Continental Bank's present cross-border processing approach would be seriously compromised at a loss of a very large investment in money, time, and committed resources.

Two: Legislation in this area varies from country to country, which results in a patch quilt of varying and highly technical laws lying across Europe which creates a confusing and burdensome task of trying to stay informed about, to interpret, and to comply with the multiple requirements of the host countries throughout the world.

Three: We are concerned that some countries may attempt to exercise extraterritorial control over data originating from their countries by mandating that the data carry with them the legal requirements of the laws of that country of their origin. This balkanization of laws could result in a catch-22 for banks in the United States having to meet the variegated requirements of different countries' laws and regulations.

Four: Artificial tariff barriers, through increasing higher charges for foreign communication lines and facilities, may become a critical inhibiting factor or even block the flow of data and centralized international processing.

Testimony, March 10, 1980, U.S. Congress, 96th, 2nd session, House of Representatives, International Data Flow. Hearings...., (Washington, D.C.: Government Printing Office, 1981), pp. 113-114.

737. REVOLUTION IN CONSUMER FINANCIAL SERVICES (1981)

Since the 1960s, the traditional division of labor in the field of consumer financial services has begun to disappear. The onetime unchallenged supremacy of the commercial bank has abated, older financial institutions have taken on new functions, and enterprises once completely removed from these consumer services have become leading factors. Somewhat defensively, a spokesman for the banking community, Walter B. Wriston, chairman of Citicorp, puts the case for restoring at least some of the ancient competitive position of the banks. His chart, "Who Does What," is an excellent graphic summary of the changes he describes.

We have heard arguments that despite banks' protestations,
regulation has not caused them to become a shrinking or less important part of the financial and credit markets , and regulation therefore little needs reform.

I find this an astonishing perception of reality.

Banks bear serious competitive disadvantages, like the cost of
reserves and insurance, and the impact of outdated legal and regulatory constraints, in their serving large corporate customers--
"big business," if you will. Literally billions of dollars of
business are bypassing the domestic banking system--not because
banks are unwilling to compete, but because regulatory burdens often
make alternate sources less expensive and more adequate.

Yet, it is when it comes to indiviuals, consumers, and small
business, that the laws really cripple the ability of banks to compete, and in this we are falling far behind.

In consumer financial services, the only ones suffering more
than the banks that are prevented from delivering services they're
best qualified to deliver, are the individuals and small businesses
that are prevented from enjoying these services.

We have also heard that inflation is the underlying cause of
the crisis engulfing traditional consumer banking institutions, and
that when inflation returns to normal, so will the industry.

This overlooks several conspicuous changes. One is the creation of revolutionary technology that the banking laws of the 30s
could never have contemplated, but that society today expects and
demands.

Another is the fact that for the past dozen years, "normal"
inflation has been a series of skyrocketing rises and precipitous
declines, with each decline setting a higher base for the next rise.

No, curing inflation will solve many problems, but will not
solve the problem we are discussing here.

The causes of the revolution in the delivery of consumer financial services today--and I say this with respect and no little
envy--are sitting with me at this table.

If and when inflation goes away, they stay.

If I may spare a thousand words, I would like to picture my
message on a chart. This chart, which appears in a tongue-in-cheek
booklet you have received, is not a legal document, with elaborate
footnotes and exhaustive qualifications. But it does the job of
illustrating today's competitive picture as we see it.

It shows, in the vertical column, a list of services offered
by the commercial banks and 25 non-bank businesses shown in the
horizontal column.

As you see, commercial banks are permitted to take money and
pay interest, to offer check writing, loans, mortgages, and credit
cards to consumers.

If these are the services that more or less define consumer
banking, let's look at what other companies meet this definition.

They include, of course, the companies represented at this
table: American Express, Merrill Lynch, Prudential Insurance,
and Benefical Finance.

As you know, Sears, which also fits this definition of banking,
had hoped to be with us today, but could not, because it is in the

process of buying a securities firm and real estate company, which
other banks, of course, are prohibited from doing.

As you see, other companies that offer all the consumer services of banks include Household Finance, Gulf and Western, and
National Steel.

I will not read the whole chart to you, Senators. That would
be not only superfluous from your point of view, but painful from
mine. I will, however, point out several of its more poignant
features.

You will note that the vertical line titled "Commercial Banks"
terminates after the fifth entry, while the others continue long
after.

The horizontal line titled "Interstate Branches" has only one
empty space, under banks. Sears may sell money funds nationwide,
but if Citibank puts one of our computer terminals that accept or
dispense cash in Jersey, we're in violation of the law.

Four lines are devoted to forms of insurance: life, property,
casualty, and mortgage. Fourteen companies shown--not counting
Prudential--sell all four kinds of insurance. Of the 25 companies
shown, only two sell no insurance at all, and that's by choice,
not law. Large signs in windows of savings banks in New York advertise Savings Bank Life Insurance, proscribed to commercial banks.

This raises a disturbing point. In a bill whose fundamental
thrust is to remove restraints on competition, one solidary provi-
sion--the prohibition on insurance--flies in the face of this
intent. In a bill designed to reverse the 1930's pattern of statutory business prohibitions and protected markets, one provision
could reanimate that spirit.

The effect would be simply to restrict banks from offering
their customers a service all these companies and others already
offer theirs, depriving cunsumers of a broader range of services,
and banks of the ability to compete more fully.

In accordance with our oft-expressed belief that the free
market serves the consumer best, we would not support such a provision in an otherwise excellent bill.

In conclusion, may I repeat my gratitude and relief that we
are finally taking the first steps in addressing this crucial
situation, and let me express the hope that the legislation that
you will enact this year and in the years ahead will finally fill
in all the blanks in this chart, not just for banks, but for all.

Thank you.

WHO DOES WHAT

WHO DOES WHAT	Take Money/Pay Interest	Check Writing	Loan	Mortgage	Credit Card	Interstate Branches	Money Market	Securities	Life Insurance	Property Insurance	Casualty Insurance	Mortgage Insurance	Buy-Rent Real Estate	Cash Management Account	Travel Agency/Service	Car Rental	Data Processing/(General)	Telecommunications
J. C. PENNY					✓	✓			✓	✓	✓			✓				
ITT			✓	✓	✓				✓	✓	✓	✓					✓	✓
ARMCO			✓	✓	✓				✓	✓	✓	✓	✓					
WESTINGHOUSE			✓	✓	✓								✓				✓	✓
NATIONAL STEEL	✓	✓	✓	✓	✓								✓					
GENERAL ELECTRIC	✓		✓	✓		✓			✓	✓	✓	✓					✓	✓
LOWES			✓	✓		✓			✓	✓	✓	✓						
DANA	✓	✓	✓	✓	✓	✓	✓		✓	✓	✓	✓	✓					
AVCO			✓	✓		✓			✓	✓	✓	✓	✓	✓	✓		✓	✓
GENERAL MOTORS		✓			✓					✓	✓		✓					
EQUITABLE LIFE	✓	✓	✓	✓			✓	✓	✓		✓		✓			✓		
GREYHOUND		✓			✓					✓	✓	✓				✓	✓	
E. F. HUTTON	✓	✓	✓		✓		✓	✓					✓					
CONTROL DATA	✓		✓	✓	✓				✓	✓	✓	✓	✓				✓	
AMERICAN GENERAL	✓	✓	✓	✓		✓	✓	✓	✓	✓	✓	✓	✓					
GULF & WESTERN	✓	✓	✓	✓	✓	✓			✓	✓	✓	✓	✓			✓		
HOUSEHOLD	✓	✓	✓	✓	✓	✓			✓						✓			
RCA			✓	✓	✓	✓			✓		✓	✓			✓			
BALDWIN PIANO	✓	✓	✓	✓	✓	✓	✓		✓	✓	✓	✓	✓		✓			✓
TRANSAMERICA	✓	✓	✓	✓			✓	✓	✓	✓	✓	✓	✓			✓		
BENEFICIAL	✓	✓	✓	✓	✓	✓			✓	✓	✓	✓	✓		✓			
SEARS	✓	✓	✓	✓	✓	✓	✓	✓	✓	✓	✓	✓	✓	✓	✓	✓		
PRUDENTIAL	✓	✓	✓	✓	✓	✓	✓	✓	✓	✓	✓	✓	✓	✓				
MERRILL LYNCH	✓	✓	✓	✓	✓	✓	✓	✓		✓	✓	✓						
AMERICAN EXPRESS	✓	✓	✓	✓	✓	✓	✓	✓	✓	✓	✓	✓			✓		✓	✓
COMMERCIAL BANK	✓	✓	✓	✓	✓													

Testimony, October 28, 1981, U.S. Congress, 97th, 1st session, Senate, Committee on Banking, Housing, and Urban Affairs, Financial Institutions Restructuring and Services Act of 1981. Hearings...., (Washington, D.C.: Government Printing Office, 1981), pp. 561-564.

738. HIGH INTEREST RATES AND AUTOMOBILE DEALERS (1981)

In addition to foreign competition, American car
dealers faced a second depressive factor -- high interest
rates. In a market dominated by sales on credit, the
level of interest rates was of critical importance. Here
Mike Shore, an official of Sharp Ford Motor, Inc. of
Indianapolis, testifies on the problem.

We are the largest Ford dealership in the Indianapolis district. The district consists of 175 dealers in Indiana and
Illinois. We sell approximately one out of every five Fords sold
in the Indianapolis metro area. Our dealership has been in business since 1937 and has been at our present location on the south
side of Indianapolis for the last 15 years.

We finance our new vehicle inventories through a large local
bank at a rate of one-half percent over prime, which is better than
most dealers. Most are faced with 1 or 2 percent over prime to
finance their inventories. That is called floor planning. In the
first 7 months of 1979 our average floor plan expense on $3,287,231
of inventory was $32,801, or $9.98 per $1,000 on the 483 units we
carried in stock; in 1980 it was $30,398, or $12.85 per $1,000 on
$2,364,788 of inventory on 349 units; and in 1981 it is $38,050 or
$16.56 per $1,000 on $2,298,095 of inventory with 295 units.

As illustrated by these figures you can see the two problems
we face. We are forced to carry much smaller inventories. At the
same time, our cost of carrying the lower inventory is much greater. The lower inventory levels have been forced upon dealers by
the higher cost of borrowing. This has also caused the manufacturers to lay off many thousands of workers at the various plants
because we cannot buy their product. As the manufacturers tell
us, the dealer is the only customer. We are the only ones that
buy from the factory. We have also been forced to reduce our number of employees and lower our expenses in an effort to compensate
for the higher cost of the floor plan. In our dealership we have
reduced our staff from 110 employees to 75 employees since January
1980.

Higher floor plan expense, along with reduced sales, has
caused many dealers to close their doors, resulting in the loss of
a great number of jobs. In 1980 there were 1,600 dealers across
the country who closed their doors.

The second part of the problem is our customers are greatly
affected by prolonged periods of high interest rates. In 1979 a
customer could finance $5,000 at 9.5 percent for $125 a month.
Today to finance that same $5,000 he will pay 17 percent for $144
a month. This is a difference of $19 per month for the same amount
of money borrowed, or a total of $912 over the 48 months of the
contract.

At our dealership approximately 85 percent of all cars purchased are financed in some manner, and the higher rates alone
have taken a great number of these buyers out of the market for a

new car, simply because they cannot afford the monthly payments.

A recent change has occurred that has many of my fellow dealers concerned. We seem to sense a change in our business relationships with our local banks. The banks have virtually stopped loaning money to consumers for the purchase of new or used vehicles.
Their attitude seems to be that their funds are better invested
in places other than consumer loans. The large majority of all
our customers are now being financed through the manufacturer's
finance arm, Ford Motor Credit. This trend is not unique to
just our market but seems to be happening nationwide, judging by
my conversations with other dealers at a recent dealer meeting.
We need our local banks as business partners, not just as money
brokers. Example: As late as March of this year our bank financed
100 contracts for us--last month they financed 7. The rest went to
Ford Motor Credit. This trend seems to be the worst by-product
of the higher interest rates.

Testimony, August 14, 1981, U.S. Congress, 97th, 1st session,
House of Representatives, Committee on Banking, Finance, and Urban
Affairs, Subcommittee on Economic Stabilization, Revitalization
and the U.S. Economy. Hearings...., Part 3, (Washington, D.C.:
Government Printing Office, 1981), pp. 362-363.

K.

THE GOVERNMENT AS PIVOT

739. TARIFF INSURES THE HOME MARKET (1900)

A tariff excluded or minimized foreign competition
at home and it enabled foreign sales to be made at lower-
than-domestic prices.

Q. (By Mr. PHILLIPS.) Had the tariff anything to do with
extending the growth of your industry?--A. Yes.
Q. Could it have been maintained and assumed its present
position without any tariff?--A. No; the tariff has given us the
advantage of a home market. As long as we secure largely the
home market--the inventive genius of the American is ahead of any
country on earth. As soon as we commenced to improve machinery
we found we could not only hold our own markets, but make inroads
to some extent in foreign countries. The foreign trade I speak
of is South America, and we had the Spanish islands, Cuba, Africa,
and Australia largely, because we were almost as near to these
places as Belgium was. In some cases, however, we were at a disadvantage in shipping and transportation, because we had to pay
ocean freights and reship our goods from Liverpool. Still we
thought it was better to sell at almost no profit at all and keep
our factories running for the benefit of labor. That is why we
are increasing it as much as possible. In a dull time we sell
everything we can export, even if we do not get a cent of profit
on it, so the workmen get their money.

Testimony, Henry Clay Fry, September 20, 1900, U.S. Congress,
56th, 2nd session, House of Representatives, Document No. 495,
Report of the Industrial Commission on the Relations and Conditions
of Capital and Labor...., VII, p. 903.

740. PRESSURES FOR POLITICAL CONTRIBUTIONS (1905)

Following is an illustration of the saying that
politics is a two-way street. Being questioned are
Thomas Platt, boss of the New York state Republican
party machine and a member of the State Senate, and
John McCall, president of the New York Life Insurance
Company.

[PLATT]
Q. If you have any opinion, of course we should be glad to
have it, but the point that I want particularly to get at is this,
what suggestion was there to the insurance companies of any quid
pro quo, what was the insurance company to get out of the fact
that they had made the contribution? A. There was not any
suggestion of any sort.
Q. What advantage really could they get? A. They get it
through me being connected with the State Committee.
Q. How would they get it through you? A. Well, they would
suppose that I would be very likely to defend them at any time
when it was necessary, if I had occasion to do it.
Q. What would that extend to, what would you mean by defend-
ing them if occasion made it necessary? A. I don't know.
Q. What had you in mind in saying that? A. That they would
expect me to support them naturally in anything that they naturally
thought was right and what they were for.
Q. And have they ever requested such support in any manner?
A. They never have.
Q. No company has? A. No company has ever asked my support.
Q. In what matters could you properly give a support to the
companies in return for such contributions? A. Oh, I don't know.
Q. I understand you to say that they would expect you would
support them or defend them. What class of possibilities had you
in mind in saying that? A. I did not have any class of possi-
bilities in mind at all--where their interests were largely in-
volved and they might come to me for help.
Q. To see that the legislature, for example, did not enact
legislation which they thought hostile to their policyholders?
A. That is what it would amount to.
Q. That is what it would amount to. How could you control
that situation? A. I could not control it.
Q. How could you in any way influence it? A. I might have
some influence.
Q. Through the disposition of the moneys in the election
of legislators? A. Well, I could not say that.
Q. Is not that the way it really comes about, Senator, that
the use of these contributions in the election of candidates to
office puts the candidates under more or less of a moral obligation
not to attack the interests supporting? A. That is what would
naturally be involved.

Q. That is really what is involved, is it not? A. I should think so.

Q. And that is what you meant when you said that they would expect you, through your relations to the State Committee, to defend them? A. Yes.

. . . .

[McCall]

Q. I should like to know Mr. McCall, who have solicited campaign contributions from you in these various campaigns? A. They are so numerous I could not tell you.

Q. They are so numerous you could not tell. Do you remember any one? A. That solicited campaign funds?

Q. Yes. A. Yes, I do, I know a great many.

Q. Why are they? A. Well, I would rather not tell you, Mr. Hughes. I would rather you would not press that. I will say that I have been solicited very often, not by members of the Legislature, and no State official.

Q. And no State Official? A. No. In various ways, leaders of halls, and leaders of organizations.

Q. Representatives of both parties? A. Absolutely.

Testimony, Thomas C. Platt, November 21, 1905, and John A. McCall, November 27, 1905, Testimony Taken Before the [Armstrong] Joint Committee, IV, pp. 3396-3397; V, pp. 3885-3886.

741. A RELUCTANT REGULATOR (1905)

The New York Department of Insurance had jurisdiction over 433 insurance companies. The life insurance companies had over $7 billion of insurance in force; the fire insurance companies, over $15 billion. State regulation operated at a very minimal level. This is illustrated by the testimony of Francis Hendricks, New York State Superintendent of Insurance.

Q. Well, is it fair to say, Mr. Hendricks, that if the department was satisfied that a company was solvent it paid virtually no attention to the question whether the management of the company was economical or extravagant? A. Not unless they were on the-- they were likely to impair their solvency.

Q. Well, if a company, for example, had a surplus apparently of $40,000,000 or $50,000,000 then would it make no difference to the department how extravagant its management was? A. I do not think--since I have been in there I have never attempted to manage the companies. I have believed that it would not be wise for that State to undertake to manage the companies; that that must be left to the directors of the company, necessarily. And--

Q. Don't you draw a distinction between the active management of a company and supervision and criticism of the management?
A. Yes, I think there might be.

Q. Did you understand that it was your duty as Superintendent
of Insurance if you came across irregularities in management to
report them to the Attorney General?   A.   Yes.

Q. Did you not think it proper in order that remedies might
be involved that extravagance or malversation of funds should be
brought to the attention of the proper officers of the State?
A. Yes, if we found them.

Q. But did you look for them?   A.   As I have said, we have
never found them.   It would be almost impossible to find them if
we tried in any of the large companies; that is if the Insurance
Department is to undertake the management, the only way they could
profit in my opinion would be to have the power to appoint their
officers and remove them at will.   I do not think we could in any
way manage a company without.

Q. You do not ascribe then as much virtue as some do to publicity?   A.   Why, I think publicity would be helpful.   I think
publicity would be helpful.

Q. Yes.   A.   But what I am going to say is this, what you
have developed is dishonesty in these companies.   Now I do not
believe that you can make men honest by any amount of examination.
If you could, why then the national banks, supervision would make
the banks.   They have two examinations a year and file reports,
and yet the amount of dishonesty that is in sight is a good deal
more than you have developed in this examination.   The trouble is,
you know, in the business morals of the people.

Q. Is it a great aid, however, to have exposure of irregularities?   A.   Oh, I think so.   I think that does good.

Q. You think that almost every one needs something of a
check?   A.   There ain't any doubt about that.

Testimony, Francis Hendricks, December 21, 1905, Testimony
Taken Before the [Armstrong] Joint Committee, pp. 5631-5633.

742.   RADIO REQUIRES GOVERNMENT REGULATION (1909)

Eighteen years later, in 1927, Congress passed
the Federal Radio Act, largely in response to the
following problem explained by Lee De Forest.

That at least as early as 1909 there were a sufficient number
of radio "hams" with transmitters to cause very bothersome interference wtih wireless communication, as evidenced by a letter
appearing in Modern Electrics addressed to the Wireless Association

of America, to which organization I had recently been elected
honorary president. In this letter I warned that
    If the present promiscuous working of unlisted sending sta-
tions continues as it has, means effective and drastic will certainly be taken to remedy this evil.
    Without question Congress will be asked to pass legislation
requiring licenses for all transmitting stations, limited their
number in given districts, limited their power, and prescribing
the wave length that may be employed.
    All stations not belonging to the Government or to legitimate
commercial companies will doubtless be absolutely prohibited by
law if the present inconsiderate interferences are continued.
    Transmitting stations of more than one-quarter horsepower,
except those with very carefully tuned radiating circuits using
very weakly damped oscillations, should be at once discontinued
if within fifty miles of Government stations.
    Disregard of such warnings, whether or not you consider them
right and just, will certainly result in drastic prohibitive
legislation at a not far-distant rate.

De Forest, Father of Radio, p. 259.

            743.   "THE SHERMAN ACT IS A HUMBUG" (1910)

        A leading American jurist traditionally regarded
        as anti-monopoly, muddles his way through to a denun-
        ciation of anti-monopoly laws. Oliver Wendell Holmes
        was an Associate Justice of the Supreme Court; he writes
        to Sir Frederick Pollock, a former jurist and legal
        writer, who was serving as Bencher of Lincoln's Inn.

    I am just too late to get the return mail in answer to yours
but I hasten to reply, partly because I have just received a semi-
request to send you the accompanying paper. I know the writer
only by correspondence. He seems to me half crank, and yet I am
told that he has done things in former days in connection with
news, and he seems to me to have ideas....His contempt for government interference with rates etc., and his belief in the validity
of the outside organizations I confess I share to a great extent.
Of course I enforce whatever constitutional laws Congress or anybody else sees fit to pass--and do it in good faith to the best
of my ability--but I don't disguise my belief that the Sherman Act
is a humbug based on economic ignorance and incompetence, and my
disbelief that the Interstate Commerce Commission is a fit body
to be entrusted. The Commission naturally is always trying to
extend its power and I have written some decisions limiting it
(by construction of statutes only). However I am so sceptical as

to our knowledge about the goodness or badness of laws that I have
no practical criticism except what the crowd wants. Personally
I bet that the crowd if it knew more wouldn't want what it does--
but that is immaterial.

Letter, Oliver Weldell Holmes to Sir Frederick Pollock.
April 23, 1910, Mark De Wolfe Howe (ed.), Holmes-Pollock Letters.
The Correspondence of Mr. Justice Holmes and Sir Frederick Pollock
1874-1932, I, (Cambridge, Massachusetts: Harvard University Press,
1944), p. 163.

744.   KNIGHT OR INDICT BUSINESSMAN? (1912)

This witness, George Perkins, proposed the setting
up of a business court, made up of experienced businessmen, within the Department of Commerce and Labor. The
court would license corporations doing interstate and
international business, lay down very broad rules of
business practice, and make individual officers but not
the corporation liable for violations. He hoped Congress
would consider changing the Sherman Act to permit this.

I believe that a commission composed of such men would accomplish a good many things. We have in this country no goal for the
business man in the way of preferment, or honorable mention, so to
speak, unless he eventually goes out of business into public life.
Now, Europe does very differently. In Germany, for instance, a
captain of industry is knighted and here he is indicted. I believe
that if we establish a business court of that sort that it would
gradually come to be the goal of the young man who is going into
business. They would say, "Some day or another I may be called
to serve on this commission or court." I think it would be a
steadying influence on that man's whole business career, and he
would look forward to it like the lawyer does to the Supreme Court
as possible preferment, and that man would give up almost any business calling finally to be a member of such a commission. There
is not a lawyer, I suppose, in the country who would not give up
any lucrative practice for an appointment on the Supreme Bench,
because that has come to be the goal--the highest degree of honor--
and if it is said that it would be turning business over, or turning
the Government over to business, I do not think that holds, because we have not found it in any respect, certainly not in regulation of our railroads. Take another instance. Our Presidents
select officials from corporation life, like Mr. Knox and Mr.
Wickersham, and they gave up lucrative businesses and went into
these offices, and have stood an immense amount of abuse from
their old friends and colleagues and associates. Yet they have
discharged their oath of office as they saw it in the interest

of the people.   I believe the business men would adopt the same
course.

. . . .

I certainly would give the court the right to revoke the
license with the right of appeal, but I would make that almost
the last resort; that is, I would in that respect control the
corporations as we do our banks.   I would punish the individual
and exhaust all those channels before I actually injured the existence of the company itself, because we must remember that the
company can not do anything wrong.   It is not a live thing; it is
a creation of man, and there is no use injuring an innocent third
party and disturbing our business because some man does something
that is not right.

Testimony, George W. Perkins, December 13, 1911, U.S.
Congress, 62nd, Senate, Committee on Interstate Commerce, Hearing.
. .Pursuant to S. Res. 98, pp. 1122-1123, 1126.

745.   EMPLOYMENT OF EX-GOVERNMENT OFFICIALS (1913)

Government regulation and supervision of economic
affairs resulted in training large numbers of officials
who were then employed directly by the economic interests
they had lately been regulating and supervising.

Mr. POWELL.   I am in Washington, Senator, representing...the
Citrus Protective League of Califoriia.   The Citrus Protective
League is a voluntary organization which represents the different
citrus-fruit growing and shipping interests in handling railroad-
rate cases and various questions that affect the industry outside
of marketing the fruit.   I was formerly manager of the Citrus
Protective League, from January 1, 1911, to September, 1912.
The CHAIRMAN.   Who compose the Citrus Protective League?
Mr. POWELL.   The Citrus Protective League comprises about 80
per cent of all the shipping and growing interests in the citrus-
growing industry in California, the orange and lemon industry, and,
as I say, it handles railroad-rate cases and all questions affecting the industry outside of marketing the fruit.
On September 1, 1912, I became general manager of the California Fruit Growers' Exchange, and while manager of the Citrus
Protective League I had made for the league investigations of the
cost of producing citrus fruits in California, both oranges and
lemons, and an investigation of the status of the citrus industries
of European countries--in Italy and in Spain--and at the request
of the directors of the Citrus Protective League I came to
Washington shortly after the tariff had left the Democratic caucus
of the House of Representatives, and have been in Washington since
that time.

The CHAIRMAN. What did you come to Washington for?

Mr. POWELL. I came to Washington for the purpose of present-ing to the Finance Committee certain briefs and statements regard-ing the citrus industry, and to be in Washington until the tariff bill passed out of the caucus in the Senate, in order to be able to give to our California Senators and Representatives, and also such other Senators as might be interested in having the data, such information as they might desire.

. . . .

Mr. POWELL. I was for 10 years in the Department of Agricul-ture for the first 9 years in charge of the cold-storage and transportation investigations affecting plant products and for the last year Assistant Chief of the Bureau of Plant Industry and acting chief in the absence of the chief of the bureau.

The CHAIRMAN. In what year was it you severed your connection with that department?

Mr. POWELL. I severed my connection with that department December 31, 1910, and then became manager of the Citrus Protective League of California, I having in my Federal service for six years at least been investigating the citrus-fruit industries in Europe and this country and having prepared and published a number of publications which were issued from the Department of Agriculture.

The CHAIRMAN. What was your salary as a Government official?

Mr. POWELL. $4,000.

The CHAIRMAN. What was your salary as manager of the Citrus Protective League?

Mr. POWELL. $25,000, under contract for a three-year term.

The CHAIRMAN. $25,000 a year?

Mr. POWELL. For three years; and I severed by connection with the Citrus Protective League, with the mutual consent of the League and myself, in order to become manager of the California Fruit Growers' Exchange.

Thw CHAIRMAN. Did you have any increase of salary?

Mr. POWELL. I entered into a contract with the exchange, for a two-years' service, of $27,000 for the two years, $12,000 payable the first year and $15,000 the second year. The California Fruit Growers' Exchange is an organization which handles from $15,000,000 to $20,000,000 worth of citrus fruits annually, and the Fruit Growers' Supply Co., of which I am selling manager, handles about $2,500,000 worth of supplies for the packing houses and citrus-fruit growers.

The CHAIRMAN. Do you get any salary as selling manager?

Mr. POWELL. Yes; that is a part of the salary I speak of.

The CHAIRMAN. And your total salary is what?

Mr. POWELL. $27,000 for two years, payable $12,000 the first year and $15,000 the second year.

The CHAIRMAN. When does that expire?

Mr. POWELL. September 1, 1914.

Testimony, G. Harold Powell, July 3, 1913, U.S. Congress, 63rd, 1st session, Senate, Committee on the Judiciary, Maintenance of a Lobby to Influence Legislation, II, pp. 1854-1855, 1855-1856.

746. AFL OPPOSES SOCIAL LEGISLATION (1914)

The American Federation of Labor favored labor-
welfare goals only as these could be achieved by workers
organized into craft unions affiliated with the AFL.
Laws which would realize these goals for union and nonunion members alike were not favored. Included were laws
for shorter hours, minimum wages, and unemployment insurance. Gompers was president of the AFL and Morris Hillquit,
the questioner, was a leader of the Socialist Party.

[Mr. GOMPERS....] As a matter of fact, the unions themselves
undertake the work of accomplishing the shorter workday. Say,
for instance, that the International Typographical Union undertook
a movement, giving employers more than a year's notice in advance,
that on a certain day they would no longer work more than eight
hours in each day. Almost immediately a large number of employers
acceded to the request. Others refused. The men struck. Covering
a period of more than a year, employers in numbers and individual
firms came to an agreement acceding to the eight-hour day, and
enforcing it, and finally the eight-hour day has been accomplished
not only by the printers, the International Typographical Union,
but the eight-hour day prevails now generally in the printing
trades; and that is true in many others, in the building trades.
It did not require any law for the printers; it did not require
any law for the granite cutters; it did not require any law for
the Cigar Makers' International Union, of which I have the honor
to be a member. There was not any requirement in the law in the
building trades, and many others, to introduce the eight-hour
workday....
    Mr. HILLQUIT. Well, now, let's understand that well, Mr.
Gompers, for the record. Your opinion is that if there were a
movement and a possibility of establishing a shorter workday, say,
an eight-hour workday, by legal enactment throughout the land,
and a minimum wage in the same way, the federation would be
opposed to such measures?
    Mr. GOMPERS. It would; because it has in a large measure
accomplished it and will accomplish it by the initiative of the
association, the organization, and the grit and courage of the
manhood and womanhood of the men and women in the American Federation of Labor.
    Mr. HILLQUIT. And if that grit and courage should express
itself by forcing the legislatures of the various States to enact
such a law and if the execution and performance of the law were
backed by a strong labor organization in each State, with the
same grit and courage, you would not object to it?
    Mr. GOMPERS. Well, your hypothesis is entirely groundless.
    Mr. HILLQUIT. Why, Mr. Gompers?
    Mr. GOMPERS. When the organizations of labor, as I have
already said, have accomplished that to a large extent, and propose

to accomplish it again, further, on their own initiative and by
their own voluntary association, it precluded the question of
having a legal enactment for that purpose.

Testimony, Samuel Gompers, May 22, 1914, U.S. Congress, 64th,
1st session, Senate, Document No. 415, Final Record and Testimony
Submitted to Congress by the Commission on Industrial Relations,
II, pp. 1501, 1502.

747. THIS BILL MUST PASS (1933)

The National Industrial Recovery bill suspended
the anti-trust laws so as to permit businessmen to
confer and fix output, prices, and wages in their
industries. The administration looked to the projected
program as a source of rising prices and thus economic
recovery. Harriman was president of the U.S. Chamber
of Commerce.

Under normal conditions I doubt very much whether the Chamber
of Commerce would desire me to come before you and approve a bill
with such drastic conditions as this. A man said to me today,
"Where are we going to if this bill is not passed?" I said, "I do
not think we can go on very much longer with millions of men out of
work and with commodities at prices which pay no return on capital
and pay almost no return for the human labor that is involved.".....
Now, whatever the exact figures may be, it is perfectly evident that we cannot have a return to prosperity until the price
level of general commodities has moved substantially upward and
until many millions of these men who are now unemployed are put
back to work. And the object of this bill which is before you is
to accomplish those two results.
Whenever there is a great surplus of labor, whenever we are
passing through a period of great depression, we always have cutthroat competition. It is inevitable. One man takes an order at a
slightly less price than his competitor. In order to have a chance
to break even on that low price he must not only use all the skill
that he has but he must cut the pay of his working people. Then
the other man, not to be outdone, cuts his prices and lower wages,
and lower wages and lower prices.
I believe the time has come when we must take out of competition the brutality of competition. We must take of competition the
right to cut wages to a point which will not given an American
standard of living, and we must recognize that capital is entitled
to a fair and reasonable return, and that therefore goods must be
sold at a price which will enable the manufacturer to pay a fair
price for his raw material, to pay fair wages to his men, and to
pay a fair dividend on his investment.

The anti-trust laws were rightly enacted to prevent monopoly;
but they have gone far beyond that. They have prevented agreements
between parties which would make it possible to stop this cutthroat
and deflationary process.

Now, I am not for one moment in favor of abolishing our antitrust laws. I believe that they should be retained on our statute
books as a guarantee against the return of unregulated monopoly.
On the other hand, I think the time has come when we should ease up
on these laws and, under proper governmental supervision, allow
manufacturers and people in trade to agree among themselves on
these basic conditions of a fair price for the commodity, a fair
wage, and a fair dividend.

That, gentlemen, is the object of this bill. It does not
propose any repeal of our antitrust laws. It simply provides that
when groups of men in trade associations or otherwise have come
together and entered into an agreement, and the Government has
found that agreement to be in the public interest, that in such a
case the antitrust laws should not prevent such contracts from
going into effect.

Testimony, Henry I. Harriman, May 19, 1933, U.S. Congress,
73rd, 1st session, House of Representatives, Committee on Ways and
Means, National Industrial Recovery, pp. 133, 134.

748. RECRUITING GOVERNMENT ADVISERS (1940)

When the federal government wished to appoint industrial leaders to administrative posts, it solicited
recommendations from executives of leading firms. In
aluminum, that meant ALCOA. Arthur Davis, who testifies,
was chairman of the board of directors of the Aluminum
Company of America.

The CHAIRMAN. Mr. Davis, I have been told that you were
responsible for the appointment of the Priorities Committee in
O. P. M. [Office of Production Management]. Is that true?

Mr. DAVIS. No, sir.

The CHAIRMAN. Did you make the recommendation for the
Priorities Committee?

Mr. DAVIS. No, sir. That is not true. But I should tell
you, if I may, what the facts are.

The CHAIRMAN. I would like to know them.

Mr. DAVIS. And you can make your own conclusions. Mr.
Folsom, who at that time had charge of the aluminum industry in
O. P. M., asked me to give him the names of a number of people
prominent in the industry. At that time Mr. Folsom explained to
me that the program would be to appoint a disinterested outstanding

man as the chairman of each committee and that there would be four
other members of the committee, one from the Army, one from the
Navy, one to represent the industry, and one to represent the
consumer. I remember I told Mr. Folsom that I could speak for the
outstanding man right now and I would like Owen Young, and he said,
"Owen Young has already been spoken for by the Steel Corporation,"
so I made no further suggestions for the chairmanship. Then I did
give Mr. Folsom some few days afterward a list of, I would say, 30
men of standing and ability and worth in the industry. He made no
comment on them, but out of those he did pick one, I think, for one
of the committees, Mr. Farrell, the vice president of the Fairmont
Aluminum Co., who was on this list that I gave him. You understand,
my list contained no recommendations: it was merely a list of
people that were prominent and solid in the industry.
     The CHAIRMAN. I just wanted to find out what the facts are.
I wanted to know if the Aluminum Co. of America had appointed the
Priorities Committee for O. P. M. We had some argument about the
priorities as they were distributed in O. P. M., and it looked to
me very much as if there had been decided favoritism in the allocation of these priorities. I was just trying to find out what was
the cause of that situation.
     Mr. DAVIS. May I add, Mr. Chairman, that in this list of 30
there was nobody connected with the Aluminum Co. of America. I
carefully avoided putting any of our own people on this list.

     Testimony, Arthur V. Davis, May 15, 1941, U.S. Congress,
77th, 1st session, Senate, Special Committee Investigating the
National Defense Program, Investigation of the National Defense
Program, III, pp. 943-944.

749.   CORPORATIONS AND GOVERNMENT (1941)

     In the age of defense contracts, political contacts
became a valuable business asset. Thomas Corcoran, who
had served as counsel to the Reconstruction Finance
Corporation from 1932 to 1940, gives this account of the
situation. He was presently a private attorney specializing in representing private businesses in their relation
to the federal government.

     Senator BALL. Seriously, Mr. Corcoran, I would like to ask
you one question going to the ethics of this picture. You have
made quite a point of the fact that your efforts on behalf of your
clients expedited the defense program. It seems to me rather a
reflection on our set-up down here that any corporation or business
that is organized to contribute to the defense program had to
obtain the services of one as skillful as I think we all recognize

you to be, in order to get action to help the defense program.
Obviously, you can't handle all the concerns that come down here
looking for defense contracts or defense business, directly or
indirectly, and doesn't it put the other concerns who may have just
as much to offer to the defense program, if they can't possibly
obtain the services of Tommy Corcoran, at a little disadvantage?
Shouldn't this expediting be in the Government and not outside?
. . . .

Mr. CORCORAN. Senator, what impreses me about the relationships of corporations to the Government in the defense effort is not
that they need anybody in relation to the Government but that they
do need somebody to help them determine their own policy inside
themselves. We are going through a period of enormous transition.
The average corporation board of directors, because it doesn't live
in this atmosphere and know the enormous changes that are taking
place and how everything is centralizing under the control of
Government administrative agencies, is normally unconvinced, in
time, of the way in which it has to move so that its plans will mesh
with plans down here. For instance, when you talk with a corporation board of directors and you try to make them understand that it
is going to take so many weeks and so many months for something to
happen, which in the much smaller scope of their relations to
private enterprise could happen the next day, they can't believe
you.

When you are dealing with the enormities that Washington is
dealing with there are reasons why things can't happen the next day.
But the average corporation doesn't realize that Washington can't
deal with its situation in particular; that Washington has to work
through, and with, regulations, generalizations, and categories.
Because the people down here have to deal with such enormous responsibilities, they can't move as quickly as a corporation official with whom my corporation would do business tomorrow morning.
There are, therefore, miscalculations on the part of private managers. Unless some adviser not only knows what will happen, but
has the ability to convince those managers of what will happen, of
things that are otherwise incredible to them, they just simply
can't gear themselves to the direction of things.

Senator Brewster has remarked that I have been suspected of
driving things down here. I have likewise been suspected in many a
corporation board meeting of driving things unnecessarily because
I knew things had to be done at a certain time or that things could
not be expected from Washington for another time. And so far as
unfair competition is concerned, I think, Senator, the point is to
get the stuff out and not to preserve competition at the speed of
the slowest train like the train schedules to the Northwest.

Testimony, Thomas G. Corcoran, December 16, 1941, U.S.
Congress, 77th, 1st session, Senate, Special Committee Investigating
the National Defense Program, Investigation of the National Defense
Program, X, pp. 3923, and 3924-3925.

750.   GOVERNMENT AS WAR SPENDER (1941-1945)

Defense Plant Corporation built productive facili-
ties and leased them to private operators at a nominal
or low rental. During 1940-1945, it spent $9.2 billion.
Jesse Jones also supervised expenditures of the Defense
Plant Corporation, a subsidiary of the Reconstruction
Finance Corporation.

About half the Defense Plant Corporation's huge outlays flowed
directly or indirectly into aviation. To build aircraft, their
engines and parts--from bolts to bomb sights, gas tanks to shimmy
dampeners--the Corporation directly invested $2,600,000,000 in land,
buildings, machines, and other equipment in several hundred new
plants. Of the fifteen largest airplane engine plants put up during
the war, fourteen were wholly or partly financed by the Corporation.
Another quarter of a billion dollars constructed and equipped forty-
five plants which produced high-octane aviation gasoline exclusively.
And aviation got the lion's share of aluminum and magnesium. Into
the expansion of these two industries we put about $1,500,000,000.
To assist the War Department's pilot-training program, the
Corporation bought and enlarged sixty-two flying schools and provided planes and housing for the cadets, all at a cost of
$41,000,000. We leased the schools to private operators, who billed
the War Department for their work.
    Enlarging steel and pig-iron capacity took almost another
billion out of the Corporation's purse. It was necessary to produce
shiploads of scrap which had been sold to foreign customers--includ-
ing our future enemies--in the years just before the war. When we
first approached the steel companies with our propositions, months
before Pearl Harbor, they were reluctant to undertake extensive
enlargements. Most steel executives felt the country did not need
any more capacity in their line. They had a natural fear that
abnormal expansion would plague them once the emergency ended.
. . . .
    The Corporation allotted many millions for plants and machin-
ery which made tanks, guns, bombs, shells, and a thousand other
implements of war. It also financed the building of ships and dry
dock facilities. Tens of millions went to enlarge production of
chemicals and synthetics, from old-fashioned bleaching powder to
ultramodern plexiglas.
    To stimulate production of machine tools we made advances to
manufacturers against purchase orders up to 30 per cent of the
delivery price. These agreements, instituted the day after Pearl
Harbor, were in effect underwritings. The machine-tool commitments
ultimately aggregated almost $2,000,000,000. They provided tool
manufacturers with supplementary capital.
    For machinery to equip one hundred and nineteen new plants
assigned to make lenses for optical instruments Defense Plant spent
$217,000,000. Transportation projects took $335,000,000. Notable

in that category were the Big Inch and Little Big Inch pipe lines
through which petroleum and its products were pumped from Texas to
the New Jersey seaboard, thus freeing tankers from the coastal runs
to vital overseas services for the armed forces. The Corporation
also financed tugboats and barges for river transportation to take
some of the War Department's load off the overburdened railroads.

Jones, Fifty Billion Dollars, pp. 316-317, 317-318.

751. "HOPE DEFERRED MAKETH THE HEART SICK" (1943)

Whether it healed the ailing heart or not, however, economic inequality did decrease somewhat during
the war years. Increased employment was basic to the
improvement, while taxation was far more important than
renegotiation of war contracts in reducing extremes of
income. John Lewis, president of the United Mine
Workers of America, testifies in the following.

Mr. LEWIS. In my opinion, we will not be able to restrain
inflation to the degree that we would wish as long as the Government
has two policies with respect to inflation.
The CHAIRMAN. What are those two policies?
Mr. LEWIS. On the one hand, the Government superinduces inflation by the excessive rewards to industry for producing essential
war commodities. Now, on the other hand, the Government seeks to
fight inflation by saying to 50,000,000 workers in America gainfully employed and largely in war industries, "We cannot do for you
what we are doing for industry because that would cause inflation.
You must not ask for a wage increase above and beyond a certain
formula which we have arbitrarily computed; and as a patriotic duty
you cannot expect your wages to keep pace with the rising cost of
living. As a citizen you must make sacrifices in the interests of
the whole nation and the war effort." There is an implication that
the individual worker is unpatriotic if he asks the same consideration as industry from his Government.
Senator BREWSTER. Mr. Lewis----
Mr. LEWIS. Let me follow out, if you will, Senator, and I
will gladly yield to any questions.
Senator BREWSTER. Under the existing tax legislation and
proposed tax legislation and under renegotiation which we have been
giving a great deal of attention to recently, we still hope that
the rich would not be getting richer out of this war. We, of
course, haven't achieved it completely but we felt as though we
had done somewhat of a job.

Mr. LEWIS. We all hope with you, but hope deferred maketh
the heart sick.

Testimony, John L. Lewis, March 26, 1943, U.S. Congress, 78th,
1st session, Senate, Special Committee Investigating the National
Defense Program, Investigation of the National Defense Program,
XVIII, pp. 7396-7397.

752. SELLING AIRCRAFT TO THE GOVERNMENT (1940's)

An experienced industrialist, Howard Hughes,
describes how his firm utilized personal contacts,
through wining and dining of government officials, to
win military contracts. In the process, he sketched
a general industrial picture. Hughes was president of
the Hughes Tool Company.

Senator FERGUSON. Did you think it was a good procurement
policy for men in the United States Government service, in the
Army, to require entertainment and accept entertainment and expense
items in order that the businessmen of America be able to get
contracts or carry on their relations with the Air Service?
Mr. HUGHES. Senator, I will try to answer that if you will
give me a chance.
Senator FERGUSON. Yes; I certainly will.
Mr. HUGHES. Now, we in this country have a capitalistic system, if you want to use that word. There is not much capital left,
but we call it that. Any way, we have a private-enterprise competitive system, if you want to call it that. The Government buys
material from private companies and corporations.
These companies are all in competition with one another and
that competition does stimulate a better product and a cheaper
price. There is no question about that.
However, there is competition in more than one way. There
is competition to produce the best product, and there is also competition to sell it; and almost every corporation in this country
has a sales department and the aircraft companies in that respect
are no exception.
Lockheed, for example, has Carl Squire, sales chief, who gets
well over $50,000 a year, I believe; and all of the companies--
Boeing has a very high-powered vice president in charge of sales,
and all of the other companies have a pretty expensive and pretty
capable sales manager, together with a large force of assistants
and salesmen.
During the war all of that sales effort was directed toward
the Government, because the airplane companies were selling to the

Government. My company, which was very small and never enjoyed the
growth during the war of the others, was never able to support or
at least I did not employ such high-pressured salesmen, and I had
no $50,000-a-year sales manager, and I had no sales force, and
in that way my sales effort was not comparable to the others. All
of these companies expended sales effort; whether it consisted of
passing a cigar to somebody, or buying his lunch, or buying his
dinner, or buying him a drink or giving him a drink out of the
cabinet when he came to the office.

But in any event, all of these companies expended sales efforts;
maybe it was in the form of some favor or service that the sales
manager did for an Army officer 3 or 4 years ago, and in that way
the Army officer became his friend, or he later called on him to
return that friendship, without saying so. But at least the friendship gave him an entree and, in any event, certainly in business in
this country there is such a thing as salesmanship, whether it consists of arguing, convincing, showing pretty pictures, passing out
cigars, or whatever it is. There is something called sales effort.

Now, I do not think that Mr. Johnny Meyer [employed by Hughes],
with his small salary, even though he did considerable entertaining,
I do not think he exerted any more sales pressure than Mr. Carl
Squire, a high-powered $50,000-a-year salesman, pushing ball-point
fountain pens into the hands of a man and giving him a contract with
a dotted line and saying, "Sign here." I think that sales pressure
is sales pressure. It certainly existed throughout.

You asked me if I think that is a good condition. Well, I do
not know how to avoid it, and I think that as long as the companies,
the various companies doing business with the Government, compete
in a fair manner with one another, then the result should be the
purchase by the Government of a fairly representative piece of
material, at a fairly representative price.

In other words, if these companies all expend somewhere near
the same type of effort, and if they compete with one another in a
fair manner, then I do not think the result is going to come out
in favor of one particularly more than another.

In any event, you asked me if I think it is a good system. I
do not know whether it is a good system. I do not know whether
it is a good system or not, but I do not know how to avoid it.

Now, the system did exist, and it certainly would not have been
fair for all of these other companies to entertain and have their
high-pressure salesmen working on the Government, while I sat back
and ignored the Government and ignored its officials and made no
effort whatsoever to be polite to them, or to do business with
them.

Testimony, Howard R. Hughes, November 10, 1947, U.S. Congress,
80th, 1st session, Senate, Special Committee Investigating the
National Defense Program, Investigation of the National Defense
Program, XLIII, pp. 26466-26467.

753. THE NAVY INDUSTRIAL ASSOCIATION (1943-1944)

Secretary Forrestal, whose background was in law
and banking, initiated the proposal for the formation
of a private association of suppliers. After some months,
the proposal was effectuated. Fechteler was Chief of
Naval Operations during 1951-1953. At the time he testified, he was retired and was employed as a consultant,
long-range planning, in the Atomic Products Division of
General Electric Co. Forrestal was Secretary of the Navy,
and after the War became the first Secretary of Defense.
Felton was vice-president of Revere Copper & Brass, Inc.

[FECHTELER]
Historically, the Navy and the Department of Defense have
invited continuing contacts between industry and Government.
There are in Washington two associations, the American
Ordnance Association, and the National Security Industrial Associa-
tion. I am a member of both.
The American Ordnance Association was organized shortly after
World War I as the Army Ordnance Association. On the advent of
unification, the name was changed to the American Ordnance Association.
The idea of a Navy Industrial Association was first voiced by
the late James Forrestal when he was Secretary of the Navy in 1943.
The association came into being the next year.
Here, then, is an example of a businessman in Government service urging the formation of an organization which, as Mr. Forrestal
believed, could be of value to the Navy both in war and peace. It
is concrete evidence of the realization of the part of the Navy
that the closest partnership between the armed services and industry
is essential to the security of our Nation.
On the event of unification, the name of Mr. Forrestal's organization was changed to the National Security Industrial Association.
Both of these associations conduct symposiums organized jointly
by the Navy and themselves. I attend as many such meetings as
possible. They constitute forums at which the Navy lays before
industry its capabilities, its limitations and its requirements
toward overcoming those limitations. They are classified meetings.
As a sidelight on the extent of my influence since I retired, I
mention the fact that I had difficulty in gaining admission to an
NSIA-Navy symposium on research and development last fall because
I did not have a Navy secret clearance. After some delay I obtained a clearance.
It seems clear from these and other activities that Department
of Defense is anxious to maintain the closest liaison with
industry.
. . . .

[FORRESTAL]

I am pleased to know that a group is meeting with you on
Monday to consider formation of a Navy Industrial Association.
Such a private organization, I believe, could be of immeasurable
value to the Navy in war and in peace.

The future welfare of our Nation requires that the Navy not
lose touch with the manufacturers and businessmen who have contributed so much to the technical advance of the Navy during the past
4 years. We need a group of patriotic men through whom the Navy
can learn of the most advanced industrial and commercial techniques
and to whom we can turn for disinterested advice on research,
manufacturing, and procurement.

Therefore, I wanted you to know that your project has my personal support and good wishes.

Testimony, William M. Fechteler, September 1, 1959; letter,
James Forrestal to C. C. Felton, June 9, 1944; U.S. Congress, 86th,
1st session, House of Representatives, Committee on Armed Services,
Subcommittee for Special Investigations, Employment of Retired
Military and Civilian Personnel by Defense Industries, pp. 1046-
1047, 374.

754. "A LONG FUSE INTO THE PENTAGON?" (1958)

Two journalists, Drew Pearson and Jack Anderson,
had accused a large defense contractor of helping arrange
a private dinner for the Army general in charge of
research. The implication was that contracts were being
obtained through political influence rather than by merit.
Dan Kimball, who discusses this here, was president of
Aerojet-General, employing 24,000 persons. In 1942, he
had become executive vice-president of Aerojet. In 1943,
he became Assistant Secretary of the Navy for Air; later,
he became Secretary of the Navy and held this office until
January, 1953.

We at Aerojet and I personally have always been ready to talk
freely, discuss any situation, and to provide all the facts within
our knowledge and within the bounds of security, to any responsible
representatives of the press or magazines, radio, and television.
We recognize them as an important factor in our democratic way of
life.

It was not my intention to reopen the matter of a dinner
planned for General Schriever several weeks ago, but Mr. Anderson
in his testimony implied that other military persons and especially
some general other than General Schriever had been invited and I
may have deceived this committee by not having another general on

the list of invitees which the committee obtained. This is a very
serious charge even if again made only by innuendo.

I am aware that the answer Mr. Anderson gave you to the question was that he didn't know whether I was deceiving you or whether
the general intended to crash the party, but it is pretty plain to
me that he intended to put over before this committee and presumably
to the public as well that I had somehow falsified a list provided
to this committee. When you questioned him closely on this matter
the only answer was the usual one that he had only the word of
sources he considered reliable, but which he couldn't reveal.

I think the nub of the entire Pearson-Anderson testimony is
summed up in the exchange which took place between the chairman and
Mr. Anderson as the testimony concluded:

Mr. Hebert said to Mr. Anderson:

But you do not have any knowledge of it of your own except from
these unidentified sources?

Mr. Anderson. That is correct.

This takes care of the major items I want to handle personally.
The outstanding false impression left with this committee by
Messrs. Pearson and Anderson concerns Aerojet's technical ability
and historical facts. I am going to let a real expert. . .tell you
about these in his own words, and let you judge for yourself whether
we were pioneers in solid rocket work or just a firecracker factory
with a long fuse into the Pentagon.

Testimony, Dan A. Kimball, August 28, 1959, U.S. Congress,
86th, 1st session, House of Representatives, Committee on Armed
Services, Subcommittee for Special Investigations, Employment of
Military and Civilian Personnel by Defense Industries, p. 1020.

755. "A MOST PRODUCTIVE RELATIONSHIP" (1959)

The Martin Company of Baltimore, Maryland, a large
defense contractor, maintained an account at the Cotton
Bay Club in the Bahamas Islands to which the company invited guests and paid their bills. Among the guests from
the Air Force were: 4 generals, 4 major-generals, 1
lieutenant-general, and 1 colonel. From the Navy: 1
vice admiral, 8 rear admirals, 4 captains, 2 colonels,
and 1 lieutenant-colonel. The company was accused of
influence-buying. George Bunker, chairman of the
board of directors of the Martin Company, attempts to
explain.

To me it is very unfortunate that. . .the public impression
has been given that military officers of the highest caliber have
been subjected to undue influence as a result of their having been

guests of the Martin Co. One of the grave questions facing us
today is: Can our capitalistic system, fundamentally divided as it
is into private enterprises competing with each other, excel the
performance of another part of the world where Communist philosophy
has produced scientific advances that have astonished the world?
It will be tragic indeed if in future years Mr. Khrushchev's claim
that the Communist economic and political system can make progress
faster than ours if proven correct.

The Martin Co. is today one of the largest manufactures of
missiles and weapons systems in the Western World. As its chairman
I feel in common with my counterparts in industry the tremendous
responsibility which is ours. The eyes of the democratic world are
on us who are bent on proving, if we possibly can, that our system
of government works not only best for the development of human
values but for scientific progress as well.

We can succeed only through the most intimate relationship
between all segments of the Defense Department and private industry.
This is one of the most productive relationships this country has
ever conceived. This joint effort won two World Wars and is
responsible for our strong defense posture today. It has been made
possible not by edict but by people who have learned to think, work,
and relax together so that their total capabilities can be released
for the job.

If the way the Martin Co. or any other defense contractor has
handled the sensitive relationships with military or Government
officials gives rise to any possible misunderstanding, then that
way must be changed. There has been no violation of business or
political or military ethics that I know about in the relationships
between the Government and private industry in the current defense
program. It has been too grim an affair for energies to be diverted
from the supreme goal we must achieve. There can be no excuse for
unethical practices, and to my knowledge there has been none.

Press release, George M. Bunker, September 10, 1959, U.S.
Congress, 86th, 1st session, House of Representatives, Committee
on Armed Services, Subcommittee for Special Investigations,
Supplemental Hearings Released From Executive Session Relating to
Entertainment Furnished by the Martin Company of Baltimore, Md.,
of [to] U.S. Government Officers, p. 39.

756. PROTECTING BUSINESSMEN FROM BUSINESSMEN (1959)

The Federal Trade Commission Act of 1914 was part
of the protection-of-business program of the Wilson
administration. Over the years, the original purpose of
the law continued in force. Kintner was chairman of the
Federal Trade Commission and had been on the Commission's
legal staff for five years, and then was general legal
counsel for FTC for six more years. His testimony follows.

Mr. ROGERS. You do take the position that the FTC was set up,
not only for the purpose of protecting the individual, the American
public from fraud and deception, but also to maintain a balance of
fairness and a code of ethics or standards as between businessmen
in commerce generally, do you not?

Mr. KINTNER. Indeed, I think the latter was the primary
objective of the Federal Trade Commission Act.

Mr. ROGERS. You mean you think that the people were just
incidental to this situation?

Mr. KINTNER. The main thrust of the act is the protection of
the competitive free enterprise system. To the extent that system
is protected, the people are also protected.

Of course, we have the 1938 Wheeler-Lea amendment, which deals
directly with falsifying, and that protects both the businessman
and the consumer.

. . . .

I indicated that basically I thought the purpose of the
Federal Trade Commission Act was to protect the free enterprise
competitive system, to keep the channels of business free and clear
against practices which were prohibited by law. We have, I am sure,
an incidental purpose even in our antimonopoly work of protecting
the consumers. With respect to the false and misleading advertising
work that we do, we protect directly, I believe, both the consumers
and competing businessmen. With respect to our labeling statutes,
we certainly do protect most directly the consumers. But again the
purpose of the labeling statutes was to protect the scrupulous
businessman against the practices of the unscrupulous businessman.

Testimony, Earl W. Kintner, October 12, 1959, U.S. Congress,
86th, 1st session, House of Representatives, Committee on Interstate and Foreign Commerce, Special Subcommittee on Legislative
Oversight, Investigation of Television Quiz Shows, I, pp. 560,
595.

757. "THE MILITARY-INDUSTRIAL COMPLEX" (1961)

An interesting, if unexpected, alarum on an
important economic-political tendency. President Dwight
Eisenhower speaks in his Farewell Address.

Our military organization today bears little relation to that
known of any of my predecessors in peacetime--or, indeed, by the
fighting men of World War II or Korea.

Until the latest of our world conflicts, the United States
had no armaments industry. American makers of plowshares could,
with time and as required, make words as well.

But we can no longer risk emergency improvisation of national defense. We have been compelled to create a permanent armaments industry of vast proportions. Added to this, three and a half million men and women are directly engaged in the defense establishment. We annually spend on military security alone more than the net income of all United States corporations.

Now this conjunction of an immense military establishment and a large arms industry is new in the American experience. The total influence--economic, political, even spiritual--is felt in every city, every state house, every office of the Federal Government. We recognize the imperative need for this development. Yet we must not fail to comprehend its grave implications. Our toil, resources and livelihood are all involved; so is the very structure of our society.

In the councils of Government, we must guard against the acquisition of unwarranted influence, whether sought or unsought, by the military-industrial complex. The potential for the disastrous rise of misplaced power exists and will persist.

We must never let the weight of this combination endanger our liberties or democratic processes. We should take nothing for granted. Only an alert and knowledgeable citizenry can compel the proper meshing of the huge industrial and military machinery of defense with our peaceful methods and goals, so that security and liberty may prosper together.

Akin to, and largely responsible for the sweeping changes in our industrial-military posture has been the technological revolution during recent decades.

In this revolution research has become central. It also becomes more formalized, complex and costly. A steadily increasing share is conducted for, by, or at the direction of the Federal Government.

Today the solitary inventor, tinkering in his shop, has been overshadowed by task forces historically the fountainhead of free ideas and scientific discovery has experienced a revolution in the conduct of research. Partly because of the huge costs involved, a Government contract becomes virtually a substitute for intellectual curiosity.

For every old blackboard there are now hundreds of new electronic computers.

The prospect of domination of the nation's scholars by Federal employment, project allocations and the power of money is ever present, and is gravely to be regarded.

Yet, in holding scientific research and discovery in respect, as we should, we must also be alert to the equal and opposite danger that public policy could itself become the captive of a scientific-technological elite.

President Dwight D. Eisenhower, Farewell Address, January 17, 1961.

758. DEFENSE COSTS AND CONTRACTS (1969)

In the late 1960s, defense expenditures related
to the Vietnam War rose sharply. The General Accounting
Office (GAO) undertook an inquiry into the costs of producing major weapon systems during the years 1964-1968.
A study was made of 131 major programs whose aggregate
cost was $141 billions. A good deal of cost overrun --
or cost growth -- occurred. In 38 systems, costs ended
up being 50 percent over planned amounts. In a large
number of cases, time lags of from six months to over
three years occurred. The underlying causes of these and
other shortcomings, according to GAO, included unrealistic
cost estimates, excessive "concurrency of development and
production," "lack of administrative discipline," factors
beyond control of the Department of Defense, and other
factors. Robert F. Keller, Assistant Comptroller General
of the United States, and Hassell B. Bell, Associate
Director, Defense Division of the GAO, are questioned by
Sen. William Proxmire, chairman of the Joint Economic
Committee, in the following interchange.

Chairman PROXMIRE. Can you explain why the program has
increased in cost by $1.3 billion?
Mr. BELL. I can give you the Navy's explanation as shown on
the SAR [Selective Acquisitions Report]. Approximately $800 million
of the $1.3 billion is explained on the SAR as being due to a com-
bination of inflation and over- and under-estimates with no breakdown as to----
Chairman PROXMIRE. Let's see if we can separate those two.
How much of this is inflation and how much is a matter of over- or
under-estimate?
Mr. BELL. We could not get those details at the time we were
making this analysis.
Chairman PROXMIRE. This is one of the most significant and
largest overruns we have in any weapons systems and it seems to me
the Congress and the public had a right to have the details on
this. It is an enormous amount of money.
Mr. BELL. I discussed this with the officials of this particular program, and they are in the process of developing this but
they tell me there are thousands and thousands of individual actions
that contributed to this, and they didn't give me an estimate as to
when this job would be completed....
Mr. KELLER. Yes, sir, in discussing cost growth we believe it
is important to recognize that not all cost growth can reasonably
be prevented and that some cost growth, even though preventable,
may be desirable. Unusual periods of inflation, for instance,
result in cost growth. Changes in the state of the art make it
possible to incorporate modifications that result in an overall
increase in the cost effectiveness of the system. Such cost growth
cannot always be anticipated, particularly where a weapons system

is in development and production over a long period of time. We
believe that the greatest concern should be with cost growth that
results from such things as faulty planning, poor management, bad
estimating, or deliberate underestimating. Our analysis of the
cost growth that has occurred in the weapons systems we reviewed is
not as yet complete and we are, therefore, unable to segregate cost
growth by its various causes. To be fully meaningful such analysis
is essential so that the undesirable and preventable can be identified. The cost growth discussed here today includes all cost growth
that has been identified. It is not necessarily all preventable or
even undesirable.

Chairman PROXMIRE. Let me ask you at this point, Mr. Keller,
have you agreed to permit the Pentagon to solve the cost overrun
problem by exterminating the words "cost overrun" and substituting
the word "growth"?

Mr. KELLER. I don't think it really solves the problem,
Mr. Chairman. I think our feeling is that perhaps----

Chairman PROXMIRE. Why shouldn't you use "cost overrun"? Why
isn't that a good term?

Mr. KELLER. (continuing). It is a term that implies that
everything that happened was preventable, which isn't always the
case.

Chairman PROXMIRE. Why does it imply that? Cost overrun, it
seems to me that is about as neutral a description as you can have,
the cost overran, the cost was higher. When you say "cost growth,"
however, there are several semantic advantages that cost growth has
for the Pentagon. For one thing we are all for growth, growth of
the economy, growth of our children, growth of our moral stature,
and so forth. Growth is a good word and growth is something that
sounds as if it is wholesome and logical and necessary. It seems
to me the "overrun" is by far the more accurate descriptive term.

Mr. KELLER. Well, it may be. Perhaps we can compromise and
use both of them.

Chairman PROXMIRE. I notice in your statement you refer to
"underruns." This is an interesting word in view of your recent
elimination of the word "overruns."

Mr. KELLER. Perhaps we might have said "under growth."

Chairman PROXMIRE. You might have said "cost shrinkage" instead of underruns as we are now being taught to say "cost growth"
instead of "cost overruns."

Go right ahead.

COST "GROWTH" TOTALS

Mr. KELLER. Comparing the estimates through program completion, that is, the current estimate--and I am again referring to
tables I and II--with earlier estimates prepared on the basis of
(1), (2), and (3) above, we found that the 38 systems show a cost
growth of $20.919 billion or 49.85 percent from original planning
estimates; $13.051 billion or 26.2 percent from planned costs at
current quantity estimates.

Chairman PROXMIRE. Let me say at this point these overall
figures don't include the blanks that you had to leave out; it does
not include the $30 million.

Mr. KELLER. No, sir; we did not have all the figures and
they are not included.

Chairman PROXMIRE. Once again I think this is a conservative statement of the overruns.

Mr. KELLER. I think it has a value, but I think without it you don't have the reasons for the cost growth or cost overrun, whatever you want to call them.

Chairman PROXMIRE. At least you don't have an understanding.

Mr. KELLER. That is right.

Chairman PROXMIRE. Explanation.

Mr. KELLER. Where dollars were identified, the reasons most frequently cited were inflation, capability increases, contract cost increases, quantity increases, and poor estimating of expected cost and program stretchouts.

Of particular significance is the effect quantity or capability increases or decreases have on costs over the life of a program. These often times do vary and do have significant impact on total program cost. A determination of cost growth should take into consideration changes in quantities and capability as well as changes in dollars....

Chairman PROXMIRE. Are you telling us that they are the same, the contract price and the contract definition are the same?

Mr. BELL. No, sir, it is not the same.

Chairman PROXMIRE. It is not the same.

Mr. BELL. It isn't the same. In one of the programs I looked at last week the amount of the prime contract was only five-twelfths of the cost of the program. The other seven-twelfths of the costs of the program were represented by other types of costs and perhaps even contracts with different contractors to supply certain types of equipment.

Chairman PROXMIRE. So the contract, what do you use, contract definition is that what you call it?

Mr. BELL. Contract definition is their term.

Chairman PROXMIRE. The contract price is only a fraction of your total contract definition.

CONTRACT DEFINITION

Mr. BELL. Contract definition, Mr. Chairman, is a kind of state of mind. It is a point in time in which the managers feel they have worked out a good number of the technical bugs, they have a pretty firm idea of what it is they want to build and how many they want and are now ready to start to negotiate a contract or a series of contracts to get them.

Chairman PROXMIRE. What's the difference between that and the contract price? Tell us what this very large proportion is that is not part of the contract price but is part of contract definition, you said about five-twelfths.

Mr. BELL. In one particular contract. Associating contract price with contract definition is something I have difficulty doing. Contract definition is a point in time in which they are ready to proceed on a certain program.

Chairman PROXMIRE. It includes the contract price?

Mr. BELL. Not yet.

Chairman PROXMIRE. What other elements?

Mr. BELL. At this point in time they are ready to start to negotiate a price with a contractor or with a group of contractors,

and the price that they eventually negotiate may be quite different
from the price that they have established.

Chairman PROXMIRE.   It could be more?

Mr. BELL.   It could be more, it could be less.   You will notice
in our schedule a couple of Navy programs they have excluded the
current estimate total program.

Chairman PROXMIRE.   Why not use the contract price for the
whole program?

Mr. KELLER.   Well, there are many costs over and above the
contract.

Mr. BELL.   Right.

Chairman PROXMIRE.   Many costs in addition to the contract cost,
such as the cost over 5 years such as you gave us in the rescue
vehicle.

Mr. KELLER.   Yes.

Testimony, December 29, 1969, U.S. Congress, 91st, 1st session,
Joint Economic Committee, The Acquisition of Major Weapons Systems.
Hearings...., Part 1, (Washington, D.C.:   Government Printing
Office, 1970), pp. 28-31, 38.

759.   POOR BUSINESS AT THE PENTAGON (1970)

The Joint Economic Committee of Congress was investigating costs in defense contracts.   One of the chief witnesses it invited was Robert N. Anthony, former Assistant
Secretary of Defense, Comptroller and present professor of
management control at Harvard Business School.   He was asked
to comment on seven issues: (1) causes and remedies of
cost overruns, (2) concurrency: premature production,
(3) overhead costs too high, (4) inadequate cost accounting
standards, (5) profits as a percentage of costs, (6) performance measurement, and (7) lack of interest in cost
control.   With respect to number 7, Anthony pointed out
that "many persons, including some senior officials take the
position" that if the article meets performance specifications and is delivered on time that cost is relatively unimportant.   "It is extremely difficult to change the current
attitude," commented Anthony.   He doubted improvement would
come without "a basic change within the [Defense] Department."   Following is a statement by F. Trowbridge vom Baur,
former general counsel of the Department of the Navy and
presently a lawyer.

I do not believe that it is commonly understood, particularly
by the public, that the Department of Defense is considerably more
than just a military organization.   The fact is that it is also a
tremendous business organization.   And I submit to you that this

business side of the Department of Defense can only be effectively managed by the application of business, rather than military principles.

The nub of the problem, however, has been that the Department of Defense is seriously out of balance, in my opinion, because it is influenced by an overemphasis on what might be described as purely military thinking.

I do not mean to be critical of the emphasis on military thinking, for, of course, it is a paramount consideration. But the extent to which the business side of the Navy has been downgraded, in my opinion, sir, has had serious results.

Procurement and contract administration are just supposed to rock along as second- or third-class functions. And in my opinion the people in the business side of the Department of Defense are inadequately recognized, inadequately staffed, inadequately housed, and inadequately paid, in relation to the inherent role which they do play in the administration of government, and in relation to the staggering amounts of dollars for whose disbursement they are responsible.

They are, in my opinion, the orphaned stepchildren, the poor relations of the Department of Defense.

Now, let me pass on to say that the overall result of all this is that in my opinion there are simply great quantities of mistakes and errors which are made by people in the business side of the Department of Defense which are tremendously expensive for the Government, which do delay the delivery of ships and other hardware, but which simply do not have to be made.

In my judgment these unnecessary mistakes cost the Government and the good old taxpayer something like 25 to 30 percent of the procurement budget.

Now, the procurement budget for defense is presently running, as I understand it, at about $40 billion, meaning that, in my opinion, some $10 to $12 billion a year is wasted through this downgrading of the business side of the Department of Defense.

Now, I have some specific examples which I will pass over lightly, Mr. Chairman. Again we come back to these nitty-gritty little items, perhaps, defective specs, delays in delivery of GFP, delivery of defective GFP, suspensions of work, et cetera.

Now, one of the things that concerns me about all this is that with the downgrading of procurement and contract administration in the Department of Defense, few people at high levels in the past have seemed to think that these items have had any real importance. And very frankly, the usual high-level reactions appear to me to have been something along this line. "Well, OK, but don't bother me to have all this, this is just low-level stuff, these are just a bunch of dull, grubby, nit-picking items, let's change the subject and pass on to something more deserving of high-level attention."

The fact is that these undoubtedly are dull, grubby, and nit-picking items. But from the taxpayer's standpoint, Mr. Chairman, they are items of tremendous importance, if for no other reason than that unnecessary mistakes in these areas have been wasting the taxpayer's money in my judgment, to the tune of something like $10 to $12 billion a year....

Perhaps you have heard, Mr. Chairman, that there is an old saying that the Army is run by sergeants and privates. In any event, when it comes to procurement, procurement and contract administration are really run to a very large extent by so-called sergeants and privates. Indeed, literally billions of dollars are spent not only by contracting officers but also by contract administrators, contract negotiators, inspectors, and believe it or not, by Government engineers and technical people.

With respect to inspectors, a single inspector, for instance, may reject items of hardware moving along a production line, where delays are very expensive, unless some change in the hardware is made. Yet the inspector may not realize that he is interpreting specifications and making legal decisions and perhaps issuing constructive change orders which may prove to be very expensive for the Government....

Systems are entrenched. People like to go on doing things in the same old way. And frankly, very few people in the Department have ever been energetically interested in reform. The great bulk of them just like to rock along on a day-to-day basis. They prefer, as some people say, to "keep the papers moving" rather than to make the strenuous efforts necessary for change and improvement.

Testimony, May 20, 1970, U.S. Congress, 91st, 2nd session, Joint Economic Committee, Subcommittee on Economy in Government, The Acquisition of Weapons Systems. Hearings....., Part 2, (Washington, D.C.: Government Printing Office, 1970), pp. 285-287.

760. A DANGEROUS GAME (1977)

Early in the 19th Century, American courts did not quite know how to conceive of the "personality" of a corporation. Was the corporation a person, a collectivity without individuality, or simply an organization led by individuals? During the 1840s and for the next half century, federal courts chose to conceive of the corporation as artificial persons, separate from the personal actions of its officers. Here is a protest against that conception, formulated by Admiral Hyman G. Rickover, pioneer in the use of nuclear submarines.

Today the privileged members of American society are engaged in a dangerous game. They are undermining the law; yet their existence depends upon the law. Contracts are no longer agreements to perform work or services, but have become armories from which highly paid lawyers find weapons to wage courtroom battles in a

campaign to increase profits. Within the last few weeks I have seen
in newspapers example after example of alleged wrongdoing by business.

There is a distinction between profit and profiteering.
Businessmen complain about overregulation, yet it is the acts of
some of them that have made the regulation necessary. Professional
societies, while proclaiming their mission is to maintain ethical
standards, are silent.

Individual pursuit of self-advancement in our commercial society is beginning to burst its efficient bounds. Unless we act
now to relieve the resulting tensions, the commercial institutions
themselves will be jeopardized.

Myopia, along with hypocrisy, is usually self-defeating.
Adolf Berle made the perceptive observation that when business
threatens to engulf the state, it forces the state to engulf business.

The 14th amendment was first applied to a corporation in 1886.
It was in a famous case--Santa Clara County v. Southern Pacific
Railroad. But the idea had been developing for several years before
that decision was delivered.

In 1873 the Supreme Court, in the Slaughter-House cases had
held that the 14th amendment did not apply to corporations; that
the word "person" in the phrase "nor shall any State deprive any
person of life, liberty, or property without due process of law"--
which was copied from the fifth amendment--was intended to protect
the newly emancipated slaves. "We are convinced," said Mr. Justice
Miller, speaking for the court, "that the sole 'pervading purpose'
of this and the other war amendments was "the freedom of the slave
race'."

The judges of the court were contemporaries of Congress and
the State legislatures enacting the amendment and, therefore,
more familiar than later courts with what the amendment was intended
to accomplish. Yet for 90 years now, the Supreme Court has taken
the opposite view, holding that a corporation, being a "person" in
law, is entitled to the protection of the 14th amendment.

I submit that if a corporation is to be assimilated to a
natural person for purposes of protection under the 14th amendment,
then all the obligations incumbent on "natural persons" ought also
to be binding on the corporation. And, since the corporation acts
through its officials, these should be held personally liable for
illegal corporate acts. Woodrow Wilson stated the issue most
clearly:

> I regard the corporation as indispensable
> to modern business enterprise. I am not jealous
> of its size or might, if you will but abandon at the
> right points the fatuous, antiquated, and quite unnece-
> ssary fiction which treats it as a legal person; if you
> will but cease to deal with it by means of your law as
> if it were a single individual not only, but also--what
> every child may perceive it is not--a responsible indi-
> vidual.

I have had experience with corporate behavior which by a
"natural person" would be considered illegal. It would seem to me

that where officials of a corporation, acting for it, commit the
corporation to illegal acts they should be held personally
accountable.

I cannot see how a corporation can be compelled to act as a
"responsible individual," to use Wilson's phrase, unless this
responsibility is attached to the human beings who speak and act
for it.

The officials who act for the corporation ought to be held
personally responsibile if by their acts the corporation breaks
the law.

It seems to me that the law must prevail and that no techni-
cality ought to stand in the way. Niether nolo contendere or consent decrees should be permitted for corporation officials. Nor
should fines for illegal acts be used to reduce corporate taxable
profit by calling them "expenditures," thereby negating the punitive
aspects. Legal concepts ought not to be twisted so as to allow
those guilty of illegal acts to escape the legal consequences of
their wrongdoings.

The Santa Clara County decision and the cases that followed
it prevented the States from taxing or regulating the corporations
whenever a court held that the corporation had been denied "due
process." Most courts at that time were heavily oriented in favor
of business, so the corporations ran pretty much unchecked. That
eventually led to the Sherman Anti-Trust Act. However, the corporations retained the rights of individuals under the law, but they
are not required to accept the same responsibilities.

An illustration of the corporations' personal rights are: The
tax advantage it has over individuals; the persistent efforts of
corporations to limit their normal responsibility under the law for
the safety and operation of their products. The officials of one
large corporation even arranged for its stockholders to indemnify
the corporate officers in defense of criminal and civil suits brought
against them. An individual cannot free himself of such responsibilities.

As a consequence of actions by corporate officers, they have,
in actuality, arrogated to themselves rights which make them supercitizens.

Since there are more than 2 million corporations in the United
States, there are at least 4 million corporate officers. These
are the supercitizens who constitute a privileged group, not
accountable in the same manner required of ordinary human citizens.
They are analogous to the aristocrats of old, with their special
privileges. Their existence is contrary to the basis of our
Government.

I firmly believe in the capitalist system under which, if it
is not perverted, there is greater freedom and opportunity than
under any other political system. To preserve this capitalist system businesses must maintain their integrity. If they cannot or
will not, Government will be compelled to do it for them.

I believe that the position which must be held on the hard
issue of personal responsibility should not collapse under the
sanctuary of the 14th amendment. I also believe we should not have
superior citizenship for a small, wealthy, powerful minority.

The only substantive answer, both in respect to antitrust laws
and others aimed at corporate activities, is to rid American juris-
prudence of the myth that corporations are beings subject to the
same civil codes and procedures as are afforded human beings.

Testimony, June 14, 1977, U.S. Congress, 95th, 1st session,
Senate, Committee on Banking, Housing, and Urban Affairs, Extension
of the Renegotiation Act. Hearings...., (Washington, D.C.:
Government Printing Office, 1977), pp. 508-510.

761. CLEANING UP THREE MILE ISLAND (1981)

Nuclear power is one of the most heavily government-
subsidized industries in the American economy. Most of the
research underlying the feasibility of nuclear power was
financed by the federal government as was the early development of nuclear facilities. Expenses involved in the
regulation of the construction, operation, and maintenance
of nuclear reactors were borne almost wholly by the federal
government. Much training of industry personnel was done
in federal research installations or research facilities
financed by federal funds. When a nuclear accident
occurred at Three Mile Island in 1979, industry representatives contended the federal government should bear much
of the expense of cleaning up. Here J. Hugh Devlin,
managing director of Morgan Stanley & Co., Inc., a large
investment banking house, testifies. Devlin is in
charge of the firm's business with the public utilities
industry.

My comments today are an update of remarks I made to the subcommittee on a similar subject in September 1979, about 6 months
after the TMI accident.
     Since that time, there has been significant deterioration
in the health of the electric utility industry coupled with little,
if any, progress in resolution of the TMI problem.
     It is my view that this makes the situation much more serious
today, and that it must be addressed in the Federal legislative
arena.
     Investors perceive that the financial condition of the electric
utility industry today is extremely weak.
     The industry has suffered from the high inflation and large
construction programs of the 1970's, and is at an all-time low.
     At the same time, the industry faces record high and, in
many cases, still increasing capital requirements—much of which is
necessary to complete the 82 nuclear units currently under construction.

Investors are increasingly selective in their investment decisions. Utilities must compete for investment funds with other segments of the economy, including industrial companies and the
Federal Government.

The access of the electric utility industry to the capital
markets will depend directly on the confidence of investors in the
industry's future viability.

This investor confidence, however, is extremely fragile.

There is no doubt in my mind that it would be dealt a serious
blow if GPU were to be allowed to go bankrupt from the burden of
the TMI cleanup.

I believe that a bankruptcy of GPU would have severe reper-
cussions for electric utilities on the financial markets.

If investors experience a problem with one nuclear company,
they may well be unwilling to take the risk of investing in any
nuclear utilities, even in those with the best operating records.

They do not believe they are being compensated for the risk of
potential bankruptcy from an accident and substantial loss of their
investment.

There are too many other investments with commensurate or
higher returns available to them which have less risk.

Increasingly, however, we see investors focusing on the
exposure of utilities with existing nuclear units.

As the costs of TMI cleanup have been escalating, there has
been growing awareness of the potential impact of even one nuclear
unit on the financial well-being of a company.

As long as an answer to TMI cleanup is now known, GPU is likely
to have periodic crises and close calls with bankruptcy such as
occurred this April.

Each of these crises increases the awareness of investors and
potentially decreases the industry's access to the capital markets.

Investors do not have the solution to the TMI cleanup problem,
nor have we at Morgan Stanley reviewed the various proposals to deal
with the problem.

I do believe that investors would look favorably on an overall
formula to handle the cleanup.

It is logical to have the cleanup expense shared by all parties, including GPU customers, whose rates are still low relative
to many parts of the Nation.

An important element to the solution must be the early return
of TMI-1 to commercial operation and to rate base treatment by the
Pennsylvania and New Jersey commissions.

It is my view that the TMI cleanup is a national problem.

Testimony, May 4, 1981, U.S. Congress, 97th, 1st session,
House of Representatives, Committee on Interior and Insular Affairs,
Subcommittee on Energy and the Environment, Financial Implications
of the Accident at Three Mile Island. Oversight Hearings,
(Washington, D.C.: Government Printing Office, 1981), pp. 58-59.

762.   ILLUSORY COMPETITION IN DEFENSE CONTRACTING (1981)

While the federal government spent over $315 billion
during World War II, contracting with more than 18,000
firms for military goods, nearly half the contracts went
to just 30 firms; two-thirds went to a slightly larger
number -- 100 firms.   Twenty-four years after the war, ten
of the top defense contractors had been among the top 20
during World War II.   Such concentration reflected the
general character of the economy rather than political
favoritism.   Whether the product was electronics or heavy
manufacturers, the span of choice among producers was
slight.   Attesting to the truth of this fact is the
following statement by Admiral Hyman G. Rickover, Deputy
Commander for Nuclear Propulsion, Naval Sea Systems Command,
Department of the Navy.

Competition in defense procurement is often more illusory than
real.   While 35 percent of the defense procurement budget is spent
under contracts the Defense Department considers competitive, only
about 8 percent is spent on formally advertised procurements--that
is where any company may submit a bid and the contract must be
awarded to the lowest responsible bidder.   In some competitive
procurements only two or three firms are asked to bid.   In other so-
called competitive procurements the competition is not based on
price but on design or other technical factors.   Sixty-five percent
of the defense procurement budget is awarded in contracts which the
Defense Department itself labels as noncompetitive....

Some believe that all defense contractors can be counted upon
to exercise self restraint.   Here are some examples to the contrary:

One: One sole source contractor typically negotiates a target
profit equal to 10 percent of the estimated cost of the work.   The
work is done under risk-free, cost-plus-incentive-fee contracts.
After the contract is completed and all changes have been negotiated, he ends up making, on the average, a 17.5 percent profit on
his actual incurred costs.

Two: One contractor has made profits as high as 36 percent on
some firm fixed price contracts for ship repair work.   The contractor has averaged a 21 percent profit on these contracts, even though
his risk has been negligible.

Three: A company that manufactures high pressure air flasks
for Trident submarines insisted on a profit between 27 and 38 percent of estimated cost.

Four: A sole source supplier of special material used in
nuclear propulsion plants demands a profit of 25 percent of his
estimated cost.

Five: A sole source supplier of special material used for
large valves in nuclear-powered ships initially refused to submit
the cost and pricing data required by law in the Truth in Negotiations Act.   The order was placed contingent upon his agreement to
provide this data.   After the contract award, the company

submitted cost data which showed a 66 percent profit in his price.
...

Although the Defense Department evaluates and negotiates profits as a percentage of cost, we cannot always tell whether or not
excessive profits exist just by looking at contractor profit expressed as a percentage of cost. If the dollars he invested are
small in relation to his profit, return on this investment will
naturally be high. For this reason when a contractor has high
costs and small investment, 5 percent profit on cost can be very
lucrative....

We all know what the defense contractor lobbyists have been
trying to achieve. In the 1960's they worked to block establishment of the Cost Accounting Standards Board on the basis that the
Renegotiation Board adequately protected the public against excessive profits. Then, after Congress established the Cost Accounting
Standards Board, they lobbied to abolish the Renegotiation Board,
citing the Cost Accounting Standards Board as the safeguard that
made Renegotiation unnecessary.

Again, when the Renegotiation Board went out of existence,
they set their sights on abolishing the Cost Accounting Standards
Board, or at least transferring it to the executive branch where
they would have a better chance to water down the standards.

Today both the Renegotiation Board and the Cost Accounting
Standards Board are out of business. The next objective apparently
is to eliminate the sole remaining form of profit-limiting legislation, the Vinson-Trammel Act, and block efforts to replace it
with a more effective substitute.

There is very little true competition in defense procurement.
For the most part the prices are negotiated between the Government
and the contractor. In negotiated procurements the Government often
has little choice but to give in to the contractor's demands. If
the Government will not pay the contractor's price, the Government
will not obtain the supplies and equipment it requires.

There is not much that can be done to preclude contractors
from negotiating high contract prices. The only way to insure
excessive profits will not occur is for the Government to strictly
enforce effective profit-limiting legislation.

Members of my organization have been involved all morning in
the Naval Sea Systems Command's attempts to negotiate a nuclear
submarine contract with a large shipbuilder who continues to fight
Navy efforts to limit after-the-fact claims submissions. The shipbuilder wants practically a limitless time in which to submit
claims. We say no, because we know that shipbuilders can identify
and price out claims promptly. Any going business can tell at the
end of the day just where they stand, but when it comes to doing
Government work, shipbuilders say they need years to determine
if they overspent and why.

Testimony, February 25, 1980, U.S. Congress, 97th, 1st session,
House of Representatives, Committee on Armed Services, Subcommittee
on Procurement and Military Nuclear Systems, Vinson-Trammell Act of
1934 and the Necessity for Profit Limitations on Defense Contracts
in the Current Contracting Environment. Hearings...., (Washington,
D.C.: Government Printing Office, 1981), pp. 64-68.

L.

INDUSTRIAL RESEARCH

763. PREJUDICE AGAINST AMERICAN-MADE INSTRUMENTS (1900)

The backwardness of American science created its
own prejudice against American-made scientific equipment.
John Gordon Gray was associated with A. Queen and Co., a
manufacturing and importing firm, specializing in
electrical and optical instruments. He was also secretary
of the Manufacturers' Club of Philadelphia.

Q. Do you as merchants deal in goods produced by other
American manufacturers?--A. To some extent; yes.
Q. What proportion of the goods that you sell is imported?--
A. I suppose not more than 20 per cent.
Q. Why do you import any?--A. Because in certain lines we
can import rather cheaper than we can make, and because for certain
things there is an established demand, and also largely because,
dealing as we do with American colleges and universities, there is
a demand for foreign instruments which could be fully met by
American instruments if these same college professors would take
them; but many of the younger professors have studied abroad and
have become imbued with the idea that it is the proper thing to
have European-made instruments, and they insist upon having instruments made by certain makers abroad, whereas instruments of the
same class and of equal quality are made here and actually exported.
In other words, we are importing things which can be gotten better
and cheaper here to satisfy the idea or fancy of certain individuals.

Q. That is one of the disadvantages of a foreign education, then?--A. Precisely.

Testimony, John Gordon Gray, December 17, 1900, U.S. Congress, 57th, 1st session, House of Representatives, Document No. 183, Report of the Industrial Commission on the Relations of Capital and Labor Employed in Manufactures and General Business, XIV, pp. 208-209.

764. ARE CONSULTANT AND CORPORATION COMPATIBLE? (1900)

The following is an interesting speculation by George Rockwood, an engineer from Worcester, Massachusetts, on the probable role of "outside" consultant engineers in the modern corporation. In the event, they were compatible.

In regard to the education of the consulting engineer, I feel strongly myself that the engineer of the future is not, for one thing, to be submerged in great corporations. I think it is a fair question, an open question, whether these great corporations themselves are going to last, although perhaps that may prove to be the ultimate method of business. Nevertheless, it seems to me reasonable to believe that the consulting engineer as a species is not to become extinct in consequence of these corporations. There are too many places and positions and "jobs" which he can do in an independent capacity, which he cannot do if in the employ of a corporation. Nearly all street-railway work, nearly all power-plant work, nearly all mill engineering and mill architecture, nearly all "civil engineering," must be done by an independent engineer or firm of engineers; and these requirements alone will always, it seems to me, sustain the consulting engineer in an independent position, free of corporations; so that the manufacturing engineer is not really taking the place of the consulting mechanical engineer who did nothing but design machines; perhaps there are such men, but my conception of the consulting mechanical engineer is that he deals, for the most part, in broad questions of policy and administration, and of the arrangement and also detail of machinery and buildings.

George I. Rockwood, Transactions, American Society of Mechanical Engineers, XXI (1900), p. 1139.

765.   THE BUSINESS OF INNOVATING (1901)

Here is one of the earliest examples of an innovator
of innovations on a business basis. The speaker is
Isaac Rice. Rice's other business affiliations included
directorships in five southern railroads, foreign representative in Europe for the Philadelphia and Reading Railroad
Company, reorganizer of the Reading Company, co-former of
the anthracite combination. Altogether Rice was a rare
combination of technical innovator, monopolist, and
financier.

Q. (By Mr. RIPLEY.) Will you state your full name, occupation, and address?--A. My name is Isaac Leopold Rice.
Q. And occupation?--A. My occupation is difficult to define.
I am president of a number of companies engaged in developing inventions, such as the Electric Boat Company, which included the Holland
submarine boat. I suppose you have heard of the Consolidated Equipment Company, which produces electricity for lighting trains from
the motion of the wheels? I am also president of the Consolidated
Rubber Tire Company, and I am vice-president of the Casein Company
of America which is developing a new raw material in milk which is
entering largely into industries now, such as the paint industry,
paper sizing, glue, sugar or milk, and other cognate industries.
All of these are based on patents granted by the United States
Government.
Q. In the organization of companies based upon patents, what
is your practice respecting capitalization?--A. Well, the usual
practice is this: The working capital is provided by the preferred
stock, which is paid for in cash, and by means of which the patents
are developed. The patents themselves are valued in common stock.
Q. Do you mean that the preferred stock is equal to the actual
value of the tangible, physical plant, machinery, building, supplies,
and so forth?--A. Well, in new invention, as a rule, they have no
tangible plant. That all has to be provided out of the capital
which is subscribed. Take, for instance, the electric-vehicle
industry. I am the father of that industry in the United States.
I secured a lot of cash in that industry, about $12,000,000, when
practically there was not a plant in existence, simply for the
purpose of developing the business. Take the Electric Storage
Battery Company. I am founder of that industry in the United
States, and we started with the mere patents; the money first has
to be raised to develop the industry.
Q. What is the usual process of promotion in case of companies
of that kind? Is the money usually advanced by an underwriting
syndicate of bankers?--A. Well, in my case I have no syndicate,
but I have a number of friends who have confidence in my judgement,
and if I tell them that it is a good thing they will subscribe the
money. I usually head the list by the largest subscription, very
much the largest. My friends follow with whatever may be necessary
to continue the business; it may be $1,000,000, or, as it was in

the vehicle business, $12,000,000; it depends on the amount actually required to develop it.

Q. Are most of those companies of which you speak owned broadly throughout the country, or are they owned by a few people? --A. Owned broadly.

Q. They are, therefore, listed on the exchange?--A. No; they are not listed on the exchange, but are dealt in without being listed. I myself am not what is called a promoter at all. I take these things with the intention of developing the industry, and the people aid as they please with their stock subscriptions. I never have anything to do with manipulating the stock or anything of that kind. I have never done that; it is not in my line at all; people buy and sell the stocks according to the value that they believe them to have.

Testimony, Isaac Leopold Rice, May 11, 1901, U.S. Congress, 57th, 1st session, House of Representatives, Document No. 178, Report of the Industrial Commission on Transportation, IX, p. 732.

766. "THERE ARE BUT FEW PIONEER INVENTIONS" (1906)

A full-bodied statement on invention stressing both the collective and the individual aspects.

As to the question of giving the credit to the inventor--I speak not of those broad and radical inventions, which are rare and far between, but of by far the largest number of patents--it must be considered that in most cases the problem was put before the inventor by some one else, or as part of his professional work; it was solved by the use of a vast amount of experience gathered by others, without which he could not proceed a single step, and very frequently that step which constitutes invention would be of no value whatever, except in connection with the rest of the work, and even then a great amount of development work may be needed to reduce the invention to practical value. That is, the new idea, while it is an invention, requires a great deal more, before it is of commercial utility, and to claim for the inventor all the credit for the advance in the art resulting from the invention, is as unjust as it would be not to give any credit for inventive origin-ality.

I repeat, most inventions are engineering steps, part of the regular work of the successful engineer, who must possess not only the knowledge to use old ways and methods, but also the originality to find new ways when required to solve the problem before him.

There are but few pioneer inventions. It occasionally happens that inventions are made which open up an entirely new field, establish a new industry, as the invention of the incandescent lamp,

of the wireless telegraph, of the polyphase system. And frequently
it is difficult to state the exact feature of which the invention
consists, especially when after the lapse of years the inventor's
work has become commonplace to the world. Take for instance the
case of the Edison incandescent lamp. This is one of the most useful, important, and radical inventions. It perhaps can be said to
be the foundation of the electrical engineering industry. Before
that, electrical engineering was only the art of telegraphy; after
that electric power became a quantity to consider. But before
Edison people had run filaments in a vacuum. Carbon filaments had
been proposed. The high-resistance-feature of the filament is
difficult to consider as an essential distinction, since it is
merely a quantitative difference: as long as the source of electric
power was a primary battery of low voltage, a high-resistance filament would have been decidedly disadvantageous--low resistance
wanted; that was self-evident, especially after Edison had done it.
To lead the current into a bulb, platinum wires had probably been
used before Edison. So you may ask: What is meant by the invention of the incandescent lamp? That is a question for lawyers to
discuss; and since the patents have expired, the details are of no
further interest. But before Edison, incandescent lighting did not
exist. As the result of Edison's work on the incandescent lamp,
an industry of vast importance has been created, and a revolution
brought about in the methods of illumination. The importance of
the problem was realized before Edison. But whatever may be the
details of the work, nobody did it before, and to the one who made
the incandescent lamp what it is to-day, the historian gives the
credit.

Charles Proteus Steinmetz, May 30, 1906, *Transactions*,
American Institute of Electrical Engineers, XXV (1906), pp. 542-
543.

767.   TRADE SECRECY IN THE ART OF CUTTING METALS (1906)

For twenty-six years, beginning in 1880, a group of
gifted engineers and mechanics under the leadership of
Frederick W. Taylor experimented on the cutting of metals
and came to a number of novel conclusions. One example:
"In 1881, the discovery that a round-nosed tool could be
run under given conditions at a much higher cutting speed
and therefore turn out much more work than the old-fashioned
diamond-pointed tool."

Throughout the whole 26 years we have succeeded in keeping
almost all of these laws secret, and in fact since 1889 this has
been our means of obtaining the money needed to carry on the work.

We have never sold any information connected with this art for cash, but we have given to one company after another all of the data and conclusions arrived at through our experiments in consideration for the opportunity of still further continuing our work. In one shop after another machines have been fitted up for our use, workmen furnished us to run them, and especially prepared tools, forgings and castings supplied in exchange for the data which we had obtained to date; and we have the best indication that they received full value for the money spent from the fact that the same company fitted up for us at intervals of several years three sets of apparatus, the additional knowledge obtained each time evidently warranting them in making the added outlay.

During this period all of the companies who were given this information, and all of the men who worked upon the experiments, were bound by promises to the writer not to give any of this information away nor to allow it to be published. Most of these promises were verbal; and in this day when there is so much talk about dishonesty and graft in connection with some of our corporations and prominent business men, it is a notable fact that through a period of 26 years it has not come to our knowledge that any one of the many men or companies connected with this work has broken a promise. The writer has his doubts whether any other country can produce a parallel record of such widespread good faith among its engineers and mechanics.

It seems to us that the time has now come for the engineering fraternity to have the results of our work, in spite of the fact that this will cut off our former means of financing the experiments. However, we are in hopes that the money required to complete this work may be obtained from some other source.

Frederick Winslow Taylor, "On the Art of Cutting Metals," Transactions, American Society of Mechanical Engineers, XXVIII (1907), p. 36.

768. EXPERIMENTATION WILL LEAD TO IMPROVED MACHINERY (1908)

The American textile-machinery industry was notably unprogressive. (See Source No. 382). Following, however, is a statement by William Draper, the head of an unusually innovative machinery firm. At the time, his firm's Northrup-Draper automatic loom was sweeping the industry. He was president of George Draper & Son, a large and progressive textile-machinery manufactory.

Our business for fifty years or more has not been based on the manufacture of "standard" machinery; but upon experiments, resulting in improvements, which we introduced and made "standard" if

successful. We further bought and developed [more] inventions of
others in textile machinery, and cloth than any other establishment
in that line of business. In fact, it is not egotism to say that we
did more in that direction than all our competitors added together.

This, of course, introduced complication into our affairs,--it
being necessary to study faults, and develop remedies,--then to
test the remedies,--then to secure them by letters patent,--and
later, to protect our rights by litigation,--in addition to the
buying and selling and manufacturing incident to mechanical work.

Up to the consolidation of our various companies in 1896 I gave
attention to all departments of the business, and for ten years
before that time all were under my control. My ambassadorship nec-
essitated a change, and after my return in 1900 I confined myself
to the special departments above mentioned,--outside of serving as
President and giving general advice as a senior director, and the
largest stockholder.

My special duties covered invention, experiment, purchase of
improvements, tests to determine value, securing patents, and litigation. As our new patents aggregated a hundred or more per annum,
and as experiments and litigation were always in progress, I was
sufficiently occupied with congenial work, and not as closely confined as if I had looked after the more ordinary detail.

This experimenting to keep at the front was, and must be, expensive and sometimes unfruitful; but improvements were the foundation of our business and the basis for the larger percentage of
gain which we earned, as compared with the results of ordinary
manufacture.

My brothers, however, did not fully sympathize either with
this view or with my expensive and exhaustive manner of conducting
experiments. For several years after my return from Europe they
acquiesced in my mode of action, but finally, and to me unexpected-
ly, in the winter of 1906, they secured a vote in the Board of
Directors which brought about a change of policy, and removed the
experimental department from my control. Believing that this was
an error, and that it would, as patents expired, change our business
to the mere making of standard machines, I sold the greater part of
my stock and invested elsewhere.

I believed that the change would, in the course of years,
diminish the profits of the business; but even if it did not, I had
reached the point where I cared more for advancing the textile art,
to which I had devoted so much of my life, than I did for the merely
profitable manufacture of standard articles. I wish my associates
all success in their new departure and believe that the enterprise
will continue; but there will hereafter, I fear, be less reason for
personal pride in the Draper Company as a prominent factor in
textile improvement.

William F. Draper, Recollections of a Varied Career, (Boston,
Massachusetts: Little, Brown, and Co., 1908), pp. 375-377.

769. FURNACE DOCTORS IN NEW JERSEY (1910)

Another evidence of the persistence of artisan
craft mysteries in the machine age written by John
Keenan, who was working for a small firm, the Wharton
Iron Company, near Dover, New Jersey.

In those days blast furnaces still held most of their secrets.
They hold some of them today. Two furnaces built side by side,
identical in construction, can be as different in operation as day
from night. One will break records and be called a 'sweet thing.'
The other may never behave. That kind of furnace is always termed
an 'old bitch.' And when those old furnaces went on the rampage,
they were man killers. Such a furnace is said to be 'sick,' and
as late as 1910 there were still some furnace 'doctors' operating
in New Jersey and Pennsylvania, men who were called in to take
complete charge until the sick furnace was in condition again. One
doctor, I remember, also ran a blacksmith shop where he made shoes
for draft horses and mine mules. He did odd jobs of dynamiting,
too, when required. It doesn't seem possible now [1943] that only
thirty-odd years ago. . .we in America were relying on people like
that part-time horseshoer and dynamiter to doctor our sick furnaces.
It's human enough to resist change, and lots of experienced men in
the business mistrusted the trend toward science in steel making
which began after the invention of the open-hearth steel process in
1878. . . .I believe Carl Langrebe, now vice-president of the
Tennessee Coal and Iron Company, was the first American college
graduate to break into the blast-furnace field. Before his time
most of the furnace superintendents, even along the Atlantic
seabord, were not Americans, but Englishmen who had had some
university training.

John L. Keenan, with collaboration of Lenore Sorsby, A Steel
Man in India, (New York: Duell, Sloan, and Pearce, 1943), pp. 12-
14.

770. THREE TYPES OF INVENTION (1919)

How would a socialist society affect inventions?
Here is an answer by a prominent inventor, Charles
Steinmetz, Consulting Engineer to the General Electric
Company, and former president of the American Institute
of Electrical Engineers.

Roughly, inventions may be divided into three groups:

(1) Fundamental or basic inventions which create new fields for human effort, or even a new era in the world's history, such as the invention of the steam engine, steamship and locomotive; of the cotton gin, which created the cotton industry, of the alternating current transformer, which made modern electrical development possible.

(2) Inventions which are merely steps in the design and development of things, such as a new form of gear shift in the automobile, or a new way of winding an electric motor.

(3) Incidental or accidental inventions, such as a new puzzle, which strikes the popular fancy.

Consider first the second group, since it represents by far the largest majority of the many thousands of inventions patented annually in the United States, and since, while individually these inventions are not radical and revolutionary and usually not thought of in the layman's discussion of inventions and inventors, in their bulk they represent the industrial progress of the country.

In the successive steps of his work, the engineer, designer or constructor devises means to accomplish the desired result, drawing upon his knowledge, skill and ability. Where these means are new, they constitute a patentable invention, and invention thus is an integral part of the routine of the engineer's work. That is, the engineer lacking in originality and limited in his work to the known means, finds himself seriously handicapped, and originality and inventive ability are essential for the successful engineer or designer.

With the progress of the world's industrial development towards organization into larger and larger corporations, steadily the number of independent engineers is decreasing and more and more find it to their advantage to enter the employ of the corporations.

In corporation employment of the engineer, it is, however, to a large extent the custom that the inventions made by the engineer, and the patents covering them, belong to the company, and not to the inventor, and the inventor thus derives no direct financial benefit from his individual invention. This practice is increasing, as experience proves it to be the most satisfactory. Morally, there is much justification in this arrangement. Usually the problem which the engineer solved by his invention has been brought before him by his work for the company, and the data and information which enabled him to solve the problem, to a considerable extent made available, and the means to develop the invention supplied by the corporation, so that outside the corporation the engineer probably would not have met the problem, and if he had met it, would have been unable to solve it. The engineer's compensation then is his pay, which covers the products of his knowledge as well as his originality and inventive skill, and the reputation he derives as an inventor. It is interesting to note that experience shows corporation engineers working under this arrangement to be on the average more prolific in useful inventions than independent engineers-- probably due to the more numerous and greater problems they meet, the better facilities they have to solve them and the satisfaction from the larger field of application of their inventions. But this arrangement is just as barren of the direct individualistic profit, so frequently considered as the essential incentive of invention, as any we would meet in socialistic society.

Thus, the evidence of experience is that this most numerous and in their aggregate most important class of inventions would not be decreased by the socialization of society; organized society would simply take the place of the present day industrial corporations and the prolificness of the inventors would still further increase by the increased opportunities and facilities.

Coming now to the third class of inventions, such as a new puzzle, a new drink, which strikes the popular fancy, and thus makes its inventor rich. These we may almost call "gambling inventions," since the profits have no relation to the value of the thing, or to the mental and intellectual work of the inventor, inasmuch as equally meritorious inventions may be an entire failure or a great financial success, almost like a stock speculation. It is not probable that in a socialist society, or in any other form of well-organized society, such conditions would exist. However, it is hard to say how this could have much effect on such accidental inventions, or if they should decrease, that the world would lose much by it.

There remains thus the first class of inventions, the great radical or basic inventions which the layman has in mind when discussing inventions or inventors. Would the withdrawal of the possibility of vast financial profits interfere with them?

First, the number of great radical inventions is much less than appears, since the outsider usually only sees the final product, and the man identified with it, but does not see the many steps preceding it, the many inventors, on whose shoulders the last one stood, as I illustrated in the preceding on the invention of the steam locomotive.

Furthermore, does modern capitalistic society hold out great financial rewards for the inventor? I know of no great inventor who has become very rich. Edison is very well to do, but far less due to his inventions than to his sharing in the industrial exploitation of them, and a small part of his genius and intellect, in the pursuit of Wall Street activities, might have made him a multi-millionaire. There is rather more truth in the statement--though wildly exaggerated--that most of the great inventors die in the poorhouse.

Usually, the statement of the "poor inventor" is backed by the statement that he has been defrauded of his dues by the corporation which acquired and manufactured his invention, and that, if he had his rights, he would have become vastly rich. Without doubting that in a few instances this may have been true, it can easily be seen that in general it is not true, but that the relatively meager return of great inventions is the inevitable consequence of our industrial organization.

Charles P. Steinmetz, "Socialism and Inventor," The Socialist Review, (New York: December, 1919), pp. 4-6.

771. "WE WERE SICK. . .OF GOING TO EUROPE" (1929)

Veblen had called chemistry and physics the mother
sciences of modern industry. In the case of the latter
field, few offspring had been produced. Here I. I. Rabi
testifies. Rabi was a Nobel Laureate in Physics; he
taught physics at Columbia University, was chairman of
the General Advisory Committee to the U.S. Atomoc Energy
Commission, and member of the Scienfific Advisory Committee
to the Ballistic Research Laboratory at Aberdeen Proving
Ground. He had known Oppenheimer since 1928. Gordon
Gray was chairman of the Personnel Security Board.

[Mr. GRAY]. As of today would you expect Dr. Oppenheimer's
loyalty to the country to take precedence over loyalty to an
individual or to some other institution?
The WITNESS. I just don't think that anything is higher in
his mind or heart than loyalty to his country. This sort of desire
to see it grow and develop. I might amplify my other statement in
this respect, and that is something we talked of through the years.
When we first met in 1929, American physics was not really very
much, certainly not consonant with the great size and wealth of the
country. We were very much concerned with raising the level of
American physics. We sere sick and tired of going to Europe as
learners. We wanted to be independent. I must say I think that
our generation, Dr. Oppenheimer's and my other friend and I can
mention, did that job, and that 10 years later we were at the top
of the heap, and it wasn't just because certain refugees came out
of Germany, but because of what we did here. This was a conscious
motivation. Oppenheimer set up this school of theoretical physics
which was a tremendous contribution. In fact, I don't know how
we could have carried out the scientific part of the war without
the contributions of the people who worked with Oppenheimer. They
made their contributions very willingly and very enthusiastically
and singlemindedly.

Testimony, I. I. Rabi, April 21, 1954, Personnel Security
Board, United States Atomic Energy Commission, In the Matter of J.
Robert Oppenheimer. Transcript of Hearing, (Washington, D.C.:
Government Printing Office, 1954), pp. 464-465.

772. NOT ALL LABS ARE RESEARCH LABS (1932)

The scientific illiteracy of the public made it
possible for "science" to be presented as things done
by men in white coats. Willis Whitney and L. A. Hawkins

comments. Whitney was vice-president and director
of research for the General Electric Company; Hawkins
was Executive Engineer of the same firm's research
laboratory.

There is some danger in America of overpopularizing industrial
research, and also of overdoing the use of the term. The result of
attracting special attention to research may be to suggest something
essentially false--like a general panacea for work or a cure for
all economic ills, and so induce unprepared people to undertake
ill-advised work.

Not all laboratories are research laboratories. An industry
may require scientific control of factory processes. It may need
acceptance tests of raw materials; metallurgists to control its
foundry; chemists to control the production of products; it may
need a development laboratory to improve its apparatus and to
find new applications for its products.

Yet none of these things is research.

All these activities--testing, factory process control, standardization and development--are the applications of existing
knowledge to the problems of industry.

Research, on the contrary, has to do with generic facts or
principles. It is essentially pure science. . .until engineering
steps in to apply it.

Engineering development and research have the same ultimate
objective--the enlargement of sales by the improvement or extension
of application of the product. But, whereas engineering seeks the
best utilization of existing knowledge, research seeks new knowledge
for future utilization.

Just as a tire manufacturer may start new plantations of rubber
trees to insure a future supply, so an industry may start a research
laboratory to insure a supply of scientific knowledge for its
future engineering development.

Science is systematized knowledge. Research is a systematized
search, and whether or not what it finds is eventually applied has
nothing to do with the nature of the search itself. Suppose a new
element is found. It may find an immediate use, or may find none
at all; but the character of the research which led to the discovery
can hardly be affected by the possible practical utility of the
discovery.

Willis R. Whitney and L. A. Hawkins, "Research in Pure
Science," Malcolm Ross (ed.), Profitable Practice in Industrial
Research, (New York: Harper and Bros., 1932), pp. 244-245.

773.   PHYSICISTS IN DISGUISE (1936)

Lacking the economic incentive of contracts for
sophisticated electronic weaponry, industry had little
conception of the usefulness of physicists. The statement is that of Eli Ginzberg who was an economist at
Columbia University.

Dr. Pegram, the former dean at Columbia, who had a lot to do
with getting the atomic bomb work started, told me that in the
late 1930's he was unable to place in American industry a physicist;
he usually had to classify him as a chemist in order to get him a
job because American industry, as late as 1936-38, with few exceptions, was not hiring physicists.

Eli Ginzberg, U.S. Congress, 84th, 2nd session, Joint
Committee on Atomic Energy, Subcommittee on Research and Development, Shortage of Scientific and Engineering Manpower, p. 395.

774.   GOVERNMENT, NOT INDUSTRY, MUST SPUR PURE
RESEARCH (1937)

Pure science was conceded to be a matter of public
interest. Industry shied away from spending on it because
of indefiniteness of outcome. So, however, did government.
As a result, pure science languished. Karl T. Compton,
president of Massachusetts Institute of Technology, who
served as chairman of the U.S. Science Advisory Board from
1933 to 1935, writes to Jennings Randolph. Randolph was a
representative from West Virginia and was sponsoring a bill
to establish a federal Scientific Research Commission to
stimulate scientific and technological research.

There is a striking peculiarity of scientific research which
makes its support peculiarly a matter for public support rather
than for support by individual industries. This peculiarity lies
in the fact that it is generally impossible to predict the direction in which practical results will follow from any given line
of scientific research. For example, if a group of engineers, 100
years ago, had been asked to devise means for improving illumination they would have undoubtedly concentrated attention on the
study of the processes of oil lamps and candles, rather than on a
study of electricity and magnetism, or the nature of tungsten wire
or the passage of electric currents through gases. It is after
rather than before the scientific discoveries are made that some

inventive or engineering genius discovers some way of using them
to accomplish some desirable purpose, and thereby creates a new
industrial activity.

For this reason, I have frequently heard industrialists question the justification for their supporting any very extensive
program of pure research in such fields as chemistry, physics,
or biology. If this is supported by the electrical industry, for
example, it may turn out that the most useful results are applicable
in the field of chemistry or food technology, and vice versa.

Thus, while the interests of the public require that scientific
research be carried on vigorously and while all experience indicates that support of research is a very worth-while investment for
the future benefit of both industry and the general public, nevertheless no one industry or group can logically defend a large expenditure for work in pure science. The support of science is
therefore a legitimate community investment.

Letter, Karl T. Compton to Representative Jennings Randolph,
July 16, 1937, U.S. Congress, 75th, 1st session, House of Repre-
sentatives, Committee on Interstate and Foreign Commerce,
Engineering, Scientific, and Business Research, p. 14.

775. NEED FOR INDUSTRIAL MATHEMATICIANS (1940)

According to the prediction, by 1954 some 280 pure
mathematicians would be employed in private industry.
According to the National Register of Scientific and
Technical Personnel, in 1954-1955 there were 394--a
41% margin of error. In view of the great expansion of
scientific work, such an error ranks as quite small.
Thornton Fry, Mathematical Research Director, Bell
Telephone Laboratories, makes the prediction.

The number of mathematicians employed in communications,
electrical manufacturing, petroleum, and aircraft, is estimated at
about 100. The number employed in other places is no doubt somewhat less, but it is probably not an insignificant part of the
whole, since mathematicians are found here and there in some very
small industries. For example, the Brush Development Company with
a total engineering force of only 17, has found it desirable to
supplement this group with a man hired specifically as a consultant
in mathematics.

It is perhaps not too wide of the mark to estimate the total
number at 150, not including actuaries and statisticans.
. . . .
Direct evidence exists in certain industries, notably aircraft,
where many of the major research problems are generally recognized

to be more readily accessible to theoretical than experimental
study, and in certain others, such as industrial chemistry, where
one may reasonably assume that modern molecular physics will soon
begin to play an important part in determining speeds of reaction.
There as also the general alertness of executives to the dollar
value of a theoretical framework in planning expensive experiments
and the gradually changing attitude toward mathematics that stems
from it.

. . . .

If, therefore, the estimate of 150 mathematicians in industry
at present is realistic, it may not be too wide of the mark to
forecast several times that number a decade or so hence.

Based on these estimates, a demand for new personnel of the
order of 10 a year may be predicted. This number sounds small; but
if we reiterate that mediocrity has no place in the consulting
field, and that these 10 must be exceptional men, it does not
seem unreasonable to ask where they may be found.

. . . .

Fifty years ago America was so backward in the field of mathematics that there was not even a national association of mathematicians. A quarter of a century later it was just coming of age in
mathematics and was properly, if not indeed necessarily, devoting
its entire attention to improving the quality of instruction in
the "pure" field. The first faint indications that industrial
mathematics might some day become a career had indeed begun to
appear, but they were not impressive enough to attract attention
of university executives.

Today we lead the world in pure mathematics, and perhaps also
in that other field of mathematics which has somehow come to be
known as modern physics. We have strong centers of actuarial and
statistical training. But in the field of applied mathematics,
which is the particular subject of this report, we stand no further
forward than at the turn of the century, and far behind most
European countries.

A quarter of a century ago it would have been difficult to
find suitable teachers. Just now it could be done, primarily because a number of European scholars of the right type have been
forced to come here and a few others have developed spontaneously
within our own borders. There are perhaps half a dozen of them,
but they are so scattered, sometimes in such unpropitious places,
as to have little influence on the development of industrial
personnel.

It is unfortunate that no university with strong engineering
and science departments has seen fit to bring this group together
and establish a center of training in industrial mathematics. We
have estimated a demand of about 10 exceptional graduates per year.
If that estimate is even remotely related to the facts, such a
department would have a most important job to do.

Thornton C. Fry, "Industrial Mathematics," U.S. National Re-
sources Committee, Science Committee, Research--A National Resource.
II. Industrial Research, (Washington, D.C.: National Planning
Board, 1941), pp. 272-273.

776.   RESEARCH, A LABORATORY SIDELINE (1943)

The distinction between "commercial work" and
"research work" is significant. Very little free-
ranging research can occur in a contract-research
organization. Roy Cross, a consulting chemist who
performed contract research for various industries,
makes the following statement.

In about thirty-five years of operation of a commercial laboratory, there are times when the owner has felt that he had better
abandon the business and get a job. The writer has often been discouraged by the lack of business and the lack of appreciation on
the part of the public that the public needs chemical services.
During these times, if he is able to pay the rent, he makes an
analysis of his business and has time for possibly some original
thinking. During this time he has always made it a point to keep
his employees busy. When no commercial work was in the laboratory, it was necessary to put that time on research. Strangely
enough the real profits from the laboratory have come from research
work rather than from the commercial work. Therefore, that lack
of business often begets profitable business.

Roy Cross, From a Chemist's Diary, (Kansas City, Missouri:
Kansas City Testing Laboratory, Cross Laboratories, 1943), p. 236.

777.   DEFENSE ABSORBS SCIENTIFIC PERSONNEL (1958)

A disproportionately large part of scientific
and technical personnel was devoted to defense production.
C. W. La Pierre, vice-president and group executive,
electronic, atomic, and defense systems group, General
Electric Co., discusses the situation.

I would like to make four points about General Electric's
participation in meeting the needs of defense....
   1. The needs of defense are changing in nature, and not just
in degree. An essential need today is for technological innovation
to keep us out in front for the future. In World War II, we had
lots of planes, lots of tanks, lots of rifles, lots of ships. Now,
the whole defense of the country may hinge upon a single new
system, as complex as a nation wide electric power system.
   2. It is General Electric's policy to concentrate its efforts
in those areas in which we feel we can make a distinct technical
contribution, generally advanced weapons system and components,
and the tough unsolved problems in military technology.

3. This defense work represents at the present time approximately 24 percent of the company's sales—the remaining 76 percent coming largely from the sales of equipment for the generation, transmission, distribution, and utilization of electricity. However, we regard defense business as an important responsibility of corporate citizenship, and we have tried to bring to it the full breadth and depth of our corporate skills and technical resources, and to conduct it on a business-like basis—organizing and planning for it on a continuing long-range basis.

4. It is characteristic of the work of technical innovation in defense that it requires a disproportionate amount technical manpower. Although our prime defense departments account for only about 24 percent of General Electric sales, the company's defense work employs nearly 65 percent of the company's 22,000 scientists and engineers.

I have cited these characteristics about the nature of General Electric's defense business in order to try to place in perspective the need for people who have training and experience in ascertaining and meeting the requirements of the military.

Testimony, C. W. La Pierre, August 11, 1959, U.S. Congress, 86th, 1st session, House of Representatives, Committee on Armed Services, Subcommittee for Special Investigation, Employment of Retired Military and Civilian Personnel by Defense Industries, p. 664.

778. APPEAL FOR BASIC RESEARCH IN AMERICAN CHEMISTRY (1959)

Few of the more than 85,000 members of the American Chemical Society were employed in basic research. Here is an analysis of the situation in terms of "tragedy" and "desperation." It was made by Walter Murphy, Editorial Director of applied journals of the American Chemical Society.

One of America's most renowned chemists recently commented to us that in the field of pure chemical research the U.S. is tragically weak and little is being done to correct the situation. The same comment has been made by many others for years. How, then, have we managed to build the largest chemical industry in the world?

The answer is simple. Many of the fundamental ideas in the industry have come from Europe. A few months ago, Sydney Steele, director of public relations for Atlas Powder, spoke at the Franklin Institute in Philadelphia. To prove several points he enumerated the basic chemical discoveries which have come from European laboratories. The list is impressive and disturbing.

Can we continue to operate successfully in the future, depending to such a great extent on pure research done abroad? Steele has serious doubts. He said:

"In years past, European industry has been too restricted to make effective use of these basic discoveries. Our ability to supply capital, plus large-scale manufacturing know-how, plus a large 'captive market,' has enabled us to benefit from European inventions."

Steele and many others see in the new European Common Market far stronger competition from abroad--a situation unlike anything we have faced before.

What practical steps must be taken to correct this weakness? There are quite a number, but first we should take inventory of what is now being done.

Really, little is known about the extent to which basic chemical research is being carried on here. The figure of $6 to 7 billion spent for research and development is impressive until it is analyzed. Then it becomes apparent that most of it is applications research and development.

Perhaps the American Chemical Society and the Manufacturing Chemists' Association should join hands in a study of what should and must be done to increase the attention given to basic research. However, there will have to be a considerable change of attitude in many areas for tangible results to take place. The basic researcher is often thought of in disparaging terms. We will have to make it far more attractive to the truly competent individual to do basic research. This means prestige; it means better remuneration.

Probably it will be necessary to define the term "fundamental research" again, because it means different things to different people.

A number of chemical companies support basic research in one way or another, largely through scholarships and fellowships. In recent years some of these companies have greatly increased amounts given, without strings attached.

However, all the evidence shows that amounts given are small in relationship to the size and growth needs of the chemical field. Ways must somehow be found to increase the amount of basic research going on and to give it more continuity--perhaps in the form of more privately supported research institutes. But their very purpose will be defeated if any sizable part of their efforts goes into applied research.

We don't have all the answers, but action is desperately needed--this is obvious.

Walter J. Murphy, "The Case for More Basic Research," Chemical and Engineering News, XXXVII (January 19, 1959), p. 7.

779.   COMPARATIVE QUALITY OF AMERICAN TECHNOLOGY (1959)

Below is a rare effort to make an overall comparison of international technological levels. The effort appears in a book on military affairs, written by Oskar Morgenstern who was an economist at Princeton University, co-editor of Naval Research Logistics Quarterly, and consultant on military problems to the Congressional Joint Committee on Atomic Energy and to the Atomic Energy Commission, as well as to Convair.

There are two widespread beliefs current throughout the country. . .:
(a) we are technologically more advanced than any other country;
(b) technological changes and improvements always work to our advantage.
Both beliefs are false.
To prove the falsity of these two statements in detail would require a great effort and much more space than is at our disposal. Regarding the first some illustrations may suffice: French electronics is at least as good as ours and in many ways far more advanced than ours; British jet engines surpass most of ours by a wide margin; Japanese optics is better than German, which in turn is better than ours; Swiss pharmaceutical products, Belgian color film, Swiss watches, British bicycles, German cameras are an easy match for the best we have to offer; Danish Diesel engines are unsurpassed anywhere in the world. The area of technological achievement where foreign developments are at least as good is of course much larger. If we look at military equipment there is ample evidence that British planes equal ours, the Belgian infantry rifle is superior to our Army's, the French artillery is superior to any we can muster.
Let us include Russia in the picture: it produces greater thrust for rockets than any other country; excellent radar equipment, in many respects surpassing ours; tanks that have no match in propulsion, armor or fire power anywhere; jet planes that are at least the equals of ours; fighter planes that in Korea outperformed those we could at first muster against them; electronic computers that are at par with our best. And this list could be lengthened.
American technological superiority exists but in two different directions; we are on the average better, and we can produce great quantities of good products after standardization has been achieved. Even this superiority is sometimes less the result of ingenuity than of the ample supply of raw materials which so far has permitted essentially wasteful production and consumption habits. One may say further than while other countries excel technologically in a few lines over the United States, this country is on the average or in the aggregate superior to all of them (though even in this sense the case is debatable regarding Switzerland). Clearly we too

have technological superiority to show--but not in missiles; perhaps
in nuclear weapons (But who can know the facts here and in Russia?
Has anyone actually dismantled nuclear weapons of Russian origin
and compared them with ours?), and probably in nuclear reactors.

We should contemplate these facts soberly in order to come to
a proper understanding of our position. These facts will make it
clear that in our great struggle we are not simply sitting on top
of the world. Too many of our leaders tell us this too often.
Repetition does not make it true. We are at best on a broad
plateau peopled by many nations. To be sure, I am not referring to
total brute strength or aggregate wealth. In both of these we now
outdo any other nation. I am talking about the state of accomplished
technology.

Oskar Morgenstern, The Question of National Defense, (New
York: Random House, 1959), pp. 160-162.

780. POLYMER CHEMISTRY IN THE U.S. AND U.S.S.R. (1959)

An unusual occasion to examine two similar scientific
enterprises comparatively. C. E. H. Bawn, who was
professor of Physical Chemistry at the University of
Liverpool, England, makes this comment.

Since my return from Moscow, I have had the opportunity of
attending polymer conferences in the U.S.A. and of visiting many of
the leading scientific and industrial laboratories working the same
fields of chemistry as those I saw in the U.S.S.R. It may be of
value to compare the progress and organization of research in the
two countries in one particular branch of science.

In the U.S.A. most of the research in polymer chemistry is
carried out by the major chemical, oil and rubber companies. The
over-all effort is considerably greater than that in the U.S.S.R.
but the quality of the Russian research was as good as any I saw
in the U.S.A. and the approach, if anything, was more fundamental.
American research is largely directed towards practical ends and
this idea has permeated into much university work. More than is
desirable of university research in the U.S.A. is sponsored by
industry and carried out with a definite industrial application in
mind. This is partly a result of shortage of adequate funds for
basic research, although steps have now been taken to rectify
this situation.

The greatest contrast between the two countries, however, is in
the organization and direction of research. The immense competition between the large chemical companies in the U.S.A. requires
that each carries a very large research department which prosecutes
very similar and often almost identical work. Any new idea or discovery immediately after its announcement is evaluated by innumerable

companies, and the same fields of research are explored over and
over again. The requirements of scientific manpower in this competitive business are enormous and one wonders if some other form
for the effective utilization of limited numbers of highly trained
scientists might be eventually devised. The U.S.S.R., on the other
hand, functions as one large company. Research is reasonably well-
coordinated but the direction is not so rigid as to preclude basic
long-range investigations. The modest needs of basic research are
used to identify and select the fields for development which require
large capital. In this way, the U.S.S.R. seems to be making the
maximum available use of its scientific and technical manpower. It
may well be that with the rapid growth of industry the central
coordination of research may become too difficult but there seems
to be no reason why this should happen in clearly delineated fields
of development.

C. E. H. Bawn, "Some Impressions of Soviet Science," American
Scientist, XXXXVIII (March, 1960), p. 50.

781. THE MECHANISMS OF TECHNOLOGY ASSESSMENT (1969)

In 1972, Congress passed the Technology Assessment
Act which created the Office of Technology Assessment
(OTA). Its basic function was "to provide early indications of the probable beneficial and adverse impacts of
the applications of technology and to develop other
coordinate information which may assist the Congress."
During its first three years of full operation (1974-
1976) OTA was called upon 175 times to assess various
matters. Two-thirds of all the relevant committees of
Congress used this service, some more than once. A
number of bills had directed that OTA perform some
specific task. Average cost per assessment ran around
$250,000. Topics of reports have ranged from the effects
of limited nuclear warfare to coal slurry pipelines --
in which coal is liquified and forced through pipelines --
to oil shale technologies and others. Following is a
commentary by John R. Pierce, executive director, Research,
Communication Services Division of Bell Telephone
Laboratories, and a member of both the National Academy
of Sciences and National Academy of Engineering.

From my experience and observation, several things come to mind
in connection with mechanisms of assessment.
It would be foolish to believe that there is any new art of
assessment which will enable people of moderate ability to assess
by rote very complicated situations of which they know little.

Any technological assessment will continue to be a chancy business which can succeed only through the work of very able and knowledgeable people. Successful technological assessment must be done by experts in relevant areas of knowledge and action. Experts may sometimes be blind, but ignorance is even blinder.

By experts, I mean people who have clearly succeeded in an area related to science and technology. I mean men who have made socially valuable scientific discoveries, or men who have made socially valuable inventions, or men who have led effective, productive industrial, educational or Government organizations in which science and technology are important, or men who have clearly contributed to the establishment of new, successful, social or governmental or educational or industrial organizations. It is by their success that experts are to be known. As Charlie Brown has said, success may not be everything, but failure isn't anything....

The usefulness of an assessment will depend partly on the quality of personnel and organization, but also partly on the tractability of the problem. Problem-oriented assessments are more likely to succeed than technology-oriented assessments. One has a fair chance of estimating what it would cost various sectors of society to reduce by various means the annoyance and/or damage due to aircraft noise. One can also reach plausible conclusions about specific areas of pollution. These are problem-oriented assessments.

On the other hand, it would have been hard, if not impossible, to have predicted, at the time of its invention, that one chief contribution of the transistor would be the growth and effects of the electronic computer, and another, growth in the technological economies of Japan, Hong Kong, Korea and Taiwan. It would have been hard to predict when the maser was invented that a chief effect would be the invention of the optical maser or laser. It would be economically important in piercing diamond dies, drilling holes in porcelain and cutting sheets of ceramic. Problems draw technologies convergingly toward their solution. Important technological advances diverge: They spread out through industry and life in a way it is hard to predict.

Let me now turn to considerations of another sort. It appears to me that any successful new process of technological assessment must be responsible to some person, agency or organization that needs and will value and make important use of the results of assessments.

Such a responsible authority must choose, with expert help, areas for assessment and must evaluate, over the years, again with expert help, the validity and value of such assessments as have been made. Such an authority must judge fairly the success and failure of assessment activities. Assessments made for people who don't care, or who don't follow through and continue to care, are almost sure to become routine and irresponsible.

Our technology is so wide ranging that the experts who make assessments must be wisely chosen, with expert help, from among all areas of successful technology and related work.

Somewhere between the responsible authority which assessment serves and the outside experts who make assessments there must be a responsible staff, whose continued welfare depends on bringing desired and valuable assessments to the responsible authority.

To summarize briefly:

Technological assessment must take into account the actions and interactions of science, industry, Government and the people these all affect.

Various existing mechanisms of assessment have various strengths and weaknesses.

Assessments must be made by experts; that is, by people who have demonstrated substantial contributions to technology and technologically related areas.

Assessments cost money and will not always be successful. They should not be undertaken lightly.

One important step in assessment is to determine the present state of affairs, which is usually not well known or understood.

Problem-oriented assessments are more likely to succeed than are technology-oriented assessments.

If an assessment mechanism is to remain honest and effective, it must serve some responsible authority which judges assessments and values and makes effective use of good assessments.

An assessment mechanism needs a responsible staff whose continued welfare depends on the successful production of pertinent, valuable assessments....

It isn't foolproof. It does require, as you said earlier, a certain amount of intuitive evaluation by people who are experts, and those people have to be drawn from all sorts of places: government laboratories, universities, and also industries and industrial laboratories.

The reason for this is that the known state of technology, as it is written down, is usually several years behind the actual state of technology, which is not written down, in a popular form and which may not even be known to a group of people. It may be hiding away in corners. That is the reason why you have to call on people whom I describe as experts. By that I mean people who are really in the thick of the work in particular areas and know how not only what has been written and laid down as gospel in popular or even technological journals, but also what is actually happening....

I think that unless people, experts or otherwise, are working for somebody whom they believe to have a real need for the result, and who will be apt to act on it, what they will produce will be generalities, and really, irresponsible generalities.

Although I am in research, I am sure that people in all of industry take more seriously putting a product or service on the market than they take predicting the future 15 or 25 years from now. That isn't going to do anything to anyone in the immediate future. I am sure, also, that people who really believe they were giving factual knowledge to the Congress, on the basis of which action might be taken--perhaps because action had been taken on such advice in the past--will behave more responsibly than people who just think they are writing a glowing testimonial to the future....

I think this is an important part. . .of the whole development
of technology. You see, I am trying to say how broadly you have to
take things into account. For example, in Europe, from a very
early time, motor cars were taxed on the cylinder capacity. That
led to fast running, small cars with fast running, noisy engines.
I am not making a point this is good or bad. I am merely saying a
Government action, in this case in the field of taxation, had an
important influence in shaping the development of the European
motor car, as opposed to the American motor car.

In assessing technology, most people don't understand the
present state. The present state has usually been influenced by
invention and discovery, by enterpreneurship, by public acceptance,
and by past government actions. Somehow, you have to look at where
and why things have got to where they are, and then ask where they
may go if government action isn't taken or if different government
action is taken.

Testimony, December 8, 1969, U.S. Congress, 91st, 1st session,
House of Representatives, Committee on Science and Astronautics,
Subcommittee on Science, Research, and Development, Technology
Assessment. Hearings...., (Washington, D.C.: Government Printing
Office, 1970), pp. 211-215.

782. DON'T SCUTTLE THE SHUTTLE (1973)

In 1962, Congress passed the Communications Satellite
Act and chartered the Communications Satellite Corporation
(Comsat). Operation of the first commercial satellite,
however, began in 1974 by Western Union. Seven years later,
the U.S. space shuttle Columbia made its first flight test.
The orbiter, designed to be used on 100 flights, could
carry payloads of satellites to be launched in outer space.
In time it was expected to carry laboratories to conduct
experimental work under conditions of weightlessness and
high purity. A year after Columbia's first flight, in mid-
1982, firms had booked one-third of flights scheduled over
the next five years. By 1982, also Columbia carried its
first secret military payload. Brig. Gen. Bernard P.
Randolph, Air Force director of space systems, said: "Space
is the modern equivalent of the 'high ground' that military
leaders have for centuries sought out and exploited to
their advantage." Endorsing the concept of the shuttle is
Wernher von Braun, pioneer in development of liquid-fueled
rocket engines. Now corporate vice-president for Engineering and Development of Fairchild Industries, he had managed
the Nazi government's rocket program during the 1930s and
World War II. During the years following the war's end he
worked on the space projects of the U.S. government.

It is sad to say, but there are some who even now would scuttle the Shuttle. In my opinion, this would be a disastrous mistake because it would deprive this country of many of the economical and social space benefits now becoming available to us as a result of our previous national multibillion-dollar space investment. Antagonists of the Shuttle say that we should not spend hard-earned tax money on such a costly new technology program as long as we are still surrounded by so many crying social needs. But, we should never forget that it is in the nature of all social programs that they are wealth consuming. The Space Shuttle, with all it can do for man down here on Earth, is a good example of a wealth-producing program. And we will continue to need promising wealth-producing programs to support our direly needed social programs. There is an old Chinese proverb that illustrates the situation quite well: "Give a boy a fish and you feed him a meal. Teach a boy to fish and you feed him for a lifetime." I also cannot emphasize too strongly how unfortunate I feel it is that budget limitations seem to be forcing NASA to abandon its 15-year involvement in the further development of advanced technology for communications satellites. Caught in a budget pinch, even inside NASA the argument has been made occasionally that communications satellites have developed into such an industrial success story that private enterprise should be able to raise enough R. & D. money to experiment with more advanced but still unproven communications technologies. From my new vantage point in a private corporation which is deeply involved with advanced communications satellites, let me assure you, gentlemen, that this is wishful thinking. Customers, whether domestic or international, want satellite communications channels with a guaranteed revenue-producing life of 7 years or more, and they don't care a hoot what technology you use, as long as it is well-proven. On the other hand, the potential of technological advancement in this new field, whose surface we have hardly scratched, is almost unlimited. There is great potential in the use of higher frequencies, in laser beams communications, in switching satellite beams by ground signal from one ground target to another, in increasing satellite transmitting power so the cost of ground stations can be drastically reduced, to name just a few. In the fiercely competitive environment of the rapidly expanding communications satellite market, no private company can take the gamble of offering unproven technologies to its customers. The few commercial giants in the communications fields may indeed be the only ones who can afford to sink a few million dollars here and there in a little experimentation with new-fangled ideas, but their overall record in advancing the field of communications satellites has been so disappointing that the Federal Communications Commission wisely decided to open up the field to a pack of lively, smaller, and less sated competitors. If NASA were to permanently discontinue its pioneering technology work in the communications satellite area, it would virtually reverse that FCC policy and give the game back to the established monopolies who, in view of their vast investments in old-fashioned wire communications, never had much of an incentive to explore the satellite potential in the first place.

The space program has done a lot of wonderful things for the human spirit, for the advancement of science and for the direct benefits of man. Only history can properly assess the lasting

significance of these contributions to the human spirit and to
science. When it comes to the direct benefits, however, we can
make some judgment now, and I would give the highest rating to the
communications satellite.

Testimony, September 27, 1973, U.S. Congress, 93rd, 1st
session, Senate, Committee on Aeronautical and Space Sciences,
State of the Aerospace Industry. Hearings...., (Washington, D.C.:
Government Printing Office, 1973), pp. 204-205.

783. THE GROWING GAP BETWEEN SCIENCE AND ENGINEERING (1980)

Historically, American science and engineering have
developed fairly independently of one another. The artisan
nature of early American technology called forth little
systematic inquiry. Imported technology also discouraged
the search for fundamental physical and biological knowledge. These existing tendencies were accentuated by
short-run perspectives that were endemic in industrial
laboratories of the late 19th and early 20th centuries.
Only during the past half-century can one speak meaning-
fully of indigenous American theoretical sciences. That
recent tradition lacks the solid moorings that can remain
undisturbed in the face of insistent industrial motivation.
Academic science has been losing out recently to highly
concrete engineering tasks in industry. Following is a
commentary on these trends by Bruno O. Weinschel, chairman
of the Engineering Affairs Council of the American Association of Engineering as well as a secretary of the Institute
of Electrical Electronics Engineers, and head of Weinschel
Engineering Co. in Gaithersburg, Maryland.

In the last 20 years in the United States there has arisen an
artificial segmentation of science and engineering. In contrast,
the German efforts are mission oriented; problems are not arbitrarily segmented into basic research, applied research, development,
and pilot production.
They are mission oriented. This also leads to greater job
satisfaction and recognition by the lay public.
Unfortunately, when you talk to many deans of engineering
schools--some of our leading deans, some of our best engineering
schools--they are not orienting their graduates towards industry.
Their staff fails to transmit any respect for the need to
design products competitively, reliably, and attractively. This,
again, is in great contrast to the engineering schools of our
successful trading partners, typically West Germany and Japan.
This is another reason why we need a focal point to remedy certain
omission in our engineering education....

A 4-year education in engineering is a core curriculum which just teaches the graduate the fundamentals. He really needs either a few years of graduate study or he needs an educational buffer before he can become effective in industry.

Our large corporations, such as General Electric, Westinghouse, IBM, and the Bell System especially, have established their own educational buffer systems.

Some of them are very elaborate, and they bridge the gap between the undergraduate core education and industrial requirements.

We learned from statistics published by the National Science Foundation that small business is highly innovative and its innovation is more cost effective--for example by a factor of 24--comparing firms up to 1,000 employees with those having over 10,000 employees.

Small business cannot finance such a buffer system, and what we in small business do--I employ almost 400 people, we pirate to the extent possible suitable engineers who have benefitted from these buffer systems in large companies. There is only a small supply available, so one of the things which I suggest: There is a need to establish in the educational community an additional buffer system bridging the gap between an undergraduate engineering education and the industry's needs.

This can be a continuing education program; it could be an evening program; but I think it will require the equivalent of 1 to 2 years of full-time study.

We learned that our graduate engineering students contain about 37 percent of foreign nationals, the Ph.D. candidates about 40 percent; the masters candidates about 34 percent.

The engineers completing graduate programs are our prime source of future professors, and we have many openings in our engineering schools. People who come, from instance, from a Far Eastern culture, while they are excellent in their capabilities for solving theoretical problems, find great difficulty in understanding how our industry works. They usually have not been accustomed to getting their hands dirty. An American boy gets underneath his car, changes the oil, fixes the engine; many of the foreign students come from very well-to-do families. They have never seen their father fix an automobile; and as I recall my own experience as an employer, I find that they are not as likely to get their hands dirty as an American engineering graduate does.

I personally do not think it is good for the future health of engineering education to have professors as examples, who are not very familiar with and attuned to our industrial culture. This is a very sensitive subject which many people will shy away from, but I think it is important to spell it out.

When you talk to the presidents of colleges and universities, they will complain about the relatively high expense of an engineering program because engineers do not use just paper as in English literature, but they use a lot of expensive equipment. A lot of this equipment is obsolete.

We are educating many of our graduates on equipment which is one or two generations old. So, when they get in industry they

find equipment they have never seen. This can be helped by greater
emphasis on cooperative courses where study and work in industry
is alternated. We also notice that the starting academic salaries
are completely noncompetitive compared with industry.

A typical B.S. graduate had an average starting salary in
electrical engineering of $20,000 in 1980. This is about the
salary of a junior professor who has an advanced degree. One of
the solutions which we have considered is to cut the engineering
schools loose from the salary structure of the universities, just
as the medical or law schools.

There must be a sound relationship between the remuneration of
a professor for a specialty with the salary his graduate will command when he gains employment. This is a very important consideration. We must cut the engineering schools loose from the salary
structure of the universities so that they are more in line with
the industrial community.

If we fail to do that, we may attract and retain some second-
rate professors who cannot get industrial jobs. There must be a
proper financial recognition of the importance of the engineering
educator.

This, I think is an important underlying problem in our productivity lag. Even if immediate remedial steps are taken, the
result would not show for over 5-10 years.

In the last 20 years we observed that the Federal Government
gave excellent support to those portions of engineering specialties
which served the Federal needs, be it aeronautics, or electronics.
This made the universities, to some extent, more independent of
industry.

One can turn this around. If there would be no Federal support
to engineering schools, it would force the universities to work
much closer with industry. It may therefore be undesirable to have
the Federal Government spend more money in the engineering
universities.

The additional money must come more from industry so that
there is a more effective linkage with industrial requirements.

By making engineering schools independent of industry, one
divorces them from one another.

Testimony, September 10, 1980, U.S. Congress, 96th, 2nd
session, House of Representatives, Committee on Science and
Technology, Subcommittee on Science, Research and Technology,
National Technology Foundation Act of 1980. Hearings....,
(Washington, D.C.: Government Printing Office, 1980), pp. 494-496.

784. RESEARCH IN PHARMACEUTICALS (1980): (A)

Modern pharmaceuticals are a product of the 20th
century and depended upon prior development of synthetic
organic chemistry, physiology, pathology and pharmacology.
Production of sulfanilamide in 1936 set off the contemporary phase of the drug industry. Discovery of sulfamilamide
resulted not from deliberate research but by accident. With
the immense growth of fundamental biological knowledge,
financed largely by the federal government, the scientific
base of pharmaceuticals proceeds far more readily than
early in the present century. Commercial pharmaceutical
research seeks a product that will either sell because of
its therapeutic novelty or its resemblence to an already-
successful product. Much of the industry's research effort
is thus duplicative or of limited efficacy, while a substantial portion is devoted to sales promotion of completed
products. Following are statements by (A) Pindaros Roy
Vagelos, president of Merck, Sharp & Dohme Research Laboratories, and (B) Baruj Benacerraf, chairman of the Department of Pathology of Harvard Medical School and president
of the Sidney Farber Cancer Institute, who also is a Nobel
laureate in medicine.

The pharmaceutical industry thrives on innovation and discovery. It is one of the most research intensive of all U.S. industries. Overall, on average, U.S. pharmaceutical companies spend 6
percent of their total sales on research and development, compared
to 2 percent of all industry. We at Merck spend more.
Reduced health care cost through both prevention and treatment
of illness by drugs has almost incalculable economic benefit. For
example, Americans spend in excess of $1 billion a year treating
pneumococcal pneumonia; the average hospital cost per patient in
1976 was about $1,600.
A new Merck vaccine, sold for approximately $5 per dose, should
enable the Nation to reduce these costs substantially. The pharmaceutical industry also contributes positively to our balance of
trade, adding $1.15 billion in 1979.
Merck is one of the U.S. pharmaceutical firms whose major emphasis is on research to invent and develop new pharmaceuticals.
Our research and development budget has increased for 25 consecu-
tive years. In the past decade, we spent nearly $1.2 billion.
In 1979, we spent an amount equivalent to two-thirds of our net
income on research and development. This year, we will spend $227
million. In a word, our business strategy is innovation.
Merck's commitment to research is credited with achievements
in sulfa drugs, streptomycin, cortisone, vitamin B^{12} thiazide
diuretics, and nonsteroidal anti-inflammatories. Our most recent,
Timoptic, is typical of those in which we take pride. Timoptic is
the most widely prescribed drug for the treatment of glaucoma;

and it has vastly improved the treatment for this disease which is
the leading cause of blindness in the United States.

These achievements of Merck research and many others from
other members of the U.S. pharmaceutical industry have been truly
spetacular....

As the president of Merck, Sharp & Dohme Research Laboratories,
I head a group of more than 2,300 biochemists, physicians, biolo-
gists, and other research scientists.

To attract and support the work of such scientists, we must
be able to fund the most modern laboratory facilities and instruments. This necessitates large investments of capital, such as
the $100 million Merck has just spent and the $50 million we have
committed for the near term.

Good laboratories are, however, only places where work can be
done. Pharmaceutical research and development requires a commitment of people and funds for projects which may take a decade or
more to reach fruition. In 1962, it took about 2 years and $4
million to bring a new pharmaceutical product from discovery to
marketing; now, it takes about 8 years and $50 million.

The commitment of such funds is made with no guarantees as
to result. In the 10-year period 1966-76, Merck invested over
$800 million in research and development and introduced only one
major new marketable drug. If our management had not had great
confidence that economically important new products would result
from the work then underway in our laboratories, they could not
have justified that large ongoing expense....

Testimony, April 15, 1980, U.S. Congress, 96th, 2nd session,
House of Representatives, Committee on the Judiciary, Subcommittee
on Courts, Civil Liberties, and the Administration of Justice,
Industrial Innovation and Patent and Copyright Law Amendments.
Hearings...., (Washington, D.C.: Government Printing Office, 1980),
pp. 48-49.

RESEARCH IN PHARMACEUTICALS (1981):   (B)

The other issue is why doesn't industry carry its research
more originally and the issue is that research is a very hazardous
process. All researchers know that, particularly those who are
interested in solving the most difficult problems. The chance that
you will solve it is very, very small and the answer is not foreseen.

Recently, I have had to deal with industry in my capacity as
president of a cancer institute to find out if we could interest
them in common projects. I dealt with several different companies.
I found that they are very reluctant to be involved in anything
which doesn't have very practical and foreseeable returns, as soon
as I say well I don't know what is going to happen, if we investigate this, we might get some answers. Well, no one in the corporate

structure is willing to take that kind of a risk with any substantial sums of money.

However, when the path has been opened with public funds and it is foreseeable that the technology will be financially rewarding, if it is refined, they are exceedingly good at that, far better than the universities.

So what you are asking really is how to build a true partnership so that Government-supported research carries out such research that opens up the vistas in new areas and as soon as practicable in combination with private industry the next step is brought forward and a much more rapid practical development will result....

[Pharmaceutical firms] are forced to not share their research, but I would venture to say that the large majority of the inventions are not made by the pharmaceutical companies in terms of what are the true breakthroughs precisely because of the attitude they have. They are shortsighted in their goals. They are jealous in the way they protect themselves. And as a consequence of that they don't make breakthroughs. They are excellent for exploitation of other people's breakthroughs.

U.S. Congress, 96th, 2nd session, House of Representatives, Committee on Science and Technology, Outlooks from Nobel Prize Winners. Hearings...., (Washington, D.C.: Government Printing Office, 1981), pp. 18, 22.

785. THE CHEMICAL ABSTRACTS SERVICE (1981)

The first general abstracting journal was published in France in 1665 whence it spread to Germany, England, and other European countries. During the following century, specialized abstracting journals relating to scientific literature made great headway in Germany. Because of the growing scope of scientific literature, learned societies or commercial publishers undertook the task of compilation and publication. Industry became the principal source of financial support and thus determined the fields to be covered. The 20th century introduced international abstracting services as well as government participation in financing. More recently, ever more specialized works are being published. The proliferation of both scientific literature and its abstracting has meant that very few abstract journals cease publication since without them researchers would drown under waves of journals and books. Here is an account of one world-renowned abstract service by Dale B. Baker, director of Chemical Abstracts Service and Chief Operating Officer of the Columbus, Ohio office of the American Chemical Society.

The Chemical Abstracts Service of the American Chemical Society is the only comprehensive abstracting and indexing service in chemistry and chemical engineering outside of the Soviet Union. Most of the world depends on our publications and services for access to the literature of chemical science and technology. About three-quarters of the material abstracted and indexed comes from outside of the U.S., and two-thirds of the circulation of our largest printed publication, Chemical Abstracts, is overseas.

CAS, now in its 75th year, is a financially self-contained unit of a non-profit educational and scientific society chartered by the U.S. Congress in 1937. We earn all operating funds by selling and licensing printed publications, microforms, and computer-readable files and services. That amount is approaching $50 million per year. Our staff of 1200 in two buildings in Columbus, Ohio, includes more than 650 technical specialists in various fields of science and technology, including computer systems. We have published nearly 9 million abstracts since 1907, and are adding to our computer-readable data base analyses of about 500,000 new documents per year. Our computer registry of chemical materials contains more than 5 million unique substances and more than 7 million corresponding names that have been used for these substances. We are identifying and registering about 350,000 new substances every year. We have a 75-year record of comprehensiveness, quality, timeliness, and dependability. Our services are used by industries, academic institutions and governments the world over. We are currently spending in the range of $5 million per year of GAS funds in research and development to improve our service.

Testimony, June 9, 1981, U.S. Congress, 97th, 1st session, House of Representatives, Committee on Science and Technology, Subcommittee on Science, Research and Technology, The Information Science and Technology Act. Hearings...., (Washington, D.C.: Government Printing Office, 1981), p. 236.

BIBLIOGRAPHY

494 Dersch, Virginia J. "Copper Mining in Northern Michigan: A
         Social History." Michigan History 61 (1977): 290-321.
     Fell, James E., Jr. Ores to Metals, The Rocky Mountain Smelt-
         ing Industry. Lincoln, NB: U. of Nebraska Press, 1980.
     Hayes, Samuel P. Conservation and the Gospel of Efficiency
         (1959).
     Langton, H. H. James Douglas, a Memoir (1940).

495 Davis, E. W. Pioneering With Taconite. St. Paul, MN:
         Minnesota Historical Society, 1964.
     Kelton, D. H. Sault Ste. Marie Canal (1888).
     Mills, J. C. Our Inland Seas (1910).

496 Cameron, Jenks. The Development of Governmental Forest Control
         in the United States. Baltimore, MD: Johns Hopkins U.
         Press, 1928.
     Hurst, James Willard. Law and Economic Growth: The Legal
         History of the Lumber Industry in Wisconsin, 1836-1915.
         Cambridge, MA: Harvard U. Press, 1964.
     McGeary, M. Nelson. Gifford Pinchot, Forester, Politician
         (1960).
     Wyant, William K. Westward in Eden: The Public Lands and
         the Conservation Movement. Berkeley, CA: U. of California
         Press, 1982.

497 Cameron, Jenks. The Development of Governmental Forest Control
         in the United States. Baltimore, MD: Johns Hopkins U.
         Press, 1928.
     Cox, Thomas R. Mills and Markets: A History of the Pacific
         Coast Lumber Industry to 1900. Seattle, WA: U. of
         Washington Press, 1974.
     Jensen, Vernon H. Lumber and Labor (1945).
     Larson, Agnes M. History of the White Pine Industry (1949).

498 Clawson, Marion. "Forests in the Long Sweep of American
         History." Science 204 (1979): 1168-1174.
     Hidy, Ralph W., Hill, F. E. and Nevins, Allan. Timber and Men:
         The Weyerhaeuser Story (1963).

499 Cooley, Richard A. Politics and Conservation: The Decline of
       the Alaska Salmon (1963).
     Dodds, Gordon B. The Salmon King of Oregon: R. D. Hume and
       the Pacific Fisheries (1963).

500 Arrington, Leonard J. The Changing Economic Structure of the
       Mountain West, 1850-1950 (1963).
     Kracht, Shannon. "Wendling, A Company Town." Lane County
       Historian 20 (1975): 3-16.
     Mosgrove, Jerry L. The Malheur National Forest: An Ethnogra-
       phic History. Portland, OR: USDA Forest Service, 1980.
     Richardson, Elinor R. The Politics of Conservation: Crusades
       and Controversies, 1897-1913 (1962).

501 Henderson, James M. and Kruger, Anne O. National Growth and
       Economic Change in the Upper Midwest (1965).
     Walker, David A. Iron Frontier: The Discovery and Early
       Development of Minnesota's Three Ranges. St. Paul, MN:
       Minnesota Historical Society Press, 1979.
     Wirth, Fremont P. The Minnesota Iron Lands (1937).

502 Bowles, Isaac A., Sturgill, Bascom and Hale, Zelda. History
       of Letcher County, Kentucky (1949).
     Bowman, Mary Jean and Haynes, W. Warren. Resources and People
       in East Kentucky: Problems and Potentials of a Lagging
       Economy (1963).
     "Images of Letcher County, Kentucky." Media and Methods 14
       (February 1978): 41-43.

503 Brantly, John Edward. History of Oil Well Drilling. Houston,
       TX: Gulf, 1971.
     Sanders, M. Elizabeth. The Regulation of Natural Gas: Policy
       and Politics, 1938-1978. Philadelphia, PA: Temple U.
       Press, 1981.

504 U.S. Office of Technology Assessment. Energy from Biological
       Processes. Washington, D.C.: G.P.O., July 1980.

505 Chandler, Alfred D., Jr. "Anthracite Coal and the Beginnings
       of the Industrial Revolution in the United States."
       Business History Review 46 (Summer 1972): 141-181.
     Powell, H. Benjamin. "The Pennsylvania Anthracite Industry,
       1769-1976." Pennsylvania History 47 (1980): 3-27.

506 Culhane, Paul J. Public Lands Politics: Interest Group Influ-
       ence on the Forest Service and the Bureau of Land Manage-
       ment. Baltimore, MD: Johns Hopkins U. Press, 1981.
     La Lande, Jeffrey M. Medford Corporation: A History of an
       Oregon Logging and Lumber Company. Medford, OR: Klocker,
       1979.
     Miyata, Edwin S. and Steinhilb, Helmuth M. Logging System Cost
       Analysis: Comparison of Methods Used. St. Paul, MN:
       North Central Forest Experiment Station, Foret Service,
       U.S. Department of Agriculture, 1981.

507 Cannon, J. "Oligopoly in Western Coal." Business and Society
        Review 41 (Spring 1982): 12-15.
     Committee on Ground-Water Resources in Relation to Coal Mining.
        Coal Mining and Ground-Water Resources in the United States:
        A Report. Washington, D.C.: National Academy Press, 1981.
     Probert, Alan (ed.). Mining in the West. Manhattan, KS:
        Sunflower U. Press, 1981.

508 Edwards, G. "Cost Disadvantages of Expanding the Nuclear Power
        Industry [in Canada]." Canadian Business Review 9 (Spring
        1982): 19-30.
     Hellman, Richard and Hellman, Caroline J. C. The Competitive
        Economics of Nuclear and Coal Power. Lexington, MA:
        Lexington Books, 1982.
     Jeffs, E. "Twenty-Five Years of Nuclear Electricity." Modern
        Power Systems 1 (October 1981): 44-46.
     Reynolds, Andrew W. Projected Costs of Electricity from
        Nuclear and Coal-fired Power Plants. Washington, D.C.:
        G.P.O., 1982.

509 Tinkle, Lon. Mr. De: A Biography of Everette Lee De Golyer.
        Boston, MA: Little, Brown, 1970.
     Williamson, Harold F. and others. The American Petroleum In-
        dustry, Vol. II: The Age of Energy, 1899-1959. Evanston,
        IL: Northwestern U. Press. 1963.

510 Adler, Jacob. "The Maui Land Deal: A Chapter in Claus
        Spreckels' Hawaiian Career." Agricultural History 39
        (1965).
     Heathcote, Lesley M. "The Montana Arid Land Grant Commission,
        1895-1903." Agricultural History 38 (1964).
     Malin, James. The Grassland of North America (1947).

511 Lampen, Dorothy. Economic and Social Aspects of Federal Re-
        clamation (1930).
     Schlebecker, John T. "The World Metropolis and the History
        of American Agriculture." Journal of Economic History XX.

512 Gray, L. C. "Trend in Farm Ownership." American Academy of
        Political and Social Science Annals CXLII.
     Saloutos, Theodore. "Land Policy and its Relation to Agricul-
        tural Production and Distribution, 1862 to 1933." Journal
        of Economic History 22 (December 1962): 445-460.
     Whitaker, James W. (ed.). Farming in the Midwest, 1840-1900.
        Washington, D.C.: Agricultural History Society, 1974.

513 Lenin, V. I. "Capitalism and Agriculture in the United States
        of America," in Selected Works XII (1943).

514 Fite, Gilbert C. "John A. Simpson: The Southwest's Militant
        Farm Leader." Mississippi Valley Historical Review XXXV.
     Hoffsommer, Harold (ed.). The Social and Economic Significance
        of Land Tenure in the Southwestern States (1950).

515 Dana, Samuel T. Forest and Range Policy. Its Development in
     the United States (1956).
     Schlebecker, John T. Cattle Raising on the Plains, 1900-1961
     (1963).

516 Karolevitz, Robert F. This Was Trucking: A Pictorial History
     of the First Quarter Century of Commercial Motor Vehicles.
     Seattle, WA: Superior Publishing, 1966.
     Roberts, Merrill J. "The Motor Transportation Revolution."
     Business History Review (March 1956).
     Yarnell, Duane. Auto Pioneering; a Remarkable Story of the
     Father of the Oldsmobile and Reo (1949).

517 Broehl, Wayne G., Jr. Trucks, Trouble and Triumph: The Nor-
     walk Truck Line Company (1954).
     Rae, John B. American Automobile Manufacturers: The First
     Forty Years (1959).

518 Casson, Herbert N., Hutchinson, Rollin W., Jr., and Ellis, L.
     W. Horse, Truck, and Tractor: The Coming of Cheaper Power
     for City and Farm (1913).
     Larson, Henrietta M. The Wheat Market and the Farmer in
     Minnesota, 1858-1900 (1926).
     Peters, Kenneth E. The Good-Roads Movement and the Michigan
     State Highway Department, 1905-1917. Doctoral disserta-
     tion, U. of Michigan, 1972.
     White, John H., Jr. "The Narrow Gauge Fallacy." Railroad
     History 141 (1979): 77-96.

519 Hartsough, Mildred L. The Development of the Twin
     Cities [St. Paul and Minneapolis] as a Metropolitan
     Market (1925).
     Taylor, Charles H. History of the Board of Trade of the City
     of Chicago. 3 vols. (1917).

520 Mansfield, Harold. Vision: A Saga of the Sky (1956).
     Rae, John B. Climb to Greatness: The American Aircraft
     Industry, 1920-1960. Cambridge, MA: MIT Press, 1968.
     _____. "Financial Problems of the American Aircraft Industry,
     1906-1940." Business History Review 39 (1965): 99-114.
     Wilson, Eugene E. Slipstream; the Autobiography of an Air
     Craftsman (1950).

521 Moulton, H. G. Waterways vs. Railways (1912).
     Quick, Herbert. American Inland Waterways (1909).
     Van Syckle, Edwin. The River Pioneers: Early Days on Grays
     Harbor. Edited by James, Dave. Seattle, WA: Pacific
     Search Press, 1982.
     Winther, Oscar O. The Transportation Frontier: Trans-
     Mississippi West, 1865-1890. New York: Holt, Rinehart and
     Winston, 1964.

522 Norton, S. V. The Motor Truck As An Aid to Business Profits
        (1918).
     Montville, John B. Mack. Newfoundland, N.J.: Haessner, 1973.
     White Company. A Quarter Century of White Transportation,
        1900-1925 (1925).

523 Bilstein, Roger E. "Technology and Commerce: Aviation in the
        Conduct of American Business, 1918-29." Technology and
        Culture 10 (July 1969): 392-411.
     Holland, R. S. Historic Airship (1928).
     Holmes, Donald B. Air Mail: An Illustrated History, 1793-
        1981. Edited by Svatos, Ladislav. New York: Clarkson
        N. Potter, 1981.
     Josephson, Matthew. Empire of the Air: Juan Trippe and the
        Struggle for World Airways (1944).

524 Fuess, Charles M. Joseph B. Eastman: Servant of the People
        (1952).
     Latham, Earl. The Politics of Railroad Coordination (1959).

525 Abbey, Wallace W. and others. Our GM Scrapbook. Milwaukee,
        WI: Kalmbach, 1971.
     Davies, W. J. K. Diesel Rail Traction: An Illustrated History
        of Diesel Locomotives, Rail-cars and Trains. London:
        Almark, 1973.
     Morgan, David P. "Diesel Traction in North America," in
        Ransome-Wallis, P. (ed.), The Concise Encyclopedia of World
        Railway Locomotives, Chapter 2 (1959).
     Munger, W. P., Jr. "The Development of the Diesel Locomotive
        in America." Diesel Power and Diesel Transportation
        (November 1942).
     Staff, Virgil. D-Day on the Western Pacific: A Railroad's
        Decision to Dieselize. Glendale, CA: Interurban Press,
        1982.

526 Morgan, David P. (ed.) Steam's Finest Hour (1959).
     Reck, Franklin M. The Dilworth Story: the Biography of
        Richard Dilworth, Pioneer Developer of the Diesel Locomo-
        tive (1954).
     Tuplin, William A. The Steam Locomotive: Its Form and Func-
        tion. New York: Scribner's, 1974.
     White, John H., Jr. American Locomotives: An Engineering
        History, 1830-1880. Baltimore, MD: Johns Hopkins Press,
        1968.

527 Harper, Donald V. Economic Regulation of the Motor Trucking
        Industry by the States (1959).
     Paxson, Frederic L. "The American Highway Movement, 1916-
        1935." American Historical Review LI.

528 Office of Defense Transportation. Civilian War Transport
        (G.P.O., 1948).

Rose, Joseph R. _American Wartime Transportation_ (1953).

529 Allhands, James L. _Tools of the Earth Mover, Yesterday and Today, Preserved in Pictures_ (1951).
Williamson, Harold F. and Myers, Kenneth H., Jr. _Designed for Digging--the First 75 Years of Bucyrus-Erie Company_ (1955).

530 Busbey, K. G. _Home Life in America_ (1910).
Cummings, Richard O. _The American and His Food: a History of Food Habits in the United States_ (1940).
Hewlett, Richard G. and Duncan, Francis. _Nuclear Navy, 1946-1962_. Chicago, IL: U. of Chicago Press, 1974.

531 Breyer, Stephen. _Regulation and Its Reform_. Cambridge, MA: Harvard U. Press, 1982.
Hoogenboom, Ari and Olive. _A History of the ICC: From Panacea to Palliative_. New York: Norton, 1976.
National Research Council. _Economic, Social, and Energy Effects of Highway Transportation_. Washington, D.C.: National Academy of Sciences, 1981.

532 Comptroller General of the U.S. _Effects of Regulatory Reform on Unemployment in the Trucking Industry_. Washington, D.C.: General Accounting Office, 1982.
U.S. Congress, Congressional Budget Office. _The Impact of Trucking Deregulation on Small Communities: A Review of Recent Studies_. Washington, D.C.: The Office, 1980.

533 Phillips, Richard and others. _Auto Industries of Europe, U.S., and Japan to 1990_. Cambridge, MA: Abt Books, 1982.
Ronstadt, Robert C. Associates, Inc. _Multinational Activities of Major U.S. Automotive Producers_. 5 vols. Springfield, VA: National Technical Information Service, 1978.
Shimokawa, Koichi. "Marketing History in the Automobile Industry: The United States and Japan," _in_ Okochi, Akio and Shimokawa, Koichi (eds.), _Development of Mass Marketing: The Automobile and Retailing Industries_. Tokyo, Japan: University of Tokyo Press, 1981.

534 Jordan, William A. _Air Line Regulation in America: Effects and Imperfections_. Baltimore, MD: Johns Hopkins Press, 1970.
Robertson, T. S. and others. "Deregulation: Surviving the Transition." _Harvard Business Review_ 60 (July-August 1982).

535 Aitken, Hugh G. J. _Syntony and Spark: The Origins of Radio_. New York: Wiley, 1976.
Lichty, Lawrence W. and Topping, Malachi C. (comps.). _American Broadcasting: A Source Book on the History of Radio and Television_. New York: Hastings House, 1975.
Maclaurin, W. Rupert. _Invention and Innovation in the Radio Industry_ (1949).

Reich, Leonard S.   "Research, Patents, and the Struggle to
     Control Radio: A Study of Big Business and the Uses of
     Industrial Research."   Business History Review 51 (1977):
     208-235.
Sturmey, S. G.   The Economic Development of Radio (1958).

536 Greenwald, W. I.   "The Impact of Sound Upon the Film Industry:
     A Case Study in Innovation."   Explorations in Entrepreneur-
     ial History, 1st ser. IV.
Jacobs, Lewis.   The Rise of the American Film (1939).

537 Everson, George.   The Story of Television;   the Life of Philo
     T. Farnsworth (1949).
Garratt, G. R. M. and Mumford, A. H.   "A History of T.V."
     Proceedings of the Institution of Electrical Engineers,
     Part III A, Television 99 (1952).
Udelson, Joseph H.   The Great Television Race: A History of
     the Television Industry, 1925-1941.   University, ALA:
     U. of Alabama Press, 1982.

538 Archer, Gleason L.   Big Business and Radio (1939).
Barnouw, Erik.   A Tower in Babel: A History of Broadcasting
     in the United States.   New York: Oxford, 1966.
Lessing, Lawrence P.   Man of High Fidelity: Edwin H. Armstrong
     (1956).
Smart, James R. (comp.)   Radio Broadcasts in the Library of
     Congress, 1924-1941:   A Catalog of Recordings.   Washington,
     D.C.:   G.P.O., 1982.

539 Edelson, Burton I. and Cooper, Robert S.   "Business Use of
     Satellite Communications."   Science 215 (February 1982):
     837-842.
U.S. Congress, 97th, 1st session, House of Representatives,
     Committee on Energy and Commerce, Subcommittee on Tele-
     communications, Consumer Protection, and Finance.
     Satellite Communications/ Direct Broadcast Satellites:
     Hearings....   Washington, D.C.:   G.P.O., 1982.

540 Barnouw, Erik.   The Image Empire: A History of Broadcasting
     in the United States.   3 vols.   New York: Oxford
     U. Press, 1966-70.
Weinberg, Meyer.   TV in America: The Morality of Hard Cash.
     New York: Ballantine, 1962.

541 Gould, Peter C. and Gross, Stephen H. (eds.)   Legal and
     Business Aspects of the Magazine Industry, 1982.   New York:
     Practising Law Institute, 1982.
Tebbel, John.   A History of Book Publishing in the United
     States.   3 vols.   New York: Bowker, 1972-1978.

542 Compaine, Benjamin M. and others.   Who Owns the Media?   Con-
     centration of Ownership in the Mass Communications Indus-
     try.   2nd ed.   White Plains, N.Y.:   Knowledge Industry
     Publications, 1982.

Kindem, Gorham (ed.). The American Movie Industry. The
    Business of Motion Pictures. Carbondale, IL: Southern
    Illinois U. Press, 1982.

543 U.S. Federal Communications Commission. The Historical Evolu-
    tion of the Commercial Network Broadcast System.
    Washington, D.C.: FCC, October 1979.
    _____. The Market for Television Advertising. Washington,
    D.C.: FCC, 1980.

544 "How Cable Television Was Born." Duns Business Month 118
    (November 1981).

545 Kempner, Isaac H. Recalled Recollections (1961).
    Laughlin, J. L. "A National Reserve Association and the Move-
    ment of Cotton in the South." Journal of Political Economy
    XX.

546 Ballagh, James C. (ed.) "Economic History, 1865-1909." The
    South in the Building of the Nation VI (1909).
    Sitterson, Joseph C. "Expansion, Reversion, and Revolution
    in the Southern Sugar Industry: 1850-1910." Business
    History Review XXVII.

547 Fite, Gilbert C. American Farmers: The New Minority.
    Bloomington, IN: Indiana U. Press, 1981.
    Krause, Kenneth R. and Kyle, Leonard R. "Economic Factors
    Underlying the Incidence of Large Farming Units: The
    Current Situation and Probable Trends." American Journal
    of Agricultural Economics 52 (December 1970).
    Schmidt, Louis B. "The International Grain Trade of the
    United States." Iowa Journal of History and Politics XVIII,
    XIX, and XX.
    U.S. Department of Agriculture. Marketing (G.P.O., 1954).

548 Coman, K. "The Negro as a Peasant Farmer." Journal of the
    American Statistical Association IX.
    Gray, Lewis C. "Southern Agriculture, Plantation System, and
    the Negro Problem." American Academy of Political and
    Social Science, Annals XL.
    Shifflet, Crandall A. Patronage and Poverty in the Tobacco
    South. Louisa County, Virginia, 1860-1900. Knoxville,
    TN: U. of Tennessee Press, 1982.

549 Gray, L. C. "Disadvantaged Rural Classes." Journal of Farm
    Economics XX.
    Shannon, Fred A. The Farmer's Last Frontier...1860-1897,
    Chapters 4, 15 (1945).

550 Anderson, Wilbert L. The Country Town (1906).
    Wilson, Harold F. The Hill Country of Northern New England:
    Its Social and Economic History, 1790-1930 (1936).

551 Black, John D. "Social Implications of the Restriction of
        Agricultural Output." American Economic Review XXI.
     Fite, Gilbert C. "Voluntary Attempts to Reduce Cotton Acreage
        in the South, 1914-1933." Journal of Southern History XIV.

552 Brown, Harry B. Cotton (1927).
     Higgs, Robert. "The Boll Weevil, the Cotton Economy, and Black
        Migration, 1910-1930." Agricultural History 50 (1976).
     Hunter, Walter D. Mexican Cotton-Boll Weevil (G.P.O., 1912).
     Mandle, Jay. The Roots of Black Poverty: The Southern Planta-
        tion Economy After the Civil War. Durham, N.C.: Duke
        University Press, 1978.

553 Ankli, Robert E. "Horses vs. Tractors on the Corn Belt."
        Agricultural History 54 (1980): 134-148.
     Cavert, William L. "The Technological Revolution in Agricul-
        ture, 1910-1955." Agricultural History (January 1956).
     Spence, Clark C. "Early Uses of Electricity in American
        Agriculture." Technology and Culture III.
     Wik, Reynold M. "Henry Ford's Tractors and American Agricul-
        ture." Agricultural History 38 (April 1964): 79-86.

554 Clark, Thomas D. "Imperfect Competition in the Southern Retail
        Trade After 1865." Journal of Economic History III.
     Hammond, Matthew B. "Agricultural Credit and Crop Mortgages
        in the South," in The South in the Building of the Nation
        V (1909).

555 Fite, Gilbert C. The Farmers' Frontier, 1865-1900. New York:
        Holt, Rinehart and Winston, 1966.
     Powell, J. C. The American Siberia; or, Fourteen Years' Exper-
        ience in a Southern Convict Camp (1891).
     Ransom, Roger L. and Sutch, Richard. "Debt Peonage in the
        Cotton South After the Civil War." Journal of Economic
        History 32 (September 1972): 641-669.
     Woodward, C. Vann. Origins of the New South, 1877-1913,
        Chapters 7 and 8 (1951).

556 Towne, C. W. and Wentworth, E. N. Shepherd's Empire (1945).
     Wentworth, E. N. America's Sheep Trails (1948).

557 Blockorby, Edward C. Prairie Rebel. The Public Life of William
        Lemke (1964).
     Drache, Hiram M. The Day of the Bonanza. Fargo, N.D.: North
        Dakota Institute for Regional Studies, 1964.
     Jorgenson, Lloyd P. "Agricultural Expansion into the Semiarid
        Lands of the West North Central States During the First
        World War." Agricultural History XXIII.
     Svobida, Lawrence. An Empire of Dust. Caldwell, KS: Caxton
        Printers, 1940.

558 Benedict, Murray R. Farm Policies of the United States, 1790-
        1950 (1953).
     Shideler, James H. Farm Crisis, 1919-1923 (1957).

559 Banfield, Edward C. "Ten Years of the Farm Tenant Purchase
        Program." Journal of Farm Economics XXXI.
     Conrad, David E. The Forgotten Farmers: The Story of Share-
        croppers in the New Deal (1965).

560 Hargreaves, Mary W. M. Dry Farming in the Northern Great
        Plains, 1900-1925 (1957).
     U.S. Department of Agriculture. Water (G.P.O., 1955).

561 Davis, J. S. Wheat and the AAA (1935).
     Leonard, William E. "The Wheat Farmer of Southeastern
        Washington." Journal of Land and Public Utility
        Economics II.

562 Conrad, David E. The Forgotten Farmers: The Story of Share-
        croppers in the New Deal. Urbana, IL: U. of Illinois
        Press, 1965.

     Frey, Fred and Smith, T. L. "The Influence of the A.A.A. Cotton
        Program upon the Tenant, Cropper, and Laborer." Rural
        Sociology I.
     Kirkendall, Richard S. Social Scientists and Farm Politics in
        the Age of Roosevelt. Columbia, MS: U. of Missouri Press,
        1966.
     Venkataramani, M. S. "Norman Thomas, Arkansas Sharecroppers,
        and the Roosevelt Agricultural Policies, 1933-1937."
        Mississippi Valley Historical Review XLVII.

563 Albertson, Dean. Roosevelt's Farmer. Claude R. Wickard in the
        New Deal (1961).
     Campbell, Christina M. The Farm Bureau and the New Deal: A
        Study of the Making of National Farm Policy, 1933-40 (1962).
     Saloutos, Theodore. The American Farmer and the New Deal.
        Ames, IA: Iowa State U. Press, 1982.

564 Fisher, Lloyd. "The Harvest Labor Market in California."
        Quarterly Journal of Economics (November 1951).
     Maika, Linda C. and Maika, Theodore J. Farm Workers, Agri-
        business, and the State. Philadelphia, PA: Temple U.
        Press, 1982.
     Musoke, Moses S. and Olmstead, Alan L. "The Rise of the Cotton
        Industry in California: A Comparative Perspective."
        Journal of Economic History 42 (June 1982): 385-412.
     Scruggs, O. M. "Evolution of the Mexican Farm Labor Agreement
        of 1942." Agricultural History (July 1960).

565 Gold, Bela. Wartime Economic Planning in Agriculture (1949).
     Wilcox, Walter W. The Farmer in the Second World War,
        Chapter 17 (1947).

566 Fleisig, Heywood. "Mechanizing the Cotton Harvest in the
        Nineteenth-Century South." Journal of Economic History
        (December 1965).

Fite, Gilbert. "Mechanization of Cotton Production since
    World War II." Agricultural History 54 (1980): 190-207.
Sayre, Charles R. "Cotton Mechanization since World War II."
    Agricultural History 53 (1979): 105-124.
Street, James H. The New Revolution in the Cotton Economy
    (1956).

567 Bachman, Kenneth L. "Changes in Scale in Commercial Farming
        and their Implications." Journal of Farm Economics XXXIV.
    Emerson, Peter M. Corporations in Farming. Washington, D.C.:
        Congressional Budget Office, 1980.
    Friedland, William H. and others. Manufacturing Green Gold:
        The Conditions and Social Consequences of Lettuce Harvest
        Mechanization. Davis, CA: Department of Applied Behavior-
        al Sciences, U. of California, 1978.
    Taylor, Paul S. "Plantation Agriculture in the United States:
        Seventeenth to Twentieth Centuries." Land Economics XXX.

568 Castle, E. N. and Hoch, I. "Farm Real Estate Price Components,
        1920-78." American Journal of Agricultural Economics 64
        (February 1982): 8-18.
    U.S. Congress, 97th, 1st session, Senate, Committee on Govern-
        mental Affairs, Subcommittee on Energy, Nuclear Prolifera-
        tion, and Government Processes. Growing Agricultural Trade
        Protectionism in Europe: Hearings.... Washington, D.C.:
        G.P.O., 1982.

569 Hinds, Dudley S. and Ordway, Nicholas. International Real
        Estate Investment. Chicago, IL: Real Estate Education
        Co., 1983.
    Rasmussen, Wayne D. "The Mechanization of Agriculture."
        Scientific American 247 (September 1982): 76-89.
    Raup, Phillip. "Corporate Farming in the United States."
        Journal of Economic History 33 (March 1973): 274-290.
    Ricks, David A. and Racster, Ronald L. "Foreign Ownership of
        U.S. Real Estate." Real Estate Review (Spring 1980): 111-
        15.

570 Shideler, James H. (ed.). Agriculture in the Development
        of the Far West. Washington, D.C.: Agricultural History
        Society, 1975.
    Ward, Ralph E. "Wheat in Montana: Determined Adaptation."
        Montana, the Magazine of Western History 25 (October 1975):
        16-37.

571 Pollard, R. W. and others. "Farmers' Experience with Conserva-
        tism Tillage: A Wisconsin Survey." Journal of Soil and
        Water Conservation 34 (September 1979): 215-19.
    "Public Attitudes Revealed on Soil and Water Conservation."
        Soil and Water Conservation News 1 (April 1980): 6-7.

    Timmons, J. F. "Protecting Agriculture's Natural Resource
        Base." Journal of Soil and Water Conservation 35
        (January 1980): 5-11.

572 Lewin, Leonard (ed.). Telecommunications in the U.S.:
       Trends and Policies. Dedham, MA: Artech, 1981.
     Pool, Ithiel deSola (ed.). The Social Impact of the Telephone.
       Cambridge, MA: M.I.T. Press, 1977.

573 Boore, James P. The Seamless Story: A History of the Seamless
       Steel Tube Industry in the United States (1951).
     Hogan, William T. Economic History of the Iron and Steel
       Industry in the United States. 5 vols. Lexington, MA:
       Lexington Books, 1971.
     Mackintosh-Hemphill Co. Rolling Mills, Rolls, and Roll Making
       (1953).
     Rosenberg, Nathan. "Technological Change in the Machine Tool
       Industry, 1840-1910." Journal of Economic History 23
       (December 1963): 414-443.

574 Clark, Victor S. History of Manufactures in the United States
       III, Chapters 5 and 20 (1929).
     Littauer, Sebastian B. "The Development of Statistical Quality
       Control in the United States." American Statistician
       (December 1950; February 1951).
     Petik, Ferenc. "The Development of Material Testing Machines."
       Technikatorteneti Szemle 11 (1979): 217-232.

575 Habakkuk, H. J. American and British Technology in the Nine-
       teenth Century, Chapters 5 and 6 (1962).
     Montgomery, David. "The 'New Unionism' and the Transformation
       of Workers' Consciousness in America, 1909-22." Journal
       of Social History 7 (1974): 508-529.
     _____. Workers' Control in America: Studies in the History of
       Work, Technology, and Labor Struggles. New York: Cambridge
       U. Press, 1979.
     Orsagh, Thomas J. "Progress in Iron and Steel: 1870-1913."
       Comparative Studies in Society and History III.

576 National Industrial Conference Board. Mergers in Industry
       (1929).
     Nelson, Ralph L. Merger Movements in American Industry, 1895-
       1956 (1959).

577 Pulos, Arthur J. American Design Ethic. A History of
       Industrial Design. Cambridge, MA: MIT Press, 1983.
     Heskett, John. Industrial Design. New York: Oxford, 1981.
     Kaufmann, Edgar, Jr. "Industrial Design in American Museums."
       Magazine of Art XXXXII.
     Richards, Charles R. Art in Industry (1922).

578 Chandler, Alfred D., Jr. "The Beginnings of 'Big Business' in
       American Industry." Business History Review XXXIII.
     Friedland, Seymour. "Turnover and Growth of the Largest Indus-
       trial Firms, 1906-1950." Review of Economic Studies
       (February 1957).
     Hacker, Louis M. The World of Andrew Carnegie, 1865-1901.
       Philadelphia, PA: Lippincott, 1968.

Lewis, W. David. Iron and Steel in America. Greenville, DE:
    Eleutherian Mills-Hagley Foundation, 1976.

579 Dewing, A. S. The Financial Policy of Corporations (1934).
    Robinson, Maurice H. "The Distribution of Securities in the
        Formation of the United States Steel Corporation." Politi-
        cal Science Quarterly XXX.

580 Du Boff, Richard B. "The Introduction of Electric Power in
        American Manufacturing." Economic History Review 20, 2nd
        series (December 1967): 509-518.
    Passer, Harold C. The Electrical Manufacturers, 1875-1900,
        Chapters 14-21 (1953).
    Sharlin, Harold I. The Making of the Electrical Age. New York:
        Abelard-Schuman, 1964.

581 Chandler, Alfred D., Jr. and Salsbury, Stephen. Pierre S.
        duPont and the Making of the Modern Corporation. New York:
        Harper & Row, 1971.
    Chandler, Alfred D., Jr. Strategy and Structure: Chapters in
        the History of Industrial Enterprise (1962).
    Flint, Charles R. Memories of an Active Life (1923).
    Litterer, Joseph A. "Systematic Management: Design for Organ-
        izational Recoupling in American Manufacturing Firms."
        Business History Review 37 (1963): 369-391.

582 Adams, Walter and Dirlam, Joel B. "Big Steel, Invention, and
        Innovation." Quarterly Journal of Economics 80 (May 1966):
        167-189.
    American Institute of Metallurgical Engineers. A History of
        Iron and Steelmaking in the United States (1961).
    Clark, Victor S. History of Manufactures in the United States
        III, Chapter 5 (1928).
    Wertime, Theodore A. The Coming of the Age of Steel. Chicago,
        IL: U. of Chicago Press, 1962.

583 Crow, Carl. The City of Flint Grows Up (1945).
    Pound, Arthur. The Turning Wheel; the Story of General Motors
        ...1908-1933 (1934).

584 Habakkuk, H. J. American and British Technology in the Nine-
        teenth Century. New York: Cambridge U. Press,
    Strassman, W. Paul. Risk and Technological Innovation (1959).

585 Saul, S. B. "The American Impact on British Industry, 1895-
        1914." Business History III.
    Steeds, William. A History of Machine Tools, 1700-1910.
        Oxford: Clarendon Press, 1969.
    Strassman, W. Paul. "Creative Destruction and Partial Obsoles-
        cence in American Economic Development." Journal of
        Economic History XIX.

Wagoner, Harless D. The U.S. Machine Tool Industry from
    1900 to 1950. Cambridge, MA: M.I.T. Press, 1968.

586 Clark, Victor S. History of Manufactures in the United States
    III, Chapter 9 (1929).
    Einstein, S. "Machine Tool Milestones--Past and Present."
    Mechanical Engineering (November 1930).

587 Chapin, Ned. "The Development of the Break-Even Chart."
    Journal of Business (April 1955).
    Hawkins, David F. "The Development of Modern Financial
    Practices among American Manufacturing Corporations."
    Business History Review 37 (1963): 135-168.
    Johnson, H. Thomas. "Management Accounting in an Early Multi-
    divisional Organization: General Motors in the 1920s."
    Business History Review 52 (1978): 490-517.
    Metcalf, Captain Henry. The Cost of Manufactures. 3rd ed.
    (1894).
    Previts, Gary John and Merino, Barbara Dubis. A History of
    Accounting in America. New York: Wiley, 1979.

588 Jerome, Harry. Mechanization in Industry (1934).
    Love, John W. Elwell-Parker Electric Company, Lengthened
    Shadows; Recounting the Development of Industrial Load
    Transportation (1943).

589 Livesay, Harold C. and Porter, Patrick G. "Vertical Integra-
    tion in American Manufacturing, 1899-1948." Journal of
    Economic History 29 (September 1969): 494-500.
    Veblen, Thorstein. The Theory of Business Enterprise,
    Chapter 3 (1904).
    Willoughby, W. F. "Integration of Industry." Quarterly
    Journal of Economics XVI.
    Yeager, Mary A. The Development of Oligopoly in the Meat
    Packing Industry. Greenwich, CT: JAI Press, 1981.

590 Arnold, Horace L. and Faurote, Fay L. Ford Methods and the
    Ford Shops (1915).
    Woodworth, Joseph V. American Tool Making and Interchangeable
    Manufacturing (1911).

591 Aitken, Hugh G. J. Taylorism at Watertown Arsenal: Scientific
    Management in Action, 1908-1915 (1960).
    Strassman, W. P. "Interrelated Industries and the Rate of
    Technological Change." Review of Economic Studies (October
    1959).

592 Payne, W. F. Business Behavior, 1919-22 (1942).
    Soule, George. Prosperity Decade...1917-1929, Chapters 2-5
    (1947).

593 Ratner, Sidney (ed.). New Light on the History of Great
    American Fortunes: American Millionaires of 1892 and 1902
    (1953).

Smith, Richard A. "The Fifty-Million Dollar Man." Fortune
    LVI.

594 Abramovitz, Moses. Inventories and Business Cycles, With
         Special Reference to Manufacturers' Inventories (1950).
     Stanback, Thomas M., Jr. Postwar Cycles in Manufacturers'
         Inventories (1962).

595 Broude, Henry W. Steel Decisions and the National Economy
         (1963).
     Lewis, H. Gregg. "The Nature of Demand for Steel." Journal
         of the American Statistical Association XXXVI.

596 Lauderbaugh, Richard A. American Steel Makers and the Coming
         of the Second World War. Ann Arbor, MI: UMI Research
         Press, 1980.
     Mason, E. S. "The Impact of the War on American Commodity
         Prices." Review of Economics and Statistics XXI.
     Mitchell, Broadus. Depression Decade, 1929-1941, Chapter 11
         (1947).

597 Barloon, M. J. "Institutional Foundations of Pricing Policy
         in the Steel Industry." Business History Review XXVIII.
     Berglund, A. "Organization in the Steel Industry and Price
         Policy." Harvard Business Review IX.

598 Holley, I. B., Jr. "The Management of Technological Change:
         Aircraft Production in the United States during World War
         II." Aerospace Historian 22 (September 1975): 161-165.
     Lilley, Tom et al. Problems of Accelerating Aircraft Produc-
         tion (1947).
     Simonson, G. R. "The Demand for Aircraft and the Aircraft
         Industry, 1907-1953." Journal of Economic History XX.
     _____. The History of the American Aircraft Industry: An
         Anthology. Cambridge, MA: M.I.T. Press, 1968.

599 Gilbert, H. N. "The Emergency in Aircraft Manufacture."
         Harvard Business Review XIX.
     _____. "The Expansion of Shipbuilding." Harvard Business
         Review XX.

600 Bain, Joe S. Barriers to New Competition (1956).
     Carroll, John M. and Schneider, Richard P. Historical Finan-
         cial Data: Domestic Automobile Manufacturers.
         Springfield, VA: National Technical Information Service,
         1979.
     Cassella, M. A. and Rabe, F. T. The Relationship of Automo-
         bile Characteristics to List Prices and Profit Margins.
         Springfield, VA: National Technical Information Service,
         1978.
     Vatter, Harold G. Small Enterprise and Oligopoly (1955).

601 Brancato, Carolyn K. Merger Tactics and Public Policy.
         Washington, D.C.: G.P.O., 1982.
     Nelson, Ralph L. Concentration in the Manufacturing Industries
         of the United States. New Haven, CT: Yale U. Press, 1963.

602 Engelberger, Joseph F. Robotics in Practice. Avebury,
         England: Kogan Page Press, 1980.
     Levitan, S. A. and Johnson, C. M. "Future of Work: Does It
         Belong to Us or to the Robots?" Monthly Labor Review 105
         (September 1982): 10-14.
     Office of Technology Assessment. Exploratory Workshop on the
         Social Impacts of Robotics. Washington, D.C.: G.P.O.,
         1982.
     Vedder, Richard K. Robotics and the Economy. Washington,
         D.C.: G.P.O., 1982.

603 Frantzich, Stephen E. Computers in Congress: The Politics of
         Information. Beverly Hills, CA: Sage, 1982.
     Schiller, Daniel. Telematics and Government. Norwood, N.J.:
         Ablex, 1982.
     Stern, Nancy and Stern, Robert A. Computers in Society.
         Englewood Cliffs, N.J.: Prentice-Hall, 1983.

604 Buss, M. D. J. "Managing International Information Systems."
         Harvard Business Review 60 (September-October 1982): 153-
         162.

605 Douglas, Paul H. American Apprenticeship and Industrial
         Education (1921).
     Motley, James M. Apprenticeship in American Trade Unions
         (1907).

606 Carlton, David L. Mill and Town in South Carolina, 1880-
         1920. Baton Rouge, LA: Louisiana State U. Press, 1982.
     Davidson, E. H. Child Labor Legislation in Southern Textile
         States (1939).
     de Graffenried, Clare. "The Georgia Cracker in the Cotton
         Mill." Century Magazine, n.s., XIX.
     Eller, Ronald D. Miners, Millhands, and Mountaineers. Indus-
         trialization of the Appalachian South, 1880-1930.
         Knoxville, TN: U. of Tennessee Press, 1982.

607 Mitchell, Broadus. Rise of Cotton Mills in the South (1921).
     Thompson, Holland. From Cotton Field to Cotton Mill (1906).

608 Blumer, Herbert. "Paternalism in Industry." Social Process
         in Hawaii (Univ. of Hawaii) XV.
     Davidson, Elizabeth H. "The Child Labor Problem in North
         Carolina, 1883-1903." North Carolina Historical Review
         XIII.

609 Greene, Lorenzo J. and Woodson, Carter G. The Negro Wage
         Earner (1930).

Wesley, Charles H. Negro Labor in the United States (1927).

610 Brody, David. The Steelworkers in America; The Nonunion Phase
        (1960).
     Eggert, Gerald G. Steelmasters and Labor Reform, 1886-1923.
        Pittsburgh, PA: U. of Pittsburgh Press, 1981.
     Garraty, John A. "The U.S. Steel Corporation versus Labor:
        the Early Years." Labor History I.

611 Balch, Emily J. Our Slavic Fellow Citizens (1910).
     Body, Paul and Boros-Kazai, Mary. Hungarian Immigrants in
        Greater Pittsburgh, 1880-1980 (1981). ERIC ED 219 344.
     Foerster, Robert F. The Italian Immigration in our Times
        (1919).
     Hannon, Joan Underhill. "City Size and Ethnic Discrimination:
        Michigan Agricultural Implements and Iron Working
        Industries, 1890." Journal of Economic History 42
        (December 1982): 825-845.

612 Hourwich, I. S. Immigration and Labor (1912).
     Rosenblum, G. Immigrant Workers, Their Impact on American
        Labor Radicalism. New York: Basic Books, 1973.
     Taylor, Joseph H. "The Restriction of European Immigration and
        the Concept of Race." South Atlantic Quarterly L.

613 Michelbacker, G. F. and Niel, T. M. Workmen's Compensation
        Insurance (1925).
     Van Doren, D. H. Workmen's Insurance (1918).

614 Millis, Harry (ed.). How Collective Bargaining Works (1942).
     Novack, David E. and Perlman, Richard. "The Structure of Wages
        in the American Iron and Steel Industry, 1860-1890."
        Journal of Economic History 22 (September 1962): 334-347.
     O'Connor, Harvey. History of the Oil Workers International
        Union (1950).

615 Grant, Madelaine P. Alice Hamilton, Pioneer Doctor in Indus-
        trial Medicine. New York: Abelard-Shuman, 1967.
     Hazlett, Theodore L. and Hummell, W. W. Industrial Medicine
        in Western Pennsylvania, 1850-1950 (1957).
     Selleck, Henry B. Occupational Health in America (1962).

616 Jenks, Jeremiah W. and Lauck, W. Jett. The Immigrant Problem.
        6th ed. (1926).
     Leiserson, William M. Adjusting Immigrant and Industry (1924).
     Shergold, Peter R. "Relative Skill and Income Levels of Native
        and Foreign Born Workers: A Reexamination." Explorations
        in Economic History 13 (October 1976): 451-461.

617 Couch, Stephen R. "Selling and Reclaiming State Sovereignty:
        The Case of Coal and Iron Police." Insurgent Sociologist
        10 (Summer-Fall 1981).

Green, Fletcher M. "Home Aspects of the Convict Lease System
    in the Southern States," in Green, F. M. (ed.), Essays in
    Southern History Presented to Joseph Gregoire de Roulhac
    Hamilton (1949).
Zimmerman, J. "The Convict Lease System in Arkansas and the
    Fight for Abolition." Arkansas Historical Quarterly VIII.

618 Foner, Philip S. History of the Labor Movement in the United
        States II, Chapter 15 (1955).
     McKelvey, Blake. "The Prison Labor Problem: 1875-1900."
        Journal of the American Institute of Criminal Law and
        Criminology XXV.

619 Alford, Leon P. Henry Lawrence Gantt (1934).
     Berck, Peter. "Hard Driving and Efficiency: Iron Production
        in 1890." Journal of Economic History 38 (December 1978):
        879-900.
     Nadworny, Milton J. "Frederick Taylor and Frank Gilbreth:
        Competition in Scientific Management." Business History
        Review XXXI.
     Nelson, Daniel. Frederick W. Taylor and the Rise of Scientific
        Management. Madison, WI: U. of Wisconsin Press, 1980.

620 Cahill, M. C. Shorter Hours: A Study of the Movement Since
        the Civil War (1932).
     Haber, Samuel. Efficiency and Uplift: Scientific Management
        in the Progressive Era, 1890-1920. Chicago, IL: U. of
        Chicago Press, 1964.
     Zeisel, J. S. "The Workweek in American Industry, 1850-1956."
        Monthly Labor Review (January 1958).

621 Cordulack, John H. The Artisan Confronts the Machine Age:
        Bureau County, Illinois, 1850-1880. Doctoral dissertation,
        U. of Illinois, 1975.
     Davis, Pearce. The Development of the American Glass Industry
        (1949).
     Minton, Lee W. Flame and Heart: A History of the Association
        of the United States and Canada Glass Bottle Blowers (1961).

622 Buttrick, John. "The Inside Contract System." Journal of
        Economic History XII.
     Vauclain, Samuel. Steaming up! (1930).
     White, John H., Jr. Cincinnati Locomotive Builders 1845-1868.
        Washington, D.C.: Smithsonian Institution, 1965.

623 Jensen, Vernon H. Hiring of Dock Workers and Employment Prac-
        tices in the Ports of New York, Liverpool, London, Rotter-
        dam, and Marseilles (1964).
     Rathbone, Eleanor F. Report of an Inquiry into the Conditions
        of Dock Labour at the Liverpool Docks (1904).

624   Jensen, Vernon H. Lumber and Labor (1945).
      Todes, Charlotte. Labor and Lumber (1931).

625   Fine, Sidney. The Automobile Under the Blue Eagle: Labor,
          Management, and the Automobile Manufacturing Code (1963).
      Haber, W. "Fluctuations in Employment in Detroit Factories,
          1921-1931." Journal of the American Statistical Associa-
          tion XXVII.
      Rae, John B. The American Automobile: A Brief History.
          Chicago, IL: U. of Chicago Press, 1965.

626   Auerbach, Jerold S. Labor and Liberty: The La Follette
          Committee and the New Deal. Indianapolis, IN: Bobbs-
          Merrill, 1966.
      Bernstein, Irving. The New Deal Collective Bargaining Policy
          (1950).
      Morris, James O. Conflict Within the AFL: A Study of Craft
          versus Industrial Unionism, 1901-1938 (1958).

627   Fine, Sidney. Sit-Down: The General Motors Strike of 1936-
          1937. Ann Arbor, MI: U. of Michigan Press, 1969.
      Friedlander, Peter. The Emergence of a UAW Local, 1936-1939:
          A Study in Class and Culture. Pittsburgh, PA: U. of
          Pittsburgh Press, 1975.
      Harris, Herbert. Labor's Civil War (1940).
      Levinson, Edward. Labor on the March (1938).

628   Gomberg, William. A Trade Union Analysis of Time Study. 2nd
          ed. (1955).
      Walker, Charles R. and Guest, Robert R. The Man on the Assembly
          Line (1952).

629   Fine, Sidney. "President Roosevelt and the Automobile Code."
          Mississippi Valley Historical Review XLV.
      _____. "The Origins of the United Automobile Workers, 1933-
          1935." Journal of Economic History XVIII.
      Meyer, Stephen III. Mass Production and Human Efficiency:
          The Ford Motor Company, 1908-1921. Doctoral dissertation,
          Rutgers University, 1977.

630   Cobb, James C. The Selling of the South: The Southern Crusade
          for Industrial Development, 1936-1980. Baton Rouge, LA:
          Louisiana State U. Press, 1982.
      Mitchell, George S. "The Negro in Southern Trade Unionism."
          Southern Economic Journal II.
      Spero, Sterling D. and Harris, Abram L. The Black Worker
          (1931).

631   Boylan, Myles G., Jr. Economic Effects of Scale Increases in
          the Steel Industry: The Case of U.S. Blast Furnaces.
          New York: Praeger, 1975.
      Brooks, R. R. R. As Steel Goes... (1940).
      Leontief, Wassily W. "The Distribution of Work and Income."
          Scientific American 247 (September 1982): 188-204.

Sherman, Herbert L. Arbitration of the Steel Wage Structure
    (1961).

632 Cherrix, C. C. Women Telephone Workers and Changing Technology
        (G.P.O., 1963).
    Erickson, Ethel. The Woman Telephone Worker (G.P.O., 1946).

633 Brophy, John. A Miner's Life. Ed. by Hall, John O. P.
        Madison, WI: U. of Wisconsin Press, 1964.
    Corbin, David Alan. Life, Work, and Rebellion in the Coal
        Fields. Urbana, IL: U. of Illinois Press, 1981.
    Lester, Richard. "Trends in Southern Wage Differentials Since
        1890." Southern Economic Journal XI.
    [Mooney, Fred]. Struggle in the Coal Fields: The Autobio-
        graphy of Fred Mooney. Ed. by Hess, J. W. Morgantown,
        W.VA.: West Virginia U. Library, 1967.
    Seidman, Joel I. American Labor from Defense to Reconversion
        (1953).

634 Baratz, Morton S. The Union and the Coal Industry (1955).
    Dubofsky, Melvyn and Van Tine, Warren. John L. Lewis: A
        Biography. New York: Quadrangle, 1977.
    Hevener, John W. Which Side Are You On? The Harlan Coal
        Miners, 1931-39. Urbana, IL: U. of Illinois Press, 1978.
    Hoover, Calvin B. and Ratchford, B. U. Economic Resources and
        Policies of the South, Chapter 8 (1951).

635 Greenberg, Simon S. "Welding Comes of Age Through Standards."
        Standards World I.
    Jefferson, T. B. (ed.). Welding Encyclopedia, 13th ed. (1951).

636 Brady, Robert A. Organization, Automation, and Society. The
        Scientific Revolution in Industry (1961).
    Hafez, E. S. and others. In Vitro Fertilization and Embryo
        Transfer. New York: A. R. Liss, 1981.
    Singer, Peter and Walters, William (eds.). Test Tube Babies.
        Oxford U. Press, 1982.

637 Backman, Jules. The Economics of the Electrical Machinery
        Industry (1962).
    Vatter, Harold G. The U.S. Economy in the 1950's (1963).

638 Buss, Terry F. and Redburn, F. Stevens. Shutdown in Youngstown:
        Public Policy for Mass Unemployment. Albany, N.Y.: State
        U. of New York Press, 1982.
    Employment Effects of Multinational Enterprises in Industrial-
        ised Counties. Geneva: International Labour Office, 1981.
    Sheingold, Steven. Dislocated Workers: Issues and Federal
        Options. Washington, D.C.: G.P.O., 1982.

639 Fay, Betsy A. and Billings, Charles E. Index of Signs and
        Symptoms of Industrial Diseases. Rockville, MD: National
        Institute of Occupational Safety and Health, 1981.

Goldberg, Marcia. A Workers' Guide to Winning at the Occupa-
     tional Safety and Health Review Commission. Rev. ed.
     Washington, D.C.: Health Research Group, 1981.
McCaffrey, David P. OSHA and the Politics of Health Regulation.
     New York: Plenum Press, 1982.

640 Lichtenstein, Nelson. "Auto Workers Militancy and the Structure
        of Factory Life, 1937-1955." Journal of American History
        67 (1980): 335-353.
     Peterson, J. S. "Auto Workers and their Work, 1900-1933."
        Labor History 22 (Spring 1981).

641 Cobb, James C. The Selling of the South: The Southern Crusade
        for Industrial Development, 1936-1980. Baton Rouge, LA:
        Louisiana State U. Press, 1982.
     Hall, Bob. "Bucking the System." Southern Exposure 10
        (September-October 1982): 66-73.
     Raynor, Bruce. "Unionism in the Southern Textile Industry:
        An Overview," in Fink, Gary M. and Reed, Merl E. (eds.),
        Essays in Southern Labor History. Westport, CT:
        Greenwood, 1977.
     Reed, Merl E. and others (ed.). Southern Workers and Their
        Unions, 1880-1975. Westport, CT: Greenwood, 1981.
     Wilson, Kinsey and Askin, Steve. "Secrets of a Union Buster."
        Nation 232 (June 1981): 725-728.

642 Graebner, William. Coal-Mining Safety in the Progressive
        Period: The Political Economy of Reform. Lexington, KY:
        U. Press of Kentucky, 1976.
     Nagy, John. The Explosion Hazard in Mining. Pittsburgh, PA:
        U.S. Department of Labor, Mine Safety and Health Adminis-
        tration, 1981.

643 Brill, Steven. The Teamsters. New York: Simon and Schuster,
        1978.

644 Bluestone, Barry and Harrison, Bennett. The Deindustrializa-
        tion of America: Plant Closings, Community Abandonment,
        and the Dismantling of Basic Industries. New York:
        Basic Books, 1982.
     Lynd, Staughton. The Fight Against Shutdowns. San Pedro,
        CA: Singlejack Books, Box 1906, 1982.
     McKenzie, Richard B. (ed.) Plant Closings: Public or Private
        Choices? Washington, D.C.: Cato Institute, 1982.
     Rainer, John C. and others (eds.). Community and Capital in
        Conflict: Plant Closings and Job Loss. Philadelphia,
        PA: Temple U. Press, 1982.

645 Terry, S. L. "Unemployment and Its Effect on Family Income
        in 1980." Monthly Labor Review 105 (April 1982): 35-43.

646 Hower, Ralph M. The History of an Advertising Agency: N. W.
        Ayer & Son at Work, 1869-1949, rev. ed. (1949).

Pease, Otis. _The Responsibilities of American Advertising. Private Control and Public Influence, 1920-1940_ (1958).

647 Presbrey, Frank. _History and Development of Advertising_ (1929).
     Sherman, S. A. "Advertising." American Statistical Association _Publications_ VII.

648 Markin, Rom J. _The Supermarket: An Analysis of Growth, Development, and Change_ (1963).
     Palamountain, Joseph C., Jr. _The Politics of Distribution_ (1955).

649 Appel, Joseph H. _The Business Biography of John Wanamaker_ (1930).
     Hower, Ralph M. _History of Macy's of New York, 1858-1919_ (1943).

650 Endicott, William. "Reminiscences of Seventy-Five Years." Massachusetts Historical Society _Proceedings_ XXXXVI.
     Nystrom, Paul H. _Economics of Retailing_ I (1930).

651 Fenin, George N. and Everson, William K. _The Western: From Silents to Cinerama_ (1962).

652 Brown, Harold. _Franchising: Realities and Remedies_, rev. ed. New York: Law Journal Seminars-Press, 1981.
     Sanders, Harland. _Finger Lickin' Good_. Carol Stream, IL: Creation House, 1974.

653 "Cash Flow Horrors and Bankruptcies Mount in Distributor Margin and Supply Squeeze." _National Petroleum News_ 74 (July 1982): 25-29.
     Crouse, W. H. _Automotive Service Business_. New York: McGraw-Hill, 1973.
     Globerman, S. "Self-service Gasoline Stations: A Case-Study of Competitive Innovation." _Journal of Retailing_ 54 (Spring 1978): 75-86.
     Howard, M. C. _The Marketing of Petroleum Products_. New York: Arno Press, 1979.
     Mitchel, E. J. "Recent Changes in Gasoline Retailing: An Economic Interpretation." _Journal of Retailing_ 56 (Winter 1980): 5-22.

654 Barmash, Isadore. _More Than They Bargained For: The Rise and Fall of Korvettes_. New York: Lebhar-Friedman, 1982.
     "General Merchandise Industry Profiles." _Chain Store Age Executive_ 58 (July 1982): 26-73.
     Super Market Institute. "The Untold Story of SMI: 1937-1962." _Super Market Merchandising_ 27 (May 1962): 61-130.

655 Bruchey, Stuart M. (ed.) _Small Business in American Life_. New York: Columbia U. Press, 1980.

Cochran, A. B. "Small Business Mortality Rates: A Review of the Literature." *Journal of Small Business Management* 19 (October 1981): 50-59.

656 Bloom, P. N. and Greyser, S. A. "Maturing of Consumerism." *Harvard Business Review* 59 (November-December 1981): 130-139.
Hinich, Melvin J. *Consumer Protection Legislation and the U.S. Food Industry.* New York: Permagon Press, 1980.
Pertschuk, Michael. *Revolt Against Regulation: The Rise and Pause of the Consumer Movement.* Berkeley, CA: U. of California Press, 1982.

657 Nearing, Scott and Freeman, Joseph. *Dollar Diplomacy* (1925).
Simon, Matthew and Novack, David. "Some Dimensions of the American Commercial Invasion of Europe, 1871-1914." *Journal of Economic History* (December 1964).
Wilkins, Mira. *The Emergence of Multinational Enterprise: American Business Abroad from the Colonial Era to 1914.* Cambridge, MA: Harvard U. Press, 1970.

658 Knapp, Frank A., Jr. "Precursors of American Investment in Mexican Railroads." *Pacific Historical Review* XXI.
Pletcher, David M. *Rails, Mines, and Progress: Seven American Promoters in Mexico, 1867-1911* (1959).

659 Campbell, Charles S., Jr. *Anglo-American Understanding, 1898-1903* (1957).
Gelber, L. M. *The Rise of Anglo-American Friendship, 1898-1906* (1938).

660 Campbell, Charles S., Jr. *Special Business Policy* (1951).
Ershkowitz, Herbert. *The Attitude of Business Toward Foreign Policy, 1900-1916.* University Park, PA: Pennsylvania State U., 1967.
Esthus, Raymond A. "The Changing Concept of the Open Door, 1899-1910." *Mississippi Valley Historical Review* XLVI.
La Feber, Walter. *The New Empire: An Interpretation of American Expansion, 1860-1898.* Ithaca, N.Y.: Cornell U. Press, 1963.

661 Radin, Max. *Manners and Morals of Business* (1939).
U.S. Federal Trade Commission. *Trade Practices Conferences* (various).

662 Queen, George S. "The McCormick Harvesting Machine Company in Russia." *Russian Review* (April 1964).

663 Faulkner, Harold U. *The Decline of Laissez Faire, 1897-1917,* Chapters 3 and 4 (1951).
Fisher, Richard B. "American Investments in Pre-Soviet Russia Russia." *American Slavic and East European Review* VIII.

664 Kepner, C. D. and Soothill, J. H. Banana Empire (1935).
     Knight, M. M. Americans in Santa Domingo (1928).

665 Thurber, F. B. Coffee--From Plantation to Cup (1883).
     Wakeman, Abram. History and Reminiscences of Lower Wall
        Street and Vicinity (1914).

666 Landes, David S. "Some Thoughts on the Nature of Economic
        Imperialism." Journal of Economic History XXI.
     Lewis, Cleona. America's Stake in International Investments
        (1938).

667 Phelps, Clyde W. The Foreign Expansion of American Banks
        (1927).
     Stern, Siegfried. The United States in International Banking
        (1951).

668 "America's Changing Investment Market." American Academy of
        Political and Social Science, Annals LXVII.
     Rippy, J. Fred. "Investments of Citizens of the United States
        in Latin America." Journal of Business XXII.

669 Brown, William Adams, Jr. The International Gold Standard
        Reinterpreted, 1914-1934 (1940).
     Winkler, John K. The First Billion: the Stillmans and the
        National City Bank (1934).

670 Curti, Merle E. Bryan and World Peace (1931).
     May, Ernest R. The World War and American Isolation, 1914-
        1917.
     Parrini, Carl. Heir to Empire: United States Economic Diplo-
        macy, 1916-1923. Pittsburgh, PA: U. of Pittsburgh Press,
        1969.
     Van Alstyne, R. W. "Private American Loans to the Allies."
        Pacific Historical Review II.

671 Schluter, W. C. The Pre-War Business Cycle, 1907-1914 (1923).
     Sprague, O. M. W. "The Crisis of 1914." American Economic
        Review V.

672 Birdsall, Paul. "Neutrality and Economic Pressures." Science
        and Society III.
     Link, Arthur S. Wilson: Confusions and Crises, 1915-1916.
        (1964).

673 Smith, Daniel M. Intervention, 1917: The Causes of American
        Involvement in World War I (1966).
     Wiltz, John E. In Search of Peace: The Senate Munitions
        Inquiry, 1934-36 (1963).

674 Brecher, Irving and Reisman, S. S. Canada-United States
        Relations (1957).
     Nicholson, Harold. Dwight Morrow (1935).

Wilson, Joan Hoff. American Business and Foreign Policy, 1920–1933. Lexington, KY: U. of Kentucky Press, 1971.
Wood, Bryce. The Making of the Good Neighbor Policy (1961).

683 Arey, Hawthorne. History of Operations and Policies of Export-Import Bank of Washington (1953).
Guerrant, E. O. Roosevelt's Good Neighbor Policy (1950).

684 Bonnell, Allen T. German Control over International Economic Relations, 1930–1940 (1950).
Feis, Herbert. The Diplomacy of the Dollar: First Era, 1919–1932 (1950).
Gardner, Lloyd C. Economic Aspects of New Deal Diplomacy. Madison, WI: U. of Wisconsin Press, 1964.
Grow, Michael. The Good Neighbor Policy and Authoritarianism in Paraguay: United States Economic Expansion and Great-Power Rivalry in Latin America during World War II. Lawrence, KS: Regents Press of Kansas, 1981.

685 Edwards, Corwin (ed.). International Restrictive Business Covenants (1959).
Martin, James S. All Honorable Men: The Story of the Men on both Sides of the Atlantic who Successfully Thwarted Plans to Dismantle the Nazi Cartel System (1950).
Solo, Robert. Across the High Technology Threshold: The Case of Synthetic Rubber. Norwood, PA: Norwood Editions, 1980.
Todd, Douglas. "Synthetic Rubber in the German War Economy. A Case of Economic Dependence." Journal of European Economic History 10 (Spring 1981): 153–165.
Tuttle, William M., Jr. "The Birth of an Industry: The Synthetic Rubber 'Mess' in World War II." Technology and Culture 22 (January 1981): 35–67.

686 Clarke, Richard. Anglo-American Economic Collaboration in War and Peace 1942–1949. New York: Oxford U. Press, 1982.
Lewis, Cleona. The United States and Foreign Investment Problems (1948).
Monroe, Elizabeth. Britain's Moment in the Middle East, 1914–1956 (1963).

687 Anderson, Irvine H. Aramco, the United States, and Saudi Arabia: A Study of the Dynamics of Foreign Oil Policy, 1933–1950. Princeton, N.J.: Princeton U. Press, 1981.
Miller, Aaron D. Search for Security: Saudi Arabian Oil and American Foreign Policy, 1939–1949. Chapel Hill, N.C.: U. of North Carolina Press, 1980.
Reed, Peter M. "Standard Oil in Indonesia, 1898–1928." Business History Review XXXII.

688 DeNovo, John A. American Interests and Policies in the Middle East, 1900–1939. (1963).
Moore, Frederick Lee. Origin of American Oil Concessions in Bahrein, Kuwait, and Saudi Arabia (1951).

675 Notz, William F. and Harvey, Richard S. American Foreign Trade
         as Promoted by the Webb-Pomerene and Edge Acts (1921).
     Williams, Benjamin H. Economic Foreign Policy of the United
         States (1929).

676 Nash, Gerald D. "Herbert Hoover and the Origins of the
         Reconstruction Finance Corporation." Mississippi Valley
         Historical Review XLVI.
     Williams, William A. The Tragedy of American Diplomacy,
         Chapter 4 (1959).

677 Allen, Robert C. "International Competition in Iron and Steel,
         1850-1913." Journal of Economic History 39 (December
         1979): 911-937.
     Hayne, Williams. American Chemical Industry II and III (1945).
     Trescott, Martha Moore. The Rise of the American Electrochem-
         icals Industry, 1880-1910: Studies in the American Techno-
         logical Environment. Westport, CT: Greenwood, 1981.

678 Jenks, Leland H. Our Cuban Colony (1926).
     Smith, Robert F. The United States and Cuba: A Study in
         Business and Diplomacy (1960).

679 Baack, Bennett D. and Ray, Edward John. "Tariff Policy and
         Comparative Advantage in the Iron and Steel Industry:
         1870-1929." Explorations in Economic History 11 (Fall
         1973): 3-23.
     Motherwell, Hiram. The Imperial Dollar (1929).
     Svennilson, Ingvar. Growth and Stagnation in the European
         Economy (1954).

680 Brandes, Joseph. Herbert Hoover and Economic Diplomacy.
         Department of Commerce Policy, 1921-1928 (1962).
     Silverman, Dan P. Reconstructing Europe After the Great
         War. Cambridge, MA: Harvard U. Press, 1982.
     Wilkins, Mira. The Maturing of Multinational Enterprise:
         American Business Abroad from 1914 to 1970. Cambridge,
         MA: Harvard U. Press, 1974.
     _____ and Hill, Frank E. American Business Abroad: Ford on
         Six Continents (1964).

681 Aldcroft, Derek H. From Versailles to Wall Street. The Inter-
         national Economy in the 1920s. Berkeley, CA: U. of
         California Press, 1977.
     Costigliola, Frank C. "Anglo-American Financial Rivalry in
         the 1920s." Journal of Economic History 37 (December
         1977): 911-934.
     Dunning, John H. American Investment in British Manufacturing
         Industry (1958).
     Southard, F. A. American Industry in Europe (1931).

682 Gardner, Lloyd C. Economic Aspects of New Deal Diplomacy
         (1964).

689   Bradshaw, Marie T. and Lechter, Max. "Expansion of Exports
         Supports Domestic Business." Survey of Current Business XL.
      Burns, Arthur F. "World Competition and the American Economy."
         Political Science Quarterly LXXVI.
      Gimbel, John. The Origins of the Marshall Plan. Stanford, CA:
         Stanford U. Press, 1976.
      Scammell, W. M. The International Economy since 1945. New
         York: St. Martin's Press, 1980.

690   Hanson, Simon G. "The End of the Good-Neighbor Policy."
         Inter-American Economic Affairs VII.
      Haring, Clarence H. "Latin American Dictatorship and the
         United States." Massachusetts Historical Society
         Proceedings (1957).

691   Eckes, Alfred E., Jr. A Search for Solvency: Bretton Woods
         and the International Monetary System, 1941-1971. Austin,
         TX: U. of Texas Press, 1975.
      Gardner, Richard N. Sterling-Dollar Diplomacy: Anglo-
         American Collaboration in the Reconstruction of Multilater-
         al Trade, 1941-1947 (1956).
      Horsefield, J. K. and others. The International Monetary Fund,
         1945-1965: Twenty Years of International Monetary
         Cooperation. Washington, D.C.: IMF, 1969.
      Polk, Judd. Sterling: Its Meaning in World Finance (1956).

692   Biggs-Davison, John Alec. The Uncertain Ally (1957).
      Ferguson, J. H. "Anglo-American Financial Agreement." Yale
         Law Journal LV.

693   de Looper, J. H. C. "Recent Latin American Experience with
         Bilateral Trade and Payments Agreements." International
         Monetary Fund, Staff Papers IV.
      Glickman, D. L. "The British Imperial Preference System."
         Quarterly Journal of Economics LXI.

694   Garceau, Frederick H. "Morgenthau's Plan for Industrial
         Disarmament of Germany." Western Political Quarterly (June
         1961).
      U.S. Department of State. Cartels and Combines in Occupied
         Areas (G.P.O., 1947).

695   Baldwin, David A. "The International Bank in Political
         Perspective." World Politics (October 1965).
      Kaufman, Burton I. Trade and Aid: Eisenhower's Foreign
         Economic Policy, 1953-1961. Baltimore, MD: Johns Hopkins
         U. Press, 1982.
      Rippy, J. Fred. "U.S. Postwar Aid to Latin America." Inter-
         American Economic Affairs (Spring 1961).

696   Kobrin, Stephen J. Managing Political Risk Assessment:
         Strategic Response to Environmental Change. Berkeley, CA:
         U. of California Press, 1982.

Moran, Theodore H. Multinational Corporations and the Politics
     of Dependence: Copper in Chile. Princeton, N.J.:
     Princeton U. Press, 1974.
Sigmund, Paul E. The Overthrow of Allende and the Politics
     of Chile, 1964-1976. Pittsburgh, PA: U. of Pittsburgh
     Press, 1977.
Uribe, Armando. The Black Book of American Intervention in
     Chile. Translated by Casart, Jonathan. Boston, MA:
     Beacon Press, 1975.

697 Johnson, Chalmers. MITI and the Japanese Miracle. The Growth
     of Industrial Policy 1925-1975. Stanford, CA: Stanford
     U. Press, 1982.
Johnston, R. Barry. The Economics of the Euro-Market. New
     York: St. Martin's Press, 1982.
U.S. Congress, 97th, 1st session, Joint Economic Committee,
     Subcommittee on Monetary and Fiscal Policy. Japanese
     and American Economic Policies and U.S. Productivity.
     Hearings.... Washington, D.C.: G.P.O., 1981.

698 Neale, A. D. and Goyder, D. G. The Antitrust Laws of the
     United States of America. 3rd ed. New York: Cambridge
     U. Press, 1980.

699 Gray, E. "Shotgun Wedding." Canadian Business 55 (March
     1982): 96-101.
Moss, Norman. The Politics of Uranium. New York: Universe
     Books, 1982.

700 Aho, C. Michael and Carney, Richard D. An Empirical Analysis
     of U.S. Manufacturing Trade, 1964-1976. Springfield, VA:
     National Technical Information Service, 1980.
Braun, Ernest and MacDonald, Stuart. Revolution in Miniature.
     The History and Impact of Semiconductor Electronics.
     2nd ed. New York: Cambridge U. Press, 1982.

701 Adler, Cyrus. Jacob H. Schiff; His Life and Letters. 2 vols.
     (1929).
Kahn, Otto H. Reflections of a Financier (1921).

702 Babson, Roger W. Actions and Reactions: An Autobiography
     (1935).
Rose, Arnold M. "Rumor in the Stock Market." Public Opinion
     Quarterly XV.

703 Clough, Shepard B. A Century of American Life Insurance: A
     History of the Mutual Life Insurance Company of New York,
     1843-1943 (1946).
Keller, Morton. The Life Insurance Enterprise, 1885-1910
     (1963).

704 Kemmerer, Donald L. "The Marketing of Securities, 1930-1952."
     Journal of Economic History XII.

North, Douglass C. "Life Insurance and Investment Banking
     at the Time of the Armstrong Investigation of 1905-1906."
     Journal of Economic History XIV.

705 Hendrick, Burton J. "Great American Fortunes and Their
        Making: Street-Railway Financiers." McClures Magazine
        XXX.
     Hirsch, M. O. William C. Whitney (1948).

706 Davis, Lance E. "The Investment Market 1870-1914: The Evo-
        lution of a National Market." Journal of Economic History
        25 (September 1965): 355-399.
     Hendrick, Burton J. The Story of Life Insurance (1907).
     Price, William H. "Life Insurance Reform in New York."
        American Economic Quarterly X.

707 Pratt, Sereno S. The Work of Wall Street. 3rd ed. (1921).
     Riefler, Winfield W. Money Rates and Money Markets in the
        United States (1930).

708 Barger, Harold. The Management of Money: A Survey of American
        Experience. Chicago, IL: Rand McNally, 1964.
     Friedman, Milton and Schwartz, Anna J. A Monetary History of
        the United States, 1867-1960. Princeton, N.J.: Princeton
        U. Press, 1963.
     Lockhart, O. C. "The Development of Interbank Borrowing in the
        National System: 1869-1914." Journal of Political
        Economy XXIX.
     Noyes, A. D. "A Year After the Panic of 1907." Quarterly
        Journal of Economics XXXII.

709 Corey, Lewis. The House of Morgan (1930).
     Noyes, A. D. "Methods and Leadership in Wall Street Since
        1893." Journal of Economic and Business History IV.

710 Conant, Charles A. "The Function of the Banker." Quarterly
        Journal of Economics XVII.
     Taylor, W. G. L. "The Source of Financial Power." Journal
        of Political Economy XIII.

711 James, John A. "The Development of the National Money Market
        1893-1911." Journal of Economic History 36 (December
        1976): 878-897.
     Kemmerer, E. W. et al. "Banking Reform in the United States."
        American Economic Review (March 1913).
     Laughlin, J. L. The Federal Reserve Act (1933).

712 Flynn, John T. Security Speculation (1934).
     Norton, Eliot. On "Short Sales" of Securities Through a
        Stockbroker (1907).

713 Gordon, Robert A. Business Leadership in the Large Corporation
        (1945).

Huebner, Solomon. "The Distribution of Stockholdings in American Railways." American Academy of Political and Social Science, Annals XXII.

714   Clapham, John H. The Economic Development of France and Germany, 1815-1914. 4th ed., Chapter 13 (1936).
Riesser, J. The German Great Banks and Their Centralization (G.P.O., 1911).

715   Link, Arthur Stanley. Wilson: The New Freedom (1956).
Warburg, P. L. The Federal Reserve System. 2 vols. (1930).

716   Wiebe, Robert H. Businessmen and Reform: A Study of the Progressive Movement. (1962).
_____. "The House of Morgan and the Executive, 1905-1913." American Historical Review LXV.

717   Haney, Lewis H. "Farm Credit Conditions in a Cotton State [Texas]." American Economic Review (March 1914).
Pope, J. E. "Agricultural Credit in the United States." Quarterly Journal of Economics XXVIII.

718   Corey, Lewis. The House of Morgan (1930).
Satterlee, Herbert L. J. Pierpont Morgan (1939).

719   Noble, H. G. S. The New York Stock Exchange in the Crisis of 1914 (1915).
Matthews, Ada M. "New York Bank Clearings and Stock Prices, 1866-1914." Review of Economic Statistics VIII.

720   Edwards, G. W. The Evolution of Finance Capitalism (1938).
Navin, Thomas R. and Sears, Marian V. "The Rise of a Market for Industrial Securities, 1887-1902." Business History Review (June 1955).

721   Dewing, Arthur S. Corporate Promotion and Reorganization (1924).
Pearson, Henry G. Son of New England: James Jackson Storrow, 1864-1926 (1932).

722   Chandler, Lester V. Benjamin Strong, Central Banker (1958).
Harris, Seymour E. Twenty Years of Federal Reserve Policy. 2 vols. (1933).

723   Galbraith, John K. The Great Crash, 1929 (1955).
Wicker, Elmus R. "Federal Reserve Monetary Policy, 1922-23. A Reinterpretation." Journal of Political Economy (August 1965).

724   Harrod, Roy F. The Dollar (1954).
Pontecorvo, Giulio. "Investment Banking and Security Speculation in the Late 1920's." Business History Review XXXII.
Sobel, Robert. The Great Bull Market: Wall Street in the 1920s. New York: Norton, 1968.

725   Awalt, Francis G.   "Recollections of the Banking Crisis in
         1933." Business History Review 43 (1969): 347-371.
      Burns, Helen M. The American Banking Community and the New
         Deal Banking Reforms, 1933-1935. Westport, CT:
         Greenwood, 1974.
      Kennedy, Susan E. The Banking Crisis of 1933. Lexington, KY:
         U. Press of Kentucky, 1973.
      Secrist, Horace. National Bank Failures and Non-Failures
         (1938).
      Willis, H. P. and Chapman, J. M. The Banking Situation (1934).

726   Jones, Lawrence A. and Durand, David. Mortgage Lending Exper-
         ience in Agriculture (1954).
      Upham, C. B. and Lamke, Edwin. Closed and Distressed Banks
         (1934).

727   Carosso, Vincent P. Investment Banking in America: A History
         Cambridge, MA: Harvard U. Press, 1970.
      Krooss, Herman B. and Blyn, Martin R. A History of Financial
         Intermediaries. New York: Random House, 1971.
      Pecora, F. Wall Street Under Oath (1939).
      Robbins, S. M. "Competitive Bidding in Sale of Securities."
         Harvard Business Review XXVII.

728   Goldsmith, Raymond W. Financial Intermediaries in the American
         Economy Since 1900 (1958).
      Waterman, Merwin H. Investment Banking Functions: Their Evo-
         lution and Adaptation to Business Finance (1958).

729   Cowles, A., 3rd. "Can Stock Market Forecasters Forecast?"
         Econometrica I, V.
      Stewart, B. "The Profits of Professional Speculators."
         Economic Journal XXXXIV.

730   Beckhart, Benjamin H. Federal Reserve System. New York:
         American Institute of Banking, 1972.
      Clifford, A. Jerome. The Independence of the Federal Reserve
         (1965).
      Kindleberger, Charles P. and Laffargue, Jean-Pierre. Financial
         Crises: Theory, History, and Policy. New York: Cambridge
         U. Press, 1982.

731   Reagan, Michael D. "The Political Structure of the Federal
         Reserve System." American Political Science Review LX.
      Veblen, Thorstein. The Engineers and the Price System,
         Chapter 2 (1921).

732   Ernst, Martin L. "The Mechanization of Commerce." Scientific
         American 247 (September 1982): 132-145.
      Sobel, Robert. N.Y.S.E.: A History of the New York Stock
         Exchange 1935-1975. New York: Weybright and Talley, 1975.

733 Baylis, R. M. "Salesmen and the Institutional Investment
     Process." Financial Analysts Journal 36 (September-
     October 1980): 25-27.
     Klemkosky, R. C. and Wright, D. J. "Changing Structure of
     the Stock Market: The National Market System." Business
     Horizons 24 (August 1981): 10-20.

734 Hamilton, J. L. "Marketplace Fragmentation Competition, and
     the Efficiency of the Stock Exchange." Journal of Finance
     34 (March 1979): 171-187.
     Melton, W. C. "Corporate Equities and the National Market
     System." Federal Reserve Bank of New York, Quarterly
     Bulletin 3 (Winter 1978-79): 13-25.

735 Sinkey, Joseph F., Jr. Problem and Failed Institutions in
     the Commercial Banking Industry. Greenwich, CT: JAI
     Press, 1979.
     Spero, Joan E. The Failure of the Franklin National Bank:
     Challenge to the International Banking System. New York:
     Columbia U. Press, 1980.

736 Crawford, Malcolm and Poole, James (eds.). Ten Years of Multi-
     national Business. Cambridge, MA: Abt Books, 1982.
     Mayo, John S. "Evolution of the Intelligent Telecommunications
     Network." Science 215 (February 1982): 831-837.
     Pastre, Olivier. Multinationals: Bank and Corporation Rela-
     tionships. Greenwich, CT: JAI Press, 1981.
     Sigel, Efrem (ed.). The Future of Videotext. White Plains,
     N.Y.: Knowledge Industry Publications, 1982.
     U.S. Congress, 97th, 1st session, Senate, Committee on
     the Judiciary. Monopolization and Competition in the
     Telecommunications Industry: Hearings.... Washington,
     D.C.: G.P.O., 1982.

737 Carron, Andrew S. The Plight of the Thrift Institutions.
     Washington, D.C.: Brookings Institution, 1982.
     Michelman, Irving S. Consumer Finance: A Case History in
     American Business. New York: Frederick Fell, 1966.

738 Congressional Budget Office. Current Problems of the U.S.
     Automobile Industry and Policies to Address Them.
     Washington, D.C.: Natural Resources and Commerce Division,
     C.B.O., July 1980.

739 Berglund, Abraham and Wright, Philip G. The Tariff on Iron
     and Steel (1929).
     Faulkner, Harold U. The Decline of Laissez Faire, 1897-1917,
     Chapter 3 (1951).
     Terrill, Tom E. The Tariff, Politics, and American Foreign
     Policy, 1874-1901. Westport, CT: Greenwood, 1973.
     Yusuf, Abdulqawi. Legal Aspects of Trade Preferences for
     Developing States: A Study in the Influence of Develop-
     ment Needs on the Evolution of International Law.
     Boston, MA: M. Nyhoff, 1982.

740   Gosnell, Harold F. Boss Platt and the New York Machine (1924).
       Steffens, Lincoln. Autobiography (1931).

741   Bernstein, Marver H. Regulating Business by Independent
           Commission (1955).
       Patteron, Edwin W. The Insurance Commissioner in the United
           States (1927).

742   Rosen, Philip T. The Modern Stentors: Radio Broadcasters
           and the Federal Government, 1920-1934. Westport, CT:
           Greenwood, 1980.
       White, Llewellyn. American Radio (1947).

743   Letwin, William. "The First Decade of the Sherman Act: Early
           Administration." Yale Law Journal (January 1959).
       Thorelli, Hans B. The Federal Antitrust Policy (1955).

744   Garraty, John A. Right-Hand Man (1960).
       Kolko, Gabriel. The Triumph of Conservatism--A Reinterpreta-
           tion of American History, 1900-1916 (1963).
       Miller, Arthur Selwyn. The Modern Corporate State: Private
           Governments and the American Constitution. Westport, CT:
           Greenwood, 1976.

745   Association of the Bar of the City of New York. Conflict of
           Interest and Federal Service (1961).
       Schwartz, Bernard. The Professor and the Commissions (1959).

746   Rogin, Michael. "Voluntarism: The Political Functions of an
           Antipolitical Doctrine." Industrial and Labor Relations
           Review XV.
       Taft, Philip. The A. F. of L. in the Time of Gompers (1957).

747   Bellush, Bernard. The Failure of the N.R.A. New York:
           Norton, 1975.
       Himmelberg, Robert F. The Origins of the National Recovery
           Administration: Business, Government, and the Trade
           Association Issue, 1921-1933. New York: Fordham U.
           Press, 1976.
       Lyon, Leverett S. et al. The National Recovery Administration
           (1935).
       Swope, Gerard. The Swope Plan (1931).

748   Harvard Business School. Businessmen in Government (1958).
       Wildavsky, Aaron. Dixon-Yates: A Study in Power Politics
           (1962).

749   Hamilton, Walton. The Politics of Industry (1957).
       Nash, Gerald D. "The Managerial State: Government and
           Business since 1940," in Weible, Robert and others (eds.),
           Essays from the Lowell Conference on Industrial History,
           1980 and 1981. Lowell, MA: Lowell Conference on Indus-
           trial History, 1981.

Schwartz, Jordan A. <u>Bernard M. Baruch in Washington, 1917-</u>
<u>1965</u>. Chapel Hill, N.C.: U. of North Carolina Press,
1980.

Spero, Herbert. <u>Reconstruction Finance Corporation Loans</u>
<u>to Railroads, 1932-1937</u> (1939).

750 Cain, Louis and Neumann, George. "Planning for Peace: The
Surplus Property Act of 1944." <u>Journal of Economic</u>
<u>History</u> 41 (March 1981): 129-135.

Shannon, Fred A. <u>America's Economic Growth</u>. 3rd ed., Chapter
42 (1951).

White, Gerald T. <u>Billions for Defense: Government Financing</u>
<u>by the Defense Plant Corporation during World War II</u>.
University, ALA: U. of Alabama Press, 1980.

_____. "Financing Industrial Expansion for War: The Origin
of the Defense Plant Corporation Lease." <u>Journal of</u>
<u>Economic History</u> IX.

751 Catton, Bruce. <u>The War Lords of Washington</u> (1948).

Montgomery, David. "'Liberty and Union': Workers and Government in America, 1900-1940" <u>in</u> Weible, Robert and others
(eds.), <u>Essays from the Lowell Conference on Industrial</u>
<u>History, 1980 and 1981</u>. Lowell, MA: Lowell Conference
on Industrial History, 1981.

Toulmin, Aubrey, Jr. <u>Diary of Democracy: Senate War Investi-</u>
<u>gating Committee</u> (1947).

752 Hatfield, D. D. <u>Howard Hughes H-4 "Hercules."</u> Los Angeles,
CA: Historical Airplanes, 1972.

Holley, Irving B., Jr. <u>Buying Aircraft: Material Procurement</u>
<u>for the Army Air Forces</u> (G.P.O., 1964).

Rutkowski, Edward H. <u>The Politics of Military Aviation</u>
<u>Procurement, 1926-1934</u> (1965).

753 Albion, Robert G. and Connery, Robert H., with Pope, Jennie B.
<u>Forrestal and the Navy</u> (1962).

Connery, R. H. <u>The Navy and Industrial Mobilization in World</u>
<u>War II</u> (1951).

754 Dupre, J. Stefan and Gustafson, W. Eric. "Contracting for
Defense: Private Firms and the Public Interest."
<u>Political Science Quarterly</u> (June 1962).

Geelhoed, E. Bruce. <u>Charles E. Wilson and Controversy at the</u>
<u>Pentagon, 1953 to 1957</u>. Detroit, MI: Wayne State U.
Press, 1979.

Peck, Merton J. and Scherer, Frederick M. <u>The Weapons Acquisi-</u>
<u>tion Process</u> (1962).

755 Cook, Fred J. <u>The Warfare State</u> (1962).

Striner, Herbert E. <u>et</u> <u>al</u>. <u>Defense Spending and the U.S.</u>
<u>Economy</u>. 2 vols. Operations Research Office, Johns
Hopkins University (1959).

756   Alexander, George J. Honesty and Competition: False-Adver-
        tising Law and Policy under FTC Administration. Syracuse,
        N.Y.: Syracuse U. Press, 1967.
      Hall, Hugh M., Jr. "The Investigatory Function of the Federal
        Trade Commission, 1933-1952," in Redford, E. S. (ed.),
        Public Administration and Policy Formation, Chapter 5
        (1956).
      Miller, John Perry. Unfair Competition (1941).

757   Blaisdell, Donald C. American Democracy Under Pressure (1957).
      Griffith, Robert. "Dwight D. Eisenhower and the Corporate
        Commonwealth." American Historical Review 87 (February
        1982): 87-122.
      Koistinen, Paul A. C. The Military-Industrial Complex: A
        Historical Perspective. New York: Praeger, 1980.
      Mills, C. Wright. The Power Elite (1956).

758   Adams, Gordon. The Politics of Defense Contracting: The Iron
        Triangle. New Brunswick, N.J. Transaction, 1982.
      Agapos, A. M. Government-Industry and Defense: Economics and
        Administration. University, ALA: U. of Alabama Press,
        1975.

759   Comptroller General of the United States. Defense Budget
        Increases: How Well Are They Planned and Spent?
        Washington, D.C.: General Accounting Office, 1982.
      _____. Who is Watching the Defense Dollars? Washington, D.C.:
        General Accounting Office, 1982.

760   U.S. Panel on Government and the Regulation of Corporate and
        Individual Decisions. Government and the Regulation of
        Corporate and Individual Decisions in the Eighties.
        Washington, D.C.: G.P.O., 1981.

761   Chernick, P. L. and others. Design, Costs, and Acceptability
        of an Electric Utility Self-Insurance Pool for Assuring
        the Adequacy of Funds for Nuclear Power Plant Decommission-
        ing Expense. Springfield, VT: National Technical Informa-
        tion Service, 1982.
      U.S. Congress, 97th, 1st session, House of Representatives,
        Committee on Energy and Commerce, Subcommittee on Over-
        sight and Investigations. Cleanup Efforts at Three Mile
        Island: Hearing.... Washington, D.C.: G.P.O., 1982.
      _____. 2nd session, Senate, Committee on Environment and
        Public Works. Nuclear Property Insurance Act of 1981:
        Hearing.... Washington, D.C.: G.P.O., 1982.
      _____. 2nd session, House of Representatives, Committee on
        Government Operations, Environment, Energy, and Natural
        Resources Subcommittee. Nuclear Safety--Three Years After
        Three Mile Island: Joint Hearings.... Washington, D.C.:
        G.P.O., 1982.
      Wood, W. C. "Nuclear Liability after Three Mile Island."
        Journal of Risk and Insurance 48 (September 1981): 450-
        464.

762 Gansler, Jacques S. The Defense Industry. Cambridge, MA:
        M.I.T. Press, 1980.
     U.S. Congress, 97th, 2nd session, Senate, Committee on
        Governmental Affairs. Competition in the Federal Procure-
        ment Process: Hearing.... Washington, D.C.: G.P.O.,
        1982.
     _____. 2nd session, Joint Economic Committee. Economics
        of Defense Policy: Adm. H. G. Rickover: Hearing....
        6 vols. Washington, D.C.: G.P.O., 1982.

763 Perazich, George, Schimmel, H. and Rosenburg, B. Industrial
        Instruments and Changing Technology (G.P.O., W.P.A., 1940).
     White, Frederick A. American Industrial Research Laboratories
        (1961).

764 Kirkland, Edward C. Industry Comes of Age...1860-1897,
        Chapter 8 (1961).
     Rae, John B. "The Engineer as Business Man in American
        Industry: A Preliminary Analysis." Explorations in Entre-
        preneurial History VII.

765 Maclaurin, W. Rupert. "The Sequence from Invention to Innova-
        tion and Its Relation to Economic Growth." Quarterly
        Journal of Economics LXVII.
     Slichter, Sumner H. "The Industry of Discovery." Science
        CXXVII.

766 Bright, Arthur A., Jr. The Electric Lamp Industry: Technolog-
        ical Change and Economic Development from 1800 to 1947
        (1949).
     Josephson, Matthew. Edison: A Biography (1959).

767 Bartlett, Howard R. "The Development of Industrial Research
        in the United States," in National Resources Planning
        Board, Research--A National Resource II (G.P.O., 1941).
     Leontief, Wassily W. "Introduction," in Silk, Leonard S.,
        The Research Revolution (1960).

768 Feller, Irwin. "The Draper Loom in New England Textiles, 1894-
        1914: A Study of Diffusion of an Innovation." Journal of
        Economic History 26 (September 1966): 320-347.
     Gibb, George S. The Saco-Lowell Shops (1950).
     Williamson, H. F. "Management and Innovations: the Winchester
        Repeating Arms Company, A Case Study." Business History
        Review XXV.

769 American Institute of. Metallurgical Engineers. A History of
        Iron and Steelmaking in the United States (1961).
     Steinmetz, Charles P. "Scientific Research in Relation to the
        Industries." Journal of the Franklin Institute CLXXXII.

770 Brittain, James E. "C. P. Steinmetz and E. F. W. Alexanderson:
        Creative Engineering in a Corporate Setting." Institute
        of Electrical and Electronic Engineers, Proceedings 64
        (September 1976): 1413-1417.
     Hammond, J. W. Charles Proteus Steinmetz, A Biography (1924).
     Jewkes, John, Sawers, David, and Stillerman, Richard. The
        Sources of Invention (1958).
     Layton, Edwin T. The Revolt of the Engineers: Social Respon-
        sibility and the American Engineering Profession.
        Cleveland, OH: Case Western Reserve U., 1971.
     Noble, David F. America by Design. Science, Technology, and
        the Rise of Corporate Capitalism. New York: Knopf, 1977.

771 Newcomb, Simon. "Conditions Which Discourage Scientific Work
        in America." North American Review CLXXIV.
     Stuewer, Roger H. (ed.) Nuclear Physics in Retrospect.
        Proceedings of a Symposium on the 1930s. Minneapolis, MN:
        U. of Minnesota Press, 1979.
     The Autobiography of Robert A. Milliken, Chapters 2, 3, and 8
        (1951).

772 Broderick, John T. Willis Rodney Whitney, Pioneer of Indus-
        trial Research (1945).
     Hall, Courtney R. History of American Industrial Science
        (1954).

773 Compton, Karl T. et al. Physics in Industry (1937).
     Feiss, Julian W. "New and Changing Activities of Scientists
        and the Implications," in National Science Foundation,
        Scientific Manpower--1957 (G.P.O., 1958).
     Kevles, Daniel J. The Physicists: The History of a Scientific
        Community in Modern America. New York: Knopf, 1978.

774 Gershinowitz, Harold. "Industrial Research Programs and
        Academic Research." American Scientist XXXXVI.
     Kistiakowski, George B. The Private Diary of President
        Eisenhower's Special Assistant for Science and Technology.
        Cambridge, MA: Harvard U. Press, 1976.
     Wilson, Robert E. "Support of Basic Research by Industry,"
        in Wolfle, Dael (ed.), Symposium on Basic Research (1959).

775 Merrill, Theodore B., Jr. "The Case of Transistors," in
        Silk, Leonard S., The Research Revolution, Chapter 4 (1960).
     Wiener, Norbert. I Am a Mathematician (1956).

776 Melman, Seymour. The Impact of the Patent System on Research
        (G.P.O., 1958).
     Solo, Robert O. Synthetic Rubber: A Case Study in Technologi-
        cal Development Under Government Direction (G.P.O., 1959).

777 Machlup, Fritz. "The Supply of Inventors and Inventions."
        Weltwirtschaftlichesarchiv LXXXV.
     Marcson, Simon. The Scientist in American Industry (1960).

778   Shryock, Richard H.   "American Indifference to Basic Science
           during the Nineteenth Century."   Archives internationales
           d' histoire des sciences (Archeion) (1948).
       Tuve, Merle A.   "Basic Research in Private Research Institutes,"
           in Wolfle, Dael (ed.), Symposium on Basic Research (1959).

779   Kilgour, Frederick G.   "How Good Are Our Science and
           Engineering?"   Yale Review (Summer 1955).
       Snyder, Carl.   "America's Inferior Position in the Scientific
           World."   North American Review CLXXIV (1902).

780   Bright, James R.   Research Development and Technological
           Innovation (1965).
       Solo, Robert A.   "Research and Development in the Synthetic
           Rubber Industry."   Quarterly Journal of Economics LXVIII.

781   Armstrong, Joe E. and Harman, W. H.   Strategies for Conducting
           Technology Assessments.   Boulder, CO: Westview Press,
           1980.
       Gold, Bela and others.   Evaluating Technological Innovations.
           Lexington, MA: Lexington, MA: Lexington Books, 1980.
       O'Brien, David M. and Marchand, Donald A. (eds.)   The Politics
           of Technology Assessment: Institutions, Processes, and
           Policy Disputes.   Lexington, MA: Lexington Books, 1982.
       Porter, Alan and others.   A Guidebook for Technology Assess-
           ment and Impact Analysis.   New York: Elsevier/North-
           Holland, 1979.

782   Bergaust, Erik.   Wernher von Braun.   Washington, D.C.:
           Stackpole Press, 1979.
       The Satellite Communications Market in North America, 1981-
           1991 (1981).   Frost and Sullivan, 106 Fulton Street,
           New York, N.Y. 10038.

783   "Few Recent Ph.Ds. on Science Faculties."   Chemical and
           Engineering News 60 (February 1982):   32.
       Fodella, Gianni.   "Narrowing the Gap among Pure Research,
           Applied Research and Technological Diffusion: The Japanese
           Experience."   Rivista Internazionale di Scienze 28 (July-
           August 1981).
       Main, Jeremy.   "Why Engineering Deans Worry a Lot."   Fortune
           (January 11, 1982):   84-90.

784   Egan, John W.   Economics of the Pharmeceutical Industry.
           New York: Praeger, 1982.

785   Chemical Abstracts Service.   CAS Today.   Facts and Figures
           About Chemical Abstracts Service.   Columbus, OH:
           Chemical Abstracts Service, 1980.
       Computer-based Information Systems: Technology and Public
           Policy Issues.   Washington, D.C.:   Office of Technology
           Assessment, 1981.

Dertouzos, Michael L. and Moses, Joel (eds.). The Computer
    Age: A Twenty-Year View. Cambridge, MA: M.I.T. Press,
    1979.
"Foreign Countries Help Pay 'Chem Abstracts' Costs."
    Library Journal 103 (April 15, 1978): 807.

INDEX

About the Author

MEYER WEINBERG has had a distinguished career as a teacher, editor, and author. Currently he is both a Professor at the University of Massachusetts, Amherst, and Director of the Horace Mann Bond Center for Equal Education. His writings include *Race and Place: A Legal History of the Neighborhood School*, *The Search for Quality Integrated Education*, and an essay on American economic development in V. B. Singh's collective volume of comparative economic history. His award-winning two-volume work, *The Education of Poor and Minority Children: A World Bibliography*, was published by Greenwood Press in 1981. He has taught courses in American economic history and the general history of the United States.